Primacy and Its Discontents:
American Power and International Stability

International Security Readers

Strategy and Nuclear Deterrence (1984)

Military Strategy and the Origins of the First World War (1985)

Conventional Forces and American Defense Policy (1986)

The Star Wars Controversy (1986)

Naval Strategy and National Security (1988)

Military Strategy and the Origins of the First World War,
revised and expanded edition (1991)

—published by Princeton University Press

Soviet Military Policy (1989)

Conventional Forces and American Defense Policy, revised edition (1989)

Nuclear Diplomacy and Crisis Management (1990)

The Cold War and After: Prospects for Peace (1991)

America's Strategy in a Changing World (1992)

The Cold War and After: Prospects for Peace, expanded edition (1993)

Global Dangers: Changing Dimensions of International Security (1995)

The Perils of Anarchy: Contemporary Realism and International Security (1995)

Debating the Democratic Peace (1996)

East Asian Security (1996)

Nationalism and Ethnic Conflict (1997)

America's Strategic Choices (1997)

Theories of War and Peace (1998)

America's Strategic Choices, revised edition (2000)

Rational Choice and Security Studies: Stephen Walt and His Critics (2000)

The Rise of China (2000)

Nationalism and Ethnic Conflict, revised edition (2001)

Offense, Defense, and War (2004)

New Global Dangers: Changing Dimensions of International Security (2004)

Primacy and Its Discontents: American Power and International Stability (2009)

—published by The MIT Press

Primacy and Its Discontents

American Power and International Stability

AN *International Security* READER

EDITED BY

Michael E. Brown
Owen R. Coté Jr.
Sean M. Lynn-Jones
and Steven F. Miller

THE MIT PRESS
CAMBRIDGE, MASSACHUSETTS
LONDON, ENGLAND

The contents of this book were first published in *International Security* (ISSN 0162-2889), a publication of the MIT Press under the sponsorship of the Belfer Center for Science and International Affairs at Harvard University. Copyright in each of the following articles is owned jointly by the President and Fellows of Harvard College and of the Massachusetts Institute of Technology.

William C. Wohlforth, "The Stability of a Unipolar World," 24:1 (Summer 1999); Barry R. Posen, "Command of the Commons: The Military Foundations of U.S. Hegemony," 28:1 (Summer 2003); Christopher Layne, "The Unipolar Illusion: Why New Great Powers Will Rise," 17:4 (Spring 1993); Kenneth N. Waltz, "Structural Realism after the Cold War," 25:1 (Summer 2000); G. John Ikenberry, "Institutions, Strategic Restraint, and the Persistence of the American Postwar Order," 23:3 (Winter 1998/99); John M. Owen IV, "Transnational Liberalism and U.S. Primacy," 26:3 (Winter 2001/02); Robert A. Pape, "Soft Balancing against the United States," 30:1 (Summer 2005); T.V. Paul, "Soft Balancing in the Age of U.S. Primacy," 30:1 (Summer 2005); Stephen G. Brooks and William C. Wohlforth, "Hard Times for Soft Balancing," 30:1 (Summer 2005); Keir A. Lieber and Gerard Alexander, "Waiting for Balancing: Why the World Is Not Pushing Back," 30:1 (Summer 2005).

Selection, foreword, preface, and Christopher Layne, "The Unipolar Illusion Revisited: The Coming End of American Hegemony," copyright © 2008 by the President and Fellows of Harvard College and of the Massachusetts Institute of Technology.

Library of Congress Cataloging-in-Publication Data

Primacy and its discontents : American power and international stability / edited by Michael E. Brown . . . [et al.].
    p.   cm. — (International security readers)
  Includes bibliographical references.
  ISBN 978-0-262-52455-1 (pbk. : alk. paper)
  1. United States—Foreign relations. 2. Balance of power. I. Brown, Michael E. (Michael Edward), 1954–
JZ1480.P747 2009
327.73—dc22
                              2008038270

Contents

The Contributors

GRAHAM ALLISON is Director of the Belfer Center for Science and International Affairs and Douglas Dillon Professor of Government at Harvard University's John F. Kennedy School of Government.

MICHAEL E. BROWN is Dean of the Elliott School of International Affairs and Professor of International Affairs and Political Science at The George Washington University.

OWEN R. COTÉ JR. is Editor of *International Security* and Associate Director of the Security Studies Program at the Massachusetts Institute of Technology.

SEAN M. LYNN-JONES is Editor of *International Security* and a Research Associate at the Belfer Center for Science and International Affairs (BCSIA), John F. Kennedy School of Government, Harvard University.

STEVEN E. MILLER is Editor-in-Chief of *International Security* and Director of the International Security Program at the Belfer Center.

GERARD ALEXANDER is Associate Professor of Politics at the University of Virginia.

STEPHEN G. BROOKS is Assistant Professor of Government at Dartmouth College.

G. JOHN IKENBERRY is Professor of Politics and International Affairs at Princeton University.

CHRISTOPHER LAYNE is Mary Julia and George R. Jordan Professor of International Affairs at the Bush School of Government and Public Service at Texas A&M University.

KEIR A. LIEBER is Assistant Professor of Political Science at the University of Notre Dame.

JOHN M. OWEN IV is Associate Professor of International Relations at the University of Virginia.

ROBERT A. PAPE is Professor of Political Science at the University of Chicago.

T.V. PAUL is James McGill Professor of International Relations at McGill University.

BARRY R. POSEN is Ford International Professor of Political Science and Director of the Security Studies Program at the Massachusetts Institute of Technology.

KENNETH N. WALTZ is Emeritus Ford Professor of Political Science at the University of California, Berkeley.

WILLIAM C. WOHLFORTH is Professor of Government at Dartmouth College.

Acknowledgments

The editors gratefully acknowledge the assistance that has made this book possible. A deep debt is owed to all those at the Belfer Center for Science and International Affairs, Harvard University, who have played an editorial role at *International Security*. We are grateful for support from the Carnegie Corporation of New York. Special thanks go to Diane McCree, Sarah Buckley, and Katherine Bartel for their invaluable help in preparing this volume for publication.

Foreword | Graham Allison

$\mathbf{F}$our months after U.S. troops marched into Baghdad, Harvard University President Larry Summers and I convened a study group to investigate the unwieldy, but looming topic of "American Primacy and its Discontents." Initially, we sought to understand the extent of U.S. primacy, its dimensions, sources, and sustainability. We analyzed the structural consequences of the United States' position as a unipolar power: the inevitable resentment and resistance that such overarching power causes in other states. We also explored ways in which U.S. words and actions can either exaggerate and exacerbate, or alternatively mitigate and contain, negative reactions to American primacy.

The study group gathered a distinguished group of faculty from across the Harvard community: from the Kennedy School of Government, the Law School, the Business School, the Faculty of Arts and Sciences, and even colleagues from MIT. Presentations, participant publications, and background readings are available at http://belfercenter.ksg.harvard.edu/project/42.

Discussions at these sessions inspired and informed an impressive collection of subsequent articles and books, including: Niall Ferguson, *Colossus: The Rise and Fall of the American Empire*; Michael Ignatieff's edited volume, *American Exceptionalism and Human Rights*; Charles Maier, *Among Empires: American Ascendancy and Its Predecessors*; Joseph Nye, *Soft Power: The Means to Success in World Politics*; and Stephen Walt, *Taming American Power: The Global Response to U.S. Primacy*. Participants also produced a number of essays and papers, some of which became the basis for *International Security* articles that are reprinted in this volume, including the contributions by Barry Posen and Stephen Brooks and William Wohlforth.

From our deliberations, three major themes emerged. First, *structure,* the distribution of power among states along all dimensions, compels a reaction by other states to U.S. primacy. It does not, however, determine either whether that reaction is positive or negative, or the magnitude of the reaction. Realist theory predicts a powerful tendency to counterbalance overwhelming power to restore a "balance of power." But where one state is so powerful that it cannot feasibly be matched, or where it exercises power in a way that provides rather than threatens security and offers other benefits, "bandwagoning" is also possible.

Second, the *substance* of policies pursued by the United States thus shapes to a considerable extent the reactions of other states to U.S. preponderance. Here deeds speak much more loudly than words. In the aftermath of World War II, the United States was also a dominant state, but the combination of postwar magnanimity (the Marshall Plan), and inventiveness in creating international institutions such as the International Monetary Fund and the World Bank that advanced the interests of all parties, succeeded, with a critical assist by an emerging Soviet threat, in organizing what came to be called the "Free World."

Third, *style,* the way a dominant power acts to advance its interests in international affairs, also matters. To the extent that the dominant power is prepared to listen, to take into account other states' perceptions of their interests, and to persuade them that what it wants is also in their own interest, it can lead. To the extent it projects disregard for their views, an unwillingness to defer to their interests, and a determination to act unilaterally, it will foster pushback.

At the beginning of what became an American century, President Theodore Roosevelt wisely counseled, "Speak softly and carry a big stick." Had candidate George W. Bush's 2000 proposal that the United States adopt a "humble" foreign policy become the hallmark of his administration's actions in the opening decade of the twenty-first century, the United States' standing in the world and support from other states need not have undergone such a precipitous decline.

In the spirit of our study group on "American Primacy and its Discontents," I welcome this *International Security* reader on the sources, limits, and prospects of U.S. primacy and recommend it for careful reading and vigorous debate.

Preface | *Sean M. Lynn-Jones*

When the Cold War ended, many commentators declared that the United States was the "sole surviving superpower." Others hailed the beginning of a "unipolar moment" in international politics. During the 1990s the United States appeared to enjoy unchallenged global primacy. Some countries complained about excessive U.S. power, but most seemed to grudgingly accept that the United States was, in the words of Secretary of State Madeleine Albright, "the Indispensable Nation." In the new millennium, however, global resentment of U.S. power grew as the George W. Bush administration responded to the terrorist attacks of September 11, 2001, with a series of unilateral and military actions. In many countries, the public and the government sought ways to counter the exercise of U.S. power.

This volume focuses on three key questions. First, what are the sources, limits, and prospects of U.S. primacy? Second, will other countries attempt to balance the power of the United States by forming alliances and building up their own capabilities? Third, have other countries already started to engage in "soft balancing" against the United States? These questions lie at the intersection of theory and policy. They are not the only questions raised by the emergence of U.S. primacy, but they are likely to be at the center of discussions of the structure of international politics and the global role of the United States for many years.

The first two essays in this volume examine the sources, implications, and durability of U.S. primacy. In "The Stability of a Unipolar World," William Wohlforth argues that the United States enjoys an unprecedented margin of superiority over its potential great-power rivals and that the resulting unipolar world is both peaceful and stable. He suggests that the United States can and should adopt a grand strategy of active engagement in world politics to maintain order and to prolong unipolarity.

Wohlforth contends that the current international system is "unambiguously unipolar." Although many commentators have argued that the United States lacks the power to shape world politics decisively, Wohlforth presents evidence to show that the United States has extraordinary advantages over all other major states. No great power in the past two centuries has enjoyed such a wide advantage in every component of power—economic, military, technological, and geopolitical. The U.S. lead appears even wider when measured against information-age indicators such as high-technology manufacturing and research and development. The "unipolar moment" that emerged at the end of the Cold War may well become a unipolar era.

Several scholars have argued that unipolarity is inherently unstable, conflict-ridden, and transitory, because other great powers will challenge the preponderant power.[1] Wohlforth, however, contends that unipolarity is peaceful and stable, for two reasons. First, because the United States has such a large advantage in raw power, no other state can hope to challenge it. Hegemonic rivalry will not emerge in the current international system; no major power can afford to incur U.S. enmity. In addition, the other major powers are unlikely to go to war or engage in intense security competitions because the United States has the capabilities to ease and prevent local security conflicts.

Second, unipolarity is peaceful because in a unipolar world states never miscalculate or misperceive the resolve of alliances or the distribution of power. In multipolar systems, the complexity and uncertainty of alliance systems and the importance of shifts in relative power often cause leaders to blunder into war. When one state is dominant, however, other states cannot form alliances against it, so there is no need to assess the resolve, power, and solidarity of rival alliances. In conflicts, the side that the dominant state takes will probably prevail.

Wohlforth argues that unipolarity is likely to last. In addition to having an overwhelming advantage in raw power, the United States is in the favorable position of being the only actual or potential pole that is not in or around Eurasia. This geographical fact means that other potential poles that seek to increase their power will provoke nearby countries to balance against them. If, for example, Germany, Japan, or Russia were to attempt to challenge U.S. preeminence, their geographical neighbors would resist this attempt—much as they have resisted earlier German, Japanese, and Russian bids for hegemony.

Some observers believe that other states are already balancing against what they see as the arrogance of U.S. power,[2] but Wohlforth points out that most of this balancing remains rhetorical. States may complain about U.S. preponderance, but in the late 1990s, at least, most of them reduced their military spending and aligned themselves implicitly or explicitly with the United States.

U.S. preeminence will not last forever, but U.S. policymakers should focus on strategies for a unipolar world instead of making premature plans for a transition to a new international system. Wohlforth recommends that the United States should attempt to prolong unipolarity by playing a major role in

---

1. See, for example, the essays by Christopher Layne and Kenneth Waltz in this volume.
2. The essays by Robert Pape and T.V. Paul in this volume argue that other countries are already engaging in "soft balancing" against the United States. Stephen Brooks and Wohlforth present their rebuttal of this argument in their essay, as do Keir Lieber and Gerard Alexander in their essay.

providing regional security, thereby forestalling the emergence of great struggles for power and security. Although some critics of U.S. foreign policy complain that the United States intervenes in too many overseas conflicts, Wohlforth argues that the United States should continue to use its capabilities to provide order and security. This strategy need not be too costly, because it does not require limitless commitments. The United States should focus on "managing the central security regimes in Europe and Asia, and maintaining the expectation on the part of other states that any geopolitical challenge to the United States is futile."

In "Command of the Commons: The Military Foundation of U.S. Hegemony," Barry R. Posen develops an innovative argument about the sources, nature, limitations, and implications of U.S. military hegemony. Whereas Wohlforth looks at the economic, military, technological, and geopolitical sources of U.S. power, Posen focuses exclusively on military capabilities. One of the keys to U.S. military preeminence, Posen says, is the country's unprecedented "command of the commons—command of the sea, space, and air." Although command of the commons gives the United States tremendous strategic advantages, it does not mean that the United States will go unchallenged everywhere. Posen notes that adversaries will be able to fight U.S. forces with "some hope of success" in several contested zones. These are arenas—"on land, in the air at low altitudes, and at sea in the so-called littorals"—where geography, knowledge of the local terrain, strong political motivations, and access to weaponry will enable adversaries to mount stiff resistance to U.S. military actions.

Posen argues that the U.S. command of the commons and the persistence of contested zones have important implications for U.S. grand strategy: "Even before the September 11 terrorist attacks, the foreign policy debate had narrowed to a dispute between primacy and selective engagement, between a nationalist, unilateralist version of hegemony, and a liberal, multilateral version of hegemony. U.S. command of the commons provides an impressive foundation for selective engagement. It is not adequate for a policy of primacy." The Bush administration's embrace of primacy is problematic, Posen argues, because it creates unease among allies and "may cause others to ally against the United States." A policy of selective engagement, on the other hand, would be more effective and more sustainable because it would help to "make U.S. military power appear less threatening and more tolerable."

The next four essays in this volume offer contending perspectives on whether other countries are likely to balance against the United States, either by forming anti-U.S. alliances or by building up their own military capabilities. They contribute to a long-standing debate over the balance of power in international relations theory. Do countries attempt to balance the power of states that threaten them? Do they balance against threat or against power? Do balances form rapidly and reliably? Does a balance of power foster peace and stability? These questions have been central in realist theories of international relations and most realists have upheld the validity of balance of power theory. Two authors—Christopher Layne and Kenneth Waltz—argue that the predictions of realist theory will be realized: other countries will sooner or later align against the United States and begin to develop the capabilities to challenge U.S. primacy.

In "The Unipolar Illusion: Why New Great Powers Will Rise," Christopher Layne explores in detail the implications of the United States' predominant international position in the aftermath of the Cold War. Unlike Wohlforth, Layne argues that a "strategy of predominance," aimed at perpetuating the singular status of the United States in the new international order, is unlikely to succeed and could be counterproductive. The reason, Layne suggests, is that both theory and history indicate that "unipolar moments" are fleeting: new great powers inevitably rise to challenge the power and standing of the hegemon.

The theoretical underpinnings of this argument are grounded in realism. Layne notes that differential economic growth rates result over time in substantial shifts in relative power—shifts that are usually reflected in the conduct of international diplomacy and eventually in the structure of the international system. He emphasizes also the structural incentives for states that have the potential to do so to seek great power status, and the tendency for other states to attempt to balance against the power of the hegemon, even if the hegemon is relatively benign. In the post–Cold War era, Layne argues, these factors will act to erode U.S. predominance. He augments this theoretical argument with historical evidence that leads to the same conclusion: both French hegemony in the late seventeenth century and British hegemony in the mid-nineteenth century were completely undermined within a few decades. In Layne's view, just as earlier unipolar moments were temporary, so too will U.S. hegemony wither with the passage of time.

Layne believes that the United States is mistakenly pursuing a strategy of preponderance, attempting to preserve its "benign hegemony." The inevitable rise of new great powers—notably Germany and Japan—dooms this approach to failure, and the aggressive quest to preserve primacy could provoke and hasten the unavoidable challenges to U.S. power. Layne advocates instead an approach that combines a focus on correcting internal sources of relative decline with an international strategy that takes multipolarity as its starting point. A multipolar world can be difficult and potentially dangerous, and Layne refuses to dismiss the possibility even of great power war. But if multipolarity is inescapable, as Layne asserts, then the United States must adapt to it. Accordingly, he urges that U.S. strategy concentrate first on preserving U.S. interests during the transition from the unipolar to the multipolar world, and second on maximizing U.S. prospects in a multipolar world.

Layne's "Unipolar Illusion" was published in 1993. In a new postscript, "The Unipolar Illusion Revisited: The Coming End of American Hegemony," Layne considers how well the arguments have stood the test of time.[3] He recognizes that he exaggerated the power of Japan and concedes that his prediction of a multipolar world in 2010 is unlikely to be borne out. Layne nevertheless argues that new great powers are emerging to challenge the United States. China, India, and the European Union will become strong enough to make the international system multipolar.

According to Layne, the United States is too powerful to be regarded as a benign hegemon, even if it repeatedly proclaims its benevolent intentions. The war in Iraq makes clear that the United States can and will act essentially unilaterally in the face of significant international opposition. Other countries are likely to mistrust and fear the United States. Some, including China, India, and Russia, are already starting to balance against U.S. power by building up their own economic and technological capabilities, which can eventually be converted into military power. Members of the European Union are developing the military capability to act autonomously against the United States.

Layne concludes that U.S. hegemony will not last forever. The only question is, when will it end?

In "Structural Realism after the Cold War," Kenneth Waltz offers a general defense of realist theory against several varieties of criticism and then provides a realist analysis of the likely pattern of international politics in the era of unipolarity. Waltz notes that criticisms of realism often emerge when "peace breaks out," as it did for a time after the end of the Cold War. He argues that realist theory remains the best guide to understanding international politics and the future of U.S. primacy.

---

3. For a longer version of Layne's arguments, see Christopher Layne, "The Unipolar Illusion Revisited: The Coming End of the United States' Unipolar Moment," *International Security*, Vol. 31, No. 2 (Fall 2006), pp. 7–41.

Waltz defends realist theory by refuting several of the major theoretical challenges to realism. He contends that the democratic peace thesis, which argues that democracies have never gone to war with one another and are unlikely to do so, is a flawed challenge to realism.[4] In his view, many of the causes of war are rooted in the anarchic structure of the international system. Changing the domestic political systems of states by turning them all into democracies will not eliminate war. Waltz accepts that "democracies seldom fight democracies," but points out that wars between democracies have been few. Citing the example of perceptions of Germany before and after the beginning of World War I, he notes that countries defined as democracies are quickly redefined as nondemocracies when they go to war with democracies. Waltz also notes that democracies are often more likely to initiate wars against nondemocracies, because they believe that they need to defeat nondemocratic states and make them democratic. The spread of democracy may thus increase the amount of war in the world.

Waltz argues that a second challenge to realist theory—the claim that economic interdependence promotes peace—is flawed. He notes that close interdependence can breed war as well as peace. Moreover, economic interdependence has weak effects. Economic interdependence reached high levels in the nineteenth century, but in 1914 quickly collapsed into war, autarky, and more war. In international politics, strong states are not losing control to global economic markets.

Turning to the claim that the rise of international institutions challenges realist theory, Waltz argues that the structure of power in the international system determines the role of institutions. NATO, for example, is often cited as a significant institution that outlived its original anti-Soviet purpose to play an important post–Cold War role. In Waltz's view, however, the continued existence of NATO "nicely illustrates how international institutions are created and maintained by stronger states [e.g., the United States] to serve their perceived and misperceived interests." Waltz sees NATO's expansion not as evi-

---

4. The literature on the democratic peace thesis is large and continues to grow. For a selection of early articles on both sides on this issue, see Michael E. Brown, Sean M. Lynn-Jones, and Steven E. Miller, *Debating the Democratic Peace* (Cambridge, Mass.: MIT Press, 1996). For a more recent debate between proponents of the democratic peace thesis and a critic, see Sebastian Rosato, "The Flawed Logic of Democratic Peace Theory," *American Politcal Science Review*, Vol. 97, No. 4 (November 2003), pp. 585–602, and the subsequent forum of articles: David Kinsella, "No Rest for the Democratic Peace"; Branislav L. Slantchev, Anna Alexandrova, and Erik Gartzke, "Probabilistic Causality, Selection Bias, and the Logic of the Democratic Peace"; Michael W. Doyle, "Three Pillars of the Democratic Peace"; and Sebastian Rosato, "Explaining the Democratic Peace," *American Political Science Review*, Vol. 99, No. 3 (August 2005), pp. 453–472.

dence of the institution's strength, but as another example of how the United States can act foolishly in the era of primacy: "In the absence of counterweights, a country's internal impulses prevail, whether fueled by liberal or by other urges." More generally, any effects attributed to international institutions "are but one step removed from the capabilities and intentions of the major state or states that gave them birth and sustain them."

Waltz then turns to the question of international politics in a unipolar world and applies realist theory to understand the future of U.S. primacy. He argues that the unipolarity that began with the demise of the Soviet Union will not last, for two reasons. First, dominant powers such as the United States weaken themselves by misusing their power internationally. During the Cold War, the Soviet threat constrained U.S. policy. In the absence of any major threat, the United States has "wide latitude in making policy choices" and may act capriciously on the basis of "internal political pressure and national ambition."

Second, even if the United States acts with moderation, other states will worry about U.S. behavior and therefore balance against it. Waltz points out that "unbalanced power leaves weaker states feeling uneasy and gives them reason to strengthen their positions." The leading candidates to become great powers are China, Japan, and the European Union, although Europe is unlikely to become a great power unless Germany decides to lead. China and Japan already have begun to take steps to counter U.S. power.

Waltz concludes that "the American aspiration to freeze historical development by working to keep the world unipolar is doomed. . . . Multipolarity is developing before our eyes."

The next two essays in this volume offer perspectives on U.S. primacy through the lens of liberal theories of international relations. Most liberal theories recognize that power matters in international politics, but they also point to the importance of international institutions, economics, and states' forms of government.

In "Institutions, Strategic Restraint, and the Persistence of American Postwar Order," John Ikenberry offers an institutional argument for why other great powers did not balance against the United States after the end of the Cold War. In his view, realist predictions of great power balancing have not been borne out because after World War II the United States decided to engage in strategic restraint and thereby reassured weaker states that it was more interested in cooperation than in domination. This reassurance enabled weaker states to participate in the postwar order. The institutions created and supported by the United States limited the opportunities for the United States to exploit its power for momentary advantages. Although the United States could have unilaterally exploited its huge advantage in power during the immediate post-1945 years, it instead decided to "lock in" its advantage by creating a durable institutional order based on U.S. restraint. Weaker states agreed to participate in this order because it limited the U.S. exercise of power.

The institutions of the postwar order have served to reduce the returns to power in international politics, "which lowers the risks of participation by strong and weak states alike." Institutions not only provide a functional basis for cooperative solutions to international problems by reducing uncertainty and lowering transactions costs, but also mitigate the security dilemma and restrain the arbitrary exercise of power.

Ikenberry argues that the liberal basis of U.S. hegemony made it easier for other countries to accept the postwar order. Because the United States has an open and transparent domestic political system, it has been able to remain at the center of "a large and expanding institutionalized and legitimate political order." The postwar order actually has become more stable over time, and its institutions have become "firmly embedded in the wider structures of politics and society."

Ikenberry's analysis finds that "the United States agrees to operate within an institutionalized political process and, in return, its partners agree to be willing participants." Writing in 1998, he suggests that the postwar order had remained remarkably stable in the face of repeated shocks such as the 1956 Suez crisis, the 1970s energy crisis, and the controversy over U.S. "Euro-missiles" in the 1980s.

Ikenberry concludes that "American hegemony is reluctant, open, and highly institutionalized—or in a word, liberal." In his view, these features increase the likelihood that it will endure: "Short of large-scale war or a global economic crisis, the American hegemonic order appears to be immune to would-be hegemonic challengers."

In "Transnational Liberalism and U.S. Primacy," John Owen offers another liberal explanation for why the rest of the world has not formed a balancing coalition to counter U.S. power. He accepts that U.S. primacy and the unipolar structure of the international system is likely to endure because the United States enjoys a large advantage in economic and military power.[5] It may take many years for other countries to catch up. Nevertheless, the magnitude of

---

5. On this point, Owen agrees with Wohlforth, "On the Stability of a Unipolar World," in this volume.

U.S. power does not fully explain why the rest of the world is not counterbalancing the United States. Owen notes that several major powers are showing signs of such balancing. China's increased military spending is partly directed against the United States and grew after U.S. military successes in Iraq in 1991 and Kosovo in 1999. Russia also has opposed U.S. policies and has cooperated with China to limit U.S. influence. For Owen, the key question is why some countries have engaged in incipient balancing against the United States while others have not.

Owen argues that "the degree to which a state counterbalances U.S. power is a function of how politically liberal that state is." He defines liberalism as "an ideology that seeks to uphold individual autonomy and prescribes a particular set of domestic institutions as a means to that end" and he distinguishes between liberalism and the related concept of democracy, which is "the rule of the majority." In Owen's view, the absence of an anti-U.S. counterbalancing coalition suggests that most potential challenger states are at least somewhat liberal and therefore believe the United States is relatively unthreatening. For their part, U.S. leaders regard liberal regimes as benign. On the other hand, states that are not liberal consider the United States a potential threat, and the United States reciprocates this suspicion.[6] Thus disagreements between the United States and liberal states do not provoke military counterbalancing, unlike similar disagreements between the United States and countries with antiliberal regimes.

Owen cites the pattern of military spending in the 1990s to support his argument. In Britain, France, and Germany, military spending remained constant or fell, indicating that these countries are not counterbalancing U.S. power. Japanese military spending followed a similar pattern in the 1990s, during which Japan also strengthened its alliance with the United States. According to Owen, European and Japanese acquiescence to U.S. power reflects the predominance of liberalism in each society. Although their governments may criticize U.S. policy, they do not regard the United States as a military threat.

When countries do not share liberal values, the pattern becomes more complicated. Owen points out that Russia's military spending declined in the late 1990s, but Russian policies became more anti-Western on issues such as Kosovo. He argues that these ambiguous policies reflect Russia's oscillations between authoritarianism and democracy under Presidents Boris Yeltsin and

---

6. For an argument that world politics will feature rivalry between liberal democracies and autocracies, see Robert Kagan, *The Return of History and the End of Dreams* (New York: Alfred A. Knopf, 2008.)

Vladimir Putin. As liberals have lost influence in Russia, relations with the United States have deteriorated, and Russia has attempted to frustrate U.S. policies in the Balkans.

Owen regards China's foreign policy in the 1990s as a prime case of antiliberal counterbalancing. China's military spending increased during the 1990s as China acquired new capabilities that appeared to be directed against the United States. China's institutions remained antiliberal. Although China has abandoned Marxist ideology, the ruling elite remains committed to a single-party dictatorship. Support for political liberalization has waned, partly because China's rulers have seen how reform led to the collapse of the communist system in the Soviet Union. Chinese elites fear transnational liberalism and U.S. military power. The United States' anti-Chinese rhetoric and its commitment to Taiwan's security reinforce these fears.

Owen considers several objections to his arguments. First, he examines the claim that hostile policies—not regime type—account for the relatively poor relations between the United States and China. Owen suggests that the divergent ideologies of the two countries explain why, for example, the May 1999 U.S. bombing of the Chinese embassy in Belgrade was regarded so differently in each country.

Second, Owen responds to the argument that the European Union is balancing against the United States by forming a rapid reaction force. He argues that the force was created not to counter U.S. power, but to intervene in the Balkans at a time when the United States seemed reluctant to do so.

Third, in response to claims that French leaders complain about American "hyperpower" because they are deeply concerned about U.S. primacy, Owen points out that such complaints have been prominent in French foreign policy for years. They reflect a desire for cultural independence and a strong tradition of nationalism, but they have not led to actual policies that would balance U.S. power.

Fourth, Owen notes that some scholars argue that China is not actually balancing against the United States. He asserts that China's current relative weakness and need to cooperate economically with the United States do not mean that China is not an antiliberal revisionist power.

Finally, in response to claims that liberal India is counterbalancing the United States, Owen (writing in 2001) detects the beginnings of a potential strategic partnership between the two countries. Even in 2001, Indian concerns about U.S. hegemony seemed much more muted than those of France.

Owen recommends several steps that the United States should take to preserve its preponderance of power. Most important, it should try to maximize the "number and influence of liberal elites in potential challenger countries." The United States will need to help liberalism preserve its promises. In practice, this means maintaining prosperity in Western Europe and Japan and encouraging liberalism in Russia, even if its prospects seem bleak. In addition, the United States should avoid threatening the vital interests of potential challengers. Doing so could encourage antiliberals in such countries or even turn liberals against the United States. Given China's illiberalism and apparent absence of domestic liberals, however, the United States will need to adopt a realpolitik approach to China and treat it as "any adversary with whom cooperation is possible, but alignment is not." Owen concludes that attempting to preserve U.S. primacy to advance the cause of liberalism and maintain U.S. security is worthwhile, even if the ultimate triumph of global liberalism would remove the rationale for U.S. primacy.

The final four essays in this volume examine whether the rest of the world already has started to balance against the United States. Theories of international relations offer different predictions about whether other countries will engage in balancing. These essays present empirical and analytical assessments of how the world is actually reacting to U.S. power. The first two assert that "soft balancing," in which states seek to undermine and restrain a potential hegemon in ways that fall short of traditional military balancing, against the United States already has begun.

In "Soft Balancing against the United States," Robert Pape argues that other countries' soft balancing is a response to the George W. Bush administration's "profoundly new U.S. national security strategy." Pape argues that the Bush strategy is one of the most aggressively unilateral U.S. postures ever taken. Since 2001 U.S. unilateral actions have included abandoning the Kyoto accords on global warming, rejecting participation in the International Criminal Court, pulling out of the Antiballistic Missile treaty, and, most significantly, invading Iraq in 2003. Pape contends that the United States now asserts that it has the right to attack and conquer sovereign countries that pose no observable threat, and to do so without international support. In his view, these new policies will have momentous long-term implications.

Pape argues that the Bush administration's aggressive unilateralism is changing the international reputation of the United States. Other countries previously believed that the United States had nonaggressive intentions. Even though the United States has been powerful for decades and has fought numerous wars, it was regarded as a benign force in world politics and few states balanced against it. In a unipolar world such as the one that emerged after the end of the Cold War, perceptions of the leading power are crucial in determining how other countries will react. There is little doubt that the United States enjoys a large advantage in power, but there is much more uncertainty about U.S. intentions. Whether other countries will balance against the United States depends on whether U.S. policies are seen as benign or threatening. As Pape puts it, "Because the United States is already so powerful, even a small change in how others perceive the aggressiveness of U.S. intentions can cause other major powers to be concerned about their security." Public opinion polls suggest that the populations of other countries, including many long-time U.S. allies such as Britain, France, Germany, and Italy, have a much less favorable image of the United States. This change is largely the result of the Bush administration's foreign and security policies—particularly its willingness to resort to unilateral preventive war in Iraq and its decision to build a national missile defense system.

Pape sees ample evidence that other countries are starting to balance against the United States. This balance has not taken the traditional forms of military buildups and alliances, because directly confronting the United States remains too risky. Instead, countries are resorting to soft balancing to delay, frustrate, and undermine U.S. policies. States that opposed the U.S. invasion of Iraq acted to ensure that the United States lacked the legitimacy that would have been conferred by United Nations Security Council support. Countries such as Saudi Arabia and Turkey refused to allow the United States to use their territory for U.S. ground forces that were deployed in the Iraq war. China and South Korea have played an expanded diplomatic role in negotiations on North Korea's nuclear status. In the short run, soft balancing can make it harder for the United States to use its extraordinary power. In the longer run, this form of balancing might establish the basis for more forceful opposition to the United States.

Soft balancing against the United States will become more intense if Washington continues to pursue aggressively unilateral security policies. According to Pape, "Unless the United States radically changes its avowed national security strategy, it risks creating a world in which a broad, if loose, coalition of major powers (including most of its nominal allies) is more motivated to constrain the United States than to cooperate with it." To avoid this outcome, the United States should renounce the systematic use of preventive war, as well as other aggressive unilateral military policies; return to its traditional policy governing the use of force; and participate vigorously in multipolar diplomatic initiatives to resolve critical security problems.

T.V. Paul offers another perspective in "Soft Balancing in the Age of U.S. Primacy." Paul argues that second-tier powers such as China, France, Germany, India, and Russia have not resorted to traditional balancing—arms buildups and alliance—against the United States because they believe that they are safe from direct U.S. attacks. They have, however, begun to form diplomatic coalitions against the United States.

Paul begins by refuting the common explanations for the lack of balancing against the United States. He disputes the liberal argument that other liberal states do not balance against the United States because they do not fear a liberal superpower. This argument assumes that states prefer wealth acquisition over military security or status, but this may not be true. Moreover, a liberal superpower might abandon its liberal ideals and become a threat if left unchecked.

Paul notes the realist arguments that other states eventually balance against preponderant powers or that such powers suffer from overstretch and decline as their commitments exceed their capabilities. He faults the realist arguments for indeterminacy and points out that leading powers may be able to stave off decline for decades or even centuries. The United States, in particular, enjoys a significant lead in modern weapons systems that will not be challenged in the near future.

Paul argues that other states are not engaging in traditional balancing against the United States because they do not believe that it threatens their sovereignty and territorial integrity. Until the George W. Bush administration, at least, the United States had not sought to expand its power through direct conquest. It may not be a benign hegemon, but it has not been a major military threat. The United States rarely has needed to conquer territory to achieve its economic goals; it has not supported secessionist movements in Russia and China; and second-tier powers can rely on nuclear deterrence to constrain it.

Since the terrorist attacks of September 11, 2001, the United States has adopted a doctrine of preventive and preemptive war that challenges the norm of territorial integrity. This doctrine, which is exemplified by the invasion of Iraq, has not provoked other states to balance militarily against the United States, but it has prompted them to adopt soft-balancing strategies. Most of this type of balancing has consisted of coalition building and diplomatic bargaining within international institutions. Actions taken by others—particularly China and Russia—in response to U.S. military intervention in the Kosovo conflict of 1999 and the Iraq war of 2003 offer examples of soft balancing against the United States.[7]

The next two essays in this volume take issue with the arguments of Pape and Paul. These essays contend that the rise of soft balancing is greatly exaggerated.

In "Hard Times for Soft Balancing," Stephen Brooks and William Wohlforth point out that the development of the concept of soft balancing is an attempt to stretch balance of power theory to encompass an international system in which traditional counterbalancing among the major powers is absent. They reject the claim that soft balancing is a new manifestation of the old pattern of balance of power politics. In their view, "balancing is action taken to check a potential hegemon. It reflects systemic incentives to rebalance power, rather than the specifics of a given issue. . . . The key point is that balance of power theory is not relevant to state behavior unrelated to systemic concentrations of power, which is arguably much of what goes on in international politics."

Having defined balancing behavior, Brooks and Wohlforth argue that many attempts to complicate U.S. foreign policy should not be regarded as balancing, soft or otherwise. At least four alternative explanations account for "unipolar politics as usual." First, states may attempt to hinder U.S. foreign policy to advance their economic interests. Second, regional security concerns and the desire for regional policy coordination may drive states to reduce U.S. freedom of action. Third, states may disagree with U.S. policy and oppose it because they think it is misguided, not because they think it threatens their security or because they think that resistance will limit U.S. power in the long run. Fourth, domestic factors may be the source of policies that complicate U.S. foreign policy: "Opposing the United States may be strongly compatible with long-standing historical, political, or cultural understandings—either for the nation as a whole or for individual political parties—that predate any recent shift in U.S. foreign policy, or indeed the rise of unipolarity."

Brooks and Wohlforth contend that their four alternative explanations account for what other analysts claim is soft balancing. A detailed comparison of soft balancing and the four alternative explanations in the main cases highlighted by proponents of the concept—Russia's strategic partnerships with China and India, Russian assistance to Iran's nuclear program, the European Union's efforts to enhance its defense capability, and opposition to the U.S.-led

---

7. For further arguments on this point, see the letters of Robert J. Art, Stephen G. Brooks and William C. Wohlforth, and Keir A. Lieber and Gerard Alexander, in "Correspondence: Striking a Balance," *International Security*, Vol. 30, No. 3 (Winter 2005/06), pp. 177–196.

Iraq war in 2003—reveals no empirical support for the soft-balancing explanation. The lack of evidence for the relevance of balancing dynamics in contemporary great-power relations indicates that further investments in adapting balance of power theory to today's unipolar system will not yield analytical dividends.

Brooks and Wohlforth conclude that soft balance is not taking place. States are engaging in diplomacy and bargaining; they are not responding to a perceived U.S. threat to their security in a way that balance of power theory would predict. Attempts to constrain the United States do not vindicate balance of power theory. Nevertheless, the United States needs to heed the views of other major powers. It cannot deal with issues such the environment, weapons of mass destruction, disease, migration, and the global economy on its own. In many cases, the United States will need to act with restraint, but this imperative for restraint reflects U.S. self-interest, not a response to expected counterbalancing.

Keir Lieber and Gerard Alexander offer additional reasons for skepticism about whether soft balancing is taking place. In "Waiting for Balancing: Why the World Is Not Pushing Back," they note that many observers predicted a rise in balancing against the United States after the collapse of the Soviet Union and that some claim that soft balancing emerged after the U.S. invasion of Iraq in 2003. These claims are rooted in traditional theories of international politics.

Lieber and Alexander find little credible evidence that major powers are engaging in either hard or soft balancing against the United States. Other states have the economic capability to engage in military balancing, but they have not increased their military spending in recent years. They also have not formed new alliances against the United States. According to Lieber and Alexander, the absence of hard balancing is explained by the lack of underlying motivation to compete strategically with the United States under current conditions.

Lieber and Alexander evaluate claims that soft balancing is taking place against the United States. They find that specific predictions of soft balancing are not supported by the evidence. Other states are not seeking to entangle the United States in a web of international institutions. No efforts are being made to exclude it from regional economic cooperation. Notwithstanding Turkey's decision to deny U.S. forces transit rights for the 2003 invasion of Iraq, the overall status of U.S. overseas basing rights seems to look brighter than it did a few years ago. Finally, other states are not aligning with rogue states to oppose the United States.

Lieber and Alexander also argue that the soft balancing argument is flawed conceptually and amounts to much ado about nothing. The concept is difficult to define or operationalize, and the behavior seems identical to traditional diplomatic friction. Lieber and Alexander conclude that balancing against the United States is not occurring because contemporary U.S. grand strategy, despite widespread criticism, poses a threat to only a very limited number of regimes and terrorist groups. Most countries either share U.S. strategic interests in the war on terrorism or do not have a direct stake in the conflict. As such, balancing behavior is likely only among a narrowly circumscribed list of states and actors being targeted by the United States.

The essays in this volume do not exhaust the debate over U.S. primacy and its implications for international politics. For many years—perhaps decades—the question of U.S. power will dominate the headlines and the pages of scholarly journals. We hope that these essays frame the important issues and will serve as a basis for further discussion and analysis. The suggested readings at the end of the volume provide a brief list of additional works for those who want to explore these topics further.

Part I:
The Sources and Prospects of American Primacy

The Stability of a Unipolar World

William C. Wohlforth

$\mathbf{T}$he collapse of the Soviet Union produced the greatest change in world power relationships since World War II. With Moscow's headlong fall from superpower status, the bipolar structure that had shaped the security policies of the major powers for nearly half a century vanished, and the United States emerged as the sole surviving superpower. Commentators were quick to recognize that a new "unipolar moment" of unprecedented U.S. power had arrived.[1] In 1992 the Pentagon drafted a new grand strategy designed to preserve unipolarity by preventing the emergence of a global rival.[2] But the draft plan soon ran into controversy, as commentators at home and abroad argued that any effort to preserve unipolarity was quixotic and dangerous.[3] Officials quickly backed away from the idea and now eschew the language of primacy or predominance, speaking instead of the United States as a "leader" or the "indispensable nation."[4]

The rise and sudden demise of an official strategy for preserving primacy lends credence to the widespread belief that unipolarity is dangerous and unstable. While scholars frequently discuss unipolarity, their focus is always on its demise. For neorealists, unipolarity is the least stable of all structures because any great concentration of power threatens other states and causes them to take action to restore a balance.[5] Other scholars grant that a large

William C. Wohlforth is Assistant Professor of International Relations in the Edmund A. Walsh School of Foreign Service at Georgetown University.

I am indebted to Stephen G. Brooks, Charles A. Kupchan, Joseph Lepgold, Robert Lieber, and Kathleen R. McNamara, who read and commented on drafts of this article.

1. Charles Krauthammer, "The Unipolar Moment," *Foreign Affairs*, Vol. 70, No. 1 (Winter 1990/1991), pp. 23–33.
2. Patrick Tyler, "The Lone Superpower Plan: Ammunition for Critics," *New York Times*, March 10, 1992, p. A12.
3. For the most thorough and theoretically grounded criticism of this strategy, see Christopher Layne, "The Unipolar Illusion: Why New Great Powers Will Arise," *International Security*, Vol. 17, No. 4 (Spring 1993), pp. 5–51; and Layne, "From Preponderance to Offshore Balancing: America's Future Grand Strategy," *International Security*, Vol. 22, No. 1 (Summer 1997), pp. 86–124.
4. The phrase—commonly attributed to Secretary of State Madeleine Albright—is also a favorite of President Bill Clinton's. For example, see the account of his speech announcing the expansion of the North Atlantic Treaty Organization in Alison Mitchell, "Clinton Urges NATO Expansion in 1999," *New York Times*, October 23, 1996, p. A20.
5. Kenneth N. Waltz, "Evaluating Theories," *American Political Science Review*, Vol. 91, No. 4 (December 1997), pp. 915–916; Layne, "Unipolar Illusion"; and Michael Mastanduno, "Preserving

International Security, Vol. 24, No. 1 (Summer 1999), pp. 5–711
© 1999 by the President and Fellows of Harvard College and the Massachusetts Institute of Technology.

concentration of power works for peace, but they doubt that U.S. preeminence can endure.[6] Underlying both views is the belief that U.S. preponderance is fragile and easily negated by the actions of other states. As a result, most analysts argue that unipolarity is an "illusion," a "moment" that "will not last long," or is already "giving way to multipolarity."[7] Indeed, some scholars question whether the system is unipolar at all, arguing instead that it is, in Samuel Huntington's phrase, "uni-multipolar."[8]

Although they disagree vigorously on virtually every other aspect of post–Cold War world politics, scholars of international relations increasingly share this conventional wisdom about unipolarity. Whether they think that the current structure is on the verge of shifting away from unipolarity or that it has already done so, scholars believe that it is prone to conflict as other states seek to create a counterpoise to the overweening power of the leading state. The assumption that unipolarity is unstable has framed the wide-ranging debate over the nature of post–Cold War world politics. Since 1991 one of the central questions in dispute has been how to explain continued cooperation and the absence of old-style balance-of-power politics despite major shifts in the distribution of power.[9]

---

the Unipolar Moment: Realist Theories and U.S. Grand Strategy after the Cold War," *International Security*, Vol. 21, No. 4 (Spring 1997), pp. 44–98. Although I differ with Waltz on the stability of unipolarity, the title of this article and much of its contents reflect intellectual debts to his work on system structure and stability. See Waltz, "The Stability of a Bipolar World," *Daedalus*, Vol. 93, No. 3 (Summer 1964), pp. 881–901.

6. See Charles A. Kupchan, "After Pax Americana: Benign Power, Regional Integration, and the Sources of Stable Multipolarity," *International Security*, Vol. 23, No. 3 (Fall 1998), pp. 40–79. Samuel P. Huntington maintained this position in Huntington, "Why International Primacy Matters," *International Security*, Vol. 17, No. 4 (Spring 1993), pp. 63–83, but he has since abandoned it. A more bullish assessment, although still more pessimistic than the analysis here, is Douglas Lemke, "Continuity of History: Power Transition Theory and the End of the Cold War," *Journal of Peace Research*, Vol. 34, No. 1 (February 1996), pp. 203–236.

7. As Glenn H. Snyder puts it, the international system "appears to be unipolar, though incipiently multipolar." Snyder, *Alliance Politics* (Ithaca, N.Y.: Cornell University Press, 1997), p. 18. The quoted phrases in this sentence appear in Charles A. Kupchan, "Rethinking Europe," *National Interest*, No. 56 (Summer 1999); Kupchan, "After Pax Americana," p. 41; Layne, "Unipolar Illusion"; and Waltz, "Evaluating Theories," p. 914. Although Charles Krauthammer coined the term "unipolar moment" in his article under that title, he argued that unipolarity had the potential to last a generation.

8. Samuel P. Huntington, "The Lonely Superpower," *Foreign Affairs*, Vol. 78, No. 2 (March/April 1999), p. 36. For similar views of the post–Cold War structure, see Aaron L. Friedberg, "Ripe for Rivalry: Prospects for Peace in a Multipolar Asia," *International Security*, Vol. 18, No. 3 (Winter 1993/94), pp. 5–33; and Josef Joffe, "'Bismarck' or 'Britain'? Toward an American Grand Strategy after Bipolarity," *International Security*, Vol. 19, No. 4 (Spring 1995), pp. 94–117.

9. The assumption that realism predicts instability after the Cold War pervades the scholarly debate. See, for example, Sean M. Lynn-Jones and Steven E. Miller, eds., *The Cold War and After: Prospects for Peace—An International Security Reader* (Cambridge, Mass.: MIT Press, 1993); and

In this article, I advance three propositions that undermine the emerging conventional wisdom that the distribution of power is unstable and conflict prone. First, the system is unambiguously unipolar. The United States enjoys a much larger margin of superiority over the next most powerful state or, indeed, all other great powers combined than any leading state in the last two centuries. Moreover, the United States is the first leading state in modern international history with decisive preponderance in *all* the underlying components of power: economic, military, technological, and geopolitical.[10] To describe this unprecedented quantitative and qualitative concentration of power as an evanescent "moment" is profoundly mistaken.

Second, the current unipolarity is prone to peace. The raw power advantage of the United States means that an important source of conflict in previous systems is absent: hegemonic rivalry over leadership of the international system. No other major power is in a position to follow any policy that depends for its success on prevailing against the United States in a war or an extended rivalry. None is likely to take any step that might invite the focused enmity of the United States. At the same time, unipolarity minimizes security competition among the other great powers. As the system leader, the United States has

David A. Baldwin, ed., *Neorealism and Neoliberalism: The Contemporary Debate* (New York: Columbia University Press, 1993). For more varied perspectives on realism and unipolarity, see Ethan B. Kapstein and Michael Mastanduno, eds., *Unipolar Politics: Realism and State Strategies after the Cold War* (New York: Columbia University Press, 1999). Explanations for stability despite the balance of power fall roughly into three categories: (1) liberal arguments, including democratization, economic interdependence, and international institutions. For examples, see Bruce M. Russett, *Grasping the Democratic Peace* (Princeton, N.J.: Princeton University Press, 1993); John R. Oneal and Bruce M. Russett, "The Classical Liberals Were Right: Democracy, Interdependence, and Conflict, 1950–1985," *International Studies Quarterly*, Vol. 41, No. 2 (June 1997), pp. 267–294; G. John Ikenberry, "Institutions, Strategic Restraint, and the Persistence of the American Postwar Order," *International Security*, Vol. 23, No. 3 (Winter 1998/99), pp. 43–78. (2) Cultural and ideational arguments that highlight social learning. See John Mueller, *Retreat from Doomsday: The Obsolescence of Major War* (Rochester, N.Y.: University of Rochester Press, 1989); and Alexander Wendt, *Social Theory of International Politics* (Cambridge: Cambridge University Press, 1999), chap. 6. (3) Arguments that highlight systemic and material factors other than the balance of power, such as globalization, the offense-defense balance, or nuclear weapons. See Stephen G. Brooks, "The Globalization of Production and the Changing Benefits of Conquest," *Journal of Conflict Resolution*, Vol. 43, No. 5 (October 1999); and Stephen Van Evera, "Primed for Peace: Europe after the Cold War," in Jones and Miller, *Cold War and After*.

10. I focus on material elements of power mainly because current scholarly debates place a premium on making clear distinctions between ideas and material forces. See Wendt, *Social Theory of International Politics*; and Jeffrey Legro and Andrew Moravscik, "Is Anybody Still a Realist?" *International Security*, Vol. 24, No. 2 (Fall 1999). Many nonmaterial elements of power also favor the United States and strengthen the argument for unipolarity's stability. On "soft power," see Joseph S. Nye, Jr., *Bound to Lead: The Changing Nature of American Power* (New York: Basic Books, 1990).

the means and motive to maintain key security institutions in order to ease local security conflicts and limit expensive competition among the other major powers. For their part, the second-tier states face incentives to bandwagon with the unipolar power as long as the expected costs of balancing remain prohibitive.

Third, the current unipolarity is not only peaceful but durable.[11] It is already a decade old, and if Washington plays its cards right, it may last as long as bipolarity. For many decades, no state is likely to be in a position to take on the United States in any of the underlying elements of power. And, as an offshore power separated by two oceans from all other major states, the United States can retain its advantages without risking a counterbalance. The current candidates for polar status (Japan, China, Germany, and Russia) are not so lucky. Efforts on their part to increase their power or ally with other dissatisfied states are likely to spark local counterbalances well before they can create a global equipoise to U.S. power.

The scholarly conventional wisdom holds that unipolarity is dynamically unstable and that any slight overstep by Washington will spark a dangerous backlash.[12] I find the opposite to be true: unipolarity is durable and peaceful, and the chief threat is U.S. failure to do enough.[13] Possessing an undisputed preponderance of power, the United States is freer than most states to disregard the international system and its incentives. But because the system is built around U.S. power, it creates demands for American engagement. The more efficiently Washington responds to these incentives and provides order, the more long-lived and peaceful the system. To be sure, policy choices are likely to affect the differential growth of power only at the margins. But given that

---

11. I define "stability" as peacefulness and durability. Kenneth Waltz first conflated these two meanings of stability in "The Stability of a Bipolar World." He later eliminated the ambiguity by defining stability exclusively as durability in *Theory of International Politics* (Reading, Mass.: Addison-Wesley, 1979). I avoid ambiguity by treating peacefulness and durability separately. Durability subsumes another common understanding of stability: the idea of a self-reinforcing equilibrium. To say that an international system is durable implies that it can experience significant shifts in power relations without undergoing fundamental change. See Robert Jervis, *Systems Effects: Complexity in Political and Social Life* (Princeton, N.J.: Princeton University Press, 1997), chap. 3.

12. Because overwhelming preponderance favors both peace and durability, stability is less sensitive to how the United States defines its interests than most scholars assume. In contrast, many realists hold that stability is strictly contingent upon Washington's nonthreatening or status quo stance in world affairs. See Mastanduno, "Preserving the Unipolar Moment." Similarly, Kupchan, "After Pax Americana," argues that the United States' "benign" character explains stability.

13. This was Krauthammer's original argument in "The Unipolar Moment." For a comprehensive review of the debate that reflects the standard scholarly skepticism toward the stability of unipolarity, see Barry R. Posen and Andrew L. Ross, "Competing Visions for U.S. Grand Strategy," *International Security*, Vol. 21, No. 2 (Winter 1996/97), pp. 5–54.

unipolarity is safer and cheaper than bipolarity or multipolarity, it pays to invest in its prolongation. In short, the intellectual thrust (if not the details) of the Pentagon's 1992 draft defense guidance plan was right.

I develop these propositions in three sections that establish my central argument: the current system is unipolar; the current unipolarity is peaceful; and it is durable. I then conclude the analysis by discussing its implications for scholarly debates on the stability of the post–Cold War order and U.S. grand strategy.

Lonely at the Top: The System Is Unipolar

Unipolarity is a structure in which one state's capabilities are too great to be counterbalanced.[14] Once capabilities are so concentrated, a structure arises that is fundamentally distinct from either multipolarity (a structure comprising three or more especially powerful states) or bipolarity (a structure produced when two states are substantially more powerful than all others). At the same time, capabilities are not so concentrated as to produce a global empire. Unipolarity should not be confused with a multi- or bipolar system containing one especially strong polar state or with an imperial system containing only one major power.[15]

---

14. This definition flows from the logic of neorealist balance-of-power theory, but it is consistent with classical balance-of-power thinking. See Layne, "Unipolar Illusion," p. 130 n. 2; Snyder, *Alliance Politics*, chap. 1; Morton Kaplan, *System and Process in International Politics* (New York: Wiley, 1957), pp. 22–36; Harrison Wagner, "What Was Bipolarity?" *International Organization*, Vol. 47, No. 1 (Winter 1993), pp. 77–106; and Emerson M.S. Niou, Peter C. Ordeshook, and Gregory F. Rose, *The Balance of Power: Stability in International Systems* (New York: Cambridge University Press, 1989), p. 76.

15. Germany was clearly the strongest state in Europe in 1910, and the United States was generally thought to be the strongest state in the world in 1960, but neither system was unipolar. One of Waltz's most widely accepted insights was that the world was bipolar in the Cold War even though the two poles shared it with other major powers such as France, Britain, West Germany, Japan, and China. In the same vein, a system can be unipolar, with unique properties owing to the extreme concentration of capabilities in one state, and yet also contain other substantial powers. Cf. Huntington, "Lonely Superpower," who defines unipolarity as a system with only one great power. Throughout this article, I hew as closely as possible to the definitions of central terms in Waltz, *Theory of International Politics*, as they have gained the widest currency. Although the distinction between bipolarity and multipolarity is one of the most basic in international relations theory, scholars do debate whether bipolar structures are more durable or peaceful than multipolar ones. For a concise discussion, see Jack S. Levy, "The Causes of War and the Conditions of Peace," *Annual Review of Political Science*, Vol. 1 (1998), pp. 139–165. There are good reasons for analyzing tripolarity as a distinct structure. See Randall L. Schweller, *Deadly Imbalances: Tripolarity and Hitler's Strategy of World Conquest* (New York: Columbia University Press, 1998).

Is the current structure unipolar? The crucial first step in answering this question is to compare the current distribution of power with its structural predecessors. The more the current concentration of power in the United States differs from past distributions, the less we should expect post–Cold War world politics to resemble that of earlier epochs. I select two cases that allow me to compare concentrations of power in both multipolar and bipolar settings: the Pax Britannica and the Cold War.[16] Within these two cases, I highlight two specific periods—1860–70 and 1945–55—because they reflect the greatest concentrations of power in the system leader, and so have the greatest potential to weaken the case for the extraordinary nature of the current unipolarity. I also include a second Cold War period in the mid-1980s to capture the distribution of power just before the dramatic changes of the 1990s.

QUANTITATIVE COMPARISON

To qualify as polar powers, states must score well on *all* the components of power: size of population and territory; resource endowment; economic capabilities; military strength; and "competence," according to Kenneth Waltz.[17] Two states measured up in 1990. One is gone. No new pole has appeared: $2 - 1 = 1$. The system is unipolar.

The reality, however, is much more dramatic than this arithmetic implies. After all, the two superpowers were hardly equal. Writing in the late 1970s, Waltz himself questioned the Soviet Union's ability to keep up with the United States.[18] The last time the scholarly community debated the relative power of the United States was the second half of the 1980s, when the United States was widely viewed as following Great Britain down the path of relative decline. Responding to that intellectual climate, several scholars undertook quantitative analyses of the U.S. position. In 1985 Bruce Russett compared the U.S. position of the early 1980s with that of the British Empire in the mid-nineteenth century. His conclusion: "The United States retains on all indicators a degree of dominance reached by the United Kingdom at no point" in the nineteenth century.[19]

---

16. Another useful comparison pursued by Layne, "Unipolar Illusion," is the Hapsburg ascendancy in sixteenth- and seventeenth-century Europe. I omit it for space reasons (the comparison to pre-Westphalian international politics is especially demanding) and because of limited data.
17. Waltz, *Theory of International Politics*, p. 131.
18. Writing of the United States in the 1960s, Waltz notes, "Never in modern history has a great power enjoyed so wide an economic and technological lead over the only other great power in the race." Ibid., p. 201. Throughout he is more concerned about the United States' *surplus* power and its associated temptations than about the rising power of any other states.
19. Bruce M. Russett, "The Mysterious Case of Vanishing Hegemony. Or, Is Mark Twain Really Dead?" *International Organization*, Vol. 39, No. 2 (Spring 1985), p. 211. See also Samuel P. Hunt-

In 1990 both Joseph Nye and Henry Nau published detailed studies of the U.S. position in world politics and the international political economy. Their conclusions mirrored Russett's: 1980s' America was a uniquely powerful hegemonic actor with a much more complete portfolio of capabilities than Britain ever had.[20]

In the years since those assessments were published, the United States' main geopolitical rival has collapsed into a regional power whose main threat to the international system is its own further disintegration, and its main economic rival has undergone a decade-long slump. The United States has maintained its military supremacy; added to its share of world product, manufactures, and high-technology production; increased its lead in productivity; and regained or strengthened its lead in many strategic industries.[21] Although recent events do remind us that the fortunes of states can change quickly in world politics even without war, the brute fact of the matter is that U.S. preeminence is unprecedented.

Table 1 shows how U.S. relative power in the late 1990s compares with that of Britain near its peak, as well as the United States itself during the Cold War. The United States' economic dominance is surpassed only by its own position at the dawn of the Cold War—when every other major power's economy was either exhausted or physically destroyed by the recent world war—and its military superiority dwarfs that of any leading state in modern international history. Even the Correlates of War (COW) composite index—which favors states with especially large populations and industrial economies—shows an improvement in the United States' relative position since the mid-1980s.[22]

ington, "The U.S.: Decline or Renewal?" *Foreign Affairs*, Vol. 67, No. 2 (Winter 1988/1989), pp. 76–96; and Susan Strange, "The Persistent Myth of Lost Hegemony," *International Organization*, Vol. 41, No. 4 (Autumn 1987), pp. 551–574.

20. Nye, *Bound to Lead*; and Henry R. Nau, *The Myth of America's Decline: Leading the World Economy into the 1990s* (New York: Oxford University Press, 1990).

21. By the 1980s, U.S. productivity growth had fallen to 1 percent a year. Since 1992 the rate of increase has been as high as 3 percent a year. See Nicholas Valéry, "Innovation in Industry," *Economist*, February 20, 1999, p. 27. For comparisons that show the increased productivity gap in favor of the United States among Organization for Economic Cooperation and Development (OECD) countries, see European Bank for Reconstruction and Development, *Transition Report 1997* (London: EBRD, 1997).

22. The COW index combines the following indicators with equal weights: total population, urban population, energy consumption, iron and steel production, military expenditures, and military personnel. As noted in Table 1, 1996 data were compiled by the author from different sources; COW methodology may lead to different results. I include the COW measure not because I think it is a good one but because it has a long history in the field. Quantitative scholars are increasingly critical of all such composite indexes. Gross domestic product (GDP) is becoming the favored indicator, a trend started by A.F.K. Organski in *World Politics*, 2d ed. (New York: Knopf, 1965): pp. 199–200, 211–215, and furthered by Organski and Jacek Kugler in *The War Ledger* (Chicago:

Table 1. Comparing Hegemonies.

a. Gross Domestic Product as Percentage of "Hegemon"

Year	United States	Britain	Russia	Japan	Austria	Germany	France	China
1870	108	100	90	n.a.	29	46	75	n.a.
1950	100	24	35	11	n.a.	15	15	n.a.
1985	100	17	39	38	n.a.	21	18	46
1997(PPP)	100	15	9	38	n.a.	22	16	53
1997 (exchange rate)	100	16	5	50	n.a.	25	17	10

b. Military Expenditures as Percentage of "Hegemon"

Year	United States	Britain	Russia	Japan	Austria	Germany	France	China
1872	68	100	120	n.a.	44	65	113	n.a.
1950	100	16	107	n.a.	n.a.	n.a.	10	n.a.
1985	100	10	109	5	n.a.	8	8	10
1996	100	13	26	17	n.a.	14	17	13

c. Power Capabilities (COW) as Percentage of "Hegemon"

Year	United States	Britain	Russia	Japan	Austria	Germany	France	China
1872	50	100	50	n.a.	27	50	60	n.a.
1950	100	37	103	n.a.	n.a.	3	21	n.a.
1985	100	22	167	56	n.a.	28	22	156
1996	100	14	43	36	n.a.	21	18	118

SOURCES: GDP figures, 1870–1985, from Angus Maddison, *Monitoring the World Economy, 1820–1992* (Paris: Organization for Economic Cooperation and Development, 1995). GDP figures, 1997 (PPP [purchasing power parity]), from Central Intelligence Agency (CIA) *World Factbook, 1998* (http://www.odci.gov/cia/publications/factbook/index.html). GDP figures, 1997 (exchange rate), from Economist Intelligence Unit, *World Outlook, 1998* (London: EIU, 1998). Military expenditures and COW, 1872–1985, from J. David Singer (University of Michigan) and Melvin Small (Wayne State University), "National Material Capabilities Data, 1816–1985" (computer file) (Ann Arbor, Mich.: Inter-University Consortium for Political and Social Research). Military Expenditures, 1997: International Institute of Strategic Studies, *The Military Balance 1997/98* (London: IISS, 1998). COW, 1996, compiled from IISS, *Military Balance 1997/98;* American Iron and Steel Institute, *Annual Statistical Report, 1997* (Washington, D.C.: AISI, 1998); World Bank, *World Development Indicators, 1998* (Washington, D.C.: International Bank for Reconstruction and Development, 1998); and United Nations, *UN Demographic Yearbook, 1996* (New York: United Nations, 1998).

NOTES: n.a.: Data not available or country not classed as a major power for given year. Germany = Federal Republic of Germany and Russia = Soviet Union in 1950 and 1985. a. Maddison's estimates are based on states' modern territories, tending to understate Austrian GDP in 1870. I added Maddison's estimates for Austria, Hungary, and Czechoslovakia. (In Russia's case, I added Finland; no data were available for Poland in 1870.) For comparison, see Paul Bairoch, "Europe's Gross National Product, 1800–1975," *Journal of Economic History,* Vol. 5, No. 2 (Fall 1976), pp. 273–340, whose estimates for 1860 give Austria 62 percent of Britain's GNP, and Russia 92 percent. According to the CIA, the PPP estimate for 1997 may overstate the size of China's economy by 25 percent. b. China's and Russia's military expenditures for 1996 are estimated using PPP ratios. c. 1996 index compiled by author using sources different from Singer and Small; it is representative of what such a composite index would yield but is not directly comparable to other COW figures.

Figure 1 presents the three measures of capabilities as a distribution among the great powers. It highlights the contrast between the extraordinary concentration of capabilities in the United States in the 1990s and the bipolar and multipolar distributions of the Cold War and the Pax Britannica. Never in modern international history has the leading state been so dominant economically and militarily.

In short, the standard measures that political scientists traditionally use as surrogates for capabilities suggest that the current system is unipolar.[23] But it takes only a glance at such measures to see that each is flawed in different ways. Economic output misses the salience for the balance of power of militarized states such as Prussia, pre–World War II Japan, Nazi Germany, or the Soviet Union, and, in any case, is very hard to measure for some states and in some periods. Military expenditures might conceal gross inefficiencies and involve similar measurement problems. Composite indexes capture the conventional wisdom that states must score well on many underlying elements to qualify as great powers. But any composite index that seems to capture the sources of national power in one period tends to produce patently absurd results for others.

Disaggregating the COW index reveals that Britain's high score in 1870 is the result of its early industrialization (high levels of iron production and coal consumption), the Soviet Union's strong showing in the late Cold War is driven by its massive military and heavy-industrial economy, and China's numbers are inflated by its huge population, numerous armed forces, and giant steel industry.[24] A roughly comparable index (Table 2) shows a more complicated

University of Chicago Press, 1980). Given its weighting of energy consumption, steel production, and military personnel, for example, the COW index had the Soviet Union surpassing U.S. power in 1971. Indeed, despite the fact that the Soviet Union produced, at best, one-third of U.S. GDP in the 1980s, it decisively surpassed the United States on *every* composite power indicator. See John R. Oneal, "Measuring the Material Base of the Contemporary East-West Balance of Power," *International Interactions,* Vol. 15, No. 2 (Summer 1989), pp. 177–196.

23. The only major indicator of hegemonic status in which the United States has continued to decline is net foreign indebtedness, which surpassed $1 trillion in 1996. For a strong argument on the importance of this indicator in governing the international political economy, see Robert Gilpin, *The Political Economy of International Relations* (Princeton, N.J.: Princeton University Press, 1987). There are other power indexes—many of which are linked to highly specific theories—that show continued U.S. decline. See George Modelski and William R. Thompson, *Leading Sectors and World Powers: The Coevolution of Global Economics and Politics* (Columbia: University of South Carolina Press, 1996); and Karen A. Rasler and William R. Thompson, *Great Powers and Global Struggle, 1490–1990* (Lexington: University Press of Kentucky, 1994). By most other measures of naval power or industrial competitiveness, however, the U.S. position has improved in the 1990s.

24. According to the COW index, Britain's relative power peaked in 1860, with a 36 percent share. In that year, Britain consumed 50 percent more energy and produced 35 percent more iron than all the other great powers (including the United States) combined; its urban population was twice

Figure 1.   Comparing Concentrations of Power: Distribution (percentage) of GDP, Military Outlays, and COW Index among the Major Powers: 1870–72, 1950, 1985, and 1996–97.

a. Pax Britannica, 1870–72

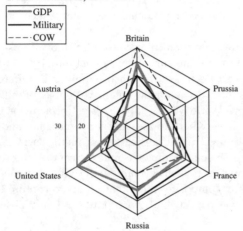

Country	GDP	Military	COW
Britain	24	20	30
Prussia	11	13	15
France	18	22	18
Russia	21	24	15
United States	24	13	15
Austria	6	9	8

b. Early Bipolarity, 1950

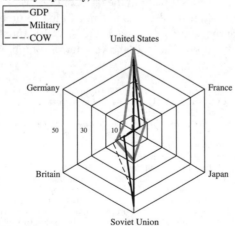

Country	GDP	Military	COW
United States	50	43	38
France	8	4	8
Japan	5	0	0
Soviet Union	18	46	39
Britain	12	7	14
Germany	7	0	1

c. Late Bipolarity, 1985

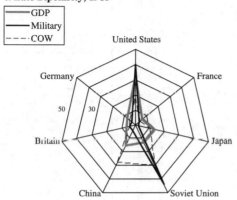

Country	GDP	Military	COW
United States	33	40	18
France	6	3	4
Japan	13	2	10
Soviet Union	13	44	30
China	15	4	28
Britain	6	4	4
Germany	7	3	5

d. Unipolarity, 1996–97

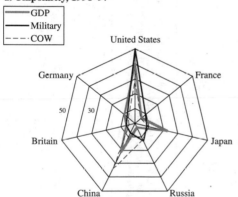

Country	GDP	Military	COW
United States	40	50	28
France	6	9	5
Japan	22	8	10
Russia	3	13	12
China	21	7	33
Britain	6	6	4
Germany	9	7	6

SOURCES: Compiled from data in Table 1.

NOTE: GDP for 1997 is based on PPP exchange rates.

Table 2. Disaggregated COW-Style Indicators for the Major Powers, 1995–97.

	Population (1996, percentage)	Per Capita GDP (1997, PPP)	Manufacturing Production (1995, percentage)	Commercial Energy Use (1996, percentage)	Military Expenditures (1996, percentage)	Military Personnel (1996, percentage)
United States	13	30.2	37	41	52	18
China	62	3.5	8	21	7	36
Japan	6	24.5	27	10	6	3
Germany	4	20.8	14	7	7	5
Russia	7	4.7	n.a.	12	13	30
Britain	3	21.2	6	5	6	3
France	3	22.7	7	5	9	5

SOURCES: Central Intelligence Agency, *World Factbook, 1998* (http://www.odci.gov/cia/publications/factbook/index.html); International Institute of Strategic Studies, *The Military Balance 1997/98* (London: IISS, 1998); World Bank, *World Development Indicators, 1999* (Washington, D.C.: International Bank for Reconstruction and Development, 1999); and National Science Foundation, *Science and Technology Indicators, 1998* (http://www.nsf.gov/sbe/srs/seind98/start.html).

NOTE: n.a.: Data not available.

picture than that conveyed by simple comparisons of gross economic output or military expenditures. But even this comparison reveals that unlike Britain at its peak, the United States currently leads in every key indicator of power except population and military personnel.[25]

The specific problem with the COW index is its implicit assumption that the wellsprings of national power have not changed since the dawn of the industrial age. Updating such an index to take account of the post–industrial revolution in political economy and military affairs would inevitably be a subjective procedure. By most such "information-age" measures, however, the United States possesses decisive advantages (Table 3). The United States not only has the largest high-technology economy in the world by far, it also has the greatest concentration in high-technology manufacturing among the major powers.[26] Total U.S. expenditures on research and development (R&D) nearly equal the combined total of the rest of the Group of Seven richest countries (and the G-7 accounts for 90 percent of world spending on R&D). Numerous studies of U.S. technological leadership confirm the country's dominant position in all the key "leading sectors" that are most likely to dominate the world economy into the twenty-first century.[27]

The U.S. combination of quantitative and qualitative material advantages is unprecedented, and it translates into a unique geopolitical position. Thanks to a decades-old policy of harnessing technology to the generation of military power, the U.S. comparative advantage in this area mirrors Britain's naval

---

as large as that of the next most urban power (France). This is the indicator Layne, "Unipolar Illusion," uses to make his case for Britain's status as a unipolar power. For more on measuring relative power, polarity, and concentration of capabilities over time, see J. David Singer and Paul F. Diehl, eds., *Measuring the Correlates of War* (Ann Arbor: University of Michigan Press, 1990).

25. Table 2 substitutes per capita gross domestic product for urban population (which was supposed to capture modernization) and manufacturing production for steel production (which was supposed to capture industrial power).

26. OECD, *Science, Technology, and Industry: Scoreboard of Indicators 1997* (Paris: OECD, 1997). By one estimate, the United States accounted for 35.8 percent of total world spending on technology in 1997. Japan accounted for 17.6 percent, Germany 6.6 percent, Britain 5.7 percent, France 5.1 percent, and China 1.6 percent. Mark Landler, "When the Dragon Awakes . . . and Finds That It's Not 1999 Anymore," *New York Times*, May 11, 1999, p. C1.

27. These studies do forecast *future* challenges—as they have since the 1970s. The incentives of nearly all data-gathering agencies are to emphasize U.S. vulnerability, yet as good social scientists, the authors of these studies acknowledge the country's decisive current advantages. See, for example, U.S. Department of Commerce, Office of Technology Policy, *The New Innovators: Global Patenting Trends in Five Sectors* (Washington, D.C.: OTP, 1998). Similarly, according to Valéry, "Innovation in Industry," p. 27, "By 1998, the Council on Competitiveness, an industry think tank in Washington set up to fathom the reasons for the country's decline, concluded that America had not only regained its former strengths, but was now far ahead technologically in the five most crucial sectors of its economy."

preeminence in the nineteenth century. At the same time, Washington's current brute share of great power capabilities—its aggregate potential compared with that of the next largest power or all other great powers combined—dwarfs Britain's share in its day. The United States is the only state with global power projection capabilities; it is probably capable, if challenged, of producing defensive land-power dominance in the key theaters; it retains the world's only truly blue-water navy; it dominates the air; it has retained a nuclear posture that may give it first-strike advantages against other nuclear powers; and it has continued to nurture decades-old investments in military logistics and command, control, communications, and intelligence. By devoting only 3 percent of its gross domestic product (GDP) to defense, it outspends all other great powers combined—and most of those great powers are its close allies. Its defense R&D expenditures are probably greater than those of the rest of the world combined (Table 3). None of the major powers is balancing; most have scaled back military expenditures faster than the United States has. One reason may be that democracy and globalization have changed the nature of world politics. Another possibility, however, is that any effort to compete directly with the United States is futile, so no one tries.

QUALITATIVE COMPARISON

Bringing historical detail to bear on the comparison of today's distribution of power to past systems only strengthens the initial conclusions that emerge from quantitative comparisons. Two major concentrations of power over the last two centuries show up on different quantitative measures of capabilities: the COW measure picks Britain in 1860–70 as an especially powerful actor, and the GDP measure singles out the post–World War II United States. These indicators miss two crucial factors that only historical research can reveal: the clarity of the balance as determined by the events that help decisionmakers define and measure power, and the comprehensiveness of the leader's overall power advantage in each period.[28] Together these factors help to produce a U.S. preponderance that is far less ambiguous, and therefore less subject to challenge, than that of previous leading states.

The end of the Cold War and the collapse of the Soviet Union were much more effective tests of material power relationships than any of the systemic

---

28. This is based on the neoclassical realist argument that power is important to decisionmakers but very hard to measure. See, for a general discussion, Gideon Rose, "Neoclassical Realism and Theories of Foreign Policy," *World Politics*, Vol. 51, No. 1 (October 1998), pp. 144–172.

Table 3. Information-Age Indicators for the Major Powers, 1995–97.

	High-Technology Manufacturing (1995, percentage)	Total R&D Expenditures (1995, percentage)	Defense R&D Expenditures (1995–96, percentage)	Utility Invention Patents Granted in the United States (1997, thousands)	PCs per 10,000 People (1997)	Internet Hosts per 1,000 People (July 1998)	Scientists and Engineers in R&D per Million People (1985–95)
United States	41	53	80	61	407	976	3,732
Britain	6	6	7	2	242	201	2,417
Japan	30	22	2	23	202	107	5,677
France	5	8	8	n.a.	174	73	2,537
Germany	10	11	3	6.8	255	141	3,016
China	8	n.a.	n.a.	n.a.	6	.16	537
Russia	n.a.	n.a.	n.a.	n.a.	32	9	4,358

SOURCES: World Bank, *World Development Indicators, 1999* (Washington, D.C.: International Bank for Reconstruction and Development, 1999); National Science Foundation, *Science and Technology Indicators, 1998* (http://www.nsf.gov/sbe/srs/seind98/start.htm); Organization for Economic Cooperation and Development, *Science, Technology, and Industry: Scoreboard of Indicators, 1997* (Paris: OECD, 1997); and Michael B. Albert, Phyllis Ganther Yoshida, and Debra van Opstal, *The New Innovators: Global Patenting Trends in Five Sectors* (Washington, D.C.: U.S. Department of Commerce, Office of Technology Policy, September 1993).

NOTES: n.a.: Data not available. Russia's R&D as a percentage of GDP has fallen to below 0.75. According to Albert, Yoshida, and van Opstal, *The New Innovators*, utility invention patents granted in the United States to nationals of a given country is the best measure of national trends in industrial and technological innovation. Nationals of all European Union states combined were granted 16,400 such patents in 1997. Because the domain name and physical location of internet hosts do not always correlate, data on internet hosts should be considered approximate.

wars of the past two centuries.[29] One reason is simple arithmetic. The greater the number of players, the more difficult it is for any single war or event to clarify relations of power throughout the system. Even very large wars in multipolar systems do not provide unambiguous tests of the relative power of the states belonging to the victorious coalition. And wars often end before the complete defeat of major powers. The systemic wars of the past left several great states standing and ready to argue over their relative power. By contrast, bipolarity was built on two states, and one collapsed with more decisiveness than most wars can generate. The gap between the capabilities of the super-powers, on the one hand, and all other major powers, on the other hand, was already greater in the Cold War than any analogous gap in the history of the European states system. Given that the United States and the Soviet Union were so clearly in a class by themselves, the fall of one from superpower status leaves the other much more unambiguously "number one" than at any other time since 1815.

Moreover, the power gap in the United States' favor is wider than any single measure can capture because the unipolar concentration of resources is *symmetrical*. Unlike previous system leaders, the United States has commanding leads in all the elements of material power: economic, military, technological, and geographical. All the naval and commercial powers that most scholars identify as the hegemonic leaders of the past lacked military (especially land-power) capabilities commensurate with their global influence. Asymmetrical power portfolios generate ambiguity. When the leading state excels in the production of economic and naval capabilities but not conventional land power, it may seem simultaneously powerful and vulnerable. Such asymmetrical power portfolios create resentment among second-tier states that are powerful militarily but lack the great prestige the leading state's commercial and naval advantages bring. At the same time, they make the leader seem vulnerable to pressure from the one element of power in which it does not excel: military capabilities. The result is ambiguity about which state is more powerful, which is more secure, which is threatening which, and which might make a bid for hegemony.

Britain's huge empire, globe-girdling navy, and vibrant economy left strong imprints on nineteenth-century world politics, but because its capabilities were

---

29. The relationship between hierarchies of power revealed by systemic wars and the stability of international systems is explored in Robert Gilpin, *War and Change in World Politics* (Cambridge: Cambridge University Press, 1981). On wars as power tests, see Geoffrey Blainey, *The Causes of War* (New York: Free Press, 1973).

always skewed in favor of naval and commercial power, it never had the aggregate advantage implied by its early industrialization. Indeed, it was not even the international system's unambiguous leader until Russia's defeat in Crimea in 1856. The Napoleonic Wars yielded *three* potential hegemons: Britain, the decisive naval and financial power; Russia, the preeminent military power on the continent; and France, the state whose military prowess had called forth coalitions involving all the other great states. From 1815 to 1856, Britain had to share leadership of the system with Russia, while the power gap between these two empires and France remained perilously small.[30] Russia's defeat in Crimea punctured its aura of power and established Britain's uncontested primacy. But even after 1856, the gap between London and continental powerhouses such as France, Russia, and Prussia remained small because Britain never translated its early-industrial potential into continental-scale military capabilities. The Crimean victory that ushered in the era of British preeminence was based mainly on *French* land power.[31] And Britain's industrial advantage peaked before industrial capabilities came to be seen as the sine qua non of military power.[32]

---

30. It goes without saying that the nineteenth-century international system was perceived as multipolar, although Russia and Britain were seen as being in a class by themselves. See R.W. Seton-Watson, *Britain in Europe, 1789–1914: A Survey of Foreign Policy* (Cambridge: Cambridge University Press, 1937). To gain a sense of Russia's power in the period, it is enough to recall Czar Nicholas's dispatch of 400,000 troops to crush the 1848 revolt in Hungary—and his simultaneous offer to send another contingent across Europe to establish order in Paris should it be necessary. On Russia as Europe's hegemon, see M.S. Anderson, *The Rise of Modern Diplomacy, 1450–1919* (London: Longman, 1993); Adam Watson, "Russia in the European States System," in Watson and Hedley Bull, eds., *The Expansion of International Society* (Oxford: Clarendon, 1984). On Russia and Britain as (rivalrous) "cohegemons," see Paul W. Schroeder, *The Transformation of European Politics* (London: Oxford University Press, 1993); and Gordon A. Craig, "The System of Alliances and the Balance of Power," in J.P.T. Bury, ed., *New Cambridge Modern History*, Volume 10: *The Zenith of European Power, 1830–70* (Cambridge: Cambridge University Press 1960). The best, concise discussion of the nature and limitations of British power in this period is Paul Kennedy, *The Rise and Fall of British Naval Mastery* (London: Macmillan, 1983), chap. 6.
31. For an excellent account of the British debate on the lessons of Crimea, see Olive Anderson, *A Liberal State at War: English Politics and Economics during the Crimean War* (New York: St. Martin's, 1967).
32. Thus the COW measure suffers from a hindsight bias that accords importance to industrial capabilities before their military significance was appreciated. Cf. William B. Moul, "Measuring the 'Balance of Power': A Look at Some Numbers," *Review of International Studies*, Vol. 15, No. 2 (April 1989), pp. 101–121. On the conservatism of nineteenth-century military assessments, see B.H. Liddell-Hart, "Armed Forces and the Art of War: Armies," in Bury, *New Cambridge Modern History*. On the slowly growing perceptions of industrialization and its implications for war, see William H. McNeil, *The Pursuit of Power: Technology, Armed Force, and Society since A.D. 1000* (Chicago: University of Chicago Press, 1982); Dennis Showalter, *Railroads and Rifles: Soldiers, Technology, and the Unification of Germany* (Hamden, Conn.: Archer, 1975); Paul Kennedy, *The Rise of the Anglo-German Antagonism, 1860–1914* (London: Allen and Unwin, 1980); and Kennedy, *Rise and Fall of British Naval Mastery*.

The Cold War power gap between the United States and the Soviet Union was much smaller. World War II yielded ambiguous lessons concerning the relative importance of U.S. sea, air, and economic capabilities versus the Soviet Union's proven conventional military superiority in Eurasia.[33] The conflict clearly showed that the United States possessed the greatest military potential in the world—if it could harness its massive economy to the production of military power and deploy that power to the theater in time. Despite its economic weaknesses, however, Stalin's empire retained precisely those advantages that Czar Nicholas I's had had: the ability to take and hold key Eurasian territory with land forces. The fact that Moscow's share of world power was already in Eurasia (and already in the form of an armed fighting force) was decisive in explaining the Cold War. It was chiefly because of its location (and its militarized nature) that the Soviet Union's economy was capable of generating bipolarity. At the dawn of the Cold War, when the United States' economy was as big as those of all other great powers combined, the balance of power was still seen as precarious.[34]

In both the Pax Britannica and the early Cold War, different measures show power to have been concentrated in the leading state to an unusual degree. Yet in both periods, the perceived power gaps were closer than the measures imply. Asymmetrical power portfolios and small power gaps are the norm in modern international history. They are absent from the distribution of power of the late 1990s. Previous postwar hegemonic moments therefore cannot compare with post–Cold War unipolarity. Given the dramatically different power distribution alone, we should expect world politics to work much differently now than in the past.

---

33. I discuss these lessons in Wohlforth, *Elusive Balance: Power and Perceptions during the Cold War* (Ithaca, N.Y.: Cornell University Press, 1993). A much fuller analysis is available in recent historical works. For the U.S. side, see Marc Trachtenberg, *A Constructed Peace: The Making of the European Settlement, 1945–1963* (Princeton, N.J.: Princeton University Press, 1999); and Melvyn P. Leffler, *A Preponderance of Power: National Security, the Truman Administration, and the Cold War* (Stanford, Calif.: Stanford University Press, 1992). And for the view from Moscow, see Vladislav M. Zubok and Constantine Pleshakov, *Inside the Kremlin's Cold War* (Cambridge, Mass.: Harvard University Press, 1996); and Vojtech Mastny, *The Cold War and Soviet Insecurity: The Stalin Years* (New York: Oxford University Press, 1996).

34. As Marc Trachtenberg summarizes the view from Washington in 1948: "The defense of the West rested on a very narrow base. Even with the nuclear monopoly, American power only barely balanced Soviet power in central Europe." See Trachtenberg, *A Constructed Peace*, p. 91. Cf. Leffler, *A Preponderance of Power*, who is more critical of U.S. officials' power assessments. Nevertheless, Leffler's narrative—and the massive documentary evidence it relies on—would not be possible had the Soviet potential to dominate Eurasia not been plausible.

Unipolarity Is Peaceful

Unipolarity favors the absence of war among the great powers and comparatively low levels of competition for prestige or security for two reasons: the
leading state's power advantage removes the problem of hegemonic rivalry
from world politics, and it reduces the salience and stakes of balance-of-power
politics among the major states. This argument is based on two well-known
realist theories: hegemonic theory and balance-of-power theory. Each is controversial, and the relationship between the two is complex.[35] For the purposes
of this analysis, however, the key point is that both theories predict that a
unipolar system will be peaceful.

HOW TO THINK ABOUT UNIPOLARITY

Hegemonic theory has received short shrift in the debate over the nature of
the post–Cold War international system.[36] This omission is unwarranted, for
the theory has simple and profound implications for the peacefulness of the
post–Cold War international order that are backed up by a formidable body
of scholarship. The theory stipulates that especially powerful states
("hegemons") foster international orders that are stable until differential
growth in power produces a dissatisfied state with the capability to challenge
the dominant state for leadership. The clearer and larger the concentration of
power in the leading state, the more peaceful the international order associated
with it will be.

---

35. For simplicity, I treat only Waltz's neorealist version of balance-of-power theory. By
"hegemonic theory," I mean the theory of hegemonic war and change in Gilpin, *War and Change
in World Politics,* as well as power transition theory, which is sometimes applied to pairs of states
other than hegemon and challenger. In addition to Organski, *World Politics,* and Organski and
Kugler, *War Ledger,* see Jacek Kugler and Douglas Lemke, eds., *Parity and War: Evaluation and
Extension of the War Ledger* (Ann Arbor: University of Michigan Press, 1996); and the chapters by
George Modelski and William R. Thompson, Manus I. Midlarsky, and Jacek Kugler and A.F.K.
Organski in Midlarsky, ed., *Handbook of War Studies* (London: Unwin, 1989). Theories of the balance
of power and hegemony are often thought to be competing. I maintained this position in *Elusive
Balance,* chap. 1. In many instances, however, they are complementary. See Randall L. Schweller
and William C. Wohlforth, "Power Test: Updating Realism in Response to the End of the Cold
War," *Security Studies* (forthcoming). For an interesting synthesis with some points of contact with
the analysis here, see William R. Thompson, "Dehio, Long Cycles, and the Geohistorical Context
of Structural Transition," *World Politics,* Vol. 45, No. 1 (October 1992), pp. 127–152; and Rasler and
Thompson, *Great Powers and Global Struggle.*
36. Exceptions include Lemke, "Continuity of History"; and Mark S. Sheetz, "Correspondence:
Debating the Unipolar Moment," *International Security,* Vol. 22, No. 3 (Winter 1997/1998), pp. 168–
174.

The key is that conflict occurs only if the leader and the challenger disagree about their relative power. That is, the leader must think itself capable of defending the status quo at the same time that the number two state believes it has the power to challenge it. The set of perceptions and expectations necessary to produce such conflict is most likely under two circumstances: when the overall gap between the leader and the challenger is small and/or when the challenger overtakes the leader in *some* elements of national power but not others, and the two parties disagree over the relative importance of these elements. Hence both the overall size and the comprehensiveness of the leader's power advantage are crucial to peacefulness. If the system is unipolar, the great power hierarchy should be much more stable than any hierarchy lodged within a system of more than one pole. Because unipolarity is based on a historically unprecedented concentration of power in the United States, a potentially important source of great power conflict—hegemonic rivalry—will be missing.

Balance-of-power theory has been at the center of the debate, but absent so far is a clear distinction between peacefulness and durability. The theory predicts that any system comprised of states in anarchy will evince a tendency toward equilibrium. As Waltz puts it, "Unbalanced power, whoever wields it, is a potential danger to others."[37] This central proposition lies behind the widespread belief that unipolarity will not be durable (a contention I address below). Less often noted is the fact that as long as the system remains unipolar, balance-of-power theory predicts peace. When balance-of-power theorists argue that the post–Cold War world is headed toward conflict, they are not claiming that unipolarity causes conflict. Rather, they are claiming that unipolarity leads quickly to bi- or multipolarity. It is not unipolarity's peacefulness but its durability that is in dispute.

Waltz argued that bipolarity is less war prone than multipolarity because it reduces uncertainty. By the same logic, unpolarity is the least war prone of all structures.[38] For as long as unipolarity obtains, there is little uncertainty re-

---

37. Waltz, "Evaluating Theories," p. 915.
38. The connection between uncertainty, the number of principal players, and war proneness has been questioned. The key to most recent criticisms of neorealist arguments concerning stability is that the distribution of capabilities alone is insufficient to explain the war proneness of international systems. Ancillary assumptions concerning risk attitudes or preferences for the status quo are necessary. See Levy, "The Causes of War"; Bruce Bueno de Mesquita, "Neorealism's Logic and Evidence: When Is a Theory Falsified?" paper prepared for the Fiftieth Annual Conference of the International Studies Association, Washington, D.C., February 1999; and Robert Powell, "Stability and the Distribution of Power," *World Politics*, Vol. 48, No. 2 (January 1996), pp. 239–267, and

garding alliance choices or the calculation of power. The only options available to second-tier states are to bandwagon with the polar power (either explicitly or implicitly) or, at least, to take no action that could incur its focused enmity. As long as their security policies are oriented around the power and preferences of the sole pole, second-tier states are less likely to engage in conflict-prone rivalries for security or prestige. Once the sole pole takes sides, there can be little doubt about which party will prevail. Moreover, the unipolar leader has the capability to be far more interventionist than earlier system leaders. Exploiting the other states' security dependence as well as its unilateral power advantages, the sole pole can maintain a system of alliances that keeps second-tier states out of trouble.[39]

Until the underlying distribution of power changes, second-tier states face structural incentives similar to those of lesser states in a region dominated by one power, such as North America. The low incidence of wars in those systems is consistent with the expectations of standard, balance-of-power thinking. Otto von Bismarck earned a reputation for strategic genius by creating and managing a complex alliance system that staved off war while working disproportionately to his advantage in a multipolar setting. It does not take a Bismarck to run a Bismarckian alliance system under unipolarity. No one credits the United States with strategic genius for managing security dilemmas among American states. Such an alliance system is a structurally favored and hence less remarkable and more durable outcome in a unipolar system.

In sum, both hegemonic theory and balance-of-power theory specify thresholds at which great concentrations of power support a peaceful structure. Balance-of-power theory tells us that smaller is better.[40] Therefore one pole is best, and security competition among the great powers should be minimal. Hegemonic theory tells us that a clear preponderance in favor of a leading state with a comprehensive power portfolio should eliminate rivalry for primacy. Overall, then, unipolarity generates comparatively few incentives for security or prestige competition among the great powers.

---

sources cited therein. These analyses are right that no distribution of power rules out war if some states are great risk takers or have extreme clashes of interest. The greater the preponderance of power, however, the more extreme the values of other variables must be to produce war, because preponderance reduces the uncertainty of assessing the balance of power.

39. The sole pole's power advantages matter only to the degree that it is engaged, and it is most . likely to be engaged in politics among the other major powers. The argument applies with less force to potential security competition between regional powers, or between a second-tier state and a lesser power with which the system leader lacks close ties.

40. Three may be worse than four, however. See Waltz, *Theory of International Politics*, chap. 9; and Schweller, *Deadly Imbalances*.

THE MISSING SYSTEMIC SOURCES OF CONFLICT

Unipolarity does not imply the end of all conflict or that Washington can have its way on all issues all the time. It simply means the absence of two big problems that bedeviled the statesmen of past epochs: hegemonic rivalry and balance-of-power politics among the major powers. It is only by forgetting them that scholars and pundits are able to portray the current period as dangerous and threatening.

To appreciate the sources of conflict that unipolarity avoids, consider the two periods already discussed in which leading states scored very highly on aggregate measures of power: the Pax Britannica and the Cold War. Because those concentrations of power were not unipolar, both periods witnessed security competition and hegemonic rivalry. The Crimean War is a case in point. The war unfolded in a system in which two states shared leadership and *three* states were plausibly capable of bidding for hegemony.[41] Partly as a result, neither the statesmen of the time nor historians over the last century and a half have been able to settle the debate over the origins of the conflict. The problem is that even those who agree that the war arose from a threat to the European balance of power cannot agree on whether the threat emanated from France, Russia, or Britain.[42] Determining which state really did threaten the equilibrium—or indeed whether any of them did—is less important than the fact that the power gap among them was small enough to make all three threats seem plausible at the time and in retrospect. No such uncertainty—and hence no such conflict—is remotely possible in a unipolar system.

Even during the height of its influence after 1856, Britain was never a major land power and could not perform the conflict-dampening role that a unipolar state can play. Thus it would be inaccurate to ascribe the two, long nineteenth-century periods of peace to British power. From 1815 to 1853, London exercised influence in the context of the Concert of Europe, which was based on a Russo-British cohegemony. But because each of these competitive "bookend

---

41. See Schroeder, *Transformation of European Politics*, Paul W. Schroeder, *Austria, Britain, and the Crimean War: The Destruction of the European Concert* (Ithaca, N.Y.: Cornell University Press, 1972); Adam Watson, *The Evolution of International Society* (London: Routledge, 1992); and William E. Echard, *Napoleon III and the Concert of Europe* (Baton Rouge: Louisiana State University Press, 1983), chaps. 1–2.

42. Cf. David M. Goldfrank, *The Origins of the Crimean War* (London: Longman, 1994); Norman Rich, *Why the Crimean War? A Cautionary Tale* (London: University Press of America, 1985); Ludwig Dehio, *The Precarious Balance: Four Centuries of the European Struggle* (New York: Knopf, 1962), chap. 4; David Wetzel, *The Crimean War: A Diplomatic History* (New York: Columbia University Press, 1985); and A.J.P. Taylor's account in Taylor, *The Struggle for Mastery in Europe* (Oxford: Oxford University Press, 1954).

empires" was in possession of a different mix of power resources whose ultimate superiority had not been tested, great power cooperation was always vulnerable to hegemonic rivalry—a problem that helped destroy the concert in the Crimean War. With Britain in "splendid isolation" after 1856, Prussia violently refashioned the balance of power in Europe without having to concern itself greatly about London's preferences. After 1871 Bismarck's diplomacy, backed up by Germany's formidable power, played the crucial role in staving off violent competition for power or security on the continent. Owing to differences in the system structure alone, the long periods of peace in the nineteenth century are much more remarkable achievements of statesmanship than a similarly lengthy peace would be under unipolarity.

Similar sources of conflict emerged in the Cold War. The most recent and exhaustively researched accounts of Cold War diplomacy reveal in detail what the numerical indicators only hint at: the complex interplay between U.S. overall economic superiority, on the one hand, and the Soviet Union's massive conventional military capabilities, on the other.[43] This asymmetrical distribution of power meant that the gap between the two top states could be seen as lopsided or perilously close depending on one's vantage. The fact that the United States was preeminent only in nonmilitary elements of power was a critical factor underlying the Cold War competition for power and security. To produce a military balance, Washington set about creating a preponderance of other capabilities, which constituted a latent threat to Moscow's war planners and a major constraint on its diplomatic strategy. Hence both Moscow and Washington could simultaneously see their rivalry as a consequence of the other's drive for hegemony—sustaining a historical debate that shows every sign of being as inconclusive as that over the origins of the Crimean War. Again, no such ambiguity, and no such conflict, is likely in a unipolar system.

Both hegemonic rivalry and security competition among great powers are unlikely under unipolarity. Because the current leading state is by far the world's most formidable military power, the chances of leadership conflict are more remote than at any time over the last two centuries. Unlike past international systems, efforts by any second-tier state to enhance its relative position can be managed in a unipolar system without raising the specter of a power transition and a struggle for primacy. And because the major powers face

---

43. Trachtenberg, *A Constructed Peace*; Leffler, *A Preponderance of Power*; John Lewis Gaddis, *We Now Know: Rethinking Cold War History* (Oxford: Oxford University Press, 1997); Mastny, *The Cold War and Soviet Insecurity*; and Zubok and Pleshakov, *Inside the Kremlin's Cold War*.

incentives to shape their policies with a view toward the power and preferences of the system leader, the likelihood of security competition among them is lower than in previous systems.

Unipolarity Is Durable

Unipolarity rests on two pillars. I have already established the first: the sheer size and comprehensiveness of the power gap separating the United States from other states. This massive power gap implies that any countervailing change must be strong and sustained to produce structural effects. The second pillar—geography—is just as important. In addition to all the other advantages the United States possesses, we must also consider its four truest allies: Canada, Mexico, the Atlantic, and the Pacific. Location matters. The fact that Soviet power happened to be situated in the heart of Eurasia was a key condition of bipolarity. Similarly, the U.S. position as an offshore power determines the nature and likely longevity of unipolarity. Just as the raw numbers could not capture the real dynamics of bipolarity, power indexes alone cannot capture the importance of the fact that the United States is in North America while all the other potential poles are in or around Eurasia. The balance of power between the sole pole and the second-tier states is not the only one that matters, and it may not even be the most important one for many states. Local balances of power may loom larger in the calculations of other states than the background unipolar structure. Efforts to produce a counterbalance globally will generate powerful countervailing action locally. As a result, the threshold concentration of power necessary to sustain unipolarity is lower than most scholars assume.

Because they fail to appreciate the sheer size and comprehensiveness of the power gap and the advantages conveyed by geography, many scholars expect bi- or multipolarity to reappear quickly. They propose three ways in which unipolarity will end: counterbalancing by other states, regional integration, or the differential growth in power. None of these is likely to generate structural change in the policy-relevant future.[44]

---

44. Here I depart from Waltz, *Theory of International Politics*, pp. 161–162, for whom a stable system is one with no "consequential variation" in the number of poles (e.g., changes between multi-, tri-, bi-, or unipolarity). In the European states system, multipolarity obtained for three centuries. While the multipolar structure itself was long lived, however, the identity of its members (the leading states in the system) changed with much greater frequency—a matter of no small consequence for the governments concerned. By this measure (change in the identity, as opposed to the number, of the states that define the structure), bipolarity had a typical life span. See Bueno de Mesquita, "Neorealism's Logic and Evidence." I expect that the unipolar era will be of comparable duration.

ALLIANCES ARE NOT STRUCTURAL

Many scholars portray unipolarity as precarious by ignoring all the impediments to balancing in the real world. If balancing were the frictionless, costless activity assumed in some balance-of-power theories, then the unipolar power would need more than 50 percent of the capabilities in the great power system to stave off a counterpoise. Even though the United States meets this threshold today, in a hypothetical world of frictionless balancing its edge might be eroded quickly.[45] But such expectations miss the fact that alliance politics always impose costs, and that the impediments to balancing are especially great in the unipolar system that emerged in the wake of the Cold War.

Alliances are not structural. Because alliances are far less effective than states in producing and deploying power internationally, most scholars follow Waltz in making a distinction between the distribution of capabilities among states and the alliances states may form.[46] A unipolar system is one in which a counterbalance is impossible. When a counterbalance becomes possible, the system is not unipolar. The point at which this structural shift can happen is determined in part by how efficiently alliances can aggregate the power of individual states. Alliances aggregate power only to the extent that they are reliably binding and permit the merging of armed forces, defense industries, R&D infrastructures, and strategic decisionmaking. A glance at international history shows how difficult it is to coordinate counterhegemonic alliances. States are tempted to free ride, pass the buck, or bandwagon in search of favors from the aspiring hegemon. States have to worry about being abandoned by alliance partners when the chips are down or being dragged into conflicts of others' making.[47] The aspiring hegemon, meanwhile, has only to make sure its domestic house is in order. In short, a single state gets more bang for the buck than several states in an alliance. To the extent that alliances are inefficient at pooling power, the sole pole obtains greater power per unit of aggregate capabilities than any alliance that might take shape against it. Right away, the odds are skewed in favor of the unipolar power.

The key, however, is that the countercoalitions of the past—on which most of our empirical knowledge of alliance politics is based—formed against cen-

---

45. I do not deny the utility of making simplifying assumptions when speculating about the balance of power. For one such analysis, see Michael W. Doyle, *Ways of War and Peace: Realism, Liberalism, and Socialism* (New York: W.W. Norton, 1997), pp. 456–473.
46. Waltz, *Theory of International Politics;* and Snyder, *Alliance Politics.*
47. See Snyder, *Alliance Politics;* and Thomas J. Christensen and Jack Snyder, "Chain Gangs and Passed Bucks: Predicting Alliance Patterns in Multipolarity," *International Organization,* Vol. 44, No. 1 (Winter 1990), pp. 137–168.

trally located land powers (France, Germany, and the Soviet Union) that constituted relatively unambiguous security threats to their neighbors. Coordinating a counterbalance against an *offshore* state that has *already* achieved unipolar status will be much more difficult.[48] Even a declining offshore unipolar state will have unusually wide opportunities to play divide and rule. Any second-tier state seeking to counterbalance has to contend with the existing pro-U.S. bandwagon. If things go poorly, the aspiring counterbalancer will have to confront not just the capabilities of the unipolar state, but also those of its other great power allies. All of the aspiring poles face a problem the United States does not: great power neighbors that could become crucial U.S. allies the moment an unambiguous challenge to Washington's preeminence emerges. In addition, in each region there are smaller "pivotal states" that make natural U.S. allies against an aspiring regional power.[49] Indeed, the United States' first move in any counterbalancing game of this sort could be to try to promote such pivotal states to great power status, as it did with China against the Soviet Union in the latter days of the Cold War.

NEW REGIONAL UNIPOLARITIES: A GAME NOT WORTH THE CANDLE
To bring an end to unipolarity, it is not enough for regional powers to coordinate policies in traditional alliances. They must translate their aggregate economic potential into the concrete capabilities necessary to be a pole: a defense industry and power projection capabilities that can play in the same league as those of the United States. Thus all scenarios for the rapid return of multipolarity involve regional unification or the emergence of strong regional unipolarities.[50] For the European, Central Eurasian, or East Asian poles to measure up to the United States in the near future, each region's resources need to fall under the de facto control of one state or decisionmaking authority. In the near term, either true unification in Europe and Central Eurasia (the European Union [EU] becomes a de facto state, or Russia recreates an empire) or unipolar dominance in each region by Germany, Russia, and China or Japan, respectively, is a necessary condition of bi- or multipolarity.

---

48. The key here is that from the standpoint of balance-of-power theory, we are dealing with a structural fait accompli. Of the two powers that made up the bipolar order, one collapsed, leaving the other at the center of a unipolar system. A situation has arisen in which the theory's central tendency cannot operate. Many readers will perceive this state of affairs as a testimony to the weakness of balance-of-power theory. I agree. The weaker the theory, the longer our initial expectations of unipolarity's longevity.
49. On "pivotal states," see Robert Chase, Emily Hill, and Paul Kennedy, *The Pivotal States: A New Framework for U.S. Policy in the Developing World* (New York: W.W. Norton, 1999).
50. Kupchan, "Pax Americana," advocates just such a system.

The problem with these scenarios is that regional balancing dynamics are likely to kick in against the local great power much more reliably than the global counterbalance works against the United States. Given the neighborhoods they live in, an aspiring Chinese, Japanese, Russian, or German pole would face more effective counterbalancing than the United States itself.

If the EU were a state, the world would be bipolar. To create a balance of power globally, Europe would have to suspend the balance of power locally. Which balance matters more to Europeans is not a question that will be resolved quickly. A world with a European pole would be one in which the French and the British had merged their conventional and nuclear capabilities and do not mind if the Germans control them. The EU may move in this direction, but in the absence of a major shock the movement will be very slow and ambiguous. Global leadership requires coherent and quick decisionmaking in response to crises. Even on international monetary matters, Europe will lack this capability for some time.[51] Creating the institutional and political requisites for a single European foreign and security policy and defense industry goes to the heart of state sovereignty and thus is a much more challenging task for the much longer term.[52]

The reemergence of a Central Eurasian pole is more remote. There, the problem is not only that the key regional powers are primed to balance against a rising Russia but that Russia continues to decline. States do not rise as fast as Russia fell. For Russia to regain the capability for polar status is a project of a generation, if all goes well. For an Asian pole to emerge quickly, Japan and China would need to merge their capabilities. As in the case of Europe and Central Eurasia, a great deal has to happen in world politics before either Tokyo or Beijing is willing to submit to the unipolar leadership of the other.

Thus the quick routes to multipolarity are blocked. If states value their independence and security, most will prefer the current structure to a multipolarity based on regional unipolarities. Eventually, some great powers will have the capability to counter the United States alone or in traditional great power

---

51. See Kathleen R. McNamara, "European Monetary Union and International Economic Cooperation," a report on a workshop organized by the International Finance Section, Princeton University, April 3, 1998. Cf. Kupchan, "Rethinking Europe," who contends: "Assuming the European Union succeeds in deepening its level of integration and adding new members, it will soon have influence on matters of finance and trade equal to America's. A more balanced strategic relationship is likely to follow." Many Europeans see a contradiction between widening and deepening the EU.
52. This is why many Americans support an EU "security identity." If all goes well, Europe will become a more useful and outward-looking partner while posing virtually no chance of becoming a geopolitical competitor. See, for example, Zbigniew Brzezinski, *The Grand Chessboard: American Strategy and Its Geostrategic Imperatives* (New York: Basic Books, 1997), chap. 3.

alliances that exact a smaller price in security or autonomy than unipolarity does. Even allowing for the differential growth in power to the United States' disadvantage, however, for several decades it is likely to remain more costly for second-tier states to form counterbalancing alliances than it is for the unipolar power to sustain a system of alliances that reinforces its own dominance.

THE DIFFUSION OF POWER

In the final analysis, alliances cannot change the system's structure. Only the uneven growth of power (or, in the case of the EU, the creation of a new state) will bring the unipolar era to an end. Europe will take many decades to become a de facto state—if it ever does. Unless and until that happens, the fate of unipolarity depends on the relative rates of growth and innovation of the main powers.

I have established that the gap in favor of the United States is unprecedented and that the threshold level of capabilities it needs to sustain unipolarity is much less than the 50 percent that analysts often assume. Social science lacks a theory that can predict the rate of the rise and fall of great powers. It is possible that the United States will decline suddenly and dramatically while some other great power rises. If rates of growth tend to converge as economies approach U.S. levels of per capita GDP, then the speed at which other rich states can close the gap will be limited. Germany may be out of the running entirely.[53] Japan may take a decade to regain the relative position it occupied in 1990. After that, if all goes well, sustained higher growth could place it in polar position in another decade or two.[54] This leaves China as the focus of current expectations for the demise of unipolarity. The fact that the two main contenders to polar status are close Asian neighbors and face tight regional constraints further reinforces unipolarity. The threshold at which Japan or

---

53. See Max Otte, *A Rising Middle Power? German Foreign Policy in Transformation, 1988–1998* (New York: St. Martin's, forthcoming), chap. 3.

54. Assessments of Japan's future growth in the late 1990s are probably as overly pessimistic as those of the 1980s were overly optimistic. According to Peter Hartcher, "Can Japan Recover?" *National Interest*, No. 54 (Winter 1998/1999), p. 33, "Japan's Ministry of International Trade and Industry (MITI) estimates that even if the country manages to emerge from recession, its maximum potential growth rate until the year 2010 is a pathetic 1.8 percent, and a miserable 0.8 percent thereafter. And that is one of the more optimistic estimates." If, in contrast to these assumptions, the Japanese economy recovers in 2000 and grows at a robust annual average rate of 5 percent, while the U.S. economy grows at 2 percent, Japan's economy would surpass the United States' around 2025 (2033 using PPP estimates of the size of the two economies in 1997).

China will possess the capabilities to face the other *and* the United States is very high. Until then, they are better off in a unipolar order.

As a poor country, China has a much greater chance of maintaining sustained high growth rates. With its large population making for large gross economic output, projections based on extrapolating 8 percent yearly growth in GDP have China passing the United States early in the twenty-first century.[55] But these numbers must be used with care. After all, China's huge population probably gave it a larger economy than Britain in the nineteenth century.[56] The current belief in a looming power transition between the United States and China resembles pre–World War I beliefs about rising Russian power. It assumes that population and rapid growth compensate for technological backwardness. China's economic and military modernization has a much longer road to travel than its gross economic output suggests.[57] And managing the political and social challenges presented by rapid growth in an overpopulated country governed by an authoritarian regime is a formidable task. By any measure, the political challenges that lie athwart Beijing's path to polar status are much more substantial than those that may block Washington's efforts to maintain its position. Three decades is probably a better bet than one.

Thus far I have kept the analysis focused squarely on the distribution of material capabilities. Widening the view only slightly to consider key legacies of the Cold War strengthens the case for the robustness of unipolarity. The United States was the leading state in the Cold War, so the status quo already reflects its preferences. Washington thus faces only weak incentives to expand, and the preponderance of power in its control buttresses rather than contradicts the status quo. This reduces the incentives of others to counterbalance the United States and reinforces stability.[58] Another important Cold War legacy

---

55. These calculations are naturally heavily dependent on initial conditions. Assuming the Chinese economy grows at 8 percent a year while the U.S. economy grows at a 2 percent rate, China would surpass the United States in about 2013, extrapolating from 1997 PPP exchange-rate estimates of the two economies' relative size; 2020 if the PPP estimate is deflated as suggested by Central Intelligence Agency economists; and 2040 if market exchange rates are used. On measuring China's economic output, see Angus Maddison, *Monitoring the World Economy, 1820–1992* (Paris: OECD, 1995), appendix C.

56. Ibid., Table C-16e.

57. A balanced appraisal is Avery Goldstein, "Great Expectations: Interpreting China's Arrival," *International Security*, Vol. 22, No. 3 (Winter 1997/98), pp. 36–73.

58. A preponderance of power makes other states less likely to oppose the United States, but it could also tempt Washington to demand more of others. Because an overwhelming preponderance of power fosters stability, the clash of interests would have to be extreme to produce a counterbalance. In other words, the United States would have to work very hard to push all the other great powers and many regional ones into an opposing alliance. The point is important in theory

is that two prime contenders for polar status—Japan and Germany (or Europe)—are close U.S. allies with deeply embedded security dependence on the United States. This legacy of dependence reduces the speed with which these states can foster the institutions and capabilities of superpower status. Meanwhile, the United States inherits from the Cold War a global military structure that deeply penetrates many allied and friendly states, and encompasses a massive and complex physical presence around the world. These initial advantages raise the barriers to competition far higher than the raw measures suggest. Finally, the Cold War and its end appear to many observers to be lessons against the possibility of successful balancing via increased internal mobilization for war. The prospect that domestic mobilization efforts can extract U.S.-scale military power from a comparatively small or undeveloped economy seems less plausible now than it did three decades ago.

THE BALANCE OF POWER IS NOT WHAT STATES MAKE OF IT

For some analysts, multipolarity seems just around the corner because intellectuals and politicians in some other states want it to be. Samuel Huntington notes that "political and intellectual leaders in most countries strongly resist the prospect of a unipolar world and favor the emergence of true multipolarity."[59] No article on contemporary world affairs is complete without obligatory citations from diplomats and scholars complaining of U.S. arrogance. The problem is that policymakers (and scholars) cannot always have the balance of power they want. If they could, neither bipolarity nor unipolarity would have occurred in the first place. Washington, Moscow, London, and Paris wanted a swift return to multipolarity after World War II. And policymakers in all four capitals appeared to prefer bipolarity to unipolarity in 1990–91. Like its structural predecessor, unipolarity might persist despite policymakers' wishes.

Other scholars base their pessimism about unipolarity's longevity less on preferences than on behavior. Kenneth Waltz claims that "to all but the myopic,

---

but moot in practice. Because the post–Cold War world is already so much a reflection of U.S. interests, Washington is less tempted than another state might be to make additional claims as its relative power increases. The result is a preponderance of power backing up the status quo, a condition theorists of many stripes view as an augury of peace and stability. For different perspectives, see E.H. Carr, *The Twenty Years' Crisis: 1919–1939: An Introduction to the Study of International Relations* (London: Macmillan, 1951); Organski, *World Politics;* Gilpin, *War and Change in World Politics;* Powell, "Stability and the Distribution of Power"; and Randall L. Schweller, "Neorealism's Status Quo Bias: What Security Dilemma?" *Security Studies,* Vol. 5, No. 3 (Spring 1996), pp. 225–258.
59. Huntington, "Lonely Superpower," p. 42.

[multipolarity] can already be seen on the horizon. . . . Some of the weaker states in the system will . . . act to restore a balance and thus move the system back to bi- or multipolarity. China and Japan are doing so now."[60] This argument is vulnerable to Waltz's own insistence that a system's structure cannot be defined solely by the behavior of its units. Theory of course cannot predict state action. Whether some states try to enhance their power or form a counterbalancing alliance is up to them. But theory is supposed to help predict the outcome of such action. And if the system is unipolar, counterbalancing will fail. As the underlying distribution of power changes, the probability increases that some states will conclude that internal or external counterbalancing is possible. But there is no evidence that this has occurred in the 1990s. On the contrary, the evidence suggests that states are only now coming to terms with unipolarity.

Most of the counterbalancing that has occurred since 1991 has been rhetorical. Notably absent is any willingness on the part of the other great powers to accept any significant political or economic costs in countering U.S. power. Most of the world's powers are busy trying to climb aboard the American bandwagon even as they curtail their military outlays. Military spending by all the other great powers is either declining or holding steady in real terms. While Washington prepares for increased defense outlays, current planning in Europe, Japan, and China does not suggest real increases in the offing, and Russia's spending will inevitably decline further.[61] This response on the part of the other major powers is understandable, because the raw distribution of power leaves them with no realistic hope of counterbalancing the United States, while U.S.-managed security systems in Europe and Asia moderate the demand for more military capabilities.

The advent of unipolarity does not mean the end of all politics among great powers. Elites will not stop resenting overweening U.S. capabilities. Second-tier great powers will not suddenly stop caring about their standing vis-à-vis other states. Rising states presently outside the great power club will seek the prerequisites of membership. We should expect evidence of states' efforts to explore the new structure and determine their place in it. Most of the action since 1991 has concerned membership in the second tier of great powers. Some seek formal entry in the second tier via nuclear tests or a permanent seat on the United Nations Security Council. Existing members fear a devaluation of

---

60. Waltz, "Evaluating Theories," pp. 915–916.
61. International Institute of Strategic Studies, *The Military Balance 1998/99* (London: IISS, 1999).

their status and resist new aspirants. All of this requires careful management. But it affects neither the underlying structure nor the basic great power hierarchy.

The fact that some important states have more room to maneuver now than they did under bipolarity does not mean that unipolarity is already giving way to some new form of multipolarity.[62] The end of the bipolar order has decreased the security interdependence of regions and increased the latitude of some regional powers. But polarity does not refer to the existence of merely regional powers. When the world was bipolar, Washington and Moscow had to think strategically whenever they contemplated taking action anywhere within the system. Today there is no other power whose reaction greatly influences U.S. action across multiple theaters. China's reaction, for example, may matter in East Asia, but not for U.S. policy in the Middle East, Africa, or Europe. However, *all* major regional powers do share one item on their political agenda: how to deal with U.S. power. Until these states are capable of producing a counterpoise to the United States, the system is unipolar.

The key is that regional and second-tier competition should not be confused with balancing to restructure the system toward multipolarity. If the analysis so far is right, any existing second-tier state that tries such balancing should quickly learn the errors of its ways. This is indeed the fate that befell the two powers that tried (hesitantly, to be sure) to counterbalance: Russia and China. Foreign Minister Yevgeny Primakov's restless "multipolar diplomacy" had run out of steam well before Russia's financial collapse. And Russia's catastrophic decline also derailed China's efforts at creating some kind of counterpoise to the United States. As Avery Goldstein shows, the costs of Beijing's "multipolar diplomacy" dramatically outweighed the benefits. Russia was weak and getting weaker, while the United States held the economic and security cards. Even fairly careful Chinese moves produced indications of a strong local counterbalancing reaction before they showed any promise of increased autonomy vis-à-vis Washington. As a result, the Chinese rethought their approach

---

62. The enhanced autonomy of many regions compared to the bipolar order has given rise to an important new research agenda. See Etel Solingen, *Regional Orders at Century's Dawn* (Princeton, N.J.: Princeton University Press, 1998); and David A. Lake and Patrick N. Morgan, eds., *Regional Orders: Building Security in a New World* (University Park: Pennsylvania State University Press, 1997). This evidence of new regional security dynamics leads many to view the current structure as a hybrid of unipolarity and multipolarity. See Huntington, "Lonely Superpower"; and Friedberg, "Ripe for Rivalry."

in 1996 and made a concerted effort to be a "responsible partner" of the Americans.[63]

Neither the Beijing-Moscow "strategic partnership" nor the "European troika" of Russia, Germany, and France entailed any costly commitments or serious risks of confrontation with Washington. For many states, the optimal policy is ambiguity: to work closely with the United States on the issues most important to Washington while talking about creating a counterpoise. Such policies generate a paper trail suggesting strong dissatisfaction with the U.S.-led world order and a legacy of actual behavior that amounts to band-wagoning. These states are seeking the best bargains for themselves given the distribution of power. That process necessitates a degree of politicking that may remind people faintly of the power politics of bygone eras. But until the distribution of power changes substantially, this bargaining will resemble real-politik in form but not content.

Conclusion: Challenges for Scholarship and Strategy

The distribution of material capabilities at the end of the twentieth century is unprecedented. However we view this venerable explanatory variable, the current concentration of power in the United States is something new in the world. Even if world politics works by the old rules—even if democracy, new forms of interdependence, and international institutions do not matter—we should not expect a return of balance-of-power politics à la multipolarity for the simple reason that we are living in the modern world's first unipolar system. And unipolarity is not a "moment." It is a deeply embedded material condition of world politics that has the potential to last for many decades.

If unipolarity is so robust, why do so many writers hasten to declare its demise? The answer may lie in the common human tendency to conflate power *trends* with existing relationships. The rush to proclaim the return of multipo-larity in the 1960s and 1970s, to pronounce the United States' decline in the 1980s, to herald the rise of Japan or China as superpowers in the 1980s and 1990s, and finally to bid unipolarity adieu after the Cold War are all examples. In each case, analysts changed reference points to minimize U.S. power. In the

---

63. Avery Goldstein, "Structural Realism and China's Foreign Policy: A Good Part of the Story," paper prepared for the annual conference of the American Political Science Association, Boston, Massachusetts, September 3–6, 1998.

bipolarity debate, the reference point became the extremely tight alliance of the 1950s, so any disagreement between the United States and Europe was seen as a harbinger of multipolarity. In the 1980s, "hegemony" was defined as "the U.S. position circa 1946," so the recovery of Europe and Japan appeared as fatal threats to the United States' position. Many analysts have come to define unipolarity as an imperial system such as Rome where there is only one great power and all other states are satrapies or dependencies. As a result, each act of defiance of Washington's preferences on any issue comes to be seen as the return of a multipolar world.

One explanation for this tendency to shift reference points is that in each case the extent of U.S. power was inconvenient for the scholarly debate of the day. Scholars schooled in nineteenth-century balance-of-power politics were intellectually primed for their return in the 1960s. In the 1980s, continued cooperation between the United States and its allies was a more interesting puzzle if the era of U.S. hegemony was over. In the 1990s, unipolarity is doubly inconvenient for scholars of international relations. For neorealists, unipolarity contradicts the central tendency of their theory. Its longevity is a testament to the theory's indeterminacy. For liberals and constructivists, the absence of balance-of-power politics among the great powers is a much more interesting and tractable puzzle if the world is multipolar. The debate would be far easier if all realist theories predicted instability and conflict and their competitors predicted the opposite.

Today's distribution of power is unprecedented, however, and power-centric theories naturally expect politics among nations to be different than in past systems. In contrast to the past, the existing distribution of capabilities generates incentives for cooperation. The absence of hegemonic rivalry, security competition, and balancing is not necessarily the result of ideational or institutional change. This is not to assert that realism provides the best explanation for the absence of security and prestige competition. Rather, the conclusion is that it offers an explanation that may compete with or complement those of other theoretical traditions. As a result, evaluating the merits of contending theories for understanding the international politics of unipolarity presents greater empirical challenges than many scholars have acknowledged.

Because the baseline expectations of all power-centric theories are novel, so are their implications for grand strategy. Scholars' main message to policymakers has been to prepare for multipolarity. Certainly, we should think about how to manage the transition to a new structure. Yet time and energy are limited. Constant preparation for the return of multipolarity means not gearing up intellectually and materially for unipolarity. Given that unipolarity is prone to peace and the probability that it will last several more decades at least, we should focus on it and get it right.

The first step is to stop calling this the "post–Cold War world." Unipolarity is nearing its tenth birthday. Our experience with this international system matches what the statesmen and scholars of 1825, 1928, and 1955 had. The key to this system is the centrality of the United States. The nineteenth century was not a "Pax Britannica." From 1815 to 1853, it was a Pax Britannica et Russica; from 1853 to 1871, it was not a pax of any kind; and from 1871 to 1914, it was a Pax Britannica et Germanica. Similarly, the Cold War was not a Pax Americana, but a Pax Americana et Sovietica. Now the ambiguity is gone. One power is lonely at the top. Calling the current period the true Pax Americana may offend some, but it reflects reality and focuses attention on the stakes involved in U.S. grand strategy.

Second, doing too little is a greater danger than doing too much. Critics note that the United States is far more interventionist than any previous system leader. But given the distribution of power, the U.S. impulse toward interventionism is understandable. In many cases, U.S. involvement has been demand driven, as one would expect in a system with one clear leader. Rhetoric aside, U.S. engagement seems to most other elites to be necessary for the proper functioning of the system. In each region, cobbled-together security arrangements that require an American role seem preferable to the available alternatives. The more efficiently the United States performs this role, the more durable the system. If, on the other hand, the United States fails to translate its potential into the capabilities necessary to provide order, then great power struggles for power and security will reappear sooner. Local powers will then face incentives to provide security, sparking local counterbalancing and security competition. As the world becomes more dangerous, more second-tier states will enhance their military capabilities. In time, the result could be an earlier structural shift to bi- or multipolarity and a quicker reemergence of conflict over the leadership of the international system.

Third, we should not exaggerate the costs. The clearer the underlying distribution of power is, the less likely it is that states will need to test it in arms races or crises. Because the current concentration of power in the United States is unprecedentedly clear and comprehensive, states are likely to share the expectation that counterbalancing would be a costly and probably doomed venture. As a result, they face incentives to keep their military budgets under control until they observe fundamental changes in the capability of the United

States to fulfill its role. The whole system can thus be run at comparatively low costs to both the sole pole and the other major powers. Unipolarity can be made to seem expensive and dangerous if it is equated with a global empire demanding U.S. involvement in all issues everywhere. In reality, unipolarity is a distribution of capabilities among the world's great powers. It does not solve all the world's problems. Rather, it minimizes two major problems—security and prestige competition—that confronted the great powers of the past. Maintaining unipolarity does not require limitless commitments. It involves managing the central security regimes in Europe and Asia, and maintaining the expectation on the part of other states that any geopolitical challenge to the United States is futile. As long as that is the expectation, states will likely refrain from trying, and the system can be maintained at little extra cost.

The main criticism of the Pax Americana, however, is not that Washington is too interventionist. A state cannot be blamed for responding to systemic incentives. The problem is U.S. reluctance to *pay up*. Constrained by a domestic welfare role and consumer culture that the weaker British hegemon never faced, Washington tends to shrink from accepting the financial, military, and especially the domestic political burdens of sole pole status. At the same time, it cannot escape the demand for involvement. The result is cruise missile hegemony, the search for polar status on the cheap, and a grand global broker of deals for which others pay. The United States has responded to structural incentives by assuming the role of global security manager and "indispensable nation" in all matters of importance. But too often the solutions Washington engineers are weakened by American reluctance to take any domestic political risks.

The problem is that structural pressures on the United States are weak. Powerful states may not respond to the international environment because their power makes them immune to its threat. The smaller the number of actors, the greater the potential impact of internal processes on international politics. The sole pole is strong and secure enough that paying up-front costs for system maintenance is hard to sell to a parsimonious public. As Kenneth Waltz argued, "Strong states . . . can afford not to learn."[64] If that was true of the great powers in multi- or bipolar systems, it is even truer of today's unipolar power. The implication is that instead of dwelling on the dangers of overinvolvement and the need to prepare for an impending multipolarity,

---

64. Waltz, *Theory of International Politics*, p. 195.

scholars and policymakers should do more to advertise the attractions of unipolarity.

Despite scholars' expectations, it was not the rise of Europe, Japan, and China that ended bipolarity. The monodimensional nature of the Soviet Union's power and the brittleness of its domestic institutions turned out to be the main threats to bipolar stability. Similarly, a uniting Europe or a rising Japan or China may not become the chief engines of structural change in the early twenty-first century. If the analysis here is right, then the live-for-today nature of U.S. domestic institutions may be the chief threat to unipolar stability. In short, the current world order is characterized not by a looming U.S. threat that is driving other powers toward multipolar counterbalancing, but by a material structure that presupposes and demands U.S. preponderance coupled with policies and rhetoric that deny its existence or refuse to face its modest costs.

Command of the Commons

Barry R. Posen

The Military Foundation of U.S. Hegemony

Since the end of the Cold War, scholars, commentators, and practitioners of foreign policy have debated what structure of world power would follow the bipolar U.S.-Soviet competition, and what U.S. foreign policy would replace containment. Those who hypothesized a long "unipolar moment" of extraordinary U.S. relative power have proven more prescient than those who expected the relatively quick emergence of a multipolar world.[1] Those who recommended a policy of "primacy"—essentially hegemony—to consolidate, exploit, and expand the U.S. relative advantage have carried the day against those who argued for a more restrained U.S. foreign policy.[2] One can argue that the jury is still out, the

Barry R. Posen is Professor of Political Science at the Massachusetts Institute of Technology and a member of its Security Studies Program. During the past academic year, he was a Transatlantic Fellow of the German Marshall Fund of the United States.

The author would like to thank Robert Art, Owen Coté, Etienne de Durand, Harvey Sapolsky, and the anonymous reviewers for their comments on earlier drafts of this article. Previous versions were presented at the U.S. Naval War College Current Strategy Forum, the Weatherhead Center Talloires conference "The Future of U.S. Foreign Policy," the Institut Français des Relations Internationales, the Centre for Defence Studies at King's College, and the European University Institute. An earlier version of this article, entitled "La maîtrise des espaces, fondement de l'hégémonie des Etats-Unis," appears in the spring 2003 issue of *Politique étrangère*, pp. 41–56.

1. The most comprehensive analysis of the extraordinary relative power position of the United States is William C. Wohlforth, "The Stability of a Unipolar World," *International Security*, Vol. 24, No. 1 (Summer 1999), pp. 5–41.
2. Barry R. Posen and Andrew L. Ross, "Competing Visions of U.S. Grand Strategy," *International Security*, Vol. 21, No. 3 (Winter 1996/97), pp. 5–53, summarizes the initial phase of the post–Cold War U.S. grand strategy debate. In that article, we discussed a policy called "primacy," a then popular term in U.S. foreign policy discourse. Primacy is one type of hegemony. A distinction should be made between a description of the structure of world politics—that is, the distribution of power among states—and the policies of a particular nation-state. The United States has more power in the world than any other state, and by a substantial margin. Wohlforth, "The Stability of a Unipolar World." This has become clear over the last decade. Thus it is reasonable to describe the world as "unipolar." Though this much power sorely tempts a state to practice a hegemonic foreign and security policy—that is, to further expand and consolidate its power position and to organize the world according to its own preferences—this is not inevitable. In terms of its potential capabilities, the United States has been a great power for at least a century, but it has followed foreign policies of varying activism. The U.S. national security elite (Democratic and Republican) did, however, settle on a policy of hegemony sometime in the late 1990s. The people of the United States did not play a significant role in this decision, so questions remained about how much they would pay to support this policy. The attacks of September 11, 2001, and the subsequent war on terror, have provided an important foundation of domestic political support for a hegemonic foreign policy. Debates between Democrats and Republicans now focus on the modalities of hegemony—whether

International Security, Vol. 28, No. 1 (Summer 2003), pp. 5–46
© 2003 by the President and Fellows of Harvard College and the Massachusetts Institute of Technology.

"moment" will soon pass, and the policy of hegemony enabled by great power will be fleeting. But the evidence does not support such predictions. Unipolarity and U.S. hegemony will likely be around for some time, though observers do suggest that the United States could hasten its own slide from the pinnacle through indiscipline or hyperactivity.[3]

The new debate on U.S. grand strategy is essentially about which variant of a hegemonic strategy the United States should pursue. The strategy proposed by President George W. Bush is, in caricature, unilateral, nationalistic, and oriented largely around the U.S. advantage in physical power, especially military power.[4] This is "primacy" as it was originally conceived. The last years of Bill Clinton's administration saw the emergence of a strategy that also depended heavily on military power, but which was more multilateral and liberal, and more concerned with international legitimacy. It aimed to preserve the dominant U.S. global position, including its military position, which was understood to be an essential underpinning of global activism.[5] That strategy has recently been elaborated, formalized, and defended under the rubric of "selective engagement" by Robert Art.[6] Though this is too big an argument to settle

---

the United States should work through multilateral institutions to exercise and increase its power or work outside them.

3. Stephen G. Brooks and William C. Wohlforth, "American Primacy," *Foreign Affairs*, Vol. 81, No. 4 (July/August 2002), pp. 20–33.

4. To be fair, Bush's *National Security Strategy of the United States of America* contains many allusions to alliances, cooperation, liberal values, and economic and political development. Nevertheless, the oldest and most powerful U.S. allies—the Europeans—are hardly mentioned in the document. Even allowing for the need for stern language to mobilize public support for the war on terror, the document has a martial tone—and is strongly committed to a wide variety of proactive uses of force. Also, the document has a vaguely nationalist flavor: "The U.S. national security strategy will be based on a distinctly American internationalism that reflects the union of our values and our national interests." Perhaps to drive home this point, the document devotes an entire paragraph to disassociating the United States from the International Criminal Court. President George W. Bush, *The National Security Strategy of the United States of America* (Washington, D.C.: White House, September 20, 2002), p. 30.

5. Posen and Ross, "Competing Visions of U.S. Grand Strategy," pp. 44–50, dubbed this strategy "selective (but cooperative) primacy."

6. Robert J. Art, *A Grand Strategy for America* (Ithaca, N.Y.: Cornell University Press, 2003). In the mid-1990s, most proponents of selective engagement had in mind a less ambitious strategy than Art now proposes. Formerly, the criteria for selective engagement were clear: Does an international problem promise significantly to increase or decrease the odds of great power war? Now the purpose of the strategy is to retain U.S. alliances and presence in Europe, East Asia, and the Persian Gulf "to help mold the political, military, and economic configurations of these regions so as to make them more congenial to America's interests." Included in the goals of the strategy are protection of the United States from grand terror attack, stopping the proliferation of weapons of mass destruction (nuclear, chemical, and biological), preserving peace and stability in Eurasia, securing access to oil, maintaining international economic openness, spreading democracy, protecting human rights, and avoiding severe climate change. Art does propose priorities among these objectives. See ibid., chap. 7.

on the sole basis of a military analysis, the understanding of U.S. military power developed below suggests that selective engagement is likely to prove more sustainable than primacy.

One pillar of U.S. hegemony is the vast military power of the United States. A staple of the U.S. debate about the size of the post–Cold War defense budget is the observation that the United States spends more than virtually all of the world's other major military powers combined, most of which are U.S. allies.[7] Observers of the actual capabilities that this effort produces can focus on a favorite aspect of U.S. superiority to make the point that the United States sits comfortably atop the military food chain, and is likely to remain there. This article takes a slightly different approach. Below I argue that the United States enjoys command of the commons—command of the sea, space, and air. I discuss how command of the commons supports a hegemonic grand strategy. I explain why it seems implausible that a challenge to this command could arise in the near to medium term. Then I review the arenas of military action where adversaries continue to be able to fight U.S. forces with some hope of success—the "contested zones." I argue that in the near to medium term the United States will not be able to establish command in these arenas. The interrelationship between U.S. command of the commons and the persistence of the contested zones suggests that the United States can probably pursue a policy of selective engagement but not one of primacy.

I purposefully eschew discussing U.S. military power in light of the metrics of the current and previous administrations. The Clinton administration planned to be able to fight two nearly simultaneous major theater wars; the Bush administration's emerging, and even more demanding, metric is the "4-2-1" principle—that is, deter in four places, counterattack in two, and if necessary, go to the enemy's capital in one of the two.[8] These metrics obscure the foundations of U.S. military power—that is, all the difficult and expensive things that the United States does to create the conditions that permit it to even consider one, two, or four campaigns.[9]

---

7. According to the Center for Defense Information, the fiscal year 2003 budget request of $396 billion "is more than the combined spending of the next 25 nations." See www.cdi.org/issues/wme.

8. U.S. Department of Defense, *Quadrennial Defense Review Report* (Washington, D.C.: U.S. Department of Defense, September 30, 2001), pp. 20–21.

9. This article does not review three military theoretical terms that have absorbed much attention over the last decade: the revolution in military affairs, net-centric warfare, and military transformation. To do so would require a major digression. I am trying to build an understanding of the overall U.S. military position and its strategic implications on the basis of a small number of empirical observations about familiar categories of conventional military activity.

Command of the Commons

The U.S. military currently possesses command of the global commons. Command of the commons is analogous to command of the sea, or in Paul Kennedy's words, it is analogous to "naval mastery."[10] The "commons," in the case of the sea and space, are areas that belong to no one state and that provide access to much of the globe.[11] Airspace does technically belong to the countries below it, but there are few countries that can deny their airspace above 15,000 feet to U.S. warplanes. Command does not mean that other states cannot use the commons in peacetime. Nor does it mean that others cannot acquire military assets that can move through or even exploit them when unhindered by the United States. Command means that the United States gets vastly more military use out of the sea, space, and air than do others; that it can credibly threaten to deny their use to others; and that others would lose a military contest for the commons if they attempted to deny them to the United States. Having lost such a contest, they could not mount another effort for a very long time, and the United States would preserve, restore, and consolidate its hold after such a fight.[12]

Command of the commons is the key military enabler of the U.S. global power position. It allows the United States to exploit more fully other sources

---

10. Kennedy distinguishes "naval mastery" from temporary, local naval superiority, or local command of the sea. "By . . . the term 'naval mastery', however, there is meant here something stronger, more exclusive and wider-ranging; namely a situation in which a country has so developed its maritime strength that it is superior to any rival power, and that its predominance is or could be exerted far outside its home waters, with the result that it is extremely difficult for other, lesser states to undertake maritime operations or trade without at least its tacit consent. It does *not* necessarily imply a superiority over all other navies combined, nor does it mean that this country could not temporarily lose local command of the sea; but it does assume the possession of an overall maritime power such that small-scale defeats overseas would soon be reversed by the dispatch of naval forces sufficient to eradicate the enemy's challenge. Generally speaking, naval mastery is also taken to imply that the nation achieving it will usually be very favourably endowed with many fleet bases, a large merchant marine, considerable national wealth, etc., all of which indicates influence at a global rather than a purely regional level." Paul M. Kennedy, *The Rise and Fall of British Naval Mastery* (London: Macmillan, 1983, first published in 1976 by Allen Lane), p. 9 (emphasis added).
11. Alfred Thayer Mahan called the sea "a wide common." Ibid., p. 2.
12. As is the case with much analysis of conventional military issues, for the sake of analytic simplicity, I do not treat the implications of the proliferation of weapons of mass destruction. Insofar as the main accomplishment of weapons of mass destruction is to increase significantly the costs and risks of any hegemonic foreign policy, the proliferation of these weapons for U.S. grand strategy should be considered independently of a treatment of their narrow tactical military utility. That said, broadly speaking the limited diffusion of these kinds of weapons would likely make the contested zone even more contested before they affect command of the commons.

of power, including its own economic and military might as well as the economic and military might of its allies. Command of the commons also helps the United States to weaken its adversaries, by restricting their access to economic, military, and political assistance. Command of the commons has permitted the United States to wage war on short notice even where it has had little permanent military presence. This was true of the 1991 Persian Gulf War, the 1993 intervention in Somalia, and the 2001 action in Afghanistan.

Command of the commons provides the United States with more useful military potential for a hegemonic foreign policy than any other offshore power has ever had. When nineteenth-century Britain had command of the sea, its timely power projection capability ended at the maximum range of the Royal Navy's shipboard guns. The Royal Navy could deliver an army many places around the globe, but the army's journey inland was usually difficult and slow; without such a journey, Britain's ability to influence events was limited. As the nineteenth century unfolded, the industrialization of the continental powers, improvements in land transportation, and the development of coastal warfare technologies such as the torpedo and mine reduced the strategic leverage provided by command of the sea.[13]

The United States enjoys the same command of the sea that Britain once did, and it can also move large and heavy forces around the globe. But command of space allows the United States to see across the surface of the world's landmasses and to gather vast amounts of information. At least on the matter of medium-to-large-scale military developments, the United States can locate and identify military targets with considerable fidelity and communicate this information to offensive forces in a timely fashion. Air power, ashore and afloat, can reach targets deep inland; and with modern precision-guided weaponry, it can often hit and destroy those targets. U.S. forces can even more easily do great damage to a state's transportation and communications networks as well as economic infrastructure. When U.S. ground forces do venture inland, they do so against a weakened adversary; they also have decent intelligence, good maps, and remarkable knowledge of their own position from moment to moment. Moreover, they can call on a great reserve of responsive, accurate, air-delivered firepower, which permits the ground forces considerable freedom of action. Political, economic, and technological changes since the 1980s have thus partially reversed the rise of land power relative to sea power that

---

13. Ibid., chap. 7.

occurred in the late nineteenth century and helped to erode Britain's formal and informal empire.

THE SOURCES OF COMMAND

What are the sources of U.S. command of the commons? One obvious source is the general U.S. superiority in economic resources. According to the Central Intelligence Agency, the United States produces 23 percent of gross world product (GWP); it has more than twice as many resources under the control of a single political authority as either of the next two most potent economic powers— Japan with 7 percent of GWP and China with 10 percent.[14] With 3.5 percent of U.S. gross domestic product devoted to defense (nearly 1 percent of GWP), the U.S. military can undertake larger projects than any other military in the world. The specific weapons and platforms needed to secure and exploit command of the commons are expensive. They depend on a huge scientific and industrial base for their design and production. In 2001 the U.S. Department of Defense budgeted nearly as much money for military research and development as Germany and France together budgeted for their entire military efforts.[15] The military exploitation of information technology, a field where the U.S. military excels, is a key element. The systems needed to command the commons require significant skills in systems integration and the management of large-scale industrial projects, where the U.S. defense industry excels. The development of new weapons and tactics depends on decades of expensively accumulated technological and tactical experience embodied in the institutional memory of public and private military research and development organizations.[16] Finally, the military personnel needed to run these systems are among the most highly skilled and highly trained in the world. The barriers to entry to a state seeking the military capabilities to fight for the commons are very high.

---

14. I calculated these percentages from the country entries in Central Intelligence Agency, *The World Factbook, 2001* (Washington, D.C.: CIA, 2001). The purchasing power parity method used by the CIA creates an exaggerated impression of China's current economic and technological capability. Measured by currency exchange rates, the United States had 29.5 percent of gross world product in 1999, Japan had 14 percent, and China had only 3.4 percent. See "World Gross Domestic Product by Region," *International Energy Outlook, 2002,* Report DOE/EIA-0484 (Washington, D.C.: Energy Information Administration, 2002), Table A3, Appendix A.

15. International Institute for Strategic Studies, *The Military Balance, 2002–2003* (London: IISS, 2002), pp. 241, 252–253. My colleague Harvey Sapolsky called this to my attention.

16. Harvey M. Sapolsky, Eugene Gholz, and Allen Kaufman, "Security Lessons from the Cold War," *Foreign Affairs,* Vol. 78, No. 4 (July/August 1999), pp. 77–89.

COMMAND OF THE SEA

U.S. nuclear attack submarines (SSNs) are perhaps the key assets of U.S. open-ocean antisubmarine warfare (ASW) capability, which in turn is the key to maintaining command of the sea.[17] During the Cold War, the Soviet Union challenged U.S. command of the sea with its large force of SSNs. The U.S. Navy quietly won the "third battle of the Atlantic," though the Soviet successes in quieting their nuclear submarines in the 1980s would have necessitated another expensive and difficult round of technological competition had the Cold War not ended.[18] At more than $1 billion each (more than $2 billion each for the new U.S. SSN), modern nuclear submarines are prohibitively expensive for most states. Aside from the United States, Britain, China, France, and Russia are the only other countries that can build them, and China is scarcely able.[19] Several partially built nuclear attack submarines remained in Russian yards in the late 1990s, but no new ones have been laid down.[20] Perhaps 20–30 Russian nuclear attack submarines remain in service.[21] Currently, the U.S. Navy has 54 SSNs in service and 4 under construction. It plans to build roughly 2 new boats every three years. It also has a program to convert 4 Ohio-class Trident ballistic missile submarines into nonnuclear cruise missile–carrying submarines for land attack. The U.S. Navy also dominates the surface of the oceans, with 12 aircraft carriers (9 nuclear powered) capable of launching high-performance aircraft.[22] The Soviet Union was just building its first true aircraft carrier when its political system collapsed. Aside from France,

---

17. The actual wartime missions of SSNs in the canonical major regional contingencies—aside from lobbing a few conventional cruise missiles and collecting electronic intelligence close to shore—are murky at best.
18. Owen R. Coté Jr., *The Third Battle: Innovation in the U.S. Navy's Silent Cold War Struggle with Soviet Submarines* (Newport, R.I.: Naval War College, 2003), pp. 69–78.
19. Construction of a new Chinese nuclear attack submarine has been delayed many times, and one is not expected to be completed until 2005. France does not have a nuclear attack submarine under construction, but it has a program planned for the 2010s. Britain has ordered three new nuclear attack submarines, and one is currently under construction. See A.D. Baker III, "World Navies in Review," *Naval Institute Proceedings,* Vol. 128 (March 2002), pp. 33–36.
20. According to A.D. Baker III, "Submarine construction in Russia had all but halted by the fall of 1998." At the time, there were four incomplete Akula-class nuclear attack submarines and one incomplete new-design attack submarine in Russian yards. Baker, "World Navies in Review," *Naval Institute Proceedings,* Vol. 125 (March 1999), pp. 3–4. See also Baker, "World Navies in Review," March 2002, pp. 35–36. One of the Akulas was finally commissioned at the end of 2001. One more may yet be completed.
21. IISS, *Military Balance, 2002–2003,* p. 113, suggests 22. Baker, "World Navies," (March, 2002), suggests about 30. I count Oscar-class cruise missile submarines as attack submarines.
22. For figures on the U.S. Navy and Marine Corps, see IISS, *Military Balance, 2002–2003,* pp. 18–21.

which has 1, no other country has any nuclear-powered aircraft carriers. At $5 billion apiece for a single U.S. Nimitz-class nuclear–powered aircraft carrier, this is no surprise.[23] Moreover, the U.S. Navy operates for the Marine Corps a fleet of a dozen large helicopter/VSTOL carriers, each almost twice the size of the Royal Navy's comparable (3 ship) Invincible class. To protect its aircraft carriers and amphibious assets, the U.S. Navy has commissioned 37 Arleigh Burke–class destroyers since 1991—billion-dollar multimission platforms capable of antiair, antisubmarine, and land-attack missions in high-threat environments.[24] This vessel is surely the most capable surface combatant in the world.

COMMAND OF SPACE

Though the United States is not yet committed to actual combat in or from space, it spends vast amounts on reconnaissance, navigation, and communications satellites.[25] These satellites provide a standing infrastructure to conduct military operations around the globe. According to Gen. Michael Ryan, the chief of staff of the U.S. Air Force, the United States had 100 military satellites and 150 commercial satellites in space in 2001, nearly half of all the active satellites in space.[26] According to Air Force Lt. Gen. T. Michael Moseley, air component commander in the U.S.-led invasion of Iraq in March 2003, more than 50 satellites supported land, sea, and air operations in every aspect of the campaign.[27] Secretary of Defense Donald Rumsfeld plans to emphasize the military exploitation of space, and has set the military the mission of "space

---

23. For costs of current U.S. warships, see Office of the Comptroller, U.S. Department of Defense, "Shipbuilding and Conversion," *National Defense Budget Estimates for the Amended FY 2002 Budget (Green Book), Procurement Programs (P1)*, pp. N. 17–18.
24. See http://www.globalsecurity.org/military/systems/ship/ddg-51-unit.htm.
25. The Pentagon has been hinting for some time that it would like to put weapons into space both for antisatellite attacks and for attacks on terrestrial targets. Many independent space policy analysts oppose this because the United States gets more out of space than any other state. They acknowledge that this makes U.S. space assets an attractive target, but they argue that hardening satellites, ground stations, and the links between them makes more sense than starting an expensive arms competition in space. Implicitly, they also rely on deterrence—the superior ability of the U.S. military to damage the other side's ground stations, links, and missile launch facilities, as well as to retaliate with nascent U.S. antisatellite systems against the other side's satellites. See, for example, Theresa Hitchens, *Weapons in Space: Silver Bullet or Russian Roulette* (Washington, D.C.: Center for Defense Information, April 19, 2002); Michael Krepon with Christopher Clary, *Space Assurance or Space Dominance? The Case against Weaponizing Space* (Washington, D.C.: Henry L. Stimson Center, 2003), chap. 3; and Charles V. Pena and Edward L. Hudgins, *Should the United States "Weaponize" Space?* Policy Analysis No. 427 (Washington D.C.: Cato Institute, March 18, 2002), pp. 5–10.
26. Vernon Loeb, "Air Force's Chief Backs Space Arms," *Washington Post*, August 2, 2001, p. 17.
27. Jim Garamone, "Coalition Air Forces Make Ground Gains Possible," American Forces Press Service, April 5, 2003, http://www.defenselink.mil/news/APR2003/n04052003_200304053.html.

control."[28] For fiscal years 2002–07, the Pentagon plans to spend $165 billion on space-related activities.[29]

Other states can and do use space for military and civilian purposes. Though there is concern that some commercial satellites have military utility for reconnaissance and communications, many belong to U.S. companies or U.S. allies, and full exploitation of their capabilities by U.S. enemies can be severely disrupted.[30] The NAVSTAR/GPS (global positioning system) constellation of satellites, designed and operated by the U.S. military but now widely utilized for civilian purposes, permits highly precise navigation and weapons guidance anywhere in the world. Full exploitation of GPS by other military and civilian users is permitted electronically by the United States, but this permission is also electronically revocable.[31] It will not be easy for others to produce a comparable system, though the European Union intends to try. GPS cost $4.2 billion (in 1979 prices) to bring to completion, significantly more money than was originally projected.[32]

---

28. According to the 2001 *Quadrennial Defense Review Report*, "The ability of the United States to access and utilize space is a vital national security interest." Moreover, "the mission of space control is to ensure the freedom of action in space for the United States and its allies and, when directed, to deny such freedom of action to adversaries." According to the report, "Ensuring freedom of access to space and protecting U.S. national security interests are key priorities that must be reflected in future investment decisions." Ibid., p. 45

29. General Accounting Office, *Military Space Operations: Planning, Funding, and Acquisition Challenges Facing Efforts to Strengthen Space Control*, GAO-02-738 (Washington, D.C.: GAO, September 2002), p. 3. It appears that U.S. military spending on space has nearly doubled since 1998, when it was estimated at $14 billion. See John Pike, "American Control of Outer Space in the Third Millennium," November 1998, http://www.fas.org/spp/eprint/space9811.htm.

30. Pike, "American Control of Outer Space."

31. The United States formerly corrupted the GPS satellite signals to reduce the accuracy that a nonmilitary user terminal could achieve. On May 1, 2000, President Clinton ended this policy due to the vast commercial possibilities of highly accurate positional information. At that time, the U.S. government believed that it could employ new techniques to jam the GPS signals regionally in a way that would prevent an adversary from exploiting them, but not dilute the accuracy elsewhere. See President Bill Clinton: "Improving the Civilian Global Positioning System (GPS)," May 1, 2000, http://www.ngs.noaa.gov/FGCS/info/sans_SA/docs/statement.html.

32. This is the cost of the development and deployment of the system, and the acquisition of sufficient satellites (118), to achieve and sustain a 24-satellite array. By 1997, $3 billion had been spent on "user equipment," the military terminals that calculate location on the basis of the satellites' signals. See U.S. Department of Defense, "Systems Acquisition Review Program Acquisition Cost Summary as of June 30, 1997." See also General Accounting Office, *Navstar Should Improve the Effectiveness of Military Missions—Cost Has Increased*, PSAD-80-91 (Washington, D.C.: GAO, February 15, 1980), p. 14. The European Union has decided to produce a competing system to GPS, called Galileo. It is estimated that 3 billion euros will be required to buy and operate 30 satellites. European advocates of Galileo explicitly argue that Europe must have its own satellite navigation systems or lose its "autonomy in defense." See Dee Ann Divis, "Military Role for Galileo Emerges," *GPS World*, Vol. 13, No. 5 (May 2002), p. 10.

The dependence of the United States on satellites to project its conventional military power does make the satellites an attractive target for future U.S. adversaries.[33] But all satellites are not equally vulnerable; low earth orbit satellites seem more vulnerable to more types of attack than do high earth orbit satellites.[34] Many of the tactics that a weaker competitor might use against the United States would probably not be usable more than once—use of space mines, for example, or so-called microsatellites as long-duration orbital interceptors. The U.S. military does have some insurance against the loss of satellite capabilities in its fleet of reconnaissance aircraft and unmanned aerial vehicles. A challenge by another country could do some damage to U.S. satellite capabilities and complicate military operations for some time. The United States would then need to put a new generation of more resilient satellites in orbit. One estimate suggests that the exploitation of almost every known method to enhance satellite survivability would roughly double the unit cost.[35]

The United States has had a number of antisatellite research and development programs under way for many years, and some are said to have produced experimental devices that have military utility.[36] The planned U.S. ballistic missile defense system will also have some antisatellite capability. U.S. conventional military capabilities for precision attack, even without the support of its full panoply of space assets, are not trivial. It is quite likely that an opponent's own satellites, and its ground stations and bases for attacking U.S. satellites, would quickly come under sustained attack. The most plausible outcome of a war over space is that the United States would, after a period of difficulty, rebuild its space assets. The fight would not only leave the adversary devoid of space capability, but would also cause the United States to insist on the permanent antisatellite disarmament of the challenger, which it would try to enforce. Finally, the United States would probably assert some special interest in policing space.

33. Tom Wilson, Space Commission staff member, "Threats to United States Space Capabilities," prepared for the *Report of the Commission to Assess United States National Security Space Management and Organization* (Washington, D.C.: Government Printing Office [GPO], January 11, 2001). Secretary of Defense Donald Rumsfeld chaired this commission.
34. A technically competent country with limited resources may be able to develop a capability to damage or destroy U.S. reconnaissance satellites in low earth orbit. See Allen Thomson, "Satellite Vulnerability: A Post–Cold War Issue," *Space Policy*, Vol. 11, No. 1 (February 1995), pp. 19–30.
35. This is based on my simple addition of the maximum estimated cost increases associated with hardening satellites, providing them the capability for autonomous operations, giving them some onboard attack reporting capability, making them maneuverable, supplying them with decoys, and providing them with some self defense capability. See Wilson, "Threats to United States Space Capabilities," p. 6.
36. Pike, "American Control of Outer Space in the Third Millennium."

COMMAND OF THE AIR

An electronic flying circus of specialized attack, jamming, and electronic intelligence aircraft allows the U.S military to achieve the "suppression of enemy air defenses" (SEAD); limit the effectiveness of enemy radars, surface-to-air missiles (SAMs) and fighters; and achieve the relatively safe exploitation of enemy skies above 15,000 feet.[37] Cheap and simple air defense weapons, such as antiaircraft guns and shoulder-fired lightweight SAMs, are largely ineffective at these altitudes. Yet at these altitudes aircraft can deliver precision-guided munitions with great accuracy and lethality, if targets have been properly located and identified. The ability of the U.S. military to satisfy these latter two conditions varies with the nature of the targets, the operational circumstances, and the available reconnaissance and command and control assets (as discussed below), so precision-guided munitions are not a solution to every problem. The United States has devoted increasing effort to modern aerial reconnaissance capabilities, including both aircraft and drones, which have improved the military's ability in particular to employ air power against ground forces, but these assets still do not provide perfect, instantaneous information.[38] Confidence in the quality of their intelligence, and the lethality and responsiveness of their air power, permitted U.S. commanders to dispatch relatively small numbers of ground forces deep into Iraq in the early days of the 2003 war, without much concern for counterattacks by large Iraqi army units.[39]

The U.S. military maintains a vast stockpile of precision-guided munitions and is adding to it. As of 1995, the Pentagon had purchased nearly 120,000 air-launched precision-guided weapons for land and naval attack at a cost of $18 billion.[40] Some 20,000 of these weapons were high-speed antiradiation missiles

---

37. Barry R. Posen, *Inadvertent Escalation: Conventional War and Nuclear Risks* (Ithaca, N.Y.: Cornell University Press, 1992), pp. 51–55. For a detailed description of a suppression operation, see Barry D. Watts and Thomas A. Keaney, *Effects and Effectiveness: Gulf War Air Power Survey*, Vol. 2, Pt. 2 (Washington, D.C.: GPO, 1993), pp. 130–145.

38. During Desert Storm, the United States employed one experimental JSTARS (joint surveillance target attack radar system) aircraft, a late Cold War project to develop an airborne surveillance radar capable of tracking the movements of large enemy ground forces at ranges of hundreds of kilometers. The U.S. Air Force has 15 such aircraft. Similarly, U.S. forces employed few if any reconnaissance drones in Desert Storm; the U.S. Air Force now operates both high- and low-altitude reconnaissance drones. Under the right conditions, drones allow U.S. forces to get a close and persistent look at enemy ground forces. For current U.S. Air Force holdings, see IISS, *Military Balance, 2002–2003*, pp. 22–23.

39. Lt. Gen. James Conway, U.S. Marine Corps, "First Marine Expeditionary Force Commander Live Briefing from Iraq," May 30, 2003, U.S. Department of Defense news transcript, http://www.defenselink.mil/transcripts/2003/tr20030530–0229.html.

40. General Accounting Office, *Weapons Acquisition: Precision-Guided Munitions in Inventory, Production, and Development*, GAO/NSIAD-95–95 (Washington, D.C.: GAO, June 1995), p. 12.

(HARMs), designed to home in on the radar emissions of ground-based SAM systems, a key weapon for the SEAD campaign. Thousands of these bombs and missiles were launched in Kosovo, Afghanistan, and Iraq, but tens of thousands more have been ordered.[41]

The capability for precision attack at great range gives the United States an ability to do significant damage to the infrastructure and the forces of an adversary, while that adversary can do little to harm U.S. forces.[42] Air power alone may not be able to determine the outcome of all wars, but it is a very significant asset. Moreover, U.S. air power has proven particularly devastating to mechanized ground forces operating offensively, as was discovered in the only Iraqi mechanized offensive in Desert Storm, the battle of al-Khafji, in which coalition air forces pummeled three advancing Iraqi divisions.[43] The United States can provide unparalleled assistance to any state that fears a conventional invasion, making it a very valuable ally.

THE INFRASTRUCTURE OF COMMAND
Two important Cold War legacies contribute to U.S. command of the commons—bases and command structure. Though the United States has reduced the number of its forces stationed abroad since the Cold War ended, and has abandoned bases in some places (such as Panama and the Philippines), on the whole the U.S. Cold War base structure remains intact.[44] Expansion of the

---

41. The U.S. military says that it needs 200,000 GPS satellite-guided bombs, the joint direct attack munition or JDAM—7,000 of which were used in the Afghan War. Six thousand five hundred JDAMs were used in the Iraq war. See Lt. Gen. T. Michael Moseley, commander, United States Central Command Air Forces, "Operation Iraqi Freedom—By the Numbers," Assessment and Analysis Division, USCENTAF, April 30, 2003, p. 3, http://www.iraqcrisis.co.uk/downloads/resources/uscentaf_oif_report_30apr2003.pdf. Boeing is producing this weapon at the rate of 2,000 per month, and the military wants to increase production to 2,800 per month. See Nick Cook, "Second-Source JDAM Production Line Moves Closer," *Jane's Defense Weekly*, October 16, 2002, p. 5.
42. Daryl G. Press, "The Myth of Air Power in the Persian Gulf War and the Future of Warfare," *International Security*, Vol. 26, No. 2 (Fall 2001), pp. 5–44, carefully and convincingly demonstrates that despite weeks of bombing, Iraqi mechanized ground forces in Kuwait and southern Iraq were still largely intact when the United States opened its ground attack. Perhaps 40 percent of Iraqi fighting vehicles were destroyed or immobilized by the air campaign, prior to the start of ground operations. Nevertheless, once the coalition ground operation began, Iraqi mechanized units managed to maneuver in the desert, in spite of U.S. command of the air. They did not suffer much damage from U.S. fixed-wing air attacks during the ground campaign. These forces were destroyed or enveloped by U.S. and allied mechanized ground forces. It should be noted, however, that army and marine attack helicopters destroyed much Iraqi armor.
43. Ibid., p. 12; and Michael R. Gordon and Bernard E. Trainor, *The Generals' War: The Inside Story of the Conflict in the Gulf* (Boston: Little, Brown, 1995), pp. 267–288.
44. The United States currently has military installations in three dozen foreign countries or special territories. See Office of the Deputy Undersecretary of Defense (Installations and Environ-

North Atlantic Treaty Organization has given the United States access to additional bases in eastern and southern Europe. These bases provide important stepping-stones around the world. The Pentagon has also improved the U.S. military's access in key regions. After the 1991 Gulf War, the United States developed a network of air base, port, and command and control facilities throughout the Persian Gulf, and cycled troops and aircraft through these bases. This base structure allowed the United States to attack Iraq successfully in 2003, despite the unwillingness of long-time NATO ally Turkey to permit the use of its territory to add a northern thrust to the effort. Though U.S. leaders were disappointed by Turkey's stance, it is noteworthy that sufficient bases were available in any case. After September 11, 2001, the U.S. government negotiated access to former Soviet air bases in the now independent states of Kyrgyzstan, Tajikistan, and Uzbekistan.[45]

The U.S. military has taken a number of other steps to improve its ability to send large forces across great distances. Munitions, support equipment, and combat equipment are prepositioned around the world, ashore and afloat. For example, the equivalent of 3 1/3 divisions' (10 brigades') worth of army and marine equipment was prepositioned at key spots in Asia, Europe, and the Persian Gulf during the 1990s. Perhaps 5 brigades of this equipment were employed in March 2003. In a crisis, troops fly to designated airfield-port combinations to marry up with this equipment. Since 1991 the United States has built

---

ment), Department of Defense, "Summary," *Base Structure Report (A Summary of DoD's Real Property Inventory), Fiscal Year 2002 Baseline,* http://www.defenselink.mil/news/Jun2002/basestructure2002.pdf.This report counts only installations in which the United States has actually invested federal dollars. Missing from the list are Kuwait and Saudi Arabia, so a peculiar definition of U.S. base must guide the report. Unfortunately, comparable time series data do not exist to permit comparison to the last days of the Cold War. Secretary of Defense William S. Cohen noted in 1997 that although the DoD had reduced active-duty military forces by 32 percent, it had reduced its domestic and overseas base structure by only 26 percent. See Secretary of Defense William S. Cohen, *Report of the Quadrennial Defense Review* (Washington, D.C.: Department of Defense, May 1997). The vast majority of overseas installations that were either reduced or closed, 878 out of 952, were in Europe. See Department of Defense, "Additional U.S. Overseas Bases to End Operations," Department of Defense, news release, April 27, 1995. From 1988 to 1997, the number of U.S. troops stationed abroad (on land) dropped from 480,000 to 210,000; 80 percent of the reduction came in Europe. See Secretary of Defense William S. Cohen, *Annual Report to the President and the Congress, 2000* (Washington, D.C.: Department of Defense, 2000), Appendix C, p. C-2.

45. Other post–Cold War allies offering overflight, port, or actual basing contributions to the war on terrorism include, among others, Albania, Bulgaria, the Czech Republic, Djibouti, Estonia, Ethiopia, Latvia, Lithuania, Pakistan, and Slovakia. See U.S. Department of Defense, *International Contributions to the War against Terrorism,* fact sheet, June 7, 2002. See also William M. Arkin, "Military Bases Boost Capability but Fuel Anger," *Los Angeles Times,* January 6, 2002, p. A-1, noting that U.S. military personnel were working at thirteen new locations in nine countries in support of the war on terror.

a fleet of 20 large, medium-speed, roll-on/roll-off military transport ships, to facilitate the movement of military matériel. Each ship can carry nearly 1,000 military vehicles and can off load this equipment at austere ports, if necessary.[46] These ships were extensively employed in the mobilization for the war to topple the Iraqi Ba'ath regime. Similarly, the United States has modernized its fleet of long-range airlift aircraft; 90 C17s of 180 on order have been delivered.[47] These aircraft are capable of carrying tank-sized cargo into relatively mediocre airfields. They in turn are supported by a fleet of aerial tankers. Finally, it is easy to forget that since World War II the U.S. Marine Corps has specialized in putting large ground and air forces ashore against opposition. The Marine Corps alone has as many personnel as the combined land and air forces of the United Kingdom, and the U.S. Navy operates almost 40 special-purpose combat ships for amphibious operations, roughly the same number of major surface combatants as the entire Royal Navy.[48]

Finally, all this capability is tied together by a seldom-mentioned Cold War legacy: the Unified Command Plan through which the U.S. military organizes the entire world for war. The U.S. military divides the world into both functional and regional commands. In most cases, the regional command elements are based in the theaters in which they would fight. PACOM is based in Hawaii and oversees U.S. forces in the Pacific. EUCOM, based in Europe, manages U.S. forces committed to NATO. CENTCOM oversees the Persian Gulf and Indian Ocean, but does so formally from Florida. Also in Florida, SOUTH-COM oversees Central and South America. These commands are each led by a four-star commander in chief (formerly referred to as a "CinC," pronounced "sink," they are now called "combatant commanders"). These are large multifunction military headquarters, to which are often attached significant operational forces. They engage in military diplomacy among the countries in

---

46. Military Sealift Command, U.S. Navy, fact sheet, "Large, Medium-Speed, Roll-on/Roll-off Ships (LMSRs)," October 2002. Thirty-three ships of various types, including 9 of the LMSRs, are employed to preposition equipment, ammunition, and fuel. See also Military Sealift Command, U.S. Navy, fact sheet, "Afloat Prepositioning Force," April 2003. A total of 87 dry cargo ships of various kinds, including 11 LMSRs and many other roll-on roll-off ships are based in the United States.
47. "Boeing and U.S. Air Force Sign $9.7 Billion C-17 Contract," news release, Boeing Corporation, August 15, 2002, http://www.boeing.com/news/releases/2002/q3/nr_020815m.html. This follow-on procurement contract added 60 C-17 Globemaster III transport aircraft to the 120 already on order.
48. IISS, *The Military Balance, 2002–2003*, pp. 18–21, 60–63. It is worth noting that Britain and France are the only two countries in the world, aside from the United States, with any global power projection capability.

their command and arrange joint exercises. They integrate the products of U.S. command of space, with the permissive conditions of command of the air and sea, to develop responsive war plans that can generate significant combat power in the far corners of the world on relatively short notice. That the geographical commands were barely touched by the passing of the Cold War is mute testimony to the quiet consensus among the foreign and security policy elite that emerged soon after the passing of the Soviet Union: The United States would hold on to its accidental hegemony.[49]

MAINTAINING COMMAND

U.S. command of the commons is the result of a Cold War legacy of both capabilities and bases, married to the disparity in overall economic power between the United States and its potential challengers. This disparity permits the United States to sustain a level of defense expenditure that dwarfs the spending of any of the world's other consequential powers. If grand strategists wish to pursue an activist global foreign policy, then they must preserve command of the commons. What then must the United States do? In the very long term, if a country comes to rival the United States in economic and technological capacity, it will be difficult to prevent a challenge, though it may be possible to out-compete the challenger. But in the short and medium terms, a successful challenge can be made highly impractical. In the short term, there is not much any other country can do to challenge the United States. In the medium term, through careful attention and resource allocation, the United States should be able to stay comfortably ahead of possible challengers. Indeed some of the more grandiose aspirations of the Pentagon may be realized: Pentagon documents in the early 1990s talked about deterring any effort to build a capability to challenge the United States.[50] The first full statement of the grand strategy of

---

49. Ronald H. Cole, Walter S. Poole, James F. Schnabel, Robert J. Watson, and Willard J. Webb, *The History of the Unified Command Plan, 1946–1993* (Washington, D.C.: Joint History Office, Office of the Chairman of the Joint Chiefs of Staff, 1995), http://www.dtic.mil/doctrine/jel/history/ucp.pdf; see especially pp. 107–117.

50. George H.W. Bush's administration reportedly issued draft defense planning guidance to the Pentagon in March 1992 with this objective. "Excerpts from Pentagon's Plan: 'Prevent the Emergence of a New Rival,'" *New York Times*, March 8, 1992, p. 14. For reportage, see Patrick E. Tyler, "U.S. Strategy Plan Calls for Insuring No Rivals Develop," *New York Times*, March 8, 1992, pp. 1, 14; and Barton Gellman, "The U.S. Aims to Remain First among Equals," *Washington Post National Weekly Edition*, March 16–22, 1992, p. 19. For examples of contemporary commentary, see Leslie Gelb, "They're Kidding," *New York Times*, March 9, 1992, p. A17; James Chace, "The Pentagon's Superpower Fantasy," *New York Times*, March 16, 1992, p. 17; and Charles Krauthammer, "What's Wrong with the 'Pentagon Paper'?" *Washington Post*, March 13, 1992, p. A25.

the administration of George W. Bush also declares, "Our forces will be strong enough to dissuade potential adversaries from pursuing a military build-up in hopes of surpassing, or equaling, the power of the United States."[51] This objective goes well beyond the traditional U.S. goal of deterring attacks. Yet it may be possible to create barriers to entry into the global military power club that are so high as to seem insurmountable.

MAINTAINING COMMAND AT SEA

Though the United States does not face a significant naval challenge to its supremacy in the open ocean, it should nevertheless preserve a scientific and technical capability to resume a sustained, large-scale, open-ocean anti-submarine warfare contest. Similarly, though the United States may not need the numbers of SSNs that it had during the Cold War, or even that it has today, it must nevertheless remain on the cutting edge of SSN design and production.

MAINTAINING COMMAND IN SPACE

In space, the United States has a more complicated political-military task. It benefits from the fact that those states capable of space activities have eschewed putting weapons in space. The United States has made the same decision, on the assumption that if it did, so would others. Ultimately the United States has more to lose than to gain from such a competition. The military does need to work aggressively on techniques to harden, hide, and maneuver satellites in case an adversary does try to interfere. An ability quickly to reconstitute some space capabilities should also be maintained, as should alternative reconnaissance means—aircraft and drones. The United States should also maintain some counteroffensive capabilities for purposes of deterrence and defense. The United States can leverage its long-range conventional attack capabilities to deny others the free use of space if they attack U.S. assets, and to reduce their offensive capabilities—mainly through direct and electronic attacks on an adversary's space launch, ground control, and tracking facilities. The United States should also maintain some antisatellite weapons research and development programs.

---

51. Bush, *The National Security Strategy of the United States of America*, p. 30. Accoding to the 2001 *Report of the Quadrennial Defense Review*, p. 12, "Well targeted strategy and policy can therefore dissuade other countries from initiating future military competitions"; see also ibid., p. 36.

MAINTAINING COMMAND OF THE AIR

Perhaps the most contested element of U.S. command of the commons is command of the air. Here, the air force buys weapons as if the principal challenge is adversary fighter aircraft. The U.S. Air Force, Navy, and Marine advantage in air-to-air combat is nearly overwhelming, however. It will be easier for others to challenge U.S. access above 15,000 feet with ground-based surface-to-air missiles of advanced design. The late–Cold War Soviet designs, and their follow-on systems, the so-called double-digit SAMs (with the SA-10 the best known and most lethal system) can offer real resistance to the U.S. military.[52] Fortunately for the United States, these systems are expensive, and Russian manufacturers sell only to those who can pay cash. China has purchased a significant number from Russia, and other countries will likely follow.[53] U.S. SEAD capabilities do not seem to be keeping up with this threat, much less staying ahead of it. The Pentagon needs to put more effort into SEAD if it hopes to retain command of the air.

Command of the commons is the military foundation of U.S. political preeminence. It is the key enabler of the hegemonic foreign policy that the United States has pursued since the end of the Cold War. The military capabilities required to secure command of the commons are the U.S. strong suit. They leverage science, technology, and economic resources. They rely on highly trained, highly skilled, and increasingly highly paid military personnel. On the whole, the U.S. military advantage at sea, in the air, and in space will be very difficult to challenge—let alone overcome. Command is further secured by the worldwide U.S. base structure and the ability of U.S. diplomacy to leverage other sources of U.S. power to secure additional bases and overflight rights as needed.

Command of the commons is so much a part of U.S. military power that it is seldom explicitly acknowledged, under this rubric or any other. And

---

52. Owen R. Coté Jr., "The Future of the Trident Force, Security Studies Program," Massachusetts Institute of Technology, May 2002, pp. 25–29, discusses air defense suppression generally, and the significant problems posed by the SA-10, specifically. See also Owen R. Coté Jr., "'Buying . . . From the Sea': A Defense Budget for a Maritime Strategy," in Cindy Williams, ed., *Holding the Line: U.S. Defense Alternatives for the Early Twenty-first Century* (Cambridge, Mass.: MIT Press, 2001), pp. 146–150.

53. IISS, *The Military Balance, 2002–2003*, p. 148, credits China with 144 SA-10s. This implies perhaps a dozen batteries. SA-10 is a NATO designation; Russia calls the weapon S-300. See Federation of American Scientists, "SA-10 Grumble," http://www.fas.org/nuke/guide/russia/airdef/s-300pmu.htm.

far too little attention is paid to the strategic exploitation of command of the commons. For example, many U.S. defense policy documents in recent years allude to the need for speed of deployment to distant theaters of operations and speed of decision in the theater contingency.[54] Among other things, this has caused the U.S. Army to become obsessed with "lightening" itself up, to better travel by air and to limit its logistics tail in the theater. This interest in speed seems misplaced. It underexploits the possibilities provided by command of the commons—the ability of the United States to muster great power; to militarily, economically, and politically isolate and weaken its adversaries; and to probe, study, and map the dimensions of the adversary to better target U.S. military power when it is applied. Full exploitation of command of the commons is rendered doubly necessary by the real problems presented once U.S. forces get close to the adversary. Below 15,000 feet, within several hundred kilometers of the shore, and on the land, a contested zone awaits them. The U.S. military hopes that it can achieve the same degree of dominance in this zone as it has in the commons, though this is unlikely to happen.

The Contested Zone

The closer U.S. military forces get to enemy-held territory, the more competitive the enemy will be. This arises from a combination of political, physical, and technological facts. These facts combine to create a contested zone—arenas of conventional combat where weak adversaries have a good chance of doing real damage to U.S. forces. The Iranians, the Serbs, the Somalis, and the still unidentified hard cases encountered in Operation Anaconda in Afghanistan have demonstrated that it is possible to fight the U.S. military. Only the Somalis can claim anything like a victory, but the others have imposed costs, preserved at least some of their forces, and often lived to tell the tale—to one another. These countries or entities have been small, resource poor, and often

---

54. The 2001 *Quadrennial Defense Review Report* seems to be preoccupied with swiftness: For example, the DoD seeks forces to "swiftly defeat aggression in overlapping major conflicts" (p. 17); "The focus will be on the ability to act quickly. U.S. forces will remain capable of swiftly defeating attack against U.S. allies and friends in any two theaters of operation in overlapping time frames" (p. 21); and "One of the goals of reorienting the global posture is to render forward forces capable of swiftly defeating an adversary's military and political objectives with only modest reinforcement" (p. 25; repeated on p. 26).

militarily "backward." They offer cautionary tales. The success of the 2003 U.S. campaign against the Ba'athist regime in Iraq should not blind observers to the inherent difficulty of fighting in contested zones.

Most of the adversaries that the United States has encountered since 1990 have come to understand U.S. military strengths, and have worked to neutralize them. The U.S. military often uses the term "asymmetric" threats to encompass an adversary's use of weapons of mass destruction, terrorism, or any mode of conventional warfare that takes into account U.S. strengths. This category is a kind of trap: Smart enemies get a special term, but by subtraction, many are expected to be stupid. This is unlikely to prove true; in any case it is a dangerous way to think about war.

The essential facts are as follows. First, local actors generally have strong political interests in the stakes of a war—interests that may exceed those of the United States. Their willingness to suffer is therefore often greater. Second, however small the local actors are, they usually have one resource in more plentiful supply than the all-volunteer U.S. military—males of fighting age. Though young men are no longer the most important ingredient of land warfare, they do remain critical, particularly in cities, jungles, and mountains. Third, local actors usually have some kind of "home-court advantage." Just as the U.S. military has built up an institutional memory over decades that has helped it to preserve command of the commons, local actors have often built up a similar institutional memory about their own arenas. They have intimate knowledge of the terrain and the meteorology and may have spent years adapting their military tactics to these factors. This advantage is magnified because the local actors are often on the defense, which permits their military engineers to disperse, harden, and camouflage their forces, logistics, and command and control. Fourth, foreign soldiers have studied how the U.S. military makes war. The Cold War saw a great deal of foreign military education as a tool of political penetration by both the U.S. and Soviet blocs. Potential adversaries have been taught Western tactics and the use of Western weaponry. There are even reports that those who have fought the U.S. forces share information on their experiences. Fifth, the weaponry of the close fight—on land, in the air at low altitudes, and at sea in the so-called littorals—is much less expensive than that required for combat in the commons. A great deal of useful weaponry was left over from the Cold War, especially Warsaw Pact designs, which are particularly cheap. Demand for weaponry has diminished greatly since the Cold War ended, so there is plenty of manufacturing capability looking for markets.[55] Moreover, the diffusion of economic and technological capabilities in the civil sector is paralleled in the military sector. New manufacturers are emerging, who themselves will seek export markets. Finally, weaponry for close-range combat is also being continuously refined. Old weapons are becoming more lethal because of better ammunition. New versions of old weapons are also more lethal and survivable. Because these weapons are relatively inexpensive, even some of the newer versions will find their way into the hands of smaller and poorer states.

Taken together, these mutually reinforcing factors create a "contested zone." In this zone, encounters between U.S. and local forces may result in fierce battles. This is not a prediction of U.S. defeat. The United States will be able to win wars in the contested zone, as it did in Afghanistan in 2002 and Iraq in 2003. It is a prediction of adversity. It is a prediction of a zone in which the U.S. military will require clever strategies and adroit tactics. It is a zone in which the U.S. military must think carefully and candidly about its own strengths and weaknesses, and how to leverage the former and buffer the latter.

LIMITS TO AIR POWER

Though U.S. aircraft possess significant potential destructive capacity, clever defenders can make it difficult to realize this potential. A combination of large numbers of inexpensive low-altitude air defense weapons; small numbers of intelligently organized and operated medium-altitude weapons; and systematic efforts at camouflage, protection, and concealment have permitted ground forces to survive the onslaught of modern U.S. air power under some circumstances.

Inexpensive weaponry drives U.S. fighters to high altitudes, where their effectiveness against ground forces is reduced. Below 15,000 feet, expensive tactical fighter aircraft are vulnerable to inexpensive weaponry—light-to-medium automatic cannon (antiaircraft artillery, or AAA) and relatively small and inexpensive short-range SAMS (mainly portable infrared-guided systems similar to the U.S. Stinger). Although some kinds of decoys work against some of the low-altitude SAMs, the effectiveness of AAA is essentially a function of how many weapons the adversary possesses, their location relative to important targets, and how much ammunition they are able and willing to expend. AAA is best thought of as a kind of aerial minefield. Vast numbers of AAA weapons

---

55. Daniel Williams and Nicholas Wood, "Iraq Finds Ready Arms Sellers from Baltic Sea to Bosnia," *International Herald Tribune*, November 21, 2002.

were built during the Cold War, especially by the Warsaw Pact, but also in the West. They seem not to wear out.[56] The majority of U.S. aircraft and helicopters lost in the Vietnam War were brought down by AAA.[57] Though coalition aircraft losses in the 1991 Persian Gulf War were very low, AAA and short-range infrared SAMs caused 71 percent of the attrition.[58] Currently, the U.S. military reports only 7 aircraft lost to enemy fire in the 2003 war—6 attack helicopters and an A-10. It is likely that all were victims of short-range air defense weapons.[59] In the only major success for Iraqi air defenses, 27 of 35 U.S. Army attack helicopters were damaged and one was lost in a single raid—all to AAA.[60] Even in South Vietnam, where North Vietnamese and Vietcong units had no radars for early warning, these weapons brought down 1,700 helicopters and aircraft between 1961 and 1968.[61] Generally, it is now the strategy of U.S. and

---

56. Prior to the start of the third Gulf War in March 2003, Iraq was reported to have had 3,000 antiaircraft guns. Many of Iraq's air defense duels with U.S. aircraft in the no-fly zones during the preceding decade depended on antiaircraft artillery. Iraq did not shoot down any Western aircraft before the war, but U.S. airmen nevertheless viewed these guns as a serious threat: "For years, the Iraqis used antiaircraft artillery (AAA), unguided rockets, and surface-to-air missiles against coalition aircraft in both the northern and southern no-fly zones. In fact, they started firing at our aircraft in 1992, and over the last three years Iraqi AAA has fired at coalition aircraft over 1,000 times, launched 600 rockets and fired nearly 60 SAMs." Secretary of Defense Donald H. Rumsfeld and Gen. Richard Myers, chairman, Joint Chiefs of Staff, news briefing, September 30, 2002. See IISS, *The Military Balance, 2002–2003*, p. 106, for Iraq's AAA inventory.

57. According to Kenneth P. Werrell, "Between 1965 and 1973 flak engaged one-fourth of all flights over North Vietnam and accounted for 66% of U.S. aircraft losses over the North." Werrell, *Archie, Flak, AAA, and SAM: A Short Operational History of Ground-Based Air Defense* (Maxwell Air Force Base, Ala.: Air University Press, 1988), p. 102.

58. Thomas A. Keaney and Eliot A. Cohen, *Gulf War Air Power Survey Summary Report* (Washington, D.C.: GPO, 1993), pp. 61–62. Thirty-eight aircraft were lost, and 48 were damaged. In explaining these low losses, Keaney and Cohen note: "Although some crews initially tried NATO-style low-level ingress tactics during the first few nights of Desert Storm, the sheer volume and ubiquity of barrage antiaircraft artillery, combined with the ability of Stinger-class infrared SAMs to be effective up to 12,000–15,000 feet, quickly persuaded most everyone on the Coalition side to abandon low altitude, especially for weapon release." See also General Accounting Office, *Operation Desert Storm: Evaluation of the Air Campaign*, GAO/NSIAD-97–134 (Washington, D.C.: GAO, June, 1997), Table II.7, p. 94. Fourteen aircraft were destroyed or damaged by radar SAMs, 28 by infrared SAMS, and 33 by AAA. AAA was much more likely than the other systems to damage rather than destroy a successfully engaged target.

59. Moseley, "Operation Iraqi Freedom—By the Numbers."

60. Rowan Scarborough, "Apache Operation a Lesson in Defeat," *Washington Times*, April 22, 2003, p. 1. This was apparently a clever Iraqi ambush. An Iraqi observer watched the helicopters take off and used a cell phone to alert some air defense units. On a prearranged signal, the local power grid was turned off for a few seconds to alert the rest. See Lt. Gen. William Scott Wallace, U.S. Army, "Fifth Corps Commander Live Briefing from Baghdad," May 7, 2003, U.S. Department of Defense news transcript, http://www.defenselink.mil/transcripts/2003/tr20030507-0157html.

61. Between 1961 and 1968, 1,709 U.S. aircraft were lost over South Vietnam, of which 63 percent were helicopters and the rest fixed-wing aircraft. During this period, AAA was the only air defense weapon available to the communists in the South. Werrell, *Archie, Flak, AAA, and SAM*, p. 112.

Western air forces to fly above 15,000 feet to avoid AAA. This reduces losses, but it also significantly reduces a pilot's ability to locate enemy forces on the ground, to distinguish targets from decoys, to distinguish undamaged targets from damaged ones, and more generally to develop a feel for the ground situation. A mobile adversary, with some knowledge of camouflage and deception, operating in favorable terrain, can exploit these problems. Thus inexpensive and simple air defense weapons help to protect ground forces even when they do not down many aircraft.

Operations above 15,000 feet can be further complicated by an integrated air defense system (IADS), which combines a communications system, early warning radars and signals intelligence collection devices, and medium-to-high-altitude SAM systems, as well as AAA.[62] An IADS does not have to shoot down many aircraft to lend assistance to ground forces. As discussed earlier, U.S. aircraft leverage technological advantages to suppress these integrated air defenses by jamming their radars and communications, by targeting SAMs with radar homing missiles, and by attacking communications nodes. More often than not, direct attacks on SAMs cause the gunners to shut down their radars, which makes the SAMs ineffective. At the same time, it usually ensures that the radar homing missiles fail to destroy the launchers—hence the term SEAD (suppression of enemy air defenses). Since 1972 both the Israeli air force and the U.S. air force(s) have proven this tactic, but it comes at a cost. It is safe to enter enemy airspace only when a host of expensive and scarce special assets are assembled.

Though the United States can command enemy airspace when it musters its SEAD capabilities, it cannot do so without them, and thus an adversary gets three benefits.[63] First, the scarcity of suppression assets slows the overall rate of

---

62. Passive electronic intelligence collection consists of radio receivers that track both radio and radar emissions. Without information on the precise content of coded communications, such systems may still develop an understanding of certain patterns of communications that are associated with certain kinds of operations. Occasional lapses in communications security may provide the actual content of communications to the receiver. Radio direction finding can provide indications of where certain patterns of electronic emissions occur, and where they are going. These can be cross-referenced with what radars may observe. The reports of spies and observers can also be integrated with this information. Over time, a competent adversary may build up a picture of U.S. procedures and tactics, which can prove invaluable. It is likely that this is how the Serbs were able to shoot down a U.S. F-117 stealth fighter in 1999. Because the Serbs destroyed so few U.S. aircraft, the magnitude of this particular achievement is underappreciated.

63. Some believe that the advent of stealth obviates this statement, but that does not seem to be the case. Stealth aircraft missions are generally planned to benefit from air defense suppression, though it appears that these missions rely on somewhat less direct suppressive support than do conventional bombing missions. Little more can be said, as the tactics of stealth missions are highly classified.

U.S. attack to the rate at which they can be assembled and organized.[64] Second, it is not safe to remain in airspace that is defended by an IADS, because it is difficult to sustain enough pressure to keep the defender's radars "off the air" for more than a short time. Finally, it seems that suppression operations generate lots of patterned activity—much of it emitting electronic signals. A dense network of reasonably good radars and passive electronic intelligence capabilities can develop a picture of such patterned activities, and thus provide early warning of U.S. attacks. Married to a decent communications system, the adversary's forces in the field can be alerted to take cover.[65] The defender may not shoot down many U.S. or other Western aircraft with this system; indeed the harder it tries, the more likely it is to suffer destruction. But by playing a game of cat and mouse, the defender can survive and achieve its minimum objective—it can ration U.S. attacks and gain useful early warning of those attacks. If patient, the defender may from time to time encounter tactical situations where it can score a kill.

In 1999 the Serb army demonstrated that AAA at low altitudes and a well-constructed, if obsolescent, IADS at medium to high altitudes can offer powerful assistance to an adversary ground force as it attempts to survive the attacks of U.S. air forces. NATO did little damage against Serb field forces in Kosovo in 1999.[66] It was no doubt discouraging to the adversary's air defense troops that they shot down so few U.S. aircraft. Nevertheless, when air defenses successfully defend key assets, they have done their job. Serbian forces presented a large array of small mobile targets. The adversary could easily camouflage tanks, tracks, and guns and could also offer a wide variety of decoys to attract the attention of U.S. pilots. Serbia's mobile SAMS also largely survived U.S. attempts to destroy them, so the United States was forced to continue mounting

---

64. Relying on accounts by Adm. James Ellis, commander in chief of Allied Forces Southern Europe during the Kosovo war, Timothy L. Thomas reports the Serbian strategy: "To prevent its air defense assets from being neutralized, the Serbian armed forces turned their assets on only as needed. They therefore presented a 'constant but dormant' threat. This resulted in NATO using its most strained assets (e.g., JSTARS, AWACS, or airborne warning and control system) to conduct additional searches for air defense assets and forced NATO aircraft to fly above 15,000 feet, making it difficult for them to hit their targets. Ellis noted that NATO achieved little damage to the Serbian integrated air defense system." see Thomas, "Kosovo and the Current Myth of Information Superiority," *Parameters*, Vol. 30, No. 1 (Spring 2000), pp. 14–29; quotation on p. 8 of the web version.
65. As Thomas notes, "Their [Serbian] offsets included deception, disinformation, camouflage, the clever use of radar, spies within NATO, helicopter movement NATO couldn't detect, and the exploitation of NATO's operational templating of information dominance activities (e.g., satellites, reconnaissance flights). See ibid., pp. 3, 9 of the web version.
66. On Serbia's air and ground strategies, as well as Serbia's tactical successes, see Barry R. Posen, "The War for Kosovo: Serbia's Political-Military Strategy," *International Security*, Vol. 24, No. 4 (Spring 2000), pp. 54–66.

elaborate suppression operations, providing the Serbs with useful early warning.

There were obvious limits to Serbian success. Large, fixed transportation targets (such as bridges) and economic infrastructure targets (such as power stations) cannot be moved, and they cannot easily be camouflaged. Only truly modern SAMs can possibly defend such targets from high-altitude aircraft armed with precision-guided munitions. In the end, it was the U.S. ability and demonstrated willingness to destroy Serbia's infrastructure and economy that coerced Slobodan Milošević into accepting a deal that satisfied NATO's war aims, but that deviated in important ways from NATO's original demands. The cautionary lesson is that a well-operated, if obsolescent, integrated air defense system can defend a ground force skilled at camouflage and deception.[67]

Iraqi air defenses and ground forces were apparently less successful at this game in 2003 than the Serbs were in 1999. Information is still limited, but several explanations seem plausible. First, Iraqi air defenses were in very poor shape on March 19, when the war officially began. The Iraqi air defense system was badly damaged in the 1991 war, damaged further during eleven years of engagements with U.S. and other Western air forces in the northern and southern no-fly zones, and largely prevented from replacing its losses or improving its technology by the twelve-year arms embargo. Existing Iraqi SAMs also seem to have been in disrepair, perhaps due to their age, the embargo, or operator incompetence.[68] Second, it appears that Iraqi SAM opera-

---

67. For a collection of deception tactics and countermeasures that the Serbs are said to have employed, see "Tactics Employed by the Yugoslav Army to Limit NATO Air Strikes' Effectiveness," Associated Press, November 18, 2002. Daryl Press notes that even in the deserts of Kuwait and southern Iraq, U.S. fighter aircraft experienced difficulties attacking a dug-in, camouflaged, ground force. See Press, "The Myth of Air Power in the Persian Gulf War," pp. 40–42. As of this writing, insufficient information has emerged to determine the effectiveness of these techniques in the U.S.-led war with Iraq that began in March 2003.
68. Lt. Gen. T. Michael Moseley, "Coalition Forces Air Component Command Briefing," April 5, 2003, U.S. Department of Defense news transcript, http://www.defenselink.mil/news/Apr2003/t04052003_t405mose.html, alludes to enforcement of the no-fly zones as an opportunity to degrade the Iraqi air defense system. He reports that after the first three or four days of the war, his flyers were able to switch from suppression to destruction of Iraqi air defenses, which suggests that the defenders suffered heavy losses in the early days, perhaps because they turned their radars on too often. Finally he said that "every time they move one of those things [a SAM or radar] they have a tendency to break something on them," which suggests unreliable and/or poorly maintained equipment. After the conventional phase of the war ended, an Iraqi air defense officer, Gen. Ghanem Abdullah Azawi, declared: "There has been practically no air defense since 1991. Nobody rebuilt it. We didn't receive any new weapons." Quoted in William Branigin, "A Brief, Bitter War for Iraq's Military Officers: Self-Deception a Factor in Defeat," *Washington Post*, April 27, 2003, p. A25.

tors were more aggressive in the early days of the war than was sensible, giving U.S. and British pilots excellent engagement opportunities. Third, Iraqi ground forces appear not to have enjoyed as much success at cover, concealment, and camouflage as did the Serbs. The terrain south of Baghdad may not have been favorable to such tactics, though opportunities did exist and much Iraqi equipment survived U.S. and British air attacks.[69] Perhaps as important, Iraqi forces had to concentrate and sometimes chose to maneuver en masse to try to meet U.S. ground attacks, creating better targets for U.S. aircraft.[70] Serb ground forces faced neither the necessity to concentrate nor the temptation to maneuver on a large scale because they faced no risk of a NATO ground attack.

The 1999 Kosovo war may provide other lessons as well. Militaries that have fought, or think they might fight, the United States now exchange lessons and technology. Serbs and Iraqis discussed tactics before the war in Kosovo began.[71] Iraq sought commercial communications technology to increase the re-

---

69. One journalist who toured Iraqi defenses south of Baghdad either in late March or early April reports that Iraqi units were well dispersed, dug in, and camouflaged. He saw some damaged equipment but more that had survived. Robert Fisk, "Saddam's Masters of Concealment Dig In, Ready for Battle," *Independent*, April 3, 2003, p. 1. On April 5, U.S. troops "found herds of tanks abandoned by the Iraqi Army and Republican Guard" in Karbala. See Jim Dwyer, "In Karbala, G.I.'s Find Forsaken Iraqi Armor and Pockets of Resistance," *New York Times*, April 6, 2003, sec. B, p. 4. One postwar report suggests that "fewer than 100 Republican Guard tanks were knocked out in the battles around Baghdad, so coalition officers say hundreds of modern T-72 main battle tanks and BMP infantry fighting vehicles are still to be found." Tim Ripley, "Building a New Iraqi Army," *Jane's Defence Weekly*, April 16, 2003, p. 3. Other journalists toured the same area after the end of conventional fighting and reported the existence of vast, but entirely unused, prepared defensive positions and the destruction of many reasonably well-camouflaged Iraqi combat vehicles, though they kept no count. They note little evidence of dead Iraqi soldiers and suggest that many units melted away. Terry McCarthy, "What Ever Happened to the Republican Guard?" *Time*, May 12, 2003, pp. 24–28. On the whole, it seems that large quantities of Iraqi armored vehicles and weapons survived concentrated Western air attacks, but Iraqi troops abandoned their equipment. One cannot know if better-led, more tactically proficient, and more politically committed troops would have found ways to employ this surviving equipment to offer stronger resistance to U.S. ground forces.
70. William M. Arkin, "Speed Kills," *Los Angeles Times*, June 1, 2003, pt. M, p. 1, suggests that the Iraqis suffered grievous damage when they tried to maneuver under cover of a late-March sandstorm. More generally, a U.S. Marine noncommissioned officer declared, "Every time they try to move their tanks even 100 yards, they get it from our aircraft. We are everywhere." See Matthew Fisher, "Skirmishes in Baghdad: Marines Blow Up Scores of Abandoned Iraqi Tanks and Armoured Vehicles," *Times Colonist* (Victoria, Canada), April 7, 2003, p. A5.
71. Philip Shenon, "The Iraqi Connection: Serbs Seek Iraqi Help for Defense, Britain Says," *New York Times*, April 1, 1999, p. A 16. This appears to have been two-way commerce. Until very recently, any companies in the former Yugoslavia apparently exported military equipment to Iraq in violation of the UN arms embargo. See Williams and Wood, "Iraq Finds Ready Arms Sellers from Baltic Sea to Bosnia."

silience of its air defense communications network.[72] This assistance seems to have come from Chinese firms, which suggests that Serb, Iraqi, and Chinese air defense experts have compared notes.[73] Serbia's mobile SA-6s largely survived NATO attacks, but its immobile SA-3s fared poorly.[74] Formerly immobile, obsolescent Iraqi SA-3 missiles turned up in domestically built mobile versions on the backs of trucks prior to the 2003 war.[75] The fact that Iraq did not profit from its contacts with Serbia does not undermine the central point—past and potential U.S. adversaries may exchange information. The Iraqis themselves demonstrated in the 1991 Gulf War that mobility pays: Though coalition forces chased Iraqi truck-mounted Scud surface-to-surface missiles all over the desert, it seems clear that none were destroyed during that war.[76] Scuds made no appearance in the 2003 war, but Iraq did possess many smaller, short-range tactical ballistic missiles. Though these were priority targets for U.S. forces because of their presumed ability to deliver chemical weapons, many of these systems survived attack. Indeed, on April 7, 2003, after nearly nineteen days of combat, a missile struck the headquarters of the Second Brigade of the 3d Infantry Division, just south of Baghdad.[77]

THE LIGHT INFANTRY CHALLENGE

The 1991 and 2003 Gulf Wars strongly suggest that there are few, if any, ground forces in the world that can challenge the U.S. Army in tank warfare in open country. But there are other possible ground fights—in cities, mountains, jungles, and marshes. And the United States needs to be cognizant of some of the difficulties that may lie ahead. The first is sheer numbers. The two remaining designated members of the "axis of evil," Iran and North Korea, have conscript

---

72. A fiber-optic network was reportedly added to Iraq's air defense command and control system. See IISS, *The Military Balance, 2002–2003*, p. 98.
73. Andrew Koch and Michael Sirak, "Iraqi Air Defences under Strain," *Jane's Defence Weekly*, February 28, 2001. The article also notes that while some Serbs have reportedly helped Iraq militarily over the years, others reportedly provided intelligence about Iraq to the United States and Britain.
74. Department of Defense, news briefing, June 10, 1999. See the slide "Air Defense BDA," http://www.defenselink.mil/news/Jun1999/990610-J-0000K-008.jpg.
75. IISS, *The Military Balance 2002–2003*, p. 98.
76. For reviews of the evidence supporting this point, see William Rosenau, *Special Operations Forces and Elusive Enemy Ground Targets: Lessons from Vietnam and the Persian Gulf War*, MR-1408-AF (Santa Monica, Calif.: RAND, 2001), pp. 40–44; and "The Great Scud Hunt: An Assessment," Centre for Defence and International Security Studies, Lancaster University, 1996, http://www.cdiss.org/scudnt6.htm.
77. Two soldiers and two journalists were killed, fifteen soldiers were wounded, and 17 military vehicles were destroyed. Steven Lee Myers, "A Nation at War: Third Infantry Division; Iraqi Missile Strike Kills Four at Tactical Operations Center," *New York Times*, April 8, 2003, sec. B, p. 3.

armies: Together these two countries have 13 million males between the ages of 18 and 32.[78] They do not train all these men for war; the training their soldiers get is almost certainly uneven; and for local political reasons, some of these young men would not necessarily fight. But this total does give some idea of the potentials: These men are an important military resource. This pattern can be expected elsewhere. The world's population is expected to grow from 6 billion to 8 billion by 2025, with most of that growth in the developing world.[79] Moreover, ground troops should have no trouble finding infantry weapons. According to one study, there are perhaps 250 million military and police small arms in the world, including mortars and shoulder-fired antitank weapons.[80]

U.S. strategists must also be cognizant of the significant police problem that would arise in the event the United States tried to conquer and politically reorganize some of these populous countries. The historical record suggests that stability operations require between two and twenty soldiers and/or policemen per 1,000 individuals, depending on the level of political instability.[81] The low figure is consistent with average U.S. police presence; the high figure with the height of the Troubles in Northern Ireland. Prior to the commencement of hostilities against Iraq in March 2003, many warned that the postwar occupation of the country could require significant troops. Gen. Eric Shinseki, then chief of staff of the U.S. Army, estimated before the Congress in late February 2003 that several hundred thousand troops would be required for several years to occupy Iraq with its 22 million people. Undersecretary of Defense Paul Wolfowitz derided this estimate.[82] By the end of April 2003, Pentagon planners were projecting that a force of 125,000 would be needed for at least a year.[83] As of early June, plans to withdraw troops of the hardworking 3d Infantry Divi-

---

78. IISS, *The Military Balance, 2002–2003*, pp. 103–105, 153–154, 279, 299. Nearly 10 million are in Iran, which conscripts perhaps only 125,000 of its 950,000 eligible males annually. North Korea appears to conscript virtually all of its eligible males.
79. U.S. Commission on National Security/21st Century, *New World Coming: American Security in the 21st, Supporting Research and Analysis*, September 15, 1999, p. 40.
80. Alexander Higgins, "UN-Backed Study Estimates 639 Million Small Arms in World," Associated Press, June 24, 2002; see also "Red Flags and Buicks: Global Firearm Stockpiles," chapter summary, *Small Arms Survey*, 2002, http://www.smallarmssurvey.org/Yearbook/EngPRkitCH2_11.06.02.pdf.
81. James T. Quinlivan, "Force Requirements in Stability Operations," *Parameters*, Vol. 25, No. 4 (Winter 1995–1996), p. 61.
82. Eric Schmitt, "Pentagon Contradicts General on Iraq Occupation Force's Size," *New York Times*, February 28, 2003, p. 1.
83. Tom Squitieri, "Postwar Force Could Be 125,000," *USA Today*, April 28, 2003, p. 1.

sion, which spearheaded the drive to Baghdad, had been shelved due to the deteriorating security situation, leaving 128,000 U.S. Army troops in Iraq and 45,000 more in Kuwait performing logistics functions. Perhaps another 30,000 U.S. Marines and British troops were also in Iraq. One unnamed U.S. Army officer averred that he has not seen the army so stretched in his thirty-one years of military service.[84] Yet with nearly 160,000 troops in Iraq, Maj. Gen. Tim Cross, the British deputy head of Reconstruction and Humanitarian Assistance, agreed that there were too few troops to keep order.[85]

U.S. military personnel, however, have almost become too expensive to hire. The Department of Defense completed a detailed study in summer 2002 suggesting that the military services cut 90,000 uniformed personnel.[86] It considered asking the army to cut one of its ten active divisions. At the time, the U.S. defense budget was going up, and the United States was already heavily engaged in the war on terror. The U.S. government had defined this war broadly, and the Pentagon civilian leadership favored extending it to Iraq. The demand for U.S. personnel would likely rise. Yet the sheer expense of uniformed personnel caused the Defense Department to briefly consider reducing the size of the armed forces.[87] This suggests that the United States must avoid lengthy military operations that require a large number of ground troops.

It is tempting to believe that heavily armed, high-technology ground forces can easily defeat large numbers of enemy infantry. But two vignettes, one from Somalia and the other from Afghanistan, suggest a different lesson. Elite U.S. Special Operations forces suffered high casualties in a mission gone awry in Mogadishu in 1993.[88] They were in part a victim of their own mistakes. But Somali gunmen fought with courage, and some skill, and were assisted by the ur-

---

84. Bradley Graham, "Iraq Stabilization Impinges on Army Rotation, Rebuilding," *Washington Post*, June 6, 2003, p. A21.
85. "'Too Few Troops' in Iraq," *BBC News*, May 26, 2003, http://news.bbc.co.uk/go/pr/fr/-/2/hi/middle_east/2938176.stm.
86. Tom Bowman, "Pentagon to Consider Large-Scale Troop Cuts," *Baltimore Sun*, July 10, 2001, p. 1A. A reduction of almost 90,000 soldiers, sailors, airmen, and marines is contemplated because "with personnel eating up a significant portion of the defense budget, and with Rumsfeld and his aides eager to harness the latest technology and weaponry, the Pentagon has begun to focus on cutting jobs among the 1.4 million people on active duty." See also Robert S. Dudney, "Hyperextension," *Air Force Magazine*, August 2002, p. 2, noting Secretary of Defense Rumsfeld's reluctance to add manpower, which he considered to be "enormously expensive."
87. The final defense authorization for fiscal year 2003 approved a modest increase in the size of the U.S. active force.
88. Mark Bowden, *Black Hawk Down: A Story of Modern War* (New York: Atlantic Monthly Press, 1999), is the source for what follows.

ban environment. They clearly had "gone to school" on U.S. forces in preceding weeks, learning their patterns and tactics.[89] Their local intelligence apparatus may have provided some warning of the U.S. raids, and a crude communications system allowed them to mobilize and coordinate the movement of their forces.[90] The Somalis reportedly altered simple, Soviet-pattern RPG-7·antitank rockets to make them more effective weapons against U.S. helicopters.[91] Some observers suggest that al-Qaeda taught them this trick. Soviet AK-47 assault rifles, RPG-7 antitank rocket launchers, and ammunition for both appear to have been plentiful. And no wonder—millions of AK-47s had been manufactured and could be had for as little as $200 dollars apiece in Somalia.[92] The Somalis did, however, suffer grievous casualties, perhaps thirty times the eighteen U.S. dead.[93] The Somalis may be among the most individually courageous fighters U.S. soldiers have encountered since the North Vietnamese. But even better prepared and better armed urban infantry combatants do exist, as the Russians discovered in Grozny in 1995.

In recent years, the U.S. military has been working assiduously to improve its urban combat capability, but soldiers still expect fights against competent defenders in cities to be costly and difficult.[94] A military rule of thumb is that it takes one company, one day, and 30–40 percent casualties to take one well-

---

89. Ibid., p. 21.
90. Ibid., pp. 31, 230.
91. Ibid., pp. 110–111. The RPG-7, intended as a point-detonated antitank projectile, reportedly also has a time fuse to ensure that it will explode somewhere in the midst of the enemy in the event that the shooter misses his target. The Somalis may have somehow shortened the time setting on this fuse, to cause the projectile to burst in the air at relatively short range—essentially turning it into a medium-caliber antiaircraft artillery round. Alternatively, the Somalis may simply have learned the range at which this explosion would normally occur and fired at least some of their RPGs at helicopters at the appropriate range.
92. Ibid. p. 109.
93. Ibid. p. 333.
94. The 1968 Battle for Hue in South Vietnam offers a cautionary tale that is much studied by the U.S. military. Hue was not a particularly large city, with 140,000 people on sixteen square kilometers, though its heavy stone construction provided excellent defensive positions. It took twenty-five days for 11 South Vietnamese and 3 U.S. Marine Corps infantry battalions, with vastly superior firepower, to evict 16 to 18 Vietcong and North Vietnamese infantry battalions from the city. U.S. Army units assisted with critical supporting attacks outside the city. The U.S. and South Vietnamese troops suffered 600 killed and 3,800 wounded and missing to do so, and the fighting destroyed much of the city. Estimates of communist dead range from 1,000 to 5,000, out of a force of perhaps 12,000. See Abbott Associates, *Modern Experience in City Combat*, Technical Memorandum 5–87, AD-A180 999 (Aberdeen, Md.: U.S. Army Human Engineering Laboratory, 1987), pp. 67–68. Casualty estimates are from Jack Shulimson, Lt. Col. Leonard A. Blasiol, Charles R. Smith, and Captain David Dawson, *U.S. Marines in Vietnam: The Defining Year, 1968* (Washington, D.C.: History and Museums Division, Headquarters, U.S. Marine Corps, 1997), p. 213.

defended city block, which would usually be defended by a platoon one-third its strength.[95] It is generally believed that casualties of this magnitude would render a unit combat ineffective for some period. After two fights of this kind, it would likely take months to rebuild the unit's combat power—even if the infantry replacements could be found, which seems difficult given the U.S. voluntary recruitment system. The entire U.S. active Army has only about 60 infantry battalions (180 companies), so it would be stressed if it stumbled into a major, extended, urban campaign against an army of even modest size. Saddam Hussein's regime did not prepare to wage such a campaign in Baghdad in 2003, allowing its best units to be destroyed outside of the city.[96] But Iraqi infantry experienced their only successes in smaller cities across southern Iraq, most notably in an-Nasiriya, where they fought bloody battles with the U.S. Marines.[97] The marines suffered more than half of the U.S. casualties in the war, though they provided about a third of the ground forces. Their commander, Lt. Gen. James Conway, explained this anomaly as follows: "The forces that we had come up against were pretty much in the villages and towns along the single avenues of approach that we had that led into Baghdad. It was close-quarter fighting, in some cases hand-to-hand fighting."[98]

Captured documents from al-Qaeda training bases in Afghanistan show how competent infantry can be trained with relatively low-technology techniques.[99] Al-Qaeda trainers, many of whom appear to have served in regular

95. Barry R. Posen, "Urban Operations: Tactical Realities and Strategic Ambiguities," in Michael C. Desch, ed., *Soldiers in Cities: Military Operations on Urban Terrain* (Carlisle, Pa.: Strategic Studies Institute, U.S. Army War College, 2001), pp. 153 154. See also *Combined Arms Operations in Urban Terrain*, FM 3–06.11 (Washington, D.C.: Headquarters, Department of the Army, February 28, 2002), secs. 4–13, 4–37, 5–12.

96. According to Gen. Alaa Abdelkadeer, a Republican Guard officer interviewed after the war, the Iraqis had discussed the details of an urban defense of Baghdad before the war, "but none of this was carried out." Robert Collier, "Iraqi Military Plans Were Simplistic, Poorly Coordinated," *San Francisco Chronicle*, May 25, 2003, p. A-19.

97. Peter Baker, "A 'Turkey Shoot,' but with Marines as the Targets," *Washington Post*, March 28, 2003, p. A1; Dexter Filkins and Michael Wilson, "A Nation At War: The Southern Front; Marines, Battling in Streets, Seek Control of City in South," *New York Times*, March 25, 2003, p. A1; John Roberts, "On the Scene: A Formidable Foe," March 26, 2003, http://www.cbsnews.com/stories/200 . . . 6/iraq/scene/printable546258.shtml; and Andrew North, "Nasiriya, 0941 GMT, " in "Reporters' Log: War in Iraq," *BBC News*, March 31, 2003, http://www.bbc.co.uk/reporters.

98. Conway, "First Marine Expeditionary Force Briefing."

99. Anthony Davis, "The Afghan Files: Al-Qaeda Documents from Kabul," *Jane's Intelligence Review*, Vol. 14, No. 2 (February 2002), p. 16. Davis visited Kabul shortly after its fall and collected many al-Qaeda documents. According to Davis, "Much of the literature also underlines the extent to which al-Qaeda was a highly organized military undertaking as well as a committed terrorist network. Detailed training manuals and student notebooks indicate that theoretical and on-the-job training involved not only small arms and assault rifles but a range of heavier weapons, including

forces, gathered tactical manuals from various armies. They distilled the information from these manuals into a syllabus. They lectured from the syllabus and insisted that each aspirant take copious notes, in effect copying a manual for himself. All procedures appear then to have been carefully drilled in the field. Bases were decorated with large training posters on various subjects.

Operation Anaconda (March 2–18, 2002) provides a sense of the success of this training, though it is unclear whether the adversary consisted entirely of al-Qaeda troops trained in Afghanistan.[100] Given the obvious skill of the defenders, it may be that these were the instructors, and not the troops, waging the fight. The adversary proved extremely skillful at camouflage; a motorized column of Afghan allies was ambushed at close range.[101] U.S. forces, though supported by reconnaissance and intelligence assets of all kinds, probably located not more than half of al-Qaeda's prepared positions in the Shah-e-Kot valley.[102] In at least one case, U.S. Special Forces helicopters landed practically on top of some of these positions, and were quickly shot up with heavy machine gun and RPG fire.[103] One Chinook transport helicopter was destroyed and another severely damaged. Every U.S. attack helicopter supporting the operation was peppered with bullet holes; four of seven AH-64s were damaged so severely that they ceased to fly sorties.[104] U.S. infantry were often brought under accurate mortar fire, which produced most of the two dozen U.S. casual-

---

12.7 millimeter machine guns, AGS-17 automatic grenade launchers, mortars, and even 107 mm BM-1 and BM-12 rocket systems." Ibid., p. 18

100. The section that follows relies largely on journalistic accounts of the battle. I have supplemented these accounts with some information gleaned in private conversations with U.S. military officers. See also the excellent study by Stephen Biddle, *Afghanistan and the Future of Warfare: Implications for Army and Defense Policy* (Carlisle, Pa.: U.S. Army Strategic Studies Institute, U.S. Army War College, November 2002), pp. 28–37.

101. Richard T. Cooper, "The Untold War: Fierce Fight in Afghan Valley Tests U.S. Soldiers and Strategy," *Los Angeles Times*, March 24, 2002, p. 1.

102. In the case of one communications bunker, an army intelligence specialist noted: "You wouldn't see it unless you looked directly on it. Predator wouldn't have been able to see it." The bunker contained a radio set up with "low probability of intercept techniques," which would have made it very difficult for U.S. electronic intelligence assets to detect its presence. See Thomas E. Ricks, "In Mop Up, U.S. Finds 'Impressive' Remnants of Fallen Foe," *Washington Post*, March 20, 2002, p. 1.

103. Cooper, "The Untold War," p. 1; see also Department of Defense, "Background Briefing on the Report of the Battle of Takur Ghar," May 24, 2002.

104. According to one reporter, "Five [AH-64] Apaches were present at the start of the battle, a sixth arrived later that morning and a seventh flew up from Kandahar to join the fight that afternoon. None of the helicopters was shot down, but four were so badly damaged they were knocked out of the fight. The fire the Apaches braved was so intense that when the day was over, 27 of the 28 rotor blades among the seven helicopters sported bullet holes," said Lt. Col. James M. Marye, the commander of the 7th Battalion, 101st Aviation Regiment." Sean D. Naylor, "In Shah-E-Kot, Apaches Save the Day—and Their Reputation," *Army Times*, March 25, 2002, p. 15.

ties on the first day of the fight.[105] After several days of combat, many al-Qaeda troops withdrew under cover of poor weather.[106] Few bodies were discovered in the valley, though U.S. officers believe that many al-Qaeda were killed and obliterated by powerful bombs. As far as one can tell, al-Qaeda waged this fight with the ubiquitous Soviet-pattern AK-47 assault rifle, RPG-7 shoulder-fired antitank grenade launcher, PKM medium machine gun, 12.7-millimeter DShK heavy machine gun, and 82-millimeter medium mortar. (There were no reliable reports of infrared-guided short-range air defense missiles fired, though a good many of them seem to have been found in Afghanistan.) Pictures of caches in Afghan caves often show crates of ammunition for these weapons stacked floor to ceiling.[107] It is important to note that better ammunition for existing Warsaw Pact–pattern infantry weapons will surely appear. Sophisticated, lightweight fire control systems, which can radically increase the lethality of such weapons, have also been designed. In addition, new generations of affordable infantry weapons will start reaching potential adversaries. Even in the Anaconda battle, night-vision devices were reportedly found in abandoned enemy positions.[108] If true, an important U.S. technical and tactical advantage has already waned. In short, large numbers of males of military age, favorable terrain, solid training, and plentiful basic infantry weapons can produce significant challenges for the U.S. military.

LITTORAL COMBAT

Since the Cold War ended, the U.S. Navy has been keen to show that it is relevant to the problems of the day. Thus, early in the 1990s it began to reorient it-

---

105. Sean D. Naylor, "What We Learned from Afghanistan," *Army Times*, July 29, 2002, p. 10. It appears to me that a problem with al-Qaeda mortar fuses saved some American lives; Soviet shells with point-detonated fuses occasionally bored into the mud without exploding. Western time or proximity fuses would not have had this problem and would have produced a more lethal explosion.
106. Walter Pincus, "Attacks on U.S. Forces May Persist, CIA, DIA Chiefs Warn of Afghan Insurgency Threat," *Washington Post*, March 20, 2002, p. 1. The director of the CIA, George Tenet, testified to Congress, "There are many, many points of exit that people in small numbers can get out. We're frustrated that people did get away." Quoted in ibid.
107. Ricks, "In Mop Up, U.S. Finds 'Impressive' Remnants of Fallen Foe" reports "sheaves of rocket-propelled grenades." Commenting on the lessons of the 2003 Iraq war, Col. Mike Hiemstra, director of the Center for Army Lessons Learned, notes, "The Proliferation of rocket-propelled grenades [RPGs] across the world continues to be huge." See "More 'Must-Have' Answers Needed," *Jane's Defence Weekly*, April 30, 2003, p. 25. The RPG was widely used by the Iraqis in the 2003 war; it seems to have been their only effective antiarmor weapon.
108. Ibid.; and Cooper, "The Untold War," p. 1, report night-vision devices being found in two separate al- Qaeda positions.

self toward affecting military matters ashore, insofar as it barely had any enemies left at sea. Its first public statements about this project were *From the Sea* and *Forward . . . From the Sea*.[109] The chief of naval operations reemphasized the navy's mission close to the adversary's shore as part of his *Sea Power 21* concept.[110] Though the navy leadership understands that combat in the littorals is a different kind of mission from its past specialization, and that this requires different assets and skills, not much progress has been made in the last decade.[111]

A properly constructed sea-denial capability in littoral combat combines several elements: bottom mines; diesel electric submarines; small, fast, surface attack craft; surveillance radars; passive electronic intelligence collectors; long-range mobile land-based SAMs; and long-range, mobile, land-based antiship missiles. Aircraft and helicopters also play important roles. These systems are inexpensive relative to the cost of U.S. warships and aircraft. There are a number of militaries worldwide with expertise in littoral combat.[112] Germany, Israel, Sweden, and perhaps South Korea are probably the best in terms of combining the most modern relevant technology and weaponry, with good training and appropriate tactics. (Only Germany and Sweden organized themselves to fight a superpower navy, however.) China, Iran, North Korea, and

---

109. U.S. Department of the Navy, . . . *From the Sea, Preparing the Naval Service for the 21st Century,* White Paper (Washington, D.C.: U.S. Department of the Navy, September 1992). See also *Forward . . . from the Sea,* U.S. Naval Institute Proceedings (Washington, D.C.: U.S. Department of the Navy, December 1994), pp. 46–49.

110. Adm. Vern Clark, U.S. Navy, "Sea Power 21 Series—Part I," National Institute *Proceedings,* Vol. 128, No. 196 (October 2002). The Pentagon recognizes the special problems of littoral warfare: "Anti-ship cruise missiles, advanced diesel submarines, and advanced mines could threaten the ability of U.S. naval and amphibious forces to operate in littoral waters." *Quadrennial Defense Review Report,* p. 31; see also p. 43. Recognition is not the same as solution, however. They recognized the problem in 1992: "Some littoral threats . . .tax the capabilities of our current systems and force structure. Mastery of the littoral should not be presumed. It does not derive directly from command of the high seas. It is an objective which requires our focused skills and resources." U.S. Department of the Navy, *Forward . . . From the Sea,* p. 4. Yet progress has been slow. According to the General Accounting Office, the Navy, "does not have a means for effectively breaching enemy sea mines in the surf zone; detecting and neutralizing enemy submarines in shallow water; defending its ships against cruise missiles, or providing adequate fire support for Marine Corps amphibious landings and combat operations ashore." General Accounting Office, *Navy Acquisitions: Improved Littoral War-Fighting Capabilities Needed,* GAO/NSIAD-01–493 (Washington, D.C.: GAO, May 2001), p. 2.

111. The problem of inexpensive technology complicating great power naval operations in the littorals is not new. This was a key fact of late nineteenth- and early twentieth-century naval life, which ended the practice of the "close blockade." See Kennedy, *The Rise and Fall of British Naval Mastery,* pp. 199–200.

112. This is my personal assessment. For suggestive, supporting material, see the various country entries in IISS, *The Military Balance, 2002–2003.*

Taiwan have all developed a considerable littoral capability, though each suffers some shortfalls. In recent years no great power has actually fought a first-class littoral navy, but there are examples of how damaging the various elements of littoral warfare can be.

Naval mines are very lethal and difficult to find and eliminate.[113] Iraq nearly blew the U.S. cruiser *Princeton* in half during Desert Storm with two modern bottom mines.[114] A more primitive Iraqi moored contact mine badly damaged and nearly sank the amphibious landing ship LPH *Tripoli* in the same engagement. In 1987 a $1,500, World War I–design, Iranian floating mine nearly sank the U.S. frigate *Samuel Roberts*.[115] Iraq still possessed some naval mines in the 2003 war, but few were deployed. Nevertheless, it took nearly a week for a combined force of British, U.S., and Australian mine-hunting units to clear the channel to the port of Umm Qasr of what was subsequently discovered to have been a total of eleven mines. It was learned, however, that the Iraqis had been preparing to lay another seventy-six mines as the war began, and commanders were very relieved that the outbreak of the war forestalled this action.[116]

Mobile land-based antiship missiles might prove as difficult to find as mobile Scuds or mobile SAMs. An improvised, land-based French-built Exocet badly damaged a British destroyer during the 1982 Falklands War.[117] Land-based Iranian Silkworm antiship missiles, of Chinese manufacture, damaged two tankers at a Kuwaiti oil terminal in 1987, from nearly 80 kilometers away.[118] Similar missiles were fired by Iraq in the same area in the 2003 war, though no shipping was hit and no serious damage was done. Iraqi antiship missiles instead struck a harborside shopping mall in Kuwait City on March

---

113. See Gregory K. Hartmann and Scott C. Truver, *Weapons That Wait: Mine Warfare in the U.S. Navy* (Annapolis, Md.: Naval Institute Press, 1991), pp. 254–262. These authors note that naval mine warfare has usually proven to be very cost effective. During World War II, U.S. forces damaged or sank five to nine Japanese ships per $1 million dollars of mine warfare expenditure. Ibid., pp. 236–237. See also "Appendix A: Mine Threat Overview," *U.S. Naval Mine Warfare Plan*, 4th ed., Programs for the New Millennium.

114. The mine was an Italian-manufactured "Manta," which cost perhaps $10,000. Edward J. Marolda and Robert J. Schneller Jr., *Shield and Sword: The United States Navy and the Persian Gulf War* (Washington, D.C.: Naval Historical Center, Department of the Navy, 1998), p. 267.

115. Ibid., p. 37.

116. "Minister of State for the Armed Forces and the First Sea Lord Admiral Sir Alan West: Press Conference at the Ministry of Defence," London, April 11, 2003, http://www.operations.mod.uk/telic/press_11april.htm.

117. Max Hastings and Simon Jenkins, *The Battle for the Falklands* (New York: W.W. Norton, 1983), pp. 296–297.

118. Robert W. Love, *A History of the U.S. Navy, 1942–1991* (Harrisburg, Pa.: Stackpole, 1992), p. 784.

29, and then struck near Umm Qasr on April 1. U.S. and British ground and air forces had been in southern Iraq for more than a week, yet these systems had eluded detection.[119] Antiship missiles fired from surface vessels and aircraft have damaged or sunk several large naval vessels. Two Exocets fired from an Iraqi aircraft nearly sank the U.S. frigate *Stark* in 1987, killing thirty-seven sailors.[120] Air-launched Exocets sank the British destroyer *Sheffield* and the container ship *Atlantic Conveyor* in the 1982 Falklands War.[121] U.S. ship-launched Harpoons sank two Iranian ships in Operation Praying Mantis in April 1988. Two Iranian ships managed to fire missiles in the same engagement, but neither was successful.[122]

Though they did not prove lethal against large ships, lightly armed (Swedish-built) Iranian Boghammer speedboats proved a nuisance in the Persian Gulf during the 1980–88 Iraq-Iran War. Their main mission was machine gun and rocket attacks on ships trading with the gulf states, especially Kuwait, which provided the money that fueled Saddam Hussein's war machine. Because the shallow waters of the northern gulf were considered too dangerous for large warships, due to mines and presumably land-based antiship missiles, the U.S. Navy built two floating bases aboard large, leased, commercial barges and used them for special operations helicopters and patrol boats to deal with this threat.[123] They did this successfully, though at some risk. The use of a small motorboat by suicide bombers against the U.S. destroyer *Cole* on October 14, 2000, has added a new dimension to this threat. Moreover, much more sophisticated fast-attack aircraft can be built.[124] Major navies now feel compelled to devise new weaponry to counter these cheap, nimble, and potentially deadly attackers. In a recent U.S war game, a defending "red force" navy con-

---

119. Paul Lewis and Steward Penney, "Timeline: Week Two," *Flight International*, April 8, 2003, p. 11.
120. Marolda and Schneller, *Shield and Sword*, p. 36.
121. Hastings and Jenkins, *Battle for the Falklands*, pp. 153–156, 227–228.
122. Love, *A History of the U.S. Navy*, pp. 787–789.
123. David B. Crist, "Joint Special Operations in Support of Earnest Will," *Joint Forces Quarterly*, No. 29 (Autumn/Winter 2001–02), pp. 15–22. Crist notes some forty-three attacks in 1986, though only one actually sank a ship.
124. Richard Scott, "UK Plans to Counter Threat of Terrorists at Sea," *Jane's Defence Weekly*, June 19, 20002, p. 8. According to Scott, "Staff in the UK Ministry of Defence's Directorate Equipment Capability . . . have identified a significant gap in the capability of ships to adequately defend themselves against fast attack craft (FACS) fast inshore attack craft (FIACS), and acknowledge a capability upgrade as an urgent priority." Ibid. In an act of perhaps unintentional irony, the second story on the same page of the magazine is "Taiwan to Launch Prototype Stealth PCFG," or fast- attack missile patrol boat. If Taiwan can build stealthy small craft, then so can many other small and middle-sized countries, and the threat can be expected to grow.

sisting of small boats and some aircraft, attacked the simulated U.S. Navy task force entering the Persian Gulf and sent much of it to the bottom.[125]

Finally, though modern diesel electric submarines have not sunk any major surface combatants of late, they have proven extremely difficult to catch. Hunting for diesel electric submarines in coastal waters is rendered difficult by the poor acoustical transmission properties of shallow water and the background noise of coastal traffic. When running on its battery, a diesel electric submarine is naturally very quiet. When recharging the battery, its diesel sounds much like any other diesel in coastal waters. Its snorkel may generate a heat and radar signature, which ASW aircraft could exploit, but not if they can in turn be engaged by SAMs based afloat or ashore. A German-designed Argentine submarine made several unsuccessful attacks against British aircraft carriers during the Falklands War. Large quantities of ASW munitions were used against it, without scoring a hit.[126] When the Iranians took their first Soviet-designed Kilo-class submarine out for its maiden voyage several years ago, the U.S. Navy is said to have quickly lost track of it.[127]

Treated separately, these weapons are not only annoying but also potentially deadly. Deployed together, they produce synergies that can be difficult to crack. These synergies become even more deadly when the "terrain" favors the defense (i.e., in constricted waters such as the Persian Gulf). Bottom mines are difficult enough to find and disable when one is not liable to attack. If the minefield is covered by fire, if it lies within the lethal range of shore-based antiship missiles, the work could be impossible. A maximum effort by a task force of heavily armed surface vessels may with difficulty defend mine hunters

---

125. Robert Burns, "Ex-General Says Wargames Were Rigged," Associated Press, August 16, 2002.
126. John Morgan, captain, U.S. Navy "Anti-Submarine Warfare: A Phoenix for the Future," *Undersea Warfare*, Vol. 1, No. 1 (Fall 1998), http://www.chinfo.navy.mil/navpalib/cno/n87/usw/autumn98/anti.htm. Morgan warns, "Finally, ASW is hard. The *San Luis* operated in the vicinity of the British task force for more than a month and was a constant concern to Royal Navy commanders. Despite the deployment of five nuclear attack submarines, twenty-four-hour-per-day airborne ASW operations, and expenditures of precious time, energy, and ordnance, the British never once detected the Argentine submarine. The near-shore regional/littoral operating environment poses a very challenging ASW problem. We will need enhanced capabilities to root modern diesel, air-independent, and nuclear submarines out of the 'mud' of noisy, contact-dense environments typical of the littoral, and be ready as well to detect, localize, and engage submarines in deep water and Arctic environments." Ibid.
127. I have heard this from several U.S. naval officers. Iran apparently began operating its first Kilo submarine in 1993. At the time Vice Admiral Henry Chiles, commander of the Atlantic Fleet's submarine force did not consider the Iranians to be a "serious military threat." He did expect that "a year from now I think they'll have a greatly improved military capability." Quoted in Robert Burns, "Admiral Calls Iranian Subs a Potential Threat to U.S. Interests," Associated Press, August 4, 1993.

working close to shore against antiship missile attack, but this will surely produce a signature that will attract the attention of surveillance assets ashore and perhaps draw the combined attention of surface, subsurface, and land-based assets.[128] The point here is not that the U.S. Navy could not ultimately take a competent littoral defense force apart. It probably could. The point is that it could take time, and may impose considerable costs.

Thus far, the United States has been fortunate in that it has encountered adversaries with perhaps only one of these three capabilities—air, land, or sea. And even when the adversary has had one of these specializations, it has not necessarily been the best of breed. Serbian air defense troops were extremely good, but their best weaponry was at least a generation old, maybe older. The Somalis fought with great tenacity and, candidly, drove the United States from the country. But they were neither as well armed nor as well trained as the al-Qaeda troops in the Shah-e-Kot valley during Operation Anaconda in Afghanistan. The al-Qaeda troops were still not as well armed as some adversaries that U.S. forces might encounter, and there were probably not more than a few hundred of them in the fight. Finally, the U.S. Navy's littoral engagements in the Persian Gulf have been fought under fortuitous conditions. Iraq did not take littoral warfare especially seriously. The Iranian navy suffered because it had lost many of its officers in the 1979 revolution and arguably had never fully focused on the littoral mission. The shah of Iran had delusions of grandeur and sought a blue water navy.

One cannot predict whether the United States will encounter an adversary with the full panoply of capabilities that make possible the contested zone, and the United States need not take up the challenge if it is presented with such an array. A decade from now, however, it seems plausible that China and Iran will have mastered a range of air, sea, and land combat capabilities. U.S. Naval authorities are already nervous about Iran's capabilities.[129] North Korea is probably quite good in the arena of close, ground combat, but only mediocre in the

---

128. Iraq's naval tactics were not adept during Operation Desert Storm: "Fortunately for the allies, the Iraqis had failed to activate many of the weapons, and chose not to cover the minefields with aircraft, naval vessels, artillery, or missiles. More expertly laid and defended mines would have sunk ships and killed sailors and marines." Marolda and Schneller, *Shield and Sword*, p. 267.

129. "U.S. Alarmed by Growing Iranian Might: U.S. Navy Commander," Agence France-Presse, February 4, 1996. Vice Adm. Scott Redd, then commander of the U.S. Fifth Fleet, declared, "Iran now poses a threat to navigation and aircraft flying over the Gulf." Referring to then new Iranian sea-launched antiship missiles he noted, "From a military point of view, I have to warn of the new threat, which is represented by Iran's ability to launch missiles from all directions and not only from its shores." Quoted in ibid.

realm of air defense and littoral warfare.[130] Russia will probably be the source of most of the best antiaircraft systems sold around the world to possible U.S. adversaries, though China will surely enter that market as its systems improve. Russia will also produce and sell deadly weapons for littoral warfare. It is likely that Russia itself will remain a master of antiair warfare, will develop (or arguably redevelop) mastery in littoral warfare, but will have problems generating land power, especially infantry power.

Implications

Military strategy that fully exploits command of the commons is not complicated in principle. From time to time, even a policy of selective engagement may necessitate offensive engagements; indeed they may necessitate fights in the contested zone. The main point is that time is usually on the side of the United States. U.S. military power resides mainly in North America, where it is largely safe from attack. Command of the sea allows the United States to marshal its capabilities, and those of its allies, from around the globe to create a massive local material superiority.

Command of the commons also permits the isolation of the adversary from sources of political and military support, further increasing the U.S. margin of superiority and further allowing the passage of time to work in favor of the United States. This is especially useful against adversaries who depend on exports and imports. U.S. allies have large numbers of good, small-to-medium, naval surface combatants, especially appropriate for maintaining a blockade.[131] These ships play important roles in the worldwide war on terror.[132]

---

130. North Korea exports several vessels designed for coastal operations, including miniature submarines. It has sold several such vessels to Iran. See Bill Gertz, "N. Korea Delivers Semi-submersible Gunships to Iran," *Washington Times*, December 16, 2002.

131. Britain, France, Germany, and Italy together operate 99 destroyers and frigates. The U.S. Navy operates 117 cruisers, destroyers, and frigates. European surface combatants are smaller and less capable than those of the U.S. Navy, but they permit the surveillance and control of a great deal of additional sea space. Moreover, these navies either possess significant littoral combat experience, such as Britain, or build some of the world's most lethal littoral weapons, such as France (antiship missiles) and Italy (bottom mines). IISS, *The Military Balance, 2002–2003*, country entries.

132. Michael R. Gordon, "Threats and Responses: Allies—German and Spanish Navies Take on Major Role Near Horn of Africa," *New York Times*, December 15, 2002, p. 36. Task Force 150 is an 8 ship flotilla conducting patrols in the Indian Ocean in search of al-Qaeda operatives. Its first commander was German, and its second was Spanish. This is part of a larger multinational operation in the region, which includes ships from Australia, Canada, France, Germany, Greece, Italy, Japan, the Netherlands, Spain, the United Kingdom, and the United States. "Greece Contributes Frigate to Anti-Terrorism Campaign," Xinhua news agency, March 12, 2002.

They played important roles in the isolation of Iraq, which was under economic embargo from 1990. Though Iraq illegally exported some oil and illegally imported some weapons and military technology between 1990 and 2003, its military capability suffered greatly in these years. It failed to modernize in any significant way and was prevented from recovering its ability to invade its neighbors. The erosion of Iraq's conventional combat power contributed to U.S. confidence as it considered an invasion of Iraq in the autumn of 2002. Once the third Persian Gulf War began in March 2003, it rapidly became clear that Iraqi conventional weapons had on the whole not improved since 1991. Iraqi tactics improved slightly, in part because U.S. forces could not avoid the contested zones. Over the last decade, the U.S. Navy and allied navies quietly helped to starve Iraq's army and air force. Had they not done so, U.S. casualties in the 2003 war in Iraq would surely have been higher.

Command of space allows the close study of the adversary and the tailoring of U.S. capabilities to fight that enemy, while command of the air permits a careful wearing away of the adversary's remaining strengths. There is little that an adversary can do to erode U.S. military capabilities or political will unless the United States engages on the enemy's terms. But the United States does not need to be in any rush to launch attacks into enemy-held real estate. Instead it can probe an adversary's defenses, forcing it to elicit the information that U.S. forces need. U.S. probes can also lure the adversary into using up some of its scarce and difficult-to-replace imported munitions. At the appropriate time, if necessary, quantitatively and qualitatively superior U.S. and allied forces can directly challenge the much-weakened adversary. The fight may still prove difficult, but the United States will have significantly buffered itself against the perils of the contested zone.

In land warfare, U.S. military capabilities are particularly lethal when defending against adversaries who have to move large amounts of heavy military equipment and supplies forward over long distances. Command of space, and command of the air, permit the United States to exact an immense toll on advancing ground forces and the air forces that support them. This means that the United States should have a good chance of deterring regional aggressors, and successfully defending against them in the event that deterrence fails, if it has some forces in the theater and is permitted to mobilize more forces in a timely fashion. Command of the sea helps the U.S. keep forces forward deployed, even in politically sensitive areas, and reinforce those forces quickly. Rapid response still, however, depends on good political relations with the threatened party. On the whole, states worry more about proximate threats than they do about distant ones. But the tremendous power projection capability of the United States can appear to be a proximate threat if U.S. policy seems domineering. So command of the commons will provide more influence, and prove more militarily lethal, if others can be convinced that the United States is more interested in constraining regional aggressors than achieving regional dominance.

Command of the commons and the enduring contested zones mean that allies remain useful, more useful than current U.S. strategic discourse would suggest. The allies provide the formal and informal bases that are the crucial stepping stones for U.S. power to transit the globe. The military power of these allies contributes modestly to maintenance and exploitation of command of the commons, but can contribute significantly to the close fights and their aftermath. The NATO allies, for example, have great expertise in sea mine clearance and possess many mine hunters; Britain and France together have nearly half again as many mine-hunting vessels as the U.S. Navy.[133] Several of the allies have good ground forces, and perhaps most critically, good infantry that seem able to tolerate at least moderate casualties. The British Army and Royal Marines have 43 infantry battalions—all professionals—nearly half as many as the United States; France has another 20.[134] Given the relative scarcity of U.S. infantry, allied ground forces are also particularly useful in the postconflict peace-enforcement missions necessary to secure the fruits of any battlefield victory.

IMPLICATIONS FOR GRAND STRATEGY

The nature and scope of U.S. military power should affect U.S. grand strategy choices. U.S. military power is very great; if it were not, no hegemonic policy would be practical, but that does not mean that every hegemonic policy is practical. Today, there is little dispute within the U.S. foreign policy elite about the fact of great U.S. power, or the wisdom of an essentially hegemonic foreign policy. Even before the September 11 terrorist attacks, the foreign policy debate had narrowed to a dispute between primacy and selective engagement, between a nationalist, unilateralist version of hegemony, and a liberal, multilateral version of hegemony. U.S. command of the commons provides an impressive foundation for selective engagement. It is not adequate for a policy of primacy.

---

133. IISS, *The Military Balance, 2002–2003,* country entries.
134. Ibid.

Primacy, in particular, depends on vast, omnicapable military power, which is why the Bush administration pushes a military agenda that aims self-confidently to master the "contested zones."[135] President Bush and his advisers believe that the United States need not tolerate plausible threats to its safety from outside its borders. These threats are to be eliminated. Insofar as preventive war is difficult to sell abroad, this policy therefore requires the ability to act alone militarily—a unilateral global offensive capability. The effort to achieve such a capability will cause unease around the world and will make it increasingly difficult for the United States to find allies; it may cause others to ally against the United States. As they do, the costs of sustaining U.S. military preeminence will grow. Perhaps the first problem that primacy will create for U.S. command of the commons is greater difficulty in sustaining, improving, and expanding the global base structure that the United States presently enjoys.

Current Pentagon civilian leaders understand that they do not yet have the military to implement their policy. They hope to create it. For political, demographic, and technological reasons, the close fights in the contested zones are likely to remain difficult—especially when the adversary is fighting largely in defense of its own country. Senior civilian and military planners in the Pentagon seem to believe that somehow the technological leverage enjoyed in the commanded zone can be made to apply equally well in the contested zone if only the Pentagon spends enough money. This seems a chimera. Although one doubts that the United States would lose many fights in the contested zones, the costs in lost U.S., allied, and civilian lives of one or more such fights could be great enough to produce significant political problems at home and abroad for an activist U.S. foreign policy of any kind.

Selective engagement aims above all to create conditions conducive to great power peace on the assumption that many other benefits flow from this blessing, the foremost being U.S. security. In return for their cooperation, others get U.S. protection. Command of the commons makes this offer of protection credible. Their cooperation, in turn, makes the protection easy for the United States

---

135. The Pentagon has set the goals of "defeating anti-access and area denial threats," and "denying enemies sanctuary by providing persistent surveillance, tracking, and rapid engagement with high-volume precision strikes . . . against critical mobile and fixed targets at various ranges and in all weather and terrains." *Quadrennial Defense Review Report*, p. 30. Moreover, "Likely enemies of the United States and its allies will rely on sanctuaries—such as remote terrain, hidden bunkers, or civilian 'shields'—for protection. The capability to find and strike protected enemy forces while limiting collateral damage will improve the deterrent power of the United States and give the president increased options for response if deterrence fails." Ibid., p. 44.

to deliver. Great powers typically chafe at such dependency relationships, so U.S. diplomacy must be particularly adroit to sustain their willingness to cooperate. Command of the commons gives the United States a tremendous capability to harm others. Marrying that capability to a conservative policy of selective engagement helps make U.S. military power appear less threatening and more tolerable.

Command of the commons creates additional collective goods for U.S. allies. These collective goods help connect U.S. military power to seemingly prosaic welfare concerns. U.S. military power underwrites world trade, travel, global telecommunications, and commercial remote sensing, which all depend on peace and order in the commons. Those nations most involved in these activities, those who profit most from globalization, seem to understand that they benefit from the U.S. military position—which may help explain why the world's consequential powers have grudgingly supported U.S. hegemony.

There is little question that the United States is today the greatest military power on the planet, and the most potent global power since the dawn of the age of sail. This military power is both a consequence and a cause of the current skewed distribution of power in the world. If the United States were not the dominant economic and technological power, it would not be the dominant military power. The fact of U.S. military dominance is also a consequence of choices—the choice to spend vast sums on armaments and the choice of how to spend those sums. Nevertheless, the immense U.S. military effort has not produced military omnipotence, and it probably cannot. Policymakers need a more nuanced understanding of the favorable U.S. military position to exploit it fully and to ensure that foreign and military policy are mutually supporting.

Part II:
Primacy and Balancing in Theory and Practice

The Unipolar Illusion

Why New Great Powers Will Rise

Christopher Layne

The Soviet Union's collapse transformed the international system from bipolarity to unipolarity. To be sure, the United States has not imposed a "universal monarchy" on the international system. There are other states that are formidable militarily (Russia) or economically (Japan and Germany).[1] However, because only the United States possesses imposing strength in all categories of great power capability, it enjoys a preeminent role in international politics.[2] Following the Gulf War and the Soviet Union's collapse, many commentators suggested that America should adopt a new grand strategy that would aim at perpetuating unipolarity.[3] Belief that unipolarity favors the United States, and hence should be maintained, resonated in official Washington as well. This became apparent in March 1992, when the initial draft of the Pentagon's Defense

Christopher Layne teaches international politics at UCLA.

I am grateful to the following for their perceptive and helpful comments on the drafts of this article: John Arquilla, Ted Galen Carpenter, Kerry Andrew Chase, John Mearsheimer, Ben Schwarz, Alan Tonelson, Kenneth Waltz, and an Anonymous reviewer. I am also indebted to Harry Kreisler (Institute of International Studies, UC Berkeley) and Jed Snyder (Washington Strategy Seminar) for providing stimulating intellectual forums that helped refine my thinking about unipolarity and prompted me to write this article.

1. Germany, Japan and Russia certainly have the potential to be great powers. Germany and Japan cannot today be considered great powers, however, because they lack the requisite military capabilities, especially strategic nuclear arsenals that would give them deterrence self-sufficiency. Notwithstanding Russia's still formidable nuclear and conventional military capabilities, economic difficulties and domestic political uncertainties have undercut its great power status. China will be a strong contender for great power status if it can maintain its internal cohesion. Buoyed by its vibrant economy, China has embarked on a major modernization and expansion of its air, naval, and ground forces, including its power-projection capabilities. Nicholas D. Kristof, "China Builds Its Military Muscle, Making Some Neighbors Nervous," *New York Times*, January 11, 1993, p. A1.
2. I define a unipolar system as one in which a single power is geopolitically preponderant because its capabilities are formidable enough to preclude the formation of an overwhelming balancing coalition against it.
3. Analysts of such diverse views as the liberal internationalist Joseph S. Nye, Jr., and neoconservatives Charles Krauthammer and Joshua Muravchick agree that a unipolar world is highly conducive to American interests. See Joseph S. Nye, Jr., *Bound to Lead: The Changing Nature of American Power* (New York: Basic Books, 1990); Charles Krauthammer, "The Unipolar Moment," *Foreign Affairs: America and the World*, Vol. 70, No. 1 (1990/91) and "What's Wrong With The 'Pentagon Paper'?" *Washington Post*, March 13, 1992; Joshua Muravchick, "At Last, Pax Americana," *New York Times*, January 24, 1991, p. A19.

International Security, Vol. 17, No. 4 (Spring 1993)
© 1993 by the President and Fellows of Harvard College and the Massachusetts Institute of Technology.

Planning Guidance (DPG) for Fiscal Years 1994–99 was leaked to the *New York Times*.[4] Specifically, the document stated that, "We must account sufficiently for the interests of the large industrial nations to discourage them from challenging our leadership or seeking to overturn the established political or economic order" and that "we must maintain the mechanisms for *deterring potential competitors from even aspiring to a larger regional or global role*."[5]

The initial draft of the DPG was controversial, and a subsequent draft deleted the language referring to the goal of preserving unipolarity.[6] Nevertheless, the available evidence suggests that the DPG accurately reflected official views about unipolarity. For example, the 1991 Summer Study organized by the Pentagon's Director of Net Assessment defined a "manageable" world as one in which there is no threat to America's superpower role.[7] The main risk to American security, the study argued, is that of "Germany and/or Japan disconnecting from multilateral security and economic arrangements and pursuing an independent course."[8] During late 1992 and early 1993, the Pentagon's Joint Staff was preparing a "new NSC 68" intended to establish an intellectual framework for America's post–Cold War grand strategy. One of this document's key themes is that a multipolar world is, by definition, dangerously unstable. There is as yet no evidence that the Clinton administration's view of unipolarity will differ from the Bush administration's.[9]

Although there are shadings of difference among the various proposals for perpetuating unipolarity, it is fair to speak of a single strategy of predomi-

---

4. Patrick E. Tyler, "U.S. Strategy Plan Calls for Insuring No Rivals Develop," *New York Times*, March 8, 1992, p. A1.
5. "Excerpts From Pentagon's Plan: 'Prevent the Re-emergence of a New Rival'," *New York Times*, March 8, 1992, p. A14 (emphasis added).
6. See Leslie H. Gelb, "They're Kidding," *New York Times*, March 9, 1992, p. A15; William Pfaff, "Does America Want to Lead Through Intimidation?" *Los Angeles Times*, March 11, 1992, p. B7; and the comments of Senator Joseph Biden (D-Del.) and the Brookings Institution's John D. Steinbruner quoted in Melissa Healy, "Pentagon Cool to Sharing Its Power," *Los Angeles Times*, March 9, 1992, p. A8; Patrick E. Tyler, "Pentagon Drops Goal of Blocking New Superpowers," *New York Times*, May 24, 1992, p. A1; Melissa Healy, "Pentagon Maps Post–Cold War Defense Plans," *Los Angeles Times*, May 24, 1992, p. A1; Barton Gellman, "On Second Thought, We Don't Want to Rule the World," *Washington Post National Weekly Edition*, June 1–7, 1992, p. 31.
7. Undersecretary of Defense (Policy), *1991 Summer Study*, Organized by the Director, Net Assessment, held at Newport, R.I., August 5–13, 1991, p. 17.
8. Ibid., p. 73.
9. Post-election analyses stressed the likelihood of substantial continuity between the Clinton and Bush foreign policies. At his first post-election news conference, President-elect Clinton referred to the responsibilities imposed on the United States by virtue of its position as the "sole superpower." "Excerpts from President-Elect's News Conference in Arkansas," *New York Times*, November 13, 1992, p. A8.

nance. This strategy is not overtly aggressive; the use of preventive measures to suppress the emergence of new great powers is not contemplated. It is not, in other words, a strategy of heavy-handed American dominance. Rather the strategy of preponderance seeks to preserve unipolarity by persuading Japan and Germany that they are better off remaining within the orbit of an American-led security and economic system than they would be if they became great powers. The strategy of preponderance assumes that rather than balancing against the United States, other states will bandwagon with it. Important benefits are thought to flow from the perpetuation of unipolarity. In a unipolar system, it is argued, the United States could avoid the unpredictable geopolitical consequences that would attend the emergence of new great powers. Unipolarity would, it is said, minimize the risks of both strategic uncertainty and instability. In effect, the strategy of preponderance aims at preserving the Cold War status quo, even though the Cold War is over.

In this article, I use neorealist theory to analyze the implications of unipolarity. I argue that the "unipolar moment" is just that, a geopolitical interlude that will give way to multipolarity between 2000–2010. I start with a very simple premise: states balance against hegemons, even those like the United States that seek to maintain their preeminence by employing strategies based more on benevolence than coercion. As Kenneth N. Waltz says, "In international politics, overwhelming power repels and leads other states to balance against it."[10] In a unipolar world, systemic constraints—balancing, uneven growth rates, and the sameness effect—impel eligible states (i.e., those with the capability to do so) to become great powers. I use neorealist theory to explain the process of great power emergence.

My theoretical argument is supported by an extensive historical discussion. A unipolar world is not *terra incognita*. There have been two other comparable unipolar moments in modern international history. The evidence from those two eras confirms the expectations derived from structural realism: (1) unipolar systems contain the seeds of their own demise because the hegemon's unbalanced power creates an environment conducive to the emergence of new great powers; and (2) the entry of new great powers into the international system erodes the hegemon's relative power and, ultimately, its preeminence. In the final section of this article, I consider the policy implications,

---

10. Kenneth N. Waltz, "America as a Model for the World? A Foreign Policy Perspective," *PS*, December 1991, p. 669.

and I argue that the strategy of preponderance is unlikely to be successful.[11] It will be difficult for the United States to maintain the Cold War status quo because structural change has destroyed the bipolar foundation of the post-1945 international system. I conclude by outlining a new grand strategy that could accomplish the two main geopolitical tasks facing the United States in the years ahead: (1) managing the potentially difficult transition from unipolarity to multipolarity; and (2) advancing American interests in the multipolar world that inevitably will emerge.

Why Great Powers Rise—The Role of Systemic Constraints

Whether the United States can maintain its standing as the sole great power depends largely on whether new great powers will rise. To answer that question, we need to understand why states become great powers.[12] This is

---

11. In a sense, this article extends Mearsheimer's examination of post–Cold War Europe's geopolitical future to the global level. See John Mearsheimer, "Back to the Future: Instability in Europe After the Cold War," *International Security*, Vol. 15, No. 1 (Summer 1990), pp. 5–56. It should be noted that Mearsheimer and I come to very different policy conclusions regarding the American military commitment to Europe (and no doubt we would not agree on some of the other policy recommendations made in this article), notwithstanding the similarity of our analyses.

12. As Kenneth Waltz writes, great powers are defined by capabilities: "States, because they are in a self-help system, have to use their combined capabilities in order to serve their interests. The economic, military, and other capabilities of nations cannot be sectored and separately weighed. States are not placed in the top rank because they excel in one way or another. Their rank depends on how they score on all of the following items: size of population and territory; resource endowment; military strength; political stability; and competence." Kenneth N. Waltz, *Theory of International Politics* (Reading, Mass.: Addison-Wesley, 1979), p. 131. Because of their capabilities, great powers tend to behave differently than other states. Jack Levy writes that great powers are distinguished from others by: 1) a high level of military capability that makes them relatively self-sufficient strategically and capable of projecting power beyond their borders; 2) a broad concept of security that embraces a concern with regional and/or global power balances; and 3) a greater assertiveness than lesser powers in defining and defending their interests. Jack Levy, *War and the Modern Great Power System, 1495–1975* (Lexington: University Press of Kentucky, 1983), pp. 11–19.

Recently there have been several questionable attempts to redefine great power status. For example, Joseph S. Nye, Jr., and Samuel P. Huntington argue that only the United States has the "soft" power resources (socio-cultural and ideological attractiveness to other states) that Nye and Huntington claim are a prerequisite of great power status. Nye, *Bound to Lead*; Huntington, "The U.S.—Decline or Renewal?" *Foreign Affairs*, Vol. 67, No. 2 (Winter 1988/89), pp. 90–93. This argument has three weaknesses. First, it is far from clear that others view U.S. culture and ideology in the same positive light that Nye and Huntington do. America's racial, economic, educational, and social problems have eroded others' admiration for the United States. Second, it is not unusual for great powers to see themselves as cultural or ideological role models; examples include nineteenth-century Britain and France, pre-1914 Germany and, of course, the Soviet Union. Finally, when it comes to setting great powers apart from others, soft power may

a critical issue because the emergence (or disappearance) of great powers can have a decisive effect on international politics; a consequential shift in the number of great powers changes the international system's structure. Waltz defines a "consequential" shift as "variations in number that lead to different expectations about the effect of structure on units."[13] Examples are shifts from: bipolarity to either unipolarity or multipolarity; unipolarity to bipolarity or multipolarity; multipolarity to bipolarity or unipolarity; from a multipolar system with three great powers to one of four or more (or vice versa).[14]

Throughout modern international history, there has been an observable pattern of great power emergence. Although neorealism does not, and cannot, purport to predict the foreign policies of specific states, it can account for outcomes and patterns of behavior that happen recurrently in international politics. Great power emergence is a structually driven phenomenon. Specifically, it results from the interaction of two factors: (1) differential growth rates and (2) anarchy.

Although great power emergence is shaped by structural factors, and can cause structural effects, it results from unit-level actions. In other words, a feedback loop of sorts is at work: (1) structural constraints press eligible states to become great powers; (2) such states make unit-level decisions whether to pursue great power status in response to these structural constraints; (3) if a unit-level decision to seek great power status produces a consequential shift in polarity, it has a structural impact. Rising states have choices about whether to become great powers. However, a state's freedom to choose whether to seek great power status is in reality tightly constrained by structural factors. Eligible states that fail to attain great power status are predictably punished. If policymakers of eligible states are socialized to the inter-

---

be a helpful supplement to the other instruments of statecraft, but states with the requisite hard power capabilities (per Waltz's definition) are great powers regardless of whether they "stand for an idea with appeal beyond [their] borders."

Another popular intellectual fashion holds that Japan and Germany will carve out niches in international politics as the first "global civilian powers." Hanns Maull, "Germany and Japan: The New Civilian Powers," *Foreign Affairs*, Vol. 69, No. 5 (Winter 1990/91), pp. 91–106. As civilian powers, it is argued, they will eschew military strength in favor of economic power, work through international institutions to promote global cooperation, and "furnish international public goods, such as refugee resettlement, national disaster relief, development of economic infrastructure, and human resources improvements." Yoichi Funabashi, "Japan and America: Global Partners," *Foreign Policy*, No. 86 (Spring 1992), p. 37. In the real world, however, one does not find traditional great powers and "civilian" great powers. One finds only states that are great powers and those that are not.

13. Waltz, *Theory of International Politics*, p. 162.
14. Ibid., pp. 163–170.

national system's constraints, they understand that attaining great power status is a prerequisite if their states are to be secure and autonomous.[15] The fate that befell nineteenth-century China illustrates what can happen to an eligible state when its leaders ignore structural imperatives. But nineteenth-century China is a rather singular exception to the pattern of great power emergence. Far more typical is post-1860 Italy, a state that tried hard to attain great power status notwithstanding that it "had more in common with . . . a small Balkan state or a colony than a Great Power" in that it was economically backward, financially weak, and resource-poor.[16]

DIFFERENTIAL GROWTH RATES

The process of great power emergence is underpinned by the fact that the economic (and technological and military) power of states grows at differential, not parallel rates. That is, in relative terms, some states are gaining power while others are losing it. As Robert Gilpin notes, over time, "the differential growth in the power of various states in the system causes a fundamental redistribution of power in the system."[17] The result, as Paul Kennedy has shown, is that time and again relative "economic shifts heralded the rise of new Great Powers which one day would have a decisive impact on the military/territorial order."[18] The link between differential growth rates

15. Kenneth N. Waltz, "A Reply to My Critics" in Robert O. Keohane, ed., *Neorealism and Its Critics* (New York: Columbia University Press, 1986), p. 343.
16. R.J.B. Bosworth, *Italy, the Least of the Great Powers: Italian Foreign Policy before the First World War*(Cambridge: Cambridge University Press, 1979), p. 2. In mid to late nineteenth-century China, some attempts were made at "self-strengthening"—adoption of Western industrial, technological, and military innovations. However, the initiative for such efforts came more from regional strongmen like Li Hongzang than from the central government in Peking. Economic problems resulting from unfavorable demographics, and social and cultural factors, especially Peking's inability to mobilize the elite for a centrally-directed reform program, undercut the modernization effort. "Late imperial China experienced a profound structural breakdown brought on by traditional forces that propelled dynastic cycles. At this unfortunate juncture between dynastic breakdown and foreign intrusion, the leadership simply lacked the internal resources to protect China from other expansive nations in search of wealth and glory." June Grasso, Jay Corrin, and Michael Kort, *Modernization and Revolution in China* (Armonk, N.Y.: M.E. Sharpe, 1991), p. 69.
17. Robert Gilpin, *War and Change in World Politics* (Cambridge: Cambridge University Press, 1981), p. 13. The role of uneven growth rates in the rise of great powers is closely connected to long cycle explanations. See Joshua S. Goldstein, *Long Cycles: Prosperity and War in the Modern Age* (New Haven: Yale University Press, 1988); George Modelski, *Long Cycles in World Politics* (Seattle: University of Washington Press, 1987); and William R. Thompson, "Dehio, Long Cycles, and the Geohistorical Context of Structural Transition," *World Politics*, Vol. 45, No. 1 (October 1992), pp. 127–152.
18. Paul Kennedy, *The Rise and Fall of Great Powers: Economic Change and Military Conflict From 1500 to 2000* (New York: Random House, 1987), p. xxii.

and great power emergence has important implications for unipolarity. Unipolarity is likely to be short-lived because new great powers will emerge as the uneven growth process narrows the gap between the hegemon and the eligible states that are positioned to emerge as its competitors.

There are at least three other respects in which great power emergence is affected by differential growth rates. First, as eligible states gain relative power, they are more likely to attempt to advance their standing in the international system. As Gilpin points out, "The critical significance of the differential growth of power among states is that it alters the cost of changing the international system and therefore the incentives for changing the international system."[19] Second, Gilpin observes, rising power leads to increasing ambition. Rising powers seek to enhance their security by increasing their capabilities and their control over the external environment.[20] Third, as Kennedy explains, rising power leads also to increased international interests and commitments. Oftentimes for great powers, geopolitical and military capabilities are the consequence of a process that begins with economic expansion. Economic expansion leads to new overseas obligations (access to markets and raw materials, alliances, bases), which then must be defended.[21]

THE CONSEQUENCES OF ANARCHY: BALANCING AND SAMENESS
Because it is anarchic, the international political system is a self-help system in which states' foremost concern must be with survival.[22] In an anarchic system, states must provide for their own security and they face many real or apparent threats.[23] International politics thus is a competitive realm, a fact that in itself constrains eligible states to attain great power status. Specifically, there are two manifestations of this competitiveness that shape great power emergence: balancing and the "sameness effect."[24]

BALANCING. The competitiveness of international politics is manifested in the tendency of states to balance.[25] Balancing has especially strong explana-

---

19. Gilpin, *War and Change*, p. 95.
20. Ibid., pp. 94–95. As Gilpin notes, rising power can tempt a state to seek change in the international system, which can trigger "hegemonic war." This problem is discussed in more detail in the conclusion.
21. Kennedy, *Rise and Fall of Great Powers*, p. xxiii.
22. Waltz, *Theory of International Politics*, pp. 107, 127.
23. Kenneth N. Waltz, "The Origins of War in Neorealist Theory," in Robert I. Rotberg and Theodore K. Rabb, eds., *The Origin and Prevention of Major Wars* (Cambridge: Cambridge University Press, 1989), p. 43.
24. The phrase "sameness effect" is from Waltz, *Theory of International Politics*, p. 128.
25. For discussion of the differences between bandwagoning and balancing behavior, see Waltz,

tory power in accounting for the facts that unipolarity tends to be short-lived and that would-be hegemons invariably fail to achieve lasting dominance. Structural realism leads to the expectation that hegemony should generate the rise of countervailing power in the form of new great powers.

The reason states balance is to correct a skewed distribution of relative power in the international system. States are highly attentive to changes in their relative power position because relative power shifts have crucial security implications.[26] It is the interaction of differential growth rates—the main cause of changes in the relative distribution of power among states—and anarchy that produces important effects. In an anarchic, self-help system, states must always be concerned that others will use increased relative capabilities against them. By enhancing their own relative capabilities or diminishing those of an adversary, states get a double payoff: greater security and a wider range of strategic options.[27] The reverse is true for states that remain indifferent to relative power relationships. Thus, as Gilpin says, the international system's competitiveness "stimulates, and may compel, a state to increase its power; at the least, it necessitates that the prudent state prevent relative increase in the powers of competitor states."[28] By definition, the distribution of relative power in a unipolar system is extremely unbalanced. Consequently, in a unipolar system, the structural pressures on eligible states to increase their relative capabilities and become great powers should be overwhelming. If they do not acquire great power capabilities, they may be exploited by the hegemon. Of course, an eligible state's quest for security may give rise to the security dilemma because actions intended to bolster its own security may have the unintended consequence of threatening others.[29]

It can be argued on the basis of hegemonic stability theory and balance of threat theory that a "benign" hegemon might be able to prevent new great powers from emerging and balancing against it.[30] These arguments are unpersuasive. Although hegemonic stability theory is usually employed in the

---

Theory of International Politics, pp. 125–126; Stephen M. Walt, *The Origins of Alliances* (Ithaca: Cornell University Press, 1987), pp. 17–33.

26. Waltz, *Theory of International Politics*, p. 126.

27. Gilpin, *War and Change*, pp. 86–87.

28. Ibid., pp. 87–88.

29. John Herz, "Idealist Internationalism and the Security Dilemma," *World Politics*, Vol. 2, No. 2 (January 1950), pp. 157–180.

30. On balance of threat theory, see Walt, *The Origins of Alliances*, pp. 17–26. For an overview of the benevolent and coercive strands of hegemonic stability theory, see Duncan Snidal, "The Limits of Hegemonic Stability Theory," *International Organization*, Vol. 39, No. 4 (Autumn 1985), pp. 579–614.

context of international political economy, it can be extended to other aspects of international politics. The logic of collective goods underlying the notion of a benign hegemon assumes that all states will cooperate because they derive absolute benefit from the collective goods the hegemon provides. Because they are better off, the argument goes, others should willingly accept a benign hegemon and even help to prop it up if it is declining. However, as Michael C. Webb and Stephen D. Krasner point out, the benign version of hegemonic stability theory assumes that states are indifferent to the distribution of relative gains.[31] This is, as noted, a dubious assumption. As Joseph Grieco points out, because states worry that today's ally could become tomorrow's rival, "they pay close attention to how cooperation might affect relative *capabilities* in the future."[32] Moreover, if stability is equated with the dominant state's continuing preeminence, the stability of hegemonic systems is questionable once the hegemon's power begins to erode noticeably. As Gilpin points out, over time a hegemon declines from its dominant position because: (1) the costs of sustaining its preeminence begin to erode the hegemon's economic strength, thereby diminishing its military and economic capabilities; and (2) the hegemonic paradox results in the diffusion of economic, technological, and organizational skills to other states, thereby causing the hegemon to lose its "comparative advantage" over them.[33] Frequently, these others are eligible states that will rise to great power status and challenge the hegemon's predominance.

This last point suggests that in unipolar systems, states do indeed balance against the hegemon's unchecked power. This reflects the fact that in unipolar systems there is no clear-cut distinction between balancing against threat and balancing against power. This is because the threat inheres in the hegemon's power.[34] In a unipolar world, others must worry about the he-

---

31. Michael C. Webb and Stephen D. Krasner, "Hegemonic Stability Theory: An Empirical Assessment," *Review of International Studies*, Vol. 15, No. 2 (April 1989), pp. 184–185.

32. Joseph M. Grieco, "Anarchy and the Limits of Cooperation: A Realist Critique of the Newest Liberal Institutionalism," *International Organization*, Vol. 42, No. 3 (Summer 1988), p. 500 (emphasis in original).

33. Gilpin, *War and Change*, pp. 156–210.

34. Traditional balance-of-power theory postulates that states align against others that are excessively powerful. Stephen Walt refined balance of power theory by arguing that states actually balance against threats rather than against power *per se*. However, Walt's balance-of-threat analysis is more ambiguous than it might seem at first glance. For example, he admits that every post-1648 bid for European hegemony was repulsed by a balancing coalition. *Origins of Alliances*, pp. 28–29. Why? Because would-be hegemons were powerful or because they were threatening? He does not say directly but one suspects that his answer would be "both." Walt

gemon's capabilities, not its intentions. The preeminent power's intentions may be benign today but may not be tomorrow. Robert Jervis cuts to the heart of the matter when he notes, "Minds can be changed, new leaders can come to power, values can shift, new opportunities and dangers can arise."[35] Unless they are prepared to run the risk of being vulnerable to a change in the hegemon's intentions, other states must be prepared to counter its capabilities. Moreover, even a hegemon animated by benign motives may pursue policies that run counter to others' interests. Thus, as Waltz says, "Balance-of-power theory leads one to expect that states, if they are free to do so, will flock to the weaker side. The stronger, not the weaker side, threatens them if only by pressing its preferred policies on other states."[36]

Invariably, the very fact that others believe a state is excessively powerful redounds to its disadvantage by provoking others to balance against it. It was precisely for this reason that, responding to Sir Eyre Crowe's 1907 "German danger" memorandum, Lord Thomas Sanderson counseled that London should try hard to accommodate rising great powers while simultaneously moderating its own geopolitical demands. Showing commendable empathy for other states' views of Britain's policies and its power, he observed that it would be unwise for Britain to act as if every change in international politics menaced its interests. "It has sometimes seemed to me that to a foreigner . . . the British Empire must appear in the light of some huge giant sprawling over the globe, with gouty fingers and toes stretching in every direction, which cannot be approached without eliciting a scream."[37]

---

does not downplay the importance of power as a factor in inducing balancing behavior; he simply says it is not the *only* factor (p. 21). Indeed, power and threat blend together almost imperceptibly. Note that two of his threat variables, geographic proximity and offensive capabilities, correlate closely with military *power*. When Walt says that states do not necessarily balance against the most powerful actor in the system he essentially is equating power with GNP. When he says that states balance against threat he is saying that they balance against military power (coupled with aggressive intentions). Obviously, power is more than just GNP. What states appear to balance against in reality is actual or latent military capabilities. In a unipolar world, the hegemon's possession of actual or latent military capabilities will result in balancing regardless of its intentions. If, in a unipolar world, capabilities matter more than intentions, the U.S. monopoly on long-range power-projection capabilities—that is, its preponderance of military power—probably will be viewed by others as threatening.

35. Robert Jervis, "Cooperation Under the Security Dilemma," *World Politics*, Vol. 30, No. 2 (January 1978), p. 105.
36. Kenneth N. Waltz, "The Emerging Structure of International Politics," paper presented at the annual meeting of the American Political Science Association, San Francisco, California, August 1990, p. 32.
37. "Memorandum by Lord Sanderson," in G. P. Gooch and Harold Temperley, eds., *British Documents on the Origins of the War, 1898–1914*, Volume III (London: His Majesty's Stationery Office [HMSO], 1928), p. 430.

It is unsurprising that counter-hegemonic balancing has occurred even during periods of *perceived* unipolarity. After the 1962 Cuban missile crisis, for instance, French policy was driven by the belief that the scales of power in the U.S.-Soviet competition were weighted too heavily in America's favor. French President DeGaulle said that the United States had become the greatest power and that it was driven "automatically" to extend its influence and "to exercise a preponderant weight, that is to say, a hegemony over others."[38] DeGaulle's policy was animated by the need to redress this perceived imbalance. As Edward Kolodziej observes, "In the closing years of Gaullist rule, *the possible development of a unipolar system became one of the major concerns of the French Government.*"[39] One of the most important questions concerning international politics today is whether this pattern of balancing against the dominant power in a unipolar system (actual or perceived) will recur in the post–Cold War world.

SAMENESS. As Waltz points out, "competition produces a tendency toward sameness of the competitors"; that is, toward imitating their rivals' successful characteristics.[40] Such characteristics include not only military strategies, tactics, weaponry, and technology, but also administrative and organizational techniques. If others do well in developing effective instruments of competition, a state must emulate its rivals or face the consequences of falling behind. Fear drives states to duplicate others' successful policies because policymakers know that, as Arthur Stein observes, "failure in the anarchic international system can mean the disappearance of their states."[41] From this standpoint, it is to be expected that in crucial respects, great powers will look and act very much alike. It is also to be expected that sameness-effect imperatives will impel eligible states to become great powers and to acquire all the capabilities attendant to that status. As Waltz observes, "In a self-help system, the possession of most but not all of the capabilities of a great power leaves a state vulnerable to others who have the instruments that the lesser state lacks."[42]

Additional light is shed on the sameness effect by the "second image reversed" perspective, which posits a linkage between the international sys-

---

38. Quoted in Edward A. Kolodziej, *French International Policy Under DeGaulle and Pompidou: The Politics of Grandeur* (Ithaca: Cornell University Press, 1974), p. 91.
39. Ibid., pp. 90–91 (emphasis added).
40. Waltz, *Theory of International Politics,* p. 127.
41. Arthur Stein, *Why Nations Cooperate: Circumstance and Choice in International Relations* (Ithaca, New York: Cornell University Press, 1990), pp. 115–116.
42. Waltz, "Emerging Structure," p. 21.

tem's structural constraints and a state's domestic structure. Charles Tilly's famous aphorism, "War made the state, and the state made war" neatly captures the concept.[43] Tilly shows how the need to protect against external danger compelled states in early modern Europe to develop administrative and bureaucratic structures to maintain, supply, and finance permanent military establishments. But there is more to it than that. As is discussed below, the evidence from 1660–1713 and 1860–1910 suggests that great power emergence reflects an eligible state's adjustment to the international system's structural constraints. Otto Hinze observed that the way in which states are organized internally reflects "their position relative to each other and their overall position in the world" and that "throughout the ages pressure from without has been a determining influence on internal structure."[44]

Great powers are similar because they are not, and cannot be, functionally differentiated. This is not to say that great powers are identical. They may adopt different strategies and approaches; however, ultimately they all must be able to perform satisfactorily the same security-related tasks necessary to survive and succeed in the competitive realm of international politics. The sameness effect reflects the enormous pressure that the international system places on great powers to imitate the successful policies of others. Hinze's discussion of Prussia-Germany and England is illustrative. Their respective domestic, political and economic systems developed dissimilarly, in large part because each was affected differently by international pressures. (Maritime England was far more secure than continental Germany.) But as is true for all great powers, in other crucial respects Prussia-Germany and England were very much alike. That is, both were organized for war and trade in order to maximize their security in a competitive international environment.

Response to Unipolarity: 1660–1714

In this and the following section, I use historical evidence to test my hypotheses about great power emergence. Such a test should be especially useful because there have been two prior occasions in history similar to

---

43. Charles Tilly, "Reflections on the History of European State Making," in Charles Tilly, ed., *The Formation of National States in Western Europe* (Princeton: Princeton University Press, 1975), p. 42.
44. Otto Hinze, "Military Organization and the Organization of the State," in Felix Gilbert, ed., *The Historical Essays of Otto Hinze* (Princeton: Princeton University Press, 1975), p. 183.

today's unipolar moment. France in 1660 and Great Britain in 1860 were as dominant in the international system as the United States is today. In neither case, however, did unipolarity last beyond fifty years. France's unipolar moment ended when Britain and Austria emerged as great powers; Britain's when Germany, Japan and the United States ascended to great power status. If the emergence of those great powers correlates strongly with uneven growth rates, the sameness effect, and balancing against hegemonic power, it can be expected that the present unipolar moment will be displaced by multipolarity within a reasonably short time.

FRENCH HEGEMONY IN A UNIPOLAR WORLD

It is generally agreed that in 1660, when Louis XIV ascended the French throne, France was Europe's sole great power, "the strongest and richest state in the world"; it was "a rare situation of preeminence."[45] France's dominant position reflected her own strength and the relative weakness of Europe's other states. In 1660, France was Europe's most populous state, had Europe's most efficient centralized administration, was (by the standards of the age) rich agriculturally, and had the potential to develop a dynamic industrial base.[46] In contrast, France's rivals were declining powers (Spain), or beset by internal troubles (England), or lacked France's capabilities or the means to mobilize them (Habsburg Austria).[47]

France achieved hegemonic standing by developing the means to mobilize its assets and convert them into effective diplomatic, military, and economic power.[48] France under Louis XIV was responsible for what G.R.R. Treasure calls the *"étatisation"* of war: "the mobilization of the total resources of the state, of the economy, as well as of manpower."[49] Under War Minister Michel Le Tellier, and his son and successor Louvois, the army was brought under the administrative control of the central government and a standing professional military force was created. The Military Revolution was completed and the French army was drastically altered and improved in such areas as

---

45. G.R.R. Treasure, *Seventeenth Century France* (London: Rivingtons, 1966), pp. 257–258. Agreeing that France was Europe's only great power in 1660 are Derek McKay and H.M. Scott, *The Rise of the Great Powers, 1648–1815* (London: Longman, 1983); John B. Wolf, *Toward a European Balance of Power, 1620–1715* (Chicago: Rand McNally, 1970), p. 1.
46. McKay and Scott, *Rise of the Great Powers*, pp. 14–15.
47. Treasure, *Seventeenth Century France*, pp. 210–215, surveys the relative weakness of France's European rivals.
48. McKay and Scott, *Rise of the Great Powers*, pp. 14–15.
49. Treasure, *Seventeenth Century France*, pp. 219–220.

selection of officers, recruitment, weapons, tactics, training and logistics. Finance Minister Colbert labored to strengthen France's financial and economic base to provide the wherewithal to support its enhanced military capabilities. These military, economic, and financial initiatives were made possible by the administrative reforms that strengthened the central government's power and made it more efficient.[50]

Although France was Europe's only great power in 1660, by 1713 England and Habsburg Austria, as well as Russia, had emerged as great powers. The rise of England and Habsburg Austria—that is, the international system's transformation from unipolarity to multipolarity—is directly traceable to anarchy and its consequences: the sameness effect and balancing. Because French dominance threatened their security and autonomy, England and Austria responded by: (1) organizing the Grand Alliances that, in the Nine Years' War and War of the Spanish Succession, sought to contain France and counter its power; and (2) reorganizing themselves administratively, military, and economically to acquire great power capabilities comparable to France's. Treasure observes that, "France's example forced change on other states"; Derek McKay and H.M. Scott point out that, to compete with France, France's opponents "had begun to copy the French model."[51] The increasing power of governments was a response to external danger: "International competition and war," says William Doyle, "were the main spur to domestic innovation."[52] The danger to their security posed by French hegemony forced England and Austria to emulate France and to develop the capabilities that would enable them to stand on an equal geopolitical footing with France.

England's rise to great power status was a direct response to France's preeminent position in international politics. The English King William III was concerned with maintaining England's security by establishing a balance of power to preserve "the peace, liberties, and well-being of Europe, which happened in his lifetime to be threatened by overgrown French power."[53] In

---

50. For brief discussions of the administrative, military, and economic bases of French power, see John B. Wolf, *The Emergence of the Great Powers, 1685–1715* (New York: Harper and Brothers, 1951), pp. 97–103, pp. 181–187; Treasure, *Seventeenth Century France*, pp. 231–244, 288–320; and William Doyle, *The Old European Order, 1660–1800* (Oxford: Oxford University Press, 1978), pp. 244–245. Ultimately, of course, fiscal reforms were only partially successful and France was unable to bear the huge financial costs of the Nine Years' War and War of the Spanish Succession.
51. Treasure, *Seventeenth Century France*, p. 241; McKay and Scott, *Rise of the Great Powers*, pp. 41–42.
52. Doyle, *The Old Order*, p. 265.
53. G.C. Gibbs, "The Revolution in Foreign Policy," in Geoffrey Holmes, ed., *Britain After the Glorious Revolution, 1689–1714* (London: Macmillan, 1989), p. 61.

rising to great power status, England was balancing at least as much against France's hegemonic power as against the French threat. Indeed, the distinction between power and threat was blurred.[54] After 1688, England was at war with France almost continuously for twenty-five years and the extent of its military involvement on the continent increased dramatically. England maintained a sizeable standing army and the largest and most powerful navy in the world. The imperatives of war meant that the state had to improve its ability to extract and mobilize the nation's wealth and, as in France, England's administrative capabilities were greatly expanded for this purpose between 1688 and 1713. France's hegemonic challenge was the most powerful stimulus to the growth of power of the English state: England "became, like her main rivals, a fiscal-military state, one dominated by the task of waging war."[55]

Habsburg Austria, too, emerged as a great power in response to France's hegemonic power, and also the Ottoman threat to Austria's eastern interests. The goals of Austria's western policy were "establishment of a recognized great power position and the fight against the supremacy of France."[56] In this context, for Austria, the stakes in the War of the Spanish Succession were survival and emergence as a great power.[57] Like Britain and France, Austria undertook administrative reforms aimed at increasing the state's warmaking capabilities. "The centralizing drive of the Habsburg government, latent in the sixteenth and conscious in the seventeenth centuries, was based upon a desire to consolidate power for the purpose of state security."[58]

---

54. Secretary of State Charles Hedges said, "We are awake and sensible to the too great growth of our dangerous neighbor, and are taking vigorous measures for the preservation of ourselves, and the peace of Europe." And in June 1701, King William III instructed the Duke of Marlborough to commence negotiations for an anti-French coalition "for the Preservation of the Liberties of Europe, the Property and Peace of England, and for reducing the Exorbitant Power of France." Quoted in John B. Hattendorf, "Alliance, Encirclement, and Attrition: British Grand Strategy in the War of the Spanish Succession," in Paul Kennedy, ed., *Grand Strategy in War and Peace* (New Haven: Yale University Press, 1991), p. 16.

55. John Brewer, *The Sinews of Power: War, Money, and the English State, 1688–1783* (London: Unwin Hyman, 1989), p. 27.

56. Robert A. Kann, *A History of the Habsburg Empire* (Berkeley: University of California Press, 1974), pp. 77–78.

57. Ibid., pp. 84–85.

58. Thomas M. Barker, *Double Eagle and Crescent: Vienna's Second Turkish Siege and Its Historical Setting* (Albany: State University of New York Press, 1967), p. 19. In the administrative sphere, efforts were stepped up to subject Hungary (the bulk of which only came under firm Austrian control after the Ottomans were defeated in 1683) to Vienna's control so that Austria could draw upon its resources; a central organ, the *Hofkanzlei*, was established to conduct foreign and domestic affairs; the *Hofkammer* was established to exert central control over the finances of Habsburg Austria's possessions; and the *Hofkreigsrat* was created to administer Austria's army centrally and remodel it as a standing professional army on French lines. See Wolf, *Emergence*

Austria was considerably less successful than France and England in creating administrative mechanisms for the efficient mobilization of national resources. Nevertheless, it remains the case that the need for security in the face of French hegemony forced Austria (like England) both to emulate France and to balance against it in order to attain great power status.[59]

Response to Unipolarity: 1860–1910

In 1860, Britain was in a position of apparently unequaled dominance in an international system that has been characterized as unipolar.[60] Because it was Europe's arbiter and possessor of a worldwide and unchallenged colonial empire, "Britain could not have been met with an overwhelming balancing coalition."[61] Indeed, Britain's dominance was so pronounced that it was able in the early 1860s largely to turn its back on European security affairs and withdraw into a "splendid isolation" that lasted until the turn of the century. Britain's hegemony was a function of its naval power, its colonial empire, and its overwhelming economic and financial strength.[62] The Royal Navy was as strong as those of the next three or four naval powers combined. Britain's level of per capita industrialization was more than twice that of the

---

of the Great Powers, pp. 126–137; R.J.W. Evans, *The Making of the Habsburg Monarchy* (Oxford: Clarendon Press, 1979), pp. 148–150.

59. Although Russia's rise to great power status paralleled England's and Austria's, I do not discuss it at length because it was unconnected to the wars against French hegemony.

60. The phrase "unequaled dominance" is from Paul Kennedy, *Rise and Fall of Great Powers*, p. 152. Michael Doyle describes the international system in 1860 as "unipolar-peripheral"; that is, in the extra-European world, Britain's power was unchallenged. Doyle, *Empires* (Ithaca: Cornell University Press, 1986), p. 236. Building on Doyle, Fareed Zakaria drops the qualifier and describes the mid-nineteenth century international system as unipolar. Zakaria, "Realism and Domestic Politics: A Review Essay," *International Security*, Vol. 17, No. 1 (Summer 1992), pp. 186–187.

61. Zakaria, "Realism and Domestic Politics," p. 187. There is empirical support for Zakaria's statement. William B. Moul's measurement of the power capability shares of Europe's great powers confirms Britain's hegemonic standing. In 1860, Britain's share was 43.8 percent, while the combined shares of Prussia, France, Austria, Russia and Italy was 56.2 percent. France was the second-ranked power at 19.7 percent. Moul, "Measuring the 'Balances of Power': A Look at Some Numbers," *Review of International Studies*, Vol. 15, No. 2 (April 1989), p. 120.

62. This discussion, and the figures cited, are based on Kennedy, *Rise and Fall of Great Powers*, pp. 152–157. In the United States there is a spirited debate about the contemporary implications of Britain's decline. For contrasting views in a policy context, see Nye, *Bound to Lead*, pp. 49–68, which rejects the British analogy's relevance; and David P. Calleo, *Beyond American Hegemony: The Future of the Western Alliance* (New York: Basic Books, 1987), pp. 129–149, which sees a strong parallel between the *Pax Britannica*'s demise and the likely demise of the post-1945 *Pax Americana*.

next ranking power (France), and Britain in 1860 accounted for 53.2 percent of world manufacturing output (a bit more than America's share in 1945).

In the following discussion, I look at the great power emergence of Germany, the United States, and Japan (but not Italy's attempted rise to great power status), and analyze how each was affected by relative power shifts and the consequences of anarchy. Germany's rise to world power status was most obviously a direct response to Britain's hegemony, while in the American and Japanese cases the connection between unipolarity and great power emergence, though less direct, is still discernible.

BRITISH HEGEMONY IN A UNIPOLAR WORLD

Britain's preeminence cast a shadow over the international system. By 1880, it was widely (and correctly) perceived that the European great power system was evolving into a system of three or four "world" powers (what today are called superpowers).[63] International politics was profoundly affected by this trend, which alerted policymakers to the security and economic consequences of the relative distribution of power in the international system. After 1880, there was among statesmen "a prevailing view of the world order which stressed struggle, change, competition, the use of force and the organization of national resources to enhance state power."[64] Britain was the first world power and it was the model that other rising powers sought to imitate as they climbed to great power status. In other words, the sameness effect was very much in evidence. Speaking of Germany, Japan, and Italy, Paul Kennedy says:

In all three societies there were impulses to emulate the established powers. By the 1880s and 1890s each was acquiring overseas territories; each, too, began to build a modern fleet to complement its standing army. Each was a significant element in the diplomatic calculus of the age and, at the least by 1902, had become an alliance partner of an older power.[65]

---

63. See Kennedy, *Rise and Fall of Great Powers*, pp. 194–202. This transformation is illustrated by the great powers' respective shares of total industrial potential and world manufacturing output. In 1880 Germany, France, and Russia were tightly bunched and well behind both Britain and the United States in terms of both total industrial potential and shares of world manufacturing output. However, by 1913 Britain, the United States, and Germany had widely distanced themselves from the rest of the great power pack. In terms of total industrial potential and share of world manufacturing output, third-place Germany held nearly a 2:1 advantage over Russia, the next ranking power.
64. Ibid., p. 196.
65. Ibid., pp. 202–203.

Kennedy does not mention the United States in this passage but he could have. Although the United States did not need a large army and was able to refrain from joining a great power alliance, it followed the same pattern of building a powerful modern navy, acquiring overseas colonies, and becoming a major factor in great power diplomacy.

GERMANY'S RISE TO WORLD POWER

The effect of differential growth rates was an important factor in Germany's rise to great power status. As Paul Kennedy has pointed out, Germany's economic growth after 1860 was "explosive."[66] Between 1860 and 1913, Germany's share of world manufacturing output rose from 4.9 percent to 14.8 percent and its share of world trade from 9.7 percent to 13 percent.[67] In 1913, Germany's share of world exports was 13 percent (compared to Britain's 14 percent).[68] Germany's rising power facilitated Berlin's decision to seek change in the international system. As Kennedy observes, Germany "either already possessed the instruments of power to alter the status quo or had the material resources to create such instruments."[69] As Kurt Reiszler, political confidant of pre-World War I Chancellor Bethmann Hollweg, observed, *Weltpolitik* was tightly linked to the dynamic growth of Germany's export-driven economy.[70] Reiszler also noted how Germany's demands for power and prestige increased in proportion to its rising strength.[71] Predictably, Germany's increasing ambition reflected Berlin's concern with protecting its deepening stakes in the international system. For a rising power such behavior is typical: "In order to increase its own security, it will try to expand its political, economic and territorial control; it will try to change the international system in accordance with its particular interests."[72]

Germany's rise to world power status was a direct response to Britain's preeminence in international politics. "The Germans came to resent British power and even British efforts to maintain their position unimpaired."[73] *Weltpolitik*—Germany's push for a big navy, colonies, and equality with Brit-

---

66. Ibid., p. 210.

67. Ibid., pp. 149, 202; Paul Kennedy, *The Rise of the Anglo-German Antagonism, 1860–1914* (London: George Allen and Unwin, 1980), pp. 44, 292.

68. Kennedy, *Anglo-German Antagonism*, p. 292.

69. Kennedy, *Rise and Fall of Great Powers*, p. 211.

70. Quoted in Imanuel Geiss, *German Foreign Policy, 1871–1914* (London: Routledge and Kegan Paul, 1976), p. 9.

71. Ibid., p. 81.

72. Gilpin, *War and Change*, pp. 94–95.

73. William L. Langer, *The Diplomacy of Imperialism, 1890–1902*, 2d ed. (New York: Alfred A. Knopf, 1965), p. 416.

ain in political influence and prestige—was driven by security concerns and was a clear manifestation of the sameness effect. German leaders were concerned that unless Germany developed countervailing naval power, its independence and interests in international politics would be circumscribed by Britain.[74] Chancellor Chlodwig Hohenlohe-Schillingfurst said in 1896: "Unless we are prepared to yield at all times and to give up the role of world power, then we must be respected. Even the most friendly word makes no impression in international relations if it is not supported by adequate material strength. Therefore, a fleet is necessary in the face of other naval powers." Notwithstanding the consequences, in an anarchic world Germany had little choice but to emulate Britain by building a powerful navy.[75]

Germany's rise to world power status and the resulting Anglo-German antagonism were structurally determined. Unless Germany acquired world power capabilities, it would have been vulnerable to states like Britain that did have them.[76] William L. Langer points out that Germany's increasing international interests and the need to defend them in the face of Britain's

---

74. Grand Admiral Alfred von Tirpitz believed Germany could not remain a great power unless it developed into a first-rank maritime power. Volker R. Berghahn, *Germany and the Approach of War in 1914* (London: MacMillan, 1973), p. 29. "Naval power," Tirpitz said, "is essential if Germany does not want to go under"; Ivor Lambi, *The Navy and German Power Politics, 1862–1914* (Boston: George Allen and Unwin, 1984), p. 139.

75. Quotation from Lambi, *The Navy and German Power Politics*, p. 114. Even Sir Eyre Crowe, the British Foreign Office's leading anti-German hardliner, recognized this in his famous 1907 memorandum. Crowe conceded that it was for Berlin, not London, to determine the size of the navy necessary to defend German interests. Crowe also understood that British opposition to Germany's naval buildup would serve only to accentuate Berlin's security dilemma: "Apart from the question of right and wrong, it may also be urged that nothing would be more likely than an attempt at such dictation, to impel Germany to persevere with her shipbuilding programs." "Memorandum by Mr. [Sir] Eyre Crow," in Gooch and Temperley, *Documents on the Origins of the War*, p. 418.

76. In the late nineteenth and early twentieth century, Germany's international behavior differed little from Britain's or America's. But unlike Britain, Germany's outward thrust did not go into a geopolitical vacuum, and unlike the United States, Germany lacked a secure strategic and economic base of continental dimension. Germany was hemmed in and its rise to great power status was too rapid, and too freighted with implications for others' interests, to be accommodated. David Calleo, *The German Problem Reconsidered: Germany and the World Order, 1870 to the Present* (Cambridge: Cambridge University Press, 1978), pp. 83–84. As W.E. Mosse observes, Germany's rise to great power status "could not but affect the interests and policies of all others. It was bound to frustrate and arouse the opposition of some at least of the older powers." W.E. Mosse, *The European Powers and the German Question, 1848–1871: With Special Reference to England and Russia* (Cambridge: Cambridge University Press, 1958), p. 2. In a real sense, therefore, Germany was born encircled. Merely by existing, it posed a threat to others. There is an important lesson here. A state must decide for itself whether to strive for great power status, but success hinges on how others react. Some states (such as pre-1914 Germany) may face a difficult path to great power status, while for others (e.g., the United States) the going is relatively easy. Environmental factors, such as geographic positioning, have a lot to do with the difficulties that may confront an eligible state as it attempts to rise to great power status.

preeminence meant that Berlin was "virtually driven" into imitating London by pursuing a policy of naval and colonial expansion. Given these circumstances, "it is hard to see how Germany could have avoided colliding with England."[77] The Anglo-German rivalry was a textbook example of the security dilemma. Because Germany's rise to world power status challenged a *status quo* that primarily reflected Britain's predominance and interests, *Weltpolitik* made Britain less secure and prompted London to take counteraction. Thus, the Anglo-German rivalry illustrates that the process of great power emergence can trigger a Hertz/Avis dynamic if a rising great power emerges as the clear challenger to a preeminent state's position.[78]

Such states are fated to engage in intense competition. The effect of Germany's emergence to great power status on Anglo-German relations is suggestive. In 1880, for example, Germany's power position (measured by share of world manufacturing output and total industrial potential) was similar to that of France and Russia.[79] While London and Berlin were on close terms during the 1880s (which at times verged on *de facto* alliance), France and Russia were Britain's main rivals.[80] By 1900, however, the Anglo-German rivalry had heated up and Germany had by a decisive margin established

---

77. Langer, *Diplomacy of Imperialism*, p. 794.

78. The competition between the largest and second-largest U.S. automobile rental companies (Hertz and Avis, respectively) became famous when Avis ran an advertising campaign with the slogan, "We're number two; we try harder." The analogy of the Anglo-German rivalry to commercial competition was apparent to Tirpitz, who wrote, "the older and stronger firm inevitably seeks to strangle the new and rising one before it is too late." Paul Kennedy, "The Kaiser and German *Weltpolitik:* Reflexions on Wilhelm II's Place in the Making of German Foreign Policy," in John C.G. Röhl and Nicolaus Sombart, *Kaiser Wilhelm II: New Interpretations* (Cambridge: Cambridge University Press, 1982), p. 149.

79. In 1880, the total industrial potential of the four powers was: Britain (73.3, where Britain in 1900 is the index benchmark of 100), Germany (27.4), France (25.1), Russia (24.5). The four powers' shares of world manufacturing output were: Britain (22.9 percent), Germany (8.5 percent), France (7.8 percent), Russian (7.6 percent). Kennedy, *Rise and Fall of Great Powers*, pp. 201–202.

80. This does not contradict my argument that Germany's rise to world power status was a balancing response to Britain's hegemony. On the contrary: during the 1880s, Berlin and London were able to maintain a cordial relationship because Germany's relative power had not risen to a point that thrust Germany into the challenger's role. It should also be noted that during the 1880s the Anglo-German relationship was indirect. London was aligned not with Berlin itself but with Germany's allies, Austria-Hungary and Italy. This alignment was part of Bismarck's intricate alliance scheme and was meant to counter Russian ambitions in the Near East and Mediterranean, an objective that overlapped Britain's interests. Bismarck's system also was intended to isolate France while simultaneously keeping Berlin on friendly terms with Europe's other great powers. After 1890, the stunning rise in Germany's relative power became manifest. Inexorably, Germany was pushed down the path to world power status, and to confrontation with Britain.

itself as Europe's second-ranking power. Indeed, Germany was closing in on Britain in terms of share of world manufacturing output and total industrial potential, and by 1913, Germany would pass Britain in these two categories.[81] The dramatic change in the two states' relative power positions fueled the deterioration in Anglo-German relations, and led to a shift in European geopolitical alignments as London sought ententes with its erstwhile rivals, France and Russia, as counterweights to German power.

EMBRYONIC SUPERPOWER: AMERICA'S RISE TO WORLD POWER

It has been argued that the United States did not seek to become a great power but rather had that status thrust upon it.[82] This view does not hold up, however. By the mid-1870s, the United States was contemplating a new role in world affairs, however tentatively.[83] This outward thrust was underpinned by the effect of differential growth rates. In the decades after the War Between the States, the United States acquired enormous economic capabilities including a rapidly expanding manufacturing and industrial base, leadership in advanced technology, a highly productive agricultural sector, abundant raw materials, ample foreign (and later internally generated) capital.[84] In 1880, the United States (at 14.7 percent) ranked second behind Great Britain (at 22.9 percent) in world manufacturing output. By 1913, the United States (at 32 percent) held a commanding advantage in share of world manufacturing production over Germany (14.8 percent) and Britain (13.6 percent).[85] As Kennedy has observed, given the economic, technological, and

---

81. In 1900, the total industrial potential of the four powers was: Britain, 100; Germany, 71.3; Russia, 47.6; France, 36.8. The four powers' shares of world manufacturing output were: Britain, 18.5 percent, Germany, 13.2 percent, Russia, 8.8 percent, France, 6.8 percent. Kennedy, *Rise and Fall of Great Powers*, pp. 201–202.

82. Ernest R. May, *Imperial Democracy: The Emergence of America as a Great Power* (New York: Harcourt, Brace and World, 1961), pp. 269–270.

83. Milton Plesur, *America's Outward Thrust: Approaches to Foreign Affairs, 1865–1890* (DeKalb: Northern Illinois University Press, 1971). "Whether great power status came in the 1890s or earlier, it is certain that the United States did not make the decision for colonialism and world involvement in a sudden movement which caught the national psyche offguard. The new departure had its roots in the quiet years of the Gilded Age." Ibid., pp. 9–10. Edward P. Crapol has recently surveyed the state of the historiography of late nineteenth-century American foreign policy. Many recent works take the view that the United States consciously sought world power status. Crapol, "Coming to Terms with Empire: The Historiography of Late Nineteenth Century American Foreign Relations," *Diplomatic History*, Vol. 16, No. 4 (Fall 1992), pp. 573–597.

84. See Kennedy, *Rise and Fall of Great Powers*, pp. 178–182, 242–249.

85. Ibid., pp. 201–202.

resource advantages the United States enjoyed, there "was a virtual inevitability to the whole process" of its rise to great power status.[86]

In the late nineteenth century, the historian Frederick Jackson Turner noted that because states develop significant international political interests as their international economic interests deepen, the United States was already on the way to becoming a great power.[87] During the Benjamin Harrison administration, the United States began engaging in what Secretary of State James G. Blaine (echoing William Pitt the younger) called "the annexation of trade."[88] Focusing first on Latin America, U.S. overseas economic interests expanded later to encompass Asia and Europe as well. Like Germany, as America's overseas economic stakes grew (or were perceived to grow), its international political interests also increased.[89] Paul Kennedy observes that the "growth of American industrial power and overseas trade was accompanied, perhaps inevitably, by a more assertive diplomacy and by an American-style rhetoric of *Weltpolitik*."[90]

Again like Germany, as America's stakes in the international system deepened, Washington began acquiring the capabilities to defend its interests. As early as the 1870s, proponents of naval expansion argued that, lacking an enlarged and modernized fleet, the United States would be vulnerable and powerless to defend its interests.[91] In the 1880s, Alfred Thayer Mahan argued that attainment of world power status was the key to America's security. His arguments about the "influence of sea power upon history" displayed an intuitive understanding of the sameness effect and he presciently argued that, to become a world power, the United States would have to emulate Britain's naval, colonial, and trade policies.[92] America's naval buildup began during the Harrison administration (1889–93) when Navy Secretary Tracy

---

86. Kennedy, *Rise and Fall of Great Powers*, p. 242.
87. Quoted in Walter LaFeber, *The New Empire: An Interpretation of American Expansion, 1860–1898* (Ithaca: Cornell University Press, 1963), pp. 69–70.
88. Quoted in ibid., p. 106.
89. American policymakers believed that overseas markets were more crucial to the nation's economic health than in fact was true. By 1913, foreign trade accounted for only 8 percent of GNP, compared with 26 percent for Britain. Kennedy, *Rise and Fall of Great Powers*, p. 244.
90. Kennedy, *Rise and Fall of Great Powers*, p. 246.
91. J.A.S. Grenville and George B. Young, *Politics, Strategy, and American Diplomacy: Studies in American Foreign Policy, 1873–1917* (New Haven: Yale University Press, 1966), pp. 5–6.
92. On Mahan's views, see Harold and Margaret Sprout, *The Rise of American Naval Power, 1776–1918* (Princeton: Princeton University Press, 1944), pp. 202–222; LaFeber, *The New Empire*, pp. 80–95.

persuaded Congress to authorize construction of a modern battleship fleet.[93] This building program signalled a break with the navy's traditional strategy of protecting American commerce, in favor of one challenging rivals for command of the sea. Responding to an increasingly competitive international environment, the navy chose "to make itself into a European-style force ready for combat with the navies of the other major powers."[94] America's naval buildup was underpinned by its rising economic power. Naval expenditures as a percentage of federal spending rose from 6.9 percent in 1890 to 19 percent in 1914 and Kennedy recounts the shock of a famous British warship designer when he discovered during a 1904 visit that America's industrial capabilities were such that the United States was simultaneously building 14 battleships and 13 armored cruisers.[95]

The extent to which America's great power emergence was a direct response to unipolarity is unclear. It is apparent, however, that Britain's preeminence was at least an important factor. The impetus for America's naval buildup and growing geopolitical assertiveness was deepening apprehension about the Western hemisphere's vulnerability to European encroachment, especially if the European great powers shifted the focus of their colonial rivalries from Asia to the Americas.[96] Policymakers became convinced that "American claims in Latin America would only be as strong as the military force behind them. Consequently, as American stakes in Central and South America increased, so did American military [i.e., naval] strength."[97] Thus, America's rise to great power status was a defensive reaction to the threat posed by others to its expanding overseas interests. Until 1898, the United States regarded Britain as the main danger to its strategic and commercial interests in the Western hemispheres.[98] No doubt, American feelings toward

---

93. For a brief discussion, see Kenneth J. Hagan, *This People's Navy: The Making of American Sea Power* (New York: The Free Press, 1991), pp. 194–197.

94. Ibid., p. 186.

95. Kennedy, *Rise and Fall of Great Powers*, pp. 243, 247.

96. The relationship between security worries and American foreign and strategic policy is explored in Richard D. Challener, *Admirals, Generals and Foreign Policy, 1898–1914* (Princeton: Princeton University Press, 1973); and Grenville and Young, *Politics, Strategy and American Diplomacy.*

97. LaFeber, *New Empire*, p. 229.

98. Kinley J. Brauer has argued that between 1815 and 1860, American leaders were concerned about the implications of Britain's expanding global interests, and various strategies were contemplated to counter the threat posed by Britain's naval and economic power and its formal and informal empire. Although these proposed strategic responses to British power did not

Britain were ambivalent because not only was the United States threatened by Britain's hegemony but simultaneously it was also a major beneficiary of London's preeminence. Nevertheless, Britain's predominance was tolerated only until the United States was strong enough to challenge it. Backed by growing naval power and unlimited industrial potential, in the mid-1890s the United States launched a diplomatic offensive against Britain. In 1895–96, the United States provoked a crisis with Britain over the seemingly obscure boundary dispute between Venezuela and British Guiana.[99] London was compelled to back down and to acknowledge America's hemispheric primacy. By 1903, Britain had given in completely to American demands concerning control over the proposed isthmian canal and the boundary between Alaska and Canada. Shortly thereafter, Britain bowed to the reality of America's overwhelming regional power and withdrew its naval and military forces from North America.

JAPAN: EXTERNAL THREAT, INTERNAL RESPONSE

Japan's great power emergence differed from Germany's and America's. The effect of differential growth rates was not a factor. Between 1860 and 1938, comparative measures of great power capabilities put Japan at or near the bottom of the list. For example, between 1860 and 1938, Japan's share of world manufacturing output rose only from 2.6 percent to 3.8 percent.[100] Japan's great power emergence was, rather, driven by its extreme vulnerability. Indeed, in the 1860s, Japan's very existence as a nation-state was at risk.

Although Japan's security-driven great power emergence was not a direct response to unipolarity, here too Britain's preeminence had its effect. Specifically, it was Britain's defeat of China in the Opium Wars, and China's consequent loss of independence, that provided an object lesson for the

---

come to fruition before the War Between the States, they nevertheless laid the groundwork for America's subsequent rise to world power status. Kinley J. Brauer, "The United States and British Imperial Expansion," *Diplomatic History,* Vol. 12, No. 1 (Winter 1988), pp. 19–38.

99. For brief discussions of the Venezuela crisis, see J.A.S. Grenville, *Lord Salisbury and Foreign Policy at the Close of the Nineteenth Century* (London: Athlone Press, 1964), pp. 54–73; May, *Imperial Democracy,* pp. 35–55; LaFeber, *The New Empire,* pp. 242–283; and "The Background of Cleveland's Venezuelan Policy: A Reconsideration," *American Historical Review,* Vol. 66, No. 4 (July 1961), pp. 947–967.

100. Kennedy, *Rise and Fall of Great Powers,* pp. 198–209.

reformers who led the Maiji Restoration.[101] They were determined that Japan would not suffer China's fate. As Shumpei Okamoto notes, the Maiji reformers shared a common purpose: "Throughout the Meiji period, the aspiration and resolve shared by all those concerned with the fate of the nation were that Japan strive to maintain its independence in a world dominated by the Western powers."[102] The reformers' aim was neatly expressed in the slogan *fukoku kyohei*—"enrich the country, strengthen the army"—which "became the official program of the Meiji government, geared to achieving the strength with which Japan could resist the West."[103]

Driven by security concerns, Japan's great power emergence reflected the sameness effect. To be secure Japan needed to develop the kind of military and economic capabilities that would enable it to compete with the West. In Maiji Japan, therefore, domestic politics was shaped by foreign policy concerns.[104] The era's governmental and administrative reforms, for example, were intended to reorganize Japan's central governmental structure along Western lines; centralized government was seen to be necessary if Japan were to organize itself to defend its interests from foreign encroachment.[105] Similarly, the Imperial Edict abolishing the feudal domains (1871) justified the action by observing that Japan needed a strong central government if it was "to stand on an equal footing with countries abroad."[106]

Recognizing the link between economics and national power, the Meiji era reformers worked hard to expand Japan's industrial and commercial strength. Toshimichi Okubo said in 1874:

A country's strength depends on the prosperity of its people . . .[which] in turn depends upon their productive capacity. And although the amount of production is determined in large measure by the diligence of the people

---

101. The intellectual background of the Meiji Restoration is discussed in W.G. Beasley, *The Meiji Restoration* (Stanford: Stanford University Press, 1972), pp. 74–139.
102. Shumpei Okamoto, *The Japanese Oligarchy and the Russo-Japanese War* (New York: Columbia University Press, 1960), p. 43.
103. Beasley, *The Meiji Restoration*, p. 379.
104. See James B. Crowley, "Japan's Military Foreign Policies," in James W. Morley, ed., *Japan's Foreign Policy, 1868–1941: A Research Guide* (New York: Columbia University Press, 1974). Also see W.G. Beasley, *The Rise of Modern Japan* (London: Weidenfeld and Nicolson, 1990), p. 21, where it is similarly pointed out that the Meiji Restoration, and its consequent reforms, were based on the assumption that a causal relationship existed between modernization at home and success in foreign policy.
105. See Beasley, *Rise of Modern Japan*, pp. 68–69; and *The Meiji Restoration*, pp. 303–304.
106. Quoted in Beasley, *The Meiji Restoration*, p. 347.

engaged in manufacturing industries, a deeper probe for the ultimate determinate reveals no instance when a country's productive power was increased without the patronage and encouragement of the government and its officials.[107]

Okubo, a key figure in the early Restoration governments, had visited Europe, including Bismarckian Germany. His travels underscored for Okubo the competitive nature of international politics and "convinced him that he must establish for Japan the same bases upon which the world powers of the day had founded their wealth and strength."[108] Under his direction, the government supported the expansion of manufacturing, trade, and shipping. At all times, there was a sense of urgency about Japan's internal efforts to enhance its national security by becoming a great power. Field Marshal Aritomo Yamagata, one of the Meiji era's towering political and military figures, said in 1898 that if Japan wanted to avoid lagging behind the West, "we cannot relax for even a day from encouraging education, greater production, communications and trade."[109]

From the beginning, almost every aspect of Meiji policy was directed toward safeguarding Japan's security and to vindicating its claim to equal status with the Western powers. To this end, Field Marshal Yamagata stressed, no effort must be spared to expand Japan's army and navy and to revise the post-1853 unequal treaties that the Western powers had forced upon Tokyo. These goals had largely been accomplished by 1890. A rising Japan then began to project its power outwards. The fear that the European powers would try to deny Japan economic access to China led the Japanese leadership to conclude that Japan must establish its own sphere of influence on the mainland.[110] Japan "found that a concern with defense led easily to arguments for expansion."[111] Japan's policy led to the Sino-Japanese War of 1894–95 and eventually to the Russo-Japanese War of 1904–05. Japan's mili-

---

107. Quoted in Masakazu Iwata, *Okubo Toshimichi: The Bismarck of Modern Japan* (Berkeley: University of California Press, 1964), p. 236.
108. Ibid., p. 175.
109. Quoted in Roger F. Hackett, *Yamagata Aritomo and the Rise of Modern Japan, 1838–1922* (Cambridge: Harvard University Press, 1971), p. 195.
110. Crowley, "Japan's Military Foreign Policies," p. 14.
111. Beasley, *Rise of Modern Japan*, p. 140. Beasley's observation seems entirely correct. Fear begets expansion. And expansion has its own consequences. As John Lewis Gaddis comments, "the principal occupational hazard as a general rule of being a great power is paranoia . . . and the exhaustion it ultimately produces." "Toward the Post–Cold War World," in John Lewis Gaddis, *The United States and the End of the Cold War: Implications, Reconsiderations, Provocations* (New York: Oxford University Press, 1992), p. 215.

tary successes in these conflicts established it as the leading power in North-east Asia, and Japan's victory over Russia "secured her recognition as a major world power."[112]

HISTORY, UNIPOLARITY AND GREAT POWER EMERGENCE

There is a strong correlation between unipolarity and great power emergence. Late seventeenth-century England and Austria and late nineteenth-century Germany balanced against the dominant pole in the system. Moreover, even when great power emergence was not driven primarily by the need to counterbalance the hegemon's power, the shadow of preeminence was an important factor.[113] This is illustrated by the rise of the United States and Japan to great power status in the late nineteenth century. It is, therefore, apparent that a general tendency exists during unipolar moments: several new great powers simultaneously enter the international system. The events of the late nineteenth century also illustrate how competition from established great powers combined with challenges from rising great powers to diminish Britain's relative power and erode its primacy. During the last years of the nineteenth century, Britain, the most powerful state in the system, was the target of others' balancing policies. "The story of European international relations in the 1890s is the story of the assault of Russia and France upon the territorial position of Britain in Asia and Africa, and the story of the great economic duel between England and her all-too-efficient German rival."[114]

In the late nineteenth century, the growth of American, German, and Japanese naval power compelled Britain to forgo its policy of maintaining global naval supremacy.[115] Indeed, Britain was pressed hard by its rivals on all fronts. By 1900, it was apparent that London could not simultaneously meet the German challenge across the North Sea, defend its imperial and colonial interests from French and Russian pressure, and preserve its position in the Western hemisphere. Britain withdrew from the Western hemisphere

---

112. Ian Nish, *Japanese Foreign Policy, 1869–1942* (London: Routledge and Kegan Paul, 1977), p. 78.

113. The shadow effect is a consequence of anarchy. The unbalanced distribution of power in the hegemon's favor implicitly threatens others' security. This is because states must react to the hegemon's capabilities rather than to its intentions. In a unipolar system, concern with security is a compelling reason for eligible states to acquire great power capabilities, even if they are not immediately menaced by the hegemon

114. Langer, *The Diplomacy of Imperialism*, p. 415.

115. See Aaron L. Friedberg, *The Weary Titan: Britain and the Experience of Relative Decline, 1895–1905* (Princeton: Princeton University Press, 1988), pp. 135–208.

because London realized it lacked the resources to compete successfully against the United States and that the naval forces deployed in North American waters could better be used elsewhere.[116] The Anglo-Japanese alliance was driven, from London's standpoint, by the need to use Japanese naval power to protect Britain's East Asian interests and thereby allow the Royal Navy units in the Far East to be redeployed to home waters. Like the rapprochement with Washington and the alliance with Tokyo, the ententes with France and Russia also evidenced Britain's declining relative power. By 1907, Britain's geopolitical position "depended upon the kindness of strangers." Over the longer term, the great power emergence of the United States and Japan paved the way for Britain's eclipse, first as hegemon and then as a great power. In the 1930s, Japanese power cost Britain its Far Eastern position, and America's relative power ultimately rose to a point where it could displace Britain as hegemon. Such was the result of Britain's policy of benign hegemony, a policy that did not merely abstain from opposing, but actually had the effect of facilitating the emergence of new great powers.

After the Cold War: America in a Unipolar World?

The historical evidence from 1660–1714 and 1860–1914 strongly supports the hypothesis derived from neorealist theory: unipolar moments cause geopolitical backlashes that lead to multipolarity. Nevertheless, in principle, a declining hegemon does have an alternative to a policy of tolerating the rise of new great powers: it can actively attempt to suppress their emergence. Thus, if Washington were prepared to contemplate preventive measures (including the use of force), it might be able to beat back rising challengers.[117] But, although prevention may seem attractive at first blush, it is a stop-gap measure. It may work once, but over time the effect of differential growth rates ensures that other challengers will subsequently appear. Given its probable costs and risks, prevention is not a strategy that would lend itself to repetition.

---

116. See C.J. Lowe and M.L. Dockrill, *The Mirage of Power*, Vol. I: *British Foreign Policy, 1902–14* (London: Routledge and Kegan Paul, 1972), pp. 96–106.
117. When a hegemon finds its primacy threatened, the best strategy is "to eliminate the source of the problem." Gilpin, *War and Change*, p. 191.

THE STRATEGY OF PREPONDERANCE

In any event, the United States has chosen a somewhat different strategy to maintain its primacy. Essentially the United States is trying to maintain intact the international order it constructed in World War II's aftermath. As Melvyn Leffler points out, after 1945 American strategy aimed at achieving a "preponderance of power" in the international system.[118] Washington sought to incorporate Western Europe, West Germany, and Japan into an American-led alliance; create an open global economy that would permit the unfettered movement of goods, capital and technology; and create an international environment conducive to America's democratic values. While committed to reviving Western Europe, Germany, and Japan economically and politically, Washington also believed that "neither an integrated Europe nor a united Germany nor an independent Japan must be permitted to emerge as a third force or a neutral bloc."[119] To maintain its preeminence in the non-Soviet world, American strategy used both benevolent and coercive incentives.

In attempting to perpetuate unipolarity, the United States is pursuing essentially the same goals, and using the same means to achieve them, that it pursued in its postwar quest for preponderance.[120] The "new NSC 68" argues that American grand strategy should actively attempt to mold the international environment by creating a secure world in which American interests are protected. American alliances with Japan and Germany are viewed as an integral part of a strategy that seeks: (1) to prevent multipolar rivalries; (2) to discourage the rise of global hegemons; and (3) to preserve a cooperative and healthy world economy. The forward deployment of U.S. military forces abroad is now viewed primarily as a means of preserving unipolarity. If the United States continues to extend security guarantees to Japan and Germany, it is reasoned, they will have no incentive to develop great power capabilities. Indeed, fear that Japan and Germany will acquire independent capabilities—that is, that they will become great powers—per-

---

118. Melvyn P. Leffler, *A Preponderance of Power: National Security, the Truman Administration, and the Cold War* (Stanford: Stanford University Press, 1992).

119. Ibid., p. 17. For second-image theorists, America's rejection of a preventive war strategy is unsurprising. It has been argued that in addition to not fighting other democracies, declining democratic powers also do not engage in preventive war against rising challengers. Randall Schweller, "Domestic Structure and Preventive War: Are Democracies More Pacific?" *World Politics*, Vol. 44, No. 2 (January 1992), pp. 235–269.

120. As I discuss below, it was the bipolar structure of the postwar system that allowed Washington to pursue a strategy of preponderance successfully and thereby smother the re-emergence of Japan and Germany as great powers.

vades the thinking of American strategists. For example, a recent RAND study of American strategy in the Pacific says that Washington must manage relations with Tokyo to maintain "the current alliance and reduce Japanese incentives for major rearmament."[121] A RAND study of the future of U.S. forces in Europe suggests that American withdrawal from Europe could result in Germany reemerging as "a heavy handed rogue elephant in Central Europe" because it would drive Germany in the "direction of militarization, nuclearization, and chronically insecure policies."[122]

Inevitably, a strategy of preponderance will fail. A strategy of more or less benign hegemony does not prevent the emergence of new great powers. The fate of nineteenth-century Britain, which followed such a strategy, is illustrative. A strategy of benign hegemony allows others to free-ride militarily and economically. Over time, the effect is to erode the hegemon's preeminence. A hegemon tends to overpay for security, which eventually weakens the internal foundation of its external position. Other states underpay for security, which allows them to shift additional resources into economically productive investments. Moreover, benign hegemony facilitates the diffusion of wealth and technology to potential rivals. As a consequence, differential growth rates trigger shifts in relative economic power that ultimately result in the emergence of new great powers. No doubt, the strategy of preponderance could prolong unipolarity somewhat, as long as eligible states calculate that the benefits of free riding outweigh the constraints imposed on them by American hegemony. Over time, however, such a policy will accelerate the hegemon's relative decline.

There is another reason why a strategy of preponderance will not work. Such a strategy articulates a vision of an American-led international order. George Bush's New World Order and Bill Clinton's apparent commitment to assertive projection of America's democratic and human rights values reflect America's desire to "press its preferred policies" on others.[123] But there is more to it than that. Other states can justifiably infer that Washington's

---

121. James A. Winnefeld, et al., *A New Strategy and Fewer Forces: The Pacific Dimension*, R-4089/1-USDP (Santa Monica, Calif.: RAND 1992), p. 111.
122. Richard L. Kugler, *The Future U.S. Military Presence in Europe: Forces and Requirements for the Post–Cold War Era*, R-4194-EUCOM/NA (Santa Monica, Calif.: RAND, 1992), pp. 11, 16.
123. As Waltz points out, other states cannot trust an excessively powerful state to behave with moderation. The United States may believe it is acting for the noblest of reasons. But, he notes, America's definition of peace, justice, and world order reflects American interests and may conflict with the interests of other states. "With benign intent, the United States has behaved, and until its power is brought into some semblance of balance, will continue to behave in ways that frighten and annoy others." Waltz, "America as a Model?" p. 669.

unipolar aspirations will result in the deliberate application of American power to compel them to adhere to the United States' policy preferences. For example, in a February 1991 address to the New York Economic Club, Bush said that because the United States had taken the leader's role in the Gulf militarily, America's renewed credibility would cause Germany and Japan to be more forthcoming in their economic relations with Washington.[124] Several weeks later, Harvard professor Joseph S. Nye, Jr. suggested that the deployment of United States forces in Europe and Japan could be used as a bargaining chip in trade negotiations with those countries.[125] Such a "leverage strategy" is no mere abstraction. In February 1992, then Vice President Dan Quayle linked the continuance of America's security commitment to NATO with West European concessions in the GATT negotiations.[126]

The leverage strategy is the hegemonic stability theory's dark side. It calls for the United States to use its military power to compel other states to give in on issue areas where America has less power. It is a coercive strategy that attempts to take advantage of the asymmetries in great power capabilities that favor the United States. The leverage strategy is not new. Washington employed it from time to time in intra-alliance relations during the Cold War. However, American policies that others found merely irritating in a bipolar world may seem quite threatening in a unipolar world. For example, Japan almost certainly must realize that its lack of power projection capability renders it potentially vulnerable to leverage policies based on America's present ability to control the flow of Persian Gulf oil. Proponents of America's preponderance have missed a fundamental point: other states react to the threat of hegemony, not to the hegemon's identity. American leaders may regard the United States as a benevolent hegemon, but others cannot afford to take such a relaxed view.

REACTION TO UNIPOLARITY: TOWARDS A MULTIPOLAR WORLD

There is ample evidence that widespread concern exists today about America's currently unchallenged dominance in international politics.[127] In Sep-

---

124. Quoted in Norman Kempster, "U.S., Allies Might Help Iraq Rebuild After War, Baker Says," *Los Angeles Times*, February 17, 1991, p. A1.
125. William J. Eaton, "Democrats Groping For Image Building Issues," *Los Angeles Times*, March 9, 1991, p. A14.
126. William Tuohy, "Quayle Remarks Spark European Alarm on Trade vs. Security," *Los Angeles Times*, February 11, 1992, p. A4; Craig R. Whitney, "Quayle, Ending European Trip, Lobbies for New Trade Accord," *New York Times*, February 12, 1992, p. A4.
127. It has been suggested that the Persian Gulf War demonstrates that other states welcome, rather than fear, America's post–Cold War preeminence. However, this simply is not the case.

tember 1991, French Foreign Minister Roland Dumas warned that American "might reigns without balancing weight" and he and European Community Commission President Jacques Delors called for the EC to counterbalance the United States.[128] Some European policy analysts have said that the Soviet Union's collapse means that Europe is now threatened mainly by unchallenged American ascendancy in world politics.[129] This viewpoint was echoed in Japan in the Gulf War's aftermath. A number of commentators worried that the United States—a "fearsome" country—would impose a Pax Americana in which other states would be compelled to accept roles "as America's underlings."[130] China, too, has reacted adversely to America's post–Cold War preeminence. "Chinese analysts reacted with great alarm to President George Bush's 'New World Order' proclamations, and maintained that this was a ruse for extending U.S. hegemony throughout the globe. From China's perspective, unipolarity was a far worse state of affairs than bipolarity."[131] Similar sentiments have been echoed in the Third World. Although the reactions of these smaller states are not as significant as those of potential new great powers, they confirm that unipolarity has engendered general unease throughout the international system. At the September 1992 Nonaligned Movement Meeting, Indonesian President Suharto warned that the New World Order cannot be allowed to become "a new version of the same old

---

First, it was *after* the Persian Gulf crisis began that others began voicing their concerns about unipolarity. Second, to the extent that the Gulf War is an example of states bandwagoning with the United States, it is easily explainable. As Walt points out, weak powers threatened by a powerful neighbor will often turn to an outside great power for defensive support. Walt, *Origins of Alliances,* p. 266. Third, as Jean Edward Smith points out, the United States had to exert considerable pressure on both Egypt and Saudi Arabia to get these nations to accept the Bush administration's decision to confront Iraq militarily after the invasion of Kuwait. Jean Edward Smith, *George Bush's War* (New York: Henry Holt and Company, 1992), pp. 63–95. Finally, it should be remembered that during the war, the Arab coalition partners restrained the United States from overthrowing Saddam Hussein and that, in July and August 1992, Egypt, Turkey and Syria restrained the United States when it appeared that the Bush administration was going to provoke a military showdown over the issue of UN weapons inspectors' access to Iraq's Agricultural Ministry.

128. Quoted in "France to U.S.: Don't Rule," *New York Times,* September 3, 1991, p. A8.
129. Rone Tempest, "French Revive Pastime Fretting About U.S. 'Imperialism'," *Los Angeles Times,* February 15, 1989, p. A9.
130. See the views of Waseda University Professor Sakuji Yoshimura, quoted in Paul Blustein, "In Japan, Seeing The War On A Five-Inch Screen," *Washington Post National Weekly Edition,* February 25–March 3, 1991, and of Tokyo University Professor Yasusuke Murakami and Opposition Diet Member Masao Kunihiro, in Urban C. Lehner, "Japanese See A More 'Fearsome' U.S. Following American Success in the Gulf," *Wall Street Journal,* March 14, 1991.
131. David Shambaugh, "China's Security Policy in the Post–Cold War Era," *Survival,* Vol. 34, No. 2 (Summer 1992), p. 92.

patterns of domination of the strong over the weak and the rich over the poor." At this same meeting, UN Secretary General Boutros-Ghali warned that "the temptation to dominate, whether worldwide or regionally, remains"; Malaysian Prime Minister Mahathir Mohammed pointedly stated that a "unipolar world is every bit as threatening as a bipolar world."[132]

As has been shown, the post–Cold War world's geopolitical constellation is not unique. Twice before in international history there have been "unipolar moments." Both were fleeting. On both occasions, the effect of the entry of new great powers in the international system was to redress the one-sided distribution of power in the international system. There is every reason to expect that the pattern of the late seventeenth and nineteenth centuries will recur. The impact of differential growth rates has increased the relative power of Japan and Germany in a way that clearly marks them as eligible states. As their stakes in the international system deepen, so will their ambitions and interests. Security considerations will cause Japan and Germany to emulate the United States and acquire the full spectrum of great power capabilities, including nuclear weapons.[133] It can be expected that both will seek recognition by others of their great power status. Evidence confirming the expectation of Japan's and Germany's great power emergence already exists.

Germany is beginning to exert its leadership in European security affairs. It has assumed primary responsibility for providing economic assistance to the former Soviet Union and Eastern Europe, and took the lead in securing EC recognition of the breakaway Yugoslav republics of Croatia and Slovenia. In a sure sign that the scope of German geopolitical interests is expanding, Defence Minister Volker Rühe is advocating acquisition of large military transport aircraft.[134] Chancellor Kohl's decision to meet with outgoing Austrian President Kurt Waldheim suggests that Germany is rejecting the external constraints heretofore imposed on its behavior. Germany is also insisting that henceforth its diplomats (who had previously spoken in French or

---

132. Quoted in Charles B. Wallace, "Nonaligned Nations Question New World Order," *Los Angeles Times*, September 2, 1992, p. A4.

133. The nuclear issue is being debated, albeit gingerly, in Japan but not in Germany (or at least not openly). Nevertheless it seems to be widely understood, in the United States and in Germany and Japan, that their accession to the nuclear club is only a matter of time. See Doyle McManus, "Thinking the Once Unthinkable: Japan, Germany With A-Bombs," *Los Angeles Times* (Washington D.C. ed.), June 10, 1992, p. A8. For a discussion of a nuclear Germany's strategic implications, see Mearsheimer, "Back to the Future."

134. Terrence Roth, "New German Defense Chief Is Redefining Agency's Role," *Wall Street Journal*, August 14, 1992, p. A10.

English) will use only German when addressing international conferences.[135] Finally, Germany's open expression of interest in permanent membership on the UN Security Council is another indication that Berlin is moving toward great power status. In making Germany's position known, Foreign Minister Klaus Kinkel pointedly noted that the Security Council should be restructured because as now constituted it reflects, not the present distribution of power, but the international order that existed at the end of World War II.[136]

Notwithstanding legal and historical inhibitions, Japan is beginning to seek strategic autonomy. An important step is the decision to develop the capability to gather and analyze politico-military and economic intelligence independently of the United States.[137] Japan has also begun importing huge amounts of plutonium from Europe. The plutonium is to be used by Japan's fast breeder reactors, thereby enabling Tokyo to free itself of dependence on Persian Gulf oil and American uranium. Plutonium imports plus the acquisition of other materials in recent years mean that Japan has the capability of moving quickly to become a nuclear power.[138] After prolonged debate, Japan has finally authorized unarmed Japanese military personnel to participate in UN peacekeeping operations. This may well be the opening wedge for Japan to develop military capabilities commensurate with great power status. As a special panel of the Liberal Democratic Party argued in February 1992, "Now that we have become one of the very few economic powerhouses, it would fly in the face of the world's common sense if we did not play a military role for the maintenance and restoration of global peace."[139] As Japan becomes more active on the international stage, military power will be needed to support its policies and ensure it is not at a bargaining disadvantage in its dealings with others. Unsurprisingly, Japan has plans to build a full-spectrum

---

135. Stephen Kinzer, "Thus Sprake Helmut Kohl Auf Deutsch," *New York Times*, February 23, 1992, p. A4.
136. "Germany Seeks a Permanent Council Seat," *Los Angeles Times*, September 24, 1992, p. A9; Paul Lewis, "Germany Seeks Permanent UN Council Seat," *New York Times*, September 24, 1992, p. A1.
137. David E. Sanger, "Tired of Relying on U.S., Japan Seeks to Expand Its Own Intelligence Efforts," *New York Times*, January 1, 1992, p. A6.
138. Jim Mann, "Japan's Energy Future Linked to Risky Cargo," *Los Angeles Times*, February 23, 1992, p. A1. The initial plutonium shipment left for Japan from Cherbourg, France, in early November 1992 and arrived in Japan in early January 1993. There has been speculation that the mere fact that Japan will possess a substantial plutonium stockpile may serve as a deterrent even if Tokyo does not acquire nuclear weapons. See David Sanger, "Japan's Atom Fuel Shipment Is Worrying Asians," *New York Times*, November 9, 1992, p. A3.
139. Quoted in Teresa Watanabe, "Shift Urged on Sending Japan's Troops Abroad," *Los Angeles Times*, February 22, 1992, p. A10.

navy (including aircraft carriers) capable of operating independently of the American Seventh Fleet.[140] In January 1993, Foreign Minister Michio Watanabe openly called for Japan to acquire long-range air and naval power-projection capabilities. Japan is also showing signs of diplomatic assertiveness, and its leading role in the UN effort to rebuild Cambodia is viewed by Tokyo as the beginning of a more forceful and independent foreign policy course now that Japan no longer is constrained to "obey U.S. demands."[141] Japan's policies toward Russia, China, and Iran demonstrate a growing willingness to follow an independent course, even if doing so leads to open friction with Washington. It is suggestive of Japan's view of the evolving international system that its recently appointed ambassador to the United States has spoken of the emergence of a "multipolar world in which the United States could no longer play the kind of dominant role it used to play."[142] That Japan is measuring itself for a great power role is reflected in its expressed desire for permanent membership of the UN Security Council.[143]

Back to the Future: The Political Consequences of Structural Change

Since 1945, the West has enjoyed a Long Peace.[144] During the post–World War II era, American leadership has been maintained, Germany and Japan have been prevented from becoming great powers, a cooperative economic order has been established, and the spread of democratic values has been

---

140. This information provided by John Arquilla based on his discussions with Japanese defense analysts. See also David E. Sanger, "Japanese Discuss an Expanded Peacekeeping Role for the Military," *New York Times*, January 10, 1993, p. A9. The issue of constitutional reform and elimination of the "peace clause" has been raised again recently; Jacob M. Schlesinger, "Japan's Ruling Party Will Seek a Review of 1946 Constitution," *Wall Street Journal*, January 14, 1993, p. A13; David E. Sanger, "Japanese Debate Taboo Topic of Military's Role," *New York Times*, January 17, 1993, p. A7.

141. Quoted in Teresa Watanabe, "Putting Cambodia Together Again," *Los Angeles Times*, March 3, 1992, p. HI.

142. Quoted in Sam Jameson, "Japan's New Envoy to U.S. Sees 'Crucial Period' Ahead," *Los Angeles Times*, February 18, 1992, p. A4.

143. Sam Jameson, "Japan to Seek U.N. Security Council Seat," *Los Angeles Times*, January 29, 1992, p. A1.

144. See John Lewis Gaddis, "The Long Peace: Elements of Stability in the Postwar International System," *International Security*, Vol. 10, No. 4 (Spring 1986), pp. 99–142, where Gaddis probed for an explanation of the absence of great power war during the Cold War rivalry between the Soviet Union and the United States. Gaddis has revisited the issue and asked whether certain factors (nuclear weapons, polarity, hegemonic stability, "triumphant" liberalism, and long cycles) have implications for the possible prolongation of the Long Peace into the post–Cold War era. Gaddis, "Great Illusions, the Long Peace, and the Future of the International System," in *The United States and the End of the Cold War*.

promoted. The strategy of preponderance seeks to maintain the geopolitical status quo that the Long Peace reflects. American strategic planners and scholars alike believe the United States can successfully perpetuate this status quo. This sanguine outlook is predicated on the belief that second-image factors (economic interdependence, common democratic institutions) militate against the reappearance of traditional forms of great power competition while promoting new forms of international cooperation.[145] Neorealists, however, believe that the Long Peace was rooted primarily in the bipolar structure of the international system, although the unit-level factor of nuclear deterrence also played a role.[146] Because they expect structural change to lead to changed international political outcomes, neorealists are not sanguine that the Long Peace can endure in the coming era of systemic change. Neorealist theory leads to the expectation that the world beyond unipolarity will be one of great power rivalry in a multipolar setting.

During the Cold War era, international politics was profoundly shaped by the bipolar competition between the United States and the Soviet Union.[147] The Soviet threat to their common security caused the United States, Western Europe, and Japan to form an anti-Soviet coalition. Because of America's military preeminence in a bipolar system, Western Europe and Japan did not have to internalize their security costs because they benefited from the protective mantle of Washington's containment policy. At the same time, because Western Europe's and Japan's political and economic stability were critical to containment's success, the United States resolved the "hegemon's dilemma"

---

145. For scholarly elaborations of this viewpoint, see John Mueller, *Retreat from Doomsday: The Obsolescence of Major War* (New York: Basic Books, 1989); Richard Rosecrance, *The Rise of the Trading State: Commerce and Conquest in the Modern World* (New York: Basic Books, 1986); Robert Jervis, "The Future of World Politics: Will It Resemble the Past?" *International Security*, Vol. 16, No. 3 (Winter 1991/92), pp. 39–73; Carl Kaysen, "Is War Obsolete?" *International Security*, Vol. 14, No. 4 (Spring 1990), pp. 42–64; Charles Kupchan and Clifford Kupchan, "Concerts, Collective Security and the Future of Europe," *International Security*, Vol. 16, No. 1 (Summer 1991), pp. 114–161; Richard Rosecrance, "A New Concert of Powers," *Foreign Affairs*, Vol. 71, No. 2 (Spring 1992), pp. 64–82; James M. Goldgeier and Michael McFaul, "A Tale of Two Worlds: Core and Periphery in the Post–Cold War Era," *International Organization*, Vol. 46, No. 3 (Spring 1992), pp. 467–491. The Defense Planning Guidance and similar documents also stress that the spread of democracy and economic interdependence are crucial to the success of the strategy of preponderance. The classic discussion of the second and third images of international politics is Kenneth N. Waltz, *Man, the State, and War* (New York: Columbia University Press, 1958).
146. This argument is presented in the European context in Mearsheimer, "Back to the Future."
147. For a different view, see Ted Hopf, "Polarity, the Offense-Defense Balance, and War," *American Political Science Review*, Vol. 81, No. 3 (June 1991), pp. 475–494. Hopf argues that the international system's stability during the Cold War era was attributable to nuclear deterrence and that bipolarity was an irrelevant factor.

by forgoing maximization of its relative gains and pursuing instead a policy of promoting absolute gains for all members of the anti-Soviet coalition.[148] For strategic reasons, the United States encouraged Western Europe's economic integration and Japan's discriminatory trade and foreign investment policies, even though the inevitable consequence of these policies was to enhance Western Europe's and Japan's relative power at America's expense.

Bipolarity was the decisive variable in the West's Long Peace because it removed the security dilemma and the relative gains problem from the agenda of relations among the Western powers. Even non-neorealists implicitly acknowledge the salience of structural factors in securing the postwar "liberal peace." Michael Doyle, for example, admits that American military leadership was crucial because it dampened the need for Western Europe and Japan to become strategically independent (which would rekindle the security dilemma) and reinforced the bonds of economic interdependence (thereby alleviating the relative gains problem). Doyle says the erosion of American preeminence could imperil the liberal peace "if independent and substantial military forces were established" by Western Europe and Japan.[149] In other words, if liberated from the bipolar structural constraints that, with Washington's help, smothered their great power emergence, states like Germany and Japan might respond to new international systemic constraints by becoming—*and acting like*—great powers. Here, Doyle is correct and that is precisely the point: structure affects outcomes.

AMERICA IN A MULTIPOLAR WORLD: IMPLICATIONS AND RECOMMENDATIONS

The Cold War structure has been swept away. American policymakers must now think about international politics from a wholly new analytical framework. This will not be easy. Richard Rosecrance observed in 1976, when it was already apparent that the bipolar system was beginning to erode, that

---

148. Arthur A. Stein, "The Hegemon's Dilemma: Great Britain, the United States, and the International Economic Order," *International Organization*, Vol. 38, No. 2 (Spring 1984), pp. 355–386. Stein delineates the hegemon's dilemma as follows:

A hegemonic power's decision to enrich itself is also a decision to enrich others more than itself. Over time, such policies will come at the expense of the hegemon's relative standing and will bring forth challengers. Yet choosing to sustain its relative standing . . . is a choice to keep others impoverished at the cost of increasing its own wealth. Maintaining its relative position has obvious costs not only to others but to itself. Alternatively, maximizing its absolute wealth has obvious benefits but brings even greater ones to others.

Stein, *Why Nations Cooperate*, p. 139.

149. Michael Doyle, "Kant, Liberal Legacies and Foreign Affairs," Part I, *Philosophy and Public Affairs*, Vol. 12, No. 3 (Summer 1983), p. 233.

Washington has, since 1945, always had difficulty in understanding how Western Europe and Japan could have different interests than the United States.[150] More recently, Stephen Krasner has observed that "U.S. policymakers have paid little attention to the possibility that a loss of power *vis-à-vis* friends could present serious and unforeseen difficulties, either because friends can become enemies or because managing the international system may be more difficult in a world in which power is more evenly distributed."[151] The impending structural shift from unipolarity to multipolarity means that the security dilemma and the relative gains problem will again dominate policymakers' concerns. As Japan and Germany become great powers, the quality of their relations with the United States will be profoundly altered.[152] Relations will become significantly more competitive, great power security rivalries and even war will be likely, and cooperation will correspondingly become more difficult.

The implications of multipolarity will be especially evident in the United States-Japan relationship.[153] Summarizing his incisive analysis of the pre-1914 Anglo-German antagonism, Paul Kennedy states that the "most profound cause, surely, was *economic*."[154] By this, Kennedy does not mean the commercial competition between British and German firms, but rather that economic shifts had radically transformed the relative power relationship between Britain and Germany. Kennedy asks if the relative power relationship of two great powers has ever changed so remarkably with the span of a single lifetime. The answer may now be "yes."

There is a very good chance that early in the next decade Japan's GNP may equal or surpass America's.[155] Such an economic change would be a fact

---

150. Richard Rosecrance, "Introduction," in Rosecrance, ed., *America as an Ordinary Country* (Ithaca: Cornell University Press, 1976), p. 12.

151. Stephen Krasner, "Trade Conflicts and the Common Defense: The United States and Japan," *Political Science Quarterly*, Vol. 101, No. 5 (1986), pp. 787–806.

152. Others have argued that America's relations with Japan and Germany will become more competitive in the post–Cold War era. A notable example is Jeffrey E. Garten, *A Cold Peace: America, Japan, Germany and the Struggle for Supremacy* (New York: Times Books, 1992). Garten's argument differs from mine in two critical respects. First, Garten pinpoints the locus of rivalry in second-image factors; specifically the different cultural, political, and economic traditions of the three countries. Second, he discounts the possibility of war or of security competitions and argues that the rivalry will be primarily economic.

153. An interesting albeit flawed attempt to consider the geopolitical consequences of the altered relative power relationship of Japan and the United States is George Friedman and Meredith Lebard, *The Coming War With Japan* (New York: St. Martin's Press, 1991).

154. Kennedy, *Anglo-German Antagonism*, p. 464.

155. This is C. Fred Bergsten's projection based on the following assumptions: Japan's annual

of enormous geopolitical significance. Should this relative power shift occur, no doubt Japan would demand that power and prestige in the international system be redistributed to reflect its new status. Besides demands for UN Security Council membership, Tokyo might: (1) insist on the decisive vote in international economic institutions; (2) demand that the yen become the international economy's primary reserve currency; (3) exploit advantageous technological, economic, and fiscal asymmetries to advance its strategic interests; and (4) become a much more assertive actor geopolitically.

Whether the United States could comfortably accommodate a Japan of equal or greater power is an open question. The answer would depend on the moderation, and the moderate tone, of Japan's *desiderata* and on the willingness of the United States to make reasonable concessions gracefully. But even skillful and patient diplomacy on both sides could fail to avert conflict. In that case, the question is not so much who as *what* would be responsible for conflict between the United States and Japan: I argue that it would be the international political system's structure and the constraints it exerts on great power behavior.

Again, history may provide insight. At the turn of the century, Great Britain was able to reach an accommodation with the United States because America's ambitions did not immediately seem to threaten London's most vital security concerns.[156] On the other hand, Germany's rising power did appear to present such a threat. It is worrisome that the changing relative power relationship between the United States and Japan contains the same Hertz/Avis dynamic that fueled the Anglo-German antagonism. Thus once again, the prospect of hegemonic war, thought to have been banished from international politics, must be reckoned with even as we hope to avoid it. Indeed, it must be reckoned with *especially* if we hope to avoid it. The main point of the hegemonic war theory is that:

there is incompatibility between crucial elements of the existing international system and the changing distribution of power among the states within the system. . . . The resolution of the disequilibrium between the superstructure of the system and the underlying distribution of power is

---

growth is about 4 percent, the United States' is 2 to 2½ percent, and the yen appreciates to 100 to 1 against the dollar. Bergsten, "Primacy of Economics," *Foreign Policy*, No. 87 (Summer 1992), p. 6.

156. See Charles S. Campbell, *Anglo-American Understanding, 1898–1903* (Baltimore: The Johns Hopkins University Press, 1957); Dexter Perkins, *The Great Rapprochement: England and the United States, 1895–1914* (New York: Atheneum, 1968).

found in the outbreak and intensification of what becomes a hegemonic war.[157]

Great power war is not a certainty, because some factors could reduce the war-proneness of the coming multipolar system. At the unit level, nuclear deterrence could maintain the peace among the great powers in a multipolar system where each has nuclear weapons.[158] In such a system, great power conflict might be played out in the economic, rather than the military, arena.[159] Still, the shadow of war will loom over a multipolar system. Consequently, the United States will have to rethink the answer it gave in the late 1940s to "the hegemon's dilemma." Put another way, Washington will have to come to grips with the *declining* hegemon's dilemma. Precisely because major shifts in relative economic power presage change in the relative distribution of power geopolitically, the United States must begin to concern itself with maintaining its relative power rather than pursuing absolute gains for itself and those who are its partners today but may become its rivals tomorrow. Although states can cooperate readily to promote absolute gains

157. Robert Gilpin, "The Theory of Hegemonic War," in Rotberg and Rabb, *Origin and Prevention of Major Wars*, pp. 25–26.

158. Kenneth N. Waltz, "Nuclear Myths and Political Realities," *American Political Science Review*, Vol. 81, No. 3 (September 1991), pp. 731–746; *The Spread of Nuclear Weapons: More May Be Better*, Adelphi Paper No. 171 (London: International Institute for Strategic Studies, 1981). For a more pessimistic view of the possible consequences of the spread of nuclear weapons, see Barry R. Posen, *Inadvertent Escalation: Conventional War and Nuclear Weapons* (Ithaca: Cornell University Press, 1991).

159. If deterrence holds among the great powers in a multipolar world, the prevailing conventional wisdom is that economic competitions would replace security competitions as the primary means of great power rivalry. Under the shadow of war, trade wars that improve a state's relative position by inflicting more pain on a rival could become a rational strategy. States in a position to do so could also use their financial power or control over access to key technologies to advance their interests relative to rivals. For a suggestive first cut at the possible role of "economic statecraft" in great power relations in the emerging multipolar system, see Aaron L. Friedberg, "The Changing Relationship Between Economics and National Security," *Political Science Quarterly*, Vol. 106, No. 2 (1991), pp. 272–274.

One should be careful about assuming that economics will entirely displace military power. Deterrence rests on military strength. Moreover, it could be expected that arms races and tests of resolve would be employed by the great powers as substitutes for actual fighting. A great power nuclear stalemate could have two other important military effects. Just as the Cold War superpowers did in Korea, Vietnam, Angola and Afghanistan, the great powers in a multipolar system could wage war through proxies. Also, deterrence at the nuclear level could, notwithstanding the risk of escalation, cause the great powers to fight (or attempt to fight) limited conventional wars. Here, it may be useful to revisit the early Cold War literature on limited war. See Henry Kissinger, *Nuclear Weapons and Foreign Policy* (New York: Harper and Row, 1957); Robert E. Osgood, *Limited War* (Chicago: University of Chicago Press, 1957).

for all when the shadow of war is absent from their relations, the barriers to cooperation become formidable when the shadow of war is present.[160]

STRATEGIC INDEPENDENCE IN A MULTIPOLAR WORLD

Because multipolarity is inevitable, it is pointless to debate the comparative merits of unipolar, bipolar, and multipolar systems. Rather than vainly and counterproductively pursuing a strategy of preponderance, the United States needs to design a strategy that will (1) safeguard its interests during the difficult transition from unipolarity to multipolarity; and (2) enable the United States to do as well as possible in a multipolar world. America's optimal strategy is to make its power position similar to Goldilocks' porridge: not too strong, which would frighten others into balancing against the United States; not too weak, which would invite others to exploit American vulnerabilities; but just right—strong enough to defend American interests, without provoking others.

The transition from unipolarity to multipolarity will challenge the United States to devise a policy that will arrest its relative decline while minimizing the chances that other states will be provoked into balancing against the United States. Relative decline has internal and external causes. Relative decline can be addressed by policies that focus on either or both of these causes. It would be counterproductive for the United States to attempt to maintain its relative power position by attempting to suppress the emergence of new great powers. This approach would heighten others' concerns about the malign effects of unchecked American power, which probably would accelerate the rise of new great powers, and increase the probability that balancing behavior would be directed against the United States. American policymakers need to remember that other states balance against hegemons

---

160. Robert Powell, "The Problem of Absolute and Relative Gains in International Relations Theory," *American Political Science Review*, Vol. 81, No. 4 (December 1991), pp. 1303–1320. Joanne Gowa points out that free trade is more likely to prevail in bipolar international systems than in multipolar ones. Because the risk of exit from a bipolar alliance is less than from an alliance in a multipolar system, bipolar alignments are more stable. Consequently, bipolar alliances are better able to internalize the security externalities of free trade (the members do not need to be concerned with relative gains because today's ally is unlikely to be tomorrow's rival). Moreover, in a bipolar alliance, the dominant partner has incentives to act altruistically towards its allies because it benefits when they do. All of these incentives are reversed in multipolar systems where risks (i.e., defection of allies) and buck passing/free rider tendencies force states to ponder the relative gains problem and to think hard about the wisdom of acting unselfishly. Free trade thus is problematic in a multipolar system. Gowa, "Bipolarity, Multipolarity and Free Trade," *American Political Science Review*, Vol. 79, No. 4 (December 1989), pp. 1245–1266.

and they should not want the United States to be seen by others as a "sprawling giant with gouty fingers and toes." A policy that concentrates U.S. energies on redressing the internal causes of relative decline would be perceived by others as less threatening than a strategy of preponderance. Although vigorous internal renewal might cause frictions with others over economic policy, it is less likely to have negative geopolitical repercussions than a policy that aims at perpetuating unipolarity.

Washington also needs to remember that while the United States may regard its hegemony as benign, others will have different perceptions. The international order objectives embedded in a strategy of preponderance reinforce others' mistrust of American preeminence. The more the United States attempts to press its preferences and values on others, the more likely it is that they will react against what is, in their view, overweening American power. Moreover, policies that arouse others' fear of America today could carry over into the emerging multipolar system. It makes no sense to alienate needlessly states (such as China) that could be strategically useful to the United States in a multipolar world. To avoid frightening others, the United States should eschew a value-projection policy and moderate both its rhetoric and its ambitions.[161]

The United States must adjust to the inevitable emergence of new great powers. The primary role of forward-deployed American forces now is to dissuade Japan and Germany from becoming great powers. There are three reasons why American forward deployments in Europe and Northeast Asia should be phased out soon. First, a policy of forward deployment could unnecessarily entangle the United States in overseas conflicts where the stakes are more important to others than to itself. Second, because the United States faces severe fiscal and economic constraints, the opportunity costs of such a strategy are high. Third, such a policy cannot work. Indeed, the strategy of preponderance is probably the worst option available to the United States because it is not coercive enough to prevent Japan and Germany from becoming great powers, but it is coercive enough to antagonize them and cause them to balance against the United States. If the analysis presented in this article is correct, a policy of attempting to smother Germany's and Japan's great power emergence would be unavailing because

---

161. For a discussion of value projection as a grand strategic option see Terry L. Deibel, "Strategies Before Containment: Patterns for the Future," *International Security*, Vol. 16, No. 4 (Spring 1992), pp. 79–108.

structural pressures will impel them to become great powers regardless of what the United States does or does not do. Simply stated, the declining hegemon's dilemma is acute: neither benign nor preventive strategies will prevent the emergence of challengers and the consequent end of the hegemon's predominance in the international system.

American grand strategy must be redesigned for a multipolar world. In a multipolar system, the United States should follow a policy of strategic independence by assuming the posture of an offshore balancer.[162] Traditionally, America's overriding strategic objective has been to ensure that a hegemon does not dominate Eurasia.[163] That objective would not change under strategic independence, but the means of attaining it would. Rather than assuming primary responsibility for containing the rise of a potential hegemon, the United States would rely on global and regional power balances to attain that goal. Strategic independence is not an isolationist policy that rules out the use of American power abroad.[164] Strategic independence also differs from the selective-commitment variant of offshore balancing articulated by John Mearsheimer and Stephen Van Evera, whereby the United States would be relatively indifferent to Third World events but would remain militarily engaged in Europe and Northeast Asia in order to preserve "stability."[165] Strategic independence is a hedging strategy that would commit the United States militarily if, but only if, other states failed to balance effectively against a rising Eurasian hegemon. The United States would need to remain alert to

---

162. I first used the term "strategic independence" in 1983 and I elaborated on it in 1989. Christopher Layne, "Ending the Alliance," *Journal of Contemporary Studies*, Vol. 6, No. 3 (Summer 1983), pp. 5–31; and Layne, "Realism Redux: Strategic Independence in a Multipolar World," *SAIS Review*, Vol. 9, No. 2 (Summer–Fall 1989), pp. 19–44. Ted Galen Carpenter, who has also embraced a form of strategic independence, has acknowledged that I was the first to articulate the concept and to so name it. Ted Galen Carpenter, "Introduction," in Carpenter, ed., *Collective Defense of Strategic Independence: Alternative Strategies for the Future* (Washington, D.C.: Cato Institute, 1989), p. xx, n. 7. The most recent explication of his views on strategic independence is Carpenter, *A Search for Enemies: America's Alliances After the Cold War* (Washington, D.C.: Cato Institute, 1992).

163. See John Lewis Gaddis, *Strategies of Containment* (New York: Oxford University Press, 1982), chap. 2; George F. Kennan, *Realities of American Foreign Policy* (Princeton: Princeton University Press, 1954), pp. 63–65; Hans Morgenthau, *In Defense of the National Interest* (Lanham, Md.: University Press of America, 1982, reprint of 1951 edition), pp. 5–7; Nicholas Spykman, *America's Strategy in World Politics: The United States and the Balance of Power* (New York: Harcourt, Brace, 1942), part 1.

164. For the isolationist approach to post–Cold War American grand strategy, see Earl C. Ravenal, "The Case For Adjustment," *Foreign Policy*, No. 81 (Winter 1990/91), pp. 3–19.

165. Mearsheimer, "Back to the Future"; Stephen Van Evera, "Why Europe Matters, Why the Third World Doesn't: American Grand Strategy After the Cold War," *Journal of Strategic Studies*, Vol. 13, No. 2 (June 1990), pp. 1–51.

the events that would require a more engaged policy: (1) the appearance of a "careful" challenger able to cloak its ambitions and ward off external balancing against it; (2) a dramatic narrowing of America's relative power margin over Japan; or (3) the inability of other states to act as effective counterweights due to internal difficulties.[166]

Strategic independence aims to capitalize on America's inherent geopolitical advantages.[167] First, in a relative sense, the United States is probably the most secure great power in history because of the interlocking effects of geography, nuclear weapons, and capabilities which, although diminished relatively, are still formidable in absolute terms. Such "strategic security enables the balancer to stay outside the central balance until the moment when its intervention can be decisive."[168] America's insularity means that it can benefit strategically from geography in another way, as well. Because America is distant from the likely theaters of great power conflict, in a multipolar world others are unlikely to view it as a threat to their security. Indeed distance would enhance America's attractiveness as an ally. (In a unipolar world the United States loses this advantage because hegemons repel others rather than attracting them). Finally, because of its still considerable great power capabilities, in a multipolar world America's intervention would decisively tip the scales against an aspiring hegemon.

---

166. For a discussion of the "careful" challenger, see John Arquilla, "Balances Without Balancing," paper presented at the annual meeting of the American Political Science Association, Chicago, Illinois, September 1992.

167. It is not neorealist heresy to suggest that the United States can play an offshore balancer's role. I do not claim that there is a functionally differentiated role for a balancer in the international system. Rather, like Waltz, I am saying that under "narrowly defined and historically unlikely conditions," certain states can play this role because of their unit-level attributes (especially geography and capabilities). The United States today meets Waltz's criteria: (1) American strength added to a weaker coalition would redress the balance; (2) America has (or ought to have) no positive ends—its goal is the negative one of thwarting an aspiring hegemon; (3) America's power for the foreseeable future will be at least the equal of any other state's. Waltz, *Theory of International Politics*, pp. 163–164. It should also be noted that balancers often are attractive allies precisely because they do not have ambitions that threaten others. As George Liska notes, Britain benefited from its "attractiveness in Europe whenever she was ready to meet an actual or potential hegemonical threat" from Europe. To win allies, "Britain had only to abstain from direct acquisitions on the continent and, when called, limit voluntarily her wartime gains overseas." George Liska, *The Quest for Equilibrium: America and the Balance of Power on Land and Sea* (Baltimore: The John Hopkins University Press, 1977), p. 13. For additional discussion of the criteria that a state should meet to be an effective balancer, see Michael Sheehan, "The Place of the Balancer in Balance of Power Theory," *Review of International Studies*, Vol. 15, No. 2 (April 1989), pp. 123–133.

168. Sheehan, "The Place of the Balancer," p. 128.

An insular great power in a multipolar system enjoys a wider range of strategic options than less fortunately placed states.[169] This would certainly be true for the United States. Because of its relative immunity from external threat, in a multipolar world the United States could stand by and could rationally adopt buck-passing strategies that force others to "go first."[170] The emerging great powers are located in regions where other potentially powerful actors are present (Ukraine, Russia, China, and Korea, which probably will be reunified in the next decade) and where the potential for intense security competitions also exists. The emerging great powers (and these other actors) are likely to be kept in check by their own rivalries. There are three reasons why this situation could be beneficial to the United States. First, the fact that the emerging great powers are involved in regional rivalries will have the effect of enhancing America's relative power.[171] Second, Japan, America's most likely future geopolitical rival, could be contained by others without the United States having to risk direct confrontation. Third, if the emerging great powers are compelled to internalize their security costs, they no longer will be free to concentrate primarily on trading-state strategies that give them an advantage in their economic competition with the United States.

Strategic independence is responsive to the constraints of the impending structural changes in the international system. It is a strategy that would serve America's interests in the emerging multipolar system. It is, admittedly, a competitive strategy. But such a strategy is needed in a world where great power rivalries, with both security and economic dimensions, will be a fact of international life. At the same time, strategic independence is a restrained

---

169. Liska, *Quest for Equilibrium*, p. 12.

170. For a discussion of the "buck-passing" phenomenon see Thomas J. Christensen and Jack Snyder, "Chain Gangs and Passed Bucks: Predicting Alliance Patterns in Multipolarity," *International Organization*, Vol. 44, No. 2 (Spring 1990), pp. 137–168; Waltz, *Theory of International Politics*, p. 165. John Arquilla defines "bystanding" as a state's propensity to avoid conflicts, if it can do so, for self-preservation reasons. Arquilla, "Balances Without Balancing."

171. An offshore balancer can benefit from others' rivalries: by the mid-1890s, America's navy was powerful, though still smaller than Britain's and those of Europe's lending powers. But "such equality was not necessary. The growing instability of the European political equilibrium seriously tied the hands of the Great Powers of that Continent, and rendered progressively improbable any determined aggression from that quarter against the interests of the United States in the northern part of the Western Hemisphere. European instability, in short, enhanced the *relative* power and security of the United States." Harold and Margaret Sprout, *Rise of American Naval Power*, p. 222 (emphasis in original). Similarly, during the nineteenth century, Britain was able to enjoy a relatively high degree of security while spending proportionately less on defense than the European powers, precisely because the European states were preoccupied with security competitions among themselves.

and prudent policy that would (1) avoid provocative actions that would cause others to regard the United States as an overpowerful hegemon; (2) minimize the risks of open confrontation with the emerging great powers; and (3) attempt to enhance America's relative power indirectly through skillful manipulation of the dynamics of multipolarity.

Strategic independence is also a more realistic policy than the strategy of preponderance, which is based on preserving the status quo and on maintaining stability. "Stability" is defined as a world where the United States is unchallenged by rivals and its interests are undisturbed by international political unheaval.[172] The strategy of preponderance aims at attaining a condition that approximates absolute security for the United States. In this respect, it is another form of American exceptionalism. It is a transcendant strategy that seeks nothing less than the end of international politics. However, unwanted and unanticipated events happen all the time in international politics; in this respect, "instability" is normal. War, the security dilemma, the rise and fall of great powers, the formation and dissolution of alliances,

---

172. For a devastating critique of America's stability obsession, see Benjamin C. Schwarz, "Rights and Foreign Policy: Morality is No Mantra," *New York Times*, November 20, 1992, p. A19. The focus on instability means that the strategy of preponderance leads inexorably to the open-ended proliferation of American commitments, all of which are seen as "interdependent." The United States must, under this strategy, worry about both the rise of new great powers and turmoil in strategically peripheral areas. The latter, it is feared, could set off a cascading series of effects that would spill over and affect important American interests. There is particular concern that American economic interests could be harmed by instability. As Bush's Secretary of Defense Dick Cheney said: "We are a trading nation, and our prosperity is linked to peace and stability in the world. . . . Simply stated, the worldwide market that we're part of cannot thrive where regional violence, instability, and aggression put it at peril." Dick Cheney, "The Military We Need in the Future," *Vital Speeches of the Day*, Vol. 59, No. 1 (October 15, 1992), p. 13. For a similar argument see Van Evera, "Why Europe Matters," pp. 10–11.
This line of thinking is an ironic twist on the interdependence/trading state concept, which holds that territorial conquest does not pay because the most effective means of increasing national power is through trade, and that war is too costly to be a viable option for economically powerful states. Rather than being a stimulus for peace, under the strategy of preponderance economic interdependence means that the United States must maintain a forward military presence and be prepared to wage war, in order to ensure that it is not cut off from the markets with which it has become economically interconnected. Here, two flaws of the stability-oriented strategy of preponderance become clear. First, there is a failure to consider whether the benefits of maintaining stability outweigh the costs of attempting to do so. Admittedly, instability abroad conceivably could harm the United States. The issue, however, is whether this harm would exceed the certain costs of maintaining American forward-deployed forces and the possible costs if commitment leads to involvement in a conflict. Second, there is no consideration of alternative strategies. For example, by relying on its large domestic market (which will get bigger if the North American Free Trade Agreement goes into effect) and diversifying its overseas markets, the United States could minimize the economic disruption that could accompany possible geopolitical disturbances in Europe and East Asia.

and great power rivalries are enduring features of international politics. The goal of a unipolar world in which the United States is unthreatened and able to shape the international environment is alluring but it is a chimera. No state can achieve absolute security because no state, not even the United States, can rise above the international political system's structural constraints.

THE COMING TEST

The coming years will be ones of turmoil in international politics. Systemic change occasioned by the rise and fall of great powers has always been traumatic. No doubt neorealism's critics will continue to point to second-image factors as reasons to take an optimistic view of the future. No doubt, too, the debate between neorealists and their critics will continue. But this one is not fated to drag on inconclusively. In coming years, the international system will provide a definitive field test of the contending views of international politics offered by neorealists and their critics. Fifty years from now, and probably much sooner, we will know who was right and who was wrong. Structural realists can be confident that events will vindicate their predictions: (1) Because of structural factors, an American strategy of preponderance or an attempt to perpetuate unipolarity is doomed to failure; (2) unipolarity will stimulate the emergence of eligible states as great powers; (3) unipolarity will cause other states to balance against the United States; (4) in a multipolar system, traditional patterns of great power competition will reemerge notwithstanding the effect of second-image factors; and (5) if differential growth rate effects allow Japan to challenge America's leading position, the United States–Japan relationship will become highly competitive and the possibility of hegemonic war will be present.

The Unipolar Illusion Revisited

Christopher Layne

The Coming End of American Hegemony

"The Unipolar Illusion" appeared in the spring 1993 issue of *International Security*. Written against the backdrop of the Cold War's stunningly sudden end and the ensuing consensus in the U.S. foreign policy establishment that the central aim of the United States' post–Cold War grand strategy should be to preserve the unipolar distribution of power favoring the United States, "The Unipolar Illusion" was intended to introduce a cautionary note into the post–Cold War grand strategic debate by reminding policymakers and scholars alike that historically the pursuit of hegemony has been self-defeating.

In terms of its central arguments, "The Unipolar Illusion" has held up well with the passage of time. Of course, as the former New York Yankee baseball great Yogi Berra famously (or at least reportedly) said, "making predictions is hard, especially about the future." To be sure, "The Unipolar Illusion" got a few things wrong. Like many others in the late 1980s and early 1990s who saw Japan emerging as a challenger to U.S. preeminence, I failed to foresee the geopolitical impact of Japan's economic and demographic stagnation. My prediction that balancing against the United States would result in the emergence of a multipolar international system by 2010 also looks as if it will not be borne out.

I and other balance of power realists erred in predicting that hard balancing against the United States quickly would restore equilibrium to the distribution of power in the international system because we failed to appreciate fully the "duality of U.S. power" in a unipolar world.[1] That is, we did not give due weight to the fact that the second-tier major powers would face conflicting pressures both to bandwagon with a hegemonic United States and to balance against it. The fact that unipolarity has not given way to a new distribution of power does not mean, however, that there has been an absence of balancing against the United States since the Cold War ended. Rather, it means that balancing behavior by other states has not yet produced the desired systemic outcome. Balancing is a grand strategy pursued by individual states. States

---

1. This phrase is borrowed from Michel Fortmann, T.V. Paul, and James J. Wirtz, "Conclusions: Balance of Power at the Turn of the New Century," in Paul, Wirtz, and Fortmann, eds., *Balance of Power: Theory and Practice in the 21st Century* (Stanford: Stanford University Press, 2004), p. 366. For a very critical analysis of neorealist predictions about the Unipolar Era (including those of John Mearsheimer, Kenneth Waltz, and myself), see Christopher J. Fettweis, "Evaluating IR's Crystal Balls: How Predictions of the Future Have Withstood Fourteen Years of Unipolarity," *International Studies Review*, Vol. 6, No. 1 (March 2004), pp. 79–104.

that balance seek to create counterweights to a hegemon's power and to ultimately bring about a realignment in the distribution of power in the international system—a "balance of power," if you will. It is important, however, not to conflate balancing (which is behavior at the unit level) with the actual attainment of "balance" (which is a systemic outcome).

The key arguments and the underlying logic of "The Unipolar Illusion" remain unrefuted and valid. First, although I may have been off somewhat on the timing, my argument that unipolarity would cause new great powers to emerge to counter U.S. hegemony and restore geopolitical equilibrium was correct. Today, it is obvious that new great powers indeed are emerging, and the unipolar era's days are numbered. In its 2004 study, *Mapping the Global Future,* the National Intelligence Council states: "The likely emergence of China and India as new major global players—similar to the rise of Germany in the nineteenth century and the United States in the early twentieth century—will transform the geopolitical landscape, with impacts potentially as dramatic as those of the previous two centuries."[2] Similarly, a recent study by the CIA's Strategic Assessment Group projects that by 2020 both China (which *Mapping the Global Future* pegs as, "by any measure a first-rate military power" around 2020), and the European Union will come close to matching the United States in terms of their respective shares of world power. That is, the international system effectively will be multipolar.

Second, the United States is not a "benevolent" hegemon that is exempt from the fate of past hegemons.[3] Prophylactic multilateralism cannot inoculate the United States from counter-hegemonic balancing, because no fig leaf is big enough to cover up the fact that the United States wields enormous power. Even when the United States professes a commitment to multilateralism, everyone knows that whenever it chooses to do so, it can break free from

---

2. *Mapping the Global Future: Report of the National Intelligence Council's 2020 Project* (Washington, D.C.: U.S. Government Printing Office, December 2004), p. 47.
3. For arguments that the United States can escape the fate of hegemons because of its benevolence, see Stephen M. Walt, *Taming American Power: The Global Response to U.S. Primacy* (New York: W.W. Norton, 2005); G. John Ikenberry, "Democracy, Institutions, and American Restraint," in Ikenberry, ed., *America Unrivaled: The Future of the Balance of Power* (Ithaca, N.Y.: Cornell University Press, 2002), pp. 213–238; G. John Ikenberry, "Institutions, Strategic Restraint, and the Persistence of the Postwar Order," *International Security,* Vol. 23, No. 3 (Winter 1998/99), pp. 43–78; Michael Mastanduno, "Preserving the Unipolar Moment: Realist Theories and U.S. Grand Strategy after the Cold War," *International Security,* Vol. 21, No. 4 (Spring 1997), pp. 44–98; Stephen M. Walt, "Keeping the World 'Off-Balance': Self-Restraint and U.S. Foreign Policy," in Ikenberry, *America Unrivaled,* pp. 121–154; and Stephen M. Walt, "Beyond Bin Laden: Reshaping U.S. Foreign Policy," *International Security,* Vol. 26, No. 3 (Winter 2001/02), pp. 59–62, 56.

multilateralism's constraints, and use its power unilaterally to others' detriment.[4] In a unipolar world, others must focus on the hegemon's capabilities (which, more or less, are knowable), not its intentions (which are difficult to ascertain, and always can change).[5] If, by some chance, other states did not know this before (and it is pretty clear that many of them did), they certainly know it after the U.S. invasion of Iraq. In international politics benevolent hegemons are like unicorns—there is no such animal. Hegemons love themselves, but others mistrust and fear them—and for good reason. While Washington's self-proclaimed benevolence is inherently ephemeral, the hard fist of American power is tangible.

Third, even though a new balance of power has not yet formed, balancing against the United States has occurred since the Cold War's end. Proponents of U.S. hegemony define "balancing" as the buildup of military capabilities in direct response to an existential security threat posed by the hegemon, but this very narrow definition misses the important kinds of balancing against U.S. hegemony that have occurred since the Cold War's end. For example, some states—notably China, Russia, and India—have engaged in opaque balancing against the United States. Rather than undertaking an overt arms buildup aimed at the United States, major powers might try first to close the capabilities gap with the United States by concentrating on building up and catching up economically and technologically. Opaque balancing is inherently ambiguous, because it is difficult to determine whether its underlying purpose is to grow a state's civilian economy, or to lay the groundwork for an eventual military challenge to U.S. hegemony. This very ambiguity, however, reduces the risk that opaque balancers will be the targets of preventive U.S. military action. Looking down the road, however, they aim to convert their economic gains into the military capabilities they need to contest U.S. preponderance.

Other states also are engaged in "semi-hard" balancing against the United States. The European Union's common security and defense policy is one example. By investing themselves with the capability to act autonomously of the United States in the realm of security, the second-tier major powers can:

---

4. Others cannot afford to trust in America's benevolence, because "even if a dominant power behaves moderation, restraint, and forbearance, weaker states will worry about its future behavior." Kenneth N. Waltz, "Structural Realism after the Cold War," in Ikenberry, *America Unrivaled*, p. 53.
5. Jervis cuts to the heart of the matter when he notes, "Minds can be changed, new leaders can come to power, values can shift, new opportunities and dangers can arise." Robert Jervis, "Cooperation under the Security Dilemma," *World Politics*, Vol. 30, No. 2 (January 1978), p. 105.

constrain the United States; gain bargaining leverage vis-à-vis the United States; acquire the means to force the United States to respect their interests abroad rather than running roughshod over them; and ensure they can take care of themselves if the United States withdraws its security umbrella. This kind of balancing is "semi-hard" because it is not explicitly directed at countering a U.S. existential threat.[6] At the same time, however, semi-hard balancing is a form of insurance against a United States that might someday exercise its power in a predatory and menacing fashion, or that might decide to abandon its allies strategically in a future crisis. In a unipolar world, the creation of new poles of power in the international system, even by U.S. allies, is, in itself, semi-hard balancing against hegemonic power.

Fourth, U.S. hegemony will end in the foreseeable future. The real debate about the future of U.S. hegemony is not about *if* it will end—even unipolar optimists and agnostics concede that someday it will—but *when*. Indeed, the foundations of U.S. hegemony already are in the process of eroding because of an interactive combination of external and internal factors. First, the distribution of power in the international system will shift as new great powers (or "peer competitors") emerge to challenge the United States. Second, by succumbing to the "hegemon's temptation," the United States will become increasingly overextended abroad. Third, fiscal and economic constraints increasingly will impinge on Washington's ability to maintain the United States' overwhelming military advantage, and as the U.S. military edge declines, other major states will be emboldened to engage in hard balancing against the United States.

Even hard-core proponents of U.S. hegemony concede that unipolarity will not last indefinitely. The real debate about U.S. hegemony is about the related questions of timing, and costs. How long can the United States keep the world unipolar? Do the benefits of perpetuating unipolarity outweigh the costs of doing so? In 1993, I wrote that by 2010, unipolarity would give way to multipolarity.[7] In contrast, in 1999, William C. Wohlforth, the leading champion of "unipolar stability," stated that American hegemony was then a

---

6. As Robert Art puts it, a state engaging in semi-hard balancing "does not fear an increased threat to its physical security from another rising state; rather it is concerned about the adverse effects of that state's rise on its general position, both political and economic, in the international arena. This concern also may, but need not, include a worry that the rising state could cause security problems in the future, although not necessarily war." Robert J. Art, "Europe Hedges Its Security Bets," in Paul, Wirtz, and Fortmann, *Balance of Power*, p. 180.

7. Christopher Layne, "The Unipolar Illusion: Why New Great Powers Will Rise," *International Security*, Vol. 17, No. 4 (Spring 1993), p. 7.

decade old, and "that *if* Washington plays its cards right, it *may* last as long as bipolarity."[8] The post–World War II bipolar era lasted forty-five years (1945–1990). So by Wohlforth's calculations, American preponderance would last until around 2030. The difference in these two predictions about how long American hegemony would last was only about twenty years. Twenty years may seem like a long time, but in geopolitics it isn't because a state's power position in the international system can decline with unexpected rapidity.

It is hard to pinpoint an exact moment when a new balance of power will take shape. Contrary to my 1993 prediction, unipolarity probably will last beyond 2010. At the same time, however, it is highly doubtful that U.S. hegemony will endure until the early 2030s as Wohlforth predicted in 1999. The key question facing U.S. strategists, therefore, is whether it is worthwhile paying the price to hang on to unipolarity for, at best, another two decades? Given that U.S. hegemony is destined to end sooner rather than later, and that the costs of trying to "shape the international system" to the liking of the United States will rise—even as the benefits of doing so diminish—it would make more sense grand strategically for the United States to retrench, and husband its resources for the long haul. The United States could best do this by forsaking its current hegemonic grand strategy, and, instead adopting an offshore balancing grand strategy.[9]

---

8. William C. Wohlforth, "The Stability of a Unipolar World," *International Security*, Vol. 24, No. 1 (Summer 1999), p. 8 (emphasis added).
9. On offshore balancing, see Christopher Layne, *The Peace of Illusions: American Grand Strategy from 1940 to the Present* (Ithaca: Cornell University Press, 2006); John J. Mearsheimer, *The Tragedy of Great Power Politics* (New York: W.W. Norton, 2001); and Christopher Layne, "From Preponderance to Offshore Balancing: America's Future Grand Strategy," *International Security*, Vol. 22, No. 1 (Summer 1997), pp. 86–124.

Structural Realism after the Cold War

Kenneth N. Waltz

$\mathbf{S}$ome students of in-
ternational politics believe that realism is obsolete.[1] They argue that, although
realism's concepts of anarchy, self-help, and power balancing may have been
appropriate to a bygone era, they have been displaced by changed conditions
and eclipsed by better ideas. New times call for new thinking. Changing
conditions require revised theories or entirely different ones.

True, if the conditions that a theory contemplated have changed, the theory
no longer applies. But what sorts of changes would alter the international
political system so profoundly that old ways of thinking would no longer be
relevant? Changes *of* the system would do it; changes *in* the system would
not. Within-system changes take place all the time, some important, some
not. Big changes in the means of transportation, communication, and war
fighting, for example, strongly affect how states and other agents interact.
Such changes occur at the unit level. In modern history, or perhaps in all of
history, the introduction of nuclear weaponry was the greatest of such
changes. Yet in the nuclear era, international politics remains a self-help
arena. Nuclear weapons decisively change how some states provide for their
own and possibly for others' security; but nuclear weapons have not altered
the anarchic structure of the international political system.

Changes in the structure of the system are distinct from changes at the unit
level. Thus, changes in polarity also affect how states provide for their security. Significant changes take place when the number of great powers reduces
to two or one. With more than two, states rely for their security both on their

*Kenneth N. Waltz, former Ford Professor of Political Science at the University of California, Berkeley, is a
Research Associate of the Institute of War and Peace Studies and Adjunct Professor at Columbia University.*

I am indebted to Karen Adams and Robert Rauchhaus for help on this article from its conception
to its completion. For insightful and constructive criticisms I wish to thank Robert Art, Richard
Betts, Barbara Farnham, Anne Fox, Robert Jervis, Warner Schilling, and Mark Sheetz.

1. For example, Richard Ned Lebow, "The Long Peace, the End of the Cold War, and the Failure of
Realism," *International Organization*, Vol. 48, No. 2 (Spring 1994), pp. 249–277; Jeffrey W. Legro and
Andrew Moravcsik, "Is Anybody Still a Realist?" *International Security*, Vol. 24, No. 2 (Fall 1999),
pp. 5–55; Bruce Russett, *Grasping the Democratic Peace: Principles for a Post–Cold War Peace* (Princeton, N.J.: Princeton University Press, 1993); Paul Schroeder, "Historical Reality vs. Neo- realist Theory," *International Security*, Vol. 19, No. 1 (Summer 1994), pp. 108–148; and John A. Vasquez, "The
Realist Paradigm and Degenerative vs. Progressive Research Programs: An Appraisal of
Neotraditional Research on Waltz's Balancing Proposition," *American Political Science Review*, Vol.
91, No. 4 (December 1997), pp. 899–912.

International Security, Vol. 25, No. 1 (Summer 2000), pp. 137–173
© 2000 by the President and Fellows of Harvard College and the Massachusetts Institute of Technology.

own internal efforts and on alliances they may make with others. Competition in multipolar systems is more complicated than competition in bipolar ones because uncertainties about the comparative capabilities of states multiply as numbers grow, and because estimates of the cohesiveness and strength of coalitions are hard to make.

Both changes of weaponry and changes of polarity were big ones with ramifications that spread through the system, yet they did not transform it. If the system were transformed, international politics would no longer be international politics, and the past would no longer serve as a guide to the future. We would begin to call international politics by another name, as some do. The terms "world politics" or "global politics," for example, suggest that politics among self-interested states concerned with their security has been replaced by some other kind of politics or perhaps by no politics at all.

What changes, one may wonder, would turn international politics into something distinctly different? The answer commonly given is that international politics is being transformed and realism is being rendered obsolete as democracy extends its sway, as interdependence tightens its grip, and as institutions smooth the way to peace. I consider these points in successive sections. A fourth section explains why realist theory retains its explanatory power after the Cold War.

Democracy and Peace

The end of the Cold War coincided with what many took to be a new democratic wave. The trend toward democracy combined with Michael Doyle's rediscovery of the peaceful behavior of liberal democratic states *inter se* contributes strongly to the belief that war is obsolescent, if not obsolete, among the advanced industrial states of the world.[2]

The democratic peace thesis holds that democracies do not fight democracies. Notice that I say "thesis," not "theory." The belief that democracies constitute a zone of peace rests on a perceived high correlation between governmental form and international outcome. Francis Fukuyama thinks that the correlation is perfect: Never once has a democracy fought another democracy. Jack Levy says that it is "the closest thing we have to an empirical law

---

2. Michael W. Doyle, "Kant, Liberal Legacies, and Foreign Affairs, Parts 1 and 2," *Philosophy and Public Affairs*, Vol. 12, Nos. 3 and 4 (Summer and Fall 1983); and Doyle, "Kant: Liberalism and World Politics," *American Political Science Review*, Vol. 80, No. 4 (December 1986), pp. 1151–1169.

in the study of international relations."[3] But, if it is true that democracies rest reliably at peace among themselves, we have not a theory but a purported fact begging for an explanation, as facts do. The explanation given generally runs this way: Democracies of the right kind (i.e., liberal ones) are peaceful in relation to one another. This was Immanuel Kant's point. The term he used was *Rechtsstaat* or republic, and his definition of a republic was so restrictive that it was hard to believe that even one of them could come into existence, let alone two or more.[4] And if they did, who can say that they would continue to be of the right sort or continue to be democracies at all? The short and sad life of the Weimar Republic is a reminder. And how does one define what the right sort of democracy is? Some American scholars thought that Wilhelmine Germany was the very model of a modern democratic state with a wide suffrage, honest elections, a legislature that controlled the purse, competitive parties, a free press, and a highly competent bureaucracy.[5] But in the French, British, and American view after August of 1914, Germany turned out not to be a democracy of the right kind. John Owen tried to finesse the problem of definition by arguing that democracies that perceive one another to be liberal democracies will not fight.[6] That rather gives the game away. Liberal democracies have at times prepared for wars against other liberal democracies and have sometimes come close to fighting them. Christopher Layne shows that some wars between democracies were averted not because of the reluctance of democracies to fight each other but for fear of a third party—a good realist reason. How, for example, could Britain and France fight each other over Fashoda in 1898 when Germany lurked in the background? In emphasizing the international political reasons for democracies not fighting each other, Layne gets to the heart of the matter.[7] Conformity of countries to a prescribed

---

3. Francis Fukuyama, "Liberal Democracy as a Global Phenomenon," *Political Science and Politics*, Vol. 24, No. 4 (1991), p. 662. Jack S. Levy, "Domestic Politics and War," in Robert I. Rotberg and Theodore K. Rabb, eds., *The Origin and Prevention of Major Wars* (Cambridge: Cambridge University Press, 1989), p. 88.

4. Kenneth N. Waltz, "Kant, Liberalism, and War," *American Political Science Review*, Vol. 56, No. 2 (June 1962). Subsequent Kant references are found in this work.

5. Ido Oren, "The Subjectivity of the 'Democratic' Peace: Changing U.S. Perceptions of Imperial Germany," *International Security*, Vol. 20, No. 2 (Fall 1995), pp. 157ff.; Christopher Layne, in the second half of Layne and Sean M. Lynn-Jones, *Should America Spread Democracy? A Debate* (Cambridge, Mass.: MIT Press, forthcoming), argues convincingly that Germany's democratic control of foreign and military policy was no weaker than France's or Britain's.

6. John M. Owen, "How Liberalism Produces Democratic Peace," *International Security*, Vol. 19, No. 2 (Fall 1994), pp. 87–125. Cf. his *Liberal Peace, Liberal War: American Politics and International Security* (Ithaca, N.Y.: Cornell University Press, 1997).

7. Christopher Layne, "Kant or Cant: The Myth of the Democratic Peace," *International Security*, Vol. 19, No. 2 (Fall 1994), pp. 5–49.

political form may eliminate some of the causes of war; it cannot eliminate all of them. The democratic peace thesis will hold only if all of the causes of war lie inside of states.

THE CAUSES OF WAR

To explain war is easier than to understand the conditions of peace. If one asks what may cause war, the simple answer is "anything." That is Kant's answer: The natural state is the state of war. Under the conditions of international politics, war recurs; the sure way to abolish war, then, is to abolish international politics.

Over the centuries, liberals have shown a strong desire to get the politics out of politics. The ideal of nineteenth-century liberals was the police state, that is, the state that would confine its activities to catching criminals and enforcing contracts. The ideal of the laissez-faire state finds many counterparts among students of international politics with their yen to get the power out of power politics, the national out of international politics, the dependence out of inter- dependence, the relative out of relative gains, the politics out of international politics, and the structure out of structural theory.

Proponents of the democratic peace thesis write as though the spread of democracy will negate the effects of anarchy. No causes of conflict and war will any longer be found at the structural level. Francis Fukuyama finds it "perfectly possible to imagine anarchic state systems that are nonetheless peaceful." He sees no reason to associate anarchy with war. Bruce Russett believes that, with enough democracies in the world, it "may be possible in part to supersede the 'realist' principles (anarchy, the security dilemma of states) that have dominated practice . . . since at least the seventeenth cen- tury."[8] Thus the structure is removed from structural theory. Democratic states would be so confident of the peace-preserving effects of democracy that they would no longer fear that another state, so long as it remained democratic, would do it wrong. The guarantee of the state's proper external behavior would derive from its admirable internal qualities.

This is a conclusion that Kant would not sustain. German historians at the turn of the nineteenth century wondered whether peacefully inclined states could be planted and expected to grow where dangers from outside pressed daily upon them.[9] Kant a century earlier entertained the same worry. The

---

8. Francis Fukuyama, *The End of History and the Last Man* (New York: Free Press, 1992), pp. 254– 256. Russett, *Grasping the Democratic Peace*, p. 24.
9. For example, Leopold von Ranke, Gerhard Ritter, and Otto Hintze. The American William Gra- ham Sumner and many others shared their doubts.

seventh proposition of his "Principles of the Political Order" avers that establishment of the proper constitution internally requires the proper ordering of the external relations of states. The first duty of the state is to defend itself, and outside of a juridical order none but the state itself can define the actions required. "Lesion of a less powerful country," Kant writes, "may be involved merely in the condition of a more powerful neighbor prior to any action at all; and in the State of Nature an attack under such circumstances would be warrantable."[10] In the state of nature, there is no such thing as an unjust war.

Every student of international politics is aware of the statistical data supporting the democratic peace thesis. Everyone has also known at least since David Hume that we have no reason to believe that the association of events provides a basis for inferring the presence of a causal relation. John Mueller properly speculates that it is not democracy that causes peace but that other conditions cause both democracy and peace.[11] Some of the major democracies—Britain in the nineteenth century and the United States in the twentieth century—have been among the most powerful states of their eras. Powerful states often gain their ends by peaceful means where weaker states either fail or have to resort to war.[12] Thus, the American government deemed the democratically elected Juan Bosch of the Dominican Republic too weak to bring order to his country. The United States toppled his government by sending 23,000 troops within a week, troops whose mere presence made fighting a war unnecessary. Salvador Allende, democratically elected ruler of Chile, was systematically and effectively undermined by the United States, without the open use of force, because its leaders thought that his government was taking a wrong turn. As Henry Kissinger put it: "I don't see why we need to stand by and watch a country go Communist due to the irresponsibility of its own people."[13] That is the way it is with democracies—their people may show bad judgment. "Wayward" democracies are especially tempting objects of intervention by other democracies that wish to save them. American policy may have been wise in both cases, but its actions surely cast doubt on the democratic peace thesis. So do the instances when a democracy did fight another democ-

10. Immanuel Kant, *The Philosophy of Law*, trans. W. Hastie (Edinburgh: T. and T. Clark, 1887), p. 218.
11. John Mueller, "Is War Still Becoming Obsolete?" paper presented at the annual meeting of the American Political Science Association, Washington, D.C., August–September 1991, pp. 55ff; cf. his *Quiet Cataclysm: Reflections on the Recent Transformation of World Politics* (New York: HarperCollins, 1995).
12. Edward Hallett Carr, *Twenty Years' Crisis: An Introduction to the Study of International Relations*, 2d ed. (New York: Harper and Row, 1946), pp. 129–132.
13. Quoted in Anthony Lewis, "The Kissinger Doctrine," *New York Times*, February 27, 1975, p. 35; and see Henry Kissinger, *The White House Years* (Boston: Little, Brown, 1979), chap. 17.

racy.[14] So do the instances in which democratically elected legislatures have clamored for war, as has happened for example in Pakistan and Jordan.

One can of course say, yes, but the Dominican Republic and Chile were not liberal democracies nor perceived as such by the United States. Once one begins to go down that road, there is no place to stop. The problem is heightened because liberal democracies, as they prepare for a war they may fear, begin to look less liberal and will look less liberal still if they begin to fight one. I am tempted to say that the democratic peace thesis in the form in which its proponents cast it is irrefutable. A liberal democracy at war with another country is unlikely to call it a liberal democracy.

Democracies may live at peace with democracies, but even if all states became democratic, the structure of international politics would remain anarchic. The structure of international politics is not transformed by changes internal to states, however widespread the changes may be. In the absence of an external authority, a state cannot be sure that today's friend will not be tomorrow's enemy. Indeed, democracies have at times behaved as though today's democracy is today's enemy and a present threat to them. In Federalist Paper number six, Alexander Hamilton asked whether the thirteen states of the Confederacy might live peacefully with one another as freely constituted republics. He answered that there have been "almost as many popular as royal wars." He cited the many wars fought by republican Sparta, Athens, Rome, Carthage, Venice, Holland, and Britain. John Quincy Adams, in response to James Monroe's contrary claim, averred "that the government of a Republic was as capable of intriguing with the leaders of a free people as neighboring monarchs."[15] In the latter half of the nineteenth century, as the United States and Britain became more democratic, bitterness grew between them, and the possibility of war was at times seriously entertained on both sides of the Atlantic. France and Britain were among the principal adversaries in the great power politics of the nineteenth century, as they were earlier. Their becoming democracies did not change their behavior toward each other. In 1914, democratic England and France fought democratic Germany, and doubts about the latter's democratic standing merely illustrate the problem of definition. Indeed, the democratic pluralism of Germany was an underlying cause of the war. In response to domestic interests, Germany followed

---

14. See, for example, Kenneth N. Waltz, "America as Model for the World? A Foreign Policy Perspective," *PS: Political Science and Politics*, Vol. 24, No. 4 (December 1991); and Mueller, "Is War Still Becoming Obsolete?" p. 5.
15. Quoted in Walter A. McDougall, *Promised Land, Crusader State* (Boston: Houghton Mifflin, 1997), p. 28 and n. 36.

policies bound to frighten both Britain and Russia. And today if a war that a few have feared were fought by the United States and Japan, many Americans would say that Japan was not a democracy after all, but merely a one-party state.

What can we conclude? Democracies rarely fight democracies, we might say, and then add as a word of essential caution that the internal excellence of states is a brittle basis of peace.

DEMOCRATIC WARS

Democracies coexist with undemocratic states. Although democracies seldom fight democracies, they do, as Michael Doyle has noted, fight at least their share of wars against others.[16] Citizens of democratic states tend to think of their countries as good, aside from what they do, simply because they are democratic. Thus former Secretary of State Warren Christopher claimed that "democratic nations rarely start wars or threaten their neighbors."[17] One might suggest that he try his proposition out in Central or South America. Citizens of democratic states also tend to think of undemocratic states as bad, aside from what they do, simply because they are undemocratic. Democracies promote war because they at times decide that the way to preserve peace is to defeat nondemocratic states and make them democratic.

During World War I, Walter Hines Page, American ambassador to England, claimed that there "is no security in any part of the world where people cannot think of a government without a king and never will be." During the Vietnam War, Secretary of State Dean Rusk claimed that the "United States cannot be secure until the total international environment is ideologically safe."[18] Policies aside, the very existence of undemocratic states is a danger to others. American political and intellectual leaders have often taken this view. Liberal interventionism is again on the march. President Bill Clinton and his national security adviser, Anthony Lake, urged the United States to take measures to enhance democracy around the world. The task, one fears, will be taken up by the American military with some enthusiasm. Former Army Chief of Staff General Gordon Sullivan, for example, favored a new military "model," replacing the negative aim of containment with a positive one: "To promote democracy,

16. Doyle, "Kant, Liberal Legacies, and Foreign Affairs, Part 2," p. 337.
17. Warren Christopher, "The U.S.-Japan Relationship: The Responsibility to Change," address to the Japan Association of Corporate Executives, Tokyo, Japan, March 11, 1994 (U.S. Department of State, Bureau of Public Affairs, Office of Public Communication), p. 3.
18. Page quoted in Waltz, *Man, the State, and War: A Theoretical Analysis* (New York: Columbia University Press, 1959), p. 121. Rusk quoted in Layne, "Kant or Cant," p. 46.

regional stability, and economic prosperity."[19] Other voices urge us to enter into a "struggle to ensure that people are governed well." Having apparently solved the problem of justice at home, "the struggle for liberal government becomes a struggle not simply for justice but for survival."[20] As R.H. Tawney said: "Either war is a crusade, or it is a crime."[21] Crusades are frightening because crusaders go to war for righteous causes, which they define for themselves and try to impose on others. One might have hoped that Americans would have learned that they are not very good at causing democracy abroad. But, alas, if the world can be made safe for democracy only by making it democratic, then all means are permitted and to use them becomes a duty. The war fervor of people and their representatives is at times hard to contain. Thus Hans Morgenthau believed that "the democratic selection and responsibility of government officials destroyed international morality as an effective system of restraint."[22]

Since, as Kant believed, war among self-directed states will occasionally break out, peace has to be contrived. For any government, doing so is a difficult task, and all states are at times deficient in accomplishing it, even if they wish to. Democratic leaders may respond to the fervor for war that their citizens sometimes display, or even try to arouse it, and governments are sometimes constrained by electoral calculations to defer preventive measures. Thus British Prime Minister Stanley Baldwin said that if he had called in 1935 for British rearmament against the German threat, his party would have lost the next election.[23] Democratic governments may respond to internal political imperatives when they should be responding to external ones. All governments have their faults, democracies no doubt fewer than others, but that is not good enough to sustain the democratic peace thesis.

That peace may prevail among democratic states is a comforting thought. The obverse of the proposition—that democracy may promote war against undemocratic states—is disturbing. If the latter holds, we cannot even say for sure that the spread of democracy will bring a net decrease in the amount of war in the world.

---

19. Quoted in Clemson G. Turregano and Ricky Lynn Waddell, "From Paradigm to Paradigm Shift: The Military and Operations Other than War," *Journal of Political Science*, Vol. 22 (1994), p. 15.
20. Peter Beinart, "The Return of the Bomb," *New Republic*, August 3, 1998, p. 27.
21. Quoted in Michael Straight, *Make This the Last War* (New York: G.P. Putnam's Sons, 1945), p. 1.
22. Hans J. Morgenthau, *Politics among Nations: The Struggle for Power and Peace*, 5th ed. (New York: Knopf, 1973), p. 248.
23. Gordon Craig and Alexander George, *Force and Statecraft: Diplomatic Problems of Our Time*, 2d ed. (New York: Oxford University Press, 1990), p. 64.

With a republic established in a strong state, Kant hoped the republican form would gradually take hold in the world. In 1795, America provided the hope. Two hundred years later, remarkably, it still does. Ever since liberals first expressed their views, they have been divided. Some have urged liberal states to work to uplift benighted peoples and bring the benefits of liberty, justice, and prosperity to them. John Stuart Mill, Giuseppe Mazzini, Woodrow Wilson, and Bill Clinton are all interventionist liberals. Other liberals, Kant and Richard Cobden, for example, while agreeing on the benefits that democracy can bring to the world, have emphasized the difficulties and the dangers of actively seeking its propagation.

If the world is now safe for democracy, one has to wonder whether democracy is safe for the world. When democracy is ascendant, a condition that in the twentieth century attended the winning of hot wars and cold ones, the interventionist spirit flourishes. The effect is heightened when one democratic state becomes dominant, as the United States is now. Peace is the noblest cause of war. If the conditions of peace are lacking, then the country with a capability of creating them may be tempted to do so, whether or not by force. The end is noble, but as a matter of *right*, Kant insists, no state can intervene in the internal arrangements of another. As a matter of *fact*, one may notice that intervention, even for worthy ends, often brings more harm than good. The vice to which great powers easily succumb in a multipolar world is inattention; in a bipolar world, overreaction; in a unipolar world, overextention.

Pithy

Peace is maintained by a delicate balance of internal and external restraints. States having a surplus of power are tempted to use it, and weaker states fear their doing so. The laws of voluntary federations, to use Kant's language, are disregarded at the whim of the stronger, as the United States demonstrated a decade ago by mining Nicaraguan waters and by invading Panama. In both cases, the United States blatantly violated international law. In the first, it denied the jurisdiction of the International Court of Justice, which it had previously accepted. In the second, it flaunted the law embodied in the Charter of the Organization of American States, of which it was a principal sponsor.

If the democratic peace thesis is right, structural realist theory is wrong. One may believe, with Kant, that republics are by and large good states *and* that unbalanced power is a danger no matter who wields it. Inside of, as well as outside of, the circle of democratic states, peace depends on a precarious balance of forces. The causes of war lie not simply in states or in the state system; they are found in both. Kant understood this. Devotees of the democratic peace thesis overlook it.

The Weak Effects of Interdependence

If not democracy alone, may not the spread of democracy combined with the tightening of national interdependence fulfill the prescription for peace offered by nineteenth-century liberals and so often repeated today?[24] To the supposedly peaceful inclination of democracies, interdependence adds the propulsive power of the profit motive. Democratic states may increasingly devote themselves to the pursuit of peace and profits. The trading state is replacing the political-military state, and the power of the market now rivals or surpasses the power of the state, or so some believe.[25]

Before World War I, Norman Angell believed that wars would not be fought because they would not pay, yet Germany and Britain, each other's second-best customers, fought a long and bloody war.[26] Interdependence in some ways promotes peace by multiplying contacts among states and contributing to mutual understanding. It also multiplies the occasions for conflicts that may promote resentment and even war.[27] Close interdependence is a condition in which one party can scarcely move without jostling others; a small push ripples through society. The closer the social bonds, the more extreme the effect becomes, and one cannot sensibly pursue an interest without taking others' interests into account. One country is then inclined to treat another country's acts as events within its own polity and to attempt to control them.

That interdependence promotes war as well as peace has been said often enough. What requires emphasis is that, either way, among the forces that shape international politics, interdependence is a weak one. Interdependence within modern states is much closer than it is across states. The Soviet economy was planned so that its far-flung parts would be not just interdependent but integrated. Huge factories depended for their output on products exchanged

---

24. Strongly affirmative answers are given by John R. Oneal and Bruce Russett, "Assessing the Liberal Peace with Alternative Specifications: Trade Still Reduces Conflict," *Journal of Peace Research,* Vol. 36, No. 4 (July 1999), pp. 423–442; and Russett, Oneal, and David R. Davis, "The Third Leg of the Kantian Tripod for Peace: International Organizations and Militarized Disputes, 1950–85," *International Organization,* Vol. 52, No. 3 (Summer 1998), pp. 441–467.
25. Richard Rosecrance, *The Rise of the Trading State: Commerce and Coalitions in the Modern World* (New York: Basic Books, 1986); and at times Susan Strange, *The Retreat of the State: The Diffusion of Power in the World Economy* (New York: Cambridge University Press, 1996).
26. Norman Angell, *The Great Illusion,* 4th rev. and enlarged ed. (New York: Putnam's, 1913).
27. Katherine Barbieri, "Economic Interdependence: A Path to Peace or a Source of Interstate Conflict?" *Journal of Peace Research,* Vol. 33, No. 1 (February 1996). Lawrence Keely, *War before Civilization: The Myth of the Peaceful Savage* (New York: Oxford University Press, 1996), p. 196, shows that with increases of trade and intermarriage among tribes, war became more frequent.

with others. Despite the tight integration of the Soviet economy, the state fell apart. Yugoslavia provides another stark illustration. Once external political pressure lessened, internal economic interests were too weak to hold the country together. One must wonder whether economic interdependence is more effect than cause. Internally, interdependence becomes so close that integration is the proper word to describe it. Interdependence becomes integration because internally the expectation that peace will prevail and order will be preserved is high. Externally, goods and capital flow freely where peace among countries appears to be reliably established. Interdependence, like integration, depends on other conditions. It is more a dependent than an independent variable. States, if they can afford to, shy away from becoming excessively dependent on goods and resources that may be denied them in crises and wars. States take measures, such as Japan's managed trade, to avoid excessive dependence on others.[28]

The impulse to protect one's identity—cultural and political as well as economic—from encroachment by others is strong. When it seems that "we will sink or swim together," swimming separately looks attractive to those able to do it. From Plato onward, utopias were set in isolation from neighbors so that people could construct their collective life uncontaminated by contact with others. With zero interdependence, neither conflict nor war is possible. With integration, international becomes national politics.[29] The zone in between is a gray one with the effects of interdependence sometimes good, providing the benefits of divided labor, mutual understanding, and cultural enrichment, and sometimes bad, leading to protectionism, mutual resentment, conflict, and war.

The uneven effects of interdependence, with some parties to it gaining more, others gaining less, are obscured by the substitution of Robert Keohane's and Joseph Nye's term "asymmetric interdependence" for relations of dependence and independence among states.[30] Relatively independent states are in a stronger position than relatively dependent ones. If I depend more on you than you depend on me, you have more ways of influencing me and affecting my fate

---

28. On states managing interdependence to avoid excessive dependence, see especially Robert Gilpin, *The Political Economy of International Relations* (Princeton, N.J.: Princeton University Press, 1987), chap. 10; and Suzanne Berger and Ronald Dore, eds., *National Diversity and Global Capitalism* (Ithaca, N.Y.: Cornell University Press, 1996).
29. Cf. Kenneth N. Waltz, in Steven L. Spiegel and Waltz, eds., *Conflict in World Politics* (Cambridge, Mass.: Winthrop, 1971), chap. 13.
30. Robert O. Keohane and Joseph S. Nye, *Power and Interdependence*, 2d ed. (New York: HarperCollins, 1989).

than I have of affecting yours. Interdependence suggests a condition of roughly equal dependence of parties on one another. Omitting the word "dependence" blunts the inequalities that mark the relations of states and makes them all seem to be on the same footing. Much of international, as of national, politics is about inequalities. Separating one "issue area" from others and emphasizing that weak states have advantages in some of them reduces the sense of inequality. Emphasizing the low fungibility of power furthers the effect. If power is not very fungible, weak states may have decisive advantages on some issues. Again, the effects of inequality are blunted. But power, not very fungible for weak states, is very fungible for strong ones. The history of American foreign policy since World War II is replete with examples of how the United States used its superior economic capability to promote its political and security interests.[31]

In a 1970 essay, I described interdependence as an ideology used by Americans to camouflage the great leverage the United States enjoys in international politics by making it seem that strong and weak, rich and poor nations are similarly entangled in a thick web of interdependence.[32] In her recent book, *The Retreat of the State,* Susan Strange reached the same conclusion, but by an odd route. Her argument is that "the progressive integration of the world economy, through international production, has shifted the balance of power away from states and toward world markets." She advances three propositions in support of her argument: (1) power has "shifted upward from weak states to stronger ones" having global or regional reach; (2) power has "shifted sideways from states to markets and thus to non-state authorities deriving power from their market shares"; and (3) some power has "evaporated" with no one exercising it.[33] In international politics, with no central authority, power does sometimes slip away and sometimes move sideways to markets. When serious slippage occurs, however, stronger states step in to reverse it, and firms of the stronger states control the largest market shares anyway. One may doubt whether markets any more escape the control of major

---

31. Keohane and Nye are on both sides of the issue. See, for example, ibid., p. 28. Keohane emphasized that power is not very fungible in Keohane, ed., "Theory of World Politics," *Neorealism and Its Critics* (New York: Columbia University Press, 1986); and see Kenneth N. Waltz, "Reflection on Theory of International Politics: A Response to My Critics," in ibid. Robert J. Art analyzes the fungibility of power in detail. See Art, "American Foreign Policy and the Fungibility of Force," *Security Studies,* Vol. 5, No. 4 (Summer 1996).
32. Kenneth N. Waltz, "The Myth of National Interdependence," in Charles P. Kindleberger, ed., *The International Corporation* (Cambridge, Mass.: MIT Press, 1970).
33. Strange, *Retreat of the State,* pp. 46, 189.

states now than they did in the nineteenth century or earlier—perhaps less so since the competence of states has increased at least in proportion to increases in the size and complications of markets. Anyone, realist or not, might think Strange's first proposition is the important one. Never since the Roman Empire has power been so concentrated in one state. Despite believing that power has moved from states to markets, Strange recognized reality. She observed near the beginning of her book that the "authority—the 'power over' global outcomes enjoyed by American society, and therefore indirectly by the United States government—is still superior to that of any other society or any other government." And near the end, she remarked that the "authority of governments tends to over-rule the caution of markets." If one wondered which government she had in mind, she answered immediately: "The fate of Mexico is decided in Washington more than Wall Street. And the International Monetary Fund (IMF) is obliged to follow the American lead, despite the misgivings of Germany or Japan."[34]

The history of the past two centuries has been one of central governments acquiring more and more power. Alexis de Tocqueville observed during his visit to the United States in 1831 that "the Federal Government scarcely ever interferes in any but foreign affairs; and the governments of the states in reality direct society in America."[35] After World War II, governments in Western Europe disposed of about a quarter of their peoples' income. The proportion now is more than half. At a time when Americans, Britons, Russians, and Chinese were decrying the control of the state over their lives, it was puzzling to be told that states were losing control over their external affairs. Losing control, one wonders, as compared to when? Weak states have lost some of their influence and control over external matters, but strong states have not lost theirs. The patterns are hardly new ones. In the eighteenth and nineteenth centuries, the strongest state with the longest reach intervened all over the globe and built history's most extensive empire. In the twentieth century, the strongest state with the longest reach repeated Britain's interventionist behavior and, since the end of the Cold War, on an ever widening scale, without building an empire. The absence of empire hardly means, however, that the extent of America's influence and control over the actions of others is of lesser moment. The withering away of the power of the state,

---

34. Ibid., pp. 25, 192.
35. Alexis de Tocqueville, *Democracy in America*, ed. J.P. Mayer, trans. George Lawrence (New York: Harper Perennial, 1988), p. 446, n. 1.

whether internally or externally, is more of a wish and an illusion than a reality in most of the world.

Under the Pax Britannica, the interdependence of states became unusually close, which to many portended a peaceful and prosperous future. Instead, a prolonged period of war, autarky, and more war followed. The international economic system, constructed under American auspices after World War II and later amended to suit its purposes, may last longer, but then again it may not. The character of international politics changes as national interdependence tightens or loosens. Yet even as relations vary, states have to take care of themselves as best they can in an anarchic environment. Internationally, the twentieth century for the most part was an unhappy one. In its last quarter, the clouds lifted a little, but twenty-five years is a slight base on which to ground optimistic conclusions. Not only are the effects of close interdependence problematic, but so also is its durability.

The Limited Role of International Institutions

One of the charges hurled at realist theory is that it depreciates the importance of institutions. The charge is justified, and the strange case of NATO's (the North Atlantic Treaty Organization's) outliving its purpose shows why realists believe that international institutions are shaped and limited by the states that found and sustain them and have little independent effect. Liberal institutionalists paid scant attention to organizations designed to buttress the security of states until, contrary to expectations inferred from realist theories, NATO not only survived the end of the Cold War but went on to add new members and to promise to embrace still more. Far from invalidating realist theory or casting doubt on it, however, the recent history of NATO illustrates the subordination of international institutions to national purposes.

EXPLAINING INTERNATIONAL INSTITUTIONS

The nature and purposes of institutions change as structures vary. In the old multipolar world, the core of an alliance consisted of a small number of states of comparable capability. Their contributions to one another's security were of crucial importance because they were of similar size. Because major allies were closely interdependent militarily, the defection of one would have made its partners vulnerable to a competing alliance. The members of opposing alliances before World War I were tightly knit because of their mutual dependence. In the new bipolar world, the word "alliance" took on a different meaning. One country, the United States or the Soviet Union, provided most of the security for its bloc. The withdrawal of France from NATO's command structure and the defection of China from the Soviet bloc failed even to tilt the central balance. Early in the Cold War, Americans spoke with alarm about the threat of monolithic communism arising from the combined strength of the Soviet Union and China, yet the bloc's disintegration caused scarcely a ripple. American officials did not proclaim that with China's defection, America's defense budget could safely be reduced by 20 or 10 percent or even be reduced at all. Similarly, when France stopped playing its part in NATO's military plans, American officials did not proclaim that defense spending had to be increased for that reason. Properly speaking, NATO and the WTO (Warsaw Treaty Organization) were treaties of guarantee rather than old-style military alliances.[36]

Glenn Snyder has remarked that "alliances have no meaning apart from the adversary threat to which they are a response."[37] I expected NATO to dwindle at the Cold War's end and ultimately to disappear.[38] In a basic sense, the expectation has been borne out. NATO is no longer even a treaty of guarantee because one cannot answer the question, guarantee against whom? Functions vary as structures change, as does the behavior of units. Thus the end of the Cold War quickly changed the behavior of allied countries. In early July of 1990, NATO announced that the alliance would "elaborate new force plans consistent with the revolutionary changes in Europe."[39] By the end of July, without waiting for any such plans, the major European members of NATO unilaterally announced large reductions in their force levels. Even the pretense of continuing to act as an alliance in setting military policy disappeared.

With its old purpose dead, and the individual and collective behavior of its members altered accordingly, how does one explain NATO's survival and expansion? Institutions are hard to create and set in motion, but once created, institutionalists claim, they may take on something of a life of their own; they may begin to act with a measure of autonomy, becoming less dependent on the wills of their sponsors and members. NATO supposedly validates these thoughts.

Organizations, especially big ones with strong traditions, have long lives. The March of Dimes is an example sometimes cited. Having won the war

---

36. See Kenneth N. Waltz, "International Structure, National Force, and the Balance of World Power," *Journal of International Affairs*, Vol. 21, No. 2 (1967), p. 219.
37. Glenn H. Snyder, *Alliance Politics* (Ithaca, N.Y.: Cornell University Press, 1997), p. 192.
38. Kenneth N. Waltz, "The Emerging Structure of International Politics," *International Security*, Vol. 18, No. 2 (Fall 1993), pp. 75–76.
39. John Roper, "Shaping Strategy without the Threat," Adephi Paper No. 257 (London: International Institute for Strategic Studies, Winter 1990/91), pp. 80–81.

against polio, its mission was accomplished. Nevertheless, it cast about for a new malady to cure or contain. Even though the most appealing ones—cancer, diseases of the heart and lungs, multiple sclerosis, and cystic fibrosis—were already taken, it did find a worthy cause to pursue, the amelioration of birth defects. One can fairly claim that the March of Dimes enjoys continuity as an organization, pursuing an end consonant with its original purpose. How can one make such a claim for NATO?

The question of purpose may not be a very important one; create an organization and it will find something to do.[40] Once created, and the more so once it has become well established, an organization becomes hard to get rid of. A big organization is managed by large numbers of bureaucrats who develop a strong interest in its perpetuation. According to Gunther Hellmann and Reinhard Wolf, in 1993 NATO headquarters was manned by 2,640 officials, most of whom presumably wanted to keep their jobs.[41] The durability of NATO even as the structure of international politics has changed, and the old purpose of the organization has disappeared, is interpreted by institutionalists as evidence strongly arguing for the autonomy and vitality of institutions.

The institutionalist interpretation misses the point. NATO is first of all a treaty made by states. A deeply entrenched international bureaucracy can help to sustain the organization, but states determine its fate. Liberal institutionalists take NATO's seeming vigor as confirmation of the importance of international institutions and as evidence of their resilience. Realists, noticing that as an alliance NATO has lost its major function, see it mainly as a means of maintaining and lengthening America's grip on the foreign and military policies of European states. John Kornblum, U.S. senior deputy to the undersecretary of state for European affairs, neatly described NATO's new role. "The Alliance," he wrote, "provides a vehicle for the application of American power and vision to the security order in Europe."[42] The survival and expansion of NATO tell us much about American power and influence and little about institutions as multilateral entities. The ability of the United States to extend the life of a moribund institution nicely illustrates how international institutions are created and maintained by stronger states to serve their perceived or misperceived interests.

---

40. Joseph A. Schumpeter, writing of armies, put it this way: *"created by wars that required it, the machine now created the wars it required."* "The Sociology of Imperialism," in Schumpeter, *Imperialism and Social Classes* (New York: Meridian Books, 1955), p. 25 (emphasis in original).

41. Gunther Hellmann and Reinhard Wolf, "Neorealism, Neoliberal Institutionalism, and the Future of NATO," *Security Studies*, Vol. 3, No. 1 (Autumn 1993), p. 20.

42. John Kornblum, "NATO's Second Half Century—Tasks for an Alliance," *NATO on Track for the 21st Century*, Conference Report (The Hague: Netherlands Atlantic Commission, 1994), p. 14.

The Bush administration saw, and the Clinton administration continued to see, NATO as the instrument for maintaining America's domination of the foreign and military policies of European states. In 1991, U.S. Undersecretary of State Reginald Bartholomew's letter to the governments of European members of NATO warned against Europe's formulating independent positions on defense. France and Germany had thought that a European security and defense identity might be developed within the EU and that the Western European Union, formed in 1954, could be revived as the instrument for its realization. The Bush administration quickly squelched these ideas. The day after the signing of the Maastricht Treaty in December of 1991, President George Bush could say with satisfaction that "we are pleased that our Allies in the Western European Union . . . decided to strengthen that institution as both NATO's European pillar and the defense component of the European Union."[43]

The European pillar was to be contained within NATO, and its policies were to be made in Washington. Weaker states have trouble fashioning institutions to serve their own ends in their own ways, especially in the security realm. Think of the defeat of the European Defense Community in 1954, despite America's support of it, and the inability of the Western European Union in the more than four decades of its existence to find a significant role independent of the United States. Realism reveals what liberal institutionalist "theory" obscures: namely, that international institutions serve primarily national rather than international interests.[44] Robert Keohane and Lisa Martin, replying to John Mearsheimer's criticism of liberal institutionalism, ask: How are we "to account for the willingness of major states to invest resources in expanding international institutions if such institutions are lacking in significance?"[45] If the answer were not already obvious, the expansion of NATO would make it so: to serve what powerful states believe to be their interests.

With the administration's Bosnian policy in trouble, Clinton needed to show himself an effective foreign policy leader. With the national heroes Lech Walesa and Vaclav Havel clamoring for their countries' inclusion, foreclosing NATO membership would have handed another issue to the Republican

---

43. Mark S. Sheetz, "Correspondence: Debating the Unipolar Moment," *International Security*, Vol. 22, No. 3 (Winter 1997/98), p. 170; and Mike Winnerstig, "Rethinking Alliance Dynamics," paper presented at the annual meeting of the International Studies Association, Washington, D.C., March 18–22, 1997, at p. 23.

44. Cf. Alan S. Milward, *The European Rescue of the Nation-State* (Berkeley: University of California Press, 1992).

45. Robert O. Keohane and Lisa L. Martin, "The Promise of Institutionalist Theory," *International Security*, Vol. 20, No. 1 (Summer 1995), p. 40.

So down the predominate

Party in the congressional elections of 1994. To tout NATO's eastward march, President Clinton gave major speeches in Milwaukee, Cleveland, and Detroit, cities with significant numbers of East European voters.[46] Votes and dollars are the lifeblood of American politics. New members of NATO will be required to improve their military infrastructure and to buy modern weapons. The American arms industry, expecting to capture its usual large share of a new market, has lobbied heavily in favor of NATO's expansion.[47]

The reasons for expanding NATO are weak. The reasons for opposing expansion are strong.[48] It draws new lines of division in Europe, alienates those left out, and can find no logical stopping place west of Russia. It weakens those Russians most inclined toward liberal democracy and a market economy. It strengthens Russians of the opposite inclination. It reduces hope for further large reductions of nuclear weaponry. It pushes Russia toward China instead of drawing Russia toward Europe and America. NATO, led by America, scarcely considered the plight of its defeated adversary. Throughout modern history, Russia has been rebuffed by the West, isolated and at times surrounded. Many Russians believe that, by expanding, NATO brazenly broke promises it made in 1990 and 1991 that former WTO members would not be allowed to join NATO. With good reason, Russians fear that NATO will not only admit additional old members of the WTO but also former republics of the Soviet Union. In 1997, NATO held naval exercises with Ukraine in the Black Sea, with more joint exercises to come, and announced plans to use a military testing ground in western Ukraine. In June of 1998, Zbigniew Brzezinski went to Kiev with the message that Ukraine should prepare itself to join NATO by the year 2010.[49] The farther NATO intrudes into the Soviet Union's old arena, the more Russia is forced to look to the east rather than to the west.

The expansion of NATO extends its military interests, enlarges its responsibilities, and increases its burdens. Not only do new members require NATO's protection, they also heighten its concern over destabilizing events near their

---

46. James M. Goldgeier, "NATO Expansion: The Anatomy of a Decision," *Washington Quarterly*, Vol. 21, No. 1 (Winter 1998), pp. 94–95. And see his *Not Whether but When: The U.S. Decision to Enlarge NATO* (Washington, D.C.: Brookings, 1999).
47. William D. Hartung, "Welfare for Weapons Dealers 1998: The Hidden Costs of NATO Expansion" (New York: New School for Social Research, World Policy Institute, March 1998); and Jeff Gerth and Tim Weiner, "Arms Makers See Bonanza in Selling NATO Expansion," *New York Times*, June 29, 1997, p. I, 8.
48. See Michael E. Brown, "The Flawed Logic of Expansion," *Survival*, Vol. 37, No. 1 (Spring 1995), pp. 34–52. Michael Mandelbaum, *The Dawn of Peace in Europe* (New York: Twentieth Century Fund Press, 1996). Philip Zelikow, "The Masque of Institutions," *Survival*, Vol. 38, No. 1 (Spring 1996).
49. J.L. Black, *Russia Faces NATO Expansion: Bearing Gifts or Bearing Arms?* (Lanham, Md.: Rowman and Littlefield, 2000), pp. 5–35, 175–201.

borders. Thus Balkan eruptions become a NATO and not just a European concern. In the absence of European initiative, Americans believe they must lead the way because the credibility of NATO is at stake. Balkan operations in the air and even more so on the ground exacerbate differences of interest among NATO members and strain the alliance. European members marvel at the surveillance and communications capabilities of the United States and stand in awe of the modern military forces at its command. Aware of their weaknesses, Europeans express determination to modernize their forces and to develop their ability to deploy them independently. Europe's reaction to America's Balkan operations duplicates its determination to remedy deficiencies revealed in 1991 during the Gulf War, a determination that produced few results.

Will it be different this time? Perhaps, yet if European states do achieve their goals of creating a 60,000 strong rapid reaction force and enlarging the role of the WEU, the tension between a NATO controlled by the United States and a NATO allowing for independent European action will again be bothersome. In any event, the prospect of militarily bogging down in the Balkans tests the alliance and may indefinitely delay its further expansion. Expansion buys trouble, and mounting troubles may bring expansion to a halt.

European conditions and Russian opposition work against the eastward extension of NATO. Pressing in the opposite direction is the momentum of American expansion. The momentum of expansion has often been hard to break, a thought borne out by the empires of Republican Rome, of Czarist Russia, and of Liberal Britain.

One is often reminded that the United States is not just the dominant power in the world but that it is a *liberal* dominant power. True, the motivations of the artificers of expansion—President Clinton, National Security Adviser Anthony Lake, and others—were to nurture democracy in young, fragile, long-suffering countries. One may wonder, however, why this should be an American rather than a European task and why a military rather than a political-economic organization should be seen as the appropriate means for carrying it out. The task of building democracy is not a military one. The military security of new NATO members is not in jeopardy; their political development and economic well-being are. In 1997, U.S. Assistant Secretary of Defense Franklin D. Kramer told the Czech defense ministry that it was spending too little on defense.[50] Yet investing in defense slows economic growth. By common calculation, defense spending stimulates economic

---

50. Ibid., p. 72.

Source.

growth about half as much as direct investment in the economy.) In Eastern Europe, economic not military security is the problem and entering a military alliance compounds it.

Using the example of NATO to reflect on the relevance of realism after the Cold War leads to some important conclusions. The winner of the Cold War and the sole remaining great power has behaved as unchecked powers have usually done. In the absence of counterweights, a country's internal impulses prevail, whether fueled by liberal or by other urges. The error of realist predictions that the end of the Cold War would mean the end of NATO arose not from a failure of realist theory to comprehend international politics, but from an underestimation of America's folly. The survival and expansion of NATO illustrate not the defects but the limitations of structural explanations. Structures shape and shove; they do not determine the actions of states. A state that is stronger than any other can decide for itself whether to conform its policies to structural pressures and whether to avail itself of the opportunities that structural change offers, with little fear of adverse affects in the short run.

Do liberal institutionalists provide better leverage for explaining NATO's survival and expansion? According to Keohane and Martin, realists insist "that institutions have only marginal effects."[51] On the contrary, realists have noticed that whether institutions have strong or weak effects depends on what states intend. Strong states use institutions, as they interpret laws, in ways that suit them. Thus Susan Strange, in pondering the state's retreat, observes that "international organization is above all a tool of national government, an instrument for the pursuit of national interest by other means."[52]

Interestingly, Keohane and Martin, in their effort to refute Mearsheimer's trenchant criticism of institutional theory, in effect agree with him. Having claimed that his realism is "not well specified," they note that "institutional theory conceptualizes institutions both as independent and dependent variables."[53] Dependent on what?—on "the realities of power and interest." Institutions, it turns out, "make a significant difference in conjunction with power realities."[54] Yes! Liberal institutionalism, as Mearsheimer says, "is no longer a clear alternative to realism, but has, in fact, been swallowed up by it."[55] Indeed, it never was an alternative to realism. Institutionalist theory, as Keohane

51. Keohane and Martin, "The Promise of Institutionalist Theory," pp. 42, 46.
52. Strange, *Retreat of the State,* p. xiv; and see pp. 192–193. Cf. Carr, *The Twenty Years' Crisis*, p. 107: "international government is, in effect, government by that state which supplies the power necessary for the purpose of governing."
53. Keohane and Martin, "The Promise of Institutionalist Theory," p. 46.
54. Ibid., p. 42.
55. Mearsheimer, "A Realist Reply," p. 85.

has stressed, has as its core structural realism, which Keohane and Nye sought "to broaden."[56] The institutional approach starts with structural theory, applies it to the origins and operations of institutions, and unsurprisingly ends with realist conclusions.

Alliances illustrate the weaknesses of institutionalism with special clarity. Institutional theory attributes to institutions causal effects that mostly originate within states. The case of NATO nicely illustrates this shortcoming. Keohane has remarked that "alliances are institutions, and both their durability and strength . . . may depend in part on their institutional characteristics."[57] In part, I suppose, but one must wonder in how large a part. The Triple Alliance and the Triple Entente were quite durable. They lasted not because of alliance institutions, there hardly being any, but because the core members of each alliance looked outward and saw a pressing threat to their security. Previous alliances did not lack institutions because states had failed to figure out how to construct bureaucracies. Previous alliances lacked institutions because in the absence of a hegemonic leader, balancing continued within as well as across alliances. NATO lasted as a military alliance as long as the Soviet Union appeared to be a direct threat to its members. It survives and expands now not because of its institutions but mainly because the United States wants it to.

NATO's survival also exposes an interesting aspect of balance-of-power theory. Robert Art has argued forcefully that without NATO and without American troops in Europe, European states will lapse into a "security competition" among themselves.[58] As he emphasizes, this is a realist expectation. In his view, preserving NATO, and maintaining America's leading role in it, are required in order to prevent a security competition that would promote conflict within, and impair the institutions of, the European Union. NATO now is an anomaly; the dampening of intra-alliance tension is the main task left, and it is a task not for the alliance but for its leader. The secondary task of an alliance, intra-alliance management, continues to be performed by the United States even though the primary task, defense against an external enemy, has disappeared. The point is worth pondering, but I need to say here only that it fur-

---

56. Keohane and Nye, *Power and Interdependence*, p. 251; cf. Keohane, "Theory of World Politics," in Keohane, *Neorealism and Its Critics*, p. 193, where he describes his approach as a "modified structural research program."

57. Robert O. Keohane, *International Institutions and State Power: Essays in International Relations Theory* (Boulder, Colo.: Westview, 1989), p. 15.

58. Robert J. Art, "Why Western Europe Needs the United States and NATO," *Political Science Quarterly*, Vol. 111, No. 1 (Spring 1996).

ther illustrates the dependence of international institutions on national decisions. Balancing among states is not inevitable. As in Europe, a hegemonic power may suppress it. As a high-level European diplomat put it, "it is not acceptable that the lead nation be European. A European power broker is a hegemonic power. We can agree on U.S. leadership, but not on one of our own."[59] Accepting the leadership of a hegemonic power prevents a balance of power from emerging in Europe, and better the hegemonic power should be at a distance than next door.

Keohane believes that "avoiding military conflict in Europe after the Cold War depends greatly on whether the next decade is characterized by a continuous pattern of institutionalized cooperation."[60] If one accepts the conclusion, the question remains: What or who sustains the "pattern of institutionalized cooperation"? Realists know the answer.

INTERNATIONAL INSTITUTIONS AND NATIONAL AIMS
What is true of NATO holds for international institutions generally. The effects that international institutions may have on national decisions are but one step removed from the capabilities and intentions of the major state or states that gave them birth and sustain them. The Bretton Woods system strongly affected individual states and the conduct of international affairs. But when the United States found that the system no longer served its interests, the Nixon shocks of 1971 were administered. International institutions are created by the more powerful states, and the institutions survive in their original form as long as they serve the major interests of their creators, or are thought to do so. "The nature of institutional arrangements," as Stephen Krasner put it, "is better explained by the distribution of national power capabilities than by efforts to solve problems of market failure"[61]—or, I would add, by anything else.

Either international conventions, treaties, and institutions remain close to the underlying distribution of national capabilities or they court failure.[62] Citing examples from the past 350 years, Krasner found that in all of the instances "it was the value of strong states that dictated rules that were applied

---

59. Quoted in ibid., p. 36.
60. Robert O. Keohane, "The Diplomacy of Structural Change: Multilateral Institutions and State Strategies," in Helga Haftendorn and Christian Tuschhoff, eds., *America and Europe in an Era of Change* (Boulder, Colo.: Westview, 1993), p. 53.
61. Stephen D. Krasner, "Global Communications and National Power: Life on the Pareto Frontier," *World Politics*, Vol. 43, No. 1 (April 1991), p. 234.
62. Stephen D. Krasner, *Structural Conflict: The Third World against Global Liberalism* (Berkeley: University of California, 1985), p. 263 and passim.

in a discriminating fashion only to the weak."[63] The sovereignty of nations, a universally recognized international institution, hardly stands in the way of a strong nation that decides to intervene in a weak one. Thus, according to a senior official, the Reagan administration "debated whether we had the right to dictate the form of another country's government. The bottom line was yes, that some rights are more fundamental than the right of nations to nonintervention. . . . We don't have the right to subvert a democracy but we do have the right against an undemocratic one."[64] Most international law is obeyed most of the time, but strong states bend or break laws when they choose to.

Balancing Power: Not Today but Tomorrow

With so many of the expectations that realist theory gives rise to confirmed by what happened at and after the end of the Cold War, one may wonder why realism is in bad repute.[65] A key proposition derived from realist theory is that international politics reflects the distribution of national capabilities, a proposition daily borne out. Another key proposition is that the balancing of power by some states against others recurs. Realist theory predicts that balances disrupted will one day be restored. A limitation of the theory, a limitation common to social science theories, is that it cannot say when. William Wohlforth argues that though restoration will take place, it will be a long time coming.[66] Of necessity, realist theory is better at saying what will happen than in saying when it will happen. Theory cannot say when "tomorrow" will come because international political theory deals with the pressures of structure on states and not with how states will respond to the pressures. The latter is a task for theories about how national governments respond to pressures on them and take advantage of opportunities that may be present. One does, however, observe balancing tendencies already taking place.

Upon the demise of the Soviet Union, the international political system became unipolar. In the light of structural theory, unipolarity appears as the least durable of international configurations. This is so for two main reasons.

63. Stephen D. Krasner, "International Political Economy: Abiding Discord," *Review of International Political Economy,* Vol. 1, No. 1 (Spring 1994), p. 16.

64. Quoted in Robert Tucker, *Intervention and the Reagan Doctrine* (New York: Council on Religious and International Affairs, 1985), p. 5.

65. Robert Gilpin explains the oddity. See Gilpin, "No One Leaves a Political Realist," *Security Studies,* Vol. 5, No. 3 (Spring 1996), pp. 3–28.

66. William C. Wohlforth, "The Stability of a Unipolar World," *International Security,* Vol. 24, No. 1 (Summer 1999), pp. 5–41.

One is that dominant powers take on too many tasks beyond their own borders, thus weakening themselves in the long run. Ted Robert Gurr, after examining 336 polities, reached the same conclusion that Robert Wesson had reached earlier: "Imperial decay is . . . primarily a result of the misuse of power which follows inevitably from its concentration."[67] The other reason for the short duration of unipolarity is that even if a dominant power behaves with moderation, restraint, and forbearance, weaker states will worry about its future behavior. America's founding fathers warned against the perils of power in the absence of checks and balances. Is unbalanced power less of a danger in international than in national politics? Throughout the Cold War, what the United States and the Soviet Union did, and how they interacted, were dominant factors in international politics. The two countries, however, constrained each other. Now the United States is alone in the world. As nature abhors a vacuum, so international politics abhors unbalanced power. Faced with unbalanced power, some states try to increase their own strength or they ally with others to bring the international distribution of power into balance. The reactions of other states to the drive for dominance of Charles V, Hapsburg ruler of Spain, of Louis XIV and Napoleon I of France, of Wilhelm II and Adolph Hitler of Germany, illustrate the point.

THE BEHAVIOR OF DOMINANT POWERS

Will the preponderant power of the United States elicit similar reactions? Unbalanced power, whoever wields it, is a potential danger to others. The powerful state may, and the United States does, think of itself as acting for the sake of peace, justice, and well-being in the world. These terms, however, are defined to the liking of the powerful, which may conflict with the preferences and interests of others. In international politics, overwhelming power repels and leads others to try to balance against it. With benign intent, the United States has behaved and, until its power is brought into balance, will continue to behave in ways that sometimes frighten others.

For almost half a century, the constancy of the Soviet threat produced a constancy of American policy. Other countries could rely on the United States for protection because protecting them seemed to serve American security interests. Even so, beginning in the 1950s, Western European countries and, be-

---

67. Quoted in Ted Robert Gurr, "Persistence and Change in Political Systems, 1800–1971," *American Political Science Review*, Vol. 68, No. 4 (December 1974), p. 1504, from Robert G. Wesson, *The Imperial Order* (Berkeley: University of California Press, 1967), unpaginated preface. Cf. Paul Kennedy, *The Rise and Fall of Great Powers: Economic Change and Military Conflict from 1500 to 2000* (New York: Random House, 1987).

ginning in the 1970s, Japan had increasing doubts about the reliability of the American nuclear deterrent. As Soviet strength increased, Western European countries began to wonder whether the United States could be counted on to use its deterrent on their behalf, thus risking its own cities. When President Jimmy Carter moved to reduce American troops in South Korea, and later when the Soviet Union invaded Afghanistan and strengthened its forces in the Far East, Japan developed similar worries.

With the disappearance of the Soviet Union, the United States no longer faces a major threat to its security. As General Colin Powell said when he was chairman of the Joint Chiefs of Staff: "I'm running out of demons. I'm running out of enemies. I'm down to Castro and Kim Il Sung."[68] Constancy of threat produces constancy of policy; absence of threat permits policy to become capricious. When few if any vital interests are endangered, a country's policy becomes sporadic and self-willed.

The absence of serious threats to American security gives the United States wide latitude in making foreign policy choices. A dominant power acts internationally only when the spirit moves it. One example is enough to show this. When Yugoslavia's collapse was followed by genocidal war in successor states, the United States failed to respond until Senator Robert Dole moved to make Bosnia's peril an issue in the forthcoming presidential election; and it acted not for the sake of its own security but to maintain its leadership position in Europe. American policy was generated not by external security interests, but by internal political pressure and national ambition.

Aside from specific threats it may pose, unbalanced power leaves weaker states feeling uneasy and gives them reason to strengthen their positions. The United States has a long history of intervening in weak states, often with the intention of bringing democracy to them. American behavior over the past century in Central America provides little evidence of self-restraint in the absence of countervailing power. Contemplating the history of the United States and measuring its capabilities, other countries may well wish for ways to fend off its benign ministrations. Concentrated power invites distrust because it is so easily misused. To understand why some states want to bring power into a semblance of balance is easy, but with power so sharply skewed, what country or group of countries has the material capability and the political will to bring the "unipolar moment" to an end?

---

68. "Cover Story: Communism's Collapse Poses a Challenge to America's Military," *U.S. News and World Report*, October 14, 1991, p. 28.

BALANCING POWER IN A UNIPOLAR WORLD

The expectation that following victory in a great war a new balance of power will form is firmly grounded in both history and theory. The last four grand coalitions (two against Napoleon and one in each of the world wars of the twentieth century) collapsed once victory was achieved. Victories in major wars leave the balance of power badly skewed. The winning side emerges as a dominant coalition. The international equilibrium is broken; theory leads one to expect its restoration.

Clearly something has changed. Some believe that the United States is so nice that, despite the dangers of unbalanced power, others do not feel the fear that would spur them to action. Michael Mastanduno, among others, believes this to be so, although he ends his article with the thought that "eventually, power will check power."[69] Others believe that the leaders of states have learned that playing the game of power politics is costly and unnecessary. In fact, the explanation for sluggish balancing is a simple one. In the aftermath of earlier great wars, the materials for constructing a new balance were readily at hand. Previous wars left a sufficient number of great powers standing to permit a new balance to be rather easily constructed. Theory enables one to say that a new balance of power will form but not to say how long it will take. National and international conditions determine that. Those who refer to the unipolar moment are right. In our perspective, the new balance is emerging slowly; in historical perspectives, it will come in the blink of an eye.

I ended a 1993 article this way: "One may hope that America's internal preoccupations will produce not an isolationist policy, which has become impossible, but a forbearance that will give other countries at long last the chance to deal with their own problems and make their own mistakes. But I would not bet on it."[70] I should think that few would do so now. Charles Kegley has said, sensibly, that if the world becomes multipolar once again, realists will be vindicated.[71] Seldom do signs of vindication appear so promptly.

The candidates for becoming the next great powers, and thus restoring a balance, are the European Union or Germany leading a coalition, China, Japan, and in a more distant future, Russia. The countries of the European Union have

69. Michael Mastanduno, "Preserving the Unipolar Moment: Realist Theories and U.S. Grand Strategy after the Cold War," *International Security*, Vol. 21, No. 4 (Spring 1997), p. 88. See Josef Joffe's interesting analysis of America's role, "'Bismarck' or 'Britain'? Toward an American Grand Strategy after Bipolarity," *International Security*, Vol. 19, No. 4 (Spring 1995).
70. Waltz, "The Emerging Structure of International Politics," p. 79.
71. Charles W. Kegley, Jr., "The Neoidealist Moment in International Studies? Realist Myths and the New International Realities," *International Studies Quarterly*, Vol. 37, No. 2 (June 1993), p. 149.

been remarkably successful in integrating their national economies. The achievement of a large measure of economic integration without a corresponding political unity is an accomplishment without historical precedent. On questions of foreign and military policy, however, the European Union can act only with the consent of its members, making bold or risky action impossible. The European Union has all the tools—population, resources, technology, and military capabilities—but lacks the organizational ability and the collective will to use them. As Jacques Delors said when he was president of the European Commission: "It will be for the European Council, consisting of heads of state and government . . . , to agree on the essential interests they share and which they will agree to defend and promote together."[72] Policies that must be arrived at by consensus can be carried out only when they are fairly inconsequential. Inaction as Yugoslavia sank into chaos and war signaled that Europe will not act to stop wars even among near neighbors. Western Europe was unable to make its own foreign and military policies when its was an organization of six or nine states living in fear of the Soviet Union. With less pressure and more members, it has even less hope of doing so now. Only when the United States decides on a policy have European countries been able to follow it.

Europe may not remain in its supine position forever, yet signs of fundamental change in matters of foreign and military policy are faint. Now as earlier, European leaders express discontent with Europe's secondary position, chafe at America's making most of the important decisions, and show a desire to direct their own destiny. French leaders often vent their frustration and pine for a world, as Foreign Minister Hubert Védrine recently put it, "of several poles, not just a single one." President Jacques Chirac and Prime Minister Lionel Jospin call for a strengthening of such multilateral institutions as the International Monetary Fund and the United Nations, although how this would diminish America's influence is not explained. More to the point, Védrine complains that since President John Kennedy, Americans have talked of a European pillar for the alliance, a pillar that is never built.[73] German and British leaders now more often express similar discontent. Europe, however, will not be able to claim a louder voice in alliance affairs unless it builds a platform for giving it expression. If Europeans ever mean to write a tune to go with their libretto, they will have to develop the unity in foreign and military affairs that they are achieving in economic matters. If French and British leaders decided

---

72. Jacques Delors, "European Integration and Security," *Survival*, Vol. 33, No. 1 (March/April 1991), p. 106.
73. Craig R. Whitney, "NATO at 50: With Nations at Odds, Is It a Misalliance?" *New York Times*, February 15, 1999, p. A1.

to merge their nuclear forces to form the nucleus of a European military organization, the United States and the world will begin to treat Europe as a major
force.

The European Economic Community was formed in 1957 and has grown
incrementally to its present proportions. But where is the incremental route to
a European foreign and military policy to be found? European leaders have
not been able to find it or even have tried very hard to do so. In the absence
of radical change, Europe will count for little in international politics for as
far ahead as the eye can see, unless Germany, becoming impatient, decides to
lead a coalition.

INTERNATIONAL STRUCTURE AND NATIONAL RESPONSES

Throughout modern history, international politics centered on Europe. Two
world wars ended Europe's dominance. Whether Europe will somehow, someday emerge as a great power is a matter for speculation. In the meantime, the
all-but-inevitable movement from unipolarity to multipolarity is taking place
not in Europe but in Asia. The internal development and the external reaction
of China and Japan are steadily raising both countries to the great power
level.[74] China will emerge as a great power even without trying very hard so
long as it remains politically united and competent. Strategically, China can
easily raise its nuclear forces to a level of parity with the United States if it has
not already done so.[75] China has five to seven intercontinental missiles (DF-5s)
able to hit almost any American target and a dozen or more missiles able to
reach the west coast of the United States (DF-4s).[76] Liquid fueled, immobile
missiles are vulnerable, but would the United States risk the destruction of,
say, Seattle, San Francisco, and San Diego if China happens to have a few more
DF-4s than the United States thinks or if it should fail to destroy all of them on
the ground? Deterrence is much easier to contrive than most Americans have
surmised. Economically, China's growth rate, given its present stage of economic development, can be sustained at 7 to 9 percent for another decade or
more. Even during Asia's near economic collapse of the 1990s, China's growth
rate remained approximately in that range. A growth rate of 7 to 9 percent
doubles a country's economy every ten to eight years.

---

74. The following four pages are adapted from Waltz, "The Emerging Structure of International
Politics."
75. Nuclear parity is reached when countries have second-strike forces. It does not require quantitative or qualitative equality of forces. See Waltz, "Nuclear Myths and Political Realities," *American Political Science Review*, Vol. 84, No. 3 (September 1990).
76. David E. Sanger and Erik Eckholm, "Will Beijing's Nuclear Arsenal Stay Small or Will It Mush-
room?" *New York Times*, March 15, 1999, p. A1.

Unlike China, Japan is obviously reluctant to assume the mantle of a great power. Its reluctance, however, is steadily though slowly waning. Economically, Japan's power has grown and spread remarkably. The growth of a country's economic capability to the great power level places it at the center of regional and global affairs. It widens the range of a state's interests and increases their importance. The high volume of a country's external business thrusts it ever more deeply into world affairs. In a self-help system, the possession of most but not all of the capabilities of a great power leaves a state vulnerable to others that have the instruments that the lesser state lacks. Even though one may believe that fears of nuclear blackmail are misplaced, one must wonder whether Japan will remain immune to them.

Countries have always competed for wealth and security, and the competition has often led to conflict. Historically, states have been sensitive to changing relations of power among them. Japan is made uneasy now by the steady growth of China's military budget. Its nearly 3 million strong army, undergoing modernization, and the gradual growth of its sea- and air-power projection capabilities, produce apprehension in all of China's neighbors and add to the sense of instability in a region where issues of sovereignty and disputes over territory abound. The Korean peninsula has more military forces per square kilometer than any other portion of the globe. Taiwan is an unending source of tension. Disputes exist between Japan and Russia over the Kurile Islands, and between Japan and China over the Senkaku or Diaoyu Islands. Cambodia is a troublesome problem for both Vietnam and China. Half a dozen countries lay claim to all or some of the Spratly Islands, strategically located and supposedly rich in oil. The presence of China's ample nuclear forces, combined with the drawdown of American military forces, can hardly be ignored by Japan, the less so because economic conflicts with the United States cast doubt on the reliability of American military guarantees. Reminders of Japan's dependence and vulnerability multiply in large and small ways. For example, as rumors about North Korea's developing nuclear capabilities gained credence, Japan became acutely aware of its lack of observation satellites. Uncomfortable dependencies and perceived vulnerabilities have led Japan to acquire greater military capabilities, even though many Japanese may prefer not to.

Given the expectation of conflict, and the necessity of taking care of one's interests, one may wonder how any state with the economic capability of a great power can refrain from arming itself with the weapons that have served so well as the great deterrent. For a country to choose not to become a great power is a structural anomaly. For that reason, the choice is a difficult one to sustain. Sooner or later, usually sooner, the international status of countries has risen in step with their material resources. Countries with great power economies have become great powers, whether or not reluctantly. Some countries may strive to become great powers; others may wish to avoid doing so. The choice, however, is a constrained one. Because of the extent of their interests, larger units existing in a contentious arena tend to take on systemwide tasks. Profound change in a country's international situation produces radical change in its external behavior. After World War II, the United States broke with its centuries-long tradition of acting unilaterally and refusing to make long-term commitments. Japan's behavior in the past half century reflects the abrupt change in its international standing suffered because of its defeat in war. In the previous half century, after victory over China in 1894–95, Japan pressed for preeminence in Asia, if not beyond. Does Japan once again aspire to a larger role internationally? Its concerted regional activity, its seeking and gaining prominence in such bodies as the IMF and the World Bank, and its obvious pride in economic and technological achievements indicate that it does. The behavior of states responds more to external conditions than to internal habit if external change is profound.

When external conditions press firmly enough, they shape the behavior of states. Increasingly, Japan is being pressed to enlarge its conventional forces and to add nuclear ones to protect its interests. India, Pakistan, China, and perhaps North Korea have nuclear weapons capable of deterring others from threatening their vital interests. How long can Japan live alongside other nuclear states while denying itself similar capabilities? Conflicts and crises are certain to make Japan aware of the disadvantages of being without the military instruments that other powers command. Japanese nuclear inhibitions arising from World War II will not last indefinitely; one may expect them to expire as generational memories fade.

Japanese officials have indicated that when the protection of America's extended deterrent is no longer thought to be sufficiently reliable, Japan will equip itself with a nuclear force, whether or not openly. Japan has put itself politically and technologically in a position to do so. Consistently since the mid-1950s, the government has defined all of its Self-Defense Forces as conforming to constitutional requirements. Nuclear weapons purely for defense would be deemed constitutional should Japan decide to build some.[77] As a secret report

---

77. Norman D. Levin, "Japan's Defense Policy: The Internal Debate," in Harry H. Kendall and Clara Joewono, eds., *Japan, ASEAN, and the United States* (Berkeley: Institute of East Asian Studies, University of California, 1990).

of the Ministry of Foreign Affairs put it in 1969: "For the time being, we will maintain the policy of not possessing nuclear weapons. However, regardless of joining the NPT [Non-Proliferation Treaty] or not, we will keep the economic and technical potential for the production of nuclear weapons, while seeing to it that Japan will not be interfered with in this regard."[78] In March of 1988, Prime Minister Noboru Takeshita called for a defensive capability matching Japan's economic power.[79] Only a balanced conventional-nuclear military capability would meet this requirement. In June of 1994, Prime Minister Tsutumu Hata mentioned in parliament that Japan had the ability to make nuclear weapons.[80]

Where some see Japan as a "global civilian power" and believe it likely to remain one, others see a country that has skillfully used the protection the United States has afforded and adroitly adopted the means of maintaining its security to its regional environment.[81] Prime Minister Shigeru Yoshida in the early 1950s suggested that Japan should rely on American protection until it had rebuilt its economy as it gradually prepared to stand on its own feet.[82] Japan has laid a firm foundation for doing so by developing much of its own weaponry instead of relying on cheaper imports. Remaining months or moments away from having a nuclear military capability is well designed to protect the country's security without unduly alarming its neighbors.

The hostility of China, of both Koreas, and of Russia combines with inevitable doubts about the extent to which Japan can rely on the United States to protect its security.[83] In the opinion of Masanori Nishi, a defense official, the main cause of Japan's greater "interest in enhanced defense capabilities" is its belief that America's interest in "maintaining regional stability is shaky."[84] Whether

---

78. "The Capability to Develop Nuclear Weapons Should Be Kept: Ministry of Foreign Affairs Secret Document in 1969," *Mainichi*, August 1, 1994, p. 41, quoted in Selig S. Harrison, "Japan and Nuclear Weapons," in Harrison, ed., *Japan's Nuclear Future* (Washington, D.C.: Carnegie Endowment for International Peace, 1996), p. 9.
79. David Arase, "US and ASEAN Perceptions of Japan's Role in the Asian-Pacific Region," in Kendall and Joewono, *Japan, ASEAN, and the United States*, p. 276.
80. David E. Sanger, "In Face-Saving Reverse, Japan Disavows Any Nuclear-Arms Expertise," *New York Times*, June 22, 1994, p. 10.
81. Michael J. Green, "State of the Field Report: Research on Japanese Security Policy," *Access Asia Review*, Vol. 2, No. 2 (September 1998), judiciously summarized different interpretations of Japan's security policy.
82. Kenneth B. Pyle, *The Japanese Question: Power and Purpose in a New Era* (Washington, D.C.: AEI Press, 1992), p. 26.
83. Andrew Hanami, for example, points out that Japan wonders whether the United States would help defend Hokkaido. Hanami, "Japan and the Military Balance of Power in Northeast Asia," *Journal of East Asian Affairs*, Vol. 7, No. 2 (Summer/Fall 1994), p. 364.
84. Stephanie Strom, "Japan Beginning to Flex Its Military Muscles," *New York Times*, April 8, 1999, p. A4.

reluctantly or not, Japan and China will follow each other on the route to becoming great powers. China has the greater long-term potential. Japan, with the world's second or third largest defense budget and the ability to produce the most technologically advanced weaponry, is closer to great power status at the moment.

When Americans speak of preserving the balance of power in East Asia through their military presence,[85] the Chinese understandably take this to mean that they intend to maintain the strategic hegemony they now enjoy in the *absence* of such a balance. When China makes steady but modest efforts to improve the quality of its inferior forces, Americans see a future threat to their and others' interests. Whatever worries the United States has and whatever threats it feels, Japan has them earlier and feels them more intensely. Japan has gradually reacted to them. China then worries as Japan improves its airlift and sealift capabilities and as the United States raises its support level for forces in South Korea.[86] The actions and reactions of China, Japan, and South Korea, with or without American participation, are creating a new balance of power in East Asia, which is becoming part of the new balance of power in the world.

Historically, encounters of East and West have often ended in tragedy. Yet, as we know from happy experience, nuclear weapons moderate the behavior of their possessors and render them cautious whenever crises threaten to spin out of control. Fortunately, the changing relations of East to West, and the changing relations of countries within the East and the West, are taking place in a nuclear context. The tensions and conflicts that intensify when profound changes in world politics take place will continue to mar the relations of nations, while nuclear weapons keep the peace among those who enjoy their protection.

America's policy of containing China by keeping 100,000 troops in East Asia and by providing security guarantees to Japan and South Korea is intended to keep a new balance of power from forming in Asia. By continuing to keep 100,000 troops in Western Europe, where no military threat is in sight, and by extending NATO eastward, the United States pursues the same goal in Europe. The American aspiration to freeze historical development by working to keep the world unipolar is doomed. In the not very long run, the

---

85.   Richard Bernstein and Ross H. Munro, *The Coming Conflict with China* (New York: Alfred A. Knopf, 1997); and Andrew J. Nathan and Robert S. Ross, *The Great Wall and the Empty Fortress: China's Search for Security* (New York: W.W. Norton, 1997).

86.   Michael J. Green and Benjamin L. Self, "Japan's Changing China Policy: From Commercial Liberalism to Reluctant Realism," *Survival*, Vol. 38, No. 2 (Summer 1996), p. 43.

task will exceed America's economic, military, demographic, and political resources; and the very effort to maintain a hegemonic position is the surest way to undermine it. The effort to maintain dominance stimulates some countries to work to overcome it. As theory shows and history confirms, that is how balances of power are made. Multipolarity is developing before our eyes. Moreover, it is emerging in accordance with the balancing imperative.

American leaders seem to believe that America's preeminent position will last indefinitely. The United States would then remain the dominant power without rivals rising to challenge it—a position without precedent in modern history. Balancing, of course, is not universal and omnipresent. A dominant power may suppress balancing as the United States has done in Europe. Whether or not balancing takes place also depends on the decisions of governments. Stephanie Neuman's book, *International Relations Theory and the Third World*, abounds in examples of states that failed to mind their own security interests through internal efforts or external arrangements, and as one would expect, suffered invasion, loss of autonomy, and dismemberment.[87] States are free to disregard the imperatives of power, but they must expect to pay a price for doing so. Moreover, relatively weak and divided states may find it impossible to concert their efforts to counter a hegemonic state despite ample provocation. This has long been the condition of the Western Hemisphere.

In the Cold War, the United States won a telling victory. Victory in war, however, often brings lasting enmities. Magnanimity in victory is rare. Winners of wars, facing few impediments to the exercise of their wills, often act in ways that create future enemies. Thus Germany, by taking Alsace and most of Lorraine from France in 1871, earned its lasting enmity; and the Allies' harsh treatment of Germany after World War I produced a similar effect. In contrast, Bismarck persuaded the kaiser not to march his armies along the road to Vienna after the great victory at Königgrätz in 1866. In the Treaty of Prague, Prussia took no Austrian territory. Thus Austria, having become Austria- Hungary, was available as an alliance partner for Germany in 1879. Rather than learning from history, the United States is repeating past errors by extending its influence over what used to be the province of the vanquished.[88] This alienates Russia and nudges it toward China instead of draw-

---

87. Stephanie Neuman, ed., *International Relations Theory and the Third World* (New York: St. Martin's, 1998).

88. Tellingly, John Lewis Gaddis comments that he has never known a time when there was less support among historians for an announced policy. Gaddis, "History, Grand Strategy, and NATO Enlargement," *Survival*, Vol. 40, No. 1 (Spring 1998), p. 147.

ing it toward Europe and the United States. Despite much talk about the "globalization" of international politics, American political leaders to a dismaying extent think of East *or* West rather than of their interaction. With a history of conflict along a 2,600 mile border, with ethnic minorities sprawling across it, with a mineral-rich and sparsely populated Siberia facing China's teeming millions, Russia and China will find it difficult to cooperate effectively, but the United States is doing its best to help them do so. Indeed, the United States has provided the key to Russian-Chinese relations over the past half century. Feeling American antagonism and fearing American power, China drew close to Russia after World War II and remained so until the United States seemed less, and the Soviet Union more, of a threat to China. The relatively harmonious relations the United States and China enjoyed during the 1970s began to sour in the late 1980s when Russian power visibly declined and American hegemony became imminent. To alienate Russia by expanding NATO, and to alienate China by lecturing its leaders on how to rule their country, are policies that only an overwhelmingly powerful country could afford, and only a foolish one be tempted, to follow. The United States cannot prevent a new balance of power from forming. It can hasten its coming as it has been earnestly doing.

In this section, the discussion of balancing has been more empirical and speculative than theoretical. I therefore end with some reflections on balancing theory. Structural theory, and the theory of balance of power that follows from it, do not lead one to expect that states will always or even usually engage in balancing behavior. Balancing is a strategy for survival, a way of attempting to maintain a state's autonomous way of life. To argue that bandwagoning represents a behavior more common to states than balancing has become a bit of a fad. Whether states bandwagon more often than they balance is an interesting question. To believe that an affirmative answer would refute balance-of-power theory is, however, to misinterpret the theory and to commit what one might call "the numerical fallacy"—to draw a qualitative conclusion from a quantitative result. States try various strategies for survival. Balancing is one of them; bandwagoning is another. The latter may sometimes seem a less demanding and a more rewarding strategy than balancing, requiring less effort and extracting lower costs while promising concrete rewards. Amid the uncertainties of international politics and the shifting pressures of domestic politics, states have to make perilous choices. They may hope to avoid war by appeasing adversaries, a weak form of bandwagoning, rather than by rearming and realigning to thwart them. Moreover, many states have insufficient resources for balancing and little room for maneuver. They have to jump on the wagon only later to wish they could fall off.

Balancing theory does not predict uniformity of behavior but rather the strong tendency of major states in the system, or in regional subsystems, to resort to balancing when they have to. That states try different strategies of survival is hardly surprising. The recurrent emergence of balancing behavior, and the appearance of the patterns the behavior produces, should all the more be seen as impressive evidence supporting the theory.

Conclusion

Every time peace breaks out, people pop up to proclaim that realism is dead. That is another way of saying that international politics has been transformed. The world, however, has not been transformed; the structure of international politics has simply been remade by the disappearance of the Soviet Union, and for a time we will live with unipolarity. Moreover, international politics was not remade by the forces and factors that some believe are creating a new world order. Those who set the Soviet Union on the path of reform were old Soviet apparatchiks trying to right the Soviet economy in order to preserve its position in the world. The revolution in Soviet affairs and the end of the Cold War were not brought by democracy, interdependence, or international institutions. Instead the Cold War ended exactly as structural realism led one to expect. As I wrote some years ago, the Cold War "is firmly rooted in the structure of postwar international politics and will last as long as that structure endures."[89] So it did, and the Cold War ended only when the bipolar structure of the world disappeared.

Structural change affects the behavior of states and the outcomes their interactions produce. It does not break the essential continuity of international politics. The transformation of international politics alone could do that. Transformation, however, awaits the day when the international system is no longer populated by states that have to help themselves. If the day were here, one would be able to say who could be relied on to help the disadvantaged or endangered. Instead, the ominous shadow of the future continues to cast its pall over interacting states. States' perennial uncertainty about their fates presses governments to prefer relative over absolute gains. Without the shadow, the leaders of states would no longer have to ask themselves how

---

89. Kenneth N. Waltz, "The Origins of War in Neorealist Theory," *Journal of Interdisciplinary History*, Vol. 18, No. 4 (Spring 1988), p. 628.

they will get along tomorrow as well as today. States could combine their efforts cheerfully and work to maximize collective gain without worrying about how each might fare in comparison to others.

Occasionally, one finds the statement that governments in their natural, anarchic condition act myopically—that is, on calculations of immediate interest—while hoping that the future will take care of itself. Realists are said to suffer from this optical defect.[90] Political leaders may be astigmatic, but responsible ones who behave realistically do not suffer from myopia. Robert Axelrod and Robert Keohane believe that World War I might have been averted if certain states had been able to see how long the future's shadow was.[91] Yet, as their own discussion shows, the future was what the major states were obsessively worried about. The war was prompted less by considerations of present security and more by worries about how the balance might change later. The problems of governments do not arise from their short time horizons. They see the long shadow of the future, but they have trouble reading its contours, perhaps because they try to look too far ahead and see imaginary dangers. In 1914, Germany feared Russia's rapid industrial and population growth. France and Britain suffered from the same fear about Germany, and in addition Britain worried about the rapid growth of Germany's navy. In an important sense, World War I was a preventive war all around. Future fears dominated hopes for short-term gains. States do not live in the happiest of conditions that Horace in one of his odes imagined for man:

> Happy the man, and happy he alone, who can say,
> Tomorrow do thy worst, for I have lived today.[92]

Robert Axelrod has shown that the "tit-for-tat" tactic, and no other, maximizes collective gain over time. The one condition for success is that the game be played under the shadow of the future.[93] Because states coexist in a

---

90. The point is made by Robert O. Keohane, *After Hegemony: Cooperation and Discord in the World Political Economy* (Princeton, N.J.: Princeton University Press, 1984), pp. 99, 103, 108.

91. Robert Axelrod and Robert O. Keohane, "Achieving Cooperation under Anarchy: Strategies and Institutions," in David Baldwin, .ed., *Neorealism and Neoliberalism: The Contemporary Debate* (New York: Columbia University Press, 1993). For German leaders, they say, "the shadow of the future seemed so small" (p. 92). Robert Powell shows that "a longer shadow . . . leads to greater military allocations." See Powell, "Guns, Butter, and Anarchy," *American Political Science Review*, Vol. 87, No. 1 (March 1993), p. 116; see also p. 117 on the question of the compatibility of liberal institutionalism and structural realism.

92. My revision.

93. Robert Axelrod, *The Evolution of Cooperation* (New York: Basic Books, 1984).

self-help system, they may, however, have to concern themselves not with maximizing collective gain but with lessening, preserving, or widening the gap in welfare and strength between themselves and others. The contours of the future's shadow look different in hierarchic and anarchic systems. The shadow may facilitate cooperation in the former; it works against it in the latter. Worries about the future do not make cooperation and institution building among nations impossible; they do strongly condition their operation and limit their accomplishment. Liberal institutionalists were right to start their investigations with structural realism. Until and unless a transformation occurs, it remains the basic theory of international politics.

Institutions, Strategic Restraint, and the Persistence of American Postwar Order

G. John Ikenberry

One of the most puzzling aspects of world order after the Cold War is the persistence of stable and cooperative relations among the advanced industrial democracies. Despite the collapse of bipolarity and dramatic shifts in the global distribution of power, America's relations with Europe and Japan have remained what they have been for decades: cooperative, stable, interdependent, and highly institutionalized. The Cold War is over, but the postwar order forged between the United States and its allies remains alive and well fifty years after its founding.

This is surprising. Many observers have expected dramatic shifts in world politics after the Cold War—such as the disappearance of American hegemony, the return of great power balancing, the rise of competing regional blocs, and the decay of multilateralism. Yet even without the Soviet threat and Cold War bipolarity, the United States along with Japan and Western Europe have reaffirmed their alliance partnerships, contained political conflicts, expanded trade and investment between them, and avoided a return to strategic rivalry and great power balancing.

The persistence of the postwar Western order is particularly a puzzle for neorealism. Neorealism has two clearly defined explanations for order: balance of power and hegemony. Neorealist theories of balance argue that order and cohesion in the West are a result of cooperation to balance against an external threat, in this case the Soviet Union, and with the disappearance of the threat,

G. John Ikenberry is Associate Professor of Political Science at the University of Pennsylvania and in 1998–99 Visiting Scholar at the Woodrow Wilson Center in Washington, D.C. He is author of Reasons of State: Oil Politics and the Capacities of American Government (Ithaca, N.Y.: Cornell University Press, 1988), coauthor of The State (Minneapolis: University of Minnesota, 1989), and coeditor of New Thinking in International Relations Theory (Boulder, Colo.: Westview Press, 1997). He is the author of the forthcoming book, After Victory: Institutions, Strategic Restraint, and the Rebuilding of Order after Major Wars.

I wish to thank Daniel Deudney, James Fearon, Joseph M. Grieco, John A. Hall, Charles A. Kupchan, David Lake, Keir Lieber, Charles Lipson, Michael Mastanduno, Nicholas Onuf, Duncan Snidel, and PIPES seminar participants at the University of Chicago.

International Security, Vol. 23, No. 3 (Winter 1998/99), pp. 43–78

174

alliance and cooperation will decline.[1] Neorealist theories of hegemony contend that order is a result of the concentration of material power capabilities in a single state, which uses its commanding position to create and maintain order; with the decline of hegemonic power, order will decay.[2] In this view, it is the preponderance of American power that explains order, with the United States using its material resources to co-opt, coerce, and induce European and Asian countries to cooperate.

But neorealist theories are inadequate to explain both the durability of Western order and its important features, such as its extensive institutionalization and the consensual and reciprocal character of relations within it. To be sure, decades of balancing against Soviet power reinforced cooperation among these countries, but the basic organization of Western order predated the Cold War and survives today without it. Hegemonic theory is more promising as an explanation, but the neorealist version is incomplete. It misses the remarkably liberal character of American hegemony and the importance of international institutions in facilitating cooperation and overcoming fears of domination or exploitation. It was the exercise of strategic restraint—made good by an open polity and binding institutions—more than the direct and instrumental exercise of hegemonic domination that ensured a cooperative and stable postwar order. For all these reasons, it is necessary to look beyond neorealism for an understanding of order among the advanced industrial societies.

To understand the continued durability and cohesion of the advanced industrial world, we need to turn neorealist theories of order on their head. It is actually the ability of the Western democracies to overcome or dampen the underlying manifestations of anarchy (order based on balance) and domination (order based on coercive hegemony) that explains the character and persistence of Western order. Neorealism misses the institutional foundations of Western political order—a logic of order in which the connecting and constraining effects of institutions and democratic polities reduce the incentives of Western states to engage in strategic rivalry or balance against American

1. See Kenneth N. Waltz, *Theory of International Politics* (Reading, Mass.: 1979). For extensions and debates, see Robert O. Keohane, ed., *Neorealism and Its Critics* (New York: Columbia University Press, 1986). For an extension of this basic position to the West, see John J. Mearsheimer, "Why We Will Soon Miss the Cold War," *Atlantic Monthly*, August 1990, pp. 35–50.
2. See Robert Gilpin, *War and Change in World Politics* (New York: Cambridge University Press, 1981). See also Stephen D. Krasner, "American Policy and Global Economic Stability," in William P. Avery and David P. Rapkin, eds., *America in a Changing World Political Economy* (New York: Longman, 1982); and see the debate in David Rapkin, ed., *World Leadership and Hegemony* (Boulder, Colo.: Lynne Rienner, 1990).

hegemony. The Western states are not held together because of external threats or the simple concentration of power. Rather, Western order has what might be called "constitutional characteristics"—a structure of institutions and open polities that constrain power and facilitate "voice opportunities," thereby mitigating the implications of power asymmetries and reducing the opportunities of the leading state to exit or dominate.

This is one of the great puzzles that has eluded full explanation: Why would the United States, at the height of its hegemonic power after World War II, agree to limit that power? It is equally a puzzle why weak and secondary states might agree to become more rather than less entangled with such a potential hegemon. The answer has to do with the incentives that powerful states have to create a legitimate political order, and it also has to do with the way institutions—when wielded by democracies—allow powerful states to both lock in a favorable postwar order and overcome fears of domination and abandonment that stand in the way of postwar agreement and the creation of legitimate order. Weak and secondary states get institutionalized assurances that they will not be exploited. Paradoxically, a leading or hegemonic state, seeking to hold on to its power and make it last, has incentives to find ways to limit that power and make it acceptable to other states.

This institutional explanation of Western order is developed in four steps. First, I argue that the basic logic of order among the Western states was set in place during and immediately after World War II, and it was a logic that addressed the basic problem of how to build a durable and mutually acceptable order among a group of states with huge power asymmetries. To gain the cooperation and compliance of secondary states, the United States had to engage in *strategic restraint*—to reassure weaker states that it would not abandon or dominate them. Cooperative order is built around a basic bargain: the hegemonic state obtains commitments from secondary states to participate within the postwar order, and in return the hegemon places limits on the exercise of its power. The weaker states do not fear domination or abandonment—reducing the incentives to balance—and the leading state does not need to use its power assets to enforce order and compliance.

Second, strategic restraint is possible because of the potential binding effects of international institutions. International institutions do not simply serve the functional purposes of states, reducing transaction costs and solving collective action problems, but they can also be "sticky"—locking states into ongoing and predictable courses of action. It is this lock-in effect of institutions that allows them to play a role in restraining the exercise of state power. In effect, institutions create constraints on state action that serve to *reduce the returns to power*—that is, they reduce the long-term implications of asymmetries of power. This is precisely what constitutions do in domestic political orders. Limits are set on what actors can do with momentary advantage. Losers realize that their losses are limited and temporary—to accept those losses is not to risk everything nor will it give the winners a permanent advantage. Political orders—domestic and international—differ widely in their "returns to power." The Western postwar order is so stable and mutually acceptable because it has found institutional ways to reduce the returns to power.

Third, the Western postwar order has also been rendered acceptable to Europe and Japan because American hegemony is built around decidedly liberal features. The penetrated character of American hegemony, creating transparency and allowing access by secondary states, along with the constraining effects of economic and security institutions, has provided mechanisms to increase confidence that the participating states would remain within the order and operate according to its rules and institutions. American hegemony has been rendered more benign and acceptable because of its open and accessible internal institutions.

Fourth, the Western order has actually become more stable over time because the rules and institutions have become more firmly embedded in the wider structures of politics and society. This is an argument about the *increasing returns to institutions*, in this case Western security and economic institutions. Over the decades, the core institutions of Western order have sunk their roots ever more deeply into the political and economic structures of the states that participate within the order. The result is that it is becoming increasingly difficult for "alternative institutions" or "alternative leadership" to seriously emerge. Western order has become institutionalized and path dependent—that is, more and more people will have to disrupt their lives if the order is to radically change. This makes wholesale change less likely.

Overall, the durability of Western order is built on two core logics. First, the constitution-like character of the institutions and practices of the order serve to reduce the returns to power, which lowers the risks of participation by strong and weak states alike. This in turn makes a resort to balancing and relative gains competition less necessary. Second, the institutions also exhibit an "increasing returns" character, which makes it increasingly difficult for would-be orders and would-be hegemonic leaders to compete against and replace the existing order and leader. Although the Cold War reinforced this order, it was not triggered by it or ultimately dependent on the Cold War for its functioning and stability.

The implication of this analysis is that the West is a relatively stable and expansive political order. This is not only because the United States is an unmatched economic and military power, but also because it is uniquely capable of engaging in "strategic restraint," reassuring partners and facilitating cooperation. Because of its distinctively open domestic political system, and because of the array of power-dampening institutions it has created to manage political conflict, the United States has been able to remain at the center of a large and expanding institutionalized and legitimate political order. Its capacity to win in specific struggles with others within the system may rise and fall, and the distribution of power can continue to evolve in America's favor or against it, but the larger Western order remains in place with little prospect of decline.

In the next section, I sketch the theoretical debate about American power and post–World War II order and the contending positions of neorealism and liberalism. Following this, I develop an institutional theory of order formation and the "constitutional bargain" that lies at the heart of the Western postwar political order. I then examine America's postwar strategy of hegemonic reassurance and the major institutional characteristics of this order that, in effect, "doomed" the United States to succeed in overcoming fears of domination and abandonment. Finally, I develop the argument that the postwar order has experienced an increasing returns to institutions, which in turn reinforces the underlying stability of relations between the United States and the other advanced industrial countries.

The Debate about Order

The debate over American grand strategy after the Cold War hinges on assumptions about the sources and character of Western order. Neorealism advances two clearly defined answers to the basic question of how order is created among states: balance of power and hegemony. Both are ultimately pessimistic about the future stability and coherence of economic and security relations between the United States, Europe, and Japan.[3]

---

3. For an extended critique of neorealist expectations of post–Cold War order, see Daniel Deudney and G. John Ikenberry, "Realism, Structural Liberalism, and the Western Order," in Ethan Kapstein and Michael Mastanduno, eds., *Unipolar Politics: Realism and State Strategies after the Cold War* (New York: Columbia University Press, forthcoming). For a sophisticated survey of realist and liberal theories of international order, see John A. Hall, *International Order* (Cambridge: Polity Press, 1996), chap. 1.

Balance-of-power theory explains order—and the rules and institutions that emerge—as the result of balancing to counter external or hegemonic power.[4] Order is the product of the unending process of balancing and adjustment among states under conditions of anarchy. Balancing can be pursued both internally and externally—through domestic mobilization and through the formation of temporary alliances among threatened states to resist and counterbalance a looming or threatening concentration of power. Under conditions of anarchy, alliances will come and go as temporary expedients, states will guard their autonomy, and entangling institutions will be resisted.[5]

A second neorealist theory, hegemonic stability theory, holds that order is created and maintained by a hegemonic state, which uses power capabilities to organize relations among states. The preponderance of power held by a state allows it to offer incentives, both positive and negative, to the other states to agree to participation within the hegemonic order. According to Robert Gilpin, an international order is, at any particular moment in history, the reflection of the underlying distribution of power of states within the system.[6] Over time, that distribution of power shifts, leading to conflicts and ruptures in the system, hegemonic war, and the eventual reorganization of order so as to reflect the new distribution of power capabilities. It is the rising hegemonic state or group of states, whose power position has been ratified by war, that defines the terms of the postwar settlement—and the character of the new order.

The continuity and stability of the Western postwar order is a puzzle for both varieties of neorealism. With the end of the Cold War, balance-of-power theory expects the West, and particularly the security organizations such as the North Atlantic Treaty Organization (NATO) and the U.S.-Japan alliance, to weaken and eventually return to a pattern of strategic rivalry. The "semi-sovereign" security posture of Germany and Japan will end, and these coun-

---

4. Waltz, *Theory of International Politics.* On the balance-of-threat theory, see Stephen M. Walt, *The Origins of Alliances* (Ithaca, N.Y.: Cornell University Press, 1987).
5. Three assumptions lie behind the neorealist claim that balance of power is the only real solution to the problem of order. First, all states seek security, but because other states can always become threats, that security is never absolute. Second, the intentions of other states are inherently uncertain. A state can never be absolutely certain that its current allies will remain allies in the future and not turn into adversaries. This is because all states have the capacity to threaten and their intentions are unknowable. Finally, relative capabilities are more important than absolute capabilities to ensure the security of states because security is derived from the relative strength of a state in relation to competing states.
6. Gilpin, *War and Change in World Politics.*

tries will eventually revert back to traditional great powers.[7] The Soviet threat also served to dampen and contain economic conflict within the West—and after the Cold War, economic competition and conflict among the advanced industrial societies is expected to rise.[8] Neorealist theories of hegemony also expect that the gradual decline of American power—magnified by the Cold War—should also lead to rising conflict and institutional disarray.[9] More recently, some realists have argued that it is actually the extreme preponderance of American power, and not its decline, that will trigger counterbalancing reactions by Asian and European allies.[10]

The basic thrust of these neorealist theories is that relations among the Western states will return to the problems of anarchy after the Cold War: economy rivalry, security dilemmas, institutional decay, and balancing alliances. The fact that post–Cold War relations among the Western industrial countries have remained stable and open, and economic interdependence and institutionalized cooperation have actually expanded in some areas, is a puzzle that

---

7. Kenneth N. Waltz, "The Emerging Structure of International Politics," *International Security*, Vol. 18, No. 2 (Fall 1993), pp. 44–79; John J. Mearsheimer, "Back to the Future: Instability in Europe after the Cold War," *International Security*, Vol. 15, No. 1 (Fall 1990), pp. 5–56; Mearsheimer, "Why We Will Soon Miss the Cold War"; Conor Cruise O'Brien, "The Future of the West," *National Interest*, Vol. 30 (Winter 1992/93), pp. 3–10; and Bradley A. Thayer, "Realism, the Balance of Power, and Stability in the Twenty-first Century," unpublished paper, Harvard University, 1997.

8. As Robert Lieber argues: "In the past, the Soviet threat and the existence of an American-led bloc to contain it placed limits on the degree of friction that could develop among the Western partners and Japan. The need to cooperate in the face of the Soviets meant that disagreements in economic and other realms were prevented from escalating beyond a certain point because of the perception that too bitter an intra-allied confrontation could only benefit their adversary and thus weaken common security." Lieber, "Eagle without a Cause: Making Foreign Policy without the Soviet Threat," in Lieber, ed., *Eagle Adrift: American Foreign Policy at the End of the Century* (New York: Longman, 1997), p. 10. This point is also made by Kenneth Oye in "Beyond Postwar Order and the New World Order," in Oye, Lieber, and Donald Rothchild, eds., *Eagle in a New World: American Grand Strategy in the Post–Cold War Era* (New York: HarperCollins, 1992), pp. 3–33.

9. For contrasting views, see Robert Gilpin, *The Political Economy of International Relations* (Princeton, N.J.: Princeton University Press, 1987); Paul M. Kennedy, *The Rise and Fall of the Great Powers* (New York: Random House, 1987); Joseph S. Nye, Jr., *Bound to Lead: The Changing Nature of American Power* (New York: Basic Books, 1990); Henry Nau, *The Myth of America's Decline: Leading the World Economy in the 1990's* (New York: Oxford University Press, 1990); and Susan Strange, "The Persistent Myth of Lost Hegemony," *International Organization*, Vol. 41, No. 4 (Autumn 1987), pp. 551–574.

10. See, for example, Christopher Layne, "The Unipolar Illusion: Why New Great Powers Will Arise," *International Security*, Vol. 17, No. 4 (Spring 1993), pp. 5–51; Layne, "From Preponderance to Offshore Balancing: America's Future Grand Strategy," *International Security*, Vol. 22, No. 1 (Summer 1997), pp. 86–124; and Josef Joffe, "'Bismarck' or 'Britain'? Toward an American Grand Strategy after Bipolarity," *International Security*, Vol. 19, No. 4 (Spring 1995), pp. 94–117. For a discussion of these views, see Michael Mastanduno, "Preserving the Unipolar Moment: Realist Theories and U.S. Grand Strategy after the Cold War," *International Security*, Vol. 21, No. 4 (Spring 1997), pp. 49–88.

neorealism is hard-pressed to explain. Despite sharp shifts in the distribution of power within the West, the political order among the industrial democracies has remained quite stable. Highly asymmetrical relations between the United States and the other advanced industrial countries—in the 1940s and again today—or declines in those asymmetries—in the 1980s—have not altered the basic stability and cohesion in relations among these countries.

Liberal theories provide some promising leads in explaining features of the postwar Western order, but they too are incomplete.[11] Many of these theories would also predict order and stability in the West—but their causal arguments are too narrow. The key focus of liberal institutional theory is the way in which institutions provide information to states and reduce the incentives for cheating.[12] But this misses the fundamental feature of order among the advanced industrial countries: the structures of relations are now so deep and pervasive that the kind of cheating that these theories worry about either cannot happen, or if it does it will not really matter because cooperation and the institutions are not fragile but profoundly robust. The basic problem is that these institutionalist arguments have not incorporated the structural features of Western order in their explanations. In particular, they miss the problems of order associated with the great asymmetries of power between Western states, the path-dependent character of postwar institutions, and the importance of the open and accessible character of American hegemony.

In general terms, liberal theories see institutions as having a variety of international functions and impacts—serving in various ways to facilitate cooperation and alter the ways in which states identify and pursue their inter-

---

11. No single theorist represents this composite liberal orientation, but a variety of theorists provide such aspects. On the democratic peace, see Michael Doyle, "Kant, Liberal Legacies, and Foreign Affairs," *Philosophy and Public Affairs*, Vol. 12, No. 3 (Summer 1983), pp. 205–235, 323–353. On security communities, see Karl Deutsch, *Political Community and the North Atlantic Area* (Princeton, N.J.: Princeton University Press, 1957). On the interrelationship of domestic and international politics, see James N. Rosenau, ed., *Linkage Politics: Essays on the Convergence of National and International Systems* (New York: Free Press, 1969). On functional integration theory, see Ernst Haas, *Beyond the Nation-State: Functionalism and International Organization* (Stanford, Calif.: Stanford University Press, 1964). On the fragmented and complex nature of power and interdependence, see Robert Keohane and Joseph Nye, *Power and Interdependence* (Boston: Little, Brown, 1977). On the modernization theory underpinnings of the liberal tradition, see Edward Morse, *Modernization and the Transformation of International Relations* (New York: Free Press, 1976); and James Rosenau, *Turbulence in World Politics: A Theory of Change and Continuity* (Princeton, N.J.: Princeton University Press, 1991).
12. Robert O. Keohane, *After Hegemony: Cooperation and Discord in the World Political Economy* (Princeton, N.J.: Princeton University Press, 1984); and Lisa Martin, *Coercive Cooperation: Explaining Multilateral Economic Sanctions* (Princeton, N.J.: Princeton University Press, 1992).

ests.[13] Liberal theories have also identified and stressed the importance of institutions among states that serve as foundational agreements or constitutional contracts—what Oran Young describes as "sets of rights and rules that are expected to govern their subsequent interactions."[14] Liberal institutional theories are helpful in explaining why specific institutions in the West may persist—even after the power and interests that established them have changed.[15] But there has been less attention to the ways that institutions can be used as strategies to mitigate the security dilemma and overcome incentives to balance. Liberal theories grasp the ways in which institutions can channel and constrain state actions, but they have not explored a more far-reaching view in which leading states use intergovernmental institutions to restrain the arbitrary exercise of power and dampen the fears of domination and abandonment.

The approach to institutions I am proposing can be contrasted with two alternative theories—the rationalist (or "unsticky") theory of institutions, and the constructivist (or "disembodied") theory of institutions.[16] Rationalist theory sees institutions as agreements or contracts between actors that function to reduce uncertainty, lower transactions costs, and solve collective action problems. Institutions provide information, enforcement mechanisms, and other devices that allow states to realize joint gains. Institutions are explained in terms of the problems they solve—they are constructs that can be traced to the

13. For a recent survey, see Lisa Martin, "An Institutionalist View: International Institutions and State Strategies," in T.V. Paul and John A. Hall, eds., *International Order and the Future of World Politics* (New York: Cambridge University Press, 1999). The liberal literature on international institutions and regimes is large. See Stephen D. Krasner, ed., *International Regimes* (Ithaca, N.Y.: Cornell University Press, 1981); Stephan Haggard and Beth Simmons, "Theories of International Regimes," *International Organization*, Vol. 41, No. 3 (Summer 1987), pp. 491–517; and Volker Rittberger, ed., *Regime Theory and International Relations* (Oxford: Oxford University Press, 1995).
14. Oran Young, "Political Leadership and Regime Formation: On the Development of Institutions in International Society," *International Organization*, Vol. 45, No. 3 (Summer 1991), p. 282. See also Young, *International Cooperation: Building Regimes for Natural Resources and the Environment* (Ithaca, N.Y.: Cornell University Press, 1989). The concept of constitutional contract is discussed in James M. Buchanan, *The Limits of Liberty* (Chicago: University of Chicago Press, 1975), esp. chap. 5.
15. See Robert B. McCalla, "NATO's Persistence after the Cold War," *International Organization*, Vol. 50, No. 3 (Summer 1996), pp. 445–476; Celeste Wallander and Robert O. Keohane, "When Threats Decline, Why Do Alliances Persist? An Institutional Approach," unpublished ms., Harvard University and Duke University, 1997; and John S. Duffield, "International Regimes and Alliance Behavior: Explaining NATO Conventional Force Levels," *International Organization*, Vol. 46, No. 4 (Autumn 1992), pp. 819–855.
16. For a good survey of these two alternative traditions of institutional theory, see Robert O. Keohane, "International Institutions: Two Perspectives," *International Studies Quarterly*, Vol. 32, No. 4 (December 1988), pp. 379–396.

actions of self-interested individuals or groups.[17] Constructivist theory sees institutions as diffuse and socially constructed worldviews that bound and shape the strategic behavior of individuals and states. Institutions are over-arching patterns of relations that define and reproduce the interests and actions of individuals and groups. Institutions provide normative and cognitive maps for interpretation and action, and they ultimately affect the identities and social purposes of the actors.[18] A third position advanced here sees institutions as both constructs and constraints.[19] Institutions are the formal and informal organizations, rules, routines, and practices that are embedded in the wider political order and define the "landscape" in which actors operate. As such, institutional structures influence the way power is distributed across individuals and groups within a political system—providing advantages and resources to some and constraining the options of others.[20]

---

17. The rationalist approach argues that institutions are essentially functional or utilitarian "solutions" to problems encountered by rational actors seeking to organize their environment in ways that advance their interests. Kenneth A. Shepsle describes institutions as "agreements about a structure of cooperation" that reduce transaction costs, opportunism, and other forms of "slippage." Shepsle, "Institutional Equilibrium and Equilibrium Institutions," in Herbert F. Weisberg, ed., *Political Science: The Science of Politics* (New York: Agathon, 1986), p. 74.

18. As Alexander Wendt argues, "Constructivists are interested in the construction of identity and interests and, as such, take a more sociological than economic approach" to theory. Wendt, "Collective Identity Formation and the International State," *American Political Science Review*, Vol. 88, No. 2 (June 1994), pp. 384–385.

19. This "third view" of institutions is dissatisfied with both rationalist and constructivist theory. Rationalist theory proves too "thin"—it provides too much agency and not enough structure. It is silent on what others see as the heart of how institutions matter, namely, the impact of institutional structures on the interests and goals of individuals and groups. Constructivist theory, on the other hand, is too "thick"—it does not allow enough agency, and it has problems explaining institutional change. It renders universal and deterministic what is really only a contingent outcome, namely, the impact of institutions on the way people conceive their identities and interests.

20. This theoretical view—often called "historical institutionalism"—makes several claims. First, state policy and orientations are mediated in decisive ways by political structures—such as institutional configurations of government. The structures of a polity shape and constrain the goals, opportunities, and actions of the groups and individuals operating within it. Second, to understand how these institutional constraints and opportunities are manifest, they must be placed within a historical process—timing, sequencing, unintended consequences, and policy feedback matter. Third, institutions have path-dependent characteristics—institutions are established and tend to persist until a later shock or upheaval introduces a new moment of opportunity for institutional change. Finally, institutional structures have an impact because they facilitate or limit the actions of groups and individuals—which means that institutions are never offered as a complete explanation of outcomes. The impacts of institutions, therefore, tend to be assessed as they interact with other factors, such as societal interests, culture, ideology, and new policy ideas. For surveys of historical institutional theory, see Peter A. Hall and Rosemary C.R. Taylor, "Political Science and the Three New Institutionalisms," *Political Studies*, Vol. 44, No. 5 (April 1996); and Sven Steinmo et al., *Structuring Politics: Historical Institutionalism in Comparative Analysis* (New York: Cambridge University Press, 1992).

This approach to institutions gives attention to the ways in which institutions alter or fix into place the distribution of power within a political order. It offers a more "sticky" theory of institutions than the rationalist account, but unlike constructivism, institutional stickiness is manifest in the practical interaction between actors and formal and informal organizations, rules, and routines. Because of the complex causal interaction between actors and institutions, attention to historical timing and sequencing is necessary to appreciate the way in which agency and structure matter.

Debates over post–Cold War order hinge on claims about the character of relations among the major industrial democracies. Neorealist theories trace order to the operation of the balance of power or hegemony, and they anticipate rising conflict and strategy rivalry within the West. Liberal theories are more inclined to see continuity and inertia in the institutions and relations of postwar order, even if threats disappear and power balances shift sharply. It is the sharply contrasting view of institutional "stickiness," as Robert Powell argues, that differentiates realist and liberal institutional theories.[21] The argument advanced here is that institutions are potentially even more "sticky" than liberal theories allow, capable under specific circumstances of locking states into stable and continuous relations that place some limits on the exercise of state power, thereby mitigating the insecurities that neorealism traces to anarchy and shifting power balances.

The Constitutional Bargain

The most fundamental strategic reality after World War II was the huge disparity of power among the great powers that had fought the war—and, in particular, the commanding hegemonic position of the United States. British scholar Harold Laski, writing in 1947, captured the overarching character of American power: "Today literally hundreds of millions of Europeans and Asiatics know that both the quality and the rhythm of their lives depend upon decisions made in Washington. On the wisdom of those decisions hangs the fate of the

---

21. Robert Powell, "Anarchy in International Relations Theory: The Neorealist and Neoliberal Debate," *International Organization*, Vol. 48, No. 2 (Spring 1994), pp. 313–344. For a skeptical realist view of institutions, see John J. Mearsheimer, "The False Promise of International Institutions," *International Security*, Vol. 19, No. 3 (Winter 1994/95), pp. 5–49. For a less skeptical view, see Randall L. Schweller and David Priess, "A Tale of Two Realisms: Expanding the Institutions Debate," *Mershon International Studies Review*, Vol. 41, Supplement 1 (May 1997), pp. 1–32.

next generation."[22] George Kennan, in a major State Department review of American foreign policy in 1948, pointed to this new strategic reality: "We have about 50% of the world's wealth but only 6.3% of its population. . . . Our real task in the coming period is to devise a pattern of relationships which will permit us to maintain this position of disparity without positive detriment to our national security."[23] It is the examination of the choices and options that the United States and the major European and Asian states faced after the war that allows us to see the underlying logic of postwar order.

In a commanding postwar position, the United States had three major options. It could *dominate*—use its power to prevail in the endless distributive struggles with other states. It could *abandon*—wash its hands of Europe and Asia and return home. Or it could seek to *convert* its favorable postwar power position into a durable order that commanded the allegiance of the other states within it. A legitimate political order is one in which its members willingly participate and agree with the overall orientation of the system.[24] To achieve a legitimate order means to secure agreement among the relevant states on the basic rules and principles of political order. States abide by the order's rules and principles because they accept them as their own.

To gain the willing participation of other states, the United States had to overcome their fears that America might pursue its other options: domination or abandonment. In this situation, the critical element to order formation was the ability of the United States to engage in "strategic restraint"—to convey to its potential partners credible assurances of its commitments to restrain its power and operate within the agreed-upon rules and principles of postwar order. In the absence of these assurances, the weaker states of Europe and Japan would have serious incentives to resist American hegemony and engage in strategic rivalry and perhaps counterbalancing alliances.

A durable and legitimate postwar order was possible precisely because the United States had the ability to engage in strategic restraint. In effect, the United States agreed to move toward an institutionalized and agreed-upon political process and to limit its power—made credible by "sticky" institutions and open polities—in exchange for the acquiescence and compliant par-

---

22. Quoted in Norman Graebner, *America as a World Power: A Realist Appraisal from Wilson to Reagan* (Wilmington, Del.: Scholarly Resources, 1984), p. 275.
23. George Kennan, Memorandum by the Director of the Policy Planning Staff to the Secretary of State and the Under Secretary of State Lovett, *Foreign Relations of the United States*, 1948, Vol. 1 (Washington, D.C.: Government Printing Office), February 24, 1948, p. 524.
24. See David Beetham, *The Legitimation of Power* (London: Macmillan, 1991).

ticipation of secondary states. At the heart of the Western postwar order is an ongoing trade-off: the United States agrees to operate within an institutionalized political process and, in return, its partners agree to be willing participants.[25]

More specifically, the United States had an incentive to move toward a "constitutional" settlement after the war—that is, to create basic institutions and operating principles that limit what the leading state can do with its power.[26] In effect, constitutional agreements reduce the implications of "winning" in international relations or, to put it more directly, they serve to *reduce the returns to power*. This is fundamentally what constitutions do within domestic orders. They set limits on what a state that gains disproportionately within the order can do with those gains, thereby reducing the stakes of uneven gains.[27] This means that constitutions reduce the possibilities that a state can turn short-term gains into a long-term power advantage.[28] Taken together, constitutional agreements set limits on what actors can do with momentary advantages. To lose is not to lose everything—the stakes are limited; to lose today does not necessarily diminish the possibility of winning tomorrow.[29]

The role of constitutional limits on power can be seen within domestic constitutional polities. When a party or leader wins an election and takes control of the government, there are fundamental and strictly defined limits on the scope of the power that can be exercised. A newly elected leader cannot use the military to oppress or punish his rivals, or use the taxing and law- enforcement powers of government to harm or destroy the opposition party or parties. The constitution sets limits on the use of power—and this serves to reduce the implications of winning and losing within the political system. To lose is not to lose all, and winning is at best a temporary advantage. As a result, both parties can agree to stay within the system and play by the rules.

---

25. Another recent case of strategic restraint is Germany within the European Union: here also is a powerful state that has agreed to operate within an institutionalized political process, and in return, its partners agree to be willing participants. Neorealists missed this development, and expected Germany to be a predatory power after the Cold War.
26. See Alec Stone, "What Is a Supranational Constitution? An Essay in International Relations Theory," *Review of Politics*, Vol. 56, No. 3 (Summer 1994), pp. 441–474.
27. See discussion in Jon Elster and Rune Slagstad, eds., *Constitutionalism and Democracy* (New York: Cambridge University Press, 1988).
28. See Adam Przeworski, *Democracy and the Market* (New York: Cambridge University Press, 1991), p. 36.
29. For a discussion of how formal institutions provide ways for powerful states to convey credible restraint to weaker states, see Kenneth W. Abbott and Duncan Snidal, "Why States Act through Formal International Organizations," *Journal of Conflict Resolution*, Vol. 42, No. 1 (February 1998), pp. 3–32.

Limits on power are never as clear-cut, absolute, or guaranteed in relations between states. The underlying structure, even in highly complex and integrated orders, is still anarchic. But where institutions can be established that provide some measure of mutually binding constraints on states, and where the polities of the participating states are open democracies, the conditions exist for a settlement with constitutional characteristics.

STRATEGIC RESTRAINT AND POWER CONSERVATION

Why would a newly hegemonic state want to restrict itself by agreeing to limits on the use of hegemonic power? The basic answer is that a constitutional settlement conserves hegemonic power, for two reasons. First, if the hegemonic state calculates that its overwhelming postwar power advantages are only momentary, an institutionalized order might "lock in" favorable arrangements that continue beyond the zenith of its power. In effect, the creation of basic ordering institutions are a form of hegemonic investment in the future. The hegemonic state gives up some freedom on the use of its power in exchange for a durable and predictable order that safeguards its interests in the future.

This investment motive rests on several assumptions. The hegemonic state must be convinced that its power position will ultimately decline—that it is currently experiencing a momentary windfall in relative power capabilities. If this is the state's strategic situation, it should want to use its momentary position to get what it wants. On the other hand, if the new hegemon calculates that its power position will remain preponderant into the foreseeable future, the incentive to conserve its power will disappear. Also, the hegemon must be convinced that the institutions it creates will persist beyond its own power capabilities—that is, it must calculate that these institutions have some independent ordering capacity.[30] If institutions simply are reflections of the distribution of power, the appeal of an institutional settlement will obviously decline. But if institutions are potentially "sticky," powerful states that are farsighted enough to anticipate their relative decline can attempt to institutional-

---

30. The argument that international regimes and institutions, once created, can have an independent ordering impact on states comes in several versions. The weak version of this claim is the modified structural realist position that sees lags in the shifts of regimes as power and interests change. See Stephen D. Krasner, "Structural Causes and Regime Consequences: Regimes as Intervening Variables," in Krasner, ed., *International Regimes* (Ithaca, N.Y.: Cornell University Press, 1983), pp. 1–12. The stronger version entails assumptions about path dependency and increasing returns. For a survey, see Walter W. Powell and Paul J. DiMaggio, eds., *The New Institutionalism in Organizational Analysis* (Chicago: University of Chicago Press, 1991), Introduction, pp. 1–38.

ize favorable patterns of cooperation with other states that persist even as power balances shift.

The second reason why a hegemon might want to reach agreement on basic institutions, even if it means giving up some autonomy and short-term advantage, is that it can reduce the "enforcement costs" of maintaining order. The constant use of power capabilities to punish and reward secondary states and resolve conflicts is costly. It is far more effective over the long term to shape the interests and orientations of other states rather than directly shape their actions through coercion and inducements.[31] A constitutional settlement reduces the necessity of the costly expenditure of resources by the leading state on bargaining, monitoring, and enforcement.

It remains a question why weaker states might not just resist any institutional settlement after the war and wait until they are stronger and can negotiate a more favorable settlement. Several factors might make this a less attractive option. First, without an institutional agreement, the weaker states will lose more than they would under a settlement, where the hegemonic state agrees to forgo some immediate gains in exchange for willing participation of secondary states. Without an institutional settlement, bargaining will be based simply on power capacities, and the hegemonic state will have the clear advantage. The option of losing more now to gain more later is not attractive for a weak state that is struggling to rebuild after war. Its choices will be biased in favor of gains today rather than gains tomorrow. The hegemon, on the other hand, will be more willing to trade off gains today for gains tomorrow. The difference in the two time horizons is crucial to understanding why a constitutional settlement is possible.

A second reason why weaker states might opt for the institutional agreement is that—if the hegemon is able to credibly demonstrate strategic restraint—it does buy them some protection against the threat of domination or abandonment. As realist theory would note, a central concern of weak or secondary states is whether they will be dominated by the more powerful state. In an international order that has credible restraints on power, the possibility of indiscriminate and ruthless domination is mitigated. Just as important, the possibility of abandonment is also lessened. If the hegemonic state is rendered

---

31. The argument that hegemons will want to promote normative consensus among states so as to reduce the necessity of coercive management of the order is presented in G. John Ikenberry and Charles A. Kupchan, "Socialization and Hegemonic Order," *International Organization*, Vol. 44, No. 3 (Summer 1990), pp. 283–315.

more predictable, the secondary states do not need to spend as many resources on "risk premiums," which would otherwise be needed to prepare for either domination or abandonment. In such a situation, the asymmetries in power are rendered more tolerable for weaker states.

Importantly, institutional agreement is possible because of the different time horizons that the hegemonic and secondary states are using to calculate their interests. The leading state agrees to forgo some of the gains that it could achieve if it took full advantage of its superior power position, doing so to conserve power resources and invest in future returns. The weaker states get more returns on their power in the early periods, but in agreeing to be locked into a set of postwar institutions, they give up the opportunity to take full potential advantage of rising relative power capacities in later periods. These alternative calculations are summarized in Figures 1 and 2. The leading state trades short-term gains for long-term gains, taking advantage of the opportunity to lay down a set of institutions that will ensure a favorable order well into the future. Gains in the later periods are greater than what that state's power capacities alone, without the institutional agreement, would otherwise yield. Weaker and secondary states give up some later opportunities to gain a more favorable return on their rising relative power, but in return they get a better postwar

Figure 1. Time Horizons and the Return on Power Assets: Leading State.

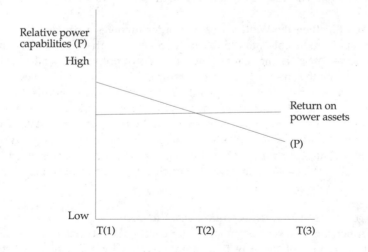

Figure 2. Time Horizons and the Return on Power Assets: Secondary State.

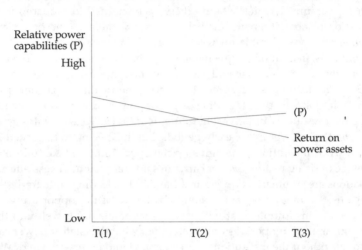

deal in the early postwar period. The option of losing more now so as to gain more later is not an attractive option for a weak state that is struggling to re-build after war. But beyond this, the weaker states also get an institutional agreement that provides some protections against the threat of domination or abandonment—if the leading state is able to credibly demonstrate strategic re-straint.

Taken together, the Western postwar order involves a bargain: the leading state gets a predictable and durable order based on agreed-upon rules and in-stitutions—it secures the acquiescence in this order of weaker states, which in turn allows it to conserve its power. In return, the leading state agrees to limits on its own actions—to operate according to the same rules and institutions as lesser states—and to open itself up to a political process in which the weaker states can actively press their interests upon the more powerful state. The he-gemonic or leading state agrees to forgo some gains in the early postwar pe-riod in exchange for rules and institutions that allow it to have stable returns later, while weaker states are given favorable returns up front and limits on the exercise of power.

STRATEGIES OF RESTRAINT: BONDING, BINDING, AND VOICE OPPORTUNITIES
The American postwar hegemonic order could take on constitutional charac-teristics because of the way institutions, created by and operated between

democratic states, could be wielded to facilitate strategic restraint. Institutions can shape and limit the way power can be used in the system, thereby rendering asymmetric postwar power relations less potentially exploitive and commitment more certain. The returns to power are reduced.[32] Where institutions create restraints on power, weaker and secondary states have less fear of abandonment, or domination is lessened. Institutions can also dampen the effects of the security dilemma and reduce the incentives for weaker and secondary states to balance against the newly powerful state. By creating a mutually constraining environment, institutions allow states to convey assurances to each other and mitigate the dynamics of anarchy.[33]

The hegemonic state has a disproportionate role in creating confidence in postwar order: it has the most capacity to break out of its commitments and take advantage of its position to dominate or abandon the weaker and secondary states.[34] As a result, in its efforts to draw other states into the postwar order, the leading state will have strong incentives to find ways to reassure these other states, to demonstrate that it is a responsible and predictable wielder of power and that the exercise of power is, at least to some acceptable degree, circumscribed. To achieve this goal, the leading state can pursue strategies that involve bonding, binding, and institutionalized voice opportunities.

Bonding means to certify state power: to make it open and predictable. A powerful leading state with a governmental decisionmaking process—and wider political system—that is open and transparent, and that operates accord-

---

32. Obviously, neorealists argue that such guarantees are never sufficient enough to go forward with far-reaching institutionalized cooperation. Under conditions of anarchy, neorealists assert, states will be reluctant to seek even mutually advantageous agreements if it leaves them vulnerable to cheating and/or the relative gains of others. In a self-help system such as anarchy, states face huge obstacles to institutionalized cooperation because the interdependence and differentiation that come with it are manifest within an anarchy as vulnerability. See Joseph M. Grieco, "Anarchy and the Limits of Cooperation: A Realist Critique of the Newest Liberal Institutionalism," *International Organization*, Vol. 42, No. 3 (Summer 1988), pp. 485–507.

33. For a discussion of the general problem of credible commitment and its importance to institutional development and the rule of law, see Barry Weingast and Douglass C. North, "Constitutions and Commitment: The Evolution of Institutions Governing Public Choice in Seventeenth-Century England," *Journal of Economic History*, Vol. 44, No. 4 (December 1989), pp. 803–832.

34. As Peter Cowhey argues, other states "will not become fully committed to working within the multilateral order unless they believe the dominant powers intend to stay within it." Cowhey, "Elect Locally—Order Globally," in John Gerard Ruggie, ed., *Multilateralism: The Theory and Practice of an Institutional Form* (New York: Columbia University Press, 1993), p. 158. Secondary states may have fewer options than the leading state, but their willingness to participate within the order—that is, to engage in voluntary compliance—will hinge on the ability of the leading state to demonstrate its reliability, commitment, and willingness of forgo the arbitrary exercise of power.

ing to predictable institutional rules and procedures, can reassure weaker and secondary states that the exercise of power will not be arbitrary or exploitive. Jon Elster argues that "bonding" is analogous to the efforts of a firm attempting to attract outside shareholders: "It must incur 'costs of bonding,' such as conservative principles of accountancy, in order to attract capital."[35] Potential shareholders are more likely to lend their capital to a firm when the firm operates according to established and reasonable methods of record keeping and accountability. Similarly, when a state is open and transparent to outside states, it reduces the surprises and allows other states to monitor the domestic decisionmaking that attends the exercise of power. The implication of this argument is that democratic states have an advantage in the process of bonding. Democratic states have a more ready capacity to incur the costs of bonding because those costs will be relatively low. Democratic states already have the decentralized and permeable institutions that provide secondary states with information, access, and ultimately reassurance.

The leading state can go beyond internal openness to establish formal institutional links with other states, limiting state autonomy and allowing other states to have institutionalized "voice opportunities" in the decisionmaking of the leading state. These institutional binding strategies have been explored by Joseph Grieco and Daniel Deudney. Grieco argues that weaker states within the European Union (EU) have had an incentive to create institutional links with stronger states so as to have a "voice" in how the strong states exercise their power, thereby preventing domination of the weaker by the stronger states. Weak states are likely to find institutionalized collaboration with stronger states attractive if it provides mechanisms to influence the policy of the stronger states. "States . . . are likely to assign great significance to the enjoyment of such effective voice opportunities in a cooperative arrangement, for it may determine whether states can obtain redress if they are concerned about such matters as the compliance of stronger partners with their commitments in the arrangement, or imbalances in the division of otherwise mutually positive gains that may be produced by their joint effort."[36] Put differently, the institutionalization of relations between weak and strong states, when it creates

---

35. Elster, "Introduction," in Elster and Slagstad, *Constitutionalism and Democracy*, p. 15.
36. Joseph M. Grieco, "State Interests and Institutional Rule Trajectories: A Neorealist Interpretation of the Maastricht Treaty and European Economic and Monetary Union," *Security Studies*, Vol. 5, No. 3 (Spring 1996), p. 288. See also Grieco, "Understanding the Problem of International Cooperation: The Limits of Neoliberalism and the Future of Realist Theory," in David A. Baldwin, ed., *Neorealism and Neoliberalism: The Contemporary Debate* (New York: Columbia University Press,

voice opportunities for the weaker states, can be a solution for these weaker states that want to work with but not be dominated by stronger states.

Deudney also describes the dynamic of binding, but emphasizes its other feature: it is a practice of establishing institutional links between the units that reduce their autonomy vis-à-vis one another.[37] In agreeing to be institutionally connected, states mutually constrain each other and thereby mitigate the problems of anarchy that lead to security dilemmas and power balancing. According to Deudney, binding practices are particularly available to and desired by democratic polities that want to resist the state-strengthening and centralizing consequences of balance-of-power orders. Binding restricts the range of freedom of states—whether weak or strong—and when states bind to each other, they jointly reduce the role and consequences of power in their relationship.

Each of these strategies involves the institutionalization of state power. Asymmetries of power do not disappear, but institutions—democratic institutions and intergovernmental institutions—channel and circumscribe the way that state power is exercised. Institutions make the exercise of power more predictable and less arbitrary and indiscriminate, up to some point. When a newly hegemonic state seeks to create a mutually acceptable order, doing so to preserve and extend the returns to its power into the future, institutions can be an attractive tool: they lock other states into the order, and they allow the leading state to reassure and co-opt other states by limiting the returns to power.

Postwar Hegemonic Reassurance

By design, inadvertence, and structural circumstance, the United States was in a position after World War II to mute the implications of unprecedented power asymmetries between itself and its postwar partners, alleviating fears of domination and abandonment. These strategies of reassurance were manifest in

---

1993), pp. 331–334; and Grieco, "The Maastricht Treaty, Economic and Monetary Union, and the Neo-Realist Research Programme," *Review of International Studies,* Vol. 21, No. 1 (January 1995), pp. 21–40. The classic formulation of this logic is Albert O. Hirschman, *Exit, Voice, and Loyalty—Responses to Decline in Firms, Organizations, and States* (Cambridge, Mass.: Harvard University Press, 1970).

37. Daniel Deudney, "The Philadelphian System: Sovereignty, Arms Control, and Balance of Power in the American States-Union," *International Organization,* Vol. 49, No. 2 (Spring 1995), pp. 191–228; and Deudney, "Binding Sovereigns: Authorities, Structures, and Geopolitics in Philadelphian Systems," in Thomas Biersteker and Cynthia Weber, eds., *State Sovereignty as Social Construct* (Cambridge: Cambridge University Press, 1996), esp. pp. 213–216.

three ways: in America's "reluctant" orientation toward hegemonic domination; in the open and penetrated character of the American polity; and in the ways postwar economic and security institutions shaped and circumscribed the exercise of American power. Together, these strategies and circumstances served to limit the returns to power in the postwar order, creating the conditions for its legitimacy and durability.

RELUCTANT HEGEMONY

Behind specific institutional strategies of reassurance, the United States exhibited a general orientation toward postwar order and the exercise of coercive hegemonic power that served to reassure other states. The United States might be seen as a "reluctant hegemon" in many respects, seeking agreement among the Western states on a mutually acceptable order, even if this meant extensive compromise, and pushing for an institutionalized order that would require little direct "management" by the United States or the active exercise of its hegemonic power. It is revealing that the initial and most forcefully presented American view on postwar order was the State Department's proposal for a postwar system of free trade. This proposal did not only reflect an American conviction about the virtues of open markets, but it also was a vision of order that would require very little direct American involvement or management. The system would be largely self-regulating, leaving the United States to operate without the burdens of direct and ongoing supervision.

This view on postwar trade reflected a more general American orientation as the war came to an end. The new hegemon wanted a world order that would advance American interests, but it was not eager to actively organize and run that order. In this sense, the United States was a reluctant superpower.[38] This general characteristic was not lost on the Europeans, and it mattered as America's potential partners contemplated whether and how to cooperate with the United States. To the extent that the United States could convey the sense that it did not seek to dominate the Europeans, it gave greater credibility to America's proposals for an institutionalized postwar order. It provided some reassurance that the United States would operate within limits and not use its overwhelming power position simply to dominate.

---

38. See Richard Holt, *The Reluctant Superpower: A History of America's Global Economic Reach* (New York: Kodansha International, 1995); see also Geir Lundestad, "An Empire by Invitation? The United States and Western Europe, 1945–1952," *Journal of Peace Research*, Vol. 23, No. 3 (September 1986).

More generally, the overall pattern of American postwar policies reflected a self-conscious effort by administration officials to infuse the postwar system with a sense of legitimacy and reciprocal consent. When American officials began to organize Marshall Plan aid for Europe, for example, there was a strong desire to have the Europeans embrace American aid and plans as their own—thus enhancing the legitimacy of the overall postwar settlement. At a May 1947 meeting, George Kennan argued that it was important to have "European acknowledgement of responsibility and parentage in the plan to prevent the certain attempts of powerful elements to place the entire burden on the United States and to discredit it and us by blaming the United States for all failures." Similarly, State Department official Charles Bohlen argued that United States policy should not be seen as an attempt "to force 'the American way' on Europe."[39] The United States wanted to create an order that conformed to its liberal democratic principles, but this could be done only if other governments embraced such a system as their own.

This orientation was also reflected in the compromises that the United States made in accommodating European views about the postwar world economy. The British and the continental Europeans, worried about postwar depression and the protection of their fragile economies, were not eager to embrace America's stark proposals for an open world trading system, favoring instead a more regulated and compensatory system.[40] The United States did attempt to use its material resources to pressure and induce Britain and the other European countries to abandon bilateral and regional preferential agreements and accept the principles of a postwar economy organized around a nondiscriminatory system of trade and payments.[41] The United States knew it held a commanding position and sought to use its power to give the postwar order a distinctive shape. But it also prized agreement over deadlock, and it

---

39. Quoted in "Summary of Discussion on Problems of Relief, Rehabilitation, and Reconstruction of Europe," May 29, 1947, *Foreign Relations of the United States,* 1947, Vol. 3, p. 235.
40. The strongest claims about American and European differences over postwar political economy are made by Fred Block, *The Origins of International Economic Disorder* (Berkeley: University of California Press, 1977), pp. 70–122.
41. The 1946 British loan deal was perhaps the most overt effort by the Truman administration to tie American postwar aid to specific policy concessions by allied governments. This was the failed Anglo-American Financial Agreement, which obliged the British to make sterling convertible in exchange for American assistance. See Richard Gardner, *Sterling-Dollar Diplomacy,* 2d ed. (New York: Columbia University Press, 1980); and Alfred E. Eckes, Jr., A Search for Solvency: Bretton Woods and the International Monetary System, 1944–71 (Austin: University of Texas Press, 1971).

ultimately moved a great distance away from its original proposals in setting up the various postwar economic institutions.[42]

OPEN HEGEMONY

A second way that the United States projected reassurance was structural—its own liberal democratic polity. The open and decentralized character of the American political system provided opportunities for other states to observe decisionmaking and exercise their "voice" in the operation of American postwar foreign policy, thereby reassuring these states that their interests could be actively advanced and that processes of conflict resolution would exist. In this sense, the American postwar order was a "liberal hegemony," an extended system that blurred domestic and international politics as it created an elaborate transnational and transgovernmental political system with the United States at its center.[43]

There are actually several ways in which America's open hegemony has reinforced the credibility of the United States' commitment to operate within an institutionalized political order. The first is simply the transparency of the system, which reduces surprises and allays worries by partners that the United States might make abrupt changes in policy. This transparency comes from the fact that policymaking in a large, decentralized democracy involves many players and an extended and relatively visible political process. However, it is not only that it is an open and decentralized system; it is also one with competing political parties and an independent press—features that serve to expose the underlying integrity and viability of major policy commitments.[44] The open and competitive process may produce mixed and ambiguous policies at times, but the transparency of the process at least allows other states to make more accurate calculations about the likely direction of American foreign policy, which lowers levels of uncertainty and provides a measure of reassurance, which—everything else being equal—creates greater opportunities to cooperate.

---

42. See John Gerard Ruggie, *Winning the Peace: America and World Order in the New Era* (New York: Columbia University Press, 1996), chap. 5.
43. This section and the next build on Daniel Deudney and G. John Ikenberry, "The Sources and Character of Liberal International Order," *Review of International Studies,* forthcoming.
44. This point is made in James Fearon, "Domestic Political Audiences and the Escalation of International Disputes," *American Political Science Review,* Vol. 88, No. 3 (September 1994), pp. 577–592.

Another way in which the open hegemonic order provides reassurances to partners is that the American system invites (or at least creates opportunities for) the participation of outsiders. The fragmented and penetrated American system allows and invites the proliferation of a vast network of transnational and transgovernmental relations with Europe, Japan, and other parts of the industrial world. Diffuse and dense networks of governmental, corporate, and private associations tie the system together. The United States is the primary site for the pulling and hauling of trans-Atlantic and trans-Pacific politics. Europeans and Japanese do not have elected officials in Washington—but they do have representatives.[45] Although this access to the American political process is not fully reciprocated abroad, the openness and extensive decentralization of the American liberal system assures other states that they have routine access to the decisionmaking processes of the United States.

The implication of open hegemony is that the United States is not as able to use its commanding power position to gain disproportionately in relations with Japan and Europe—or at least it diminishes the leverage that would otherwise exist. For example, there is little evidence that the United States has been able to bring more pressure to bear on Japanese import policy, even as its relative power capacities have seemingly increased in the 1990s with the end of the Cold War and the slump in the Japanese economy. Beginning in July 1993 with the signing of a "framework" agreement, the Clinton administration launched a series of efforts to pin Japan to numerical import targets, including threatened sanctions to boost American automobile imports. But despite repeated efforts in February 1994 and the spring of 1995, Prime Minister Morihiro Hosakawa, helped by protests from the European Union, was largely able to resist American pressure.[46] The advent of the World Trade Organization (WTO) also has provided additional ways for Japan to narrow

---

45. For the transnational political process channeled through the Atlantic security institutions, see Thomas Risse-Kappen, *Cooperation among Democracies: The European Influence on U.S. Foreign Policy* (Princeton, N.J.: Princeton University Press, 1995). On the U.S.-Japanese side, see Peter J. Katzenstein and Yutaka Tsujinaka, "'Bullying,' 'Buying,' and 'Binding': U.S.-Japanese Transnational Relations and Domestic Structures," in Risse-Kappen, ed., *Bringing Transnational Relations Back In: Non-State Actors, Domestic Structures, and International Institutions* (Cambridge: Cambridge University Press, 1995), pp. 79–111.

46. See Andrew Pollack, "U.S. Appears to Retreat from Setting Targets to Increase Japan's Imports," *New York Times*, July 10, 1993; David Sanger, "Hosakawa's Move Foils U.S. Strategy," *International Herald Tribune*, April 11, 1994; Nancy Dunne and Michito Nakamato, "Wiser U.S. to Meet Chastened Japan," *Financial Times*, May 18, 1994; and Reginald Dale, "Japan Gains the Edge in Trade War," *International Herald Tribune*, September 13, 1994.

trade disputes to specific issues, bring international procedures of review into play, and diminish the capacity of the United States to bring its hegemonic power to bear. In the recent Kodak case, for example, the WTO basically ruled against the United States in its effort to push Japan toward greater openness. After this ruling, the United States quietly lowered its voice and sat down.[47] The open and penetrated character of the United States serves to fragment and narrow policy disputes, creates a more level playing field for European and Japanese interests, and reduces the implications of hegemonic power asymmetries.

BINDING INSTITUTIONS

A final way in which reassurance has been conveyed is through the institutions themselves, which provide "lock in" and "binding" constraints on the United States and its partners, thereby mitigating fears of domination or abandonment. The Western countries have made systematic efforts to anchor their joint commitments in principled and binding institutional mechanisms. Governments might ordinarily seek to preserve their options, to cooperate with other states but to leave open the option of disengaging. What the United States and the other Western states did after the war was exactly the opposite: they built long-term economic, political, and security commitments that were difficult to retract. They "locked in" their commitments and relationships, to the extent that this can be done by sovereign states.

The logic of institutional binding is best seen in security alliances. Alliances have often been formed not simply or even primarily to aggregate power so as to balance against external threats, but rather to allow alliance partners to restrain each other and manage joint relations. Alliances have traditionally been seen as temporary expedients that bring states together in pledges of mutual assistance in the face of a common threat, a commitment specified in the *casus foederis* article of the treaty. But as Paul Schroeder and others have

---

47. As Clyde V. Prestowitz, Jr. writes: "In the past, the United States would have attempted to negotiate a bilateral settlement with the potential imposition of sanctions lurking in the background as an incentive to reach an agreement. Under the new WTO rules, however, all disputes are supposed to be submitted to the WTO for compulsory arbitration and unilateral imposition of trade sanctions is illegal....But if America then attempts to solve the problem unilaterally by imposing sanctions, Japan could have the U.S. sanctions declared illegal by the WTO. Knowing this, Japanese officials have refused even to meet with U.S. negotiators—and have effectively told the United States to buzz off." Prestowitz, "The New Asian Equation," *Washington Post*, April 14, 1996.

noted, alliances have also been created as *pacta de contrahendo*—pacts of restraint.[48] They have served as mechanisms for states to manage and restrain their partners within the alliance. "Frequently the desire to exercise such control over an ally's policy," Schroeder argues, "was the main reason that one power, or both, entered into the alliance."[49] Alliances create binding treaties that allow states to keep a hand in the security policy of their partners. When alliance treaties are *pacta de contrahendo*, potential rivals tie themselves to each other—alleviating suspicions, reducing uncertainties, and creating institutional mechanisms for each to influence the policies of the other.[50]

The practice of mutual constraint makes sense only if international institutions or regimes can have an independent ordering impact on the actions of states. The assumption is that institutions are sticky—that they can take on a life and logic of their own, shaping and constraining even the states that create them. When states employ institutional binding as a strategy, they are essentially agreeing to mutually constrain themselves. In effect, institutions specify what it is that states are expected to do, and they make it difficult and costly for states to do otherwise.[51] In this sense, institutional binding is like marriage: two individuals realize that their relationship will eventually generate conflict and discord, so they bind themselves in a legal framework, making it more difficult to dissolve the relationship when those inevitable moments arrive. In the case of international institutions, examples of binding mechanisms include treaties, interlocking organizations, joint management responsibilities, agreed-upon standards and principles of relations, and so forth. These mechanisms raise the "costs of exit" and create "voice opportunities," thereby providing mechanisms to mitigate or resolve the conflict.

---

48. See Paul W. Schroeder, "Alliances, 1815–1945: Weapons of Power and Tools of Management," in Klaus Knorr, ed., *Historical Dimensions of National Security Problems* (Lawrence: University Press of Kansas, 1975), pp. 227–262. As Schroeder notes, the internal constraint function of alliances was earlier observed by George Liska. See Liska, *Nations in Alliance: The Limits of Interdependence* (Baltimore, Md.: Johns Hopkins University Press, 1962), p. 116; *Imperial America: The International Politics of Primacy* (Baltimore, Md.: Johns Hopkins University Press, 1967); pp. 9–11, 20–21; and *Alliances and the Third World* (Baltimore, Md.: Johns Hopkins University Press, 1968), pp. 24–35.

49. Schroeder, "Alliances, 1815–1945," p. 230.

50. For a recent extension of this argument, see Patricia A. Weitsman, "Intimate Enemies: The Politics of Peacetime Alliances," *Security Studies*, Vol. 7, No. 1 (Autumn 1997), pp. 156–192.

51. This view accords with our general view of what institutions are and do. As Lorenzo Ornaghi argues: "The role of institutions in politics is to give the rules of the game, in that, by reducing the uncertain and unforeseeable character of interpersonal relations, insurance is mutually provided." Ornaghi, "Economic Structure and Political Institutions: A Theoretical Framework," in Mauro Baranzini and Roberto Scazzieri, eds., *The Economic Theory of Structure and Change* (Cambridge: Cambridge University Press, 1990), p. 27.

The Bretton Woods economic and monetary accords exhibit the logic of institutional lock-in. These were the first accords to establish a permanent international institutional and legal framework to ensure economic cooperation between states. They were constructed as elaborate systems of rules and obligations with quasi-judicial procedures for adjudicating disputes.[52] The dollar-gold standard collapsed in 1971, but the broader institutions of joint management remain. In effect, the Western governments created an array of functionally organized transnational political systems. Moreover, the democratic character of the United States and the other Western countries facilitated the construction of these dense interstate connections. The permeability of domestic institutions provided congenial grounds for reciprocal and pluralistic "pulling and hauling" across the advanced industrial world.

It was here that the Cold War's security alliances provided additional institutional binding opportunities. The old saying that NATO was created to "keep the Russians out, the Germans down, and the Americans in" is a statement about the importance of the alliance structures for locking in long-term commitments and expectations. The U.S.-Japan security alliance also had a similar "dual containment" character. These institutions not only served as alliances in the ordinary sense of organized efforts to balance against external threats, but they also provided mechanisms and venues to build political relations, conduct business, and regulate conflict.

The constitutional features of the Western order have been particularly important for Germany and Japan. Both countries were reintegrated into the advanced industrial world as "semisovereign" powers: that is, they accepted unprecedented constitutional limits on their military capacity and independence.[53] As such, they became unusually dependent on the array of Western regional and multilateral economic and security institutions. The Western political order in which they were embedded was integral to their stability and functioning. The Christian Democrat Walther Leisler Kiep argued in 1972 that "the German-American alliance . . . is not merely one aspect of modern German history, but a decisive element as a result of its preeminent place in our politics. In effect, it provides a second constitution for our coun-

---

52. See Harold James, *International Monetary Cooperation since Bretton Woods* (New York: Oxford University Press, 1995).
53. On the notion of semisovereignty, see Peter J. Katzenstein, *Policy and Politics in West Germany: The Growth of a Semi-Sovereign State* (Philadelphia: Temple University Press, 1987). For a discussion of Japanese semisovereignty and the postwar peace constitution, see Masaru Tamamoto, "Reflections on Japan's Postwar State," *Daedalus*, Vol. 125, No. 2 (Spring 1995), pp. 1–22.

try."[54] This logic of Germany's involvement in NATO and the EU was reaffirmed recently by the German political leader Voigt Karsten: "We wanted to bind Germany into a structure that practically obliges Germany to take the interests of its neighbors into consideration. We wanted to give our neighbors assurances that we won't do what we don't intend to do."[55] Western economic and security institutions provide Germany and Japan with a political bulwark of stability that far transcends their more immediate and practical purposes.

The recent revision of the U.S.-Japan security treaty in May 1996 is another indication that both countries see virtues in maintaining a tight security relationship regardless of the end of the Cold War or the rise and fall of specific security threats in the region.[56] Even though the threats in the region have become less tangible or immediate, the alliance has been reaffirmed and cooperation and joint planning have expanded. Part of the reason is that the alliance is still seen by many Japanese and American officials as a way to render the bilateral relationship more stable by binding each to the other.[57] The expansion of NATO is also, at least in part, driven by the binding aspects of the alliance. This view of NATO as "architecture" that would stabilize relations within Europe and across the Atlantic, rather than primarily an alliance to counter external threats, was first signaled in Secretary of State James Baker's famous speech in the aftermath of the fall of the Berlin Wall in 1989.[58] Some supporters of NATO expansion see it as an insurance policy against the possibility of a fu-

---

54. Quoted in Thomas A. Schwartz, "The United States and Germany after 1945: Alliances, Transnational Relations, and the Legacy of the Cold War," *Diplomatic History*, Vol. 19, No. 4 (Fall 1995), p. 555.

55. Quoted in Jan Perlez, "Larger NATO Seen as Lid on Germany," *International Herald Tribune*, December 8, 1997.

56. President Bill Clinton and Prime Minister Ryutaro Hashimoto signed a Joint Declaration on Security on April 17, 1996, which was a revision of the 1978 Guidelines for U.S.-Japan Defense Cooperation. The agreement declared that the U.S.-Japan security treaty of 1960 "remains the cornerstone" of their policies, that their combined forces in Japan would engage in policy coordination for dealing with regional crises, and on a reciprocal basis provide equipment and supplies. Overall, the Japanese made a commitment to actually move toward closer security relations with the United States.

57. Peter J. Katzenstein and Yutaka Tsujinaka argue that "the security relationship between the United States and Japan is best described by 'binding,' with the United States doing most of the 'advising' and Japan most of the 'accepting.' By and large since the mid-1970s defense cooperation has increased smoothly and apparently to the satisfaction of both militaries. Since that cooperation involved primarily governments and sub-units of governments implementing policy, 'binding' results primarily from transgovernmental relations." Katzenstein and Tsujinaka, "'Bullying,' 'Buying,' and 'Binding,'"in Risse-Kappen, *Bringing Transnational Relations Back In*, p. 80. See also Richard Finn, "Japan's Search for a Global Role," in Warren S. Hunsberger, *Japan's Quest: The Search for International Role, Recognition, and Respect* (New York: M.E. Sharpe, 1977), pp. 113–130.

58. See Michael Smith and Stephen Woolcock, *The United States and the European Community in a Transformed World* (London: Pinter/Royal Institute of International Affairs, 1993), p. 1.

ture resurgent and revisionist Russia.[59] But others, particularly in the Clinton administration, see the virtues of expansion more in terms of the stabilizing, integrating, and binding effects that come from NATO as an institution.[60]

Overall, U.S. hegemony is reluctant, open, and highly institutionalized. All these characteristics have helped to facilitate a rather stable and durable political order. American strategic restraint after World War II left the Europeans more worried about abandonment than domination, and they actively sought American institutionalized commitments to Europe. The American polity's transparency and permeability fostered an "extended" political order—reaching outward to the other industrial democracies—with most of its roads leading to Washington. Transnational and transgovernmental relations provide the channels. Multiple layers of economic, political, and security institutions bind these countries together in ways that reinforce the credibility of their mutual commitments. The United States remains the center of the system, but other states are highly integrated into it, and its legitimacy diminishes the need for the exercise of coercive power by the United States or for balancing responses from secondary states.

Increasing Returns to Postwar Institutions

The bargains struck and institutions created at the early moments of postwar order building have not simply persisted for fifty years, but they have actually become more deeply rooted in the wider structures of politics and society of the countries that participate within the order. That is, more people and more of their activities are linked to the institutions and operations of the American liberal hegemonic order. A wider array of individuals and groups, in more countries and more realms of activity, have a stake—or a vested interest—in the continuation of the system. The costs of disruption or change in this system have steadily grown over the decades. Together, this means that "competing orders" or "alternative institutions" are at a disadvantage. The system is increasingly hard to replace.

The reason institutions have a lock-in effect is primarily because of the phenomenon of increasing returns.[61] There are several aspects to increasing re-

---

59. See Zbigniew Brzezinski, "NATO—Expand or Die?" *New York Times,* December 28, 1994.
60. See Michael Cox, *U.S. Foreign Policy after the Cold War: Superpower without a Mission?* (London: Royal Institute of International Affairs), pp. 79–83.
61. Both rational choice and sociological theories of institutions offer theories of institutional path dependency—both emphasizing the phenomenon of increasing returns. See Paul Pierson, "Path Dependence and the Study of Politics," unpublished paper, Harvard University, 1996.

turns to institutions. First, there are large initial start-up costs to creating new institutions. Even when alternative institutions might be more efficient or accord more closely with the interests of powerful states, the gains from the new institutions must be overwhelmingly greater before they overcome the sunk costs of the existing institutions.[62] Moreover, there tend to be learning effects that are achieved in the operation of the existing institution that give it advantages over a start-up institution. Finally, institutions tend to create relations and commitments with other actors and institutions that serve to embed the institution and raise the costs of change. Taken together, as Douglass North concludes, "the interdependent web of an institutional matrix produces massive increasing returns."[63]

When institutions manifest increasing returns, it becomes very difficult for potential replacement institutions to compete and succeed. The logic is seen most clearly in regard to competing technologies. The history of the videocassette recorder is the classic example, where two formats, VHS and Beta, competed for standardization. The two formats were introduced roughly at the same time and initially had equal market share, but soon the VHS format, through luck and circumstances unrelated to efficiency, expanded its market share. Increasing returns on early gains tilted the competition toward VHS, allowing it to accumulate enough advantages to take over the market.[64] Even if Beta was ultimately a superior technology, a very small market advantage by VHS at an early and critical moment allowed it to lower its production costs, and the accumulation of connecting technologies and products that require compatibility made it increasingly hard for the losing technology to compete. The costs of switching to the other technology rise as production costs are lowered, learning effects accumulate, and the technology is embedded in a wider system of compatible and interdependent technologies.[65]

---

62. On sunk costs, see Arthur L. Stinchcombe, *Constructing Social Theories* (New York: Harcourt, Brace and World, 1968), pp. 108–118.
63. Douglass C. North, *Institutions, Institutional Change, and Economic Performance* (New York: Cambridge University Press, 1990), p. 95. For discussions of path dependency arguments and their implications, see Stephen D. Krasner, "Approaches to the State: Conceptions and Historical Dynamics," *Comparative Politics,* Vol. 16 (January 1984); and Paul Pierson, "When Effect Becomes Cause: Policy Feedback and Political Change," *World Politics,* Vol. 45, No. 4 (July 1993), pp. 595–628.
64. See W. Brian Arthur, "Positive Feedbacks in the Economy," *Scientific American* (February 1990), pp. 92–99. Reprinted in Arthur, *Increasing Returns and Path Dependence in the Economy* (Ann Arbor: University of Michigan Press, 1995), pp. 1–12.
65. W. Brian Arthur, "Competing Technologies, Increasing Returns, and Lock-In by Historical Small Events," *Economic Journal,* March 1989, pp. 116–131.

American postwar hegemonic order has exhibited this phenomenon of increasing returns to its institutions. At the early moments after 1945, when the imperial, bilateral, and regional alternatives to America's postwar agenda were most imminent, the United States was able to use its unusual and momentary advantages to tilt the system in the direction it desired. The pathway to the present liberal hegemonic order began at a very narrow passage where really only Britain and the United States—and a few top officials—could shape decisively the basic orientation of the world political economy. But once the institutions, such as those erected at Bretton Woods and the General Agreement on Tariffs and Trade, were established, it became increasingly hard for competing visions of postwar order to have any viability. America's great burst of institution building after World War II fits a general pattern of international continuity and change: crisis or war opens up a moment of flux and opportunity, choices are made, and interstate relations get fixed or settled for a while.[66]

The notion of increasing returns to institutions means that once a moment of institutional selection comes and goes, the cost of large-scale institutional change rises dramatically—even if potential institutions, when compared with existing ones, are more efficient and desirable.[67] In terms of American hegemony, this means that, short of a major war or a global economic collapse, it is very difficult to envisage the type of historical breakpoint needed to replace the existing order. This is true even if a new would-be hegemon or coalition of states had an interest in and agenda for an alternative set of global institutions—which they do not.[68]

While the increasing returns to institutions can serve to perpetuate institutions of many sorts, American hegemonic institutions have characteristics that particularly lend themselves to increasing returns. First, the set of principles that infuse these institutions—particularly principles of multilateralism, openness, and reciprocity—are ones that command agreement because of their seeming fairness and legitimacy. Organized around principles that are easy for

---

66. See Peter J. Katzenstein, "International Relations Theory and the Analysis of Change," in Ernst-Otto Czempiel and James N. Rosenau, eds., *Global Changes and Theoretical Challenges: Approaches to World Politics for the 1990s* (Lexington, Mass.: Lexington Books, 1989), pp. 291–304.

67. This notion of breakpoint or critical juncture is not developed in the increasing returns literature, but it is implicit in the argument, and it is very important for understanding the path dependency of American hegemony.

68. Major or great power war is a uniquely powerful agent of change in world politics because it tends to destroy and discredit old institutions and force the emergence of a new leading or hegemonic state. Robert Gilpin discusses the possibility that with the rise of nuclear weapons, this sort of pattern of global change may end, thereby leaving in place the existing hegemonic order. See Gilpin, Epilogue, *War and Change in World Politics*, pp. 231–244.

states to accept, regardless of their specific international power position, the institutional pattern is more robust and easy to expand. Moreover, the principled basis of hegemonic order also makes it more durable. This is John Ruggie's argument about the multilateral organization of postwar international institutions: "All other things being equal, an arrangement based on generalized organizing principles should be more elastic than one based on particularistic interests and situational exigencies."[69] Potential alternative institutional orders are at an added disadvantage because the principles of the current institutional order are adaptable, expandable, and easily accepted as legitimate.

Second, the open and permeable character of American hegemonic institutions also serves to facilitate increasing returns. One of the most important aspects of increasing returns is that once a particular institution is established, other institutions and relations tend to grow up around it and become interconnected and mutually dependent. A good analogy is computer software, where a software provider like Microsoft, after gaining an initial market advantage, encourages the proliferation of software applications and programs based on Microsoft's operating language. This in turn leads to a huge complex of providers and users who are heavily dependent on the Microsoft format. The result is an expanding market community of individuals and firms with an increasingly dense set of commitments to Microsoft—commitments that are not based on loyalty but on the growing reality that changing to another format would be more costly, even if it were more efficient.

The open and penetrated character of American hegemony encourages this sort of proliferation of connecting groups and institutions. A dense set of transnational and transgovernmental channels are woven into the trilateral regions of the advanced industrial world. A sort of layer cake of intergovernmental institutions extend outward from the United States across the Atlantic and Pacific.[70] Global multilateral economic institutions, such as the International Monetary Fund (IMF) and WTO, are connected to more circumscribed governance institutions, such as the Group of Seven (G-7) and the Group of Ten. Private groups, such as the Trilateral Commission and hundreds of business trade associations, are also connected in one way or another to individual

---

69. John Gerard Ruggie, "Multilateralism: The Anatomy of an Institution," in Ruggie, ed., *Multilateralism Matters: The Theory and Praxis of an Institutional Form* (New York: Columbia University Press, 1993), pp. 32–33.
70. See Cheryl Shanks, Harold K. Jacobson, and Jeffrey H. Kaplan, "Inertia and Change in the Constellation of International Governmental Organizations, 1981–1992," *International Organization*, Vol. 50, No. 4 (Autumn 1996), pp. 593–628.

governments and their joint management institutions. The steady rise of trade and investment across the advanced industrial world has made these countries more interdependent, which in turn has expanded the constituency within these countries for a perpetuation of an open, multilateral system.[71]

Not only have more and more governments and groups become connected to the core institutions of the Western order; still more are seeking to join. Almost every country in the world, including China, has now indicated a desire to join the WTO, and the line for membership in NATO stretches all the way to Moscow. In the recent Asian currency crisis, even countries with little affinity for the IMF and its operating methods have had little choice but to negotiate with it over the terms of loans and economic stabilization. Russia has joined the annual G-7 summit, turning it into the Summit of the Eight, and the eventual inclusion of China is quite likely. In the meantime, the G-7 process in the 1990s has generated an expanding array of ministerial and intergovernmental bodies in a wide variety of functional areas, tackling problems such as organized crime, energy, terrorism, the environment, aid to Ukraine, and global finance.[72] Together, relations among the advanced industrial countries since the end of the Cold War are characterized by an increasingly dense latticework of intergovernmental institutions and routinized organizational relationships that are serving to draw more governments and more functional parts of these governments into the extended postwar Western political order.

This means that great shifts in the basic organization of the Western order are increasingly costly to a widening array of individuals and groups that make up the order. More and more people have a stake in the system, even if they have no particular loyalty or affinity for the United States and even if they might really prefer a different order. As the decades have worn on, the operating institutions of the postwar Western order have expanded and deepened. More and more people would have their lives disrupted if the system were to radically change—which is another way of saying that the constituency for

---

71. This is the dynamic that Robert Keohane and Joseph Nye seek to capture in their "international organization" model. "International organization in the broad sense of networks, norms, and institutions includes the norms associated with specific international regimes, but it is a broader category than regime, because it also includes patterns of elite networks and (if relevant) formal institutions." They go on to argue that "the international organization model assumes that a set of networks, norms, and institutions, once established, will be difficult either to eradicate or drastically to rearrange. Even governments with superior capabilities—overall or within the issue area—will find it hard to work their will when it conflicts with established patterns of behavior within existing networks and institutions." See Keohane and Nye, *Power and Interdependence*, p. 55.
72. See Peter I. Hajnal, "From G7 to G8: Evolution, Role, and Documentation of a Unique Institution," unpublished paper, Centre for International Studies, University of Toronto, 1998.

preserving the postwar political order among the major industrial countries is greater than ever before. It is in this sense that the American postwar order is stable and growing.

The dominance of the United States has sparked complaints and resistance in various quarters of Europe and Asia—but it has not triggered the type of counterhegemonic balancing or competitive conflict that might otherwise be expected. Some argue that complaints about America's abuse of its commanding power position have grown in recent years.[73] Unwillingness to pay United Nations dues, the Helms-Burton Act, which inhibits trade with Cuba, and resistance to commitments to cut greenhouse gases—these and other failures are the grist of European and Asian complaints about American predominance. But complaints about the American "arrogance of power" have been a constant minor theme of postwar Western order. Episodes include the "invasion" of American companies into Europe in the 1950s, the dispute over Suez in 1953, the "Nixon shocks" in 1971 over the surprise closure of the gold window, America's failure to decontrol oil prices during the 1970s energy crisis, and the Euro-missiles controversy of the early 1980s. Seen in postwar perspective, it is difficult to argue that the level of conflict has risen. Today, as in the past, the differences tend to be negotiated and resolved within intergovernmental channels—even while the Europeans, Americans, and Japanese agree to expand their cooperation in new areas, such as international law enforcement, the environment, and nonproliferation. More important, despite complaints about the American abuse of its hegemonic position, there are no serious political movements in Europe or Japan that call for a radical break with the existing Western order organized around American power and institutions. It is the stability of the order, in spite of policy struggles and complaints, that is more remarkable than any changes in the character of the struggles or complaints.

Conclusion

The twentieth century may be ending, but the American century is in full swing. The character of American power is as interesting and remarkable as the fact of its existence. American domination or hegemony is very unusual,

---

73. A reporter for the *Washington Post* recently summarized this view: "The chorus of dismay with America's overwhelming power has grown louder lately as the United States finds itself increasingly accused of bullying the rest of the world. Indeed, the United States is discovering that its behavior has come under sharpest scrutiny from friendly nations that no longer feel prevented by Cold War loyalties from expressing their disagreements with Washington." William Drozdiak, "Even Allies Resent U.S. Dominance," *Washington Post*, November 4, 1997.

and the larger Western political order that surrounds it is unique as well. Fundamentally, American hegemony is reluctant, open, and highly institutionalized—or in a word, liberal. This is what makes it acceptable to other countries that might otherwise be expected to balance against hegemonic power, and it is also what makes it so stable and expansive.

Even with the end of the Cold War and the shifting global distribution of power, the relations between the United States and the other industrial countries of Europe and Asia remain remarkably stable and cooperative. This article offers two major reasons why American hegemony has endured and facilitated cooperation and integration among the major industrial countries rather than triggered balancing and estrangement. Both reasons underscore the importance of the liberal features of American hegemony and the institutional foundations of Western political order.

First, the United States moved very quickly after World War II to ensure that relations among the liberal democracies would take place within an institutionalized political process. In effect, the United States offered the other countries a bargain: if the United States would agree to operate within mutually acceptable institutions, thereby muting the implications of power asymmetries, the other countries would agree to be willing participants as well. The United States got the acquiescence of the other Western states, and they in turn got the reassurance that the United States would neither dominate nor abandon them.

The stability of this bargain comes from its underlying logic: the postwar hegemonic order is infused with institutions and practices that reduce the returns to power. This means that the implications of winning and losing are minimized and contained. A state could "lose" in intra-Western relations and yet not worry that the winner would be able to use those winnings to permanently dominate. This is a central characteristic of domestic liberal constitutional orders. Parties that win elections must operate within well-defined limits. They cannot use their powers of incumbency to undermine or destroy the opposition party or parties. They can press the advantage of office to the limits of the law, but there are limits and laws. This reassures the losing party; it can accept its loss and prepare for the next election. The features of the postwar order—and, importantly, the open and penetrated character of the American polity itself—has mechanisms to provide the same sort of assurances to America's European and Asian partners.

Second, the institutions of American hegemony also have a durability that comes from the phenomenon of increasing returns. The overall system—organized around principles of openness, reciprocity, and multilateralism—

has become increasingly connected to the wider and deeper institutions of politics and society within the advanced industrial world. As the embeddedness of these institutions has grown, it has become increasingly difficult for potential rival states to introduce a competing set of principles and institutions. American hegemony has become highly institutionalized and path dependent. Short of large-scale war or a global economic crisis, the American hegemonic order appears to be immune to would-be hegemonic challengers. Even if a large coalition of states had interests that favored an alternative type of order, the benefits of change would have to be radically higher than those that flow from the present system to justify change. But there is no potential hegemonic state (or coalition of states) and no set of rival principles and organizations even on the horizon. The world of the 1940s contained far more rival systems, ideologies, and interests than the world of the 1990s. The phenomenon of increasing returns is really a type of positive feedback loop. If initial institutions are established successfully, where the United States and its partners have confidence in their credibility and functioning, this allows these states to make choices that serve to strengthen the binding character of these institutions.

The postwar Western order fits this basic logic. Its open and decentralized character invites participation and creates assurances of steady commitment. Its institutionalized character also provides mechanisms for the resolution of conflicts and creates assurances of continuity. Moreover, like a marriage, the interconnections and institutions of the partnership have spread and deepened. Within this open and institutionalized order, the fortune of particular states will continue to rise and fall. The United States itself, while remaining at the center of the order, also continues to experience gains and losses. But the mix of winning and losing across the system is distributed widely enough to mitigate the interest that particular states might have in replacing it. In an order where the returns to power are low and the returns to institutions are high, stability will be an inevitable feature.

Transnational Liberalism and U.S. Primacy

John M. Owen, IV

The longer U.S. global military primacy endures, the more puzzling it becomes. If, as balance-of-power theory asserts, the international system abhors imbalances of power, why is it tolerating this particular one? How can it be that the unipolar moment is now in its second decade, with few if any concrete signs of decay?

A first step toward understanding the singularity and the causes of U.S. primacy is to note that the United States enjoys being both the only pole in the international system and on the heavy end of an imbalance of world power. In principle, a unipolar international system need not be imbalanced. Neorealism, the school of thought most concerned with power, implies that a system is unipolar when the second most powerful state cannot by itself counterbalance the most powerful state. For neorealism, only states, not alliances, may be poles.[1] But in theory a pole may be counterbalanced by an alliance of nonpolar states. Thus U.S. primacy presents two puzzles: the endurance of unipolarity and the endurance of the imbalance of power.

William Wohlforth adequately explains why unipolarity is so durable. The lead of the United States over potential challengers is so great that, barring an unlikely abrupt American collapse, it will take decades for any power to gain polar status. The scale of the imbalance is a product of a number of crucial his-

John M. Owen, IV, is Assistant Professor of Government and Foreign Affairs at the University of Virginia.

The author thanks the Sesquicentennial Fellowship and the Miller Center for Public Affairs at the University of Virginia and the Center of International Studies at Princeton University for generous support, and the Rothermere American Institute and Nuffield College at the University of Oxford for a congenial venue. He is indebted to Mark Haas, John Ikenberry, Charles Kupchan, Michael McFaul, Henry Nau, William Wohlforth, and three anonymous referees for comments on previous drafts. He also thanks Rachel Vanderhill for research assistance.

1. Kenneth N. Waltz makes this clear in his *Theory of International Politics* (Reading, Mass.: Addison-Wesley, 1979). Other realists agree; cf. Randall L. Schweller, *Deadly Imbalances: Tripolarity and Hitler's Strategy of World Conquest* (New York: Columbia University Press, 1998); and William C. Wohlforth, "The Stability of a Unipolar World," *International Security*, Vol. 24, No. 1 (Summer 1999), pp. 5–41. For Schweller (*Deadly Imbalances*, p. 17), a pole "must have greater than half the military capability of the most powerful state in the system." Schweller thus implies that a state with 51 percent of the power of the most powerful state is a pole (i.e., is able internally to counterbalance the most powerful state). This is a possible operationalization of the definition of "pole" but not a necessary one, inasmuch as it defines "balance" rather broadly.

International Security, Vol. 26, No. 3 (Winter 2001/02), pp. 117–152
© 2001 by the President and Fellows of Harvard College and the Massachusetts Institute of Technology.

torical events. The United States became the world's leading economic power in the late nineteenth century; it was compelled by World War II to channel that power into military might; during the Cold War, it continued to amass power to counter its Soviet rival, while potential great powers joined it in counterbalancing; the Soviet Union suddenly disappeared in 1991; and the United States was left as the only pole. If Robert Gilpin and other hegemonic stability theorists are correct, the putative law of uneven growth ensures that unipolarity will erode.[2] The erosion may be slow, however.

Wohlforth is less convincing on the persistence of the imbalance of international power or why the American "unipole" still faces no counterbalancing coalition.[3] The United States has the world's largest economy, accounting for 23 percent of gross world product; but the European Union (EU) accounts for 20 percent, China for 12 percent, and Japan for 7 percent.[4] The United States has no monopoly on nuclear weapons or offensive delivery systems (although in many areas it enjoys a sizable qualitative advantage). In principle, therefore, a balance of power could emerge were enough states sufficiently motivated to increase their offensive capabilities and form an alliance.

Why is the rest of the world not compelled to counterbalance the United States?[5] Wohlforth and Stephen Walt argue that geography inhibits counterbalancing. The country's physical isolation from potential challengers renders it relatively nonthreatening, and any power that counterbalanced the United States would itself be counterbalanced in its own region.[6] Other scholars offer institutional, "path-dependent" explanations for continuing U.S. predominance. John Ikenberry argues that the United States and its allies are parties to an implicit constitution that limits U.S. power in exchange for cooperation; moreover, the international institutions that the United States has constructed

---

2. Robert Gilpin, *War and Change in World Politics* (New York: Cambridge University Press, 1981); see also Charles A. Kupchan, "After Pax Americana: Benign Power, Regional Integration, and the Sources of a Stable Multipolarity," *International Security*, Vol. 23, No. 2 (Fall 1998), pp. 40–79.
3. Wohlforth, "Stability of a Unipolar World," pp. 37–41, posits an extreme definition of unipolarity, namely, a situation wherein *all* counterbalancing is impossible. This definition, however, does not follow from his assertion that "alliances are not structural," because in that case a unipole could conceivably face a counterbalancing alliance. It also begs the question by implying that unipolarity endures because it is unipolarity.
4. The figures are for 1999. Central Intelligence Agency, *World Fact Book*, http://www.cia.gov/cia/publications/factbook/geos/xx.html#Econ.
5. I reduce states' options to two: counterbalancing and acquiescence. States actually have a large number of possible responses to power imbalances; for a nuanced treatment, see Schweller, *Deadly Imbalances*.
6. Wohlforth, "Stability of a Unipolar World"; and Stephen M. Walt, "Two Cheers for Clinton's Foreign Policy," *Foreign Affairs*, Vol. 79, No. 2 (March/April 2000), pp. 63–79. Wohlforth's argument is about unipolarity, but as discussed above, he also has in mind the lack of a balance of power.

since World War II pay increasing returns, raising the costs of defection over time.[7] Charles Kupchan and Josef Joffe make similar arguments. For Kupchan the United States is a benign unipole that has offered states restraint in exchange for protection.[8] For Joffe the United States maintains primacy by following a global Bismarckian strategy, eschewing conquest in favor of making itself indispensable to order in most regions of the world.[9]

None of these arguments can explain why some states are in fact counterbalancing U.S. might. The explanations commit the fallacy of inferring behavior from outcomes: They assert an absence of counterbalancing from the absence of a balance of international power. Following convention, I define counterbalancing as taking internal or external measures, or both, to increase one's military capabilities relative to a particular state or alliance.[10] It is true that neither Western Europe nor Japan is counterbalancing. Neither the formation of an EU Rapid Reaction Force to intervene for humanitarian purposes nor French grumbling about U.S. "hyperpower" constitutes counterbalancing. Japan, meanwhile, recently renewed its U.S. alliance and is cooperating with the Americans on theater missile defense (TMD).

Russia's policy has been more ambiguous. Russia has mostly acquiesced to U.S. predominance, but since 1991 has moved haltingly from a cooperative to a testy relationship with the United States. In particular, Russia attempted to block NATO, and hence U.S., control of Kosovo in June 1999 by attempting to carve out its own zone of occupation; and in July 2001 Russia entered a "friendship pact" with China.[11] China, for its part, is clearly counterbalancing the United States. Increases in its gross military spending and attempts to modernize its navy, air force, and missile arsenal are not directed solely at the

---

7. G. John Ikenberry, "Institutions, Strategic Restraint, and the Persistence of American Postwar Order," *International Security*, Vol. 23, No. 3 (Winter 1998/99), pp. 43–78.

8. Kupchan, "After Pax Americana."

9. Josef Joffe, "How America Does It," *Foreign Affairs*, Vol. 76, No. 5 (September/October 1997), pp. 13–27. Michael Mastanduno has also published work on the persistence of unipolarity. See Mastanduno, "Preserving the Unipolar Moment: Realist Theories and U.S. Grand Strategy after the Cold War," *International Security*, Vol. 21, No. 4 (Spring 1997), pp. 49–88. But he seeks to explain how U.S. policymakers are trying to preserve unipolarity, not the outcome of unipolarity (or an imbalance of power) per se.

10. Counterbalancing is thus directed at some state or coalition; not any increase in power will do. Evidence that B is increasing its power to counterbalance A is of two types: timing (when B's power increases closely follow in time those of A), and verbal statements (when officials from B say that B's power increases are intended to counterbalance A). In keeping with the literature on international security, I refer to military power. Economic and cultural assets may also be used to influence others, and indeed America's allies are attempting to counterbalance these forms of U.S. power.

11. Patrick E. Tyler, "Russia and China Sign 'Friendship' Pact," *New York Times*, July 17, 2001, p. A1.

United States. But these efforts were accelerated following U.S. successes in the Persian Gulf War of 1991 and the Kosovo campaign of 1999. Chinese military and civilian officials openly state that they consider the United States the greatest threat to their country.[12]

If it were enough that the United States is half a world away, or exploits its allies relatively little, or includes them in institutions that pay increasing returns, or is indispensable to regional order, then China and Russia ought to act as Japan does: acquiesce to U.S. power or even become a spoke of the American hub. Kenneth Waltz at least does recognize that some states are beginning to counterbalance, but he seems to include Japan on the list (without any concrete evidence), and in any case cannot say why East Asian states are doing so while West European states are not.[13] Recent explanations for U.S. predominance fall short because they employ the standard assumption that states' domestic institutions and ideologies are unit-level variables that do not belong in a theory of international politics. They hold these variables constant and posit one or another set of incentives facing potential challengers to U.S. primacy, implying that any reasonable state would not try to counterbalance the United States. Empirically, however, the net effect of the incentives clearly varies across states. That can only result from differences among the states themselves.[14]

In this article I argue that the degree to which a state counterbalances U.S. power is a function of how politically liberal that state is, measured by the degree to which its internal institutions and practices are liberal and the degree to which liberals influence foreign policy. Political liberalism is an ideology that seeks to uphold individual autonomy and prescribes a particular set of domestic institutions as means to that end.[15] No coalition has formed to counterbal-

---

12. David Shambaugh, "China's Military Views the World: Ambivalent Security," *International Security*, Vol. 24, No. 3 (Winter 1999/2000), pp. 52–79; Alastair Iain Johnston, "China's New 'Old Thinking': The Concept of Limited Deterrence," *International Security*, Vol. 20, No. 3 (Winter 1995/96), pp. 5–42; and John Pomfret, "U.S. Now a 'Threat' in China's Eyes," *Washington Post*, November 15, 2000, p. A1.
13. Kenneth N. Waltz, "Structural Realism after the Cold War," *International Security*, Vol. 25, No. 1 (Summer 2000), pp. 5–41.
14. For the original justification of this move, see Waltz, *Theory of International Politics*. Logically, of course, there is no reason to consider power an international-systemic variable but ideology or institutions domestic; one may conceive of any of these variables in relative and hence systemic terms.
15. As I use the term, liberalism must not be conflated with democracy. The two concepts overlap in theory and practice, but democracy I take to be the rule of the majority. For more on the distinction as it applies to international relations, see John M. Owen, IV, *Liberal Peace, Liberal War: American Politics and International Security* (Ithaca, N.Y.: Cornell University Press, 1997), chap. 1; and Fareed Zakaria, "The Rise of Illiberal Democracy," *Foreign Affairs*, Vol. 76, No. 6 (November/December 1997), pp. 22–43.

ance U.S. power because political liberalism constitutes a transnational movement that has penetrated most potential challenger states at least to some degree. How liberal a state is affects both how it responds to U.S. power and policy and how the United States treats it. Liberal elites the world over tend to perceive a relatively broad coincidence of interest between their country and other liberal countries. They tend to interpret the United States as benign and devote few state resources to counterbalancing it. In turn, the liberals who govern the United States tend to treat other liberal countries relatively benignly. But antiliberal elites tend to perceive a more malign United States and devote relatively more state resources to counterbalancing; the United States meanwhile tends to treat less benignly countries governed by such elites and their favored institutions.

The interactions between the United States and a given potential challenger are mutually reinforcing, and so each relationship is on a path that is difficult to abandon. Unilateral moves by the administration of George W. Bush on issues such as the environment and missile defense may perturb and even anger U.S. allies, but should not drive them toward military counter- balancing. Similarly, U.S. policies are unlikely to cause China to abandon counterbalancing. The U.S.-Russian relationship is the least settled, in part because the Russian domestic regime is itself unsettled. Should Russia end up with an antiliberal regime, it will likely counterbalance the United States more consistently. U.S. policies toward Russia can have a marginal effect on the fate of Russian liberalism: The more objectively threatening are U.S. gestures toward Russia, the more Russian liberals lose domestic credibility and influence. In this way the power of transnational liberal identity is limited, as is the durability of U.S. primacy. If Americans want to preserve primacy—and the benefits of U.S. primacy outweigh the costs for many non-Americans as well as for Americans—their country must walk a difficult line, simultaneously preserving not only its power but transnational liberalism where it can, and yet guarding against actions that appear imperialistic to foreign elites.

In the next section, I advance an explanation for continuing U.S. primacy that turns on a notion of identity derived from the social theory of Georg Simmel. Following that, I show how the argument is consistent with the evidence in Japan, Western Europe, Russia, and China. I consider various objections to the argument. Finally, I argue that, for its own good as well as the general global good, the United States ought to try to maintain its primacy for as long as it can, including by judiciously promoting and preserving political liberalism abroad.

Ideology and Strategic Preferences

States' strategic preferences—the foreign alignments desired by their governments—are a function not only of their material power but also of the ideology and relative influence of their elites.[16] Ideology shapes strategic preferences because it gives its holders a transnational group affiliation. By transnational I simply mean crossing state boundaries; members of a transnational group may be in or out of the government of a given state.[17] Transnational affiliations provide a basis for identifying with certain foreign states and against others. If elites of one ideology control foreign policy, the state will follow one set of strategic preferences; if no ideology dominates, the state's policy will be incoherent.

POLITICAL GROUPS AND IDENTITIES

Following the German sociologist Georg Simmel, I define identity as the unique set of social groups to which an actor belongs. Conceived of spatially, the "intersection of social circles" that an actor inhabits constitutes his identity. A given person will belong to an infinite number of groups: for example, males, sociologists, Germans, Berliners, and so on. No two persons belong to precisely the same set of groups, and thus each person has his own identity.[18]

Most relevant here is a political group, that is, a group constituted by a plan for ordering social life. Any such plan is a rejection of alternative plans, and hence any political group is in competition with one or more other such groups. Because political groups compete with one another, members of a given political group derive positive utility from one another's gains vis-à-vis

---

16. Cf. Andrew Moravcsik, "Taking Preferences Seriously: A Liberal Theory of International Politics," *International Organization*, Vol. 51, No. 4 (Autumn 1997), pp. 513–553.
17. Thus my definition is more general than that employed in such works as Robert O. Keohane and Joseph S. Nye, Jr., eds., *Transnational Relations and World Politics* (Cambridge, Mass.: Harvard University Press, 1970); Thomas Risse-Kappen, ed., *Bringing Transnational Relations Back In: Non-State Actors, Domestic Structures, and International Institutions* (New York: Cambridge University Press, 1995); and Margaret Keck and Kathryn Sikkink, *Advocates beyond Borders: Advocacy Networks in International Politics* (Ithaca, N.Y.: Cornell University Press, 1998). For these scholars, at least one actor in a transnational relationship must be nongovernmental (Risse-Kappen, *Bringing Transnational Relations Back In*, p. 3); for me a transnational group could in principle comprise only members of governments. J. David Singer refers to what I call transnational groups as "extra-national entities." Singer, "The Global System and Its Subsystems: A Developmental View," in James N. Rosenau, ed., *Linkage Politics: Essays on the Convergence of National and International Systems* (New York: Free Press, 1969), pp. 21–43. In the past such groups were called *international* (e.g., the Socialist International).
18. Georg Simmel, "The Web of Group Affiliations" ("Die Kreuzung sozialer Kreise," *Soziologie* [Munich: Duncker and Humblot, 1922], pp. 305–344), trans. Reinhard Bendix, in Simmel, *Conflict and the Web of Group-Affiliations* (Glencoe, Ill.: Free Press, 1955).

opposing groups. A political group's tactics may include persuasion (which, insofar as it succeeds, expands the group's membership); alliances with other groups with which it shares an enemy; bribery; and coercion.[19]

In the modern world, virtually everyone belongs to at least one political group, namely, a nation-state. The social context for a nation-state is global. A given nation-state's plan for ordering social life is that world politics should never work to its detriment. Elites involved in the domestic politics of a given state likely belong to additional political groups, namely, factions with competing visions for ordering public life.[20] Typically these groups differ over the proper scope of state power in a given area of social life (e.g., the distribution of resources, civil rights, or the religious beliefs of citizens). Because similar ideas and social conditions often exist in more than one state at once, like-minded elites in two or more states form a transnational ideological group whose members identify with one another across state boundaries. A transnational ideological group need not be centralized or regulated, nor need its members interact with one another (although they may do so, as with the various socialist and communist internationals). What makes it a group is the intersubjective understanding that its members have one or more ideological enemies in common.

As David Skidmore writes, members of a transnational ideological group tend to derive positive utility from one another's gains vis-à-vis opposing ideological groups.[21] By contrast, they will perceive losses in their own power from increases in the power of opposing ideological groups in other states. Members of a transnational group do not simply see and act similarly; they feel solidarity for one another.[22]

---

19. For discussions of these activities and applications to international relations, see Audie Klotz, *Norms in International Relations: The Struggle against Apartheid* (Ithaca, N.Y.: Cornell University Press, 1995), especially pp. 152–164; Martha Finnemore, *National Interests and International Society* (Ithaca, N.Y.: Cornell University Press, 1996); and Thomas Risse, Stephen C. Ropp, and Kathryn Sikkink, eds., *The Power of Human Rights: International Norms and Domestic Change* (New York: Cambridge University Press, 1999), especially the introductory essay by Risse and Sikkink (pp. 1–38).
20. Cf. Carl Schmitt, *The Concept of the Political*, trans. George Schwab (New Brunswick, N.J.: Rutgers University Press, 1976). For Schmitt politics was essentially a struggle among competing ways of life.
21. David Skidmore, "Introduction: Bringing Social Orders Back In," in Skidmore, ed., *Contested Social Orders and International Politics* (Nashville: Vanderbilt University Press, 1997), pp. 5–6. Skidmore refers to competing domestic social orders whose members form cross-national coalitions, rather than to transnational ideological groups, but the concept is virtually the same.
22. Transnational ideological groups are conceptually similar to the transnational civilizations explored in Samuel P. Huntington, *The Clash of Civilizations and the Remaking of World Order* (New York: Simon and Schuster, 1996). Huntington's civilizations, however, are constituted by fundamental worldviews best described as religious. Civilizations and political ideologies may correlate

THE NATIONAL INTEREST

An elite who belongs to a transnational ideological group as well as to a nation-state will have a conception of his state's interests that integrates the visions of the two groups. The national interest for him will include the particular way of life prescribed by his ideology, and hence particular institutions, as well as security from attack. Physical security is a necessary condition for his preferred way of life, but that priority does not necessarily lead him to set aside domestic ideology when thinking about foreign policy. Rather, ideology will to a greater or lesser extent color his perception of foreign threats.

The extent to which an elite will identify threats based on ideology will vary with which component—internal or external—of his conception of the national interest is more threatened. If the greater threat is a domestic ideological enemy, he will defend his ideology more vigorously and identify more strongly with fellow ideologues in other countries. The limiting case is a civil war.[23] If the greater threat is a foreign state, he will defend his country's security more vigorously and identify more with fellow nationals of whatever ideology. The limiting case is an interstate war. When the ratio of internal to external threats approaches one to one, as when his government faces no serious internal *or* external threats, he will feel moderate solidarity with both his ideological group and his nation-state, and will tend to see no conflict between the two groups.[24]

IDENTITIES AND STRATEGIC PREFERENCES

The more a state governed by an ideology acts as an instrument of that ideology, the more members of its ideological group feel solidarity with that state. A state acts as an instrument of its governing ideology when it promotes that ideology within or without its borders. Revolutionary states are especially prone to such promotions, but normal states engage in them as well.[25] It follows that adherents to a given ideology will want to treat more kindly a state governed

---

to some extent, but political ideologies such as liberal democracy or Marxism-Leninism are trans-civilizational (and civilizations such as Islam are trans-ideological).

23. Cf. Karl Deutsch, "External Involvement in Internal War," in Harry Eckstein, ed., *Internal War: Problems and Approaches* (New York: Free Press, 1964), p. 103.

24. The process is similar to what Steven R. David has called "omnibalancing," or the balancing of domestic and foreign threats in which leaders of many third world countries engaged during the Cold War. David, however, explicitly downplays any role for ideology in the production of threats. David, *Choosing Sides: Alignment and Realignment in the Third World* (Baltimore, Md.: Johns Hopkins University Press, 1991).

25. On revolutionary states and ideological promotion, see Stephen M. Walt, *Revolution and War* (Ithaca, N.Y.: Cornell University Press, 1996); on promotion by normal states, see John M. Owen, IV, "The International Promotion of Domestic Institutions," *International Organization*, Vol. 56, No. 2 (Spring 2002).

by their ideology, particularly one that promotes it; and they will be inclined to be confrontational toward a state governed by an enemy ideology. It also follows that such adherents will derive positive utility from the gains of a state governed by their ideology, and negative utility from the gains of a state governed by an enemy ideology. As outlined above, the intensity of these preferences and utilities will vary directly with the degree to which these adherents face ideological threats in their own countries. In normal times, members of an ideological group will simply be complacent about the gains of exemplary states.

If war is what Clausewitz said it is—"an act of violence intended to compel our opponent to fulfill our will"[26]—then it is easy to see why adherents to an ideology will have little to fear from an increase in the power of a state ruled by their ideology. Across countries, members of an ideological group share the end of broadening and deepening support for their ideology. Thus the will of a state ruled by members of the group overlaps significantly with the will of group members in other countries. It would make little sense for the latter to invest many resources in counterbalancing that state. Conversely, ideological group members will have good reason to fear, and counterbalance, states governed by an opposing group.[27] The empirical record shows that victors in war often impose new domestic institutions upon states they defeat.[28]

INTERNATIONAL OUTCOMES

The longer states continue to interact in a particular pattern, be it friendly or hostile, the more their governing elites both expect the pattern to continue and act so as to perpetuate it. Departing from the predominant patterns entails var-

---

26. Carl von Clausewitz, *On War*, ed. Anatol Rapaport (New York: Penguin, 1982), Bk. 1, chap. 2, p. 101.
27. The Monroe Doctrine of December 1823 illustrates that the degree to which governments fear that foreign power depends on the purpose to which that power is likely to be put, and that purpose is often tied to ideology. "The *political system* of the allied powers is *essentially different* in this respect from that of America," declared Monroe. "We owe it, therefore, to candor and to the amicable relations existing between the United States and those powers to declare that we should consider any attempt on their part to *extend their system* to any portion of this hemisphere as dangerous to our peace and safety" (emphasis added). Monroe went on to emphasize the French imposition of absolute monarchy in Spain, which had ended a few weeks before. The text of Monroe's address is available at http://www.yale.edu/lawweb/avalon/monroe.htm.
28. Suzanne Werner, "Absolute and Limited War: The Possibility of Foreign-Imposed Regime Change," *International Interactions*, Vol. 22, No. 1 (1996), pp. 67–88; Bruce Bueno de Mesquita and Randolph Siverson, "Nasty or Nice? Political Systems, Endogenous Norms, and the Treatment of Adversaries," *Journal of Conflict Resolution*, Vol. 41, No. 1 (February 1997), pp. 175–199; and Owen, "International Promotion of Domestic Institutions." Of course, war victors often replace the leaders of states they defeat; see, for example, Henk E. Goemans, *War and Punishment: The Causes of War Termination and the First World War* (Princeton, N.J.: Princeton University Press, 2000).

ious psychic and political costs. Typically it will also entail material costs, inasmuch as prudent elites will use the state to broaden and deepen support for their strategic preferences. They will attempt to bind future governments of their country to their preferred alignments through treaties and membership in international organizations. They will create societal interests in continuing the alignment by encouraging economic interdependence with countries governed by their ideology. They will seek to discourage alignments with states having an opposing ideology by entering fewer treaties and minimizing economic interdependence with them.[29]

Of course, international alignments do change. Ideologies that stress correctness over consent, such as Marxism-Leninism, tend to yield brittle alliances; adherents to such ideologies are quick to pronounce one another heretical.[30] Liberalism, with its emphasis on choice, is less prone to heresy hunting, and hence its alliances are more robust.[31] But even liberal alliances are vulnerable to the familiar pressures of international anarchy, in particular the security dilemma, wherein steps taken by state A to enhance its security may cause B to feel less secure and thereby to take steps that make A feel less secure.[32] The

---

29. See, for example, Joanna Gowa, *Allies, Adversaries, and International Trade* (Princeton, N.J.: Princeton University Press, 1994); and Brian Pollins, "Does Trade Still Follow the Flag?" *American Political Science Review*, Vol. 83, No. 2 (June 1989), pp. 465–480. Thus the arguments of Kupchan ("After Pax Americana"), Ikenberry ("Institutions, Strategic Restraint, and the Persistence of American Postwar Order"), Joffe ("How America Does It"), and others are valid as far as they go; but they only go so far as the zone of liberal states. Put another way, the relations between the United States and its liberal allies on the one hand, and nonliberal states on the other, are "path-dependent," meaning that changing the quality of those relations becomes increasingly costly, in psychic as well as material terms, over time. On path dependence, see Paul Pierson, "Increasing Returns, Path Dependence, and the Study of Politics," *American Political Science Review*, Vol. 94, No. 2 (June 2000), pp. 251–268.
30. Cf. Chen Jian and Yang Kuisong, "Chinese Politics and the Collapse of the Sino-Soviet Alliance," in Odd Arne Westad, ed., *Brothers in Arms: The Rise and Fall of the Sino-Soviet Alliance, 1945–1963* (Washington, D.C.: Woodrow Wilson Center Press, 1998). See also the vigorous and once-secret debates between Soviet and Chinese diplomats over Stalinism, available on the web site of the Woodrow Wilson Center's Cold War International History Project, http://cwihp.si.edu. See, for example, Zhang Shu Guang and Chen Jian, eds. and trans., "The Emerging Disputes between Beijing and Moscow: Ten Newly Available Chinese Documents, 1956–1958"; and, specifically on Soviet worries about Chinese communist ideology, see V.M. Zubok, ed. and trans., "A New 'Cult of Personality': Suslov's Secret Reports on Mao, Khrushchev, and Sino-Soviet Tensions, December 1959."
31. See Stephen M. Walt, *The Origins of Alliances* (Ithaca, N.Y.: Cornell University Press, 1987), pp. 35–37; Owen, *Liberal Peace, Liberal War*, pp. 35–36; and Mark L. Haas, "Systemic Ideology and National Threat: Ideological Affinity and Threat Perception in International Relations," Ph.D. dissertation, University of Virginia, 2000, chap. 1.
32. For definitive works on the security dilemma, see John H. Herz, "Idealist Internationalism and the Security Dilemma," *World Politics*, Vol. 2, No. 2 (January 1950), pp. 157–180; and Robert Jervis, "Cooperation under the Security Dilemma," *World Politics*, Vol. 30, No. 2 (January 1978), pp. 167–214.

security dilemma is mitigated but does not disappear among elites who share an ideology but live in different countries. Even if A is a liberal exemplar, policies its government implements to enhance national security may unambiguously degrade B's security. Consider relations between the United States and India, two liberal giants, from the early 1960s through the early 1990s. China's conflicts with both the Soviet Union and India led the latter two to align, which in turn alienated the United States from India. Tensions were exacerbated in the early 1970s when Richard Nixon's administration cultivated relations with China and tilted toward Pakistan. The natural affinity between India and the United States was overshadowed by international rivalries.[33]

Even if ideological brethren do not sour on foreign ideological exemplars, their influence within their own state may shrink simply because the foreign exemplar is not conforming to their predictions. An ideology claims to explain the political world and asserts that its own adherents will act rightly, nobly, and peacefully, while adherents to opposing ideologies will act wrongly, shamefully, and aggressively. When those assertions appear falsified, the ideology's credibility is damaged and its support may decay. Like Thomas Kuhn's scientific paradigms,[34] ideologies move toward crises as anomalies accumulate. Suppose republicans in B assert that A, being a republic, is pacific (unlike monarchies, which on their reckoning are warlike). If A repeatedly displays unambiguously aggressive tendencies or aligns with B's enemy, thus appearing to threaten B's security, republicanism will have suffered a defeat within B. At that point republicans may either suffer a loss of ideological credibility or conceal their strategic preferences.[35] The case of the Italian left and the Soviet Union following World War II is illustrative. Italian communists and socialists were openly pro-Soviet and anti-American, opposing both NATO membership and Marshall Plan aid. They were poised to win the crucial April 1948 parliamentary elections until, two months before the balloting, the communists in Czechoslovakia carried out their infamous coup. When the Italian left refused

---

33. See, for example, Stephen M. Walt, "Testing Theories of Alliance Formation: The Case of Southwest Asia," *International Organization*, Vol. 42, No. 2 (Spring 1988), especially pp. 299–302. On the tilt toward Pakistan, see Henry A. Kissinger, *White House Years* (Boston: Little, Brown, 1979), chap. 21.

34. See Thomas S. Kuhn, *The Structure of Scientific Revolutions* (Chicago: University of Chicago Press, 1962).

35. On the falsification of preferences for political reasons, see Timur Kuran, "Ethnic Dissimilation and Its International Diffusion," in David A. Lake and Donald Rothchild, *The International Spread of Ethnic Conflict: Fear, Diffusion, and Escalation* (Princeton, N.J.: Princeton University Press, 1998), pp. 35–60.

to condemn this clear act of Soviet aggression, their credibility plummeted, helping the Christian Democrats to win the Italian election.[36]

Thus realist and constructivist theories that ascribe importance to international interactions are correct.[37] Treating another country as an enemy may make it into one, inasmuch as it can weaken those actors in that state who have staked their reputations on one's good intentions toward their country.[38] But contrary to the assertions of theories that ignore domestic politics, the rate at which B becomes A's enemy or friend will vary with its degree of ideological affinity with A. Hence a state can act more harshly for longer toward states governed by its own ideology without alienating them.

Transnational Liberalism and Potential Challengers

What follows is not a rigorous test of hypotheses deduced from my argument, but rather some observations on various potential challengers to U.S. primacy. My argument would attribute the persistence of the imbalance of international power to the wide distribution and influence of a particular transnational ideological group, namely, liberals. By liberals I mean elites who hold as normative the tenets of political liberalism, an ideology that asserts the autonomy of the individual as the highest good. Liberals believe that each person (minors, the mentally incapable, and felons excepted) ought to be allowed to pursue her happiness as she sees fit, so long as she does not violate the autonomy of another. Any coercion must be by an authority to which individuals have voluntarily handed over coercive power. Liberalism implies certain governmental institutions, preeminently those limiting the power of the state over the individual. Examples include freedoms of speech, the press, assembly, and religion; various juridical rights; and regularly held, competitive elections. Because they are involved in politics—a struggle for power—liberals may employ illiberal means to liberal ends. Lyndon Johnson used his power as a U.S. senator and then president to liberal ends; but to gain that power he probably

---

36. James Edward Miller, *The United States and Italy, 1940–1950: The Politics of Diplomacy and Stabilization* (Chapel Hill: University of North Carolina Press), pp. 147–150; and Donald Sassoon, "Italian Images of Russia, 1945–56," in Christopher Duggan and Christopher Wagstaff, eds., *Italy in the Cold War: Politics, Culture, and Society, 1948–58* (Oxford: Berg, 1995), p. 198.
37. Realists making this claim include Stephen Walt, *Origins of Alliances*, who argues that states judge threats based in part upon evidence of aggressive intention. Constructivists include Alexander Wendt, *Social Theory of International Politics* (New York: Cambridge University Press, 1999), who argues that the norm governing relations among states—whether competitive, cooperative, or altruistic—is built upon the quality of gestures they make toward one another.
38. Of course, treating another country as a friend when it is an ideological enemy may also be dangerous, as the British and French learned in 1939.

stole the 1948 U.S. Senate election in Texas.[39] What makes a politician liberal are his ends more than his means. At some point, however, the distinction between means and ends disappears; thus for example I do not classify as liberal former Russian President Boris Yeltsin, inasmuch as he behaved illiberally on so many occasions.[40]

Modern liberalism arose in Western Europe during the Enlightenment (seventeenth and eighteenth centuries). From the beginning liberalism was transnational, with elite propagators in Scotland, England, France, Prussia, and elsewhere. The links between liberals in France and Britain's American colonies in the late eighteenth century, brought out most starkly in the two revolutions in these lands, are perhaps the most dramatic evidence. Liberalism continued to spread until World War I, after which it retreated in many regions in the face of fascism and Marxism-Leninism. Although it vanquished each of these ideological foes during the twentieth century, liberalism is not predominant in every region of the world. For now, however, it is the "prevailing nostrum," the agenda-setting ideology that puts its competitors on the defensive in most regions.[41]

Table 1 lists military spending by the most plausible counterbalancers. As explained below, the degree of a state's liberalism correlates well with the degree to which it has been counterbalancing the United States.

THE EUROPEAN UNION AND JAPAN: LIBERAL ACQUIESCENCE

Western Europe's leading military powers, with the partial exception of France, are not counterbalancing U.S. power. Military spending in France and Germany in the latter half of the 1990s was flat, and British spending actually declined slightly (see Table 1). Far from abandoning the Atlantic alliance through which they have bandwagoned with the United States since the late 1940s, Germany, France, and Britain participated in the 1999 Kosovo air war,

---

39. The case is made forcefully in Robert Caro, *Means of Ascent: The Years of Lyndon Johnson* (New York: Vintage, 1991), Vol. 2.

40. Among Yeltsin's illiberal policies were the 1997 law restricting religious freedom and the brutal suppression of the Chechen rebellion. He also chose the competent but nonliberal Vladimir Putin as his successor. For a severe critique of Yeltsin's liberal-democratic credentials, see Lilia Shevtsova, "Yeltsin and the Evolution of Electoral Monarchy in Russia," *Current History*, Vol. 99, No. 639 (October 2000), pp. 315–320. For Yeltsin's defense of these and other policies, see Boris Yeltsin, *Midnight Diaries*, trans. Catherine A. Fitzpatrick (New York: PublicAffairs, 2000). I thank Alex Pravda and Marcia Weigle for helping me think through this issue.

41. Francis Fukuyama, *The End of History and the Last Man* (New York: Free Press, 1992); and Samuel P. Huntington, *The Third Wave* (Norman: University of Oklahoma Press, 1991), p. 33. On the near-global ascendancy of human rights norms (a subset of liberal norms), see Risse, Ropp, and Sikkink, *Power of Human Rights*.

Table 1. Military Spending, 1995–99 (in 1995 $U.S. billions).

	1995	1996	1997	1998	1999	Rank (1999)
United States	278.9	263.7	262.2	256.1	259.9	1
Japan	50.1	51.1	51.3	51.3	51.2	2
France	47.8	46.6	46.8	45.5	46.8	3
Germany	41.2	40.3	38.9	39.0	39.5	4
Great Britain	33.8	34.4	32.3	32.6	31.8	5
Russia	25.7	23.4	24.9	18.1	22.4	7
China	12.5	13.7	14.9	16.9	18.4	8
India	8.0	8.2	8.9	9.3	10.2	12

SOURCE: Stockholm International Peace Research Institute, http://projects.sipri.se/milex/mex_major_spenders.html.

one of whose purposes was to maintain NATO's credibility. Their dependence on U.S. offensive power in that war—80 percent of sorties were flown by U.S. aircraft—has led them to discuss improving their offensive capabilities.[42] That concern, in turn, has led to the creation of a 60,000-person EU Rapid Reaction Force to deal quickly with any future humanitarian crises. Only the French have portrayed this new force as independent of NATO, but at the EU summit in Nice in December 2000, even the French agreed that the Atlantic alliance would remain supreme in Western Europe.[43] Still, France is more dissatisfied with U.S. primacy than are other U.S. allies, and I discuss possible reasons for this dissatisfaction in a later section.

Neither is Japan counterbalancing the United States. Its aggregate military spending remains around 1 percent of its gross national product. It is increasing its ability to defend itself against missile attacks by building four space surveillance satellites and developing theater missile defense. These policies, however, are clearly in reaction to the North Korean launch of a Taepo-Dong missile over Japan in August 1998. Japan's TMD initiative was at the prodding of the United States itself and is a joint U.S.-Japanese venture.[44] Indeed, far from attempting to form any anti-U.S. alliance, Tokyo renewed the 1960 U.S.-Japanese security treaty in 1997. The Japanese Diet has yet to approve all of the

42. See, for example, "The Two Main Things," *Economist*, July 31, 1999, survey section, pp. 14–16.
43. "So That's All Agreed, Then," *Economist*, December 16, 2000, pp. 25–30.
44. Richard Tanter, "Japan and the Coming East Asian Explosion," *Arena*, August 1999, p. 44.

details of the new treaty, but the chances of repudiation appear nil.[45] Despite increasing domestic political costs, successive governments have continued to favor the presence of four U.S. naval bases on Japanese territory.[46]

Japanese and West European relative acquiescence to U.S. power is caused in part by the predominance of liberalism in these societies. Along with North America, Western Europe and Japan are the most liberal areas of the world. Although these countries have antiliberal elements, such as ultranationalists and communists, all are liberal democracies overwhelmingly dominated by liberal elites. To varying degrees their governments often criticize U.S. internal and external policies, even to the point where they sound anti-American. Yet elites in most of these countries do not appear to fear that the United States will use its massive power against them. Many even indirectly support U.S. primacy by asserting that in today's world military power matters little, thereby absolving their countries of the need to counterbalance.

This state of affairs is helped by the relatively benign way in which the United States treats its allies. Although most European elites believe that some U.S. policies, particularly regarding missile defense and the environment, are contrary to their countries' interests,[47] no one could reasonably construe any U.S. intention to attack or blackmail Europe or Japan. Nor have America's huge military budget, its continuing network of overseas bases, and its ability to project massive force quickly and accurately induced any such fear. In the case of Japan and Germany, this acquiescence to American power is partly the product of deliberate U.S. efforts after 1945 to reconstruct the defeated Axis powers into liberal countries that shared U.S. goals for international and domestic order.[48] Because the United States imposed its will upon them in the 1940s, they need not fear that it will do so again. Being non-Americans as well as liberals, Western European and Japanese liberals may prefer a multipolar world, but the preference is not strong enough to cause them to devote many

---

45. Yoichiro Sato, "Will the U.S.-Japan Alliance Continue?" *New Zealand International Review*, Vol. 24, No. 4 (July 1999), p. 10.

46. Lisa Troshinsky, "U.S. Navy Trying to Keep Asia-Pacific Bases Low-Key: Naval War College Guru," *Navy News & Undersea Technology*, June 26, 2000, p. 1. Waltz, "Structural Realism after the Cold War," pp. 33–35, notes increases in Japanese defensive capabilities but cites no evidence that they are reactions to U.S. power. Indeed, insofar as Japan is rearming, Waltz suggests that it is because of a fear that the United States may *decrease* its power in East Asia. That may be correct, but it would not vindicate predictions that Japan will counterbalance U.S. power.

47. The tensions surrounding President George W. Bush's June 2001 visit to Europe are illustrative. See, for example, Martin Fletcher and Giles Whittell, "Europe Vents Its Anger against Bush," *Times* (London), June 15, 2001, p. 1.

48. G. John Ikenberry and Charles A. Kupchan, "Socialization and Hegemonic Power," *International Organization*, Vol. 44, No. 3 (Summer 1990), pp. 283–315.

resources to bring that world about. Not only are they complacent regarding U.S. primacy, but they advocate aiding and abetting that primacy by continuing their alliances and, in the German and Japanese cases, hosting thousands of U.S. forces. Even French elites who carp about U.S. hyperpower and yearn for multipolarity do not call for policies that would go any way toward redressing the international imbalance of power.

That the common bond is at bottom political liberalism is evident in the NATO action in Kosovo in 1999. Here the United States and its European allies put offensive air power—at great financial and, for some, domestic political cost—at the service of liberal purposes. They even agreed that the force should be constrained according to liberal norms. For them the war was not about extending U.S. power into a region traditionally in Russia's sphere of influence. It was rather a multilateral, just use of force that would vindicate human rights in Kosovo. Robert Art argues that the Europeans continue to aid and abet U.S. power primarily out of fear of "renationalization" or a return to the destructive rivalries of the past.[49] But if that were the entire story, antiliberals in Russia, the country that lost more than any other from the twentieth century's nationalistic wars, should likewise desire to aid and abet U.S. power.

RUSSIA: AMBIGUITY FROM A DIVIDED SOCIETY

The Russian case is complicated. Russian military spending declined slightly in the latter half of the 1990s (Table 1), reflecting the dire situation of the Russian economy. Despite its massive nuclear arsenal, Russia has made no serious attempts to blackmail the United States.[50] Still, observers agree that Russian policy generally moved from pro- to anti-Western in the 1990s.[51] Two Russian policies in particular appear intended to help counterbalance the United States. First, Russia challenged NATO, and hence the United States, in the aftermath of the Kosovo war by stationing troops in Kosovo. The offensive capability of this Russian brigade is negligible, but it does serve to check Wash-

---

49. See Robert J. Art, "Why Western Europe Needs the United States and NATO," *Political Science Quarterly,* Vol. 111, No. 1 (Spring 1996), pp. 1–39.
50. Russian President Boris Yeltsin did make noises about the United States triggering World War III, but his aides quickly spun the statement into oblivion. See Dmitry Gornostayev, "Clinton 'Might Run Right into a New World War': With That Warning, Boris Yeltsin Intends to Avert Missile Strikes against Iraq," *Current Digest of the Post-Soviet Press,* Vol. 50, No. 5 (March 4, 1998), pp. 5–6.
51. Michael McFaul, "Russia's Many Foreign Policies," *Demokratizatsiya,* Vol. 7, No. 3 (Summer 1999), pp. 393–412; and Sergei Medvedev, "Power, Space, and Russian Foreign Policy," in Ted Hopf, ed., *Understandings of Russian Foreign Policy* (University Park: Pennsylvania State University Press, 1999), pp. 15–55.

ington's ability to control events in southeastern Europe. Certainly the Russian military intended the troops to counterbalance U.S. strength in the region, as seen by the troops' seizure of the Priština airport in advance of NATO forces in June 1999.[52] Second, in July 2001 the Russian and Chinese governments signed a treaty of friendship and peace. Russian and Chinese officials assert that the treaty is not directed against any third country, but the document pledges opposition to U.S. missile defense and formalizes Russian support for Chinese claims to Taiwan. Both governments clearly intend for the treaty to counter the U.S.-sponsored global order.[53]

Since 1991 the Russian polity has oscillated between authoritarianism and democracy. Political power has been dispersed among bureaus, branches of government, and geographical regions. The dispersal of power has been crucial to the ambiguity of Russian foreign policy, inasmuch as it has allowed various societal interests and ideological groups influence over particular issue areas.[54] Under Boris Yeltsin's presidency, policy fluctuated all the more because of Yeltsin's tendency to encourage and exploit factionalism within his own government.[55] Deep ideological fissures tear at Russia because it was never militarily defeated and occupied by the United States; America could not eradicate communism there after 1991 as it eradicated fascism in Japan and Germany after 1945. Russian elites thus include not only liberals—who favor eventual political as well as economic liberalization—but also ultranationalists, communists, and moderates. These factions react to U.S. primacy in predictable ways: Liberals tend to favor acquiescence, the far left and right tend to favor counterbalancing, and the center tends to cut a middle course.[56] The first observation about Russia's policy toward U.S. power, then, is that it correlates

---

52. McFaul, "Russia's Many Foreign Policies," pp. 404–408.
53. Tyler, "Russia and China Sign 'Friendship' Pact."
54. See Celeste A. Wallander, ed., *Sources of Russian Foreign Policy after the Cold War* (Boulder, Colo.: Westview, 1996); and Neil Malcolm, "Foreign Policy Making," in Malcolm, Alex Pravda, Roy Allison, and Margot Light, *Internal Factors in Russian Foreign Policy* (Oxford: Clarendon, 1996), pp. 101–168. For an argument that Russian foreign policy has been consistent, see Allen Lynch, "The Realism of Russia's Foreign Policy," *Europe-Asia Studies*, Vol. 53, No. 1 (January 2001), pp. 7–31.
55. McFaul, "Russia's Many Foreign Policies," p. 407.
56. See, for example, Malcolm et al., *Internal Factors in Russian Foreign Policy*, passim, especially the table on p. 24. On the 1992–95 period, Alex Pravda and Neil Malcolm write that Russian "preferences and stances on external issues broadly correspond to those on internal affairs." Pravda and Malcolm, "Conclusion," in ibid., p. 291; see also p. 287. See also McFaul, "Russia's Many Foreign Policies," pp. 393–412; and Elizabeth Wishnick, "Prospects for the Sino-Russian Partnership: Views from Moscow and the Russian Far East," *Journal of East Asian Affairs*, Vol. 12, No. 2 (Summer/Fall 1998), p. 421.

to Russia's domestic structure. Both its policies and its degree of liberalism lie between those of Western Europe and Japan on the one hand, and China on the other.

Second, changes in Russian politics and policy over the 1990s correlate in the same way. At the dawn of Russia's anticommunist revolution, from 1991 through late 1992, political and economic liberals had their way in the Kremlin. Yeltsin's first foreign minister, Andrei Kozyrev, wanted Russia to become like and join the West. During his early months in office, Kozyrev was almost sycophantic toward the United States, even favoring NATO's eastward expansion. A shift occurred in late 1993, when the Kremlin reversed itself on that issue.[57] In February 1994 Russia suddenly obstructed NATO's efforts to bring to heel the Bosnian Serbs besieging Sarajevo by announcing that it would send peacekeeping troops to the area.[58] Yeltsin also began to increase Russia's weapons exports to China and Iran in 1994.[59] Since then, Russia has by no means returned to the unambiguous counterbalancing policies of the Soviet era, but neither has it been as cooperative as the Japanese and West Europeans. It has sought to slow NATO expansion, although it also joined the Partnership for Peace; it has tried to limit NATO's military actions in Bosnia-Herzegovina and Kosovo, although it has done so in part by joining the Kosovo occupation force.

Coincident with Russia's shift away from acquiescence to testiness vis-à-vis U.S. power has been a general reduction in the influence of liberals within Russia itself. Liberals began to lose power at the end of 1992, when Yeltsin fired Yegor Gaidar, his unabashedly reformist prime minister, and replaced him with Viktor Chernomyrdin, a moderate former Soviet official and founder of Gazprom, the natural gas monopoly. Gaidar returned to government briefly in late 1993, but the trend away from liberalism continued as Aleksandr Korzhakov, Yeltsin's authoritarian security chief and bodyguard, began to exert increasing influence over the president due in part to the liberals' failure to end the Chechen rebellion.[60] In January 1996, a month after the communist

---

57. Paul Marantz, "Neither Adversaries nor Partners: Russia and the West Search for a New Relationship," in Roger E. Kanet and Alexander V. Kozhemiakin, eds., *The Foreign Policy of the Russian Federation* (New York: Macmillan, 1997), pp. 92–96; and Johanna Granville, "After Kosovo: The Impact of NATO Expansion on Russian Political Parties," *Demokratizatsiya*, Vol. 8, No. 1 (Winter 2000), pp. 24–45.

58. Marantz, "Neither Adversaries nor Partners," p. 89.

59. Coit D. Blacker, "Russia and the West," in Michael Mandelbaum, ed., *The New Russian Foreign Policy* (New York: Council on Foreign Relations, 1998), pp. 181–182.

60. Chrystia Freeland, *Sale of the Century: The Inside Story of the Second Russian Revolution* (Boston: Little, Brown, 2000), pp. 159–160; and Yeltsin, *Midnight Diaries*, p. 215.

electoral victory in the Duma, Yeltsin sacked the liberals Kozyrev and Anatoly Chubais, replacing the former as foreign minister with the antiliberal Yevgeny Primakov. But liberal influence increased again following Yeltsin's electoral victory, as the president fired Korzhakov and called Chubais and the liberal Boris Nemtsov into his government. In August 1998 came yet another reversal of liberal fortune, as Yeltsin named Primakov as prime minister; the latter's loyal aide Igor Ivanov became foreign minister. In May 1999 Primakov himself was replaced by the hapless Sergei Stepashin, who was in turn replaced by Vladimir Putin in August.[61] Putin, whose domestic policies suggest decidedly illiberal leanings, became acting president in January 2000 and was elected president the following March.

This riot of names and sackings suggests that liberals have not held supreme power since late 1992 but that they have nonetheless retained some influence, at least so long as Yeltsin was president. The foreign policy of Russia defies explanation by one variable as much as that of any nation. Nonetheless, evidence suggests that the Kremlin's vague policy vis-à-vis U.S. power is partially a function of the power of liberals within the Russian government. The macrotrends away from domestic liberalism and a pro-U.S. foreign policy are roughly coincident. As Alex Pravda and Neil Malcolm write of the 1991–95 period, "The phases through which Russian external policy passed broadly corresponded to stages in internal political development."[62] Efforts toward the alignment with China, for example, have accelerated since Putin became president.[63]

A third observation is that although antiliberal Russians exaggerate U.S. hostility to their country, the United States has treated Russia less kindly than it has Western Europe and Japan. The most obvious example has been Washington's refusal to support offering NATO membership to Russia. Other former communist countries—Poland, the Czech Republic, and Hungary—have been admitted. Those that have not—for example, Slovakia, Romania, and Bulgaria—are, like Russia, countries that have not demonstrated that they are stable, durable liberal democracies.[64]

---

61. The chronology is drawn from Freeland, *Sale of the Century*, pp. 340–346; and Yeltsin, *Midnight Diaries*, pp. xi–xvi.
62. Pravda and Malcolm, "Conclusion," p. 301.
63. "Partners of Inconvenience: The Russo-Chinese Partnership," *Economist*, January 20, 2001, p. 4.
64. All in all, it is wise to restrict NATO membership to stable liberal democracies. And as Michael McFaul has pointed out to me, no Russian government has ever formally asked to join NATO. Still, signaling Russia that it is not on the list for NATO membership may aggravate Russian apprehensions about U.S. intentions. For an argument that Russia should be admitted to NATO, see Bruce

A final observation is that even some U.S. policies not intended as anti-Russian have been perceived as such and may have contributed to the waning influence of liberalism in Russia. Events within the country itself are the primary causes of liberalism's decline. Economic reform failed to live up to its promises, most obviously in the August 1998 financial crash that led to the premiership of Primakov. Although recent statistics are somewhat encouraging, the country's economy has shrunk since the end of communism, corruption remains the surest path to prosperity, and average citizens' savings have been destroyed by economic crises. Yet certain U.S. moves appear to have undermined the liberals' claim that the West no longer threatens Russian security. NATO's eastward expansion and the Kosovo war—which was NATO's first use of offensive force, and that in an area of traditional Russian influence—confirmed the predictions of antiliberals and falsified those of liberals. During the Kosovo war, a common complaint among liberals was that the United States was aiding the Russian far left and far right. "Clinton Is an Honorary Member of the Russian Communist Party" may sound like a headline from America's own John Birch Society, but it actually appeared in a liberal Russian periodical.[65] Public opposition to NATO's expansion spread and deepened following Kosovo.[66]

A similar reaction has greeted accelerating U.S. plans for missile defense. The Russian fear is not simply that a successful missile defense would weaken nuclear deterrence, because the Europeans share this fear. Rather, with the decaying of its conventional forces, Russia has begun to rely on its nuclear arsenal as a war-fighting force.[67] The inference is that at least some Russian officials contemplate a future conflict with the United States. (Note, however, that the Putin government has responded favorably to U.S. proposals to include Russia

Russett and John Oneal, *Triangulating Peace: Democracy, Interdependence, and International Organizations* (New York: W.W. Norton, 2001), pp. 288–297.

65. Sarah Karush, "Kosovo Could Leave Lasting Stain on U.S. Ties," *Moscow Times,* March 30, 1999, n.p. See also Vladimir Shlapentokh, "Aftermath of the Balkan War, the Rise of Anti-Americanism, and the End of Democracy in Russia," *World and I,* Vol. 14, No. 10 (October 1999), p. 310.

66. Granville, "After Kosovo," pp. 38–39.

67. Celeste A. Wallander, "Russia's New Security Policy and the Ballistic Missile Defense Debate," *Current History,* Vol. 99, No. 639 (October 2000), pp. 339–344. For the official Russian view, see Igor Ivanov, "The Missile-Defense Mistake: Undermining Strategic Stability and the ABM Treaty," *Foreign Affairs,* Vol. 79, No. 5 (September/October 2000), pp. 15–20. Advocates of missile defense point out that it is not the comprehensive Strategic Defense Initiative or "Star Wars" envisaged by Ronald Reagan. It is limited to intercepting up to thirty missiles, and is thus designed to deter states or other actors with small nuclear arsenals. See "Talbott Predicts Russian Agreement on Missile Defense," United Press International, January 17, 2001, provided by Comtex, http://www.comtexnews.com.

in an international missile defense scheme, perhaps because of its own fears of "rogue states.")[68]

CHINA: ANTILIBERAL COUNTERBALANCING

China is the second-tier power that is most clearly trying to counterbalance the United States, albeit at a slow pace. From 1995 to 1999, Chinese military spending grew by an average of 10 percent per annum; although that is in line with the growth of China's economy, it does contrast to the *negative* relation between military and economic growth in Western Europe and the United States itself during the same period. Adjusted for inflation, real growth in Chinese military spending from 1987 to 1997 was approximately 4 percent.[69] The government recently launched a navigation positioning satellite to improve missile accuracy.[70] China is also modernizing its navy and air force, partly through purchases of foreign fighter aircraft, AWACS and in-flight refueling technology, missile guided destroyers, and submarines as quiet as those of the U.S. Navy.[71] It is also improving its medium- and possibly long-range missiles. In August 1999 China tested its DF-31 missile, with a range of up to 8,000 kilometers; the government plans to put the DF-31 into service between 2002 and 2005.[72] As discussed above, China entered a friendship pact with Russia in July 2001; its government has also courted India, with little success thus far.[73]

Many of China's military improvements are clearly better suited to the projection of power than to the defense of home territory. Doubtless Japan, India, Russia, ASEAN (Association of Southeast Asian Nations) states, and of course Taiwan are objects of these power increases. The timing of the improvements, however, suggests that their primary object is the United States. America's stunning successes in the Gulf War spurred the Chinese toward military modernization.[74] U.S. performance in the Kosovo campaign provided further impetus.[75] Chinese officials make no secret as to whom they consider their country's

---

68. See Arnaud de Borchgrave, "Analysis: Russia, NATO, and NMD," United Press International, March 11, 2001, provided by Comtex, http://www.comtexnews.com.
69. Avery Goldstein, "Great Expectations: Interpreting China's Arrival," *International Security*, Vol. 22, No. 3 (Winter 1997/98), p. 43.
70. Pomfret, "U.S. Now a 'Threat' in China's Eyes."
71. Goldstein, "Great Expectations," pp. 45–50. Goldstein argues that despite these improvements, Chinese offensive capability remains relatively low. My argument is about Chinese intentions, not the practical effect of these intentions.
72. International Institute for Strategic Studies, *The Military Balance, 1999/2000* (London: IISS, 1999), p. 171.
73. On India, see Martin Sieff, "Commentary: India Slides into Sino-Russian Orbit," United Press International, January 15, 2001, provided by Comtex, http://www.comtexnews.com.
74. Goldstein, "Great Expectations," p. 43.
75. Shambaugh, "China's Military Views the World," pp. 57–61.

primary enemy to be. People's Liberation Army (PLA) officials are especially anti-American;[76] recently the civilian side of the government has begun to publicize the same view.[77] As Avery Goldstein writes, "Early in the post–Cold War era, it would certainly appear that China and the United States rather quickly have come to focus on each other as the two key players in the game and to view each other's actions as potentially threatening. Each worries about allegedly shifting balances of military power and mutual perceptions of resolve. The early signs suggest that a bipolar East Asia would be dominated by recurrent Sino-American conflict."[78]

China's counterbalancing follows from its thoroughly antiliberal institutions and ideology. Since 1979 China has all but abandoned Marxism, yet kept Leninism. It has a partially capitalist economy and a single-party dictatorship. How long such an arrangement can last is not clear, but what is clear is that within the ruling Communist Party no political liberals are evident. Chinese elites tend to interpret U.S. power as malign. Those interpretations are a product of the ideological distance separating them from their counterparts in the United States, Japan, and Western Europe.

Observers agree that the ideological spectrum among Chinese elites today is much narrower than it was in the 1980s.[79] Having witnessed the collapse of the Soviet Union under Mikhail Gorbachev's reforms, officials in the Chinese Communist Party (CCP) are determined to retain the party's monopoly on political power, and so entertain no thoughts of meaningful political liberalization.[80] Elites do disagree, however, over the pace of economic reform and integration into the world economy. The economic (as distinguished from political) liberals, led by Premier Zhu Rongji, have labored long to gain Chinese entry into the World Trade Organization (WTO). Economic reactionaries have been much less willing to offer concessions to the United States in order to gain WTO membership and have challenged Zhu's power at times over the issue.[81]

---

76. Ibid., pp. 52–79; and Johnston, "China's New 'Old Thinking.'"
77. Pomfret, "U.S. Now a 'Threat' in China's Eyes."
78. Goldstein, "Great Expectations, " p. 64. Goldstein adds that if Asia became multipolar rather than bipolar, China's suspicions of the United States would be diluted.
79. One should note that it may have been closet liberals in the CCP who smuggled documents to the West in January 2001 that demonstrated the responsibility of specific comrades for the Tiananmen Square massacre of June 1989. For a careful assessment of the documents, see Andrew J. Nathan, "The Tiananmen Papers, an Introduction," *Foreign Affairs*, Vol. 80, No. 1 (January/February 2001), pp. 2–10.
80. Michael D. Swaine, *China: Domestic Change and Foreign Policy* (Santa Monica, Calif.: RAND, 1995), pp. 4–14.
81. David E. Sanger, "At the Last Hour, Down to the Last Trick, and It Worked," *New York Times*, November 17, 1999, p. A14.

But it is not at all clear that economic reformers oppose military balancing against the United States or have the ability to say so if they do. The leadership of the PLA, meanwhile, perceives a malevolent United States bent on world domination. The CCP itself also is evidently dominated by virulent anti-Americans, particularly since the Kosovo war. During the war the *People's Daily* "accused the United States of seeking to become 'Lord of the Earth' and compared contemporary U.S. hegemony to the aggression of Nazi Germany."[82]

Having endured year after year of threatened congressional trade sanctions, countless press attacks from the American left and right, and dozens of lectures from U.S. officials and even entertainers over their violations of human rights, Chinese officials can see clearly that America's will for China is sharply at odds with their own. Were the United States able to have its way, China would have a new, liberal-democratic regime, just as Japan and Germany got when the United States imposed its will on them. That regime would not only uphold human rights and thereby halt the building and maintenance of the Chinese state. It would also allow political competition, and thus end the CCP's fifty-two-year political monopoly on power. It could lead to the breakup of the world's last great formal empire.

Chinese officials know that liberalism is a transnational movement. The liberal student protesters at Tiananmen Square were clearly part of a group that included not only fellow Chinese students studying in the West, but also the Western publics who applauded their efforts and were horrified at their brutal suppression. Insofar as the United States is an instrument of transnational liberalism, its overwhelming military power is bound to be a source of fear to Chinese elites, and hence will generate counterbalancing. China is evidently a revisionist power, but precisely because it sees the United States as revisionist. As Steve Chan explains the Chinese view, it is the United States that seeks to violate the sovereignty of China and other states by imposing its vision for the proper ordering of society.[83]

The United States, for its part, has obliged by making more provocative gestures toward China than toward the liberal democracies. It sends spy aircraft to Chinese coastal waters to monitor naval developments. It sent two carrier battle groups to the waters near Taiwan in March 1996 (in response to Chinese live-fire exercises in the Taiwan Strait, designed to intimidate Taiwan's voters

---

82. Shambaugh, "China's Military Views the World," p. 78.
83. Steve Chan, "Chinese Perspectives on World Order," in T.V. Paul and John A. Hall, eds., *International Order and the Future of World Politics* (New York: Cambridge University Press, 1999), pp. 208–209.

into rejecting a pro-independence party).[84] Even Russia fares better than China. In his speech of May 1, 2001, announcing missile defense, President Bush devoted great attention to Russia as a partner and potential democracy, but mentioned China only in passing.[85] All in all, it is clear that profound ideological differences are at least partly responsible for the difficult Sino-American relationship, and hence for Chinese attempts to counterbalance the United States.

Objections and Replies

In this section I consider various objections to my argument. Skeptics might respond that U.S. policies are entirely responsible for Chinese and Russian hostility; that the EU is in fact counterbalancing U.S. power; that French liberals are alarmed about unipolarity; that China is not really counterbalancing; or that democratic India is doing so.

BLAME AMERICA FIRST

Balance-of-threat theory would suggest that it is sufficient to note that the United States has displayed more menacing intentions toward China and Russia than toward its allies; one need not invoke ideology to explain the outcomes.[86] This objection fails to appreciate the degree to which acts are open to interpretation: For example, what appeared to Americans an accidental and idiotic bombing of the Chinese embassy in Belgrade in May 1999 appeared to Chinese a deliberate and outrageous effort at intimidation. Furthermore, this objection would need to offer an account of why the United States treats different countries differently to begin with. Why is the United States more suspicious of China than of Japan? My argument provides an explanation. It cannot be simply that countries treat allies better than non-allies, because we would then need to ask why the liberal democracies became U.S. allies and have remained so long after the demise of the Soviet Union. That is a reformulation of the question that motivates this article. Theories emphasizing power transition

---

84. "Taiwan Votes, China Thunders," *Economist*, March 16, 1996, pp. 39–41.
85. Said Bush: "Today's Russia is not yesterday's Soviet Union. Its government is no longer Communist. Its president is elected. Today's Russia is not our enemy, but a country in transition with an opportunity to emerge as a great nation, democratic, at peace with itself and its neighbors." The implicit comparison with China was as obvious as it was devastating. See the full text at http://www.whitehouse.gov/news/releases/2001/05/20010501–10.html.
86. Balance-of-threat theory posits that a threat has four components: aggregate power, offensive power, geography, and evidence of offensive intentions. See Walt, *Origins of Alliances*, pp. 21–28. In this case the first three are held constant, leaving only the fourth as a possible explanation.

might attribute U.S. treatment of China to the normal realpolitik anxiety over a rising challenger.[87] Such anxiety is clearly present but cannot be understood apart from China's antiliberalism. Americans are apprehensive about the illiberal purposes to which China would put its power. If power differentials alone accounted for U.S. treatment of other countries, then the United States should treat Russia, a stagnant power at best, as it treats Western Europe and Japan.

It might be further objected, however, that if Americans cared so deeply about whether foreign countries were liberal, they would pour vast resources into promoting liberalism abroad, at least in Russia. In fact, the United States has promoted liberal democracy in Russia. The amount of money directly devoted to democracy promotion has admittedly been paltry. Between 1992 and 1998, the United States extended $130 million in direct democratic assistance to Russia, only 2.3 percent of the $5.4 billion offered to Russia during that period (most of the money went to denuclearization, economic reform, and humanitarian projects). But much of this $5.4 billion, plus International Monetary Fund (IMF) aid of $16.5 billion and World Bank transfers of $6 billion,[88] provided general support for the current Russian regime, which from 1993 onward faced serious challenges from the far right and the far left. The United States (not to mention other liberal states) has provided costly indirect support for political liberalization in Russia. It has not done more because liberalism in the United States itself is so secure; Americans' solidarity with Russian liberals is lower than vice versa.

THE EU IS COUNTERBALANCING THE UNITED STATES
The formation of the EU's Rapid Reaction Force of 60,000 British, French, and German troops could be interpreted as a step toward counterbalancing American power, particularly in light of French assertions that the force will be independent of NATO. Thus far, however, that interpretation is difficult to sustain. The impetus behind the emergency force was the Europeans' inability to handle the Balkan crises of the 1990s without U.S. leadership. In particular, that atrocities continued while the Europeans and Americans dithered,[89] and that once NATO did take action in Kosovo, approximately 80 percent of the

---

87. See, for example, Dale C. Copeland, *The Origins of Major War* (Ithaca, N.Y.: Cornell University Press, 2000).

88. Figures are from Michael McFaul and Sarah E. Mendelson, "Russian Democracy: A U.S. National Security Interest," *Demokratizatsiya*, Vol. 8, No. 3 (Summer 2000), p. 336.

89. Ivo Daalder and Michael O'Hanlon, *Winning Ugly: NATO's War to Save Kosovo* (Washington, D.C.: Brookings, 2000); and Tim Judah, *Kosovo: War and Revenge* (New Haven, Conn.: Yale University Press, 2000).

munitions were delivered by U.S. aircraft and missiles,[90] motivated European elites to develop a better way to handle such crises.[91] A major cause of the EU force, then, is the need to carry out liberal foreign policy more efficiently. Certainly the British and Germans show little desire to counterbalance the United States and are at pains to make clear that they intend for NATO to remain supreme in Western Europe. There remains, however, the matter of the French.

FRENCH LIBERALS ARE ALARMED AT U.S. POWER

If French elites are complacent about U.S. primacy, why do they pronounce so about American hyperpower and routinely call for a multipolar world? With liberal bona fides as strong as those of any nation (in political if not economic affairs), French elites are nonetheless rhetorically different from their German, British, and Japanese counterparts concerning U.S. military power. Most outspoken among French government officials has been Hubert Védrine, the foreign minister, who has called on Europeans and others to "steady and persevering work in favor of real multilateralism against unilateralism, for balanced multipolarism against unipolarism, for cultural diversity against uniformity."[92] Other French elites, including President Jacques Chirac and Prime Minister Lionel Jospin, have made similar statements.[93]

The French are following a Gaullist tradition of anti-Americanism that perennially irks and baffles those on the receiving end. During the Cold War France insisted upon an independent foreign policy, developing its own nuclear force, withdrawing from the integrated military command of NATO, and pursuing détente with communist countries even as it remained in the Western camp.[94] This independent tradition predates Charles de Gaulle by many centuries: Medieval popes contending with Gallicanism, the notion that the Church in France should be directed by the French king rather than Rome, would recognize France's current behavior. French discontent with U.S. primacy, then,

---

90. International Institute for Strategic Studies, *The Military Balance, 2000/2001* (London: IISS, 2000), p. 289.

91. Ibid., p. 290; see also Michael Ignatieff, *Virtual War: Kosovo and Beyond* (Toronto: Viking, 2000).

92. Quoted in John Vinocur, "To Paris, U.S. Looks Like a Hyperpower," *International Herald Tribune*, February 5, 1999, p. 5.

93. Kevin Cullen, "A Call for Limits on 'Hyperpower' U.S.: At Kosovo Talks, French Aide Urges Blunting of Nation's Will," *Boston Globe*, February 9, 1999, p. A4.

94. See, for example, Stanley Hoffmann, "Obstinate or Obsolete? France, European Integration, and the Fate of the Nation-State," in Hoffmann, *The European Sisyphus: Essays on Europe, 1964–1994* (Boulder, Colo.: Westview, 1995), pp. 71–106, especially pp. 80–81; and Philip H. Gordon, *A Certain Idea of France: French Security Policy and the Gaullist Legacy* (Princeton, N.J.: Princeton University Press, 1993), pp. 27–29.

may result from a historic attachment to national independence stronger than that of most nations. Students of French politics note the nation's unusually acute fear that its culture is being supplanted by that of the United States. They also note that France, like the United States, has long seen itself as having a *mission civilitrice*, a quasi-religious duty to bring liberty and culture to the rest of the world; perhaps the world is only big enough for one such *mission*.[95] Put succinctly, French foreign policy may be less pro-American than that of other liberal countries because French liberals, like their American counterparts, are more nationalistic than other liberals.[96] That France and the United States are so alike may account for their differences.

Notwithstanding their chafing at U.S. primacy, it is not at all evident that French elites fear that the United States will use its power to impose its will upon them, as realism predicts they should do in an anarchical international system. The most telling sign of fear would be advocacy of policies that would help correct the imbalance of power that the United States enjoys. Apart from French aspirations for the EU's tiny Rapid Reaction Force, such advocacy has not materialized.

CHINA IS NOT COUNTERBALANCING

Several Western scholars have argued that China does not threaten U.S. interests. Avery Goldstein acknowledges China's rise in power but submits that it is less steep than many have represented.[97] Andrew Nathan and Robert Ross interpret China as a defensive and still weak power, no threat to international or even regional stability.[98] Steve Chan argues that China is no revisionist power.[99] Michael Gallagher argues that even on the narrow question of the South China Sea, China is not dangerous.[100] It is clear, moreover, that under Jiang Zemin China has continued the Dengist policy of integrating itself into international society, particularly the liberal international economy. Despite its serious differences with Washington, Beijing is cooperating with the United States and the West on many matters, in contrast to its behavior under Mao Zedong during the 1950s and 1960s.

---

95. For these and other factors, see Sophie Meunier, "The French Exception," *Foreign Affairs*, Vol. 79, No. 4 (July/August 2000), pp. 104–116.
96. I have benefited from conversation with Sophie Meunier on this point.
97. Goldstein, "Great Expectations."
98. Andrew J. Nathan and Robert S. Ross, *Great Wall, Empty Fortress: China's Search for Security* (New York: W.W. Norton, 1997).
99. Chan, "Chinese Perspectives on World Order," pp. 208–209.
100. Michael G. Gallagher, "China's Illusory Threat to the South China Sea," *International Security*, Vol. 19, No. 1 (Summer 1994), pp. 169–194.

China may indeed remain relatively weak, hold defensive intentions, and aspire to mere regional dominance, yet still be counterbalancing U.S. power. As for China's cooperation with the West, it is possible to engage economically with a country while simultaneously counterbalancing it militarily. Certainly the United States did so vis-à-vis Great Britain in Latin America during the late nineteenth century. Indeed, if China does desire to increase its national power, recent Chinese history demonstrates that the Dengist route is more promising than was the disastrous Maoist route. Even the most anti-American Chinese understand that China needs capital and technology from abroad to become a great power; while military technology may come from Russia, capital must come from the United States and its allies. Thus does the United States have leverage over China, but PLA and CCP officials clearly intend for this leverage to be temporary. Only Chan really contradicts my argument. He appears to define a revisionist power as one that challenges a broad conception of world order (namely, Westphalian sovereignty), rather than as one that challenges the existing hierarchy of power and prestige. On the latter, more standard definition, it is difficult to deny that China is revisionist.

INDIA IS COUNTERBALANCING

If China is counterbalancing the United States, is not liberal India doing the same? In May 1998 India tested a nuclear device, placing itself firmly in the nuclear club and thereby boosting its deterrent power exponentially. Indian military spending steadily increased from 1995 to 1999 (Table 1), at a greater average annual rate than that of any leading power save China. India has also reciprocated Chinese interest in a security relationship, hosting dozens of Chinese officials on a nine-day visit in January 2001 to discuss cooperation.[101] As already noted, India has a history of anti-Americanism dating from the early 1970s.

In an earlier section, I explained how my argument does not rule out a security dilemma among liberal states. In the early 1960s, India's need to counterbalance China drove Indian liberals to embrace a Soviet alignment and the resulting alienation from the United States. In the early 1970s U.S. cultivation of China and Pakistan, driven by a need to contain Soviet power, deepened this alienation. With the Cold War over, it is more accurate to say that India is no longer counterbalancing the United States. Some hard-liners in the Indian military do favor developing long-range missiles that could strike the United

---

101. Sieff, "India Slides into Sino-Russian Orbit."

States, but they are losing the policy contest to those who want to target only China and Pakistan.[102] Various students of Indian politics judge that it is those two regional rivals, rather than the United States, that were the object of the nuclear tests. The tests were also a product of a long-standing desire among many elites to make India a nuclear state, coupled with a desire to end international pressure to sign the 1996 Comprehensive Test Ban Treaty by presenting the world with a fait accompli.[103]

Despite the developing Sino-Indian thaw, Indian leaders are greatly concerned about Chinese military modernization. Thus far India has decided not to join the incipient Sino-Russian alignment, and progress in Sino-Indian relations is mostly a product of China's reducing its support of Muslim terrorists.[104] China evidently has made these concessions out of increased fear of U.S. missile defense[105] coupled with recent U.S. courting of India. That courting intensified during 2000 with a long visit by President Bill Clinton to India and a reciprocal visit to the United States by Indian Prime Minister Atal Behari Vajpayee; both visits were replete with statements about common democratic purposes.[106] Although Indians, like the French, call for a multipolar world, Indian elite rhetoric is generally much less anti-American than it was in previous years. Some elites are openly pro-American,[107] and some foreign policy experts are discussing a strategic partnership with the United States.[108] Overall, Stephen Cohen likens India's attitude toward U.S. primacy to that of France: Both have a "different and not necessarily hostile view of how the world should be organized."[109] In contrast to China, then, India's increases in power are not directed primarily at the United States.

---

102. Sadanand Dhume, "Choosing the Target: Hardliners Want Nuclear Missiles That Can Hit America," *Far Eastern Economic Review,* September 16, 1999, p. 30.
103. Šumit Ganguly, "India's Pathway to Pokhran II: The Prospects and Sources of New Delhi's Nuclear Weapons Program," *International Security,* Vol. 23, No. 4 (Spring 1999), pp. 148–177; and Mohammed Ayoob, "Nuclear India and Indian-American Relations," *Orbis,* Vol. 43, No. 1 (Winter 1999), pp. 59–74.
104. "Partners of Inconvenience," *Economist,* p. 4.
105. Sieff, "India Slides into Sino-Russian Orbit."
106. Nayan Chanda and Susan V. Lawrence, "Nuclear Balancing Act: Prospects of Warming U.S.-India Ties Are Causing Unusual Concern in China," *Far Eastern Economic Review,* March 16, 2000, pp. 26–27. See also Vajpayee's address to the U.S. Congress. Atal Behari Vajpayee, "Advancing Democracy: A Natural Partnership of Shared Endeavors," *Vital Speeches of the Day,* Vol. 66, No. 24 (October 1, 2000), pp. 740–741.
107. One of the most determined is S. Prasannarajan, senior editor of *India Today.* Prasannarajan calls anti-Americanism "redundant," an "ism . . . long ago repudiated by civil society everywhere." Prasannarajan, "Redundancy of Anti-Americanism," *India Today,* September 16, 2000, http://www.india-today.com/webexclusive/columns/prasana/20000917.html.
108. Stephen P. Cohen, "India Rising," *Wilson Quarterly,* Vol. 24, No. 3 (Summer 2000), p. 46.
109. Ibid., p. 52.

Preserving Primacy

In this section I discuss how Washington might maintain the U.S. preponderance of power, and defend the notion that it ought to do so.

HOW TO PRESERVE U.S. PRIMACY

If U.S. leaders want to preserve the favorable imbalance of international power, they must not only maintain the country's prosperity and edge in offensive military technology. Because liberal elites around the world tend to acquiesce to American primacy, U.S. leaders should also try to maximize the number and influence of liberal elites in potential challenger countries. The task in Europe and Japan appears relatively simple: Do not allow liberalism to fail as it did in Germany in the 1930s. U.S. efforts to continue prosperity in Western Europe and East Asia not only help the U.S. economy directly, but also help assure the survival of political liberalism and hence U.S. primacy. The task in Russia is more difficult, as the deep economic crisis there has undermined liberalism and thus the complacency regarding U.S. primacy. The task in China is more difficult still, perhaps prohibitive.

HELP LIBERALISM FULFILL ITS PROMISES. U.S. administrations during and af-·ter World War II understood that if the Western bloc were to survive, liberal institutions had to survive; and if those institutions were to survive, they had to make good on the liberal promise of the good life for a majority of citizens. Weimar Germany had fallen in 1933 under the weight of 6 million unemployed German men. Thus Washington implemented the Bretton Woods system and the Marshall Plan, and until the 1970s tolerated persistent current account deficits with its allies in order to foster their economic recovery. Circumstances between the United States and Russia today are vastly different from those between the United States and Japan and Germany after World War II. Russians are more responsible for their country's future than West Germans or Japanese were, and it would be hubristic to think that the United States can have more than a marginal effect on the future of liberalism there.

In Russia liberalism is ailing but still has a pulse. Given the atrocious conduct of the Russian military in Chechnya, a strong moral case can be made for suspending IMF aid to Russia. Given the poor return on previous aid, a pragmatic case for the same is easy to make as well. Yet U.S. policymakers must consider the consequences for Russian liberalism of such a measure. Russia's economy trudges on but remains in deep trouble. Communist and ultranationalist politicians continue to fulminate against liberalism and the West in the State Duma. An end to IMF aid would worsen the economy and also weaken the influence of economic interests who benefit from such aid, interests who as discussed above have been pro-Western.[110]

DO NOT THREATEN VITAL INTERESTS. Other measures would also be counseled by realists and international institutionalists who stake U.S. primacy on America's moderate behavior: The United States should not threaten the vital interests of potential challengers. As argued above, such threats can strengthen antiliberals in such states and eventually turn even liberals against the United States. The probability is virtually nil that the United States would make any move that would alarm Japanese or European liberals into thinking that it intended to blackmail them or seize their sovereign territory. As already discussed, most Russians have already begun to perceive such threats from the United States. On balance, it may be worth the damage to relations with Russia to use force when humanitarian crises erupt in southeastern Europe and Central Asia in the future. But Washington should at least recognize the possibility that in the long run such policies undermine the very U.S. primacy that makes them possible.[111]

On the other hand, Vladimir Putin's own antiliberalism and attempted centralization of power may be rendering the issue moot. Putin seems a pragmatic nationalist whose main priority is making Russia more efficient. He supports market economics and a strong central government that can control the parliament, the republics, and the oligarchs. But he is evidently no political liberal. Like some of Yeltsin's old subordinates, his government has bullied the press, most clearly in the June 2000 arrest and brief detention of media baron Vladimir Gusinsky, whose outlets had been Putin's most vigorous critics.[112] He has also weakened the checks and balances of Yeltsin's Russia by forming and relentlessly subsidizing a new Unity Party, which quickly gained a majority in the Duma; by abolishing various government ministries that had independent power bases; and by reorganizing Russia into seven districts governed by his own appointees.[113] His most clearly illiberal policies have been in suppressing the rebellion in Chechnya, where Russian troops have indiscriminately used

---

110. For a vigorous and extended argument that nurturing liberalism in Russia is in the security interests of the United States, see McFaul and Mendelson, "Russian Democracy."
111. Cf. Bruce D. Porter, "Russia and Europe after the Cold War: The Interaction of Domestic and Foreign Policies," in Wallander, *Sources of Russian Foreign Policy after the Cold War*, pp. 121–145; and Michael Mandelbaum, "Introduction: Russian Foreign Policy in Historical Perspective," in Mandelbaum, ed., *The New Russian Foreign Policy* (New York: Council on Foreign Relations, 1998), pp. 14–20.
112. John Lloyd, "Vladimir Putin," *New Statesman*, July 31, 2000, p. 16.
113. Masha Gessen, "Moscow Dispatch: New Depths," *New Republic*, September 11, 2000, p. 14. On the tendency for centralized regimes to be less open to transnational influences, see Risse-Kappen, *Bringing Transnational Relations Back In*.

force against civilians and medical personnel.[114] Nonetheless, liberal reformers such as Chubais retain some influence.[115]

CHINA AND REALPOLITIK. Because China evidently has no political liberals, the United States should handle it differently from other.potential challengers. Being fundamentally opposed to America's domestic norm of political liberalism, Chinese elites are predisposed to fear any expansion of U.S. power. Their harsh reactions to the Belgrade embassy bombing in May 1999 and the U.S. EP-3 collision with a Chinese jet fighter over Hainan Island in May 2001 are symptomatic.[116] In a sense, these events confirmed a prediction of Chinese antiliberals—namely, that the United States is aggressively building a world empire—and thus undermined whatever political liberalism remains in China. Furthermore, it is difficult to find a Chinese elite who does not express a deep passion for reuniting Taiwan, long a U.S. client, with China, or who does not resent U.S. statements over his country's violations of human rights.

Inasmuch as Chinese elites seem predisposed to interpret U.S. actions as ipso facto threatening, there seems little that Washington can do to prevent Chinese counterbalancing in the long run. Conciliatory gestures may help Russian liberals, but there appear to be no Chinese liberals to help. A Gorbachevian reform movement would have to arise in China, with the attendant emergence of politically liberal elites, for Chinese views of the United States to change. And Gorbachevian reform is what the CCP is most determined to prevent. Thus for the present the United States must deal with China as with any adversary with whom cooperation is possible, but alignment is not.

WHY PRESERVE U.S. PRIMACY?
Some foreign policy experts contend that the United States ought not to try to preserve its primacy in any case. Robert Jervis writes that primacy is "a game not worth the candle." For Jervis, relative gains in today's world simply are not important enough to warrant the resources needed to pursue them. Major power war is unlikely; military power is not fungible enough to give the United States relative advantages in economic and other affairs; and global stability may be maintained by a concert as well as by a military hegemon.[117] If

---

114. McFaul and Mendelson, "Russian Democracy."
115. Chubais is director of the state-owned electricity monopoly, scheduled for privatization over the next decade. See "Russia Adopts Energy Reform Plan," United Press International, May 19, 2001, provided by Comtex, http://www.comtexnews.com.
116. On the latter incident, see "Beyond Hainan: The Worry about China," *Economist*, April 14, 2001, pp. 1–2.
117. Robert Jervis, "International Primacy: Is the Game Worth the Candle?" *International Security*, Vol. 17, No. 4 (Spring 1993), pp. 52–67.

Jervis is correct, the United States might have other reasons to promote liberalism abroad, but preserving primacy is not one of them. In a rejoinder Samuel Huntington notes that, by definition, having more power is better because it allows a state to have its way more often. Power "enables an actor to shape his environment so as to reflect his interests. In particular it enables a state to protect its security and prevent, deflect, or defeat threats to that security. It also enables a state to promote its values among other peoples and to shape the international environment so as to reflect its values."[118] Huntington's propositions are undeniable in the abstract, but in practice is Jervis correct? Are the benefits from maintaining the imbalance of international power really worth the costs?

Insofar as prestige itself is a good, there is no substitute for primacy. Liberals do not acknowledge it readily, but psychic benefits increase with one's rank in the power hierarchy. It is not only the French who pine for the days when their nation was predominant. Yet, like all positional goods, prestige is dangerous to pursue and ought not to be a state's top priority. What of more concrete interests? The interests of the United States and its liberal-democratic allies are not congruent, but as I argue above they do overlap significantly, inasmuch as their governing elites share a common vision for domestic order and thus tend to share common enemies. Were the EU or Japan to gain parity with the United States, U.S. security would not be seriously jeopardized so long as each country or bloc retained its liberalism. The United States would have to suffer the many irritations and welfare losses that come from equality or subordination, including submitting to allies' agendas and preferences, irritations that the allies themselves have endured for many decades. Coordination would become more difficult in the absence of a military hegemon or "power of last resort." Collective actions such as humanitarian intervention would thus be more difficult to carry out unless the powers, in concert-like fashion, divided the world into spheres of influence.

More dangerous would be the supplanting of U.S. primacy by a coalition of illiberal states. The most likely combination, given current trends, is a Sino-Russian alliance. Were such an alliance to form tomorrow, it would certainly not be equipped to counterbalance U.S. might, but several decades hence it might just. We know from recent history what such a balanced international system would be like. The tighter the Sino-Russian alliance, the more it would resemble the bipolar Cold War international system. Most of us do not miss the

---

118. Samuel P. Huntington, "Why International Primacy Matters," *International Security*, Vol. 17, No. 4 (Spring 1993), pp. 69–70.

Cold War.[119] Those nostalgic for the days when Americans were unified against the communist adversary have somehow forgotten the wrenching disagreements that spanned the entire Cold War period over how far to oppose that adversary, or even whether it was an adversary. National disunity was much greater between 1968 and 1975 than at any time since. We may all be Kennanites now, but we were certainly not all then.

A world in which U.S. power was balanced by a coalition of illiberal powers would be one in which the United States devoted vast resources toward the pursuit of relative gains through internal and external balancing. As in the Cold War, there would be benefits such as security-driven technological innovations that eventually increased the efficiency of the civilian economy. But the costs would almost certainly outweigh such benefits. Other bipolar international systems, such as when the Habsburgs and French dueled over Europe or Rome and Carthage vied for control of the ancient Mediterranean, were even more dangerous (in part because nuclear deterrence did not exist).[120] Better for the country, and for the world, that the U.S. preponderance of power continue. For the world, not just any primacy is better than none. German primacy under the Nazis, or Soviet primacy, would have been far worse for all than a balance of power. As Huntington writes, it matters *which* country exercises power.[121] An imbalance that favors the United States, while not without costs and humiliations to non-Americans, is on balance better for most of the world.

Conclusion

"If you want a picture of the future, imagine a boot stamping on a human face—for ever." So wrote George Orwell in 1948, when totalitarianism seemed the wave of the future. More recently, an anonymous wit has said of life in Britain under New Labour: "Imagine a velvet glove coming down to caress a human face—for ever."[122] Orwell's boot was the totalitarian model that seemed ascendant in the 1940s; the velvet glove might equally be applied to the U.S.-led world order. The United States is indeed a restrained, benign hegemon. It is far away from the countries that have any prospect of ever challenging its pri-

---

119. Cf. John J. Mearsheimer, "Why We Will Soon Miss the Cold War," *Atlantic Monthly,* August 1990, pp. 30–40; for a more scholarly version, see John J. Mearsheimer, "Back to the Future: Instability in Europe after the Cold War," *International Security,* Vol. 15, No. 1 (Summer 1990), pp. 5–56.
120. On the relative dangers of bipolarity, see Copeland, *Origins of Major War,* pp. 11–34.
121. Huntington, "Why International Primacy Matters," p. 70. For a compelling defense of U.S. primacy, see Wohlforth, "Stability of a Unipolar World."
122. Quoted in Martin Ivens, "Brown Moves Fast in the Wake of Disaster," *Sunday Times* (London), January 28, 2001, pp. 1–18.

macy. It enriches itself to be sure, but by promoting economic efficiency and thereby enriching other countries as well, rather than by conquest. It uses its power not to subjugate but to establish and uphold order via institutions that yield increasing benefits over time. If the United States is an imperial power, the world may never have known such a benevolent empire.

Yet the United States also instantiates an ideology, liberalism, that is repulsive to the actors who dominate a number of countries. America's every success—and there have been many since the early 1980s—strengthens the credibility of liberalism everywhere. Its successes thus threaten the prospects of antiliberals in their own countries. When these antiliberal actors see the United States, they see not restraint, but bullying; not benignity, but a metastasizing cancer; not a distant great power, but a vigilante able to hurt them quickly; perhaps a velvet caress with one hand, but a handcuffing with the other. To them, uses of force to vindicate human rights are hypocritical efforts to extend American power, and U.S. allies who participate in such efforts are stooges.

An explanation of why the United States retains its primacy thus must go beyond noting that benefits to its allies from the American-built world order outweigh the probable costs of building an alternative order. It must also go beyond noting that geography makes counterbalancing the United States especially difficult and unrewarding. If these explanations were sufficient, no rational state would even try counterbalancing; rather, all would seek to do as Japan and Germany did after 1945. In fact, many countries are counterbalancing, most important China. With the partial exception of France, countries are counterbalancing U.S. power in inverse proportion to the influence that liberal elites have over their foreign policies. The argument that the United States is a benign hegemon is one that only a liberal could make. Thus the lack of a balance of international power is caused in part by the widespread penetration of most potential challenger states by liberalism. Liberal elites everywhere belong to a transnational group whose members identify with one another's successes. Because the United States is the leading liberal country, its unprecedented power engenders in most non-American liberals not fear but acquiescence (actual if not rhetorical). America's postwar reconstruction of Germany and Japan into liberal democracies reflected Washington's understanding that extending liberalism meant extending U.S. power.

Domestic ideology is not everything. International interactions may reinforce or reverse the identities that membership in a transnational ideological group produce. The United States may not do whatever it likes and blithely assume that it will never generate counterbalancing. Even liberal elites are also citizens of nation-states whose interests are not fully congruent with those of the United States. Should U.S. policies degrade the security of a state, it may be compelled to counterbalance, liberals or no. Thus did India counterbalance the United States during the Cold War; thus has Russia inched toward doing in recent years. Still, those who doubt the importance of political liberalism should ask themselves whether they are genuinely indifferent toward the future of Russian or Chinese liberalism. If not—if they would prefer for Russia and China to be mature liberal democracies—they should then ask whether that preference is solely out of moral concern for Russians and Chinese, or whether it might also be out of a concern for the quality of those countries' relations with the United States.

U.S. primacy is not eternal, but it can last much longer than many believe, and the United States may act at the margin to extend its life by promoting liberalism abroad. In so doing, it faces a dilemma: Promoting liberalism further alienates antiliberals even as it empowers liberals. It is a platitude that U.S. foreign policy must be judicious, but it is nonetheless particularly true as regards the export of liberal-democratic institutions, including human rights.[123] China is the most problematic case and probably presents the most serious long-term challenge to U.S. primacy. But its very antiliberalism, and that of other states and transnational movements, helps to keep liberals elsewhere content with the current imbalance of world power. Insofar as the label "liberal" has any meaning, it requires an opposite, some concrete variety of "antiliberalism." Should antiliberal actors disappear from the world, transnational liberalism would follow, and so would U.S. primacy.[124] The United States benefits from a peculiar equilibrium. Globally, antiliberal actors are weak enough not to threaten U.S. primacy but strong enough to enable its continuance. This equilibrium cannot last forever. But Americans and others fortunate enough to enjoy the fruits of U.S. primacy should enjoy it while it lasts.

---

123. On democracy promotion, see Larry Diamond, *Developing Democracy: Toward Consolidation* (Baltimore, Md.: Johns Hopkins University Press, 1999); Thomas Carothers, *Aiding Democracy Abroad: The Learning Curve* (Washington, D.C.: Carnegie Endowment for International Peace, 1999); Michael Cox, G. John Ikenberry, and Takashi Inoguchi, eds., *American Democracy Promotion: Impulses, Strategies, and Impacts* (New York: Oxford University Press, 2000); and Gideon Rose, "Democracy Promotion and American Foreign Policy," *International Security*, Vol. 25, No. 3 (Winter 2000/01), pp. 186–203.
124. For further discussion, see Owen, *Liberal Peace, Liberal War*, pp. 234–235; and John M. Owen, IV, "Pieces of Maximal Peace: Common Identities, Common Interests," in Arie Kacowicz, Yaacov Bar-Siman-Tov, Ole Elgström, and Magnus Jerneck, eds., *Stable Peace among Nations* (Totowa, N.J.: Rowman and Littlefield, 2000), pp. 74–91.

Part III
New Responses to American Primacy

Soft Balancing against the United States

Robert A. Pape

$\mathbf{P}$resident George W. Bush and his administration are pursuing a profoundly new U.S. national security strategy. Since January 2001 the United States has unilaterally abandoned the Kyoto accords on global warming, rejected participation in the International Criminal Court, and withdrawn from the Antiballistic Missile (ABM) treaty, among other unilateralist foreign policies. Although the United States gained considerable international sympathy following the terrorist attacks of September 11, 2001, the Bush administration chose to conduct military operations against the Taliban regime in Afghanistan with the aid of only one country: Great Britain.[1] In 2002 the administration announced that it would replace the Baathist regime in Iraq, a country that posed no observable threat to attack the United States, and to do so with military force "unilaterally if necessary."[2] The United States went on to conquer Iraq in early 2003 despite vigorous efforts by many of the world's major powers to delay, frustrate, and even undermine war plans and reduce the number of countries that would fight alongside the United States. Since then, the United States has threatened Iran and Syria, reaffirmed its commitment to build an ambitious ballistic missile defense system, and taken few steps to mend fences with the international community.

The Bush strategy is one of the most aggressively unilateral U.S. national security strategies ever, and it is likely to produce important international consequences. So far, the debate has focused almost exclusively on the immediate

Robert A. Pape is Professor of Political Science at the University of Chicago.

The author would like to thank the following individuals for offering valuable comments: Kenneth Abbott, Karen Alter, Robert Art, Richard Betts, Risa Brooks, Michael Desch, Alexander Downes, Daniel Drezner, Charles Glaser, Elizabeth Hurd, Ian Hurd, Chaim Kaufmann, Charles Lipson, Michael Loriaux, John Mearsheimer, Jeremy Pressman, Sebastian Rosato, Duncan Snidal, Jack Snyder, Hendrik Spruyt, Kenneth Waltz, and Alexander Wendt. He is also grateful to the members of the Program on International Security Policy at the University of Chicago and to participants in the conference on preemption held by the Triangle Institute on Security Studies at Duke University on January 17, 2003.

1. As an unnamed senior Bush administration official said, "The fewer people you have to rely on, the fewer permissions you have to get." Quoted in Elaine Sciolino and Steven Lee Meyers, "U.S. Plans to Act Largely Alone," *New York Times*, October 7, 2001.
2. "In Cheney's Words: The Administration's Case for Replacing Saddam Hussein," *New York Times*, August 27, 2002; and George W. Bush, *The National Security Strategy of the United States* (Washington, D.C.: White House, September 2002).

International Security, Vol. 30, No. 1 (Summer 2005), pp. 7–45
© 2005 by the President and Fellows of Harvard College and the Massachusetts Institute of Technology.

consequences of individual elements of the Bush foreign policy—on abandoning the ABM treaty, conquering Iraq, or failing to accept international limits on the use of force embodied in the United Nations.[3] Despite the significance of these issues, however, the long-term consequences of aggressive unilateralism and the Bush strategy as a whole are likely to be even more momentous.

Throughout history, states that have pursued aggressive unilateral military policies have paid a heavy price. In fact, major powers have often balanced against such states, though few analysts think that this will happen to the United States.[4] Historically, major powers have rarely balanced against the United States and not at all since the 1990s when it has been the sole superpower. The conventional wisdom among policymakers is that Europe, Russia, China, Japan, and other important regional actors such as Turkey and Brazil may grumble, but they will not stand in the way of U.S. military policies and will quickly seek to mend fences once the United States imposes its will by implementing these policies.

Recent international relations scholarship has promoted the view that the United States, as a unipolar leader, can act without fear of serious opposition in the international system. In the early 1990s a number of scholars argued that major powers would rise to challenge U.S. preponderance after the collapse of the Soviet Union and that unipolarity was largely an "illusion" that will not last long.[5] By the late 1990s, however, as it became increasingly evident that

---

3. On the debate over Bush's policies on national missile defense, see Charles L. Glaser and Steve Fetter, "National Missile Defense and the Future of U.S. Nuclear Weapons Policy," *International Security*, Vol. 26, No. 1 (Summer 2001), pp. 40–92; Heritage Commission on Missile Defense, *Defending America: A Plan to Meet the Urgent Missile Threat* (Washington, D.C.: Heritage Foundation, 1999); and Philip H. Gordon, "Bush, Missile Defense, and the Atlantic Alliance," *Survival*, Vol. 43, No. 1 (Spring 2001), pp. 17–36. On Iraq, see Kenneth M. Pollack, "Next Stop Baghdad," *Foreign Affairs*, Vol. 81, No. 1 (March/April 2002), pp. 32–48; John J. Mearsheimer and Stephen M. Walt, "An Unnecessary War," *Foreign Policy*, No. 134 (January/February 2003), pp. 51–61; and Robert A. Pape, "The World Pushes Back," *Boston Globe*, March 23, 2003. On the UN, see Michael J. Glennon, "Why the Security Council Failed, *Foreign Affairs*, Vol. 82, No. 3 (May/June 2003), pp. 16–35.
4. Although most critics of the United States' unilateralist diplomatic policies present a compelling case that these policies are increasing anti-Americanism around the world, they generally stop short of outlining the full long-term risks of aggressively unilateral military policies for the position of the United States in the world. On U.S. unilateral diplomacy, see Joseph S. Nye Jr., *The Paradox of American Power: Why the World's Only Superpower Can't Go It Alone* (New York: Oxford University Press, 2002); Yu Zhou, "American Unilateral Approach Threatens International Relations," *Beijing Review*, August 16, 2001, pp. 8–10; Peter W. Rodman, "The World's Resentment," *National Interest*, No. 60 (Summer 2000), pp. 8–10; Robert J. Art, *A Grand Strategy for America* (Ithaca, N.Y.: Cornell University Press, 2003); and Stephen M. Walt, "Beyond bin Laden: Reshaping U.S. Foreign Policy," *International Security*, Vol. 26, No. 3 (Winter 2001/02), pp. 56–78.
5. Christopher Layne, "The Unipolar Illusion: Why New Great Powers Will Rise," *International Security*, Vol. 17, No. 4 (Spring 1993), pp. 5–51; Kenneth N. Waltz, "Evaluating Theories," *American Political Science Review*, Vol. 91, No. 4 (December 1997), pp. 915–916; Aaron L. Friedberg, "Ripe for

unipolarity had not immediately given way to a new round of multipolar politics, the scholarly conventional wisdom began to change. While recognizing that states have often balanced against superior power in the past, most contemporary scholars of unipolarity assert that the United States commands such a huge margin of superiority that second-class powers cannot balance against its power, either individually or collectively. As William Wohlforth writes, "The raw power advantage of the United States means that . . . second-tier states face incentives to bandwagon with the unipolar power."[6]

This article advances three propositions that challenge the prevailing view that major powers cannot balance against the United States. First, the most consequential effect of the Bush strategy will be a fundamental transformation in how major states react to future uses of U.S. power. The United States has long been a remarkable exception to the rule that states balance against superior power. Aside from the Soviet Union, major powers have rarely balanced against it. The key reason is not the United States' overwhelming power relative to that of other major powers, which has varied over time and so cannot explain this nearly constant pattern. Rather, until recently the United States enjoyed a robust reputation for nonaggressive intentions toward major powers and lesser states beyond its own hemisphere. Although it has fought numerous wars, the United States has generally used its power to preserve the established political order in major regions of the world, seeking to prevent other powers from dominating rather than seeking to dominate itself. The Bush strategy of aggressive unilateralism is changing the United States' long-enjoyed reputation for benign intent and giving other major powers reason to fear its power.

Second, major powers are already engaging in the early stages of balancing behavior against the United States. In the near term, France, Germany, Russia, China, Japan, and other important regional states are unlikely to respond with traditional hard-balancing measures, such as military buildups, war-fighting alliances, and transfers of military technology to U.S. opponents. Directly confronting U.S. preponderance is too costly for any individual state and too risky for multiple states operating together, at least until major powers become confident that members of a balancing coalition will act in unison. Instead, ma-

Rivalry: Prospects for Peace in a Multipolar Asia," *International Security,* Vol. 18, No. 3 (Winter 1993/94), pp. 5–33; and Charles A. Kupchan, "After Pax Americana: Benign Power, Regional Integration, and the Sources of a Stable Multipolarity," *International Security,* Vol. 23, No. 2 (Fall 1998), pp. 40–79.
6. William C. Wohlforth, "The Stability of a Unipolar World," *International Security,* Vol. 24, No. 1 (Summer 1999), pp. 7–8.

jor powers are likely to adopt what I call "soft-balancing" measures: that is, actions that do not directly challenge U.S. military preponderance but that use nonmilitary tools to delay, frustrate, and undermine aggressive unilateral U.S. military policies. Soft balancing using international institutions, economic statecraft, and diplomatic arrangements has already been a prominent feature of the international opposition to the U.S. war against Iraq.

Third, soft balancing is likely to become more intense if the United States continues to pursue an aggressively unilateralist national security policy. Although soft balancing may be unable to prevent the United States from achieving specific military aims in the near term, it will increase the costs of using U.S. power, reduce the number of countries likely to cooperate with future U.S. military adventures, and possibly shift the balance of economic power against the United States. For example, Europe, Russia, and China could press hard for the oil companies from countries other than the United States to have access to Iraqi oil contracts, which would increase the economic costs of U.S. occupation of the country. Europeans could also begin to pay for oil in euros rather than in dollars, which could reduce demand for the dollar as the world's reserve currency and so increase risks of inflation and higher interest rates in the United States. Most important, soft balancing could eventually evolve into hard balancing. China and European states could also increase their economic ties with Russia while the Kremlin continues or even accelerates support for Iran's nuclear program, a step that would negate U.S. economic pressure on Russia while signaling the start of hard balancing against the United States.

Soft balancing, however, is not destiny. The Bush administration's national security strategy of aggressive unilateralism is the principal cause of soft balancing and repudiating this strategy is the principal solution. In practice, this would mean an explicit rejection of the strategy's most extreme elements (e.g., unilateral preventive war), renouncement of the most serious reasons to doubt U.S. motives (e.g., unilateral control over Iraqi oil contracts), and reestablishment of the U.S. commitment to solve important international problems multilaterally (e.g., a renewed commitment to the UN). The reputation of the United States for benign intent would slowly return, and the incentives for balancing against it would markedly decline. Although rare circumstances may require the unilateral use of U.S. power in the future, the security of the United States would be significantly enhanced if the Bush administration abandoned its policy of aggressive unilateralism.

This article evaluates the Bush administration's national security strategy on its key assumption: that states will not balance against aggressive unilateral uses of U.S. power. First, it develops a theory of security in a unipolar world that lays out the logic of balancing against a sole superpower. Second, it uses this theory to explain why states have not balanced against the United States in the past. Third, it articulates why U.S. unilateralism is beginning to change these dynamics. Fourth, it outlines how the strategy of soft balancing works and its potential costs for the United States. Finally, it presents the policies most likely to diffuse incentives for major powers to balance against the United States in the future.

A Theory of Security in a Unipolar World

Although the United States is commonly described as "a unipolar super-power," a clear definition of the meaning of unipolarity remains elusive. To determine how today's structure of the international system affects the incentives and behavior of both the unipolar leader and the world's other important powers, it is important to clarify the conceptual boundary that separates unipolarity from either a multipolar or bipolar system, on the one hand, and a hegemonic or imperial system, on the other.

DEFINITION OF UNIPOLARITY
The distinct quality of a system with only one superpower is that no other single state is powerful enough to balance against it. As a unipolar leader, the United States is also more secure than any other state in the world, able to determine the outcome of most international disputes, and has significant opportunities to control the internal and external behavior of virtually any small state in the system.

A unipolar world, however, is a balance of power system, not a hegemonic one. Powerful as it may be, a unipolar leader is still not altogether immune to the possibility of balancing by most or all of the second-ranked powers acting in concert. To escape balancing altogether, the leading state in the system would need to be stronger than all second-ranked powers acting as members of a counterbalancing coalition seeking to contain the unipolar leader. The term "global hegemon" is appropriate for a state that enjoys this further increase in power, because it could act virtually without constraint by any collection of other states anywhere in the world (see Figure 1).

In a unipolar world, the extraordinary power of the leading state is a serious barrier to attempts to form a counterbalancing coalition for two reasons. First, the coalition would have to include most or possibly even all of the lesser major powers. Second, assembling such a coalition is especially difficult to coordinate. As a result, forming a balancing coalition requires the sudden solution of

Figure 1. International Systems with One Strong State

Balance of Power Systems	Hegemonic Systems
multipolarity ⟵⟶ unipolarity	hegemony ⟵⟶ empire

a difficult collective action problem in which several powers must trust one another where buck-passing by any could doom them all.

In multipolar systems, too, the strongest power may enjoy such a wide margin of superiority over all others that containing it may require a coalition of several states. This situation of "unbalanced" multipolarity, however, is distinguishable from a unipolar world by the existence of at least one state that can mount a reasonable defense, at least for a time, even against the multipolar leader. In doing so, the state can provide the public good of serving as an "anchor" for a counterbalancing coalition by shouldering the risk of containing the leading state when others are unable, unwilling, or undecided. The most famous example is Britain's role in sparking the several coalitions against Napoleonic France from 1793 to 1815. Similarly, in Europe in 1940–41, both Britain and the Soviet Union showed themselves capable of serving as an anchor against Nazi Germany until an even larger coalition could be formed.[7] Today, however, no possible rival of the United States could reasonably assume this role. The absence of such an anchor marks the critical break between today's world and the past several centuries of major power politics.

Degrees of hegemony are also distinguishable. The difference between a global hegemon and an imperial hegemon is the level of control that the most powerful state exercises over subordinate states. A global hegemon is unchallengeably powerful. An imperial hegemon exercises a measure of control over second-ranked powers, regulating their external behavior according to the established hierarchy, even to the point of enforcing acceptable forms of internal behavior within the subordinate states.[8] Further, an imperial hegemon can create and enforce rules over the use of force, norms that apply to subordinate

---

7. Strictly speaking, the Soviet Union was not fighting alone in 1941. In practice, however, Britain and the United States provided so little assistance or distraction until late 1942 that Moscow had to shoulder most of the burden of confronting German military power during this period. For a discussion of unbalanced multipolarity, see John J. Mearsheimer, *The Tragedy of Great Power Politics* (New York: W.W. Norton, 2001).
8. On the definition of empire, see Stephen Peter Rosen, "An Empire, If You Can Keep It," *National Interest*, No. 71 (Spring 2003), pp. 51–62.

states but not to the hegemon itself. As a result, it can take steps to establish a monopoly on the use of force, and even second-ranked powers can lose important aspects of their sovereignty even if they are not formally occupied.[9]

Although differences in specific systems are important, from the standpoint of a theory of unipolar politics, the key boundary is between a balance of power system and a hegemonic one. This line separates a world in which the second-ranked powers can still act to preserve their security independent of the leading state from a world in which they cannot. Once the relative power of the leading state reaches this threshold, second-ranked powers may begin to worry about the consequences this might have for their security, but they can do little about it. As a result, second-ranked powers have tremendous incentives to contain the unipolar superpower's further expansion, or even to seek a shift in the distribution of power back toward multipolarity, depending on the perceived intentions of the leading state.

CONDITIONS THAT THREATEN SECOND-RANKED POWERS
In a balance of power system, states must guard against three security problems: (1) the threat of direct attack by another major power; (2) the threat of indirect harm, in which the military actions of a major power undermine the security of another, even if unintentionally; and (3) the possibility that one major power will become a global hegemon and thus capable of many harmful actions, such as rewriting the rules of international conduct to its long-term advantage, exploiting world economic resources for relative gain, imposing imperial rule on second-ranked powers, and even conquering any state in the system.

In general, major powers have commonly balanced against indirect as well as direct threats to their security. For instance, the United States acted to balance Germany before both world wars, even though it did not pose a direct threat to the United States in either case. Although historians debate whether the United States entered World War I in 1917 in response to the spillover effects of Germany's submarine campaign against Great Britain or the general fear that a victorious Germany would become a global hegemon, no major scholar contends that Germany posed an imminent threat to the United States. In World War II, the leading realist analysis calling for U.S. intervention to bal-

---

9. A unipolar superpower, like great powers in general, could create and maintain one or several regional empires that regulate the behavior of weak states according to the established hierarchy. Arguably, the United States has done just this in Central America and may be doing this in the Persian Gulf.

ance Germany explicitly ruled out a direct threat to invade or bombard the United States, and instead justified intervention on the basis of the indirect harm to U.S. security that might occur if a victorious Germany went on to establish exclusive control over economic resources and markets in Europe, Asia, and South America.[10] The experience of the United States before both world wars was not unique, because the European balancing coalitions against Germany began to form long before the aspiring hegemon actually attacked a major power.[11]

Concerns over indirect threats are likely to be greater in unipolar systems than in other balance of power systems. A unipolar leader is so strong that it may engage in military actions in distant regions of the world that are often likely to have real, if inadvertent, consequences for the security of major powers that are geographically close or have important economic ties to the region. For instance, how the unipolar leader wages a war on transnational terrorism can reduce or improve the security of other major powers, giving them a powerful security interest in how such a war is waged. Further, there is less ambiguity in a unipolar than a multipolar world about which state can make a bid for global hegemony, and even minor steps in this direction by a unipolar leader can create a common fear among second-ranked powers. Hence, other states may have reason to oppose military action by a unipolar leader, even if it has no intention of harming them directly.

This logic implies that perceptions of the most powerful state's intentions are more important in unipolar than in multipolar worlds. Because a unipolar leader is already stronger than all individual second-ranked powers, additional increments of power are unlikely to significantly increase its ability to become a global hegemon. For this reason, although the leading state's relative power gains are viewed with suspicion, they are ultimately of secondary importance in the politics of unipolarity.

More important is how others perceive the unipolar leader's motives. The overwhelming power of the unipolar leader means that even a modest change

---

10. On the decision of the United States to balance Germany before both world wars, see Ernest R. May, *The World War and American Isolationism, 1914–1917* (Cambridge, Mass.: Harvard University Press, 1959); George F. Kennan, *American Diplomacy, 1900–1950* (New York: New American Library, 1951); Richard Ned Lebow, *Between Peace and War: The Nature of International Crisis* (Baltimore, Md.: Johns Hopkins University Press, 1981), pp. 41–56; and Nicholas John Spykman, *America's Strategy in World Politics: The United States and the Balance of Power* (New York: Harcourt, Brace, and Company, 1942).

11. V.R. Berghahn, *Germany and the Approach to War in 1914* (London: Macmillan, 1973); and Williamson Murray, *The Change in the European Balance of Power, 1938–1939* (Princeton, N.J.: Princeton University Press, 1984).

in how others perceive the aggressiveness of its intentions can significantly increase the fear that it would make a bid for global hegemony. In fact, the threshold for what counts as an "aggressive" intention by a unipolar leader is lower than for major powers in a multipolar world because its capability to become a global hegemon is given. Thus, even a unipolar leader that adopts unilateral policies that merely expand its control over small states or that make only modest relative power gains can be viewed as aggressive, because these unilateral acts signal a willingness to make gains independently, and possibly at the expense of others.

THE LOGIC OF BALANCING AGAINST A SOLE SUPERPOWER
Major states have at least as much incentive to balance against a unipolar leader that poses a direct or indirect threat to their security as they would against strong states in a multipolar world. The main question is whether they can do so, and how.

Balancing against a unipolar leader is possible, but it does not operate according to the rules of other balance of power systems. In general, states may cope with an expansionist state through either "internal" balancing (i.e., rearmament or accelerated economic growth to support eventual rearmament) or "external" balancing (i.e., organization of counterbalancing alliances). In most multipolar systems, both forms of balancing are possible.[12]

Against a unipolar leader, however, internal balancing is not a viable option because no increase in standing military forces or economic strength by just one state is adequate to the task. This follows from the definition of a unipolar world and not from specific details about individual states' capabilities. Attempts at internal balancing by any one state are also likely to lead to a prompt, harsh response by the unipolar leader; this possibility is sufficiently obvious that individual states would rarely try such efforts on their own.[13]

States concerned about a unipolar leader, thus, have only the option of external balancing, but they face serious difficulties in coordinating their efforts. As developed below, soft balancing is a viable strategy for second-ranked powers to solve the coordination problems they encounter in coping with an expan-

---

12. In bipolar systems, only internal balancing is relevant because no third state is strong enough to matter. On internal and external balancing and the logic of bipolarity, see Kenneth N. Waltz, *Theory of International Politics* (Reading, Mass.: Addison-Wesley, 1979), chap. 8.
13. The futility of internal balancing has another important implication. Although one might think that a major power's attempts to balance a unipolar leader through internal efforts would spark local counterbalancing against the major power by other major powers, the obvious weakness of individual internal balancing against a unipolar leader means that this scenario is not likely to emerge in the first place.

sionist unipolar leader. So long as the unipolar leader has not already become a global hegemon, the lesser major powers can band together to contain its predominate military power. The key question is not whether these states have the collective power to do so, but whether they can solve their collective action problem and work together to form a balancing coalition.

Scholars of international politics are used to thinking about the problem of collective action in the context of a multipolar system, where buck-passing is the main obstacle to the formation of a counterbalancing coalition. Balancing is risky business. Strong states rarely welcome others standing in their way and can impose harsh penalties on those that do. In a multipolar system, major powers have a reasonable chance of defending themselves individually against even the strongest state in the system, and so each can try to make others pay the price for confronting the revisionist state. For this reason, states in a mulitpolar system are often slow to balance against powerful rivals, and the formation of a balancing coalition is generally an incremental process in which new members are added over time.[14]

The dynamics of balancing are different in a unipolar system. Balancing against a unipolar leader cannot be done by any one state alone; it can only be done by several second-ranked states acting collectively. This means that buck-passing is not an option. Because no one state—by definition—is powerful enough to balance a sole superpower, no state is available to catch the buck. Instead, the main problem of states wanting to balance against the unipolar leader is fear of collective failure. An individual state may fear that there are not enough states to form an effective countercoalition, that it will take too long for a sufficient number to organize, or that the unipolar leader will single it out for harsh treatment before the balancing coalition has coalesced.

Thus, the logic of balancing against a sole superpower is a game of coordination in which assuring timely cooperation is the principal obstacle. In this situation, each member of a potential balancing coalition is best off cooperating with others to balance the unipolar leader. At the same time, each member's decision to balance depends on the expectation that others will also balance, which in turn depends on the others' expectations of its balancing behavior. As Thomas Schelling articulated, the outcome of coordination games

---

14. In cases of hegemonic challengers in multipolar international systems, buck-passing was a problem. Before both world wars, Great Britain, France, and Russia were slow to cooperate against the German challenge and paid stiff penalties for their foot-dragging. Members of the final coalition, however, were able to solve their buck-passing problems, with the result that balancing was late but did eventually occur.

depends on the process of converging expectations[15]—a process that is especially likely to delay hard balancing. Directly confronting the preponderant military capability of a sole superpower before the full coalition has assembled would likely lead to a quick defeat and the loss of valuable members of an effective balancing coalition. Hence, the formation of a hard-balancing coalition against a unipolar leader is likely to occur abruptly, or not at all, rather than by incrementally adding members to a balancing coalition over time.

Although a sole superpower's preponderance of strength increases the incentive for second-ranked powers to delay hard balancing until they can coordinate collective action, it does not weaken the common interest that these states have in balancing against an aggressive unipolar leader. In a unipolar system, states balance against threats, defined by the power and aggressive intentions of the revisionist state. The power of a unipolar leader may keep other states from forming a balancing coalition, but it is still a key reason why these states may wish to do so. As a result, second-ranked states that cannot solve their coordination problem by traditional means may turn to soft-balancing measures to achieve this aim.

Soft-balancing measures do not directly challenge a unipolar leader's military preponderance, but they can delay, complicate, or increase the costs of using that extraordinary power. Nonmilitary tools, such as international institutions, economic statecraft, and strict interpretations of neutrality, can have a real, if indirect, effect on the military prospects of a unipolar leader.[16]

Most important, soft balancing can establish a basis of cooperation for more forceful, hard-balancing measures in the future. The logic of balancing against a sole superpower is about coordinating expectations of collective action among a number of second-ranked states. In the short term, this encourages

---

15. Thomas C. Schelling, *The Strategy of Conflict* (Cambridge, Mass.: Harvard University Press, 1960).

16. Soft balancing differs from "soft power," which refers to the ability of (some) states to use the attractiveness of their social, cultural, economic, or political resources to encourage other governments and publics to accept policies favorable toward their state, society, and policies. Although uses of soft power are not limited to security issues, in principle a state with excellent soft-power resources might be in a better than average position to organize a balancing coalition (or to prevent the formation of one against it). Favorable perceptions of a unipolar leader's intentions are thus an important soft-power asset. If a unipolar leader's aggressive unilateralism undermines favorable perceptions of its intentions, this also has the effect of reducing its soft power to block the formation of a counterbalancing coalition. In general, however, soft power is an attribute of a state, whereas soft balancing involves the nonmilitary policies that states can use to limit and offset the leading state in the international system. On soft power, see Joseph S. Nye Jr., *Bound to Lead: The Changing Nature of American Power* (New York: Basic Books, 1990).

states to pursue balancing strategies that are more effective at developing a convergence of expectations than in opposing the military power of the leading state. Building cooperation with nonmilitary tools is an effective means for this end.

The logic of unipolarity would suggest that the more aggressive the intentions of the unipolar hegemon, the more intense the balancing by second-ranked states, to the extent balancing is possible at all. If the unipolar leader does not pursue aggressively unilateral military policies, there should be little balancing of any kind against it. If, however, the unipolar leader pursues aggressive unilateral military policies that change how most of the world's major powers view its intentions, one should expect, first, soft balancing and, if the unipolar leader's aggressive policies do not abate, increasingly intense balancing efforts that could evolve into hard balancing.

Why the United States Has Been Exempt—Until Now

Thus far, the long ascendancy of the United States has been a remarkable exception to the general rule that states balance against superior power.[17] The United States was the world's strongest state throughout the twentieth century and, since the end of the Cold War, has been the leader of a unipolar international system. The most reliable long-run measure of a state's power is the size of its gross national product, because economic strength ultimately determines the limit of a state's military potential. For the past century, the U.S. share of gross world product was often double (or more) the share of any other state: 32 percent in 1913, 31 percent in 1938, 26 percent in 1960, 22 percent in 1980, and 27 percent in 2000.[18] During this period, the United States fought numerous major wars, determining the outcomes of World Wars I and II and, more recently, fighting against Iraq in 1991, Bosnia in 1995, and Serbia in 1999. Yet aside from the Soviet Union, no major power has sought to balance against the United States.[19] Why not?

---

17. On the tendency for an international balance of power to emerge and for this tendency to increase with the relative power of the leading state, see Hans J. Morgenthau, *Politics among Nations,* 4th ed. (New York: Alfred A. Knopf, 1967); Waltz, *Theory of International Politics;* and Mearsheimer, *The Tragedy of Great Power Politics.*
18. Paul Kennedy, *The Rise and Fall of the Great Powers* (New York: Random House, 1987), pp. 202, 436; and *World Development Indicators* (Washington, D.C.: World Bank, 2000).
19. Other important exceptions include mid-nineteenth-century Britain and Germany. Moreover, many scholars have doubted the universal applicability of balance of power theory. For historical exceptions, see Brian Healy and Arthur Stein, "The Balance of Power in International History: Theory and Reality," *Journal of Conflict Resolution,* Vol. 17, No. 1 (March 1973), pp. 33–61; and Paul Schroeder, "Alliances, 1815–1945: Weapons of Power and Tools of Management," in Klaus Knorr,

Scholars of international politics have given three answers. The first is that states balance against superior power,[20] but the process is uneven and slow.[21] As Kenneth Waltz argues, the weak have a common interest in balancing against the strong, and there is little that the dominant state can do to arrest this tendency: "A dominant power may behave with moderation, restraint, and forbearance. Even if it does, however, weaker states will worry about its future behavior."[22] Yet balancing poses risks. Superior powers do not take kindly to states that oppose their will. Weak states recognize these risks and are often content to pass the buck on to others. Buck-passing explains why balancing was slow to develop against Germany before both world wars and why balancing has been slow to emerge against the United States since the end of the Cold War.

The second answer stresses the U.S. reputation for benign intentions. Stephen Walt contends that states balance not so much against power alone, as against threat—the combination of raw power and perceived aggressive intent. In his view, states may have good or bad intentions, and only states with aggressive intentions provoke others to balance against it.[23] The United States has had fairly moderate foreign policy intentions compared with those of most other great powers throughout the past two centuries, never seeking to conquer a major country that was not already at war with it or one of its allies and never seeking to build an empire or to establish a sphere of influence beyond its own region of the world.[24] Thus, during the Cold War, Western Europe and Japan sided with the stronger United States against the weaker, but more ag-

---

ed., *Historical Dimensions of National Security Problems* (Lawrence: University Press of Kansas, 1976), pp. 173–225. For a broad challenge that argues that balance of threat rather than balance of power better explains the causes of alliances, see Stephen M. Walt, *The Origins of Alliances* (Ithaca, N.Y.: Cornell University Press, 1987).

20. Why do states not bandwagon with a threat rather than balance against it? Although there are important qualifications, international relations scholarship has found that major powers have a strong preference for balancing, because bandwagoning—even for profit—still leaves them vulnerable to an expansionist power. Bandwagoning is favored overwhelmingly by small states too weak to defend themselves without a major power patron. See Walt, *The Origins of Alliances;* and Randall L. Schweller, "Bandwagoning for Profit: Bringing the Revisionist State Back In," *International Security*, Vol. 19, No. 1 (Summer 1994), pp. 72–107.

21. Waltz, *Theory of International Politics*, chap. 8.

22. Waltz, "Evaluating Theories," p. 915.

23. To be clear, a state that is seen as aggressive, even if it is not the most powerful in the system, can provoke others to balance against it. Conversely, even the most powerful state may avoid becoming the target of balancing, provided that other powerful states are seen as much more aggressive. Walt, *The Origins of Alliances*.

24. For instance, in the late 1930s when U.S.-Japanese relations deteriorated, none of the main powers in the region—Britain, the Soviet Union, the Netherlands, and China—sided with the weaker, but expansionist Japan. Similarly, during the Cold War, Western Europe and Japan sided with the stronger United States against the weaker, but more aggressive Soviet Union.

gressive Soviet Union. Despite the enormous potential threat posed by U.S. power, no one has balanced against the United States because it has generally manifested nonaggressive intentions.

The third answer focuses on U.S. grand strategy. Mearsheimer argues that the United States pursued a strategy of "offshore balancing" throughout the twentieth century, focusing on preventing strong states from dominating important regions of the world rather than dominating those regions itself.[25] It was this strategy that called the United States to the defense of its European allies in World Wars I and II, of South Korea and Vietnam during the Cold War, and of Kuwait in 1991. As a result, U.S. grand strategy has effectively reassured major powers such as Europe, Russia, Japan, and China that the United States, even as a sole superpower, poses little threat to them.[26] At least until the Bush Doctrine, U.S. grand strategy avoided giving others much reason to balance against the United States.

Scholars may argue over which of these answers is the most convincing. Each, however, has an element of truth and together explain more than any one alone. No other great power in history has been so dominant, has had such a high reputation for nonaggressive intentions, and has limited itself to offshore balancing—all at the same time. This triple combination is probably the best explanation for why the United States has gotten a pass from balance of power politics so far.

To the extent that one factor has been especially important since the United States became the sole superpower, it is probably the U.S. reputation for benign intent. Consider the evidence that would be needed to support each of the above three positions. If, as Waltz suggests, the structure of the unipolar system encourages balancing but that buck-passing will make the process slow and uneven, then evidence of either balancing or buck-passing among the major powers should exist, especially during periods when the United States used its considerable military power. If, however, Walt and Mearsheimer are correct that the United States' reputation for good intentions, bolstered by a grand strategy of offshore balancing, effectively reassures major powers, then there should be little evidence of either balancing or buck-passing.

Strikingly, from 1990 to 2000 no significant instances of balancing occurred

---

25. Mearsheimer, *The Tragedy of Great Power Politics*.
26. Mearsheimer believes that the U.S. strategy of offshore balancing is dictated more by limits in U.S. capabilities than by benign intentions. He agrees with Walt, however, on the effect of the United States pursuing a limited-aims grand strategy.

against the United States; nor was there notable buck-passing among the world's major powers in which one encouraged another to balance U.S. power. In the 1990s, resentment of U.S. preponderance led some major powers to complain of U.S. "arrogance" and to call for a new "counterweight" to American strength. Counterbalancing was limited to rhetoric, however, and it did not involve changes in military spending or opposition to U.S. uses of force, either directly or indirectly.[27] Starting in the mid-1990s, the United States began to increase its defense spending, while Europe, Japan, and China did not and Russia's military spending rapidly declined.[28] At the start of the 1990s, U.S. defense spending exceeded the next seven countries combined. By the decade's end, it exceeded the next eight.

Similarly, major powers did not act to restrain the use of U.S. military power in three extended conflicts during the period: Iraq in 1991, Bosnia in 1995, and Kovoso in 1999. Although major powers were often reluctant to join these military campaigns, in no case did they take action to impede, frustrate, or delay U.S. war plans; or actively oppose the use of U.S. military power; or discourage other states from supporting America's wars. In Iraq in 1991 and Kosovo in 1999, the United States ended with more military allies than it began. As in the Vietnam War in the 1960s and 1970s, some major states grumbled, but none took measures to contain the use of U.S. military power.

Overall, the record of the 1990s does not reflect a balancing process that was slow or erratic. The politics of unipolarity changed, however, once the United States began to act in ways that would undermine its reputation for benign intent.

Unilateralism and the United States' Changing Reputation

The Bush national security strategy asserts the right of the United States to wage unilateral preventive war against so-called rogue states and calls for a military posture that will keep U.S. preponderance beyond challenge from any state in the world. Under the Bush administration, the United States has moved vigorously to implement this game plan by waging a preventive war against Iraq and by accelerating the move toward developing a national missile defense (NMD). These military policies are creating conditions that are

---

27. In 1991 French Foreign Minister Roland Dumas warned that "[U.S.] might reigns without balancing weight," while Chinese leaders warned that "unipolarity was a far worse state of affairs than bipolarity." Quoted in Layne, "The Unipolar Illusion," p. 36.
28. International Institute of Strategic Studies, *The Military Balance, 1998/99* (London: IISS, 2000).

Table 1. Declining Image of the United States, 2000–03 (percentage favorable)

	United Kingdom	France	Germany	Italy	Spain	Russia	Turkey
U.S. Image							
1999/2000	83	62	78	76	50	37	52
July 2002	75	63	61	70	—	61	30
February 2003	48	31	25	34	14	28	12
Change 2002–03	−27	−32	−36	−36	—	−33	−18

SOURCE: Pew Global Attitudes Project, *America's Image Further Erodes, Europeans Want Weaker Ties: A Nine Country Survey* (Washington, D.C.: Pew Research Center, March 2003).

likely to fundamentally change how other major powers react to future uses of U.S. power. Although these policies may add marginally to the United States' world power position, this is not the heart of the matter. Rather, these policies are changing how other states view U.S. intentions and the purposes behind U.S. power, putting at risk the United States' long-enjoyed reputation for benign intent. If these policies continue, the damage to the image of the United States will have negative consequences for U.S. security.

THE CHANGING IMAGE OF THE UNITED STATES

The image of the United States has been plummeting even among its closest allies since preparations for preventive war against Iraq began in earnest. International public opinion polls show that the decline is especially sharp from July 2002 (the month before Bush administration officials began calling for the war) to March 2003 (the month military operations started). During this period, the percentages of the populations in Great Britain, France, Germany, Italy, Spain, Russia, and Turkey who viewed the United States favorably declined by about half, as Table 1 shows.

This decline is closely related to perceptions of rising unilateralism in U.S. foreign policy. As Table 2 shows, majorities in France, Germany, Italy, Spain, Russia, and Turkey as well as a near majority in the United Kingdom believe that U.S. foreign policy is highly unilateral and has negative consequences for their country. Table 2 also shows that these publics believe that these negative consequences are specifically due to the foreign policy of the "Bush administration" rather than to a "more general problem with America," but also that they support greater independence between their country and the United States.

Table 2. U.S. Foreign Policy and Independence from the United States, 2002–03 (percentage of respondents)

	United Kingdom	France	Germany	Italy	Spain	Russia	Turkey
U.S. foreign policy considers others							
Yes	44	21	53	36	—	21	16
No	52	76	45	58	—	70	74
Effect of U.S. foreign policy on our country							
Negative	42	71	67	52	57	55	68
Positive	30	9	11	17	9	11	14
Why U.S. policy produces a negative effect							
Bush administration	56	76	68	52	53	29	35
United States in general	31	15	30	36	33	48	48
Both	11	7	1	7	10	17	12
U.S.-European security ties							
Remain close	40	30	46	30	24	17	17
Be more independent	48	67	52	63	60	72	62

SOURCES: Pew Global Attitudes Project, *What the World Thinks in 2002* (Washington, D.C.: Pew Research Center, December 2002); and Pew Global Attitudes Project, *America's Image Further Erodes, Europeans Want Weaker Ties: A Nine Country Survey* (Washington, D.C.: Pew Research Center, March 2003).

International polls also shed light on the underlying reasons for these attitudes. As Table 3 shows, although public opinion in France, Germany, Russia, and other European states strongly supported the U.S. war against terrorism, a large majority in each country did not believe that the United States seriously considered Saddam Hussein a threat and felt that the United States' true motivation was securing access to Iraqi oil.

In addition, foreign leaders expressed concern about U.S. unilateralism during the lead-up to the war. Although individual foreign leaders occasionally made such public remarks from the late 1990s onward,[29] it was only during the fall of 2002 and winter of 2003 that many collectively declared support for

29. In 1999 French Foreign Minister Hubert Védrine described the United States as a "hyperpower"; in the same year, German Chancellor Gerhard Schröder warned that the danger of "unilateralism" by the United States was "undeniable." The January 2000 "National Security Blueprint" of the Russian Federation warned of "attempts to create an international relations structure . . . under U.S. leadership and designed for unilateral solutions (including the use of military force) to key issues in world politics." All quoted in Walt, "Beyond bin Laden," p. 60.

Table 3. International Support for War on Iraq and Terrorism, November 2002 (percentage of respondents)

	United States	United Kingdom	France	Germany	Russia
What explains U.S. use of force					
U.S. sees Saddam as threat	67	45	21	39	15
U.S. wants Iraq's oil	22	44	75	54	76
U.S. war on terrorism					
Support	89	69	75	70	73
Oppose	8	23	23	25	16

SOURCE: Pew Global Attitudes Project, *What the World Thinks in 2002* (Washington, D.C.: Pew Research Center, December 2002).

a multipolar world to limit U.S. unilateralism. In February 2003 France's foreign minister, Dominique de Villepin, asserted, "We believe that a multipolar world is needed, that no one power can ensure order through the world." Russian President Vladimir Putin agreed and went further to explain that his country's concerns served as the basis for union with European states against U.S. unilateralism. Putin stated, "We believe here, in Russia, just as French President Jacques Chirac believes, that the future international security architecture must be based on a multipolar world. This is the main thing that unites us. I am absolutely confident that the world will be predictable and stable only if it is multipolar."[30] Also during this period, it became common for foreign leaders to declare their suspicion of U.S. "ulterior motives," a phrase that evoked a rare round of applause when de Villepin uttered it at UN in February 2003.

WHY UNILATERALISM IS CHANGING THE U.S. IMAGE
The root cause of widespread opposition to U.S. military policies under President George W. Bush's administration does not lie in the political values or character of France, Germany, Russia, China, and important regional states, factors that do not point in a single direction and that have not changed significantly since July 2002.[31] Nor does it lie in a shift in U.S. relative power,

30. French Foreign Minister Dominique de Villepin, February 16, 2003, in "Poles Apart," *Le Monde*, in Foreign Broadcast Information Service (FBIS), March 17, 2003; and Russian President Vladimir Putin, Moscow Itar-Tass, in FBIS, February 9, 2003.
31. Stephen G. Brooks and William C. Wohlforth contend that opposition to the Bush strategy among various European states and Russia was driven not by incentives to balance the United States, but by the coincidence of two main factors: domestic politics, especially in the case of Ger-

which has hardly changed in this short time. Rather, the key reason is that the Bush strategy is changing the United States' long-enjoyed reputation of benign intent. Precisely because the United States is already so powerful, even a small change in how other perceive the aggressiveness of U.S. intentions can cause other major powers to be concerned about their security.

On its face, the rhetoric of the Bush strategy may appear to present few reasons for major powers and other states to change their view of U.S. intentions. Its chief objective is to stop the proliferation of weapons of mass destruction to rogue states, principally Iran, Syria, Libya, North Korea, and Iraq (before March 2003). To achieve this aim, the United States asserts the right to destroy a rogue state's military power "unilaterally if necessary," to build a national missile defense to defeat efforts by rogue states to develop long-range ballistic missiles capable of hitting the United States, and to maintain the primacy of U.S. military power to keep other states from "surpassing, or equaling, the power of the United States."[32]

The main concern of other states is not with the goals of U.S. policy, but with the means, especially with the Bush administration's willingness to use unilateral military action to achieve its otherwise acceptable goals. Such action violates long-standing international norms against the use of preventive war as a legitimate policy tool, provides important relative gains for the United States in a region of the world crucial to the economic growth of major states, and increases the United States' already considerable military advantages over major nuclear powers.

PREVENTIVE WAR. Iraq is the United States' first preventive war. Although the United States has used force to defend allies from military attack, to stop the spread of ethnic and ideological insurgencies, and to protect oppressed

---

many; and hard bargaining, particularly for Russia. Their evidence, however, shows that neither alternative factor provides much explanatory power independent of the key international pressures generated by the Bush Doctrine. Brooks and Wohlforth note that in the summer of 2002 Chancellor Schröder started to use opposition against the United States for domestic political advantage, but gained no increased German public support until Vice President Dick Cheney's public call for preventive war on Iraq on August 26. They also confirm that Russia gave up a great deal (oil contracts worth $8–$20 billion) to oppose Iraq, which should not have happened if hard bargaining to make absolute gains had been the main motive behind Russia's behavior. See Brooks and Wohlforth, "Hard Times for Soft Balancing," *International Security*, Vol. 30, No. 1 (Summer 2005), pp. 72–108.

32. Key Bush administration national security policy statements include "In Bush's Words: Substantial Advantages of Intercepting Missiles Early," *New York Times*, May 2, 2001; "President Bush's State of the Union Address," *New York Times*, January 30, 2002; "In Cheney's Words: The Administration's Case for Replacing Saddam Hussein," *New York Times*, August 27, 2002; and Bush, *The National Security Strategy of the United States*.

peoples, it had never before conquered a country to stop that state from gaining military power. Until now, many analysts have thought that democratic values and institutions would make classic territorial aggrandizement to conquer, occupy, and transform another country that does not pose an imminent military threat impossible. The U.S. conquest of Iraq, however, challenges one of the most important norms in international politics—that democracies do not fight preventive wars—and so undermines the assurance that comes from the expectation that democratic institutions can keep a sole superpower from altering the status quo to its advantage.

Officially, the Bush strategy is described as "preemption," but the strategy against rogue states fits with the more aggressive policy of preventive war, a fact recognized in the Bush administration's own national security strategy statements. What is at issue in the definition of the strategy is not simply who fires the first shot—preemption and preventive war are both policies that allow the United States to attack countries that have not opened fire against it—but whether the threat is imminent and thus whether only a military strike can respond to it.[33]

A preemptive war is fought against an opponent already in the process of mobilizing military forces for an imminent attack, usually within a matter of days. The enemy's intent to attack is not assumed or even merely expected; it is observed by concrete changes in the operational status of the enemy's military capabilities. With war under way, the incentive for preemptive attack is to deny the aggressor the advantage of completing the first move: that is, to destroy oncoming enemy forces while they are mobilizing and more vulnerable than they would be once the enemy's first strike has begun. The timing of a preemptive war is determined by observable changes in the operational readiness of the enemy's military forces.[34]

---

33. Paul W. Schroeder, "The Case against Preemptive War," *American Conservative*, October 21, 2002, pp. 19–27; Richard K. Betts, "Striking First: A History of Thankfully Lost Opportunities," *Ethics & International Affairs*, Vol. 17, No. 1 (Spring 2003), pp. 17–24; Ivo H. Daalder, James M. Lindsay, and James B. Steinberg, *The Bush National Security Strategy: An Evaluation* (Washington, D.C.: Brookings, 2002); and Chaim D. Kaufmann, "Overstretching America," paper presented to the Triangle Institute on Security Studies, Duke University, Durham, North Carolina, January 17, 2003.

34. On preemptive war, see Thomas C. Schelling, *Arms and Influence* (New Haven, Conn.: Yale University Press, 1966), chap. 6; Richard K. Betts, "Surprise Attack and Preemption," in Graham T. Allison, Albert Carnesale, and Joseph S. Nye Jr., eds., *Hawks, Doves, and Owls: An Agenda for Avoiding Nuclear War* (New York: W.W. Norton, 1985), pp. 54–79; Dan Reiter, "Exploding the Powder Keg Myth: Preemptive Wars Almost Never Happen," *International Security*, Vol. 20, No. 2 (Fall 1995), pp. 5–34; and Stephen Van Evera, *Causes of War: Power and the Roots of Conflict* (Ithaca, N.Y.: Cornell University Press, 1999), chap. 3.

In contrast, a preventive war is fought to keep an opponent from acquiring military capabilities long before—often years before—it begins to mobilize forces for an attack. Preventive war logic generally takes the opponent's intent to use newly acquired military capabilities for granted or bases such expectations on broad conclusions derived from the opponent's character or past behavior. The primary purpose of preventive war is not merely to deny the aggressor the advantage of striking first—this is a lesser included benefit. Instead, the chief purpose is to engage the adversary before it can shift the long-term military balance of power in its favor. For this reason, the timing of a preventive attack has little to do with changes in the operational status of the enemy's military forces, because the goal is to conquer the target state before it has gained those military capabilities. The war starts when the preventive attacker's forces are ready.[35]

The Bush strategy against rogue states follows the normal understanding of preventive war in substance, if not in rhetoric. In fact, *The National Security Strategy of the United States*, the principal statement of the Bush strategy, expressly redefines the meaning of "preemption" against rogue states to encompass traditional preventive war logic:

Legal scholars and international jurists often conditioned the legitimacy of preemption on the existence of an imminent threat—most often a visible mobilization of armies, navies, and air forces preparing to attack. We must adapt the concept of imminent threat to the capabilities and objectives of today's adversaries. . . . The greater the threat, the greater is the risk of inaction—and the more compelling the case for taking anticipatory action to defend ourselves, even if uncertainty remains as to the time and place of the enemies' attack. To forestall or prevent such hostile acts by our adversaries, the United States will, if necessary, act preemptively.[36]

Classic preventive war logic is also a common theme in public speeches by administration officials, including President Bush, on Iraq: "We are acting now because the risks of inaction would be far greater. In one year, or five years, the

---

35. On preventive war, see Alfred Vagts, "Preventive War," *Defense and Diplomacy* (New York: King's Crown Press, 1956), pp. 263–350; Robert Gilpin, *War and Change in World Politics* (Cambridge: Cambridge University Press, 1981); Jack Levy, "Declining Power and Preventive Motivation for War," *World Politics*, Vol. 40, No. 1 (October 1987), pp. 82–107; Van Evera, *Causes of War*, chap. 4; and Dale C. Copeland, *The Origins of Major War: Hegemonic Rivalry and the Fear of Decline* (Ithaca, N.Y.: Cornell University Press, 2000).
36. Bush, *The National Security Strategy of the United States*, p. 15. The Bush strategy against terrorist groups relies on the normal use of the concept of preemption. For a sophisticated discussion of the role of preventive war logic in the Bush administration's national security strategy, see Kaufmann, "Overstretching America."

power of Iraq to inflict harm on all free nations would be multiplied many times over."[37]

The Bush administration's strategy of preventive war represents a major departure from traditional U.S. security policy. Although the United States has historically maintained a policy of preemption—to strike first when credible evidence warned that an enemy was mobilizing military forces for an imminent attack—it has categorically ruled out preventive war on numerous occasions.[38] The United States conquered much of North America in the nineteenth century, used force to ensure that European powers could not establish a strong presence in the Caribbean Basin in the early twentieth century—including retaliation against Spain's attack on the USS *Maine*, which led to the U.S. conquest of the Philippines—and intervened to defend the political status quo numerous times in the twentieth century. In no case, however, did the United States wage a classic preventive war to conquer a sovereign country, prior to the conquest of Iraq in March 2003.[39]

The United States' traditional policy against preventive war is not unique. Over the past two centuries, no major democratic power has ever started a preventive war[40]—not Britain even at the height of its power in the nineteenth

---

37. Bush, March 17, 2003, quoted in Kaufmann, "Overstretching America."
38. During the 1950s, Dwight Eisenhower's administration authorized the Strategic Air Command to maintain the capability to turn the Soviet Union into "a smoking, radiating ruin in two hours" in response to intelligence that Soviet missiles were being fueled for an imminent attack; however, the administration ruled out initiating an attack before the Soviet Union had begun mobilizing for war. "National Security Council 68: United States Objectives and Programs for National Security (April 14, 1950)," considered one of the most aggressive U.S. official policy statements during the Cold War, categorically ruled out preventive war to stop the Soviet Union from acquiring nuclear weapons in the 1950s. Lyndon Johnson's administration considered but also ruled out preventive war against China's nascent nuclear capabilities in the 1960s. See Marc Trachtenberg, "A 'Wasting Asset': American Strategy and the Shifting Nuclear Balance, 1949–1954," *International Security*, Vol. 13, No. 3 (Winter 1988/89), pp. 5–49; and William Burr and Jeffrey T. Richelson, "Whether to 'Strangle the Baby in the Cradle': The United States and the Chinese Nuclear Program, 1960–64," *International Security*, Vol. 25, No. 3 (Winter 2000/01), pp. 54–99.
39. Max Boot contends that U.S. interventions in Latin America, Vietnam, and elsewhere have been "preemptive" and thus are consistent with the Bush Doctrine. Boot, *The Savage Wars of Peace: Small Wars and the Rise of American Power* (New York: Basic Books, 2002). Although one might doubt the wisdom of many of these small wars, Boot provides no evidence on the key point—that any of them were fought to prevent the target state from gaining military power with which to subsequently attack the United States. Moreover, a basic understanding of the main cases suggests that such preventive war motives were highly unlikely. On their own, Cuba, the Philippines, China, and Nicaragua in the late nineteenth century and North Korea and North Vietnam in the mid-twentieth century had little, if any, prospects of gaining sufficient military power to threaten the United States.
40. In the standard list of preventive wars over the past two centuries, all were started by authoritarian states: Napoleonic Wars (1793–1815), Austro-Prussian War (1866), Franco-Prussian War (1870), Russo-Japanese War (1904), World War I (1914), Germany-Soviet Union (1941), and Japan-

century,[41] or France in the twentieth century.[42] The closest any democracy has come to a preventive war was Israel's Suez campaign against Egypt in 1956, an action encouraged and supported by a majority of the world's strongest states.[43]

The Bush administration's rhetoric is not limited to Iraq, but seeks to legitimate preventive war as a "normal" tool of U.S. statecraft. Now that the United States has actually acted on the Bush preventive war strategy, other countries will have to include in their calculations the possibility that it may do so again.

For other major powers, the main threat to their security stems not from the risk that the United States will eventually pose a direct threat to attack their homelands, but that the U.S. policy of preventive war is likely to unleash violence that the United States cannot fully control and that poses an indirect threat to their security. As a result, even though the United States means them no harm, other major states must still contend with the spillover effects of U.S. unilateral uses of force. These indirect effects are especially pronounced for U.S. military adventures in the Middle East, which could stimulate a general rise in the level of global terrorism targeted at European and other major states. As the French foreign policy adviser Bruno Tertrais explains: "The implementation of the U.S. strategy [of preventive war] tends to favor, rather than reduce, the development of the principal threats to which it is addressed: terrorism and proliferation. . . . The Al Qaeda organization . . . has now reached the shores of Europe, as shown by the [terrorist attacks] in Turkey (De-

---

United States (1941). See Randall L. Schweller, "Domestic Structure and Preventive War," *World Politics*, Vol. 44, No. 2 (January 1992), pp. 235–269.
41. Britain did use force in anticipation of growing challenges to its empire. It attacked Afghanistan in 1850–55 and again in 1878–80, and it fought the Boer War in South Africa in 1899–1902. In these cases, the British acted in response to initial attacks by local, irregular forces that they feared would escalate if major powers assisted their efforts. Britain may well have faced serious preemptive incentives to destroy local resistance groups before major power patrons could arm them. These cases, however, do not qualify as preventive war in the classic sense because Britain was acting to stop the escalation of immediate, ongoing military threats, not to prevent a future threat. Once violence begins, an opponent can often mobilize still more military forces in the near term, but this is not the essence of preventive war.
42. The closest the world has come to a preventive war by a major democracy was Germany's initiation of World War I in 1914. Most observers at the time believed that Germany was on the road to developing real democratic institutions. Indeed, it was the act of starting a preventive war against Russia and France in 1914 that destroyed most British and American elites' faith that Germany would likely develop as a democracy at all. Ido Oren, "The Subjectivity of the 'Democratic' Peace: Changing U.S. Perceptions of Imperial Germany," *International Security*, Vol. 20, No. 2 (Fall 1995), pp. 147–184.
43. Michael Brecher, *Decisions in Israel's Foreign Policy* (New Haven, Conn.: Yale University Press, 1975), pp. 225–317. Israel's 1981 air attack that destroyed Iraq's nuclear power plant is an instance of a preventive strike, but it had little, if any, risk of escalating into a larger war. See Ilan Peleg, *Begin's Foreign Policy, 1977–1983* (New York: Greenwood, 1987), pp. 185–190.

cember 2003) and Spain (March 2004). The campaign conducted by the United States has strengthened the Islamists' sense of being totally at war against the rest of the world."[44]

RELATIVE GAINS. Foreign suspicion of U.S. intentions is exacerbated by the politics of oil. Conquering Iraq puts the United States in a strategic position to control virtually all of the Persian Gulf's vast oil reserves, potentially increasing its power to manipulate supply for political and even military advantage against Europe and Asia. This power could be used broadly by withdrawing Persian Gulf oil from the world market, or selectively by imposing a strategic embargo on a specific major power rival.

The main effect of U.S. control over Persian Gulf oil is to create relative, as opposed to absolute, power advantages for the United States.[45] Iraq possesses the world's second-largest oil reserves, which could provide economic returns to the United States. These benefits are unlikely to dramatically increase America's relative power position, because the United States is already the world's sole superpower and most wealthy state. Assume the extreme: that Iraqi oil production immediately ramps up to pre-1990 levels of about 3 million barrels per day and that the United States seizes fully 100 percent of these oil revenues, leaving nothing for the Iraqi population or economy and ignoring the costs of occupation. Even under these circumstances, U.S. gains from Iraqi oil revenues would total about $30 billion a year or about 1/3 of 1 percent of the United States' $10 trillion gross national product in 2003. This amount would

---

44. Bruno Tertrais, *War without End: A View from Abroad* (London: New Press, 2004), p. 85. Official French analyses agree. The first vice president of the Tribunal de Grande Instance de Paris stated, "The war in Iraq did not reduce the terrorist threat, and in fact, has increased the risk of attacks in the United States and Europe by increasing the level of Islamist and anti-American rhetoric, by diverting the attention of political leaders from the central issue of the war on terrorism, and by encouraging the view among the public that the war on terrorism is nearly won." Judge Jean-Louis Bruguière, *Terrorism and the War in Iraq* (Washington, D.C.: Center on the United States and France, U.S.-France Analysis Series, May 2003), p. 1. Given that nearly 10 percent of France's population is Muslim and that Germany was used as a staging ground for al-Qaida's September 11 attacks, it is perhaps not surprising that these two European countries were especially concerned about the consequences of the Bush strategy.

45. Absolute gains refer to the profit a state makes on a transaction independently of how others gain or lose on the deal. Relative gains refer to one state's profit compared with the profits and losses of others. Although absolute gains among states encourage cooperation, differences in relative gains make some better off than others and often explain why cooperation breaks down. Relative gains are especially problematic in cooperation over major economic or military matters that influence the long-term balance of power among states. See Joseph M. Grieco, "Anarchy and the Limits of Cooperation: A Realist Critique of the Newest Liberal Institutionalism," *International Organization*, Vol. 42, No. 3 (Summer 1988), pp. 485–508; and Robert Powell, "Absolute and Relative Gains in International Relations Theory," *American Political Science Review*, Vol. 85, No. 4 (December 1991), pp. 1303–1320.

be important to specific U.S. oil companies and their investors, but it would not make a significant difference to the balance of power among the United States, Europe, Russia, China, and Japan.

Even the value of the Persian Gulf region as a whole would add only modestly to the absolute level of U.S. power. Assuming the same standard as above, U.S. control of the region would add only about 3 percent to U.S. GNP. Moreover, a monopoly by U.S. companies over Persian Gulf oil would allow them to buy oil cheaply—because Arab producers would have nowhere else to go—resulting in lower oil prices for the United States and its major power rivals, except for Russia.[46]

Rather, the main effect would be a relative gain for the United States. Total control of Persian Gulf oil would give the United States monopoly power over a crucial source of economic growth.[47] Other states could develop new sources of oil to substitute for Persian Gulf oil, although the likely decline in oil prices following U.S. control of the Persian Gulf would make new oil development uneconomical. Most important, however, U.S. monopolization of Persian Gulf oil would be the single most significant act that the United States could take to increase its relative power, save for taking control of European or Asian resources. During the Cold War, the United States feared that Soviet conquest of the Persian Gulf would offer new political leverage against Europe and Asia. Many argued that such fears were based on unsophisticated economics, but this did not stop U.S. leaders from balancing against the Soviet threat to oil.[48]

Although many Americans doubt that the United States would use this new power, in fact it already is. For months, it has been threatening to deny oil contracts to French, Russian, and other oil companies if their countries do not co-

---

46. The losers would be Arab states, other developing-world oil producers, and Russia, which is the only industrial power that is also a net exporter of oil. The countries whose companies have the oil contracts would probably not derive long-term economic advantage from those countries as a whole. Although U.S. and British companies owned almost all of the oil contracts, which kept the price of oil low from 1945 to 1973, it did little harm to the Germans, French, or Japanese. There is no reason to think that, had these last three owned some shares, their economies would have grown faster and those of the United States and Britain slower.
47. The importance of Persian Gulf oil is not expected to change for decades. According to the Bush administration, "By 2020, Gulf oil producers are projected to supply between 54 and 67% of the world's oil. . . . By any estimation, Middle East oil producers will remain central to world oil security. The Gulf will be a primary focus of U.S. international energy policy." National Energy Policy Development Group, *National Energy Policy* (Washington, D.C.: Office of the Vice President, May 2001), chap. 8, pp. 4–5.
48. See Ray Dafter, "World Oil Production and Security of Supplies," *International Security*, Vol. 4, No. 3 (Winter 1979/80), pp. 154–176; and Robert H. Johnson, "The Persian Gulf in U.S. Strategy: A Skeptical View," *International Security*, Vol. 14, No. 1 (Summer 1989), pp. 122–160.

operate with U.S. military plans for Iraq. More important, other states may not share the confidence the United States has of its own good intentions. If the United States retains unilateral control over Iraq's oil, this is almost certain to favor U.S. companies and add to U.S. power, which is likely to magnify suspicion of the United States' power and purpose. Relative gains over economic stakes have been a principal cause of major power competition in the past.[49] U.S. unilateral preventive wars against rogue states in the Persian Gulf could create the same incentives today.

GROWING NUCLEAR ADVANTAGES. Suspicion of U.S. intentions is also aggravated by the Bush administration's nuclear policies, especially its pursuit of an ambitious system of national missile defense. Although the administration views NMD as a reasonable effort to protect the U.S. homeland from the threat of ballistic missiles from rogue states, other major powers see it as a signal of U.S. malign intent.[50]

The Bush administration appears determined to field the first-ever operational system to intercept ballistic missiles heading for the United States. Following aborted negotiations with Russia, the administration officially abandoned the ABM treaty in June 2002, authorized more than $17 billion to construct a ballistic missile defense system in Alaska in December 2002, and plans to have the initial system operational in the early years of the second administration. The plan calls for ten ground-based interceptors and accompanying radars based in Alaska and California in the first year of operation, ten more interceptors in Alaska in the second year, and more ambitious, multilayer defenses after this point.[51]

Whether this system will effectively counter ballistic missiles from rogue states is difficult to assess, in part because no rogue state has yet tested an operational missile capable of hitting the United States. Concern over the poten-

49. For evidence that concerns about relative gains impede cooperation among major powers, see Joseph M. Grieco, *Cooperation among Nations: Europe, America, and Non-tariff Barriers to Trade* (Ithaca, N.Y.: Cornell University Press, 1990); Michael Mastanduno, "Do Relative Gains Matter? America's Response to Japanese Industrial Policy," *International Security*, Vol. 16, No. 1 (Summer 1991), pp. 73–113; and John C. Matthews III, "Current Gains and Future Outcomes: When Cumulative Relative Gains Matter," *International Security*, Vol. 21, No. 1 (Summer 1996), pp. 112–146.

50. On the consequences of U.S. national missile defense for other major powers, see Glaser and Fetter, "National Missile Defense and the Future of U.S. Nuclear Weapons Policy"; Dean A. Wilkening, *Ballistic Missile Defense and Strategic Stability*, Adelphi Paper 334 (London: International Institute for Strategic Studies, May 2000); James M. Lindsay and Michael E. O'Hanlon, *Defending America: The Case for Limited National Missile Defense* (Washington, D.C.: Brookings, 2001); and Victor A. Utgoff, *Missile Defense and American Ambitions* (Alexandria, Va.: Institute for Defense Analysis, December 2001).

51. Eric Schmitt, "Antimissile System, in a Limited Form, Is Ordered by Bush," *New York Times*, December 18, 2002.

tial negative international consequences among the major powers, however, is already apparent. Most NATO members, including Great Britain, Germany, and France, have been consistently opposed to U.S. NMD.[52] Russia and China have gone further, explicitly stating their fears that it threatens their strategic nuclear capabilities. Although the United States has repeatedly declared that NMD is aimed only at North Korea and other rogue states, one Chinese government official stated, "That doesn't matter. The consequences are still terrible for us."[53] The U.S. claim that it needs missile defense to protect itself from rogue states is, according to one Russian general, "an argument for the naive or the stupid. . . . This system will be directed against Russia and against China."[54] In July 2000 China and Russia issued a joint statement declaring that U.S. NMD would have "the most grave adverse consequences not only for the security of Russia, China and other countries, but also for the security of the United States."[55]

Why is the prospect of U.S. ballistic missile defenses increasing the perception of insecurity among the world's major powers? In the nuclear age, the security of major powers depends on maintaining credible nuclear retaliatory capabilities. Even after the end of the Cold War, the United States, Great Britain, France, Russia, and China continue to believe that their security requires nuclear forces that can respond to a nuclear attack on their homelands. On any given day, the United States and Russia have some 6,000 strategic nuclear warheads deployed in a fashion that could retaliate in short order against a nuclear strike from any state in the world; Great Britain has several hundred and China several dozen.

The development of U.S. NMD is creating a classic security dilemma between the United States and other major powers, especially with Russia and China. As the United States gains the capability to intercept missiles from rogue states, its efforts are increasing fears that this limited system will expand to allow it to achieve nuclear superiority. The problem is not that the United States will actually gain nuclear superiority in the near term—the inevitable

---

52. See Stephen Cambone, *European Views of National Missile Defense* (Washington, D.C.: Atlantic Council of the United States, September 2000); and *Foreign Affairs—Eighth Report*, House of Commons, United Kingdom, November 2000, http://www.publications.parliament.uk/pa/cm199900/cmselect/cmfaff/407/40702.htm.
53. Quoted in Eric Eckholm, "What America Calls a Defense China Calls an Offense," *New York Times*, July 2, 2000.
54. Quoted in Martin Nesirky, "Interview—Russian General Slams U.S. on Missile Plan," Reuters, February 14, 2000.
55. Quoted in Ted Plafker, "China Joins Russia in Warning U.S. on Shield," *Washington Post*, July 14, 2000.

technical difficulties with a new, sophisticated military system mitigate such immediate fears. Rather, it is that U.S. efforts will continue to expand, enabling Washington to pursue meaningful nuclear advantages in the long term.

The United States' ambitious pursuit of NMD is giving major powers reason to doubt its intentions. U.S. nuclear retaliatory capabilities are already stronger than those of any other state; thus nuclear deterrence already provides robust security against deliberate missile attack. Moreover, the September 11 terrorist attacks demonstrated that rogue states would probably find covert attack more reliable than low-quality ballistic missiles as a means to deliver a nuclear weapon against the United States. Further, the technological infrastructure— sophisticated radars and command and control networks—for a limited ballistic missile defense system against a small number of missiles from rogue states has the operational capacity to expand the system to counter a larger number of missiles from major powers. Accordingly, major powers have a basis to fear that U.S. NMD could evolve into a serious effort to acquire meaningful nuclear superiority, an effort that would make sense only if the United States had expansionist rather than status quo aims.[56]

The central problem is the dual purpose inherent in the technological infrastructure for ballistic missile defense, especially in the radars. During the 1990s, ballistic missile defense became more technologically feasible in part because of a dramatic improvement in the discrimination capacity of cutting-edge radars, such as the X-band radar capable of identifying, tracking, and differentiating thousands of individual targets with perhaps a sufficiently high resolution to overcome decoys and other countermeasures. Although the initial missile defense system will have a fairly small number of interceptors, the core of the system will include one special high-resolution radar in Alaska; fifteen upgraded and new radars in the United States, Greenland, South Korea, and the United Kingdom; and a new generation of ballistic missile detection satellites. Once this technological infrastructure is in place, major powers will have to consider the possibility that the United States could rapidly increase the capability of the system by adding more interceptors or other upgrades.[57]

China's small nuclear arsenal would be the most vulnerable to this new sys-

---

56. An extremely limited NMD system, especially if confined to boost-phase intercept, would not create severe security dilemmas with Russia and China. See Glaser and Fetter, "National Missile Defense and the Future of U.S. Nuclear Weapons Policy."

57. Union of Concerned Scientists and MIT Security Studies Program, *Countermeasures: A Technical Evaluation of the Operational Effectiveness of the Planned U.S. National Missile Defense System* (Cambridge, Mass.: MIT Press, 2000); and Edward O. Rios, "A Credible National Missile Defense: Do-Able NMD," *Breakthroughs*, Vol. 8, No. 1 (Spring 1999), pp. 9–18.

tem. With only twenty single-warhead nuclear missiles capable of hitting the United States, Chinese leaders undoubtedly know that these strategic forces are vulnerable to a U.S. surprise attack. Today, even a highly successful U.S. attack that destroyed fifteen Chinese strategic nuclear missiles would still leave five nuclear warheads capable of retaliation. If, however, the United States builds a missile defense system to counter five or more ballistic missiles from a rogue state such as North Korea, leaders in Beijing are likely to fear that it is developing the capability to defeat Chinese retaliation as well.

Russia's nuclear arsenal would not be vulnerable to initial U.S. missile defenses, but the Bush administration's more ambitious plans could eventually create problems. Today, even the most effective U.S. strike that experts can imagine would still leave Russia with about 150 strategic nuclear warheads, more than enough to wreak unacceptable retaliation to deter a first strike. A missile defense designed to intercept five or so warheads from an Asian country is not likely to challenge Russia's nuclear deterrent. The Bush administration is interested in a more ambitious system, however, one that could destroy ballistic missiles from multiple rogue states and perhaps even "accidental" launches from Russia itself. Given these facts, it would be surprising if Russian security analysts did not believe that the administration's plan for a limited NMD would provide the United States with the infrastructure and experience to field a larger and more advanced system that could erode Russia's retaliatory capabilities.[58]

U.S. UNILATERALISM AND THE GLOBAL RESPONSE

The international image of the United States as a benign superpower is declining, particularly with regard to the aspects that are likely to erode its relative immunity to balance of power dynamics. Without the perception of benign intent, a unipolar leader's intervention in regions beyond its own, especially those with substantial economic value, is likely to produce incentives among the world's other major powers to balance against it. That the United States does not pose an imminent threat to attack any major power is not sufficient to prevent these incentives, because the main danger for second-ranked states is that the United States would pose an indirect threat or evolve from a unipolar leader into an unrestrained global hegemon. In a unipolar world, the response to an expansionist unipolar leader is likely to be global balancing.

---

58. Igor Ivanov, "The Missile-Defense Mistake: Undermining Strategic Stability and the ABM Treaty," *Foreign Affairs*, Vol. 79, No. 5 (September/October 2000), pp. 15–20.

The Strategy of Soft Balancing

Balancing is about equalizing the odds in a contest between the strong and the weak. States balance when they take action intended to make it hard for strong states to use their military advantage against others. The goal can be to deter a strong state from attacking or to reduce its prospects of victory in war. Traditional hard balancing seeks to change the military balance in an actual or (more often) potential conflict by contributing military capabilities to the weaker side through measures such as a military buildup, war-fighting alliance, or transfer of military technology to an ally.

HOW SOFT BALANCING WORKS

States can also seek to equalize the odds through soft balancing. Balancing can involve the utilization of tools to make a superior state's military forces harder to use without directly confronting that state's power with one's own forces. Although soft balancing relies on nonmilitary tools, it aims to have a real, if indirect, effect on the military prospects of a superior state. Mechanisms of soft balancing include territorial denial, entangling diplomacy, economic strengthening, and signaling of resolve to participate in a balancing coalition. All of these steps can weaken the military power that the superior state can bring to bear in battle.[59]

TERRITORIAL DENIAL. Superior states often benefit from access to the territory of third parties as staging areas for ground forces or as transit for air and naval forces. Denying access to this territory can reduce the superior state's prospects for victory, such as by increasing the logistical problems for the superior state or compelling it to fight with air or sea power alone, constraints that effectively reduce the overall force that a stronger state can bring to bear against a weaker one.

ENTANGLING DIPLOMACY. Even strong states do not have complete freedom to ignore either the rules and procedures of important international organizations or accepted diplomatic practices without losing substantial support for their objectives. Accordingly, states may use international institutions and ad hoc diplomatic maneuvers to delay a superior state's plan for war and so reduce the element of surprise and give the weaker side more time to prepare; delay may even make the issue irrelevant. Especially if the superior state is

---

59. Thus, soft balancing differs from everyday international diplomacy, which often seeks to resolve disputes through compromise rather than through changes in the balance of power or the use of policies that limit a strong state's military power.

also a democracy, entangling diplomacy works not only by affecting the balance of military capabilities that can be brought to bear in the dispute but also by strengthening domestic opposition to possible adventures within the superior state.

ECONOMIC STRENGTHENING. Militarily strong, threatening states that are the targets of balancing efforts usually derive their military superiority from possession of great economic strength. One way of balancing effectively, at least in the long run, would be to shift relative economic power in favor of the weaker side. The most obvious way of doing this is through regional trading blocs that increase trade and economic growth for members while directing trade away from nonmembers. If the superior state can be excluded from the most important such blocs, its overall trade and growth rates may suffer over time.

SIGNALS OF RESOLVE TO BALANCE. Second-ranked powers seeking to act collectively against a sole superpower confront intense concern that the needed collective action will not materialize. Soft balancing, in addition to its direct usefulness in restraining aggression by a unipolar leader, may also address this problem by helping to coordinate expectations of mutual balancing behavior. If multiple states can cooperate, repeatedly, in some of the types of measures listed above, they may gradually increase their trust in each other's willingness to cooperate against the unipolar leader's ambitions. Thus, a core purpose of soft balancing is not to coerce or even to impede the superior state's current actions, but to demonstrate resolve in a manner that signals a commitment to resist the superpower's future ambitions. Accordingly, the measure of success for soft balancing is not limited to whether the sole superpower abandons specific policies, but also includes whether more states join a soft-balancing coalition against the unipolar leader.

HISTORICAL PRECURSORS IN MULTIPOLAR SYSTEMS
Soft balancing is most conducive to the politics of unipolar systems, but examples of it can be found in history. Today, the U.S. strategy of containing the Soviet Union during the Cold War is thought of as a military strategy, but this is not how it started out. The crucial first step was the Marshall Plan, a massive program of U.S. economic aid to rebuild the shattered industries, agricultural areas, and cities of Europe and Japan in the aftermath of World War II. This economic instrument helped desperate states resist the temptations of communist doctrines of class struggle and revolution; it also integrated Western Europe and Japan into a North Atlantic trading network. Although the Marshall Plan did not create military forces or commit states to use force against the Soviet Union, it was the crucial long-term bond that ensured that the world's key

industrial centers would be in the Western camp and that the Soviet Union would remain permanently inferior to it.[60]

A second example is Bismarckian Germany. After Germany's victory in the Franco-Prussian war in 1870, France remained Bismarck's immediate problem, both because it retained the most latent power of any state on the continent and because it might have tried to avenge its loss. A comprehensive German-led alliance against the French, however, was not possible. Austria, Russia, and Britain were worried about France, but they were also worried about a newly unified Germany, and so could be tempted into an alliance with Paris. Bismarck's solution was to set up a series of cross-cutting alliances and contradictory international commitments that, at its peak, included half of Europe but excluded France. This system was largely useless in case of war, but that was not the point. As Josef Joffe has written, "Bismarck did not construct his system in order to aggregate power but to devalue it—balancing and stalemating à la Britain, but in totally un-British ways."[61] In other words, this new web of international cooperation isolated and balanced against a potentially superior power not through addition (amassing military forces in opposition) but through dilution (removing capabilities available to the opponent) and without confronting the power of the opponent directly.

THE START OF SOFT BALANCING AGAINST THE UNITED STATES
Soft balancing is replacing traditional hard balancing as the principal reaction of major powers to the Bush administration's preventive war doctrine. Until now, there has been no concept for this form of balancing behavior, and so it has been difficult to detect that the early stages of soft balancing against U.S. power have already started.

On August 26, 2002, Vice President Dick Cheney called for the United States to launch a preventive war to depose Saddam Hussein. In September the United States issued its new strategy, asserting the right to wage preventive war against rogue states. Shortly thereafter, European, Middle Eastern, and Asian powers undertook a series of steps to contain U.S. military power using soft-balancing instruments.

First, France, Sweden, and other European states used institutional rules and procedures in the UN to delay, if not head off completely, U.S. preventive

---

60. On the geopolitical significance of the Marshall Plan, see John Lewis Gaddis, *Strategies of Containment: A Critical Appraisal of Postwar American Security Policy* (Oxford: Oxford University Press, 1982), pp. 30–31.
61. Josef Joffe, "'Bismark' or 'Britain'? Toward an American Grand Strategy after Bipolarity," *International Security*, Vol. 19, No. 4 (Spring 1995), p. 107.

war against Iraq. In the past, the United States has often been able to legitimate foreign and military policies by gaining the approval of the UN Security Council. In September 2002 it sought to gain such sanction for war against Iraq. France, however, threatened to veto the resolution authorizing war—which would have been the first time a U.S. resolution had ever been vetoed in the Security Council—unless two conditions were met: (1) the Bush administration would have to accept a serious effort to resolve matters with Iraq through weapons inspections; and (2) it would need to wait for a resolution authorizing war until after the inspections were completed. The administration agreed, even though this meant delaying its plan for war. In March 2003 the UN's chief weapons inspector, Hans Blix, and the head of the International Atomic Energy Agency, Mohamed ElBaradei, declared that the inspections had made substantial progress but would take months longer to complete—a judgment that effectively prevented the United States from gaining the votes necessary for a Security Council resolution in support of the war.

Second, Turkey and Saudi Arabia firmly denied the United States the use of their territory for ground forces and have been ambiguous about providing basing rights for logistic efforts and airpower. Turkey is the most important case because Bush administration officials made repeated efforts to gain its cooperation. In January 2003 the administration asked Turkey to allow the deployment of between 60,000 to 90,000 U.S. ground troops who then would cross Turkish territory into Kurdish-controlled northern Iraq. Ankara balked. "The government has indicated its preparedness to meet American requests basically in all areas with the exception of the stationing of a large number of ground forces in Turkey," a Turkish official said. Turkey was strategically important to a low-cost, high-confidence strategy for defeating Iraq. The United States hoped to invade Iraq from Turkey in the north and Kuwait in the south, and so attack Saddam Hussein's overstretched military forces from different directions and quickly overwhelm them. Although U.S. officials expected that they could conduct a successful attack to conquer Iraq even without access to land bases in Turkey, they granted that such a war would be, as one ranking official put it, "harder and uglier." U.S. ships with an infantry division waited off the coast of Turkey for weeks, but the Turkish government remained firm.[62]

Third, China and South Korea are attempting to elevate their role in diplomatic negotiations over North Korea's nuclear program, making it more

---

62. Philip Stephens, "A Deadline for War Looms as Allied Enthusiasm Fades," *Financial Times,* January 10, 2003; and Michael R. Gordon, "Turkey's Reluctance on Use of Bases Worries U.S.," *New York Times,* January 9, 2003.

difficult for the United States to use force. In October 2002 North Korea admitted to having an ongoing nuclear weapons program, declaring that in response to the growing U.S. threat to its country from the Bush doctrine of preventive war, it would accelerate its efforts to build nuclear weapons. The North Korean leadership offered to halt the nuclear program if the United States would sign a nonaggression treaty agreeing not to attack their country. While the United States has refused to make this pledge, South Korea has sided with North Korea, asking the United States to sign a nonaggression treaty in return for Pyongyang's agreement to abandon nuclear development and meeting with Japanese and Russian officials to gain their support for this position. December 2002 Gallup polls show that more South Koreans had a positive view of North Korea than of the United States. Of those surveyed, 47 percent felt positively about North Korea, while 37 percent held an unfavorable view. Only 37 percent had a positive view of the United States, while 53 percent viewed it unfavorably. This represented a significant change from 1994 when 64 percent of South Koreans surveyed said they liked the United States and only 15 percent disliked it. Also in December 2002 South Korea elected a new president, Roh Moo Hyun, who advocates continuation of the sunshine policy of engagement with North Korea and who, after the election, met with military officials and instructed them to draw up plans that assume a reduction in U.S. forces stationed there. "The U.S. military presence must be adjusted," says Kim Sang-woo, a foreign policy adviser to Roh.[63]

None of these moves directly challenges U.S. military power, but they all make it more difficult for the United States to exercise that power. They impose immediate costs and constraints on the application of U.S. power by entangling the United States in diplomatic maneuvers, reducing the pressure on regional states to cooperate with its military plans, and bolstering the claims of target states that U.S. military threats justify the acceleration of their own military programs. They also establish a new pattern of diplomatic activity: cooperation among major powers that excludes the United States.

If the United States remains committed to its unilateral military policies, such soft-balancing measures are likely to become more common. Balancing against a sole superpower such as the United States will have a logic of its

---

63. Peter S. Goodman, "Anti-U.S. Sentiment Deepens in S. Korea," *Washington Post*, January 9, 2003; David J. Lynch, "Many S. Koreans Pin Blame on U.S., Not North," *USA Today*, January 6, 2003; John Burton, "Seoul May Seek U.S. Pledge on N. Korea," *Financial Times*, January 4, 2003; and John Burton, "Fears Grow over Widening Rift between Seoul and U.S.," *Financial Times*, January 13, 2003.

own, one perhaps not wholly unique, but one that is nonetheless distinctive to the condition of unipolarity.[64]

WHY SOFT BALANCING MATTERS

Soft balancing may not stop the United States from conquering a rogue state or from pursuing a vigorous nuclear buildup, but it can have significant long-term consequences for U.S. security. In the months leading up to the U.S. invasion of Iraq, soft balancing had already encouraged millions of Europeans and hundreds of thousands of Americans to protest the impending war. Such protests can have important consequences for governments that support U.S. policy—or refuse to. In recent elections, German, Turkish, and even South Korean political leaders have already learned that anti-Americanism pays. Indeed, vigorous opposition to the Bush doctrine of preventive war in September 2002 was likely the pivotal factor enabling German Chancellor Gerhard Schröder to recover from a position of almost certain defeat to win a new term. Even if the leaders of Britain and other members of the "coalition of the willing" against Iraq can avoid domestic backlash, few are likely to be willing to cooperate with future U.S. military adventures.

Soft balancing can also impose real military costs. The United States may be the sole superpower, but it is geographically isolated. To project power in Europe, Asia, and the Middle East, it depends greatly on basing rights granted by local allies. Indeed, all U.S. victories since 1990—Iraq, Bosnia, Kosovo, and Afghanistan—relied on the use of short-legged tactical air and ground forces based in the territory of U.S. allies in the region. Without regional allies, the United States might still be able to act unilaterally, but it would have to take higher risks in blood and treasure to do so.[65] Turkey's refusal to allow U.S. ground forces on its soil reduced the amount of heavy ground power available against Iraq by one-third, thus compelling the United States to significantly alter its preferred battle plan, increasing the risk of U.S. casualties in the con-

---

64. Certain actions, such as French withdrawal from operations to enforce the no-fly zones after the U.S. Desert Fox bombing campaign in December 1998, can be viewed as antecedents to the soft balancing witnessed today. The main differences are (1) merely withdrawing support for an action is not equivalent to actively seeking to stall or prevent the leading state's use of power; and (2) action by just one state is unlikely to constitute notable balancing in a unipolar system.
65. In general, regional military bases serve as force multipliers, reducing the requirements for naval ships (at the distance between the United States and Asia, by more than two-thirds), lowering the costs of air transport operations (by about half in this case), and most important, making it possible to use heavy ground forces and tactical air forces (on the Korean Peninsula and in other Asian contingencies). Michael C. Desch, "Bases for the Future: U.S. Military Interests in the Post–Cold War Third World," *Security Studies*, Vol. 2, No. 2 (Winter 1992), pp. 201–224.

quest of Iraq, and leaving fewer forces to establish stability in the country after the war.

Soft balancers may also become more ambitious. As the U.S. occupation of Iraq continues, France, Germany, Russia, and China could press hard for the UN rather than the United States to oversee the administration of oil contracts in Iraq, perhaps even working with the new Iraqi government for this purpose. Even if they did not succeed, U.S. freedom of action in Iraq and elsewhere in the region would decline. If the United States gave in, it would lose control over which companies ultimately obtain contracts for Iraq's oil, and so pay a higher price for any continued presence in the region.

Further, Europeans and others may take steps that start to shift the balance of economic power against the United States. Today Europeans buy their oil in dollars, a practice that benefits the United States by creating extra demand for dollars as the world's reserve currency. This extra demand allows the United States to run outsized trade and government budget deficits at lower inflation and interest rates than would otherwise be the case. A coordinated decision by other countries to buy oil in euros would transfer much of this benefit to Europe and decrease the United States' gross national product, possibly by as much as 1 percent, more or less permanently.[66]

Most important, soft balancing could eventually evolve into hard balancing. Now that the United States has conquered Iraq, major powers are likely to become quite concerned about U.S. intentions toward Iran, North Korea, and possibly Saudi Arabia. Unilateral U.S. military action against any of these states could become another focal point around which major powers' expectations of U.S. intentions could again converge. If so, then soft balancing could establish the basis for actual hard balancing against the United States.

Perhaps the most likely step toward hard balancing would be for major states to encourage and support transfers of military technology to U.S. opponents. Russia is already providing civilian nuclear technology to Iran, a state that U.S. intelligence believes is pursuing nuclear weapons. Such support is

---

66. Ideas for more intense soft balancing have been articulated by Chinese academics. Zhiyuan Cui, a professor at Tsinghua University in Beijing, writes that "China is naturally . . . sensitive about American aggressive unilateralism" and identifies numerous "Chinese counterbalancing efforts to set against the unipolar power of the United States . . . using China's power in the UN Security Council to seek peaceful resolutions . . . supporting the euro by diversifying China's foreign currency holding . . . developing trade and security cooperation with Russia. . . . Indeed, the increasing cooperation between China and the EU may be the most important response to the Bush Doctrine on the part of both China and the EU." Zhiyuan Cui, "The Bush Doctrine: A Chinese Perspective," in David Held and Mathias Koenig-Archibugi, eds., *American Power in the Twenty-first Century* (Cambridge: Polity, 2004), pp. 241–251.

likely to continue, and major powers may facilitate this by blocking U.S. steps to put pressure on Moscow. For instance, if the United States attempts to make economic threats against Russia, European countries might open their doors to Russia wider. If they did, this would involve multiple major powers cooperating for the first time to transfer military technology to an opponent of the United States. Collective hard balancing would thus have truly begun.

Traditional realists may be tempted to dismiss soft balancing as ineffective. They should not. In the long run, soft balancing could also shift relative power between major powers and the United States and lay the groundwork to enable hard balancing if the major powers come to believe this is necessary.

Preventing Soft Balancing in the Future

The Bush strategy of preventive war against rogue states and aggressive unilateral military policies in general are increasing the incentives for major powers to balance against the United States. Since 2002, scholars, journalists, and diplomats have witnessed the result: a profound change in the world's response to American power. They have seen not simply the reluctance of traditional allies to join the U.S. war effort against Iraq, but active efforts by many of the world's major powers to delay, frustrate, and undermine U.S. war plans and reduce the number of countries that would fight alongside the United States.

Although some observers might have thought that major powers would easily mend fences with the United States after the conquest of Iraq, in fact there are signs of growing soft balancing against it. Perhaps the most important indicator concerns U.S. allies. Key countries that sided with the United States during the war are working with France and Germany in a manner that works against further U.S. military adventures. Following the March 2004 election, Spain's newly elected prime minister, José Luis Rodriguez Zapatero, declared, "I want Europe to see us again as pro-European. The war in Iraq has been a disaster and the occupation continues to be a great disaster. Spain is going to see eye to eye with Europe again. Spain is going to be more pro-Europe than ever."[67] In September 2003 the United Kingdom joined France and Germany in an effort independent of the United States to use diplomacy and economic statecraft to persuade Iran to limit its nuclear ambitions. In February 2005 these European efforts compelled the Bush administration to declare that it

---

67. Quoted in Elaine Sciolino, "Spain Will Loosen Its Alliance with U.S., Premier-Elect Says," *New York Times*, March 16, 2004.

would not use force against Iran "at this point in time" and to support a multi-lateral approach to the issue, at least temporarily.[68]

Such widespread opposition is virtually unprecedented in U.S. history, especially by European and other major powers allied with the United States since World War II. The world is pushing back in response to the Bush administration's strategy of aggressive unilateralism. For the first time, the United States has adopted a national strategy to conquer countries that are not attacking it or its allies, at a time of its choosing, whether other states agree with U.S. policies or not. That Iraq and most other announced possible targets of this preventive war strategy are important to the control of Persian Gulf oil only makes matters worse. That the Bush strategy simultaneously calls for other aggressive unilateral military policies that will increase U.S. nuclear advantages over major powers indicates the administration's lack of concern about a backlash from these states.

Serious opposition to U.S. military policies is only likely to increase if the United States continues along its present course of aggressive unilateralism. Traditional hard balancing—military buildups, war-fighting alliances, and transfers of military technology to U.S. opponents—may not occur soon in today's world, dominated as it is by the United States' overwhelming military power. But states can dilute the U.S. advantage and contain the United States' power in other ways. Even without directly confronting U.S. military might, major powers can use soft balancing tools—international institutions, economic statecraft, and ad hoc diplomatic arrangements—to limit the use of U.S. power in the short term and establish the crucial conditions for more ambitious balancing efforts in the long term.

Without broad international support, the Bush strategy for stopping the spread of weapons of mass destruction to rogue states using preventive war and aggressive nuclear policies does not serve U.S. national security interests. Keeping nuclear weapons out of the hands of authoritarian regimes is important, but even the world's only superpower cannot afford to provoke—and, more significantly, to frighten—a majority of the major powers at once. Immediately after the September 11 terrorist attacks, the United States' NATO allies unanimously declared that the attacks were an act of aggression, and they offered to assist in joint defense. Indeed, many nations—including Germany and France—have military forces still serving in Afghanistan. But, unless the United States radically changes its avowed national security strategy, it risks

---

68. "Timeline: U.S.-Iran Ties," *BBC News*, March 12, 2005.

creating a world in which a broad, if loose, coalition of major powers (including most of its nominal allies) is more motivated to constrain the United States than to cooperate with it.

U.S. national security policy should rest on a calculation of costs and benefits about how to best defend the country and its citizens. The unilateral use of force may, on rare occasions, be the only way to prevent imminent harm to the United States, and so the benefits of an isolated use of unilateral force may overwhelm the costs of international opposition to it. A systematic U.S. policy of resolving numerous potential threats through the routine use of preventive war, however, is likely to pose far greater risks to U.S. security than it would solve. Smart unilateralism is often multilateral—especially when confronted with a spectrum of future dangers.

Soft balancing against the United States has begun, but balancing against a sole superpower is not destiny. At bottom, the world's major powers are reacting to concerns over U.S. intentions, not U.S. capabilities. Accordingly, the United States should mend fences; but after Iraq, it will take more than cheap talk to overcome the damage the Bush strategy of aggressive unilateralism is doing to America's reputation for benign intent. If the Bush administration repudiates preventive war as the centerpiece of U.S. national security strategy, vigorously participates in multilateral solutions to important international security issues such as Iran's nuclear program, strengthens international institutions by supporting the inclusion of Germany and other major powers as permanent members of the UN Security Council, and surrenders unilateral control over Iraq's oil contracts to a broader consortium of international companies, these would be meaningful steps to regain the United States' image as a benevolent superpower.

Soft Balancing in the Age of U.S. Primacy

T.V. Paul

$\mathbf{A}$ growing body of international relations literature contends that balance of power theory has become a relic of the Cold War.[1] According to this literature, second-ranking major powers such as Russia and China are abandoning balance of power strategies despite increased U.S. capabilities in almost all parameters of traditional sources of national power.[2] In every category of new weapons development and acquisition, the United States is widening its lead vis-à-vis the rest of the world. Not only does it possess global power status, but it has also been pursuing unilateralist strategies to prevent the rise of a peer competitor. Since the terrorist strikes of September 11, 2001, preventive and preemptive military actions against regional challengers seeking weapons of mass destruction (WMD) have become a key part of the United States' global strategy.[3] Certain U.S. policies, especially with respect to the Middle East and Central Asia, have made some foreign governments uneasy—among them the United States' traditional allies in Europe. Yet evidence of a balancing coalition forming against

T.V. Paul is James McGill Professor of International Relations at McGill University, Montreal, Canada. He has published eight books including Balance of Power: Theory and Practice in the 21st Century, coedited with James J. Wirtz and Michel Fortmann (Stanford, Calif.: Stanford University Press, 2004).

The author would like to thank Anne Clunan, William Hogg, Jenna Jordan, Christopher Layne, Charles Lipson, John Mueller, Baldev Raj Nayar, Norrin Ripsman, Richard Rosecrance, and Matthias Staisch, as well as participants in the University of Chicago's Program on International Politics, Economics, and Security Speaker Series and in the Mershon Center seminar series at Ohio State University for their useful comments. He also thanks Louis Blais Dumas for research assistance and the Fonds de recherche sur la société et la culture for its support.

1. See, for example, Richard Ned Lebow, "The Long Peace, the End of the Cold War, and the Failure of Realism," *International Organization*, Vol. 48, No. 2 (Spring 1994), pp. 249–277; John A. Vasquez, "The Realist Paradigm and Degenerative versus Progressive Research Programs: An Appraisal of Neotraditional Research in Waltz's Balancing Proposition," *American Political Science Review*, Vol. 91, No. 4 (December 1997), pp. 899–912; and Edward Rhodes, "A World Not in Balance: War, Politics, and Weapons of Mass Destruction," in T.V. Paul, James J. Wirtz, and Michel Fortmann, eds., *Balance of Power: Theory and Practice in the 21st Century* (Stanford, Calif.: Stanford University Press, 2004), pp. 150–176.
2. Second-tier major powers are states that possess the actual or potential capabilities to engage in balance-of-power coalition building against the United States. In addition to China and Russia, France, the United Kingdom, Germany, India, and Japan can be included in this group.
3. "Preventive military action" refers to engagement in a war before an adversary develops operational capabilities, thus forestalling future aggression. "Preemptive action" is meant to stop an attacker that is about to launch a war. Regional challengers include Iran, North Korea, and Iraq under Saddam Hussein's rule.

International Security, Vol. 30, No. 1 (Summer 2005), pp. 46–71
© 2005 by the President and Fellows of Harvard College and the Massachusetts Institute of Technology.

the United States to countervail its power or threatening behavior has been conspicuously absent.

In this article I argue that since the end of the Cold War, second-tier major powers such as China, France, Germany, India, and Russia have mostly abandoned traditional "hard balancing"—based on countervailing alliances and arms buildups—at the systemic level. This does not mean, however, that they are helplessly watching the resurgence of U.S. power. These states have forgone military balancing primarily because they do not fear losing their sovereignty and existential security to the reigning hegemon, a necessary condition for such balancing to occur. In the past, weaker states aligned themselves against the increasing power of a hegemonic state out of concern that the rising power would inevitably challenge their sovereign territorial existence. Examples include great power behavior in eighteenth- and nineteenth-century Europe as well as during the Cold War. Absent this fear, the motivations and strategies of second-tier major powers vis-à-vis the dominant state can change. The U.S. imperial strategy by indirect methods sufficiently assures these powers that they are safe from predatory attacks by the United States. Indeed, they view the United States as a constrained hegemon whose power is checked by a multitude of factors, including: internal democratic institutions, domestic politics, and above all, the possession of nuclear weapons by some second-ranking powers.

Nevertheless, second-tier major powers—barring the United Kingdom—are concerned about the increasing unilateralism of the United States and its post–September 11 tendency to intervene militarily in sovereign states and forcibly change regimes that pursue anti-U.S. policies (such as Iraq). In this new environment, the second-ranking states are taking steps—including bandwagoning, buck-passing, and free-riding—both to constrain U.S. power and to maintain their security and influence. They have also begun to engage in "soft balancing," which involves the formation of limited diplomatic coalitions or ententes, especially at the United Nations, with the implicit threat of upgrading their alliances if the United States goes beyond its stated goals.

This article begins with a discussion of the existing explanations for the absence of traditional balancing against the United States. The second section provides an overview of the key characteristics of balance of power theory and its two variants—hard balancing and soft balancing—and the conditions under which states employ these strategies. The third section analyzes two cases of attempted soft balancing: Kosovo in 1999 and Iraq in 2002–03. It then elaborates on the balancing strategies adopted by second-tier powers and their allies through the UN and other forums such as NATO and examines the outcomes. The article concludes with some thoughts for understanding state behavior in the twenty-first century given this broadened concept of balancing and its implications for U.S. foreign policy.

Explanations for the Absence of Traditional Balancing

Explanations for the lack of balancing against the United States hinge on the liberal characteristics of U.S. hegemony, the liberal-democratic political system of the United States, and the absence of a rival state or coalition of states with the military capabilities to mount a serious challenge. According to William Wohlforth, nonliberal states such as Russia and China are incapable of balancing U.S. power because they cannot find allies to join them in such an endeavor.[4] From a liberal perspective, other liberal states, such as France and Germany, do not perceive the need to counterbalance the United States because they do not consider its growing power a threat.[5] To John Ikenberry, other states—both liberal and nonliberal—have eschewed traditional balancing because of their ability to influence American foreign policy through both U.S. and international institutions.[6] To economic liberals, economic interdependence and, more recently, globalization disincline second-tier states from engaging in balance of power politics. Because these powers—especially China and increasingly Russia—are linked by trade, investment, and commercial flows with the United States, they fear that military competition with it could derail their economies.[7]

The liberal school's argument thus assumes that second-tier major powers

---

4. William C. Wohlforth, "Revisiting Balance of Power Theory in Central Eurasia," in Paul, Wirtz, and Fortmann, *Balance of Power*, pp. 214–238.

5. John M. Owen IV, "Transnational Liberalism and U.S. Primacy," *International Security*, Vol. 26, No. 3 (Winter 2001/02), pp. 117–152. For alternative views, see William C. Wohlforth, "The Stability of a Unipolar World," *International Security*, Vol. 24, No. 1 (Summer 1999), pp. 5–41; Charles A. Kupchan, "After Pax Americana: Benign Power, Regional Integration, and the Sources of a Stable Multipolarity," *International Security*, Vol. 23, No. 2 (Fall 1998), pp. 40–79; Michael Mastanduno, "A Realist View: Three Images of the Coming International Order," in T.V. Paul and John A. Hall, eds., *International Order and the Future of World Politics* (Cambridge: Cambridge University Press, 1999), pp. 19–40; and Randall L. Schweller, "Unanswered Threats: A Neoclassical Realist Theory of Underbalancing," *International Security*, Vol. 29, No. 2 (Fall 2004), pp. 159–201.

6. G. John Ikenberry, "Liberal Hegemony and the Future of American Postwar Order," in Paul and Hall, *International Order and the Future of World Politics*, pp. 123–145.

7. On this, see Edward D. Mansfield and Brian M. Pollins, eds., *Economic Interdependence and International Conflict* (Ann Arbor: University of Michigan Press, 2003); and Thomas L. Friedman, *The Lexus and the Olive Tree: Understanding Globalization* (New York: Farrar, Straus and Giroux, 2000).

are generally more interested in wealth acquisition than security or military status. In the hierarchy of national goals, however, security concerns could override wealth acquisition if the former became the predominant challenge to a major power state. Further, if a hegemonic power is left unbalanced, it may deviate from its liberal ideals, especially if it believes that any of its vital interests are at stake. Indeed, liberal states have engaged in empire building and military interventions for both ideological and economic reasons.[8] Additionally, liberal states can form balancing coalitions with nonliberal nations against other liberal states.[9] The absence of capable nonliberal states, however, does not explain the dearth of balancing efforts against the United States. Because a state cannot single-handedly balance, it needs coalition partners. Such a coalition needs only to achieve a rough equilibrium, as absolute parity is often not needed to obtain a balance of power in the nuclear age. (In this regard, it is unclear why the combined power of China and Russia cannot achieve a meaningful balance of power against the United States.)

Realists, in contrast, contend that the United States will eventually be balanced by one or more states with matching capabilities, which in turn will produce a multipolar international system.[10] Power transitions occur over time because of the changes in the military, economic, and technological capabilities of major powers.[11] The problem with the realist perspective, however, is the indeterminacy in the timing of the arrival of a countervailing power. Moreover, as mentioned earlier, second-tier major powers have in the past adopted various strategies (including bandwagoning, buck-passing, and free-riding) when faced with an ascendant or threatening power, demonstrating that the formation of balancing military coalitions is not automatic.[12]

---

8. On liberal imperialism, see Michael Doyle, "Liberalism and World Politics," *American Political Science Review*, Vol. 80, No. 4 (December 1986), pp. 1154–1155.
9. An example is the U.S.-China-Pakistan alliance versus the Russia-India quasi alliance of the 1970s.
10. Kenneth N. Waltz, "Structural Realism after the Cold War," *International Security*, Vol. 25, No. 1 (Summer 2000), pp. 5–41; and Colin Gray, "Clausewitz Rules, OK? The Future Is the Past—with GPS," *Review of International Studies*, Vol. 25, No. 5 (December 1999), p. 169; and Christopher Layne, "The War on Terrorism and Balance of Power: The Paradoxes of American Hegemony," in Paul, Wirtz, and Fortmann, *Balance of Power*, pp. 103–126.
11. For arguments for and against this thinking, see Sean M. Lynn-Jones, ed., *The Cold War and After: Prospects for Peace* (Cambridge, Mass.: MIT Press, 1991); Waltz, "Structural Realism after the Cold War"; John J. Mearsheimer, *The Tragedy of Great Power Politics* (New York: W.W. Norton, 2001), chap. 10; Robert Gilpin, *War and Change in World Politics* (Cambridge: Cambridge University Press, 1981); and Christopher Layne, "The Unipolar Illusion: Why New Great Powers Will Rise," *International Security*, Vol. 17, No. 4 (Spring 1993), pp. 5–51.
12. Paul W. Schroeder, "Historical Reality vs. Neo-realist Theory," *International Security*, Vol. 19,

A variant of the realist argument is the historical/structural perspective on the rise and fall of great powers. On the basis of its logic, some scholars argue that overspending, overstretching, and internal failures will eventually cause the United States' decline.[13] Although the historical records of past great powers (e.g., Spain and Portugal) attest to the strength of this argument, one must be cautious of its application to the United States for three reasons. First, no previous empire had the benefit of capitalism in its highly developed form as the United States enjoys today. Second, several past empires and major powers managed to persevere, albeit in a weakened form, contrary to the expectations of perspectives that focus on automatic structural change. For instance, depending on the Western or Eastern manifestation, the Roman Empire lasted from 500 to 1,100 years. The Ottoman Empire survived for more than 400 years; the Mughal Empire in India more than 300; and the British Empire more than 250. Without World War II, the British Empire would probably have lasted even longer. Third, most past great powers (e.g., Spain, Portugal, Austria-Hungary, Japan, and Germany) declined following long periods of war with other imperial powers. In the case of the United States, the low probability of a global war akin to World War II may help to prolong its hegemony. Smaller challengers could wear down the hegemon's power through asymmetric strategies; but given its technological and organizational superiority, the United States can devise countermeasures to increase its power position even if it may not fully contain such challenges. Without war as a system-changing mechanism, and with no prospects of an alternative mechanism emerging for systemic change, even a weakened hegemon could endure for a long period. Further, because economic superiority does not automatically bestow military capability, as most modern weapons systems take considerable time to develop and deploy, U.S. dominance in this area is unlikely to be challenged for some time by a potential peer competitor, such as China, even after it overtakes the United States in gross economic terms.

A closer look at balance of power theory helps to clarify why the United States has not been balanced the way realists would have expected.

No. 1 (Summer 1994), pp. 108–148; and Mark R. Brawley, "The Political Economy of Balance of Power Theory," in Paul, Wirtz, and Fortmann, *Balance of Power*, pp. 76–99.

13. Paul Kennedy, *The Rise and Fall of the Great Powers* (New York: Random House, 1987). Similarly, power transition theorists of various hues believe in the rise and fall of great powers. See A.F.K. Organski and Jacek Kugler, *The War Ledger* (Chicago: University of Chicago Press, 1980); and Jacek Kugler and Douglas Lemke, eds., *Parity and War: Evaluations and Extensions of* The War Ledger (Ann Arbor: University of Michigan Press, 1996).

The Axioms of Balance of Power Theory

Balance of power has been the bedrock of realist international relations theory. To realists, states maintain security and stability at the systemic level largely through balancing. Throughout the history of the modern international system, balancing has been the key strategy employed by major powers to achieve their security goals.[14] Traditional balance of power theory is predicated on the following four premises that are also held in realism. First, the international system is anarchic and has no central governing authority to offer protection to individual states. Second, states seek to survive as independent entities. Third, power competition is a fact of international politics, as differential growth rates and technological innovations endow one or more states with military and economic advantages over time. Hegemony is sought by the power whose expanding capabilities compel it to broaden its national interests and thereby seek more power to protect its increasing assets. Fourth, when one state attempts to become dominant, threatened states will form defensive coalitions or acquire appropriate military wherewithal through internal or external sources or, in some cases, a combination of both. In rare cases, they will resort to preventive war to countervail the power of the rising or hegemonic state.[15] If the rising power is not constrained, it will inevitably engage in aggressive behavior that could result in other states losing their sovereign existence.[16]

Thus the fundamental goal of balance of power politics is to maintain the survival and sovereign independence of states in the international system; a related objective is not allowing any one state to preponderate.[17] Great powers may also have other instrumental goals in pursuing a balancing strategy, such as maintaining the independence of other great powers. As Jack Levy puts it, from the balance of power perspective, "maintaining the independence of

---

14. On the significance of balance of power, see Hans J. Morgenthau, *Politics among Nations,* 4th ed. (New York: Alfred A. Knopf, 1967), chap. 11; David Hume, "Of the Balance of Power," in Paul Seabury, ed., *Balance of Power* (San Francisco, Calif.: Chandler, 1965), pp. 32–36; Henry A. Kissinger, *A World Restored: Metternich, Castlereagh, and the Problems of Peace* (Boston: Houghton Mifflin, 1973); and Inis L. Claude Jr., *Power and International Relations* (New York: Random House, 1962).

15. Kenneth N. Waltz, *Theory of International Politics* (New York: McGraw-Hill, 1979), p. 127.

16. In the current international system, the United States is not a rising power as described above. It is an established hegemonic power, but its power capabilities have been rapidly improving vis-à-vis other great power states, giving it the wherewithal to become an overwhelmingly preponderant state in the medium term.

17. Edward Vose Gulick, *Europe's Classical Balance of Power* (Ithaca, N.Y.: Cornell University Press, 1955), pp. 31–33.

one's own state is an irreducible national value, whereas maintaining the independence of other great powers is a means to that end, not an end in itself."[18] Even during the heyday of the balance of power system in nineteenth-century Europe, although major powers wanted to maintain the independence of most states, they were occasionally willing to sacrifice the independence of smaller ones (e.g., Poland) to advance their interests. Nevertheless, this was a rare occurrence, because when a great power occupies strategically vital smaller powers, other great powers may perceive that its ultimate goal is domination over all states.

Of the two hard-balancing instruments, the alignment of smaller states with opponents of the most powerful state is more common.[19] States, especially affected great powers, form coalitions to build both their defensive and deterrent capabilities, so as to dissuade the hegemonic power from becoming too strong or too threatening. Weaker states join coalitions to gain greater respect and appreciation from members of their peer groups. From the structural realist perspective, balancing recurs in international politics as a lawlike phenomenon.[20]

BALANCING SINCE THE END OF THE COLD WAR

Traditional balance of power theory, especially the variant that postulates balance of power as an outcome, fails to explain state behavior in the post–Cold War era. Since the end of the Cold War, the United States has been expanding both its economic and political power. More recently, it has begun to engage in increasingly unilateralist military polices. The defense expenditure of the United States for 2004–05 represented more than 47 percent of the world's military spending. In the area of research and development (R&D), the United

---

18. Jack S. Levy, "What Do Great Powers Balance Against and When?" in Paul, Wirtz, and Fortmann, *Balance of Power,* p. 32.

19. George Liska, *International Equilibrium: A Theoretical Essay on the Politics and Organization of Security* (Cambridge, Mass.: Harvard University Press, 1957), pp. 34–41; Stanley Hoffmann, "Balance of Power," in David L. Sills, ed., *International Encyclopedia of the Social Sciences,* Vol. 1 (New York: Macmillan, 1968), p. 507; Claude, *Power and International Relations,* p. 56; and Dale C. Copeland, *The Origins of Major War* (Ithaca, N.Y.: Cornell University Press, 2000).

20. Waltz, *Theory of International Politics,* pp. 126–128. Scholars disagree about whether balance of power occurs as a conscious strategy or as a law of politics. On the distinction between automatic balance of power and manual balancing, see Colin Elman, "Introduction: Appraising Balance of Power Theory," in John A. Vasquez and Elman, eds., *Realism and the Balancing of Power: A New Debate* (Upper Saddle River, N.J.: Prentice Hall, 2003), pp. 9–10. In addition, there is debate over whether balancing occurs against a rising power or a threatening power. Stephen M. Walt, "Alliance Formation and the Balance of World Power," *International Security,* Vol. 9, No. 4 (Spring 1985), pp. 3–43. Further, some scholars argue that balancing seems to occur against continental powers, such as Germany and Russia, but not against maritime powers, such as Britain and the United States. Levy, "What Do Great Powers Balance Against and When?" pp. 45–46.

States spent $56.8 billion in 2003–04, which constituted 60 percent of the world total.[21] The United States' wide network of overseas bases and its possession of advanced weapons systems (e.g., aircraft carriers, cruise missiles, stealth bombers, and precision-guided bombs) have given it an extraordinary advantage over all other powers.[22] U.S. military superiority in areas such as technology, modern industries, organization, strategic lift capabilities, and personnel quality and training has been on display most recently in Kosovo, Afghanistan, and Iraq.[23] Yet despite these growing material capabilities, major powers such as China, France, Germany, India, and Russia have not responded with significant increases in their defense spending. Nor have they formed military coalitions to countervail U.S. power, as traditional balance of power theory would predict. Even the U.S. effort to expand NATO to Eastern Europe did not elicit a strong reaction from Moscow. Similarly, the United States' ongoing plans to build national and theater missile defense systems have not produced major balancing efforts from either China or Russia. Although these systems are not yet fully operational, if they are ever successfully developed and deployed, the nuclear deterrent capabilities of both countries will be compromised.

Second-tier major powers have not balanced against the United States primarily because, unlike previous hegemonic or rising powers, it does not appear to be challenging the sovereign existence of other states, barring a few isolated regional countries (e.g., Iran). Although not stated in so many words, the military doctrines and defense plans of second-ranked powers, including those of China and Russia, rule out a major war with the United States and increasingly focus instead on regional and internal security challenges.[24] U.S. power seems to be limited by a multitude of internal and external factors, thus making the United States a "constrained hegemon." Even when pursuing quasi-imperial policies, such as in the Middle East, the United States has gen-

---

21. On comparative military spending, see Stockholm International Peace Research Institute, *SIPRI Yearbook, 2005: Armaments, Disarmament, and International Security* (Oxford: Oxford University Press, 2005), http://yearbook2005.sipri.org/ch8/ch8. On R&D spending, see Bonn International Center for Conversion, *Conversion Survey, 2004: Global Disarmament, Demilitarization, and Demobilization* (Baden-Baden, Germany: Nomos Verlagsgesellshaft, 2004).
22. For instance, the United States operates nearly 650 military bases around the world and has basing rights in more than forty countries. Jim Garrison, *America as Empire: Global Leader or Rogue Power?* (San Francisco, Calif.: Berrett-Koehler, 2004), p. 25.
23. William E. Odom and Robert Dujarric, *America's Inadvertent Empire* (New Haven, Conn.: Yale University Press, 2004).
24. For the Russian military doctrine, see http://www.armscontrol.org/act/2000_05/dc3ma00 .asp; and for the Chinese defense policy statement of 2002, see http://english.people.com.cn/ features/ndpaper2002/nd1.html.

erally been perceived as a defender of the international status quo and an opponent of forced territorial revisions. The U.S. war against terrorism and regional challengers (i.e., the so-called rogue states) does not affect most states negatively; they too feel threatened by terrorist groups and regional proliferators that are attempting to acquire weapons of mass destruction: efforts they believe upset the regional balance of power and the international nuclear order built around the nonproliferation regime.

Michael Doyle has developed a general definition of empire that helps to illuminate the peculiarities of the United States' post–September 11 imperial strategy. Doyle defines an empire as "a system of interaction between two political entities, one of which, the dominant metropole, exerts political control over the internal and external policy—the effective sovereignty—of the other in the subordinate periphery."[25] Although the United States exerts some degree of control over many secondary states, unlike previous empires it often does so through indirect means. The United States does not yet require direct conquest, unlike former European hegemonic states that needed additional land for economic or military purposes. Instead, U.S. global military power is based on nuclear and conventional weapons that can be dispatched from great distances, including from U.S. aircraft carriers and U.S. bases in the territory of allies.

Thus, a fundamental cause of hard balancing in the past—states' fear of losing their sovereign existence to a hegemonic power—has had less salience since the end of the Cold War. Great powers once engaged in intense balancing behavior because they worried that a rapidly rising power would eventually subjugate them, challenge their physical existence, or conquer their imperial domains. From the sixteenth to the mid-nineteenth centuries, European powers feared such outcomes, as is evident in the wars they fought and the intense balance of power games they played. Erstwhile European hegemons, such as the Habsburg Empire under Charles V, Spain under Philip II, France under Louis XIV and Napoleon, and Germany under Wilhelm II and Hitler, directly challenged the existence of sovereign states, especially of other great powers. The military doctrines and strategies of rising powers were often territorially revisionist, as is apparent in the policies of France under Napoleon in the nineteenth century and of Germany and Japan in the early twentieth century. Hard balancing was therefore essential if states wanted to survive against the onslaught of land-grabbing, predatory great powers. Until the mid-twentieth

---

25. Michael W. Doyle, *Empires* (Ithaca, N.Y.: Cornell University Press, 1986), p. 12.

century, land was also the source of much great power prosperity. Today, however, direct land possession is not a requirement for great powers seeking to accumulate wealth and achieve their military goals; this includes the United States.[26]

During the Cold War, however, the United States and the Soviet Union perceived that a balance of power, built around mutual nuclear deterrence, was necessary to prevent the loss of their allies' independence. The United States and its Western allies viewed the Soviet Union as a revisionist power bent on altering the sovereign state system through the spread of its communist ideology. Meanwhile, the Soviets feared that the United States and its allies had predatory intentions, and that without an arms buildup and alliances, they would lose their sovereignty and great power status.[27] The radical political and economic changes pushed through by Mikhail Gorbachev in the 1980s began to modify this vision. With the end of the Cold War, perceptions on both sides changed dramatically.

Today, even though the overwhelming power of the United States may make many countries uncomfortable, none of the major powers fears being conquered or having their territories usurped. This does not mean that the United States is a benign hegemonic power, as many liberal theorists argue. Rather, it has pursued quasi-imperial policies through indirect means, largely by helping either to install or to prop up favorable regimes in strategic regions such as the Middle East and East Asia, from where it can control the flow of goods and commodities vital for its economy as well as those of its allies. Because the United States does not engage in the kind of direct imperialism that erstwhile European colonial powers did, authors have taken to describing it as an "informal empire," "incoherent empire," "inadvertent empire," "imperial republic," and "unacknowledged empire," as well as a "reluctant superpower." Others consider the United States' dominant role in globalization, for example, as a model of "soft imperialism."[28] Yet this hegemony is not as hier-

---

26. See Richard N. Rosecrance, *The Rise of the Trading State: Commerce and Conquest in the Modern World* (New York: Basic Books, 1986), chap. 2.
27. See John Lewis Gaddis, *We Know Now: Rethinking Cold War History* (Oxford: Oxford University Press, 1997); and Deborah W. Larson, *Anatomy of Mistrust: U.S.-Soviet Relations during the Cold War* (Ithaca: N.Y.: Cornell University Press, 2000).
28. For these characterizations, see Michael Mann, *Incoherent Empire* (London: Verso, 2003); Odom and Dujarric, *America's Inadvertent Empire;* John Newhouse, *Imperial America: The Bush Assault on the World Order* (New York: Alfred A. Knopf, 2003); Garrison, *America as Empire;* and Clyde Prestowitz, *Rogue Nation: American Unilateralism and the Failure of Good Intentions* (New York: Basic Books, 2003), p. 30.

archical, deeply institutionalized, or territory bound as previous imperial orders were.

The United States' wealth derives partially from its economic interactions, especially trade, with other states. Besides oil, there are few resources it needs to acquire through overt land possession. The American population is not growing at a pace that would require the seizure of foreign territory, unlike, for example, Nazi Germany and its policy of *Lebensraum*. Although the United States has at times pursued mercantilist and protectionist policies, its economic prosperity depends on a stable international order. In every key region, the United States offers some level of protection to potential key balancers, such as the NATO member states and Japan, or economic goods to major rising powers such as China, India, and Russia. During the first decade of the post–Cold War era, U.S. policy posed only a low level of threat to major powers.

Second-tier major powers do not fear direct conquest by the United States for three reasons. First, their possession of nuclear weapons assures their existential security, which allows them to worry less about fluctuations in relative advantages in military capability and about the submerged imperial tendencies of the hegemon. Nuclear possession—even in small numbers—offers assurance to second-tier major powers that the hegemon will not directly threaten their existence as independent actors. Thus, at a minimum the existential deterrence offered by nuclear weapons provides these states with existential security.[29] Second, the United States has been careful not to intervene directly in secessionist movements in China, India, and Russia, which further assures these states that it does not want to challenge their territorial integrity. Although at times Washington may have encouraged them to negotiate with the insurgent groups, there is no evidence that it has offered material support to such groups. Third, all major powers, including the United States, seem to believe that the powerful force of nationalism and the asymmetric strategies of nationalist groups make permanent occupation of another state infeasible.[30]

---

29. Existential deterrence is based on the notion that a nuclear state can deter an attacker with a small number of nuclear weapons, but that it does not need military capabilities that would guarantee mutual assured destruction. Patrick M. Morgan, *Deterrence Now* (Cambridge: Cambridge University Press, 2003), p. 23. For an alternate view on the absence of major power war since 1945, see John Mueller, *Retreat from Doomsday: The Obsolescence of Major War* (New York: Basic Books, 1989).

30. See T.V. Paul, *Asymmetric Conflicts: War Initiation by Weaker Powers* (Cambridge: Cambridge University Press, 1994); Thomas J. Christensen, "Posing Problems without Catching Up: China's Rise and Challenges for U.S. Security Policy," *International Security*, Vol. 25, No. 4 (Spring 2001), pp. 5–40; and Ivan Arreguín-Toft, "How the Weak Win Wars: A Theory of Asymmetric Conflict," *International Security*, Vol. 26, No. 1 (Summer 2001), pp. 93–128. Even during the Cold War, a strong norm against the forcible change of state borders and the creation of new states was able to

U.S. involvement in Vietnam and the Soviet occupation of Afghanistan made clear that even superpowers cannot invade and control smaller countries for too long in the face of intense local opposition.

BALANCING SINCE THE SEPTEMBER 11 TERRORIST ATTACKS

In the aftermath of the September 11 terrorist strikes, the United States began to change its national strategy, which until then had emphasized its role as a defender of state sovereignty. The George W. Bush administration's strategic approach has become more offensive and quasi-imperial with the adoption of the preventive and preemptive doctrines that allow the United States to attack states that are suspected of developing or planning to use weapons of mass destruction. In a document titled *The National Security Strategy of the United States of America,* the administration asserts that the United States will not hesitate to act alone and, if necessary, "preemptively" to counter such threats.[31] The doctrines are recycled from the 1992 draft defense planning guidelines prepared by some of the same individuals who held positions in George H.W. Bush's administration, which had proposed elevating the objective of U.S. defense strategy to "prevent the reemergence of a new rival."[32] These doctrines, if fully implemented, will significantly challenge both sovereignty and territorial integrity norms.

Second-tier major powers (except the United States' closest ally, Britain) and a large number of smaller powers have become increasingly worried about the Bush administration's unilateralist policies—enshrined in its preemptive and preventive war doctrines—which, though mainly directed against "rogue states," nonetheless challenge the norm of territorial integrity. These powers are willing to accept the U.S. war on terrorism, especially against failed states such as Afghanistan, because they share the same overall objective. They supported U.S. military action in Afghanistan because, like the United States, they

---

emerge. For the basis of this norm, see Mark W. Zacher, "The Territorial Integrity Norm," *International Organization,* Vol. 55, No. 2 (Spring 2001), pp. 215–250.

31. George W. Bush, *The National Security Strategy of the United States of America* (Washington, D.C.: White House, September 2002), http://www.whitehouse.gov/nsc/nss.pdf, p. 15.

32. The draft was prepared under the supervision of then Undersecretary for Defense Policy Paul Wolfowitz for the Department of Defense. The forty-six-page document was leaked by the *New York Times* and the *Washington Times,* forcing President Bush to order rewriting of its key passages. The document stated that the first key objective of U.S. defense policy should be to prevent the rise of hostile powers and ensure that they never "dominat[e] a region whose resources would, under consolidated control, be sufficient to generate global power." See Frontline, "The War behind Closed Doors: Excerpts from 1992 Draft 'Defense Planning Guidance,'" http://www.pbs.org/wgbh/pages/frontline/shows/iraq/etc/wolf.html. In response to worldwide opposition, the Bush administration changed the wording of the document.

did not recognize the Taliban regime as a legitimate government.[33] But the U.S. invasion of Iraq in March 2003 and the subsequent occupation, both of which were undertaken without the consent of the UN and justified on the flimsy pretext of the war on terrorism and faulty intelligence on WMD development, are antithetical to Westphalian notions of sovereignty. Second-tier major powers have begun to detect erosion in the liberal characteristics of U.S. hegemony, which had previously allowed allies some say over American policies, especially through NATO. If the United States succeeds in Iraq, these submerged quasi-imperial forces may gather strength within the U.S. political system. If it fails, the neoconservative actors who are pushing for an imperialist strategy may be discredited. In that sense, the affected second-tier major powers' decision not to support the U.S. war in Iraq is a response to their concerns about U.S. hegemony, as success could lead to more military ventures and the expansion of U.S. power globally.

To date, however, the U.S. occupation of Iraq has not been so threatening as to prompt the second-tier major power states to balance militarily against the United States. Instead, they have opted for low-cost diplomatic strategies that essentially seek to constrain U.S. power and dim the chances of the United States becoming a more threatening hegemon. In so doing, they and their supporters believe they can once again make U.S. power institution bound and sovereignty-norm bound.

Soft Balancing: Constraining U.S. Power by Other Means

Balance of power theory, rooted in hard-balancing strategies such as arms buildups and alliance formation, does not seem to explain current great power behavior. In the post–Cold War era, second-tier great power states have been pursuing limited, tacit, or indirect balancing strategies largely through coalition building and diplomatic bargaining within international institutions, short of formal bilateral and multilateral military alliances. These institutional and diplomatic strategies, which are intended to constrain U.S. power, constitute forms of soft balancing. Second-tier states that engage in soft balancing develop diplomatic coalitions or ententes with one another to balance a powerful state or a rising or potentially threatening power. The veto power that

---

33. For instance, even China, which is usually touchy on the question of sovereignty, seemed to have viewed the U.S. action as not "constituting a technical violation of national sovereignty." Aaron L. Friedberg, "11 September and the Future of Sino-American Relations," *Survival*, Vol. 44, No. 1 (Spring 2002), p. 35.

these states hold in the UN Security Council is pivotal to this strategy. By denying the UN stamp of approval on U.S.-led interventions, these states hope to deny legitimacy to policies they perceive as imperial and sovereignty limiting.

Soft-balancing behavior occurs under the following conditions: (1) the hegemon's power position and military behavior are of growing concern but do not yet pose a serious challenge to the sovereignty of second-tier powers; (2) the dominant state is a major source of public goods in both the economic and security areas that cannot simply be replaced; and (3) the dominant state cannot easily retaliate either because the balancing efforts of others are not overt or because they do not directly challenge its power position with military means. While pursuing soft balancing, second-tier states could engage the hegemon and develop institutional links with it to ward off possible retaliatory actions.[34]

In the post–Cold War era, soft balancing has become an attractive strategy through which second-tier major powers are able to challenge the legitimacy of the interventionist policies of the United States and its allies both internationally and in U.S. domestic public opinion. There is an international consensus that foreign intervention, even for humanitarian purposes, needs the "collective legitimation" of the United Nations or a multilateral regional institution.[35] The success of a U.S.-led intervention, especially one for humanitarian purposes, depends on post-intervention peacekeeping and stabilization support offered by the UN and its members. The United States would find it difficult to obtain troops from other countries for postwar reconstruction efforts without the support of the UN Security Council.

When the United States has ignored or sidetracked the UN, as it did in the 1999 Kosovo conflict and the lead-up to the invasion of Iraq, the interventions have become more cumbersome and less legitimate. In the Iraqi case, the absence of UN approval for the invasion led many potential allies to withhold troops. UN sanction of an intervention is deemed necessary for states to transcend the sovereignty norm temporarily, with the understanding that sovereignty will be restored once the source of the problem that led to the intervention is removed. The UN is unlikely to approve the permanent occupation of a country by the intervening power or the permanent loss of its sovereign existence.

---

34. See T.V. Paul, "Introduction: The Enduring Axioms of Balance of Power Theory and Their Contemporary Relevance," in Paul, Wirtz, and Fortmann, *Balance of Power*, pp. 1–25.
35. For this concept, see Inis L. Claude Jr., *The Changing United Nations* (New York: Random House, 1967), chap. 4; and Martha Finnemore, *The Purpose of Intervention: Changing Beliefs About the Use of Force* (Ithaca, N.Y.: Cornell University Press, 2003).

THE KOSOVO CRISIS, 1999

The diplomatic efforts of Russia and China prior to and during the U.S.-led NATO offensive against Yugoslavia in March 1999 offer a case of soft balancing. The NATO intervention took place in support of Kosovar Albanians being targeted by Serbian President Slobodan Milošović for ethnic cleansing. Both Russia and China expressed concern that the intervention could establish a potentially dangerous precedent, particularly within their own countries, where ethnic groups have been attempting to secede; examples include Chechnya, Tibet, Taiwan, and Xinjiang.[36] The Kosovo intervention, they feared, would dilute the sovereignty norm and give carte blanche authority to the United States and its allies to meddle in the affairs of other countries in the name of humanitarian intervention. Russia was also opposed to the intervention because of its potential impact on Serbia's Orthodox population and President Boris Yeltsin's domestic standing. Russia was especially concerned about the unilateral nature of NATO's intervention against an independent state without UN sanction, as well as what it viewed as NATO's transformation from a Western European military alliance into one willing to deploy forces in places outside the alliance's article 5 collective-defense mandate.[37]

Although in hindsight these concerns appear exaggerated, at the time of the intervention, Russians had strong reasons to compare their situation in Chechnya with that of Yugoslavia in Kosovo. The Russian leadership feared that Western support for Albanian Muslim separatists in Kosovo would encourage similar movements by Muslim groups inside Russia and other Commonwealth of Independent States (CIS). The widespread Russian view was that NATO instigated the conflict by supporting the Kosovo Liberation Army (KLA) in an effort to expand its military presence in the Balkans. The Russian leadership detected what it believed to be similarities between the KLA and Chechen rebels: both represented local Muslim majorities persecuting a Slav minority; both emerged out of the breakup of multinational federations; and both employed terrorism as their principal means to wage war on legitimate states. To the Russians, both movements carried territorial ambitions beyond their immediate borders. The Russian military feared that Kosovo could emerge as a model for NATO intervention in similar conflicts within former

---

36. The Russian posture was driven by the assumption that Kosovo was Yugoslavia's internal affair and that centrifugal forces within Russia dictated caution. Oleg Levitin, "Inside Moscow's Kosovo Muddle," *Survival*, Vol. 42, No. 1 (Spring 2000), p. 131; and Simon Saradzhyan, "Russia Won't Back Down on Kosovo," *Moscow Times*, October 8, 1998, quoted in ibid., p. 136.

37. Ekaterina A. Stepanova, "Explaining Russia's Dissention on Kosovo," PONARS Policy Memo 57 (Washington, D.C.: Program on New Approaches to Russian Security, Center for Strategic and International Studies, March 1999).

Soviet republics and Russia, especially in the context of the appeals by Georgia and Azerbaijan for NATO intervention to quell their internal conflicts.[38]

In addition to its efforts to stall the intervention through public statements, Russia engaged in soft-balancing diplomacy at the UN with the aid of China and on its own in European multilateral institutions. Although they succeeded in preventing UN approval for the intervention, they failed to prevent NATO from taking military action, largely because it had the support of almost all of the other European states, including former Warsaw Pact allies of Russia. These actors saw the Milošović regime as a larger threat to peace and stability in Europe than a U.S./NATO-led intervention and military presence in the region. The desire to prevent another Bosnia-type situation, where Serb forces had committed ethnic cleansing of Muslims, was deep in the calculations of the European states, a concern that did not strike a chord with the Russians.

Russia continued its soft-balancing efforts even after NATO's aerial bombing had begun. Moscow suspended its participation in the Russia-NATO Founding Act and the Partnership for Peace Program; it withdrew its military mission from Brussels and suspended talks on setting up a NATO information office in Moscow; it attempted to improve its military ties with CIS allies; and it conducted joint military exercises with Armenia, Belarus, Kazakhstan, and Tajikistan.[39] Further, Russia put diplomatic pressure on the United States and its allies to accept its proposal to designate the Group of Eight (G-8) as the venue for political discussions on the conflict. This led to a G-8 meeting in Bonn on May 21, 1999, that resulted in the adoption of a protocol for negotiating an end to the conflict.[40]

Despite actions that caused temporary fissures in Russian-Western relations, Moscow engaged diplomatically to end the conflict and, in fact, helped to convince Milošević to capitulate. The process began when, on April 14, President Yeltsin dispatched former Prime Minister Viktor Chernomyrdin to serve as special envoy to Yugoslavia. Chernomyrdin worked with U.S. Deputy Secretary of State Strobe Talbott and President Martti Ahtisaari of Finland to gain Milošević's acceptance of NATO's cease-fire conditions. Russia also became involved in the postwar settlement when it sent troops to occupy Kosovo's Priština airport, an action that provoked a tense standoff between Russian and NATO troops. Russian Defense Minister Igor Sergeyev was dispatched to Hel-

---

38. For these considerations, see Oksana Antonenko, "Russia, NATO, and European Security after Kosovo," *Survival*, Vol. 41, No. 4 (Winter 1999–2000), pp. 124–144.
39. Ibid., p. 136.
40. Rebecca J. Johnson, "Russian Responses to Crisis Management in the Balkans," *Demokratizatziya*, Vol. 9, No. 2 (Spring 2001), pp. 298–299.

sinki where, on June 19, he reached an agreement with NATO officials according to which nearly 3,600 Russian troops would be deployed in Kosovo as part of NATO's KFOR mission, although they would remain under the jurisdiction of Russian commanders.[41] According to one analyst, Russian persuasion was perhaps more crucial in forcing Milošević to acquiesce than his fear of an impending NATO ground invasion.[42]

The Kosovo crisis was partially instrumental in Russia's approval of a new national security concept in January 2000. A few months later, in April the Russian government introduced a new military doctrine that places high emphasis on the role of nuclear weapons in protecting Russian sovereignty, territorial integrity, and influence in the region. The new doctrine states that although the threat of direct military aggression against Russia has declined, external and internal threats to its security, as well as to that of its allies, persist. Among these threats are territorial claims by other countries, intervention in Russia's internal affairs, attempts to ignore Russia's interests in resolving international security problems, the buildup of forces in adjacent regions, the expansion of military blocs, and the introduction of foreign troops into other states in violation of the UN charter.[43]

China also opposed the U.S.-led NATO invasion of Kosovo, arguing that it lacked UN approval.[44] Throughout the crisis, China sought to uphold the sovereignty norm, which it viewed as essential to "counter U.S. hegemony in the post–Cold War era."[45] To China, sovereignty should remain an inviolable principle to protect the weak; NATO's new intervention strategy, for reasons unrelated to the defense of its member states, was a violation of this principle.

China initially confined its soft-balancing efforts to a veto threat in the UN Security Council, in conjunction with Russia, if the United States and its Euro-

41. Ibid., p. 300.
42. Steven L. Burg, "Coercive Diplomacy in the Balkans: The Use of Force in Bosnia and Kosovo," in Robert J. Art and Patrick M. Cronin, eds., *The United States and Coercive Diplomacy* (Washington, D.C.: United States Institute of Peace, 2003), p. 100.
43. For these documents, see Alexei G. Arbatov, *The Transformation of Russian Military Doctrine: Lessons Learned from Kosovo and Chechnya*, Marshall Center Papers No. 2 (Garmisch-Partenkirchen, Germany: George C. Marshall European Center for Security Studies, 2000), http://www.eng.yabloko.ru/Brooks/Arbatov/rus-military.html.
44. Evan A. Feigenbaum, "China's Challenge to Pax Americana," *Washington Quarterly*, Vol. 24, No. 3 (Summer 2001), pp. 31–43.
45. Russell Ong, *China's Security Interests in the Post–Cold War Era* (London: Curzon, 2002), p. 142. According to one Chinese analyst, the U.S. intervention in Kosovo was part of a "python strategy" of using "its thickest body to coil tightly around the world and prevent any country from possessing the ability to stand up to it." Cheng Guangzhong, "Kosovo War and the U.S. 'Python' Strategy," *Ta Kung Pao* (Hong Kong), June 2, 1999, http://www.mtholyoke.edu/acad/intrel/cheng.htm.

pean allies introduced a resolution authorizing the use of force. On March 26 Beijing and Moscow put forward a resolution in the Security Council calling for an immediate halt to the aerial bombing, but it was rejected by a vote of twelve to three.[46] After the mistaken U.S. bombing of China's embassy in Belgrade on May 8, Beijing cut off all military exchanges and human rights dialogues with the United States and stepped up its strategic collaboration with Moscow, including the activation of a hotline.[47] Beijing desisted, however, from taking any concrete hard-balancing actions during the crisis.

Both Russia and China continued their soft-balancing efforts even after the Kosovo crisis was brought to an end. Russia, in particular, attempted to enlist India and Central Asian states in this pursuit. In the spring of 1999, Russian Prime Minister Yevgeny Primakov called for the formation of a "strategic triangle" against NATO, consisting of Russia, China, and India.[48] President Vladimir Putin visited India in October 2000 and signed a declaration of strategic partnership, among other agreements—one of which expresses both countries' opposition "to the unilateral use or threat of use of force in violation of the UN charter, and to intervention in the internal affairs of other states, including under the guise of humanitarian intervention."[49] The proposed Russia-China-India alliance ultimately failed to materialize, as the principal powers began to perceive the likelihood of "potential American military intervention in their internal wars of secession in Kashmir, Chechnya and Xinjiang" as extremely low.[50]

On July 16, 2001, Russia and China signed the Treaty of Good Neighborliness, Friendship, and Cooperation, which calls for "joint actions to offset a perceived U.S. hegemonism" and the rise of militant Islam in Asia. The treaty also includes agreements on the demarcation of their disputed 4,300-kilometer

---

46. "Security Council Rejects Russian Halt to Bombing," *CNN.com*, March 26, 1999. See also Voice of Russia, http://www.vor.ru/Kosovo/news_25_29_03_99.html; and M.A. Smith, "Russian Thinking on European Security after Kosovo" (Surrey, U.K.: Conflict Studies Research Centre, Royal Military Academy Sandhurst, July 1999), http://www.da.mod.uk/CSRC/documents/Russian/F65.

47. Yu Bin, "NATO's Unintended Consequence: A Deeper Strategic Partnership . . . or More," *Comparative Connections* (Washington, D.C.: Center for Strategic and International Studies, July 1999), p. 69.

48. Tyler Marshall, "Anti-NATO Axis Poses Threat, Experts Say," *Los Angeles Times*, September 27, 1999.

49. John Cheriyan, "A Strategic Partnership," *Frontline*, October 14–27, 2000, quoted in Julie M. Rahm, "Russia, China, India: A New Strategic Triangle for a New Cold War?" *Parameters*, Vol. 31, No. 4 (Winter 2001–02), pp. 87–97. The Russian efforts continued in 2002 when Putin visited China and India. "Putin Keen on Triangle," *Hindu* (Chennai), December 9, 2002.

50. Raju G.C. Thomas, "South Asian Security Balance in a Western Dominant World," in Paul, Wirtz, and Fortmann, *Balance of Power*, pp. 322, 324.

border; a substantial arms sale; and the supply of technology, energy, and raw materials by Russia to China.[51] In June 2001 Russia, China, and four Central Asian states—Kazakhstan, Kyrgyzstan, Tajikistan, and Uzbekistan—announced the creation of the Shanghai Cooperation Organization, a regional association designed to confront Islamic fundamentalism and promote economic development.

The Kosovo case shows that although soft-balancing efforts by second-tier major powers may not prevent an intervention, they can still influence the post-intervention settlement. Strictly speaking, although NATO's military intervention in Kosovo constituted a violation of the Westphalian sovereignty norm, there was no intention to dismember Yugoslavia further. In the cease-fire agreement, Kosovo was retained as part of the Yugoslav state. Moreover, NATO members did not want to permanently occupy Yugoslavia or Kosovo. The peacekeeping mission was expected to be temporary and to bring stability to the region. Thus, the security of the two concerned major powers, Russia and China, was challenged in only a limited and indirect way. In the absence of a direct threat, the formation of a coalition to balance against the United States and NATO was unnecessary. Kosovo was a limited operation meant to confront a threatening regime in Central Europe. The intervention was not intended either to radically alter the state system in Central or Eastern Europe or to threaten the physical security and welfare of the other major powers. Moreover, NATO's actions did not create a precedent for similar interventions in places such as Chechnya or Xinjiang; nor did it create a norm that supports secession.

THE IRAQ WAR, 2002–03

The 2002–03 lead-up to the invasion of Iraq provides another example of soft balancing by second-tier major powers against unilateral U.S. military intervention. The invasion was preceded by six months of intense efforts by the United States and Britain to gain the support of the UN Security Council to launch an attack. During this period, a coalition led by France, Germany, and Russia emerged as a strong opponent of U.S. intentions to invade a sovereign country. The opposing states engaged in intense diplomatic balancing at the UN, threatening to veto any resolution that would have authorized the use of

---

51. Ariel Cohen, "The Russia-China Friendship and Cooperation Treaty: A Strategic Shift in Eurasia," Backgrounder 1459 (Washington, D.C.: Heritage Foundation, July 18, 2001). See also Igor S. Ivanov, *The New Russian Diplomacy* (Washington, D.C.: Brookings, 2002); and J.L. Black, *Vladimir Putin and the New World Order: Looking East, Looking West?* (Lanham, Md.: Rowman and Littlefield, 2004), chap. 11.

force. In the end, the United States launched the attack without the backing of a UN resolution and thus without the international legitimacy it had earlier sought.

In the fall of 2002, when the United States attempted to gain the support of the Security Council for the invasion, the second-tier major power states tried to block UN approval. On September 12 President Bush spoke before the General Assembly, seeking a resolution to take action against Iraq for its failure to disarm. On October 22 France and Russia announced their strong opposition to the proposed resolution, arguing that it would implicitly allow the United States to use force.[52] After several weeks of deliberations and failed efforts to gain consensus, the United States formally introduced a resolution to the UN on October 25, 2002, that would have implicitly authorized the use of force. In response to U.S. pressure, however, on November 7, 2002, the Security Council unanimously approved resolution 1441, which found Iraq in "material breach" of earlier resolutions; established a new regime for inspections; and warned of "serious consequences" in the event of Baghdad's noncompliance. The resolution did not, however, explicitly threaten the use of force. Meanwhile, in a concession to France, Germany, and Russia, the United States agreed to return to the Security Council for further discussions before taking military action. At the same time, however, the Bush administration argued that resolution 1441 was an endorsement for such action. Opponents asserted that the resolution diminished the chances of war by giving the Security Council the key role in sanctioning the use of force and allowing UN inspectors more time to determine whether Iraq possessed weapons of mass destruction, as alleged by the Bush administration.[53]

France, Germany, and Russia, joined by China, demanded more time for the weapons inspectors to complete their work. Most outspoken were the French. Dominique de Villepin, France's foreign minister, told reporters on January 20, "If war is the only way to resolve this problem, we are going down a dead end." At the Security Council, several foreign ministers argued that war "would spawn more acts around the globe"; in the words of Germany's Joschka Fischer, it would have "disastrous consequences for long-term re-

---

52. Colum Lynch, "France and Russia Raise New Objections to Iraq Plan," *Washington Post*, October 23, 2002.
53. Russia's ambassador to the UN, Sergey Lavrov, stated in the Security Council that "the Resolution deflects the direct threat of war"; and according to France's UN ambassador, Jean-David Levitte, "as a result of intensive negotiations, the resolution that has just been adopted does not contain any provision about automatic use of force." Both quoted in Colum Lynch, "Security Council Resolution Tells Iraq It Must Disarm; Baghdad Ordered to Admit Inspectors or Face Consequences, *Washington Post*, November 10, 2002.

gional stability."[54] Despite this intense opposition, U.S. Secretary of State Colin Powell made the case for invasion before the Security Council on January 21 and February 5, 2003, asserting that Iraq still possessed weapons of mass destruction in breach of resolution 1441 and earlier agreements. On February 10 France, Germany, and Russia issued a joint statement calling for the strengthening of the weapons inspection process, the dispatch of additional inspectors with increased surveillance technology at their disposal, and a concerted effort to disarm Iraq through peaceful means."[55]

On February 14, 2003, the UN's chief weapons inspector, Hans Blix, reported to the Security Council that no evidence of weapons of mass destruction had been found in Iraq, although many items of concern were unaccounted for. On February 24 the United States, the United Kingdom, and Spain introduced a resolution in the Security Council declaring that, under chapter 7 of the UN charter (which deals with threats to peace), Iraq had failed its final opportunity to comply fully with resolution 1441. Nevertheless, France, Germany, and Russia increased their opposition to a U.S. invasion, especially to the new U.S. aim of achieving regime change in Iraq. Also on February 24, French President Jacques Chirac and German Chancellor Gerhard Schröder met in Paris to declare their opposition to the U.S. resolution and plans to place a deadline on Iraq for compliance. The two leaders proposed giving the inspectors at least four more months to complete their work.[56] At a meeting of their foreign ministers on March 5, France, Germany, and Russia issued a statement that read in part: "We will not let a proposed resolution pass that would authorize the use of force." The next day China declared that it was taking the same position.[57] In spite of these soft-balancing efforts, the United States continued its military buildup in the Persian Gulf.

France and Germany also used NATO to engage in soft balancing against the United States by blocking U.S. attempts to gain the alliance's involvement in the war. On January 16, 2003, U.S. Deputy Secretary of Defense Paul Wolfowitz approached NATO to request its support in the event the United States went to war. Washington wanted NATO to send AWACS surveillance planes and Patriot antimissile batteries in the defense of Turkey, a NATO member with a 218-mile border with Iraq whose bases U.S. officials were planning

---

54. Quoted in Glenn Kessler and Colum Lynch, "France Vows to Block Resolution on Iraq War," *Washington Post*, January 21, 2003.
55. Peter Finn, "U.S.-Europe Rifts Widen over Iraq," *Washington Post*, February 11, 2003.
56. Peter Finn, "Chirac, Schroeder Make Counter Proposal," *Washington Post*, February 25, 2003.
57. For a chronology of events, see Michael J. Glennon, "Why the Security Council Failed," *Foreign Affairs*, Vol. 82, No. 3 (May/June 2003), pp. 16–35.

to use as launching pads for possible air and land attacks on northern Iraqi targets. The United States also wanted to employ NATO naval forces to guard approaches to the Mediterranean, through which U.S. warships and cargo vessels would have to pass en route to the Persian Gulf, and to enlist NATO troops to help guard bases in Europe and other strategic areas.[58] On January 23 and February 12, 2003, opponents of the U.S. invasion plan vetoed a U.S.-backed proposal for NATO to support Turkey in the event of war, arguing that such support was premature before the UN Security Council reviewed the weapons inspectors' report. In the opponents' view, an endorsement of this proposal would facilitate a "rush toward hostilities" and "invite the conclusion that the alliance has accepted the inevitability of war."[59] Ultimately, however, they relented, with the knowledge that NATO's unity required support for a key member state such as Turkey in the event of an attack.

President Chirac also used the European Union as a forum for mobilizing the antiwar coalition. He pressured the EU to endorse a statement giving more time and resources to efforts to disarm Iraq peacefully; however, French opposition to allow the thirteen Eastern European states waiting for EU membership to speak on the issue led to denunciations by these states for being treated as "second-class citizens."[60] France pursued its opposition in other forums as well. On February 21, 2003, at a summit in Paris of fifty-two African countries—including three nonpermanent members of the UN Security Council (Angola, Cameroon, and Guinea)—France's opposition to military intervention in Iraq was endorsed.[61]

The French position reflected France's general foreign policy orientation. Since the end of the Cold War, France has championed the creation of a multipolar system in which Europe acts as a pole to balance against the United States. Given the military weaknesses of the EU, France has devoted considerable energy to soft-balancing measures such as using international institutions—especially the UN Security Council, NATO, and the EU—to constrain the U.S. unilateral exercise of power. Although France's primary apprehension in early 2003 hinged on the fear that a U.S. invasion of Iraq would further destabilize the Middle East and increase terrorism in the West, the na-

---

58. Bradley Graham, "U.S. Official Appeals to NATO for Military Support," *Washington Post*, January 17, 2003.
59. Keith B. Richburg, "NATO Blocked on Iraq Decision," *Washington Post*, January 23, 2003; and Peter Finn, "NATO Still at Imasse on Asssiting Turkey," *Washington Post*, February 12, 2003.
60. Keith B. Richburg, "E.U. Unity on Iraq Proves Short-lived; France Again Threatens to Veto U.N. Resolution Mandating Force," *Washington Post*, February 19, 2003.
61. Glen Frankel, "Chirac Fortifies Antiwar Caucus; 52 African Leaders Endorse French Stance toward Iraq," *Washington Post*, February 22, 2003.

tional leadership's overriding concern has been the future international order. In President Chirac's view, "The Security Council and the European Union are becoming counterweights to the United States in the post–Cold War, post–September 11 world—and in each of those bodies, France has a say greater than its size or military capability."[62]

Two days after the start of the war, President Chirac vowed to block any UN resolution authorizing the United States and the United Kingdom to administer postwar Iraq.[63] At a meeting in St. Petersburg on April 11, 2003, Chirac, Schröder, and Putin issued a call for a "broad effort under United Nations control to rebuild the shattered country but warned that the immediate tasks of quelling anarchy and preventing a civil catastrophe fell on the United States and Britain."[64]

As discussed earlier, Germany also voiced opposition to the war, despite its greater dependency than, for example, France on the United States for security and trade. Chancellor Schröder successfully used the Iraq crisis to win reelection. In campaign rallies, he called Bush's policy an "adventure."[65] Unlike the Bush administration's preference for unilateral intervention, Germany has increasingly opted for a multilateralist approach toward regional challengers. In the Iraqi case, the Germans feared that the U.S. intervention would be a distraction from the fight against global terrorism while radicalizing anti-Western opinion in the Middle East.[66] The Germans also view the UN Security Council as the legitimate authority to sanction the use of force, preferably police force.[67] The Bush administration's rationale for preemptive and preventive military strikes without UN sanction, based on anticipatory self-defense, has been less than convincing to Germany and many other European states.

From the perspective of France, Germany, and Russia, as well as a majority of other states in the international system, the U.S. intervention in Iraq posed a limited yet important challenge to the Westphalian sovereignty norm. In the

---

62. Keith B. Richburg, "French See Iraq Crisis Imperiling Rule of Law; Concern Focuses on Future International Order," *Washington Post*, March 6, 2003, p. A19.

63. Robert J. McCartney, "France Opposes New U.N. Vote," *Washington Post*, March 22, 2003.

64. Michael Wines, "3 War Critics Want U.N. Effort to Rebuild but Say Allies Must Act Now," *New York Times*, April 12, 2003.

65. Peter Finn, "U.S.-Style Campaign with Anti-U.S. Theme: German Gain by Opposing Iraq Attack," *Washington Post*, September 19, 2002.

66. Klaus Larres, "Mutual Incomprehension: U.S.-German Value Gaps beyond Iraq," *Washington Quarterly*, Vol. 26, No. 2 (Spring 2003), pp. 23–42; and Anja Dalgaard-Nielsen, "Gulf War: The German Resistance," *Survival*, Vol. 45, No. 1 (Spring 2003), pp. 99–116.

67. David B. Rivkin Jr. and Lee A. Casey, "Leashing the Dogs of War," *National Interest*, Fall 2003, pp. 57–69; and Joachim Krause, "Multilateralism: Behind European Views," *Washington Quarterly*, Vol. 27, No. 2 (Spring 2004), pp. 43–59.

perception of the concerned states, the Bush administration's case against Iraq's weapons of mass destruction and terrorist groups allegedly linked to al-Qaida was less than convincing for at least three reasons. First, they suspected that the real U.S. motive was to assert power in the region and to use Iraq as a source for its increasing oil demands. Second, they assumed that U.S. success in Iraq would increase the Bush administration's appetite for further military actions in the region against other states (e.g., Iran). Third, they wanted to restrain the United States from undertaking unilateral military action by using the veto in international institutions. Unlike the Kosovo operation, which received support from France, Germany, and other NATO members, no formal regional alliance backed the intervention against Iraq. Even without UN approval, the Kosovo intervention had partial legitimacy: it was a NATO undertaking to reestablish regional order. The intervention in Iraq, on the other hand, was essentially a U.S.-led operation, although it did receive support from the United Kingdom and other U.S. allies, including Spain, Italy, Japan, and Australia. Traditional U.S. allies such as Canada and Belgium opposed the war and refused to lend assistance by way of troops and matériel. To them, the Bush administration was "making a claim to the sovereign right to intervene to disarm and carry out regime change in other countries, subject to no external restraint."[68]

Still, opposition to the U.S.-led invasion by second-tier major powers and their allies did not result in hard balancing against the United States. The coordination of diplomatic positions at the UN and in other forums (e.g., NATO and the EU), as well as summit diplomacy involving national leaders, were the main soft-balancing tactics used by the principal second-ranking powers. These efforts did not prevent the United States from launching the offensive, but they did help to reduce the legitimacy of the U.S. military action. They also made it more difficult for the United States to gain peacekeeping forces from other countries, as they demanded UN approval before dispatching their troops. Thus, in the case of Iraq, U.S. power has been partially constrained by the soft-balancing efforts of second-tier major powers. The less-than-successful outcome of the war and the growing insurgency against the occupation make it increasingly unlikely that, at least in the short term, the United States will undertake similar regime-changing military actions against Iran, another regional challenger pursuing nuclear weapons and a member of President Bush's "axis of evil."

---

68. William Pfaff, "The Iraq Issue: The Real Issue Is American Power," *International Herald Tribune*, March 14, 2003.

Despite the opposition of France, Germany, and Russia, the United States invaded Iraq using overwhelming force and toppled the regime of Saddam Hussein within three weeks of the start of major combat operations. After the war, the three states continued their opposition by challenging U.S. efforts to gain UN support for the stabilization of the country and the legitimization of the occupation. Their soft-balancing efforts culminated in a partial victory in June 2004, when the United States agreed to adopt UN resolution 1546/2004, which returned partial sovereignty to the Iraqi government and took away some U.S. powers in the day-to-day running of the country, except in security matters. The unanimous approval of the resolution was the result of diplomatic bargaining among the United States, the United Kingdom, France, Germany, and Russia. According to the resolution, the U.S.-led coalition agreed to end its occupation of Iraq before June 30, 2004, when an interim Iraqi government would assume responsibility for, among other things, the "convening of a national conference reflecting the diversity of Iraqi society, [and the] holding of direct democratic elections to a transitional national assembly, no later than 31 January 2005." This transitional government will draft a permanent constitution leading to a democratically elected government by December 31, 2005.[69]

Conclusion

The analysis in this article suggests that in the post–Cold War era, second-tier major power states have been increasingly resorting to soft-balancing strategies to counter the growing military might and unilateralist tendencies of the United States without harming their economic ties with it. They are opting for institutionalist and diplomatic means to balance the power of the United States, although the success of such strategies remains less than certain. This does not make soft balancing a futile strategy, as the success of hard balancing is also uncertain, given the difficulty in determining when balancing has or has not occurred. If, however, the hegemonic power in response to soft-balancing efforts tempers its aggressive behavior, then one can deduce that the efforts by second-tier major power states partially succeeded.

Balance of power theory has traditionally focused on military balancing as a way to restrain the power of a hegemonic actor. This perspective held true for the European era and the Cold War period, but in the post–Cold War world, it has become a difficult strategy for second-ranking great power states to pur-

---

69. Brian Knowlton, "UN Accord Emerging on Iraqi Governance," *IHT.com,* June 7, 2004.

sue. Hard balancing no longer has an appeal for second-tier powers because they do not believe, at least as of now, that the United States is a threat to their sovereign existence. They are, however, worried about the unilateralism and interventionist tendencies in U.S. foreign policy, especially since September 11, 2001, and they have resorted to less threatening soft-balancing means to achieve their objective of constraining the power of the United States without unnecessarily provoking retribution. Thus, if balancing implies restraining the power and threatening behavior of the hegemonic actor, strategies other than military buildups and alliance formation should be included in balance of power theory.

The Bush administration's national security strategy, which was adopted following the September 11, 2001, terrorist attacks, has challenged some of the notions of second-ranking major powers about the impact of U.S. policies on their vital interests. To date, however, they have not resorted to hard balancing because none of these states fears a loss of its existential security. Still, they are concerned about the increasing imperial tendencies in U.S. strategy. The conquest of Iraq was a quasi-imperial act planned and executed by a group of ideologically oriented U.S. policymakers who operated on the basis of misinformation and miscalculations. Although some administration officials sought to pursue an overt imperial strategy, the U.S. offensive against Iraq has been primarily confined to deposing Saddam Hussein and transforming the country to suit U.S. interests in the region. If this strategy is extended to other states, however, it could raise fears that the United States is on an imperial mission.

The policy implications of these changes in world politics are abundant. Hard balancing against U.S. military power or threatening behavior is not automatic, as realists would claim. It is very much tied to the security and foreign policies of the hegemonic state. If the United States pursues its foreign policy in less threatening ways, it can avoid the rise of hard-balancing coalitions. As long as the United States abstains from empire building that challenges the sovereignty and territorial integrity of a large number of states, a hard-balancing coalition is unlikely to emerge either regionally or globally. If, however, it pursues empire building, it would no longer be a status quo power, but a revisionist state bent on forcefully altering the international order. The constraints on the United States against an overt imperial strategy are many, but the war on terrorism and the need for oil could yet push it further in this direction. An overt imperial strategy, if adopted, would eventually cause great friction in the international system, built around the independent existence of sovereign states, especially major power actors.

Hard Times for Soft Balancing

Stephen G. Brooks and William C. Wohlforth

$\mathbf{F}$rench, German, and Russian opposition to the U.S. invasion of Iraq in 2003 brought to the fore a question that has been a staple of scholarly and policy debate since the 1991 fall of the Soviet Union: Is the international system on the cusp of a new balancing order? In the early-to-mid-1990s, the issue in dispute was when to expect the return of multipolarity.[1] By the turn of the millennium, the puzzling absence of a balancing coalition against the United States became the focus of the debate.[2] Now the question is whether balance of power politics is emerging in a new and subtler guise.

It was a mistake to expect "hard balancing" to check the power of the international system's strongest state, a growing number of analysts maintain, because, under unipolarity, countervailing power dynamics first emerge more subtly in the form of "soft balancing," as it is typically called.[3] T.V. Paul pro-

Stephen G. Brooks is Assistant Professor and William C. Wohlforth is Professor in the Department of Government at Dartmouth College. They are currently writing a book on the challenge of U.S. primacy.

The authors acknowledge with thanks comments from Jeremy Pressman and Benjamin Valentino as well as the helpful critical feedback they received from participants at presentations given at the John Sloan Dickey Center for International Understanding; the John M. Olin Center at Harvard University; and the Christopher H. Browne Center for International Politics at the University of Pennsylvania; as well as from participants at the 2004 annual meeting of the American Political Science Association and the 2005 annual convention of the International Studies Association.

1. See, for example, John J. Mearsheimer, "Back to the Future: Instability in Europe after the Cold War," *International Security*, Vol. 15, No. 1 (Summer 1990), pp. 5–56; and Christopher Layne, "The Unipolar Illusion: Why New Great Powers Will Rise," *International Security*, Vol. 17, No. 4 (Spring 1993), pp. 5–51.
2. G. John Ikenberry, "Institutions, Strategic Restraint, and the Persistence of the American Postwar Order," *International Security*, Vol. 23, No. 3 (Winter 1998/99), pp. 43–78; Charles A. Kupchan, "After Pax Americana: Benign Power, Regional Integration, and the Sources of a Stable Multipolarity," *International Security*, Vol. 23, No. 2 (Fall 1998), pp. 40–79; Michael Mastanduno, "Preserving the Unipolar Moment: Realist Theories and U.S. Grand Strategy after the Cold War," *International Security*, Vol. 21, No. 4 (Spring 1997), pp. 49–88; William C. Wohlforth, "The Stability of a Unipolar World," *International Security*, Vol. 24, No. 1 (Summer 1999), pp. 5–41; Stephen G. Brooks and William C. Wohlforth, "American Primacy in Perspective," *Foreign Affairs*, Vol. 81, No. 4 (July/August 2002), pp. 20–33; Ethan B. Kapstein, and Michael Mastanduno, eds., *Unipolar Politics: Realism and State Strategies after the Cold War* (New York: Columbia University Press, 1999); and G. John Ikenberry, ed., *America Unrivaled: The Future of the Balance of Power* (Ithaca, N.Y.: Cornell University Press, 2002).
3. The best treatments of the general soft-balancing argument are Robert A. Pape, "Soft Balancing: How States Pursue Security in a Unipolar World," annual meeting of the American Political Science Association, Chicago, Illinois, September 2–5, 2004; Stephen M. Walt, "Keeping the World 'Off Balance,'" in Ikenberry, *America Unrivaled*; T.V. Paul, "The Enduring Axioms of Balance of Power Theory," in Paul, James J. Wirtz, and Michel Fortmann, eds., *Balance of Power Revisited: Theory and Practice in the Twenty-first Century* (Stanford, Calif.: Stanford University Press, 2004); and

International Security, Vol. 30, No. 1 (Summer 2005), pp. 72–108
© 2005 by the President and Fellows of Harvard College and the Massachusetts Institute of Technology.

vides a concise definition of this basic concept: "Soft balancing involves tacit balancing short of formal alliances. It occurs when states generally develop ententes or limited security understandings with one another to balance a potentially threatening state or a rising power. Soft balancing is often based on a limited arms buildup, ad hoc cooperative exercises, or collaboration in regional or international institutions; these policies may be converted to open, hard-balancing strategies if and when security competition becomes intense and the powerful state becomes threatening."[4]

For the many analysts who use the concept, soft balancing is a warning sign that the age-old counterbalancing constraint is latent but subtly operative. For them, soft balancing is not just issue-specific diplomatic wrangling but a reflection of the underlying systemic concentration of power in the United States. As Josef Joffe put it concerning the policies of France, Germany, and Russia on Iraq, "What was their purpose? To save Saddam Hussein? No, of course not. It was to contain and constrain American power, now liberated from the ropes of bipolarity."[5]

As a staple of punditry both in the United States and abroad, the balance of power metaphor has contributed significantly to the growing popularity of the soft-balancing argument in scholarly circles. Commentators hail each new coordination effort among major powers that excludes the United States as an epoch-making "axis." Indeed, the leaders of other major powers—notably the

---

Josef Joffe, "Defying History and Theory: The United States as the 'Last Superpower,'" in Ikenberry, *America Unrivaled*. The soft-balancing argument initially rose to prominence in the late 1990s, as analysts such as Stephen M. Walt and Josef Joffe sought to articulate a distinction between traditional military balancing and subtler forms of balancing. See Walt, "Keeping the World 'Off Balance'"; and Joffe "Defying History and Theory." More recently, the term "soft balancing" has described balancing efforts that fall short of military balancing. See, for example, Paul, "The Enduring Axioms of Balance of Power Theory"; Pape, "Soft Balancing"; Yuen Foong Khong, "Coping with Strategic Uncertainty: The Role of Institutions and Soft Balancing in Southeast Asia's Post–Cold War Strategy," in Allen Carlson, Peter J. Katzenstein, and J.J. Suh, eds., *Rethinking Security in East Asia: Identity, Power, and Efficiency* (Stanford, Calif.: Stanford University Press, 2004); Erik Voeten, "Resisting the Lonely Superpower: Responses of States in the United Nations to U.S. Dominance," *Journal of Politics*, Vol. 66, No. 3 (May 2004), pp. 729–754; Josef Joffe, "Gulliver Unbound: Can America Rule the World?" Twentieth Annual John Boynthon Lecture, Centre of Independent Studies, St. Leonards, New South Wales, August 5, 2003; Stephen M. Walt, "Can the United States Be Balanced? If So, How?" annual meeting of the American Political Science Association, Chicago, Illinois, September 2–5, 2004; Christopher Layne, "America as European Hegemon," *National Interest*, No. 72 (Summer 2003), pp. 17–30; Bradley A. Thayer, "The Pax Americana and the Middle East: U.S. Grand Strategic Interests in the Region after September 11," Mideast Security and Policy Studies No. 56 (Ramat Gan, Israel: Begin-Sadat Center for Strategic Studies, Bar-Ilan University, December 2003); and Ruth W. Grant and Robert O. Keohane, "Accountability and Abuses of Power in World Politics," Duke University, March 2004. The most ambitious theoretical effort to fully develop the soft-balancing concept is Pape, "Soft Balancing."
4. Paul, "The Enduring Axioms of Balance of Power Theory," p. 3.
5. Joffe, "Gulliver Unbound."

presidents of France, Russia, and China—sometimes invoke the balancing proposition themselves, arguing that their policies are intended to foster the return of a multipolar world.

This confluence of theoretical expectations, journalistic commentary, and political rhetoric lends initial plausibility to the soft-balancing proposition and partly explains its current popularity as an argument for restraint in U.S. foreign policy. The growing popularity of the soft-balancing argument raises one of the most important questions in international relations today: Are recent state actions that have the effect of constraining U.S. foreign policy an outgrowth of the systemic balancing imperative? If the soft-balancing argument is right, then the international system's current equilibrium could shift toward a rapid escalation of constraints on the United States. As Stephen Walt warns, "Successful soft balancing today may lay the foundations for more significant shifts tomorrow. If other states are able to coordinate their policies so as to impose additional costs on the United States or obtain additional benefits for themselves, then America's dominant position could be eroded and its ability to impose its will on others would decline."[6]

So far, the soft-balancing argument has only been asserted. In this article, we conduct the first rigorous evaluation of soft balancing by performing four tasks. First, we show how the high stakes involved in this debate are closely linked to its underpinnings in balance of power theory. We demonstrate the core conceptual components that a theory of soft balancing must have to yield the soft-balancing argument that is so often applied to the United States today.

Second, we address the principal analytical flaw in the arguments of soft-balancing proponents: their failure to consider alternative explanations for the state behavior they observe. Other states obviously sometimes take actions that make it harder for the United States to advance its foreign policy goals, including its military security. Yet just because other states' actions periodically constrain the United States does not mean that soft balancing explains their behavior. Analysts' failure to address alternative explanations for the constraint actions undertaken by other states biases the discussion in favor of the soft-balancing argument. We remove this bias by putting forward four obvious but nevertheless overlooked alternatives to soft balancing: economic interest, regional security concerns, policy disputes, and domestic political incentives.

Third, we redress an equally critical weakness in the case for soft balancing:

---

6. Walt, "Can the United States Be Balanced?" p. 17.

the absence of a careful empirical analysis of the phenomenon. We compare the strength of soft balancing to alternative explanations in the four most prominent cases that soft-balancing proponents have highlighted: Russian assistance to Iranian nuclear efforts; Russia's strategic partnerships with India and especially China; enhanced military coordination among members of the European Union; and opposition to the U.S.-led war in Iraq. In the fourth section, we show why it is crucial to distinguish policy bargaining from balancing.

We conclude that although states do periodically undertake actions that end up constraining the United Sates, the soft-balancing argument does not help to explain this behavior. There is no empirical basis for concluding that U.S. power, and the security threat that potentially inheres in it, has influenced recent constraint actions undertaken by the other major powers. Our examination therefore provides further confirmation of the need for analysts to move beyond the familiar but misleading precepts of balance of power theory. Instead, new theorizing is needed that is more appropriate for understanding security relations in today's unipolar era.

Beyond the theoretical stakes, our analysis has repercussions for the debate over U.S. foreign policy. Put simply, soft balancing is not a compelling argument for U.S. restraint. The champions of the soft-balancing perspective uniformly oppose the recent "new unilateralist" turn in U.S. foreign policy.[7] Although we agree with their main recommendation—that the general disposition of the United States ought to be restrained—we do not agree that this recommendation can be derived from any variant of balance of power theory.[8] We find no evidence to support the expectation that the coordinated actions of other major powers will compel the United States to be restrained. Instead, the case for restraint will hinge on convincing U.S. foreign policy makers that it serves the United States' long-term interest.

The Stakes in the Soft-Balancing Debate

No one disputes that states sometimes undertake actions that either hamper the ability of the United States to further its foreign policy aims in the short

---

7. For a discussion of this so-called new unilateralism, see Charles Krauthammer, "The Unipolar Moment Revisited," *National Interest*, No. 70 (Winter 2002/2003), pp. 5–18.
8. See the related discussion in Brooks and Wohlforth, "American Primacy in Perspective," pp. 31–33.

term or are contrary to its long-term preferences. The United States is not omnipotent, and other states' actions have clearly complicated Washington's ability to pursue its foreign policy interests effectively. The challenge is in explaining and assessing the general significance of this behavior. After all, the United States has long had to contend with actions that ran counter to its objectives, not just from its competitors but from its major allies as well. Consider, for example, what happened in the decade that followed the Cuban missile crisis in 1962: France defected from NATO's military command; the United States was unable to obtain assistance from its major European allies in conducting the Vietnam War; Germany, Japan, and other countries stubbornly resisted a devaluation of their currencies; and France sought to undermine the Bretton Woods system by purchasing large amounts of gold from the U.S. Treasury. These actions all took place in the shadow of the Cold War, which provided a reference point for judging their significance. In the bipolar standoff, the United States and the Soviet Union provided the other with a yardstick for measuring the implications and significance of policy changes by third states. As a result, it was apparent that although the United States and its major allies had a relationship that was not always harmonious, they were far from being geopolitical rivals.

In today's unipolar system, in contrast, no comparable reference point exists. When any state begins to undertake actions that are contrary to U.S. interests, it is hard to estimate exactly how far it has traveled toward becoming a geopolitical rival. In turn, no identifiable yardstick exists for assessing the negative consequences of various state policies. The soft-balancing argument is influential precisely because it provides a familiar framework for making such assessments. In a unipolar system, the argument is, actions that may appear similar to inter-allied squabbling of the bipolar era are actually early warning signs of a coming era in which the United States will face increasing, and increasingly consequential, opposition deriving not just from the specific policies it may adopt but also from the very fact of its power.

The link to balance of power theory is what gives the soft-balancing argument this dramatic punch. Take away that link, and soft balancing collapses into a portentous-sounding term to describe conventional policy disputes and diplomatic bargaining. It follows that the soft-balancing argument must share some core features with balance of power theory. The theory posits that because states in anarchy have an interest in maximizing their long-term odds of survival (security), they will check dangerous concentrations of power (hegemony) by building up their own capabilities (internal balancing) or by aggregating their capabilities with other states in alliances (external balancing). The theory sounds simple, but it is fraught with ambiguity and remains the subject of ongoing scholarly dissension.[9] Moreover, many classical and modern formulations of the theory do not apply to the United States today, and so they cannot serve as the conceptual basis for soft balancing.[10] But despite the numerous setbacks it has received in the world of academic research, the basic proposition that state systems tend toward balanced power still has a strong claim on many analysts' thinking. Two popular formulations of the theory clearly do yield implications for the United States today: Kenneth Waltz's structural variant and Stephen Walt's balance of threat version.[11]

Waltz's theory defines hegemony as "unrivaled power" and predicts a general tendency toward balance. According to his theory, U.S. hegemony is so extreme that robust predictions of balancing emerge.[12] Walt modified the theory, notably by including perceptions of intentions as a factor that influences balancing. According to Walt, the willingness of other states to bear the high costs of balancing the United States depends not only on its power but also on its intentions, as revealed to other states by its behavior.[13]

9. For a sampling of this discussion, see John A. Vasquez and Colin Elman, eds., *Realism and the Balancing of Power: A New Debate* (Saddle River, N.J.: Prentice Hall, 2003).
10. See Jack Levy, "What Do Great Powers Balance Against and When?" in Paul, Wirtz, and Fortmann, *Balance of Power Revisited*. Levy argues that "few balance of power theorists, at least in the tradition of Western international theory that includes Morgenthau, Claude, Gulick, and Dehio, would predict balancing against the United States" today. Ibid., p. 30. A prominent modern example is John J. Mearsheimer's offensive realist theory, which encompasses a version of balance of power theory that applies only to contiguous great powers and not to offshore powers such as the United States. Indeed, Mearsheimer's theory yields an explanation for the recent, more independent behavior of some U.S. allies that is the opposite of soft balancing: a response to the fear of the retraction rather than the expansion of U.S. power. "America's Cold War allies have started to act less like dependents of the United States and more like sovereign states," he writes, "because they fear that [Washington] . . . might prove to be unreliable in a future crisis." Mearsheimer, *The Tragedy of Great Power Politics* (New York: W.W. Norton, 2001), p. 391.
11. Kenneth N. Waltz, *Theory of International Politics* (Reading, Mass.: Addison-Wesley, 1979); and Stephen M. Walt, *The Origins of Alliances* (Ithaca, N.Y.: Cornell University Press, 1987).
12. To be sure, Waltz and some of his followers have claimed that their theory explains balanced outcomes without necessarily predicting balancing strategies by states. See Kenneth N. Waltz, "International Politics Is Not Foreign Policy," *Security Studies*, Vol. 6, No. 1 (Autumn 1996), pp. 54–57. This argument makes the theory exceedingly general, extremely difficult to falsify and test, and impossible to apply to any specific case. More important, accepting the contention that balance of power theory does not predict balancing would sever it from the soft-balancing argument, which is explicitly about state strategies. We can set this claim aside, however, because Waltz has stated that his theory predicts balancing against U.S. unipolarity. Hence, he expects that causal mechanism to be in play today, however subtly. See Kenneth N. Waltz, "Structural Realism after the Cold War," *International Security*, Vol. 25, No. 1 (Summer 2000), pp. 5–41; and Kenneth N. Waltz, "Evaluating Theories," *American Political Science Review*, Vol. 91, No. 4 (December 1997), pp. 913–917.
13. Walt, "Keeping the World 'Off Balance.'"

The soft-balancing argument combines elements of Waltz's structural balance of power theory and Walt's balance of threat theory. In keeping with the intellectual history of balance of power theory, both formulations are systemic when applied to the United States.[14] For each, balancing is action taken to check a potential hegemon. It reflects systemic incentives to rebalance power, rather than the specifics of a given issue. It is action, moreover, that would not have been taken in the absence of the prospect of a dangerous concentration of power in the system. The key point is that balance of power theory is not relevant to state behavior unrelated to systemic concentrations of power, which is arguably much of what goes on in international politics.

For the soft-balancing argument to have the explanatory and predictive punch its proponents advertise, it must be connected to these same underlying causal mechanisms. Soft balancing must be linked causally to the systemic concentration of power in the United States. U.S. behavior is so important only because the United States is so powerful. Soft balancing is action that would not be taken if the United States were not so powerful; it is not merely a reflection of a specific policy dispute with Washington.

In addition, soft balancing must reflect the imperative of security seeking under anarchy, something advocates of the concept are keenly aware of.[15] Soft-balancing proponents raise the concern that states will increasingly see the concentration of power in the United States as a direct security threat, especially if it comes to be seen as having malign intentions. As Walt puts it, "If the United States acts in ways that fuel global concerns about U.S. power—and in particular, the fear that it will be used in ways that harm the interests of many others—then the number of potential 'soft balancers' will grow."[16] Balancing has been muted to this point, the argument goes, for two main reasons: the Soviet Union's sudden demise left the United States in such a commanding position that putting together a balancing coalition is especially hard; and the United States had acquired a reputation for benign intentions that is only now being undermined by actions such as the war in Iraq. The prediction is that as other states gain relative capabilities and update their assessments of the U.S. threat, they will begin to take soft-balancing measures. Under the logic of soft balancing, these measures must plausibly be linked to enhancing these states'

---

14. On the intellectual history of balance of power theory, see Martin Wight, *Power Politics* (Leicester, U.K.: Leicester University Press, 1978); and Herbert Butterfield, "Balance of Power," in Philip P. Wiener, ed., *Dictionary of the History of Ideas* (New York: Scribner's, 1968).
15. For an argument stressing this point, see Pape, "Soft Balancing."
16. Walt, "Can the United States Be Balanced?" p. 18.

security vis-à-vis the U.S. threat. In undertaking these measures, states must rationally expect to constrain the threat posed by the United States and so be more secure as a result. Actions that are expected only to frustrate U.S. policies without affecting the real capability of the United States to threaten the security of other major powers fall outside the logic of soft balancing.

Alternative Explanations

How does one identify soft balancing? The answer matters greatly for both policy and theory, yet it remains elusive because soft-balancing proponents have not supplied the conceptual tools to distinguish behavior that is an outgrowth of the systemic balancing imperative from what we might call "unipolar politics as usual." Crucially missing from the literature is sufficient recognition that other explanations besides soft balancing exist for state actions that constrain the United States. As a result, analysts tend to treat nearly any behavior that complicates U.S. foreign policy as soft balancing. We remove this bias by setting out four alternative explanations.

ECONOMIC INTEREST
States may undertake actions that hamper the conduct of U.S. foreign policy not principally because they wish to do so, but rather to advance economic gains, either for the state as a whole or for powerful interest groups or business lobbies. A government's interest in fostering economic growth or obtaining revenue for itself or its constituents may be unrelated to the presence of a hegemon on the horizon or the potential security threat it poses.

REGIONAL SECURITY CONCERNS
States routinely pursue policies to enhance local security that are unrelated to constraining U.S. hegemony. For a variety of reasons, there is a greater demand for regional policy coordination than existed in the past: a vast increase in the number of states; a consequent increase in the overall number of weak or failed states; and the rise of transnational security challenges such as organized crime, terrorism, drug trafficking, and refugee flows. Major powers frequently face incentives to enhance their capabilities—often through collaboration with other regional states—in response to these local or regional concerns. These efforts may result in shifts in relative power—and perhaps in reduced U.S. freedom of action—even if constraining U.S. hegemony is not an important driver of them.

POLICY DISPUTES AND BARGAINING

Other states may undertake actions that constrain the United States not in response to the security threat presented by U.S. hegemony, but rather because they sincerely disagree with specific U.S. policies. Governments may resist a given U.S. policy because they are convinced that it is ill suited to the problem at hand or otherwise inappropriate, and not because they think it directly threatens their security or that opposition to it will reduce U.S. power over the long term. If so, then soft balancing is a misnomer, for the behavior concerned is unrelated to maximizing security under anarchy by checking a dangerous systemic concentration of power. In short, other states may push back against specific U.S. policies (pushing back because they disagree) and not against U.S. power in general (pushing back because they fear or wish to challenge U.S. hegemony). Given the reasonable expectation of future policy differences on various issues, and therefore the expectation of future policy bargaining, it follows that states may take actions intended to increase, or at least maintain, bargaining leverage over the long term. This is where policy bargaining takes forms that most closely resemble what analysts mean by soft balancing. As we show below, there are crucial analytical differences between long-term bargaining enhancement strategies and real soft balancing.

DOMESTIC POLITICAL INCENTIVES

Opposing the United States on a particular issue may be a winning strategy domestically even for leaders with no general interest in constraining U.S. power. Only domestic opposition that is an outgrowth of the security threat flowing from U.S. power can be thought of as a manifestation of soft balancing. All other ways in which the domestic politics of other countries may feed actions that complicate matters for the U.S. government fall outside the logic of soft balancing. Specifically, soft balancing does not encompass opposition to the United States that is a manifestation of the unpopularity of a particular U.S. policy. In addition, opposing the United States may be strongly compatible with long-standing historical, political, or cultural understandings—either for the nation as a whole or for individual political parties—that predate any recent shift in U.S. foreign policy, or indeed the rise of unipolarity.

SOFT BALANCING VERSUS THE ALTERNATIVES

To the degree that these other four explanations account for actions that constrain U.S. foreign policy, the soft-balancing argument is weakened. It would be surprising to find no evidence consistent with the soft-balancing explanation. Just as unlikely would be evidence that soft balancing is the only explanation in play—even though the concept's proponents essentially imply just such an expectation by failing to consider alternatives. The real issue is relative salience. Determining the strength of the various explanations, however, is no easy task.

The key cases of soft balancing are quite recent, so reliable inside information can be scarce. The chief putative soft-balancing powers—France, Russia, and China—are also not known for the transparency of their executive decisionmaking. And public rhetoric presents difficult analytical challenges. A government with a sincere interest in soft balancing may not want to advertise it. At the same time, all four other dynamics may generate balancing rhetoric from policymakers, creating prima facie evidence for a soft-balancing explanation. Leaders motivated chiefly by domestic political considerations are hardly likely to say so; they may detect domestic political advantage in touting the balancing element even if countering the threat from U.S. power is not the real issue. In turn, leaders who have sincere policy differences with the United States may talk up balancing to help build a coalition to increase their bargaining leverage. Being seen by Washington as a potential soft-balancer has risks, to be sure, but it also holds out the promise of magnifying one's bargaining influence and the significance of any concessions one might make. Governments that pursue relative economic advantages for themselves or their constituents may find it convenient to cloak the policy in high-minded talk about checking U.S. power. And the United States is so prominent on the global stage that it can potentially serve as a convenient focal point for other states that seek to cooperate on regional security issues. States will likely have strong disagreements on the specifics of how to cooperate at the regional level; a public stance against U.S. policies may be one issue they can agree on. Balancing rhetoric can thus be a useful rallying point for stimulating regional cooperation.

Balancing talk, moreover, is often as cheap as it is useful. A state can rationally be expected to address an issue only to the degree that it has the capability to do so. Actors and observers expect France to play a far more substantial role in resolving an issue in the Balkans than in North Korea, and vice versa for China. Yet because of the United States' globe-girdling capabilities, critical U.S. involvement is likely to be expected in both cases. This illustrates the immense gap between the set of issues the United States might rationally be expected to address seriously and the corresponding issue sets of the other great powers. As a result, there is a range of issues over which they can take positions without expecting to be compelled to bear the costs of their resolution. Ultimately, rhetoric is a poor indicator of the salience of soft balancing.

Perhaps recognizing these challenges, proponents of the soft-balancing concept frequently place more emphasis on its portents for the future than on its contemporary significance. For the argument to be taken seriously, however, there must be evidence for its current explanatory value.[17] Otherwise, soft balancing is not an explanation but an expectation: a mere reassertion of the well-known, neorealist prediction of the return of multipolarity that has been advanced since 1990, which is also typically formulated in an unfalsifiable manner.[18]

Although some uncertainty will always attend judgments about such recent events, there are observable implications of the differences between soft balancing and the other explanations we delineated. In assessing the competing arguments, two guidelines are most important. The first is the overall significance of the policy. Soft balancing is not an argument about symbolic action. It applies only to policies that promise to do something to increase constraints on or shift power against the United States. The second guideline is policymakers' willingness to accept trade-offs between constraints on the United States and other valued objectives. Soft balancing is not an argument about preferences but rather behavior. Many politicians in France, Russia, China, and other putative soft-balancing states periodically express a preference for what they often call "multipolarity" (although by this they usually mean multilateralism). They also express a desire for mutually beneficial partnerships with the United States, robust economic growth, prosperity, and many other values. The question is: How much are they willing to give up to obtain constraints on the United States? The United States is so powerful that no state can meaningfully seek to check it single-handedly; policymakers who wish to take this route will need to work in conjunction with other states that must also see a compelling interest in doing so—to the point that they will consistently seek opportunities to check U.S. power even when the pursuit of this goal conflicts with other priorities.

---

17. On this falsifiability issue, see Keir Lieber and Gerard Alexander, "Waiting for Balancing: Why the World Isn't Pushing Back," annual meeting of the American Political Science Association, Chicago, Illinois, September 2–5, 2004.

18. For example, Christopher Layne asserts that other states will balance the United States, but it may be fifty years before this occurs. See Layne, "The Unipolar Illusion," p. 17.

Testing Soft Balancing against Unipolar Politics as Usual

Using these guidelines, we evaluate the relative strength of soft balancing compared with the other explanations identified above in the four most prominent cases highlighted by proponents of the concept. These cases have attracted so much attention from advocates of soft balancing because they share three key characteristics: (1) they involve coordination among two or more states in areas directly related to security; (2) at least one great power, and in most cases several of them, are involved; and (3) they feature state actions that make it harder for Washington to advance its foreign policy goals.

RUSSIAN "STRATEGIC PARTNERSHIPS" WITH INDIA AND CHINA
In some respects, Russia's strategic partnerships with India and especially China represent the strongest case of soft balancing.[19] These are treaty-governed relationships that have resulted in a net shift in the distribution of military power against the United States. Russia's own military is presently unable to use most of the output of its defense industry. To the extent that its strategic partnerships with India and China permit the transfer of some of this output to militaries that can use it effectively, the net effect is a shift in relative power. Moreover, Russia-China cooperation includes the creation and promotion of a regional security organization that excludes the United States—the Shanghai Cooperation Organization (SCO). In the end, however, each of the three elements that make up the much-touted "Asian triangle"—the diplomatic relationships, the SCO, and the arms sales—defies a soft-balancing interpretation.

Although Russian, Chinese, and (to a lesser extent) Indian leaders periodically describe their diplomatic partnerships as an expression of their preference for a multipolar world, there is little evidence that balancing U.S. power is a driving force behind them. Rhetoric notwithstanding, the policies are crafted precisely to avoid the need for any of the parties to face a trade-off between their mutual partnerships and their key bilateral relationships with the United States. Russia's partnership with India amounts to a Soviet holdover based on the Friendship Treaty of 1971, whose language implied weak security obligations even in the Cold War, and the largely symbolic Declaration on Stra-

---

19. Analyses that treat these partnerships in soft-balancing terms include Paul, "Enduring Axioms"; Walt, "Can the United States Be Balanced?"; and Joffe "Defying History and Theory."

tegic Partnership signed by Russian President Vladimir Putin and Indian Prime Minister Atal Behari Vajpayee in 2000. The Russia-China Treaty on Good-Neighborliness, Friendship, and Cooperation, signed in 2001, capped more than a decade of improving bilateral ties, but it similarly lacks anything resembling a mutual defense clause.[20] While the treaty obligates the signatories in a general sense to maintain the global equilibrium and to consult each other in the event of security threats, neither it nor any other public Russo-Chinese agreement entails any observable or costly commitment to counter U.S. power. No mutual undertaking by the two powers in accordance with their partnership has involved major costs in their relationships with the United States. The same is true of Russia's cooperation with India.

This reluctance to jeopardize relations with the United States is not surprising to experts on all three countries. Russia, China, and India are pursuing grand strategies that highlight economic and institutional modernization, a goal that requires cordial relations with the United States and the global economic institutions over which it has such a strong influence. The strategy has yielded high growth rates for all three countries in recent years. Moreover, in all three cases, policymakers have explicitly reoriented their strategic priorities to emphasize regional security issues such as terrorism and weapons proliferation on which they tend to have roughly similar preferences to those of the United States.[21]

A significant constraint on the development of deep Russia-China security ties is the nature of their economic relationship: trade between the two countries remains anemic; they do not have complementary economies from which high levels of trade can develop; and both are dependent to a large degree on inward flows of capital and technology, which come mainly from the West. Even more important, Russia's willingness to commit to its Asian partnerships is limited by its perceived weakness in the region.[22] Russians remain wary of China's growing economic and diplomatic clout, and express a general prefer-

---

20. For a detailed analysis of the treaty, see Elizabeth Wishnick, "Russia and China: Brothers Again?" *Asian Survey*, Vol. 41, No. 5 (September–October 2001), pp. 797–821.

21. Ample evidence and analysis concerning these grand strategies is presented in the chapters on Russia, India, and China in Richard J. Ellings and Aaron L. Friedberg, with Michael Wills, eds., *Strategic Asia, 2002–03: Asian Aftershocks* (Seattle, Wash.: National Bureau of Asian Research, 2003). On China's grand strategy and its implications for balancing, see Avery Goldstein, "An Emerging China's Grand Strategy," in G. John Ikenberry and Michael Mastanduno, eds., *International Relations Theory and the Asia Pacific* (New York: Columbia University Press, 2002); and Alastair Iain Johnston, "Is China a Status Quo Power?" *International Security*, Vol. 27, No. 4 (Spring 2003), pp. 5–56.

22. Bobo Lo, "The Long Sunset of Strategic Partnership: Russia's Evolving China Policy," *International Affairs*, Vol. 80, No. 2 (March 2004), pp. 295–309.

ence for diversifying Russia's Asian relationships. Suspicions plague both countries, stemming partly from mutual fears that each is using the other only to gain leverage over Washington. Many Russian analysts regard their country's partnership with India as a hedge against rising Chinese power in Asia. Russia tends to sell India more advanced weapons systems than it exports to China, and the agreements on the joint design and production of weapons that Russia has signed with India also tend to be deeper and more comprehensive than the arrangements that Moscow has made with Beijing. Russian officials are quick to cite these facts when questioned by domestic critics who accuse them of mortgaging Russia's security through the arms transfers to China. ·

These background factors all help to explain the real role and limitations of the SCO. Russian and Chinese leaders have frequently used SCO gatherings to express their preference for a multipolar world, and observers sometimes see the organization as a coordinating mechanism for counterbalancing U.S. power in the region.[23] Yet an examination of the organization's real activities belies this interpretation.[24] The SCO's main initial goal was confidence building among the new states in the region, especially by resolving old Soviet-Chinese border disputes. China further sought to stabilize and secure its borders from Islamic extremism, a factor that threatened not only post-Soviet Central Asia but also the restive Xinjiang region of western China. China feared that the Uighur separatists were receiving funding and arms from Uighurs in its neighboring states, as well as from Afghanistan. Russia shared the common threat of an increasingly Islamicized Chechen separatist movement. Uzbekistan joined the SCO in 2001 as it sought a common forum for responding to the Islamic Movement of Uzbekistan (IMU)—a transnational guerrilla threat.[25] The SCO signed a declaration on June 15, 2001, expanding its mission in the region and focused increasingly on terrorist threats, religious extremism, and to a lesser extent, arms and narcotics trafficking. The organization announced the creation of a counterterrorism center in Bishkek, Kyrgyzstan, known as the Regional Antiterrorism Structure (RATS), but the project stalled and few assets were invested or resources committed.[26]

---

23. See, for example, Sergei Blagov, "Russia Seeking to Strengthen Regional Organizations to Counterbalance Western Influence," *Eurasia Insight*, December 4, 2002.

24. See Kathleen Collins and William C. Wohlforth, "Central Asia: Defying 'Great Game' Expectations," in Richard J. Ellings and Aaron L. Friedberg, with Michael Wills, eds., *Strategic Asia, 2003–04: Fragility and Crisis* (Seattle, Wash.: National Bureau of Asian Research, 2004), pp. 291–317.

25. Interview with senior analyst, Institute of Strategic Studies, Uzbekistan, Tashkent, August 2002, reported in Collins and Wohlforth, "Central Asia: Defying 'Great Game' Expectations."

26. "Declaration of the Establishment of the Shanghai Cooperation Organization, June 15, 2001," http://www.missions.itu.int/?kazaks/eng/sco/sco02.htm.

A key problem with interpreting the SCO as an example of soft balancing is that the main issue that China, Russia, and the Central Asian states agreed upon that warranted an upgrading of the organization was counterterrorism. Having coordinated the SCO around this issue, however, the members were unable to assemble the capabilities required to address it. This shortcoming was made brutally evident after the terrorist attacks of September 11, 2001, when U.S.-led Operation Enduring Freedom quickly toppled the ruling Taliban in Afghanistan and weakened the IMU—the very threats whose rise had just begun to provide the SCO's raison d'être. The U.S. deployment to Afghanistan created a contradiction between the SCO's rhetorical role as a counterbalancing mechanism and its operational role as a regional security organization. China and Russia resolved the contradiction by bandwagoning with the United States in the war on terror. Indeed, on September 14, 2001, the SCO was the first international organization to issue a formal statement condemning the attacks on the United States. An extraordinary meeting of SCO foreign ministers in Beijing in January 2002 pledged the organization's support for the UN Security Council resolutions on Afghanistan and the international war on terror.[27]

In short, pragmatic regional cooperation is the chief driver of the SCO, with soft-balancing rhetoric sometimes providing a convenient focal point for rallying greater collaboration. The real core of Russia's relationships with India and China, however, is not the diplomatic partnerships but extensive military coproduction arrangements and major arms sales. Yet Russia's interest in these exports is not driven by the need to counterbalance U.S. power but rather by a desperate need to slow the inexorable decline of its military industrial complex. Between 1992 and 1998, Russia experienced what was probably the steepest peacetime decline in military power by any major state in history.[28] Weapons procurement and spending declined dramatically after 1991, and by 2000 only 20 percent of Russia's operational weapons stocks were modern, compared with 60–80 percent in NATO countries.[29] Maintenance and training

---

27. "Joint Statement by the Ministers of Foreign Affairs of the Member States of the Shanghai Cooperation Organization," January 7, 2002, Beijing, http://russia.shaps.hawaii.edu/fp/russia/sco_3_20020107htm.

28. Christopher Hill, "Russian Defense Spending," in United States Congress, Joint Economic Committee, *Russia's Uncertain Economic Future* (Washington, D.C.: U.S. Government Printing Office, 2002), p. 168. For an excellent overview of the defense sector's dilemmas, see Christopher Davis, "Country Survey XV: The Defence Sector in the Economy of a Declining Superpower: Soviet Union and Russia, 1965–2001," *Defence and Peace Economics*, Vol. 13, No. 3 (June 2002), pp. 145–177.

29. "Only 20% of Russian Arms Are Modern," *RFE/RL Daily Report*, May 21, 2001.

are dismal; personnel problems are dire and getting worse.[30] Unable to subdue the Chechen rebels, the Russian military is beset by so many problems of such magnitude that experts agree that major reforms entailing huge expenditures are critically necessary simply to forestall its continued decline. Increased budgetary outlays and intensified reform efforts are thus driven by deep problems of decay that are unrelated to counterbalancing U.S. power.

Arms sales are a substrategy that aids Russia's more general interest in staving off further military decline. Given the collapse of domestic orders (in 2001 only 10 percent of Russian defense firms received state orders), Russia's defense sector possesses massive excess capacity.[31] Exports are a lifeline for a military industry producing less than one-third of its 1992 output, and rapidly losing technological competitiveness. Russia wants to sustain a core defense manufacturing capacity until economic growth affords it the opportunity to modernize its surviving military infrastructure and to transfer excess defense workers and production capacities into more competitive sectors. Even more immediately, exports aid a defense sector that supplies income and welfare services to hundreds of thousands of workers and their families, provides the economic lifeblood of dozens of cities, and enriches numerous managers and public officials. Military industry represents one of the few high-technology sectors in which Russians remain competitive, and they perceive a strong overall commercial interest in promoting exports.

In sum, the evidence concerning Russia's major arms relationships overwhelmingly indicates that Moscow's eagerness to sell weaponry to Beijing and New Delhi is only indirectly and marginally connected to the issue of U.S. hegemony. If the United States were to cut its defense outlays by two-thirds tomorrow, Moscow's interest in arms sales would be undiminished, as would India's demand. To be sure, China's demand for Russian military hardware is partly a response to U.S. military support for Taiwan, but China's desire to enhance its bargaining position over the Taiwan Strait has been a constant since 1949 and hence is not causally related to the advent of unipolarity after 1991 or recent U.S. security behavior. And what makes the soft-balancing argument superficially applicable to the case is not that China wants to import weapons. If the Chinese obtained weaponry from Israel or South Africa, it would hardly attract the attention of soft-balancing proponents. The arms sales seem so significant because they come from Russia, suggesting interstate coopera-

---

30. "Every Third Potential Conscript Said Not Fit for Military Service," Itar-Tass, May 23, 2002.
31. Kevin P. O'Prey, "Arms Exports and Russia's Defense Industries: Issues for the U.S. Congress," in Joint Economic Committee, *Russia's Uncertain Economic Future*, pp. 385–410.

tion to balance U.S. capabilities. Yet the evidence strongly indicates that it is regional security needs in conjunction with economic concerns, not soft balancing, that explain Russian military sales to both China and India.

THE MOSCOW-TEHRAN CONNECTION

Analysts commonly interpret great power support for states that are opponents of the United States as soft balancing. Russia's relationship with Iran is the most prominent case in point.[32] Russia has assisted Iran's nuclear program, cooperated in space technology and other high-technology areas, sold large quantities of military hardware (Iran is Russia's third largest customer, after China and India), and pursued a general policy of engagement with Iran. Such policies helped to buttress Iran against pressure from Washington for nearly a decade.

There is scant evidence, however, that a desire to balance U.S. power explains the relationship. Regional security concerns and economic incentives have remained consistently at the forefront. Russia has numerous reasons besides balancing U.S. power to seek good relations with Iran. Nuclear sales, technology transfers, and other moves that appear to bolster Iran serve as part of an engagement strategy that is itself driven by Moscow's need for Iranian cooperation in resolving a complex nexus of regional issues surrounding the exploitation of petroleum and other natural resources in the Caspian. Even regional analysts who stress the importance of geopolitics do not accord balancing the United States a significant role in explaining the Moscow-Tehran connection.[33] As in the China case, Moscow has no incentive to alienate Tehran. At the same time, the two states remained at loggerheads on local issues throughout the 1990s and early 2000s, placing limits on the scope and depth of their cooperation.

Russia's arms sales to Iran buttress this general strategy of engagement. But, as in the China and India cases, economic incentives loom large for all the reasons noted above. The issue of nuclear cooperation attracts the most attention from analysts. From the early 1990s on, Russia was the only major power openly cooperating with Iran in this area, defying occasionally intense pres-

---

32. See, for example, Pape, "Soft Balancing"; and Walt, "Can the United States Be Balanced?"
33. See, for example, Carol R. Saivetz, "Perspectives on the Caspian Sea Dilemma: Russian Policies since the Soviet Demise," *Eurasian Geography & Economics*, Vol. 44, No. 8 (December 2003), pp. 588–607; Gawdat Bahgat, "Pipeline Diplomacy: The Geopolitics of the Caspian Sea Region," *International Studies Perspectives*, Vol. 3, No. 3 (August 2002), pp. 310–327; and Douglas W. Blum, "Perspectives on the Caspian Sea Dilemma: A Framing Comment," *Eurasian Geography & Economics*, Vol. 44, No. 8 (December 2003), pp. 617–703.

sure from Washington. The chief problem with a soft-balancing interpretation is that Russia experts are virtually unanimous in regarding the Moscow-Tehran nuclear connection as driven principally by economic concerns. No one in Russia is able to develop a plausible argument for how the country's security would benefit from Iran's nuclearization. Russia's official policy is that proliferation of weapons of mass destruction "is the main threat of the 21st century."[34] The commercial interests in play are substantial enough, however, to induce Moscow to set a relatively high bar for proof of the relationship's proliferation risks.

Nuclear technology is a declining asset inherited from the Soviet Union that figures importantly in Russia's small share of high-technology exports. With abundant hydrocarbon-fueled electrical generation capacity and declining demand compared to Soviet times, the domestic market for nuclear technology has dried up. Foreign sales are vital to sustaining essentially half of the atomic energy ministry's activities, and Iran is a major market.[35] Viktor Mikhailov, Russia's atomic energy minister when the agreement with Iran was initiated, summed up the motivation succinctly: "What could Russia have brought onto world markets? We only had one strength: our scientific and technical potential. Our only chance was broad cooperation in the sphere of peaceful nuclear energy."[36]

Large sums of money for the atomic energy ministry and associated firms are at stake. Russia's construction of Iran's Bushehr reactor alone is worth up to $1 billion; reprocessing fuel is also lucrative; and more reactor projects are planned. And the Iranians, Russians stress, pay cash. Boosters of these deals claim that the total value of the long-term relationship could exceed $8 billion and involve orders for more than 300 Russian companies. Moreover, significant numbers of high-technology jobs—many located in politically crucial and economically strapped regions of Russia—are involved.[37] The Russian

---

34. Transcript of Putin's BBC interview on June 22, 2003, reprinted in Johnson's Russia List, No. 7236, June 24, 2003.
35. See Celeste A. Wallander, "Russia's Interest in Trading with the 'Axis of Evil,'" testimony given at "Russia's Policies toward the Axis of Evil: Money and Geopolitics in Iraq and Iran" hearing, House Committee on International Relations, 108th Cong., 2d sess., February 26, 2003. For an overview of the problems facing Russia's nuclear industry and its interest in foreign sales, see Igor Khripunov, "MINATOM: Time for Crucial Decisions," *Problems of Post-Communism*, Vol. 48, No. 4 (July–August 2001), pp. 49–59.
36. Quoted in Vladimir A. Orlov and Alexander Vinnikov, "The Great Guessing Game: Russia and the Iranian Nuclear Issue," *Washington Quarterly*, Vol. 28, No. 2 (Spring 2005), p. 51.
37. See Anatoly Andreev, "Mirnyi Atom dlia Bushera" [Peaceful atom for Bushehr], *Trud*, December 27, 2002, p. 1. For more on Russia's role in proliferation in Asia, see Bates Gill, "Proliferation," in Ellings and Friedberg, with Wills, *Strategic Asia, 2003–04*.

atomic energy ministry remains a formidable interest group in Moscow politics, and its lobbyists work hard to make the case publicly and in Kremlin corridors that the nuclear sector is critical to Russia's modernization drive.[38]

Russia's substantive foreign policy behavior is consistent with this analysis. When the economic and regional security incentives for engaging Iran appear to contradict Russia's general antiproliferation stance, the latter wins. The extent of Iran's nuclear weapons–related programs came to the fore in 2002–03, and they turned out to have been based not on the Russian project but on purchases from the transnational nuclear proliferation network run from Pakistan by Abdul Qadeer Khan, as well as indigenous efforts. In response to the new evidence, Moscow recalibrated its policy in 2003. Russia reaffirmed its commitment to nonproliferation and its desire to see Iran submit to robust International Atomic Energy Agency (IAEA) inspections. To allay potential IAEA concerns regarding the Bushehr reactor, Russia secured a deal with Iran on returning all fuel to Russia for reprocessing. The Russians also pressured Tehran to sign and implement the IAEA additional protocol, which imposed further restrictions and openness on the Iranian program. Ultimately, U.S. and international concerns about the proliferation risks of Russia's nuclear project eased, resulting in diminished diplomatic pressure on Moscow.

Russia's continued reluctance to adopt an American-style hard line on Iran's nuclear program is the result of the same regional security, and especially economic, incentives. In expressing their reservations concerning further pressuring of Tehran, President Putin and other top government officials stressed the fear that if Russia backed away from its contract with the Iranians, American or European companies might move in to exploit the opening. As Putin put it, "We will protest against using the theme of nuclear weapons proliferation against Iran as an instrument for forcing Russian companies out of the Iranian market."[39] Moscow wants guarantees that international efforts to compel Iran to comply with IAEA strictures do not come at the expense of Russia's commercial interests. Nor do Russian foreign policy makers want to forgo the diplomatic dividends of their position as the great power with the best ties to Tehran, unless Iranian recalcitrance vis-à-vis the IAEA forces them to.

In short, there is no basis for concluding that soft balancing plays any role in Russia's relationship with Iran. Regional security concerns figure importantly

---

38. Although the nuclear issue attracts most of the attention, a similar constellation of interests lies behind Russia's arms sales to Iran. Tor Bukkvoll, "Arming the Ayatollahs: Economic Lobbies in Russia's Iran Policy," *Problems of Post-Communism*, Vol. 49, No. 6 (November/December, 2002), pp. 29–41.
39. Quoted in Orlov and Vinnikov, "The Great Guessing Game," p. 59.

in the larger diplomatic relationship, while economic incentives are the driver behind their nuclear cooperation.

EU DEFENSE COOPERATION

Since the turn of the millennium, member states have made concerted efforts to enhance the European Union's Security and Defense Policy (ESDP), including the development of a 60,000-man rapid reaction force, a new security strategy, a defense agency to support efforts to improve military capability, and most recently, the formation of 1,500-man "battle groups" capable of higher intensity operations.[40] European officials sometimes justify these efforts by stressing that they will lay the foundation for a larger EU role in regional and global security, thus implicitly reducing U.S. influence. For many analysts, this is a clear case of soft balancing.[41] The evidence, however, does not support such an interpretation.

Far from being a response to U.S. hegemonic dominance, the EU's attempts to increase its military capability are seen by European analysts and decisionmakers as necessary to deal with the prospect of the United States' decreased presence in Europe and reduced willingness to solve Balkans-style problems for its European allies.[42] For example, in explaining the origins of the ESDP, the director of the European Union's Institute for Security Studies, Nicole Gnesotto, notes that "because American involvement in crises that were not vital for America was no longer guaranteed, . . . the Europeans had to organize themselves to assume their share of responsibility in crisis management and, in doing so, maintain or even enhance the United States' interest within the Alliance."[43] For many of the key member governments, notably the United Kingdom, the corrosive effects of European military weakness on the transatlantic alliance provided the key impetus for enhancing EU capabilities. Most analysts thus concur that EU defense cooperation can go forward only if it is seen as complementary to the alliance with the United States. That is, some degree of U.S. support is a necessary condition of the ESDP's further progress. Indeed, the forces that the Europeans are actually seeking to create complement,

---

40. For a comprehensive analysis, see Nicole Gnesotto, ed., *EU Security and Defence Policy: The First Five Years (1999–2004),* (Paris: European Union Institute for Security Studies, 2005).
41. See, for example, Robert J. Art, "Europe Hedges Its Security Bets," in Paul, Wirtz, and Fortmann, *Balance of Power Revisited;* Walt, "Can the United States Be Balanced?"; Joffe, "Defying History and Theory"; and Layne, "America as European Hegemon."
42. See, for example, Charles A. Kupchan, *The End of the American Era: U.S. Foreign Policy and the Geopolitics of the Twenty-first Century* (New York: Alfred A. Knopf, 2002).
43. Nicole Gnesotto "ESDP: Results and Prospects," in Gnesotto, *EU Security and Defence Policy,* p. 25.

rather than compete with, U.S. capabilities because they provide additional units for dealing with Balkans-style contingencies or peacekeeping missions abroad.

Moreover, the EU will be unable to measurably narrow the overall gap in military power vis-à-vis the United States in the foreseeable future. Only seven of the 1,500-man battle groups—intended for smaller stability operations along the lines of the EU's Operation Artemis in the Congo—are projected for 2007. After six years of effort, the 60,000-man rapid reaction force still faces major hurdles: an independent task force of the EU's Institute for Security Studies identifies eight key strategic deficiencies, ranging from deployability and sustainability to interoperability and strategic decisionmaking.[44] When this force will be able to operate independently from U.S. transport, communications, and other forms of logistical support remains unclear. Both the rapid reaction force and the battle groups are not standing forces but rather pools of national units on which the EU can draw if the Council decides unanimously to use military force. And as Robert Cooper points out, "There is no member state for which EDSP is central to its security policy."[45]

Even if all currently envisioned forces materialize according to plan, they will do little to create any serious ability to constrain the United States. Indeed, generating a usable force for peace enforcement may work against the development of such a potential check on U.S. power. Unless Europeans assume a much greater willingness to pursue higher defense expenditures, investments toward making the rapid reaction contingent into a credible force will have to come at the expense of developing advanced systems capable of competing with or displacing those fielded by U.S. forces. In the opinion of most military analysts familiar with developments on both sides of the Atlantic, the most likely trajectory—even if all goes well for the EU's current plans—is a widening of the gap in high-intensity military capabilities in favor of the United States.[46] Over the past three decades, the United States has spent three times

---

44. Nicole Gnesotto (chair) and Jean-Yves Haine (rapporteur), *European Defence: A Proposal for a White Paper* (Paris: European Union Institute for Security Studies, 2004). An earlier EU report noted more than forty technological shortfalls constraining the force. See Alexander Nicoll, "Spending Call for EU Rapid Reaction Force, *Financial Times*, February 8, 2002; and the discussion in Ethan B. Kapstein, "Allies and Armaments," *Survival*, Vol. 44, No. 2 (Summer 2002), pp. 141–160.
45. Quoted in Gnesotto, *EU Security and Defence Policy*, p. 189.
46. See, for example, Hans-Christian Hagman, "EU Crisis Management Capabilities," paper delivered at the conference "The European Union—Its Role and Power in the Emerging International System," Woodrow Wilson School of Public and International Affairs, Princeton University, October 3–5, 2003; and Julian Lindley-French, "In the Shadow of Locarno? Why European Defense Is Failing," *International Affairs*, Vol. 78, No. 4 (October 2002), pp. 789–811.

more than all of the EU members combined on military research and development. This gap will affect the development of assets and capabilities for decades to come.

Hence, far from sacrificing other preferences to create capabilities that might constrain the United States, the Europeans may be sacrificing limited resources that could potentially be useful for countering U.S. power to create capabilities that largely complement those of the United States.[47] Why then do leaders in Europe sometimes use balancing language when describing these new forces? To begin, the overwhelming majority of the rhetoric is about building up capabilities for reasons other than balancing the United States; indeed, much of this rhetoric is about trying to be a better partner of the United States, not a competitor.

Sometimes, however, politicians do use balancing language to describe their aims for EU military strengthening, in part because increasing EU military capabilities involves financial and other costs that many member states seem very reluctant to bear. To the extent that this force is portrayed as a means of checking U.S. power, some of this hesitance may be reduced, if only because adopting a more independent EU foreign policy is popular among the public in Europe. Paying for such independence, however, is unpopular in Europe, which is why EU aggregate defense spending has steadily declined even as European politicians' rhetoric about defense has escalated. The result is a crescendo of calls for enhanced EU military capabilities and an alphabet soup of new organizational initiatives but relatively limited operational output on the ground.

In sum, the evidence indicates that regional security needs, not soft balancing, are the principal driver of EU defense cooperation. To this point, there is also no indication of European willingness to pay the economic costs to take the necessary steps to develop military capabilities that could meaningfully reduce the gap with the United States.

OPPOSITION TO THE IRAQ WAR
Unlike Russia's Asian partnerships, opposition to the U.S. invasion of Iraq did not entail measurable shifts in hard power. It nonetheless seemed tailor-made for the soft-balancing argument. On a policy it declared vital to its national security, the United States faced opposition from key allies. The opposition was

---

47. For an analysis that captures this trade-off, see Bastian Giegerich and William Wallace, "Not Such a Soft Power: The External Deployment of European Forces," *Survival*, Vol. 46, No. 2 (Summer 2004), pp. 163–182.

not haphazard but coordinated in elaborate diplomatic exchanges. And the leaders of France, the linchpin of the "coalition of the unwilling," made a point of describing their policy as part of an overall preference for a multipolar world. Not surprisingly, such efforts propelled the soft-balancing argument to the forefront.[48]

Nevertheless, this argument dramatically oversimplifies and misrepresents what occurred. Soft balancing played no discernable role for some of the principal actors in the drama. For others, strategic calculations that superficially resemble soft balancing, but actually stem from a different logic, interacted in complex ways with other incentives that also pushed strongly toward constraining the United States. Even a generous rendering of the soft-balancing argument would accord it at best a minor role.[49]

GERMANY AND TURKEY. A central link in the complex chain of events that ended in the failure of the U.S. attempt to achieve a second UN Security Council resolution authorizing the invasion of Iraq was Germany's uncompromising opposition to U.S. policy and, as a consequence, a brief but dramatic shift in post–Cold War Franco-German relations. For the first time in more than a decade, Berlin was the supplicant in the relationship, which presented Paris with an attractive opportunity to regain its status as the EU's driver just as it was expanding to include a raft of new Central European member states.[50] This shift originated in German domestic politics. To be sure, Chancellor Schröder expressed doubts about the wisdom of invading Iraq long before Germany's election campaign got under way in the summer of 2002. But his need to recapture elements of his political base soon pointed irresistibly toward taking an especially strong stand on the issue. Running on a dismal economic record and having alienated his more left-wing supporters with tough economic proposals and a series of controversial new German military com-

---

48. See, for example, Robert Pape, "Welcome to the Era of 'Soft Balancing,'" *Boston Globe,* March 23, 2003, p. H1; and Joseph S. Nye, "The UN Is Right for the Job: Rebuilding Iraq II," *International Herald Tribune,* April 14, 2003, p. 10.
49. In reconstructing inter-allied disputes over Iraq, the best extant account is Philip H. Gordon and Jeremy Shapiro, *Allies at War: America, Europe, and the Crisis over Iraq* (New York: McGraw-Hill, 2004). Other accounts and chronologies that were critical in constructing this case study include Elizabeth Pond, *Friendly Fire: The Near-Death of the Transatlantic Alliance* (Washington, D.C.: Brookings and European Union Studies Association, 2003); Gustav Lindstrom and Burkhardt Schmidt, eds., "One Year On: Lessons from Iraq," Challiot Paper No. 68 (Brussels: EU Institute for Security Studies, March 2004); John Peterson, "Europe, America, Iraq: Worst Ever, Ever Worsening?" *Journal of Common Market Studies,* Vol. 42, No. S1 (September 2004), pp. 9–26; David Allen and Michael Smith, "External Policy Developments," *Journal of Common Market Studies,* Vol. 42, No. S1 (September 2004), pp. 95–112; and "The Divided West," pts. 1–3, *Financial Times,* May 27–30, 2003.
50. Pond, *Friendly Fire,* chap. 3.

mitments abroad, Schröder was trailing in the polls and facing near-certain defeat as the political season began to ramp up. His political advisers told him that his re-election hinged on recapturing two key left-wing constituencies, both of which had strong, long-standing antiwar preferences: core Social Democratic Party (SPD) activists, and left-wing voters in Eastern Germany who were defecting to the pacifist and anti-American Party of Democratic Socialism (the successor party of the former Communists).[51]

Then came what one Schröder operative called "the miracle" of Vice President Dick Cheney's August 26 speech calling for preventive war in Iraq and questioning a UN-based approach.[52] The speech generated intensely negative reactions throughout Europe and gave the Schröder team a chance to relaunch its re-election bid on an uncompromising antiwar platform. The campaign's tenor and dynamic changed immediately. As antiwar passions mounted, economic issues, on which the Christian Democrats' Edmund Stoiber had been campaigning effectively, receded into the background. Political incentives pushed Schröder toward an increasingly uncompromsing antiwar stand. Even after President George W. Bush moved away from Cheney's initial stance and took the Iraq matter to the UN, Schröder adopted a hard-line position, declaring his refusal to support the use of force even if sanctioned by the Security Council. Yet as strident as he became on Iraq, Schröder never expressed his opposition in balancing or multipolar terms, sticking to a script of policy opposition on strategic grounds combined with a general posture as a principled socialist heroically standing up to a U.S. president who embodies everything German leftists loathe.[53] Even so, important sectors of the socialist-leaning elite and media, to say nothing of swathes of more centrist SPD voters, were uncomfortable with Schröder's stance, preferring a more statesmanlike position that upheld the centrality of the UN.[54]

A second link in the story of constraining the United States on Iraq was Turkey's decision not to permit the U.S. military to use its territory for an assault on Saddam Hussein's army. In hindsight, the Turkish government's move did not undermine the invasion's operational effectiveness, but this was not clear at the time, and it may have affected the resolve of France and others in their

---

51. Martin Walker, "The Winter of Germany's Discontent," *World Policy Journal*, Vol. 19, No. 4 (Winter 2002/2003), p. 37.
52. Ibid.
53. See, for example, Jeffrey Herf, "The Perfect Storm and After: Retrospect and Prospect for American-German Relations," American Institute for Contemporary German Studies, July 29, 2004, http://www.aicgs.org/c/herfc.shtml.
54. Pond, *Friendly Fire*, chap. 3.

interactions with the Bush administration. Accordingly, many analysts view the Turks' decision as an example of soft balancing.[55] In this case, however, the domestic political dynamic was even more dominant than in Germany, for it overwhelmed a strategic decision to support the United States. Of key importance here was Turkey's baleful experience of the 1990–91 Persian Gulf War, which was widely perceived as an economic disaster for the Turks. Also significant was Turkey's long-standing concern that upsetting the status quo in Iraq could alter the political equation regarding the Iraqi Kurds, whose independence might incite co-nationals in Turkey itself. These two historical legacies help to explain why any Turkish government would have had to bargain hard for strong guarantees from the United States to reassure a public that was especially skeptical about the consequences of another war in the region. Negotiations with Turkey followed three tracks: political (regarding the degree of autonomy for Iraqi Kurds and the fate of Iraqis of Turkish descent); military (concerning where Turkish troops could be deployed in Iraq); and economic (compensation for the costs that a war would impose on Turkey).

Although the details of the economic package were never fully worked out, Prime Minister Tayyip Erdogan and the leadership of his Islamist Justice and Development Party ultimately supported a three-track deal to allow the United States to use Turkey as a staging ground for the invasion of Iraq and submitted a resolution to parliament asking their members to support it.[56] Erdogan and the party leadership calculated that supporting the Bush administration would best secure Turkey's interests in postwar Iraq while maximizing the economic benefits. Both the powerful Turkish military and the opposition Republican People's Party, however, opted to free ride and let the ruling party suffer the domestic political costs of pushing through the measure, assuming, as did Erdogan and most analysts, that it would pass. In the event, it did win a majority under standard rules. But under Turkish parliamentary rules, the nineteen abstentions meant that the resolution failed by three votes to win the necessary simple majority of those present. News accounts note that some parliamentarians' ignorance of this rule may have affected their votes.[57] Immediately thereafter, top generals who had previously opted to free ride sought to reverse the decision. By the time these machina-

---

55. See Pape, "Soft Balancing"; and Walt, "Can the United States Be Balanced?"
56. Mustafa Kibaroglu, "Turkey Says No," *Bulletin of the Atomic Scientists*, Vol. 59, No. 4 (July/August 2003), pp. 22–26.
57. "A Pivotal Nation Goes Into a Spin," *Economist*, March 8, 2003, p. 41. See also Gordon and Shapiro, *Allies at War*.

tions got under way, however, the rapid advance of U.S. and British forces in Iraq radically devalued the importance of the Turkish invasion route.

In sum, the behavior of both Germany and Turkey can be traced to domestic political incentives unrelated to the concentration of power in the United States. Russia and France are far more complex actors in this case because both had stated preferences for multipolarity, general policies of buttressing the role of the UN Security Council and thus the bargaining value of their veto power in that body, economic interests in play in Iraq, strong domestic incentives for standing up to Washington, and sincere policy differences with the United States over costs and benefits of a war in Iraq and its relation to the war on terrorism. The interaction among these dynamics was complicated. How did soft balancing fit into this mosaic?

RUSSIA. In Moscow President Putin and his top foreign policy aides were reluctant to take the lead in any constraint-coalition against the Bush administration, having recently reoriented Russia's grand strategy toward pragmatic cooperation with the United States.[58] At the same time, they were inclined to maintain their existing policy on Iraq, under which Russia reaped rich economic rewards. Russian firms profited handsomely under the UN's oil-for-food program, and Saddam Hussein also offered longer-term inducements that Russia could realize only if sanctions were withdrawn: a major development contract with Russia's Lukoil (valued at some $12 billion) and the prospect of settling Iraq's state debt to Russia of about $8 billion. As long as there was some possibility that the Iraq issue could be settled with the Baathist regime in power, Russia had incentives to position itself to reap these promised rewards.

Putin's initial response to these mixed incentives was to keep his options open with strategic ambiguity. While Foreign Minister Igor Ivanov made strong statements in opposition to U.S. pronouncements, Putin authorized official contacts with Iraqi opposition figures and chose to support UN Security Council resolution 1441 in November, which warned Iraq of "serious consequences" if it did not meet its disarmament obligations. Meanwhile U.S. officials sought Russian support by offering inducements—honoring Iraqi contracts with Russian oil companies and promising Russia a role in the postwar stabilization—that the United States could deliver only after a regime change

---

58. On Russia's reorientation toward the United States, see William C. Wohlforth, "Russia," in Ellings and Friedberg, with Wills, *Strategic Asia, 2002–03;* and Thomas M. Nichols, "Russia's Turn West: Sea Change or Opportunism?" *World Policy Journal,* Vol. 19, No. 4 (Winter 2002/03), pp. 13–22. On Putin's strategy and maneuverings on Iraq, see Wohlforth, "Russia's Soft Balancing Act," in Ellings and Friedberg, with Wills, *Strategic Asia, 2003–04,* pp. 165–179.

in Baghdad. Putin's most trusted aides reportedly worked hard to reach an agreement with Bush administration officials.[59] But as long as Putin remained uncertain of U.S. resolve and capability to prevail, he risked more by aligning himself prematurely with the United States than by standing aloof. If Hussein somehow survived the crisis—perhaps by satisfying the world that Iraq had disarmed—Putin would have lost the economic benefits Baghdad offered and gained nothing. Pressuring Baghdad to disarm in accordance with resolution 1441 thus had three overlapping benefits: it maintained the prestige of the Security Council (Russia's favored forum); it did not foreclose the possibility of cooperation with the United States if Hussein proved recalcitrant; and it maintained Russia's potentially profitable position in case the crisis was resolved without a full-scale invasion of Iraq.

Ultimately, Russia chose to align with France and Germany in opposing a second UN resolution authorizing an invasion. In intense diplomatic exchanges in January and February 2003, President Jacques Chirac convinced Putin that France (with Germany) would lead the campaign. With such long-time U.S. allies taking the lead, Putin could expect that the diplomatic costs of opposing Washington would be minor. Given the relatively low expected costs, a number of other factors argued strongly in favor of Putin's decision. Putin appears to have considered an invasion to be an unwise and potentially very costly strategic move that would ill serve the war on terror.[60] Strong elite and popular opinion against U.S. policy in Iraq also doubtless figured in the Russian president's calculations—parliamentary and presidential elections were forthcoming. Having just caved in to U.S. pressure on a host of salient issues ranging from the future of the Antiballistic Missile Treaty to NATO expansion, standing up to Washington was an attractive option—particularly given that Russia could follow rather than lead the opposition, thereby reducing the likelihood that its larger efforts to realign with the West would be thrown off track.

Putin worked hard to ensure that his tack toward Europe did not come at the expense of a working strategic partnership with the United States. As his foreign policy aide Sergei Prikhodko put it, "Our partnership with the United States is not a hostage of the Iraq crisis. There are far too many common values and common tasks both short term and long term. . . . Our co-operation never

---

59. Pavel Felgenhauer, "New Détente to Die Young," *Moscow Times*, May 29, 2003.
60. Reports suggest that Russia's intelligence services were feeding Putin wildly exaggerated estimates of Iraq's prospects in a war with U.S. forces. See Sergei Karaganov, "Crisis Lessons," *Moscow News*, April 23, 2003. Putin voiced skepticism regarding the strategic wisdom of U.S. policy in preinvasion interviews.

stopped, even during the Iraq crisis."[61] This was not just rhetoric; concrete co-operation continued on intelligence sharing, nuclear arms control, NATO expansion, peacekeeping in Afghanistan, and the multilateral efforts to counter the proliferation threat from North Korea—all of which helped to ensure that Russia would not jeopardize its overall relationship with the United States. And as then National Security Adviser Condoleezza Rice's famous "punish France, ignore Germany, and forgive Russia" quip indicates, this strategy worked.[62]

FRANCE. The primacy of long-standing domestic political factors in the German and Turkish cases, and Russia's extreme circumspection and unwillingness to face any significant trade-off between constraining the United States on Iraq and other goals, all serve to bring France's role to the fore. Nevertheless, soft balancing is notably absent from the three explanations for French policy upon which expert observers converge.[63]

First was the policy dispute between the French and U.S. governments. President Chirac, Foreign Minister Dominique de Villepin, and indeed most of the French policy establishment opposed regime change on a variety of grounds, chief among them their expectation that an occupation of Iraq would be so bloody and long as to worsen the problem of al-Qaida-style terrorism.[64] Given France's large Muslim population and its perceived high exposure to Islamic terrorism, the potential downsides of a contested occupation of Iraq were highly salient to French policymakers. Hence, at the outset they faced strong incentives to bargain with their U.S. allies to try to alter the Bush administration's chosen policy. Pushing for the Iraq issue to be played out in the UN

---

61. Quoted in Andrew Jack and Stefan Wagstyl, "Optimism on Russian Postwar Accord with U.S.," *Financial Times*, May 16, 2003.

62. Elaine Sciolino, "French Struggle Now with How to Coexist with Bush," *New York Times*, February 8, 2005.

63. The following sources were especially helpful in reconstructing French policymaking on Iraq: Gordon and Shapiro, *Allies at War*; Pond, *Friendly Fire*; "The Divided West," pts. 1–3; and the conference "The United States and France after the War in Iraq" (Washington, D.C.: Center for the United States and France [CUSF], Brookings, May 12, 2003), http://www.brookings.edu/fp/cusf/events/20030512cusf.htm. The assessments of motivations in these analyses correspond to those found in the wider literature. Analysts do not see economic incentives as being important in this case. See, for example, Valerie Marcel, "Total in Iraq," U.S.-France Analysis Series (Washington, D.C.: CUSF, Brookings, August 2003).

64. See, for example, "Interview Given by M. Jacques Chirac, President of the Republic, to 'TF1' and 'France2,'" March 10, 2003, http://www.elysee.fr/elysee/francais/actualites/a_l_elysee/2003/mars/interview_televisee_sur_l_iraq-page_2–2.4840.html; also indicative are the analyses of French counterterrorism expert Judge Jean-Louis Bruguière. See Bruguière, "Terrorism after the War in Iraq," U.S.-France Analysis Series (Washington, D.C.: CUSF, Brookings, May 2003), http://www.brook.edu/printme.wbs?page=/fp/cuse/analysis/bruguiere.htm. For an analysis of U.S.-European policy differences on Iraq, see Pond, *Friendly Fire*, chap 3.

reflected not only France's immediate policy interests, but also its long-term bargaining incentive to maintain the centrality of the Security Council. Once the Bush administration made it abundantly clear that it would invade Iraq no matter what, a French policy of criticizing the Iraq invasion could still be seen as an optimal response, especially given that the invasion's operational effectiveness did not depend on France's assistance. France may indeed have been successful in insulating itself from the potential downsides of the Iraq invasion: indicative in this regard is a recent PIPA poll that found that among the major powers, France is the one most widely viewed worldwide as having a positive influence.[65] Significantly, the French policy of opposing the United States on Iraq did not simply offer a potential benefit of insulation from anger emanating from the Muslim world; the expected diplomatic costs of France's opposition to the United States were also unusually low, owing to surprise decisions by two traditionally loyal U.S. allies—Germany and Turkey—to defy the Bush administration.

Second, informed accounts of French policy highlight the significance of European regional dynamics. At a time when the EU faced numerous new challenges from its inclusion of several Central European states, President Chirac could not afford to lose the policy initiative to Chancellor Schröder, whose antiwar stance was more consistent with European opinion than Chirac's initial posture. Schröder's vulnerability in the face of Washington's intense ire at his decision made him the supplicant in the bilateral relationship with France, which gave Chirac the opportunity to restart the Franco-German "motor" of the EU with himself in control. Chirac's decision in January to side with Schröder allowed him to co-opt the German leader and restore France to a more commanding role in EU affairs.

Third, observers agree that domestic politics played a role in the French president's calculations. Chirac had just weathered a touch-and-go re-election in which he won only 19 percent of the vote in the first round. True to his Gaullist roots, he clearly saw the advantage of playing to the French public's traditional appreciation of standing up to the United States. This position was particularly tempting given France's sizable Muslim minority.

In the view of most analysts, European and domestic politics were important incentives for France, but they were dominated by policy and bargaining considerations. Had the logic of policy and bargaining pointed toward French participation in the war, Chirac would likely have ignored the domestic politi-

---

65. "Who Will Lead the World?" Program on International Policy Attitudes, April 6, 2005, http://www.pipa.org/OnlineReports/europe/040605/Qnnaire04_06_05.pdf, p. 1.

cal incentives. On the other hand, the political and European dimensions may well have tipped the balance in favor of opposition beyond what might have been optimal for policy and bargaining purposes—that, at any rate, is the assessment of the numerous French critics of Chirac's and de Villepin's conduct during the crisis.[66] The critical issue, therefore, is to assess the degree to which the soft-balancing explanation captures the general UN Security Council–focused bargaining stance and how this interacted with the more immediate policy concerns swirling around the Iraq issue.

Unlike their counterparts in Moscow and Berlin, Chirac and de Villepin publicly and loudly associated their position on Iraq with their preference for a multipolar world. Although the term "multipolarity" as French statesmen use it has many meanings, none matches its definition in American political science. Judging by their public utterances, both men believe that France and the world are better off when key decisions regarding global security are arrived at multilaterally—and that the UN Security Council is an important mechanism for achieving this state of affairs.[67] This preference fits with France's conception of its identity and foreign policy traditions, but it also merges seamlessly with a rational bargaining strategy vis-à-vis the United States that exploits the fortuitous circumstance of being one of the five veto-wielding permanent members of the Security Council.[68] Given the veto, a policy preference for maintaining the prestige of the Security Council by trying to delegitimize recourse to force without its sanction marginally increases France's influence over U.S. use of force. That influence is valuable to France, given that it is incapable of either countering American power or even, in most cases, fielding forces of its own to accomplish global missions such as disarming Iraq.

The purpose of that bargaining stance, however, is not necessarily to check

---

66. See, for example, Lionel Jospin, "The Relationship between France and America," lecture delivered at Harvard University, December 4, 2003; and commentary by French participants at the conference "The United States and France after the War in Iraq."

67. To cite one example: It was widely reported that the first sentence Chirac uttered in the interview in which he announced his intention to veto the second Security Council resolution was: "We want to live in a multipolar world." This, however, was only the first clause in a sentence that continues: "i.e. one with a few large groups enjoying as harmonious relations as possible with each other, a world in which Europe, among others, will have its full place, a world in which democracy progresses, hence the fundamental importance for us of the United Nations Organization which provides a framework and gives impetus to this democracy and harmony." "Interview Given by M. Jacques Chirac." For an example of the foreign minister's thinking, see the Alastair Buchan Lecture 2003, delivered by French Foreign Minister Dominique de Villepin, International Institute for Strategic Studies, London, United Kingdom, March 27, 2003 http://www.iiss.org/conferencepage.php?confID=56.

68. Erik Voeten, "Outside Options and the Logic of Security Council Action," *American Political Science Review*, Vol. 95, No. 4 (November 2001), pp. 845–858.

U.S. power generally but to enhance France's ability to bargain over specific policy responses to global security issues. In the Iraq case, France's general stance toward bolstering the Security Council worked with its real policy preferences on Iraq. Together these incentives pushed Paris toward a position between Germany's outright opposition and the U.S.-U.K. stance. Opposition as categorical as Schröder's would push Washington toward unilateralism and thus weaken the Security Council. In late August, de Villepin repositioned France's policy on Iraq to accept the possibility of the use of force as long as it was channeled through the Security Council. After President Bush put the disarmament of Iraq before the UN in September 2002, France agreed to Security Council resolution 1441, following hard bargaining to prevent the inclusion of wording that would have given the United States and Britain a green light to topple Hussein without further Security Council say-so.

Chirac's policy may have lured the United States into the web of UN diplomacy, but only by moving France's stance much closer to Washington's and London's and actively preparing to sanction and even participate in a war against Iraq. French policymakers initially assumed that Hussein's recalcitrance would probably lead to a violation of resolution 1441 and a casus belli. Although it is impossible to know whether Chirac was sincere, the evidence suggests that France actively prepared for possible participation in a military action against Iraq, including mobilizing the carrier *Charles de Gaulle,* readying the armed forces, and initiating staff talks with the commander in chief of the U.S. Central Command, Gen. Tommy Franks, on a possible 15,000-man contribution to an allied assault on Iraq. The policy was logical, given Chirac's policy preferences and bargaining interests: France's main hope of pushing Washington and London closer to its preferred policy was by using its influence in the UN Security Council, a route that benefited the longer-term strategy of buttressing the role of that body. Given that bargaining incentives and policy preferences worked in tandem here, France did not face a trade-off between them. It is therefore hard to assign relative weight to each.

These incentives, however, do not always coincide. In one recent case where the two incentives came into conflict—Kosovo—France's position of supporting NATO military action in 1999 was consistent with its immediate policy preferences but not with the long-term bargaining incentive of maintaining the centrality of the UN Security Council. In the Iraq case, even though it served both the general bargaining interest and the immediate policy preference of the French, France's initial policy was illogical from a soft-balancing perspective because it potentially eased the diplomatic path for a massive exercise and possible expansion of U.S. power.

In January 2003 Chirac learned that the Bush administration was going to go to war regardless of what the UN weapons inspectors in Iraq uncovered. This intelligence exposed a fundamental contradiction between French and U.S.-U.K. policy preferences that had been diplomatically obfuscated until that moment. Chirac strongly preferred containment and inspections as a way of dealing with Iraq, while President Bush and Prime Minister Tony Blair just as strongly preferred regime change. The fact that the weapons inspections seemed—to the UN's Hans Blix and the French, at least—to be going so well (which Chirac frankly acknowledged was the result of U.S.-U.K. military pressure) exacerbated the contradictions between the two sides' preferred policies. The realization that the Iraq question was going to be resolved through regime change no matter what the inspectors discovered meant that the French would not participate in the coalition. The only question was how strongly to oppose the Bush administration's decision.

The French leadership much preferred a low-key approach to the Iraq issue. They tried to avoid a public showdown with the United States and the United Kingdom by urging them not to try for a second resolution—in which case, they argued in meetings with Bush officials, the French government would voice disapproval but otherwise stand aside. The Bush administration rejected Chirac's "gentlemen's agreement" out of deference to Prime Minister Blair, who believed that he needed a second Security Council resolution for domestic reasons.[69] But for this unique domestic contingency, a Washington-Paris deal might have been struck, and the most dramatic phase of the inter-allied dispute avoided. In the event, Chirac decided to work hard to deny the Americans and the British a second resolution, resulting in the well-publicized spectacle of the two sides feverishly lining up allies in the UN, France's veto threat, and the U.S.-U.K. failure to put together a majority in the Security Council.

The soft-balancing argument holds that the United States increasingly poses a direct security challenge to other states, which they respond to by seeking to constrain U.S. power and the attendant threat. Our review of the events leading up to the invasion of Iraq shows how mistaken this argument is. For France—the linchpin of the diplomatic coalition that confronted the Bush administration—policy preferences, longer-term bargaining incentives, and domestic and European politics all pushed toward constraining the United States. Even though the French leadership strongly disagreed with the Bush administration over the sagacity of invading Iraq on strategic grounds, the

---

69. This episode is detailed in Gordon and Shapiro, *Allies at War*.

most precedent-breaking aspect of French behavior—the intense campaign against the United States and Britain in the UN Security Council—was something President Chirac tried to avoid. The second UN resolution, and the attendant debate, went forward only because of complex domestic incentives acting on Prime Minister Blair. The soft-balancing argument is thus wrong to attribute the novel elements in French policy mainly to a shift in how France viewed U.S. power or the potential security threat it poses.

What is true for France also applies to the other key players. The most salient and novel behavior in the Iraq case—especially Chancellor Schröder's fateful decision to oppose the Bush administration categorically—cannot be seen as a response to the security challenges emanating from the underlying power of the United States. Great power behavior during the past two years since the invasion of Iraq provides further evidence against the soft-balancing argument. In particular, far from seeking to further distance themselves from the United States, France and Germany have rushed to pursue a rapprochement with the Bush administration during this period. Significantly, this move had already gathered substantial momentum even before President Bush extended a diplomatic olive branch after gaining re-election.

Iraq Postmortem: Soft Balancing versus Bargaining

Of all the complex motivations in play in the Iraq case, the bargaining incentive is closest to what analysts mean by "soft balancing." But the differences between balancing and bargaining are profound. Bargaining is ubiquitous in a world of self-interested states. Using the term "balancing" to describe bargaining amounts in practice to equating balancing with international relations writ large. If it becomes another word for bargaining, balancing is meaningless as an analytical concept—something that describes a constant, rather than a variable; a mundane rather than noteworthy development in international politics.

The critical need to distinguish bargaining from soft balancing becomes even clearer when one considers that bargaining incentives can sometimes drive states into behavior that is the opposite of soft balancing. In the Iraq case, for example, France's bargaining interest in maintaining the importance of the UN Security Council led it to follow a policy that held out as a real possibility a UN sanction of a U.S.-led invasion of Iraq. Pursuit of this bargaining incentive led France toward a policy that, in the end, might have helped to legitimize a potential expansion of U.S. power in the Persian Gulf—that is, the opposite of what soft balancing predicts. To call this soft balancing makes a mockery of the term. Acting to augment the role of the UN in this way made sense for a France interested in maximizing its long-term ability to influence U.S. decisions to use force globally. Had the Bush administration's actions regarding Iraq caused France to perceive a direct security threat from U.S. power, as soft-balancing proponents maintain, this behavior would have been nonsensical.

Distinguishing bargaining from soft balancing is also crucial because a key reason states may now seek greater capabilities is not to check U.S. power, but rather to be in a better position to bargain over the appropriate responses to security challenges from other states or actors. This is, for example, a major impetus for enhanced EU military capacity. It is an article of faith among many Europeans that the United States will take them seriously only if they are more capable militarily. This desire to influence Washington is understandable. On any given global security issue, each government is likely to have its own favored approach that fits with its traditions, ideas, and interests (commercial and strategic). Moreover, there are situations in which states are concerned that the manner in which the United States might address a security issue could redound negatively for their own security. Key here is that the concern is not about a direct security threat from the United States; rather, the security connection is indirect "blowback" from various U.S. policies that increase the threat from other actors (e.g., France's fear that a U.S. invasion of Iraq would only exacerbate the problem of al-Qaida-style terrorism). This threat of indirect blowback is hardly inconsequential, and it is not surprising that other great powers will sometimes bargain hard with Washington to change its approach when they see this threat emerging. States are not indifferent to how security issues are resolved, and so may be willing to invest in capabilities that give them a seat at the bargaining table.

Although this incentive for enhancing capabilities concerns security and is directly connected to U.S. policy, it has nothing to do with balancing. Balancing, whether hard or soft, is about protection from the security threat emanating directly from a potential hegemon. If it means anything, the soft-balancing argument must predict that less U.S. power and lower involvement will reduce incentives for other states to gain relative power. If bargaining rather than balancing is in play, however, then there is no reason to believe that shrinking either U.S. power or the level of its global engagement would reduce other states' incentives to build up their capabilities. On the contrary, a precipitous U.S. withdrawal from the world—as neo-isolationists are now calling for—could generate new security dynamics that produce much greater incentives for other powers to increase their capabilities.

Ultimately, what appears new about the behavior analysts are calling soft balancing is not its significance, but its perceived prominence on the agenda. What used to be considered standard diplomatic bargaining is now likely trumpeted as balancing because real balancing of the kind that has appeared so often throughout history—competing great-power alliances, arms buildups, brinkmanship crises, and the like—was cleared off the international agenda in 1989–91 with the end of the Cold War. Importantly, the concept of balancing rose to prominence in a world in which great power security relations were dominated by the direct threat that they posed to each other. Today, by contrast, the likelihood of great power war is exceedingly low. Weak states and nonstates pose the main security challenge, and the great powers argue primarily over the best way to address them. Balance of power theory has no utility in explaining great power relations in this world.

Conclusion

This article shows that the soft-balancing argument has no traction. The only reason some analysts have concluded otherwise is because they have failed to consider alternative explanations. If it were reasonable to equate soft balancing with great power policy bargaining, then balancing would figure as a contributor, but not a driver, in at least the Iraq case. As we have demonstrated, however, there are critical analytical costs to equating these two phenomena. Once the distinction between soft balancing and bargaining is recognized, the strict conclusion is that soft balancing plays no discernable role in any of the four cases we examine.

None of this should be interpreted to mean that Washington can safely ignore the views of the other major powers. The further one looks beyond the immediate short term, the clearer the issues become—among them, the environment, weapons of mass destruction, disease, migration, and the stability of the global economy. The United States cannot effectively address these issues on its own; all of them will require repeated dealings with many partners over many years. It is also clear that other states can take actions that end up constraining the United States, sometimes significantly. These constraint actions, however, are not an outgrowth of balance of power dynamics and cannot be explained by the soft-balancing amendment to that theory. The current practice of using balance of power concepts to describe and explain this behavior is costly in theoretical and policy terms.

With regard to theory, the widespread tendency to shoehorn policy disputes and bargaining dynamics into a simplistic balancing narrative has the effect of generating unwarranted support for balance of power theory. Our analysis demonstrates that even though other states sometimes undertake actions that constrain the United States, and occasionally use balancing language to describe these efforts, such behavior does not validate balance of power theory. In a unipolar world, soft balancing can be seen as the first observable implication that the world works the way balance of power theory expects it to. There is no empirical basis for the soft-balancing argument, and hence any effort to invoke it as a means of buttressing balance of power theory is fruitless.

Where should scholarly research go from here? The soft-balancing argument rose to prominence only in the past several years and has not yet been fully fleshed out theoretically. One option that might seem appealing would be to develop the theoretical logic of the argument further, as Robert Pape has done in a recent analysis.[70] Although we certainly understand the appeal of trying to explain the constraint actions of other states with a parsimonious, generalizable theory, these advantages of the soft-balancing argument in no way make up for its lack of explanatory power—even in cases that soft-balancing proponents have highlighted to try to forward their argument. Although it is bound to disappoint those who have sought to rework balance of power theory to accommodate a world without hard balancing, this result is not surprising. Balance of power theory was developed to explain the behavior of states in systems with two or more poles in which war among the great powers was an ever-present danger. Neither of those conditions applies today: the international system is unipolar, and the likelihood of war among the great powers has receded because of a host of factors, some of which are highlighted by realism (such as the geographic location of the United States and nuclear weapons) and others of which are emphasized by nonrealist theories (such as economic globalization and democracy).[71] Analysts would be wise to invest their talents in investigating the novel dynamics of great power bargaining in today's unipolar system rather than seeking to stretch old analytical concepts that were created to deal with the bipolar and multipolar systems of the past.[72]

---

70. Pape, "Soft Balancing."
71. For a general discussion, see Robert Jervis, "Theories of War in an Era of Great Power Peace," *American Political Science Review*, Vol. 96, No. 1 (March 2002), pp. 1–14. On economic globalization, see Stephen G. Brooks, *Producing Security: Multinational Corporations, Globalization, and the Changing Calculus of Conflict* (Princeton, N.J.: Princeton University Press, 2005). On geography, see William C. Wohlforth, "U.S. Strategy in a Unipolar World," in Ikenberry, *America Unrivaled*, pp. 98–120. On nuclear weapons, see Kenneth N. Waltz, "More May Be Better," in Scott D. Sagan and Waltz, *The Spread of Nuclear Weapons: A Debate Renewed* (New York: W.W. Norton, 2003). On democracy, see Bruce Russett and John R. Oneal, *Triangulating Peace: Democracy, Interdependence, and International Organizations* (New York: W.W. Norton, 2001).
72. A useful step in this direction is provided in Voeten, "Outside Options and the Logic of Security Council Action."

Regarding policy, this article reveals that supporters of a U.S. foreign policy characterized by restraint should not rely on balancing dynamics as they construct their arguments. On any given issue, the United States may take a more or less restrained stance. Much of the debate on any issue will naturally concern cost-benefit assessments specific to that issue. Nonetheless, when arguing for U.S. restraint, scholars and policy analysts routinely appeal to the staple balance-of-power proposition that the costs of a relatively unrestrained policy on some issue transcend the specifics of the case and include counterbalancing. In making this argument, they are following a venerable tradition: expected counterbalancing has historically been the strongest argument for restraint in the face of temptation. It is true that soft balancing is tailor-made as an argument for U.S. restraint; the problem is that it has no empirical support. Our examination indicates that other states are simply not going to force the United States to act in a more restrained manner by acting in a systematic, coordinated manner to check U.S. power. There are many compelling reasons why the United States should adopt this foreign policy course, but soft balancing is not among them.

Waiting for Balancing

Why the World Is Not Pushing Back

Keir A. Lieber and
Gerard Alexander

Many scholars and policy analysts predicted the emergence of balancing against the United States following the collapse of the Soviet Union and the end of the Cold War. Since then, however, great power balancing—when states seriously commit themselves to containing a threatening state—has failed to emerge, despite a huge increase in the preponderant power of the United States. More recently, the prospect and then onset of the U.S.-led invasion of Iraq in March 2003 generated renewed warnings of an incipient global backlash. Some observers claim that signs of traditional balancing by states—that is, internal defense buildups or external alliance formation—can already be detected. Others suggest that such "hard balancing" may not be occurring. Instead, they argue that the world is witnessing a new phenomenon of "soft balancing," in which states seek to undermine and restrain U.S. power in ways that fall short of classic measures. But in both versions, many believe that the wait is over and that the world is beginning to push back.

This article argues, in contrast, that both lines of argument are unpersuasive. The past few years have certainly witnessed a surge in resentment and criticism of specific U.S. policies. But great power balancing against the United States has yet to occur, a finding that we maintain offers important insights into states' perceptions and intentions. The United States' nearest rivals are not ramping up defense spending to counter U.S. power, nor have these states sought to pool their efforts or resources for counterbalancing. We argue, further, that discussion of soft balancing is much ado about nothing. Defining or operationalizing the concept is difficult; the behavior typically identified by it seems identical to normal diplomatic friction; and, regardless, the evidence does not support specific predictions suggested by those advancing the concept.

Global interactions during and after the Iraq war have been filled with both a great deal of stasis—as many states leave their policies toward the United States fundamentally unchanged—and ironies, such as repeated requests by

Keir A. Lieber is Assistant Professor of Political Science at the University of Notre Dame. He is also Faculty Fellow at the Joan B. Kroc Institute for International Peace Studies and the Nanovic Institute for European Studies at Notre Dame. Gerard Alexander is Associate Professor of Politics at the University of Virginia.

The authors thank Keven Ruby, Randall Schweller, and the participants of the Program on International Politics, Economics, and Security at the University of Chicago for comments on an earlier draft of this article. They also thank Ozlem Kayhan for her research assistance.

International Security, Vol. 30, No. 1 (Summer 2005), pp. 109–139

the United States for its allies to substantially boost their military spending and capabilities, requests that so far have gone unfilled. Moreover, U.S. relations with regional powers such as China, Russia, India, and other key states (e.g., Egypt, Jordan, Pakistan, and Saudi Arabia) have improved in recent years. These revealing events and trends are underappreciated by many, perhaps most, analyses in search of balancing.

The lack of balancing behavior against the United States constitutes a genuine puzzle for many observers, with serious implications both for theorizing and for U.S. foreign policy making, and so is a puzzle worth explaining. The next section of this article reviews approaches that predict balancing under current conditions. The second section presents evidence that classic forms of balancing are not occurring. The third section argues that claims of soft balancing are unpersuasive because evidence for them is poor, especially because they rely on criteria that cannot effectively distinguish between soft balancing and routine diplomatic friction. These claims are, in that sense, nonfalsifiable. The fourth section proposes that balancing against the United States is not occurring because the post–September 11 grand strategy designed by the George W. Bush administration, despite widespread criticism, poses a threat only to a very limited number of regimes and terrorist groups. As a result, most countries either do not have a direct stake in the "war on terror" or, often, share the U.S. interest in the reduction of threats from rogue states and terrorist groups. This line of argument refocuses analytic attention away from U.S. relations with the entire world as a disaggregated whole and toward a sharp distinction between, on the one hand, U.S. policy toward rogue states and transnational terrorist organizations and, on the other, U.S. relations with other states.

Predictions of Balancing: International Relations Theory and U.S. Foreign Policy

The study of balancing behavior in international relations has deep roots, but it remains fraught with conceptual ambiguities and competing theoretical and empirical claims.[1] Rather than offer a review of the relevant debates, we focus here on a specific set of realist and liberal predictions that states will balance

---

1. Recent surveys of balance of power theory that also include discussions of contemporary international politics include G. John Ikenberry, ed., *America Unrivaled: The Future of the Balance of Power* (Ithaca, N.Y.: Cornell University Press, 2002); John A. Vasquez and Colin Elman, eds., *Realism and the Balancing of Power: A New Debate* (Englewood Cliffs, N.J.: Prentice Hall, 2002); and T.V. Paul, James J. Wirtz, and Michel Fortmann, eds., *Balance of Power: Theory and Practice in the 21st Century* (Stanford, Calif.: Stanford University Press, 2004).

against U.S. power under current conditions. Although realists tend to see great power balancing as an inevitable phenomenon of international politics and liberals generally see it as an avoidable feature of international life, the arguments discussed below share the view that balancing is being provoked by aggressive and imprudent U.S. policies.

Traditional structural realism holds that states motivated by the search for security in an anarchical world will balance against concentrations of power: "States, if they are free to choose, flock to the weaker side; for it is the stronger side that threatens them."[2] According to Kenneth Waltz and other structural realists, the most powerful state will always appear threatening because weaker states can never be certain that it will not use its power to violate their sovereignty or threaten their survival. With the demise of the Soviet Union in 1991, the United States was left with a preeminence of power unparalleled in modern history. The criteria for expecting balancing in structural realist terms do not require that U.S. power meet a specific threshold; all that matters is that the United States is the preeminent power in the system, which it was in 1990 and clearly remains today. Consistent with earlier theorizing, prominent realists predicted at the end of the Cold War that other major powers would balance against it.[3] A decade later, Waltz identified "balancing tendencies already taking place" and argued that it was only a matter of time before other great powers formed a serious balancing coalition, although that timing is theoretically underdetermined: "Theory enables one to say that a new balance of power will form but not to say how long it will take. . . . In our perspective, the new balance is emerging slowly; in historical perspectives, it will come in the blink of an eye."[4]

John Mearsheimer's work is an important exception to the structural realist prediction of balancing against the United States. He argues that geography— specifically, the two oceans that separate the United States from the world's other great powers—prevents the United States from projecting enough military power to pursue global hegemony. Given this lack of capability, the

---

2. Kenneth N. Waltz, *Theory of International Politics* (New York: McGraw-Hill, 1979), p. 127.

3. Kenneth N. Waltz, "The Emerging Structure of International Politics," *International Security*, Vol. 18, No. 2 (Fall 1993), pp. 44–79; and Christopher Layne, "The Unipolar Illusion: Why New Great Powers Will Rise," *International Security*, Vol. 17, No. 4 (Spring 1993), pp. 5–51. John J. Mearsheimer's widely cited article about a return to multipolarity (and the dangers that would follow) was predicated on the assumption that the United States would join the Soviet Union in withdrawing its forces from Europe. See Mearsheimer, "Back to the Future: Instability in Europe after the Cold War," *International Security*, Vol. 15, No. 1 (Summer 1990), pp. 5–56.

4. Kenneth N. Waltz, "Structural Realism after the Cold War," *International Security*, Vol. 25, No. 1 (Summer 2000), pp. 27, 30.

United States must be content with regional hegemony. This means that the United States is essentially a status quo power that poses little danger to the survival or sovereignty of other great powers. Thus, according to Mearsheimer, no balancing coalition against the United States is likely to form. (For similar reasons, history's previous "offshore balancer"—Great Britain—did not provoke a balancing coalition even at the height of its power in the nineteenth century.)[5]

A distinctive strand of realist theory holds that states balance against perceived threats, not just against raw power. Stephen Walt argues that perceived threat depends on a combination of aggregate power, geography, technology, intentions, and foreign policy behavior.[6] With this theoretical modification, Walt and others seek to explain why the United States provoked less balancing in the last half century than its sheer power would suggest.[7] Although geography is important, as in Mearsheimer's explanation above, balance of threat theorists find the key to the absence of real balancing in the United States' distinct history of comparatively benign intentions and behavior, especially the absence of attempts to conquer or dominate foreign lands. As Robert Pape argues, "The long ascendancy of the United States has been a remarkable exception" to the balance of power prediction, and the main reason for this is its "high reputation for non-aggressive intentions."[8] Given the United States' long-standing power advantages, this has been partly the result of self-restraint, which Walt believes can continue to "keep the rest of the world 'off-balance' and minimize the opposition that the United States will face in the future."[9]

Now, however, many balance of threat realists predict balancing based on what amounts to an empirical claim: that U.S. behavior since the September 11, 2001, terrorist attacks is sufficiently threatening to others that it is accelerating the process of balancing. For these balance of threat theorists, U.S. policies are

---

5. John J. Mearsheimer, *The Tragedy of Great Power Politics* (New York: W.W. Norton, 2001). See also Jack S. Levy, "What Do Great Powers Balance Against and When?" in Paul, Wirtz, and Fortmann, *Balance of Power*, pp. 29–51.
6. Stephen M. Walt, *The Origins of Alliances* (Ithaca, N.Y.: Cornell University Press, 1987).
7. The United States was overwhelmingly the world's most dominant country immediately after World War II, surpassed the Soviet Union by a considerable margin in the primary indicators of national power throughout the Cold War, and was left as the sole superpower after the Cold War.
8. Robert A. Pape, "Soft Balancing: How States Pursue Security in a Unipolar World," paper prepared for the annual meeting of the American Political Science Association, Chicago, Illinois, September 2–5, 2004, pp. 11, 13.
9. Stephen M. Walt, "Keeping the World 'Off-Balance': Self-Restraint and U.S. Foreign Policy," in Ikenberry, *America Unrivaled*, p. 153.

undermining the reputation of the United States for benevolence. Walt compares the position of the United States today with that of imperial Germany in the decades leading up to 1914, when that country's expansionism eventually caused its own encirclement. According to Walt, "What we are witnessing is the progressive self-isolation of the United States."[10] Pape argues that President George W. "Bush['s] strategy of aggressive unilateralism is changing America's long-enjoyed reputation for benign intent and giving other major powers reason to fear America's power." In particular, adopting and implementing a preventive war strategy is "encouraging other countries to form counterweights to U.S. power."[11] Pape essentially suggests that the Bush administration's adoption of the preventive war doctrine in the aftermath of the September 11 attacks converted the United States from a status quo power into a revisionist one. He also suggests that by invading Iraq, the United States has become an "'on-shore' hegemon in a major region of the world, abandoning the strategy of off-shore balancing," and that it is perceived accordingly by others.[12]

Traditional structural realists agree that U.S. actions are hastening the balancing process. They argue that the United States is succumbing to the "hegemon's temptation" to take on extremely ambitious goals, use military force unselectively and excessively, overextend its power abroad, and generally reject self-restraint in its foreign policy—all of which invariably generate counterbalancing. Christopher Layne's stark portrayal is worth citing at length: "Many throughout the world now have the impression that the United States is acting as an aggressive hegemon engaged in the naked aggrandizement of its own power. The notion that the United States is a 'benevolent' hegemon has been shredded. America is inviting the same fate as that which has overtaken previous contenders for hegemony."[13] The Bush administration's decision to go to war against Iraq is singled out as a catalytic event: "In coming years, the Iraq War may come to be seen as a pivotal geopolitical event that

---

10. "Opposing War Is Not 'Appeasement': An Interview with Stephen Walt," March 18, 2003, http://www.tompaine.com/feature.cfm/ID/7431.

11. Pape, "Soft Balancing: How States Pursue Security in a Unipolar World," pp. 3, 14, 22; and Robert A. Pape, "The World Pushes Back," *Boston Globe*, March 23, 2003.

12. Robert A. Pape, "Soft Balancing: How the World Will Respond to U.S. Preventive War on Iraq," article posted on the Oak Park Coalition for Truth & Justice website, January 20, 2003, http://www.opctj.org/articles/robert-a-pape-university-of-chicago-02-21-2003-004443.html; and Pape, "Soft Balancing: How States Pursue Security in a Unipolar World," p. 24.

13. Christopher Layne, "America as European Hegemon," *National Interest*, No. 72 (Summer 2003), p. 28. See also Waltz, "Structural Realism after the Cold War," p. 29.

heralded the beginning of serious counter-hegemonic balancing against the United States."[14]

Liberal theorists typically argue that democracy, economic interdependence, and international institutions largely obviate the need for states to engage in balancing behavior.[15] Under current conditions, however, many liberals have joined these realists in predicting balancing against the United States. These liberal theorists share the view that U.S. policymakers have violated a grand bargain of sorts—one that reduced incentives to balance against preponderant U.S. power. In the most detailed account of this view, John Ikenberry argues that hegemonic power does not automatically trigger balancing because it can take a more benevolent form. Specifically, the United States has restrained its own power through a web of binding alliances and multilateral commitments infused with trust, mutual consent, and reciprocity. This U.S. willingness to place restraints on its hegemonic power, combined with the open nature of its liberal democracy, reassured weaker states that their interests could be protected and served within a U.S.-led international order, which in turn kept their expected value of balancing against the United States low. This arrangement allowed the United States to project its influence and pursue its interests with only modest restraints on its freedom of action.[16] Invoking a similar empirical claim, Ikenberry argues that U.S. policies after September 11 shattered this order: "In the past two years, a set of hard-line, fundamentalist ideas have taken Washington by storm" and have produced a grand strategy equivalent to "a geostrategic wrecking ball that will destroy America's own half-century-old international architecture."[17] This has greatly increased the incentives for weaker states to balance.[18]

These claims and predictions rest on diverse theoretical models with different underlying assumptions, and one should not conclude that all realist or liberal theories now expect balancing. But there is unusual convergence among these approaches on the belief that other countries have begun to en-

---

14. Christopher Layne, "The War on Terrorism and the Balance of Power: The Paradoxes of American Hegemony," in Paul, Wirtz, and Fortmann, *Balance of Power*, pp. 103–126 at p. 119.

15. See, for example, John M. Owen IV, "Transnational Liberalism and American Primacy," *International Security*, Vol. 26, No. 3 (Winter 2001/2002), pp. 117–152; G. John Ikenberry, "Democracy, Institutions, and American Restraint," in Ikenberry, *America Unrivaled*, pp. 213–238; and T.V. Paul, "Introduction: The Enduring Axioms of Balance of Power Theory and Their Contemporary Relevance," in Paul, Wirtz, and Fortmann, *Balance of Power*, pp. 1–25 at pp. 9–11.

16. G. John Ikenberry, *After Victory: Institutions, Strategic Restraint, and the Rebuilding of Order after Major War* (Princeton, N.J.: Princeton University Press, 2001).

17. G. John Ikenberry, "The End of the Neo-Conservative Moment," *Survival*, Vol. 46, No. 1 (Spring 2004), p. 7.

18. Ibid., p. 20; and G. John Ikenberry, "Introduction," in Ikenberry, *America Unrivaled*, p. 10.

gage in balancing behavior against the United States, whether because of the U.S. relative power advantage, the nature of its foreign policies (at least as those policies are characterized), or both.

Evidence of a Lack of Hard Balancing

The empirical evidence consistently disappoints expectations of traditional forms of balancing against the United States. This section first justifies a focus on this evidence and then examines it.

JUSTIFYING A FOCUS ON HARD BALANCING
Some international relations theorists appear to have concluded that measurements of traditional balancing behavior since September 11 are irrelevant to assessing the strength of impulses to balance the United States. They have done so because they assume that other states cannot compete militarily with the United States. Therefore, they conclude, any absence of hard balancing that may (well) be detected would simply reflect structural limits on these states' capabilities, and does not constitute meaningful evidence about their intentions. Evidence of such an absence can thus be dismissed as analytically meaningless to this topic. We dispute this and argue instead that evidence concerning traditional balancing behavior is analytically significant.

William Wohlforth argues that the United States enjoys such a large margin of superiority over every other state in all the important dimensions of power (military, economic, technological, geopolitical, etc.) that an extensive counterbalancing coalition is infeasible, both because of the sheer size of the U.S. military effort and the huge coordination issues involved in putting together such a counterbalancing coalition.[19] This widely cited argument is invoked by theorists of soft balancing to explain, and explain away, the absence of traditional balancing, at least for now.[20]

Wohlforth's main conclusion on this matter is unconvincing empirically. As a result, the claim that the absence of hard balancing does not reveal intentions is unconvincing analytically. There is certainly a steep disparity in worldwide

---

19. Additionally, "Efforts to produce a counterbalance globally will generate powerful countervailing action locally," thus undermining the effort. William C. Wohlforth, "The Stability of a Unipolar World," *International Security*, Vol. 24, No. 1 (Summer 1999), p. 28.
20. See, for example, Stephen M. Walt, "Can the United States Be Balanced? If So, How?" paper prepared for the annual meeting of the American Political Science Association, Chicago, Illinois, September 2–5, 2004, p. 14; and Pape, "Soft Balancing: How States Pursue Security in a Unipolar World," pp. 2–3. Both Walt and Pape stress the coordination aspects in particular.

levels of defense spending. Those levels fell almost everywhere after the end of the Cold War, but they fell more steeply and more durably in other parts of the world, which resulted in a widening U.S. lead in military capabilities. Even Europe's sophisticated militaries lack truly independent command, intelligence, surveillance, and logistical capabilities. China, Russia, and others are even less able to match the United States militarily. In 2005, for example, the United States may well represent 50 percent of defense spending in the entire world.

Although this configuration of spending might appear to be a structural fact in its own right, it is less the result of rigid constraints than of much more malleable budgetary choices. Of course, it would be neither cheap nor easy to balance against a country as powerful as the United States. Observers might point out that the United States was able to project enough power to help defeat Wilhelmine Germany, Nazi Germany, and Imperial Japan; it managed to contain the Soviet Union in Europe for half a century; and most recently it toppled two governments on the other side of the world in a matter of weeks (the Taliban in Afghanistan and the Baathist regime in Iraq). But it is easy to exaggerate the extent and effectiveness of American power, as the ongoing effort to pacify Iraq suggests. The limits of U.S. military power might be showcased if one imagines the tremendous difficulties the United States would face in trying to conquer and control, say, China. Whether considered by population, economic power, or military strength, various combinations of Britain, China, France, Germany, Japan, and Russia—to name only a relatively small number of major powers—would have more than enough actual and latent power to check the United States. These powers have substantial latent capabilities for balancing that they are unambiguously failing to mobilize.

Consider, for example, Europe alone. Although the military resources of the twenty-five members of the European Union are often depicted as being vastly overshadowed by those of the United States, these states have more troops under arms than the United States: 1.86 million compared with 1.43 million.[21] The EU countries also have the organizational and technical skills to excel at command, control, and surveillance. They have the know-how to develop a wide range of high-technology weapons. And they have the money to pay for them,

---

21. Of this, the fifteen countries that were EU members before May 2004 have an estimated 1.55 million active military personnel. See International Institute for Strategic Studies (IISS), *The Military Balance, 2003–2004* (London: IISS, 2003), pp. 18, 35–79.

with a total gross domestic product (GDP) greater than that of the United States: more than $12.5 trillion to the United States' $11.7 trillion in 2004.[22]

It is true that the Europeans would have to pool resources and overcome all the traditional problems of coordination and collective action common to counterbalancing coalitions to compete with the United States strategically. Even more problematic are tendencies to free ride or pass the buck inside balancing coalitions.[23] But numerous alliances have nonetheless formed, and the EU members would be a logical starting point because they have the lowest barriers to collective action of perhaps any set of states in history. Just as important, as discussed below, the argument about coordination barriers seems ill suited to the contemporary context because the other major powers are apparently not even engaged in negotiations concerning the formation of a balancing coalition. Alternatively, dynamics of intraregional competition might forestall global balancing. But this, too, is hardly a rigid obstacle in the face of a commonly perceived threat. Certainly Napoleon, Adolf Hitler, and Joseph Stalin after World War II all induced strange bedfellows to form alliances and permitted several regional powers to mobilize without alarming their neighbors.

That said, even if resources can be linked, there are typically limits to how much internal balancing can be undertaken by any set of powers, even wealthy ones, given that they usually already devote a significant proportion of their resources to national security. But historical trends only highlight the degree to which current spending levels are the result of choices rather than structural constraints. The level of defense spending that contemporary economies are broadly capable of sustaining can be assessed by comparing current spending to the military expenditures that West European NATO members—a category of countries that substantively overlaps with the EU—maintained less than twenty years ago, during the Cold War. In a number of cases, these states are spending on defense at rates half (or less than half) those of the mid-1980s (see Table 1).

Consider how a resumption of earlier spending levels would affect global military expenditures today. In 2003 the United States spent approximately $383 billion on defense. This was nearly twice the $190 billion spent by West

---

22. These figures are the Organization for Economic Cooperation and Development's estimates for 2004. See http://www.oecd.org/dataoecd/48/4/33727936.pdf. Of this, the pre–May 2004 EU members had a combined 2004 GDP of approximately $12 trillion. EU per capita income, of course, is somewhat lower than in the United States, and dollar-denominated comparisons shift with currency fluctuations.
23. Mearsheimer, *The Tragedy of Great Power Politics*, pp. 155–162.

Table 1. Military Spending as a Percentage of Gross Domestic Product, European NATO Members, 1985 and 2002

Country	1985	2002
Belgium	2.9	1.3
Denmark	2.1	1.6
France	3.9	2.5
Germany	3.2	1.5
Greece	7.0	4.4
Italy	2.2	1.9
Luxembourg	1.0	0.9
Netherlands	2.9	1.6
Norway	2.8	1.9
Portugal	3.2	2.3
Spain	2.4	1.2
United Kingdom	5.2	2.4

SOURCE: International Institute for Strategic Studies, *The Military Balance, 2003–2004* (London: IISS, 2003), p. 335.

European NATO members. But if these same European countries had resumed spending at the rates they successfully sustained in 1985, they would have spent an additional $150 billion on defense in 2003. In that event, U.S. spending would have exceeded theirs by little more than 10 percent, well within historic ranges of international military competition.[24] Moreover, this underlying capacity to fully, if not immediately, match the United States is further enhanced if one considers the latent capabilities of two or three other states, especially China's manpower, Japan's wealth and technology, and Russia's extensive arms production capabilities.

In sum, it appears that if there were a will to balance the United States, there would be a way. And if traditional balancing is in fact an option available to contemporary great powers, then whether or not they are even beginning to exercise that option is of great analytic interest when one attempts to measure the current strength of impulses to balance the United States.

International relations theorists have developed commonly accepted standards for measuring traditional balancing behavior. Fairly strictly defined and relatively verifiable criteria such as these have great value because they reveal

---

24. This estimate is calculated from individual country data on military expenditure in local currency available from the Stockholm International Peace Research Institute, http://www.sipri.org/contents/milap/milex/mex_database1.html; GDP for eurozone countries from Eurostat, http://epp.eurostat.cec.eu; and GDP for non-eurozone countries from UN Statistics Division, "National Accounts Main Aggregates Database," http://unstats.un.org/unsd/snaama/Introduction.asp.

behavior—costly behavior signifying actual intent—that can be distinguished from the diplomatic friction that routinely occurs between almost all countries, even allies.

We use conventional measurements for traditional balancing. The most important and widely used criteria concern internal and external balancing and the establishment of diplomatic "red lines." Internal balancing occurs when states invest heavily in defense by transforming their latent power (i.e., economic, technological, social, and natural resources) into military capabilities. External balancing occurs when states seek to form military alliances against the predominant power.[25] Diplomatic red lines send clear signals to the aggressor that states are willing to take costly actions to check the dominant power if it does not respect certain boundaries of behavior.[26] Only the last of these measurements involves the emergence of open confrontation, much less the outbreak of hostilities. The other two concern instead states' investments in coercive resources and the pooling of such resources.

EXAMINING EVIDENCE OF INTERNAL BALANCING

Since the end of the Cold War, no major power in the international system appears to be engaged in internal balancing against the United States, with the possible exception of China. Such balancing would be marked by meaningfully increased defense spending, the implementation of conscription or other means of enlarging the ranks of people under arms, or substantially expanded investment in military research and technology.

To start, consider the region best positioned economically for balancing: Europe. Estimates of military spending as a share of the overall economy vary because they rely on legitimately disputable methods of calculation. But recent estimates show that spending by most EU members fell after the Cold War to rates one-half (or less) the U.S. rate. And unlike in the United States, spending has not risen appreciably since September 11 and the lead-up to the Iraq war, and in many cases it has continued to fall (see Table 2).

In the United Kingdom, Italy, Spain, Greece, and Sweden, military spending has been substantially reduced even since September 11 and the lead-up to the invasion of Iraq. Several recent spending upticks are modest and predomi-

---

25. Waltz sums up the basic choice: "As nature abhors a vacuum, so international politics abhors unbalanced power. Faced with unbalanced power, some states try to increase their own strength or they ally with others to bring the international distribution of power into balance." Waltz, "Structural Realism after the Cold War," p. 28. On internal and external balancing more generally, see Waltz, *Theory of International Politics*, p. 118.
26. Mearsheimer, *The Tragedy of Great Power Politics*, pp. 156–157.

Table 2. Military Spending as a Percentage of Gross Domestic Product, 2000–03

Country	2000	2001	2002	2003
United States	3.10	3.12	3.44	4.11
Austria	0.84	0.78	0.76	0.78
Belgium	1.40	1.34	1.29	1.29
Denmark	1.51	1.59	1.56	1.57
France	2.58	2.52	2.53	2.58
Germany	1.51	1.48	1.48	1.45
Greece	4.87	4.57	4.31	4.14
Italy	2.09	2.02	2.06	1.88
Netherlands	1.61	1.62	1.61	1.60
Portugal	2.07	2.11	2.14	2.14
Spain	1.25	1.22	1.21	1.18
Sweden	2.03	1.91	1.84	1.75
United Kingdom	2.47	2.46	2.40	2.37

NOTE: Percentages were calculated with individual country data on military expenditure in local currency at current prices taken from Stockholm International Peace Research Institute, http://www.sipri.org/contents/milap/milex/mex_database1.html; and on gross domestic product at current prices from UN Statistics Division, "National Accounts Main Aggregates Database," http://unstats.un.org/unsd/snaama/Introduction.asp.

nantly designed to address in-country terrorism. Long-standing EU plans to deploy a non-NATO rapid reaction force of 60,000 troops do not undermine this analysis. This light force is designed for quick deployment to local-conflict zones such as the Balkans and Africa; it is neither designed nor suited for continental defense against a strategic competitor.

In April 2003 Belgium, France, Luxembourg, and Germany (the key player in any potential European counterweight) announced an increase in cooperation in both military spending and coordination. But since then, Germany's government has instead trimmed its already modest spending, and in 2003–04 cut its military acquisitions and participation in several joint European weapons programs. Germany is now spending GDP on the military at a rate of under 1.5 percent (a rate that is declining), compared with around 4 percent by the United States in 2003, a rate that is growing.

Alternative explanations for this spending pattern only undercut the logical basis of balancing predictions. For example, might European defense spending be constrained by sizable welfare-state commitments and by budget deficit limits related to the common European currency? Both of these constraints are self-imposed and can easily be construed to reveal stronger commitments to entitlement programs and to technical aspects of a common currency than to the priority of generating defenses against a supposed potential strategic

threat.[27] This contrasts sharply with the United States, which, having unambiguously perceived a serious threat, has carried out a formidable military
buildup since September 11, even at the expense of growing budget deficits.

Some analysts also argue that any European buildup is hampered deliber-
ately by the United States, which encourages divisions among even traditional
allies and seeks to keep their militaries "deformed" as a means of thwarting efforts to form a balancing coalition. For example, Layne asserts that the United
States is "actively discouraging Europe from either collective, or national, efforts to acquire the full-spectrum of advanced military capabilities . . . [and] is
engaged in a game of divide and rule in a bid to thwart the E.U.'s political
unification process."[28] But the fact remains that the United States could not
prohibit Europeans or others from developing those capabilities if those countries faced strong enough incentives to balance.

Regions other than Europe do not clearly diverge from this pattern. Defense
spending as a share of GDP has on the whole fallen since the end of the Cold
War in sub-Saharan Africa, Latin America, Central and South Asia, and the
Middle East and North Africa, and it has remained broadly steady in most
cases in the past several years.[29] Russia has slightly increased its share of defense spending since 2001 (see Table 3), but this has nothing to do with an attempt to counterbalance the United States.[30] Instead, the salient factors are the
continuing campaign to subdue the insurgency in Chechnya and a dire need to
forestall further military decline (made possible by a slightly improved overall
budgetary situation). That Russians are unwilling to incur significant costs to
counter U.S. power is all the more telling given the expansion of NATO to
Russia's frontiers and the U.S. decision to withdraw from the Antiballistic Missile Treaty and deploy missile defenses.

China, on the other hand, is engaged in a strategic military buildup. Although military expenditures are notoriously difficult to calculate for that
country, the best estimates suggest that China has slightly increased its share
of defense spending in recent years (see Table 3). This buildup, however, has
been going on for decades, that is, long before September 11 and the Bush administration's subsequent strategic response.[31] Moreover, the growth in Chi-

---

27. Moreover, neither constraint applies to Japan, which enjoys the second-largest economy in the
world, has been a relatively modest welfare state, and since the mid-1990s has had extensive experience with budget deficits—and yet has not raised its military expenditures in recent years.
28. Layne, "America as European Hegemon," p. 25.
29. IISS, The *Military Balance, 2004–2005* (London: IISS, 2004).
30. See William C. Wohlforth, "Revisiting Balance of Power Theory in Central Eurasia," in Paul,
Wirtz, and Fortmann, *Balance of Power*, pp. 214–238.
31. Measuring rates of military spending as a percentage of GDP as an indication of military

Table 3. Military Spending as a Percentage of Gross Domestic Product, Selected Regional Powers, 2000-03

Country	2000	2001	2002	2003
Brazil	1.27	1.45	1.56	1.52
China	2.04	2.24	2.40	2.35
India	2.33	2.31	2.25	2.29
Japan	0.96	0.98	0.99	0.99
Russia	3.73	4.09	4.06	4.30

NOTE: Percentages were calculated with individual country data on military expenditure in local currency at current prices taken from Stockholm International Peace Research Institute, http://www.sipri.org/contents/milap/milex/mex_database1.html; and on gross domestic product at current prices from UN Statistics Division, "National Accounts Main Aggregates Database," http://unstats.un.org/unsd/snaama/Introduction.asp.

nese conventional capabilities is primarily driven by the Taiwan problem: in the short term, China needs to maintain the status quo and prevent Taiwan from acquiring the relative power necessary to achieve full independence; in the long term, China seeks unification of Taiwan with the mainland. China clearly would like to enhance its relative power vis-à-vis the United States and may well have a long-term strategy to balance U.S. power in the future.[32] But China's defense buildup is not new, nor is it as ambitious and assertive as it should be if the United States posed a direct threat that required internal balancing. (For example, the Chinese strategic nuclear modernization program is often mentioned in the course of discussions of Chinese balancing behavior, but the Chinese arsenal is about the same size as it was a decade ago.[33] Moreover, even if China is able to deploy new missiles in the next few years, it is not clear whether it will possess a survivable nuclear retaliatory capability vis-à-

buildups—which is the conventional practice and a good one in the case of stable economies—can be deceptive for countries with fast-growing economies, such as China. Maintaining a steady share of GDP on military spending during a period in which GDP is rapidly growing essentially means that a state is engaging in a military buildup. Indeed, China has not greatly increased its military spending as a share of GDP, but it is conventional wisdom that the Chinese are modernizing and expanding their military forces. The point does not, however, undermine the fact that the Chinese buildup predates the Bush administration's post–September 11 grand strategy.

32. See Robert S. Ross, "Bipolarity and Balancing in East Asia," in Paul, Wirtz, and Fortmann, *Balance of Power*, pp. 267–304. Although Ross believes the balance of power in East Asia will remain stable for a long time, largely because the United States is expanding its degree of military superiority, he characterizes Chinese behavior as internal (and external) balancing against the United States.

33. Jeffrey Lewis, "The Ambiguous Arsenal," *Bulletin of the Atomic Scientists*, Vol. 61, No. 3 (May/June 2005), pp. 52–59.

vis the United States.) Thus, China's defense buildup is not a persuasive indicator of internal balancing against the post–September 11 United States specifically.

In sum, rather than the United States' post–September 11 policies inducing a noticeable shift in the military expenditures of other countries, the latters' spending patterns are instead characterized by a striking degree of continuity before and after this supposed pivot point in U.S. grand strategy.

ASSESSING EVIDENCE OF EXTERNAL BALANCING

A similar pattern of continuity can be seen in the absence of new alliances. Using widely accepted criteria, experts agree that external balancing against the United States would be marked by the formation of alliances (including lesser defense agreements), discussions concerning the formation of such alliances or, at the least, discussions about shared interests in defense cooperation against the United States.

Instead of September 11 serving as a pivot point, there is little visible change in the alliance patterns of the late 1990s—even with the presence of what might be called an "alliance facilitator" in President Jacques Chirac's France. At least for now, diplomatic resistance to U.S. actions is strictly at the level of maneuvering and talk, indistinguishable from the friction routine to virtually all periods and countries, even allies. Resources have not been transferred from some great powers to others. And the United States' core alliances, NATO and the U.S.-Japan alliance, have both been reaffirmed.

Walt recognized in 2002 that Russian-Chinese relations fell "well short of formal defense arrangements" and hence did not constitute external balancing; this continues to be the case.[34] Russian President Vladimir Putin's expressed hope that India becomes a great power to help re-create a multipolar world hardly rises to the standard of external balancing. Certainly few would suggest that the Indo-Russian "strategic pact" of 2000, the Sino-Russian "friendship treaty" of 2001, or media speculation of a Moscow-Beijing-Delhi "strategic triangle" in 2002 and 2003 are as consequential as, say, the Franco-Russian Alliance of 1894 or even the less-formal U.S.-Chinese balancing against the Soviet Union in the 1970s.[35] In 2002–03 Russia, China, and several EU members broadly coordinated diplomatically against granting

---

34. Walt, "Keeping the World 'Off-Balance,'" p. 126.
35. Arguing that a "strategic triangle" between Russia, China, and India is unlikely, in large part because U.S. ties with each of these countries are stronger than any two of them have between themselves, is Harsh V. Pant, "The Moscow-Beijing-Delhi 'Strategic Triangle': An Idea Whose Time May Never Come," *Security Dialogue*, Vol. 35, No. 3 (September 2004), pp. 311–328.

international-institutional approval to the 2003 Iraq invasion, but there is no evidence that this extended at the time, or has extended since, to anything beyond that single goal. The EU's common defense policy is barely more developed than it was before 2001. And although survey data suggest that many Europeans would like to see the EU become a superpower comparable to the United States, most are unwilling to boost military spending to accomplish that goal.[36] Even the institutional path toward Europe becoming a plausible counterweight to the United States appears to have suffered a major setback by the decisive rejection of the proposed EU constitution in referenda in France and the Netherlands in the spring of 2005.

Even states with predominantly Muslim populations do not reveal incipient enhanced coordination against the United States. Regional states such as Jordan, Kuwait, and Saudi Arabia cooperated with the Iraq invasion; more have sought to help stabilize postwar Iraq; and key Muslim countries are cooperating with the United States in the war against Islamist terrorists.

Even the loosest criteria for external balancing are not being met. For the moment at least, no countries are known even to be discussing and debating how burdens could or should be distributed in any arrangement for coordinating defenses against or confronting the United States. For this reason, the argument (discussed further below) that external balancing may be absent because it is by nature slow and inefficient and fraught with buck-passing behavior is not persuasive. No friction exists in negotiations over who should lead or bear the costs in a coalition because no such discussions appear to exist.

EVALUATING EVIDENCE OF DIPLOMATIC RED LINES
A final possible indicator of traditional balancing behavior would be states sending "clear signals to the aggressor . . . that they are firmly committed to maintaining the balance of power, even if it means going to war."[37] This form of balancing has clearly been absent. There has been extensive criticism of specific post–September 11 U.S. policies, especially criticism of the invasion of Iraq as unnecessary and unwise. No states or collections of states, however, issued an ultimatum in the matter—drawing a line in the Persian Gulf sand and warning the United States not to cross it—at the risk that confrontational steps would be taken in response.

Perhaps a more generous version of the red-lines criterion would see evi-

---

36. German Marshall Fund of the United States and the Compagnia di San Paolo, *Transatlantic Trends, 2004,* http://www.transatlantictrends.org.
37. Mearsheimer, *The Tragedy of Great Power Politics,* p. 156.

dence of balancing in a consistent pattern of diplomatic resistance, not concili-
ation. A recent spate of commentary about soft balancing does just this.

Evidence of a Lack of Soft Balancing

In the absence of evidence of traditional balancing, some scholars have advanced the concept of soft balancing. Instead of overtly challenging U.S.
power, which might be too costly or unappealing, states are said to be able to
undertake a host of lesser actions as a way of constraining and undermining it.
The central claim is that the unilateralist and provocative behavior of the
United States is generating unprecedented resentment that will make life
difficult for Washington and may eventually evolve into traditional hard balancing.[38] As Walt writes, "States may not want to attract the 'focused enmity'
of the United States, but they may be eager to limit its freedom of action, complicate its diplomacy, sap its strength and resolve, maximize their own autonomy and reaffirm their own rights, and generally make the United States work
harder to achieve its objectives."[39] For Josef Joffe, "'Soft balancing' against Mr.
Big has already set in."[40] Pape proclaims that "the early stages of soft balancing against American power have already started," and argues that "unless
the United States radically changes course, the use of international institutions, economic leverage, and diplomatic maneuvering to frustrate American
intentions will only grow."[41]

We offer two critiques of these claims. First, if we consider the specific predictions suggested by these theorists on their own terms, we do not find persuasive evidence of soft balancing. Second, these criteria for detecting soft
balancing are, on reflection, inherently flawed because they do not (and possibly cannot) offer effective means for distinguishing soft balancing from routine
diplomatic friction between countries. These are, in that sense, nonfalsifiable
claims.

---

38. Layne writes, "By facilitating 'soft balancing' against the United States, the Iraq crisis may
have paved the way for 'hard' balancing as well." Layne, "America as European Hegemon," p. 27.
See also Walt, "Can the United States Be Balanced?" p. 18; and Pape, "Soft Balancing: How States
Pursue Security in a Unipolar World," p. 27. See also Paul, "Introduction," in Paul, Wirtz, and
Fortmann, *Balance of Power*, pp. 2–4, 11–17.
39. Walt, "Keeping the World 'Off-Balance,'" p. 136; and Walt, "Can the United States Be
Balanced?"
40. Josef Joffe, "Gulliver Unbound: Can America Rule the World?" August 6, 2003, http://
www.smh.com.au/articles/2003/08/05/1060064182993.html.
41. Pape, "Soft Balancing: How States Pursue Security in a Unipolar World," p. 29; and Pape, "The
World Pushes Back."

EVALUATING SOFT-BALANCING PREDICTIONS

Theorists have offered several criteria for judging the presence of soft balancing. We consider four frequently invoked ones: states' efforts (1) to entangle the dominant state in international institutions, (2) to exclude the dominant state from regional economic cooperation, (3) to undermine the dominant state's ability to project military power by restricting or denying military basing rights, and (4) to provide relevant assistance to U.S. adversaries such as rogue states.[42]

ENTANGLING INTERNATIONAL INSTITUTIONS. Are other states using international institutions to constrain or undermine U.S. power? The notion that they could do so is based on faulty logic. Because the most powerful states exercise the most control in these institutions, it is unreasonable to expect that their rules and procedures can be used to shackle and restrain the world's most powerful state. As Randall Schweller notes, institutions cannot be simultaneously autonomous and capable of binding strong states.[43] Certainly what resistance there was to endorsing the U.S.-led action in Iraq did not stop or meaningfully delay that action.

Is there evidence, however, that other states are even trying to use a web of global institutional rules and procedures or ad hoc diplomatic maneuvers to constrain U.S. behavior and delay or disrupt military actions? No attempt was made to block the U.S. campaign in Afghanistan, and both the war and the ensuing stabilization there have been almost entirely conducted through an international institution: NATO. Although a number of countries refused to endorse the U.S.-led invasion of Iraq, none sought to use international institutions to block or declare illegal that invasion. Logically, such action should be the benchmark for this aspect of soft balancing, not whether states voted for the invasion. No evidence exists that such an effort was launched or that one would have succeeded had it been. Moreover, since the Iraqi regime was toppled, the UN has endorsed and assisted the transition to Iraqi sovereignty.[44]

If anything, other states' ongoing cooperation with the United States ex-

---

42. These and other soft-balancing predictions can be found in Walt, "Can the United States Be Balanced?"; Pape, "Soft Balancing: How States Pursue Security in a Unipolar World," pp. 27–29; and Pape, "Soft Balancing: How the World Will Respond to U.S. Preventive War on Iraq."

43. Randall L. Schweller, "The Problem of International Order Revisited: A Review Essay," *International Security*, Vol. 26, No. 1 (Summer 2001), p. 182.

44. Before the invasion, Pape predicted that "after the war, Europe, Russia, and China could press hard for the United Nations rather than the United States to oversee a new Iraqi government. Even if they didn't succeed, this would reduce the freedom of action for the United States in Iraq and elsewhere in the region." See Pape, "Soft Balancing: How the World Will Respond to U.S. Preventive War on Iraq." As we note above, the transitional process was in fact endorsed by the Bush administration, and if anything, it has pressed for greater UN participation, which China, France,

plains why international institutions continue to amplify American power and facilitate the pursuit of its strategic objectives. As we discuss below, the war on terror is being pursued primarily through regional institutions, bilateral arrangements, and new multilateral institutions, most obviously the Proliferation Security and Container Security Initiatives, both of which have attracted new adherents since they were launched.[45]

ECONOMIC STATECRAFT. Is post–September 11 regional economic cooperation increasingly seeking to exclude the United States so as to make the balance of power less favorable to it? The answer appears to be no. The United States has been one of the primary drivers of trade regionalization, not the excluded party. This is not surprising given that most states, including those with the most power, have good reason to want lower, not higher, trade barriers around the large and attractive U.S. market.

This rationale applies, for instance, to suits brought in the World Trade Organization against certain U.S. trade policies. These suits are generally aimed at gaining access to U.S. markets, not sidelining them. For example, the suits challenging agricultural subsidies are part of a general challenge by developing countries to Western (including European) trade practices.[46] Moreover, many of these disputes predate September 11; therefore, relabeling them a form of soft balancing in reaction to post–September 11 U.S. strategy is not credible. For the moment, there also does not appear to be any serious discussion of a coordinated decision to price oil in euros, which might undercut the United States' ability to run large trade and budget deficits without proportional increases in inflation and interest rates.[47]

RESTRICTIONS ON BASING RIGHTS/TERRITORIAL DENIAL. The geographical isolation of the United States could effectively diminish its relative power advantage. This prediction appears to be supported by Turkey's denial of the Bush administration's request to provide coalition ground forces with transit

---

and Russia, among others, have resisted. This constitutes resistance to U.S. requests, but it hardly constitutes use of institutions to constrain U.S. action.

45. The Proliferation Security Initiative's initial members were Australia, Britain, Canada, France, Germany, Italy, Japan, the Netherlands, Norway, Poland, Portugal, Singapore, Spain, and the United States.

46. The resistance of France and others to agricultural trade liberalization could be interpreted as an attempt to limit U.S. economic power by restricting access to their markets by highly competitive U.S. agribusiness. But then, presumably, contrasting support for liberalization by most developing countries would have to be interpreted as expressing support for expanded U.S. power.

47. For an insightful discussion of why this may well remain the case, see Herman Schwartz, "Ties That Bind: Global Macroeconomic Flows and America's Financial Empire," paper prepared for the annual meeting of the American Political Science Association, Chicago, Illinois, September 2–5, 2004.

rights for the invasion of Iraq, and possibly by diminished Saudi support for bases there. In addition, Pape suggests that countries such as Germany, Japan, and South Korea will likely impose new restrictions or reductions on U.S. forces stationed on their soil.

The overall U.S. overseas basing picture, however, looks brighter today than it did only a few years ago. Since September 11 the United States has established new bases and negotiated landing rights across Africa, Asia, Central Asia, Europe, and the Middle East. All told, it has built, upgraded, or expanded military facilities in Afghanistan, Bulgaria, Diego Garcia, Djibouti, Georgia, Hungary, Iraq, Kuwait, Kyrgyzstan, Oman, Pakistan, the Philippines, Poland, Qatar, Romania, Tajikistan, and Uzbekistan.[48]

The diplomatic details of the basing issue also run contrary to soft-balancing predictions. Despite occasionally hostile domestic opinion surveys, most host countries do not want to see the withdrawal of U.S. forces. The economic and strategic benefits of hosting bases outweigh purported desires to make it more difficult for the United States to exercise power. For example, the Philippines asked the United States to leave Subic Bay in the 1990s (well before the emergence of the Bush Doctrine), but it has been angling ever since for a return. U.S. plans to withdraw troops from South Korea are facing local resistance and have triggered widespread anxiety about the future of the United States' security commitment to the peninsula.[49] German defense officials and businesses are displeased with the U.S. plan to replace two army divisions in Germany with a single light armored brigade and transfer a wing of F-16 fighter jets to Incirlik Air Base in Turkey.[50] (Indeed, Turkey recently agreed to allow the

---

48. See James Sterngold, "After 9/11, U.S. Policy Built on World Bases," *San Francisco Chronicle*, March 21, 2004, http://www.globalsecurity.org/org/news/2004/040321-world-bases.htm; David Rennie, "America's Growing Network of Bases," *Daily Telegraph*, September 11, 2003, http://www.globalsecurity.org/org/news/2003/030911-deployments01.htm; and "Worldwide Reorientation of U.S. Military Basing in Prospect," Center for Defense Information, September 19, 2003, and "Worldwide Reorientation of U.S. Military Basing, Part 2: Central Asia, Southwest Asia, and the Pacific," Center for Defense Information, October 7, 2003, http://www.cdi.org/program/documents.cfm?ProgramID-37.

49. Strategic and economic worries are easily intertwined. In response to prospective changes in U.S. policy, the South Korean defense ministry is seeking a 13 percent increase in its 2005 budget request. See "U.S. Troop Withdrawals from South Korea," *IISS Strategic Comments*, Vol. 10, No. 5 (June 2004). Pape suggests both that Japan and South Korea could ask all U.S. forces to leave their territory and that they do not want the United States to leave because it is a potentially indispensable support for the status quo in the region. See Pape, "Soft Balancing: How States Pursue Security in a Unipolar World."

50. "Proposed U.S. Base Closures Send a Shiver through a German Town," *New York Times*, August 22, 2004.

United States expanded use of the base as a major hub for deliveries to Iraq and Afghanistan.)[51]

The recently announced plan to redeploy or withdraw up to 70,000 U.S. troops from Cold War bases in Asia and Europe is not being driven by host-country rejection, but by a reassessment of global threats to U.S. interests and the need to bolster American power-projection capabilities.[52] If anything, the United States has the freedom to move forces out of certain countries because it has so many options about where else to send them, in this case closer to the Middle East and other regions crucial to the war on terror. For example, the United States is discussing plans to concentrate all special operations and anti-terrorist units in Europe in a single base in Spain—a country presumably primed for soft balancing against the United States given its newly elected prime minister's opposition to the war in Iraq—so as to facilitate an increasing number of military operations in sub-Saharan Africa.[53]

THE ENEMY OF MY ENEMY IS MY FRIEND. Finally, as Pape asserts, if "Europe, Russia, China, and other important regional states were to offer economic and technological assistance to North Korea, Iran, and other 'rogue states,' this would strengthen these states, run counter to key Bush administration policies, and demonstrate the resolve to oppose the United States by assisting its enemies."[54] Pape presumably has in mind Russian aid to Iran in building nuclear power plants (with the passive acquiescence of Europeans), South Korean economic assistance to North Korea, previous French and Russian resistance to sanctions against Saddam Hussein's Iraq, and perhaps Pakistan's weapons of mass destruction (WMD) assistance to North Korea, Iraq, and Libya.

There are at least two reasons to question whether any of these actions is evidence of soft balancing. First, none of this so-called cooperation with U.S. adversaries is unambiguously driven by a strategic logic of undermining U.S. power. Instead, other explanations are readily at hand. South Korean economic aid to North Korea is better explained by purely local motivations: common ethnic bonds in the face of famine and deprivation, and Seoul's fears of the consequences of any abrupt collapse of the North Korean regime. The other

---

51. "Turkey OKs Expanded U.S. Use of Key Air Base," *Los Angeles Times,* May 3, 2005.
52. Kurt Campbell and Celeste Johnson Ward, "New Battle Stations?" *Foreign Affairs,* Vol. 82, No. 5 (September/October 2003), pp. 95–103.
53. "Spain, U.S. to Mull Single Europe Special Ops Base—Report," *Wall Street Journal,* May 2, 2005.
54. Pape, "Soft Balancing: How the World Will Respond to U.S. Preventive War on Iraq"; and Pape, "Soft Balancing: How States Pursue Security in a Unipolar World," pp. 31–32.

cases of "cooperation" appear to be driven by a common nonstrategic motivation: pecuniary gain. Abdul Qadeer Khan, the father of Pakistan's nuclear program, was apparently motivated by profits when he sold nuclear technology and methods to several states. And given its domestic economic problems and severe troubles in Chechnya, Russia appears far more interested in making money from Iran than in helping to bring about an "Islamic bomb."[55] The quest for lucrative contracts provides at least as plausible, if banal, an explanation for French cooperation with Saddam Hussein.

Moreover, this soft-balancing claim runs counter to diverse multilateral nonproliferation efforts aimed at Iran, North Korea, and Libya (before its decision to abandon its nuclear program). The Europeans have been quite vocal in their criticism of Iranian noncompliance with the Nonproliferation Treaty and International Atomic Energy Agency guidelines, and the Chinese and Russians are actively cooperating with the United States and others over North Korea. The EU's 2003 European security strategy document declares that rogue states "should understand that there is a price to be paid" for their behavior, "including in their relationship" with the EU.[56] These major powers have a declared disinterest in aiding rogue states above and beyond what they might have to lose by attracting the focused enmity of the United States.

In sum, the evidence for claims and predictions of soft balancing is poor.

DISTINGUISHING SOFT BALANCING FROM TRADITIONAL DIPLOMATIC FRICTION
There is a second, more important, reason to be skeptical of soft-balancing claims. The criteria they offer for detecting the presence of soft balancing are conceptually flawed. Walt defines soft balancing as "conscious coordination of diplomatic action in order to obtain outcomes contrary to U.S. preferences, outcomes that could not be gained if the balancers did not give each other some degree of mutual support."[57] This and other accounts are problematic in a crucial way. Conceptually, seeking outcomes that a state (such as the United States) does not prefer does not necessarily or convincingly reveal a desire to balance that state geostrategically. For example, one trading partner often seeks outcomes that the other does not prefer, without balancing being relevant to the discussion. Thus, empirically, the types of events used to

---

55. The importance of the sums Russia is earning, compared to its military spending and arms exports, is suggested in IISS, *Military Balance, 2003–2004*, pp. 270–271, 273.
56. European Union, "A Secure Europe in a Better World: European Security Strategy," Brussels, December 12, 2003, http://ue.eu.int/uedocs/cmsUpload/78367.pdf.
57. Walt, "Can the United States Be Balanced?" p. 14.

operationalize definitions such as Walt's do not clearly establish the crucial claim of soft-balancing theorists: states' desires to balance the United States. Widespread anti-Americanism can be present (and currently seems to be) without that fact persuasively revealing impulses to balance the United States.

The events used to detect the presence of soft balancing are so typical in history that they are not, and perhaps cannot be, distinguished from routine diplomatic friction between countries, even between allies. Traditional balancing criteria are useful because they can reasonably, though surely not perfectly, help distinguish between real balancing behavior and policies or diplomatic actions that may look and sound like an effort to check the power of the dominant state but that in actuality reflect only cheap talk, domestic politics, other international goals not related to balances of power, or the resentment of particular leaders. The current formulation of the concept of soft balancing is not distinguished from such behavior. Even if the predictions were correct, they would not unambiguously or even persuasively reveal balancing behavior, soft or otherwise.

Our criticism is validated by the long list of events from 1945 to 2001 that are directly comparable to those that are today coded as soft balancing. These events include diplomatic maneuvering by U.S. allies and nonaligned countries against the United States in international institutions (particularly the UN), economic statecraft aimed against the United States, resistance to U.S. military basing, criticism of U.S. military interventions, and waves of anti-Americanism.

In the 1950s a West Europe–only bloc was formed, designed partly as a political and economic counterweight to the United States within the so-called free world, and France created an independent nuclear capability. In the 1960s a cluster of mostly developing countries organized the Nonaligned Movement, defining itself against both superpowers. France pulled out of NATO's military structure. Huge demonstrations worldwide protested the U.S. war in Vietnam and other U.S. Cold War policies. In the 1970s the Organization of Petroleum Exporting Countries wielded its oil weapon to punish U.S. policies in the Middle East and transfer substantial wealth from the West. Waves of extensive anti-Americanism were pervasive in Latin America in the 1950s and 1960s, and Europe and elsewhere in the late 1960s and early 1970s and again in the early-to-mid 1980s. Especially prominent protests and harsh criticism from intellectuals and local media were mounted against U.S. policies toward Central America under President Ronald Reagan, the deployment of theater nuclear weapons in Europe, and the very idea of missile defense. In the Reagan era, many states coordinated to protect existing UN practices, promote the 1982 Law of the Sea treaty, and oppose aid to the Nicaraguan Contras. In the 1990s the Philippines asked the United States to leave its Subic Bay military base; China continued a long-standing military buildup; and China, France, and Russia coordinated to resist UN-sanctioned uses of force against Iraq. China and Russia declared a strategic partnership in 1996. In 1998 the "European troika" meetings and agreements began between France, Germany, and Russia, and the EU announced the creation of an independent, unified European military force. In many of these years, the United States was engaged in numerous trade clashes, including with close EU allies. Given all this, it is not surprising that contemporary scholars and commentators periodically identified "crises" in U.S. relations with the world, including within the Atlantic Alliance.[58]

These events all rival in seriousness the categories of events that some scholars today identify as soft balancing. Indeed, they are not merely difficult to distinguish conceptually from those later events; in many cases they are impossible to distinguish empirically, being literally the same events or trends that are currently labeled soft balancing. Yet they all occurred in years in which even soft-balancing theorists agree that the United States was not being balanced against.[59] It is thus unclear whether accounts of soft balancing have provided criteria for crisply and rigorously distinguishing that concept from these and similar manifestations of diplomatic friction routine to many periods of history, even in relations between countries that remain allies rather than strategic competitors. For example, these accounts provide no method for judging whether post–September 11 international events constitute soft balancing, whereas similar phenomena during Reagan's presidency—the spread of anti-Americanism, coordination against the United States in international institutions, criticism of interventions in the developing countries, and so on—do not. Without effective criteria for making such distinctions, current claims of soft balancing risk blunting rather than advancing knowledge about international political dynamics.

In sum, we detect no persuasive evidence that U.S. policy is provoking the

---

58. See, for example, Eliot A. Cohen, "The Long-Term Crisis of the Alliance," *Foreign Affairs*, Vol. 61, No. 2 (Winter 1982/83), pp. 325–343; Sanford J. Ungar, ed., *Estrangement: America and the World* (New York: Oxford University Press, 1985); and Stephen M. Walt, "The Ties That Fray: Why Europe and America Are Drifting Apart," *National Interest*, No. 54 (Winter 1998–99), pp. 3–11.
59. Walt, "Keeping the World 'Off-Balance'"; and Pape, "Soft Balancing: How States Pursue Security in a Unipolar World," p. 13.

seismic shift in other states' strategies toward the United States that theorists of balancing identify.

Why Countries Are Not Balancing against the United States

The major powers are not balancing against the United States because of the nature of U.S. grand strategy in the post–September 11 world. There is no doubt that this strategy is ambitious, assertive, and backed by tremendous offensive military capability. But it is also highly selective and not broadly threatening. Specifically, the United States is focusing these means on the greatest threats to its interests—that is, the threats emanating from nuclear proliferator states and global terrorist organizations. Other major powers are not balancing U.S. power because they want the United States to succeed in defeating these shared threats or are ambivalent yet understand they are not in its crosshairs. In many cases, the diplomatic friction identified by proponents of the concept of soft balancing instead reflects disagreement about tactics, not goals, which is nothing new in history.

To be sure, our analysis cannot claim to rule out other theories of great power behavior that also do not expect balancing against the United States. Whether the United States is not seen as a threat worth balancing because of shared interests in nonproliferation and the war on terror (as we argue), because of geography and capability limitations that render U.S. global hegemony impossible (as some offensive realists argue), or because transnational democratic values, binding international institutions, and economic interdependence obviate the need to balance (as many liberals argue) is a task for further theorizing and empirical analysis. Nor are we claiming that balancing against the United States will never happen. Rather, there is no persuasive evidence that U.S. policy is provoking the kind of balancing behavior that the Bush administration's critics suggest. In the meantime, analysts should continue to use credible indicators of balancing behavior in their search for signs that U.S. strategy is having a counterproductive effect on U.S. security.

Below we discuss why the United States is not seen by other major powers as a threat worth balancing. Next we argue that the impact of the U.S.-led invasion of Iraq on international relations has been exaggerated and needs to be seen in a broader context that reveals far more cooperation with the United States than many analysts acknowledge. Finally, we note that something akin to balancing is taking place among would-be nuclear proliferators and Islamist extremists, which makes sense given that these are the threats targeted by the United States.

THE UNITED STATES' FOCUSED ENMITY

Great powers seek to organize the world according to their own preferences, looking for opportunities to expand and consolidate their economic and military power positions. Our analysis does not assume that the United States is an exception. It can fairly be seen to be pursuing a hegemonic grand strategy and has repeatedly acted in ways that undermine notions of deeply rooted shared values and interests. U.S. objectives and the current world order, however, are unusual in several respects. First, unlike previous states with preponderant power, the United States has little incentive to seek to physically control foreign territory. It is secure from foreign invasion and apparently sees little benefit in launching costly wars to obtain additional material resources. Moreover, the bulk of the current international order suits the United States well. Democracy is ascendant, foreign markets continue to liberalize, and no major revisionist powers seem poised to challenge U.S. primacy.

This does not mean that the United States is a status quo power, as typically defined. The United States seeks to further expand and consolidate its power position even if not through territorial conquest. Rather, U.S. leaders aim to bolster their power by promoting economic growth, spending lavishly on military forces and research and development, and dissuading the rise of any peer competitor on the international stage. Just as important, the confluence of the proliferation of WMD and the rise of Islamist radicalism poses an acute danger to U.S. interests. This means that U.S. grand strategy targets its assertive enmity only at circumscribed quarters, ones that do not include other great powers.

The great powers, as well as most other states, either share the U.S. interest in eliminating the threats from terrorism and WMD or do not feel that they have a significant direct stake in the matter. Regardless, they understand that the United States does not have offensive designs on them. Consistent with this proposition, the United States has improved its relations with almost all of the major powers in the post–September 11 world. This is in no small part because these governments—not to mention those in key countries in the Middle East and Southwest Asia, such as Egypt, Jordan, Pakistan, and Saudi Arabia—are willing partners in the war on terror because they see Islamist radicalism as a genuine threat to them as well. U.S. relations with China, India, and Russia, in particular, are better than ever in large part because these countries similarly have acute reasons to fear transnational Islamist terrorist groups. The EU's official grand strategy echoes that of the United States. The 2003 European security strategy document, which appeared months after the U.S.-led invasion of Iraq, identifies terrorism by religious extremists and the proliferation of WMD as the two greatest threats to European security. In language familiar to students of the Bush administration, it declares that Europe's "most frightening scenario is one in which terrorist groups acquire weapons of mass destruction."[60] It is thus not surprising that the major European states, including France and Germany, are partners of the United States in the Proliferation Security Initiative.

Certain EU members are not engaged in as wide an array of policies toward these threats as the United States and other of its allies. European criticism of the Iraq war is the preeminent example. But sharp differences over tactics should not be confused with disagreement over broad goals. After all, comparable disagreements, as well as incentives to free ride on U.S. efforts, were common among several West European states during the Cold War when they nonetheless shared with their allies the goal of containing the Soviet Union.[61]

In neither word nor deed, then, do these states manifest the degree or nature of disagreement contained in the images of strategic rivalry on which balancing claims are based. Some other countries are bystanders. As discussed above, free-riding and differences over tactics form part of the explanation for this behavior. And some of these states simply feel less threatened by terrorist organizations and WMD proliferators than the United States and others do. The decision of these states to remain on the sidelines, however, and not seek opportunities to balance, is crucial. There is no good evidence that these states feel threatened by U.S. grand strategy.

In brief, other great powers appear to lack the motivation to compete strategically with the United States under current conditions. Other major powers might prefer a more generally constrained America or, to be sure, a world where the United States was not as dominant, but this yearning is a long way from active cooperation to undermine U.S. power or goals.

REDUCTIO AD IRAQ
Many accounts portray the U.S.-led invasion of Iraq as virtually of world-historical importance, as an event that will mark "a fundamental transformation in how major states react to American power."[62] If the Iraq war is placed

---

60. European Union, "A Secure Europe in a Better World," p. 4.
61. This was exemplified in highly uneven defense spending across NATO members and in European criticism of the Vietnam War and U.S. nuclear policy toward the Soviet Union.
62. Pape, "Soft Balancing: How the World Will Respond to U.S. Preventive War on Iraq," p. 1. See

in its broader context, however, the picture looks very different. That context is provided when one considers the Iraq war within the scope of U.S. strategy in the Middle East, the use of force within the context of the war on terror more broadly, and the war on terror within U.S. foreign policy in general.

September 11, 2001, was the culmination of a series of terrorist attacks against U.S. sites, soldiers, and assets in the Middle East, Africa, and North America by al-Qaida, an organization that drew on resources of recruits, financing, and substantial (though apparently not majoritarian) mass-level support from more than a dozen countries across North and East Africa, the Arabian Peninsula, and Central and Southwest Asia. The political leadership of the United States (as well as many others) perceived this as an accelerating threat emerging from extremist subcultures and organizations in those countries. These groupings triggered fears of potentially catastrophic possession and use of weapons of mass destruction, which have been gradually spreading to more countries, including several with substantial historic ties to terrorist groups. Just as important, U.S. leaders also traced these groupings backward along the causal chain to diverse possible underlying economic, cultural, and political conditions.[63] The result is perception of a threat of an unusually wide geographical area.

Yet the U.S. response thus far has involved the use of military force against only two regimes: the Taliban, which allowed al-Qaida to establish its main headquarters in Afghanistan, and the Baathists in Iraq, who were in long-standing defiance of UN demands concerning WMD programs and had a history of both connections to diverse terrorist groups and a distinctive hostility to the United States. U.S. policy toward other states, even in the Middle East, has not been especially threatening. The United States has increased military aid and other security assistance to several states, including Jordan, Morocco, and Pakistan, bolstering their military capabilities rather than eroding them. And the United States has not systematically intervened in the domestic politics of states in the region. The "greater Middle East initiative," which was floated by the White House early in 2004, originally aimed at profound economic and political reforms, but it has since been trimmed in accordance with

---

also Layne, "The War on Terrorism and the Balance of Power"; and Paul, Wirtz, and Fortmann, *Balance of Power*, p. 119.
63. See, for example, *The 9/11 Commission Report: Final Report of the National Commission on Terrorist Attacks upon the United States* (New York: W.W. Norton, 2004), pp. 52–55.

the wishes of diverse states, including many in the Middle East. Bigger budgets for the National Endowment for Democracy, the main U.S. entity charged with democratization abroad, are being spent in largely nonprovocative ways, and heavily disproportionately inside Iraq. In addition, Washington has proved more than willing to work closely with authoritarian regimes in Kuwait, Pakistan, Saudi Arabia, and elsewhere.

Further, U.S. policy toward the Middle East and North Africa since September 11 must be placed in the larger context of the war on terror more broadly construed. The United States is conducting that war virtually globally, but it has not used force outside the Middle East/Southwest Asia region. The primary U.S. responses to September 11 in the Mideast and especially elsewhere have been stepped-up diplomacy and stricter law enforcement, pursued primarily bilaterally and through regional organizations. The main emphasis has been on law enforcement: the tracing of terrorist financing; intelligence gathering; criminal-law surveillance of suspects; and arrests and trials in a number of countries. The United States has also pursued a variety of multilateralist efforts. Dealings with North Korea have been consistently multilateralist for some time; the United States has primarily relied on the International Atomic Energy Agency and the British-French-German troika for confronting Iran over its nuclear program; and the Proliferation and Container Security Initiatives are new international organizations obviously born of U.S. convictions that unilateral action in these matters was inadequate.

Finally, U.S. policy in the war on terror must be placed in the larger context of U.S. foreign policy more generally. In matters of trade, bilateral and multilateral economic development assistance, environmental issues, economically driven immigration, and many other areas, U.S. policy was characterized by broad continuity before September 11, and it remains so today. Government policies on such issues form the core of the United States' workaday interactions with many states. It is difficult to portray U.S. policy toward these states as revisionist in any classical meaning of that term. Some who identify a revolutionary shift in U.S. foreign policy risk badly exaggerating the significance of the Iraq war and are not paying sufficient attention to many other important trends and developments.[64]

---

64. See, for example, Ivo H. Daalder and James M. Lindsay, *America Unbound: The Bush Revolution in Foreign Policy* (Washington, D.C.: Brookings, 2003).

"ASYMMETRIC BALANCING"?

Very different U.S. policies, and very different local behavior, are of course visible for a small minority of states. U.S. policy toward terrorist organizations and rogue states is confrontational and often explicitly contains threats of military force. One might describe the behavior of these states and groups as forms of "asymmetric balancing" against the United States.[65] They wish to bring about a retraction of U.S. power around the globe; unlike most states, they are spending prodigiously on military capabilities; and they periodically seek allies to frustrate U.S. goals. Given their limited means for engaging in traditional balancing, the options for these actors are to engage in terrorism to bring about a collapse of support among the American citizenry for a U.S. military and political presence abroad or to acquire nuclear weapons to deter the United States. Al-Qaida and affiliated groups are pursuing the former option; Iran and North Korea the latter.

Is this balancing? On the one hand, the attempt to check and roll back U.S. power—be it through formal alliances, terrorist attacks, or the acquisition of a nuclear deterrent—is what balancing is essentially about. If balancing is driven by defensive motives, one might argue that the United States endangers al-Qaida's efforts to propagate radical Islamism and North Korea's and Iran's attempts to acquire nuclear weapons. On the other hand, the notion that these actors are status quo oriented and simply reacting to an increasingly powerful United States is difficult to sustain. Ultimately, the label "asymmetric balancing" does not capture the kind of behavior that international relations scholars have in mind when they predict and describe balancing against the United States in the wake of September 11 and the Iraq war.

Ironically, broadening the concept of balancing to include the behavior of terrorist organizations and nuclear proliferators highlights several additional problems for the larger balancing prediction thesis. First, the decisions by Iran and North Korea to devote major resources to their individual military capabilities despite limited means only strengthens our interpretation that major powers, with much vaster resources, are abstaining from balancing because of a lack of motivation, not a lack of latent power resources. Second, the radical Islamist campaign against the United States and its allies is more than a decade old, and the North Korean and Iranian nuclear programs began well before that, reinforcing our argument that the Bush administration's grand strategy and invasion of Iraq are far from the catalytic event for balancing that some an-

---

65. See Paul, "Introduction," in Paul, Wirtz, and Fortmann, *Balance of Power,* p. 3.

alysts have portrayed it to be. Finally, much of the criticism that current U.S. strategy is generating counterbalancing yields few policy options that would actually eliminate or reduce asymmetric balancing.

Conclusion

Major powers have not engaged in traditional balancing against the United States since the September 11 terrorist attacks and the lead-up to the Iraq war, either in the form of domestic military mobilization, antihegemonic alliances, or the laying-down of diplomatic red lines. Indeed, several major powers, including those best positioned to mobilize coercive resources, are continuing to reduce, rather than augment, their levels of resource mobilization. This evidence runs counter to ad hoc predictions and international relations scholarship that would lead one to expect such balancing under current conditions. In that sense, this finding has implications not simply for current policymaking but also for ongoing scholarly consideration of competing international relations theories and the plausibility of their underlying assumptions.

Current trends also do not confirm recent claims of soft balancing against the United States. And when these trends are placed in historical perspective, it is unclear whether the categories of behaviors labeled "soft balancing" can (ever) be rigorously distinguished from the types of diplomatic friction routine to virtually all periods of history, even between allies. Indeed, some of the behavior currently labeled "soft balancing" is the same behavior that occurred in earlier periods when, it is generally agreed, the United States was not being balanced against.

The lack of an underlying motivation to compete strategically with the United States under current conditions, not the lack of latent power potentialities, best explains this lack of balancing behavior, whether hard or soft. This is the case, in turn, because most states are not threatened by a post–September 11 U.S. foreign policy that is, despite commentary to the contrary, highly selective in its use of force and multilateralist in many regards. In sum, the salient dynamic in international politics today does not concern the way that major powers are responding to the United States' preponderance of power but instead concerns the relationship between the United States (and its allies), on the one hand, and terrorists and nuclear proliferators, on the other. So long as that remains the case, anything akin to balancing behavior is likely only among the narrowly circumscribed list of states and nonstate groups that are directly threatened by the United States.

Suggestions for Further Reading

There is a huge and growing literature on unipolarity, the responses of the rest of the world to U.S. primacy, when balancing occurs in international politics, and alternative foreign policies for the United States. The following suggested readings are only some of the more prominent contributions to this literature that were not included in this volume. To avoid repetition, all the works listed appear only once, even if they make contributions in several categories.

Unipolarity and World Politics

Kapstein, Ethan B., and Michael Mastanduno, eds. *Unipolar Politics: Realism and State Strategies after the Cold War*. New York: Columbia University Press, 1999.

Krauthammer, Charles. "The Unipolar Moment," *Foreign Affairs*, Vol. 70, No. 1 (Winter 1990/1991), pp. 23–33.

Krauthammer, Charles. "The Unipolar Moment Revisited," *National Interest*, Vol. 70 (Winter 2002), pp. 5–17.

Layne, Christopher. "The Unipolar Illusion Revisited: The Coming End of the United States' Unipolar Moment," *International Security*, Vol. 31, No. 2 (Fall 2006), pp. 7–41.

U.S. Foreign Policy in an Era of U.S. Primacy

Art, Robert J. *A Grand Strategy for America*. Ithaca, N.Y.: Cornell University Press, 2003.

Brzezinski, Zbigniew. *The Choice: Global Domination or Global Leadership*. New York: Basic Books, 2004.

Brzezinski, Zbigniew. *The Grand Chessboard: American Primacy and Its Geostrategic Imperatives*. New York: Basic Books, 1997.

Haass, Richard N. *The Opportunity: America's Moment to Alter History's Course*. New York: PublicAffairs, 2005.

Haass, Richard N. "What to Do with American Primacy," *Foreign Affairs*, Vol. 78, No. 5 (September/October 1999), pp. 37–49.

Huntington, Samuel P. "The Lonely Superpower," *Foreign Affairs*, Vol. 78, No. 2 (March/April 1999), pp. 35–49.

Layne, Christopher. "From Preponderance to Offshore Balancing: America's Future Grand Strategy," *International Security*, Vol. 22, No. 1 (Summer 1997), pp. 86–124.

Layne, Christopher. *The Peace of Illusions: American Grand Strategy from 1940 to the Present*. Ithaca, New York: Cornell University Press, 2006.

Lieber, Robert J., ed. *Eagle Rules? Foreign Policy and American Primacy in the 21st Century*. New York: Prentice-Hall and Woodrow Wilson Center, 2002.

Maier, Charles. *Among Empires: American Ascendancy and Its Predecessors*. Cambridge, Mass.: Harvard University Press, 2006.

Mastanduno, Michael. "Preserving the Unipolar Moment: Realist Theories and U.S. Grand Strategy after the Cold War," *International Security*, Vol. 21, No. 4 (Spring 1997), pp. 49–88.

Nye, Joseph S., Jr. *The Paradox of American Power: Why the World's Only Superpower Can't Go It Alone.* Oxford: Oxford University Press, 2002.

Nye, Joseph S., Jr. *Soft Power: The Means to Success in World Politics.* New York: PublicAffairs, 2004.

U.S. Unilateralism under Unipolarity

Brooks, Stephen G. and William C. Wohlforth, "International Relations Theory and the Case against Unilateralism," *Perspectives on Politics*, Vol. 3, No. 3 (September 2005), pp. 509–524.

Ignatieff, Michael, ed. *American Exceptionalism and Human Rights.* Princeton, N.J.: Princeton University Press, 2004.

Ikenberry, G. John. "Is American Multilateralism in Decline?" *Perspectives on Politics*, Vol. 1, No. 3 (September 2003), pp. 533–550.

Mahbubani, Kishore. "The Impending Demise of the Postwar System," *Survival*, Vol. 47, No. 4 (Winter 2005–06), pp. 7–18.

Malone, David M., and Yuen Foong Khong. *Unilateralism and U.S. Foreign Policy: International Perspectives.* Boulder, Colo.: Lynne Rienner, 2003.

Prestowitz, Clyde. *Rogue Nation: American Unilateralism and the Failure of Good Intentions.* New York: Basic Books, 2003.

Balancing Power in Theory and Practice

Gilpin, Robert. *War and Change in World Politics.* Cambridge: Cambridge University Press, 1981.

He, Kai, and Huiyun Feng. "If Not Soft Balancing, Then What? Reconsidering Soft Balancing and U.S. Policy Toward China," *Security Studies*, Vol. 17, No. 2 (April–June 2008), pp. 363–395.

Ikenberry, G. John, ed. *America Unrivaled: The Future of the Balance of Power.* Ithaca, N.Y.: Cornell University Press, 2002.

Levy, Jack S, and William R. Thompson. "Hegemonic Threats and Great-Power Balancing in Europe, 1495–1999," *Security Studies*, Vol. 14, No. 1 (January–March 2005), pp. 1–30.

Mearsheimer, John J. *The Tragedy of Great Power Politics.* New York: W.W. Norton, 2001.

Paul, T.V., James J. Wirtz, and Michel Fortmann, eds. *Balance of Power: Theory and Practice in the 21st Century.* Stanford, Calif.: Stanford University Press, 2004.

Posen, Barry R. "European Union Security and Defense Policy: Response to Unipolarity?" *Security Studies*, Vol. 15, No. 2 (April–June 2006), pp. 149–186.

Press-Barnathan, Galia. "Managing the Hegemon: NATO under Unipolarity," *Security Studies*, Vol. 15, No. 2 (April–June 2006), pp. 271–309.

Schroeder, Paul. "Historical Reality vs. Neo-realist Theory," *International Security*, Vol. 19, No. 1 (Summer 1994), pp. 108–148.

Schweller, Randall L. "Bandwagoning for Profit: Bringing the Revisionist State Back In," *International Security*, Vol. 19, No. 1 (Summer 1994), pp. 72–107.

Schweller, Randall L. "Unanswered Threats: A Neoclassical Realist Theory of Underbalancing," *International Security*, Vol. 29, No. 2 (Fall 2004), pp. 159–201.

Vasquez, John A., and Colin Elman, eds. *Realism and the Balancing of Power: A New Debate*. Upper Saddle River, N.J.: Prentice-Hall, 2003.

Walt, Stephen M. *Taming American Power: The Global Response to U.S. Primacy*. New York: W.W. Norton, 2005.

Walt, Stephen M. *The Origins of Alliances*. Ithaca, N.Y.: Cornell University Press, 1987.

Waltz, Kenneth N. "Evaluating Theories," *American Political Science Review*, Vol. 91, No. 4 (December 1997), pp. 913–917.

Waltz, Kenneth N. *Theory of International Politics*. Reading, Mass.: Addison-Wesley, 1979.

U.S. Grand Strategy and the Future of American Primacy

Brooks, Stephen G., and William C. Wohlforth. *World out of Balance: International Relations and the Challenge of American Primacy*. Princeton, N.J.: Princeton University Press, 2008.

Drezner, Daniel W. "The New New World Order," *Foreign Affairs*, Vol. 86, No. 2 (March/April 2007), pp. 34–46.

Ferguson, Niall. *Colossus: The Rise and Fall of the American Empire*. New York: Penguin, 2005.

Haas, Mark L. "A Geriatric Peace? The Future of U.S. Power in a World of Aging Populations," *International Security*, Vol. 32, No. 1 (Summer 2007), pp. 112–147.

Haass, Richard N. "The Age of Nonpolarity: What Will Follow U.S. Dominance," *Foreign Affairs*, Vol. 87, No. 3 (May–June 2008), pp. 44–56.

Kagan, Robert. *The Return of History and the End of Dreams*. New York: Knopf, 2008.

Kupchan, Charles A. "After Pax Americana: Benign Power, Regional Integration, and the Sources of a Stable Multipolarity," *International Security*, Vol. 23, No. 2 (Fall 1998), pp. 40–79.

Kupchan, Charles A. *The End of the American Era: U.S. Foreign Policy and the Geopolitics of the Twenty-first Century*, New York: Knopf, 2002

Kupchan, Charles A., and Peter L. Trubowitz. "Dead Center: The Demise of Liberal Internationalism in the United States," *International Security*, Vol. 32, No. 2 (Fall 2007), pp. 7–44.

National Intelligence Council. *Mapping the Global Future: Report of the National Intelligence Council's 2020 Project*. Washington, D.C.: U.S. Government Printing Office, December 2004. (http://www.dni.gov/nic/NIC_2020_project.html).

Nye, Joseph S., Jr. "Recovering American Leadership," *Survival*, Vol. 50, No. 1 (February–March 2008), pp. 55–68.

Zakaria, Fareed. "The Future of American Power: How America Can Survive the Rise of the Rest," *Foreign Affairs*, Vol. 87, No. 3 (May/June 2008), pp. 18–43.

Zakaria, Fareed. *The Post-American World*. New York: W.W. Norton, 2008.

International Security
The Robert and Renée Belfer Center for
Science and International Affairs
John F. Kennedy School of Government
Harvard University

All of the articles in this reader were previously published in **International Security,** a quarterly journal sponsored and edited by the Robert and Renée Belfer Center for Science and International Affairs at Harvard University's John F. Kennedy School of Government, and published by MIT Press Journals. To receive journal subscription information or to find out more about other readers in our series, please contact MIT Press Journals at 238 Main Street, suite 500, Cambridge, MA 02142, or on the web at http:// mitpress.mit.edu.